INTERSECTIONALITY

INTERSEC

EXPANDING FRONTIERS

INTERDISCIPLINARY APPROACHES TO STUDIES

OF WOMEN, GENDER, AND SEXUALITY

Series Editors:

KAREN J. LEONG

ANDREA SMITH

TIONALITY

Origins, Contestations, Horizons

ANNA CARASTATHIS

UNIVERSITY OF NEBRASKA PRESS | LINCOLN & LONDON

Earlier portions of chapter 1 originally appeared as "The Concept of Intersectionality in Feminist Theory" in *Philosophy
Compass* 9, no. 5 (2014): 304–13. An earlier version of chapter 2
appeared as "Basements and Intersections" in *Hypatia: A Journal
of Feminist Philosophy* 28, no. 4 (2013): 698–715. Part of chapter
3 was originally published as "Reinvigorating Intersectionality
as a Provisional Concept" in *Why Race and Gender Still Matter:
An Intersectional Approach*, edited by Namita Goswami, Maeve
O'Donovan, and Lisa Yount (London: Pickering & Chatto,
2014), 59–70, used by permission from Taylor & Francis. A portion of chapter 5 originally appeared as "Identity Categories
as Potential Coalitions" in *Signs: Journal of Women in Culture
and Society*, special issue: "Intersectionality: Theorizing Power,
Empowering Theory," edited by Kimberlé Williams Crenshaw,
Sumi Cho, and Leslie McCall, 38, no. 4 (2013): 941–65.

Library of Congress Cataloging-in-Publication Data
Names: Carastathis, Anna, 1981–
Title: Intersectionality: origins, contestations,
horizons / Anna Carastathis.
Description: Lincoln: University of Nebraska Press, 2016.
| Series: Expanding frontiers: interdisciplinary approaches
to studies of women, gender, and sexuality | Includes
bibliographical references and index.
Identifiers: LCCN 2016010867 (print)
LCCN 2016034740 (ebook)
ISBN 9780803285552 (hardback: alk. paper)
ISBN 9780803296626 (epub)
ISBN 9780803296633 (mobi)
ISBN 9780803296640 (pdf)
Subjects: LCSH: Feminist theory. | Women's studies. |
Women, Black. | African Americans—Race identity. |
BISAC: SOCIAL SCIENCE / Feminism & Feminist Theory. |
SOCIAL SCIENCE / Ethnic Studies / General.
Classification: LCC HQ1190 .C374 2016 (print) |
LCC HQ1190 (ebook) | DDC 305.4201—dc23
LC record available at https://lccn.loc.gov/2016010867

Set in Garamond Premier Pro by Rachel Gould.

To my sister, Katerina
and to my yiayia, Katerina

CONTENTS

PREFACE

At its core, this is a book about reading and listening. At times, as I wrote it, I was not sure I wanted to advance an argument to the extent it required me to shift from reading and listening to writing and speaking, and in a sense—since the argument centrally concerns the politics of interpretation and representation—to speaking for others. But since I have now done that, I want to preface what I have written with a story about the "locus of enunciation" of its author. The Cherokee-Greek writer Thomas King has said that "the truth about stories is that that's all we are." I tell this story with trepidation, vulnerability and apprehension, knowing that stories are "dangerous" as much as they are "wondrous"; we can become "chained" to them, and they cannot be called back; once told, they are "loose in the world" (King 2003).

I was born in 1981, the same year Cherríe Moraga and Gloria Anzaldúa first published *This Bridge Called My Back: Writings by Radical Women of Color*, across an ocean, on a different continent, probably in a different world. A decade later I would fly above that ocean and arrive on northeastern Turtle Island an "immigrant." Still another decade would pass. In my early twenties, attending graduate school, I would come across this book for the first time in a university library (it would be none the worse for wear) in an attempt to educate myself with respect to women-of-color feminisms in an academic context where, to my disappointment and frustration, they were institutionally, disciplinarily, and phenomenologically underrepresented. Becoming absorbed in its pages, while still standing between the stacks, sweating in my winter parka (it would be winter in Montreal, Kanien'kehá:ka-Mohawk territory), I would come across a passage. As my eyes passed over its lines, I would let out an audible gasp. It would be the first (and last) time I saw my ethnicity mentioned within a women-of-color feminist text. This was not an act of self-representation; neither was it, straightforwardly, an inclusionary gesture in the category. But it was a fleeting moment of visibility. In an essay titled "I Paid Very Hard for My Immigrant Ignorance," which instantly captured my interest, Mirtha Quintanales writes with a lot of empathy and nuance about her Greek friend, a woman who does not quite fit, a queer figure whose ambivalent, ambiguous racialization—white by U.S. Census standards, yet "loud," "aggressive," and "very Greek identified"—renders her an outsider to both hegemonic and minoritized racial groups. Quintanales reports: "The Greek woman's many attempts to 'connect with Third World lesbians and Women of Color' . . . have been met with outright rejection," rejection she faces "in white, mainstream lesbian/feminist circles as well. Clearly she does not fit there either" (1983, 150–51). I would slam the book shut, and then quickly open it again, reading and rereading these lines with astonishment, incredulity, confusion, and a strange mixture of pleasure and pain—the pleasure of recognition, the pain that this recognition is one of rejection. I would never speak about it with anyone.

I would write a dissertation on intersectionality, questioning its efficacy as a multi-axial theory of oppression. The next decade, which brings me into the present, would be one of more relocations and dislocations, which entailed a great many opportunities to learn about what had become my object of study even if I would feel unable to avow it, at least aloud, as my subjective experience. This was a decade during which my NAFTA-facilitated crossing of the Canadian-U.S. border would transform me into a nonresident alien, who would be granted the privilege to teach philosophy and women's, gender, and sexuality studies at the "Other" state university in Los Angeles. Since my "object" is critical race feminisms and postcolonial, anticolonial, and decolonial thought, I would have many conversations about intersectionality, primarily with interlocutors who were positioned as my "students"—even though I was keenly aware they were surely teaching me as much as, if not more than, I was them—as well as with colleagues and friends who would either look upon me as a three-headed monster or as amusingly naive when I would question the self-evidence of the racialized perceptions and ideologies that, somehow, always seemed ready to hand. I would learn to distrust the most "innocent" of encounters, which I found myself constantly plumbing for undercurrents and blatant statements of racism, homophobia, misogyny. I would learn about the history and reconstitution of slavery in and through the prison-industrial complex; about the U.S. version of genocidal settler colonialism (no "worse" than the Canadian version that I had already encountered but to which I could never become "accustomed"); about internally colonized groups constructed as "minorities" on their own ancestral lands, even when they numerically predominate; about the criminalization of migration and the struggles to survive of people rendered "illegal"; about the naturalization of permanent war and the state of terror it inflicted on racialized religious groups within the national territory and abroad; about the solipsistic, assimilative arrogations of whiteness, and the ambitions of some to be absorbed within it. I would begin to "deal with" my own queerness, both sexual and "racial." I think about the figure of the "Greek woman" in Quintanales's text. I do not experience rejection from women of color, but neither do I experience belonging. I feel I do not belong. I feel I do not have the right to belong. I begin to question my desire to belong, to distrust my thinking about my own identity; could the experience of "ambivalence" and "ambiguity" be just another instance of white evasion of responsibility? From what enunciatory location can I speak authentically and responsibly, and in what language? What am I doing on this continent? When I think of who and where I am, the words "dislocation," "displacement," and "dispossession" weigh on my mind. I start to feel that my very presence on these appropriated lands is untenable. I start to remember the first days after my arrival in a small city in northern Ontario, traditional territory of the Anishinaabe-Ojibwe people. I remember us silently sitting on the monkey bars with Thelma, a Native kid and an immigrant kid, the Anglo/white students spitting hatred at us, and feeling then, and now, that I should not want to belong here, that belonging was a trap. I wanted to go home. Almost twenty years later, though, a home place had ceased to exist for me.

After losing my home, I gradually lost my tongue. Unlike the "Greek woman" in Quintanales's essay, I was never very Greek-identified. Of mixed roots, born to an Irish mother—herself three times an immigrant—and a Greek father, whose parents were Egyptiot Greeks, like that poet of diasporic nostalgia and cosmopolitan queerness, Constantine Cavafy, with migratory roots from the islands and mainlands of what became the Greek nation-state. My relationship to "Greekness" was always mediated by a persistent ascription of inauthenticity. I remember, as a child, my elder relatives in Greece observing that I looked "European, not Greek." Outside Greece, I have heard countless times from acquaintances moments after meeting them that I do not "look Greek"—their perception is confirmed by hearing that my mother is Irish—and they almost always seem to mean it as a compliment. In Greece, I am often perceived as an immigrant, not an emigrant. In the diaspora, Greek identity is overdetermined by religion, nationalism, heteronormativity, and a shared language. As a queer secular anti-nationalist, losing my tongue and the fading of my (sort of Irish, sort of Greek) immigrant accent meant losing the last, tenuous claim I had on this identity. If my experience in the first decade of living in Canada was characterized by estrangement, alienation, and overt cultural racism, by the end of the second I could feel myself ever more assimilated into the Canadian settler state, a process exacerbated by migrating to the United States to work, where "Americans" would seek to define me as "Canadian"; if this is a true description of my naturalized citizenship, it made me cringe as a characterization of my ethnic identity.

Then the "crisis" occurred. Suddenly I am re-membered as Greek in the diaspora; I am asked my opinion about the profligacy of "my" government, the indolence of "my" compatriots, and the violence of their protest. I feel a need to relearn a lost language in order to read and understand, if from a distance, how austerity capitalism is being resisted in Greece, where historical experiences of war, occupation, dictatorship and imperialism are being reanimated in the present conjuncture. This is a history that my leftist parents had never allowed us to forget; yet, returning to Greece amid the crisis, I notice how one of its effects is the dispelling of a prevalent forgetting that enabled the rise of "European" aspirations along with the entrenchment of consumer capitalism. Now, as Greece is reminded that Europe is a continental, racial project to which it peripherally belongs, my own sense of belonging and desire to retrace roots in the place of my birth is reignited. I begin to relearn what I have forgotten, and for the first time in nearly a decade (and only the second time since we emigrated), return. Walking in my godmother's neighborhood on the outskirts of Athens, where asphalt roads have since been laid, I get lost and stop a neighbor to ask for directions. He looks at me suspiciously, calls me an "illegal immigrant," and sneers that I'd do better to return from whence I came.

When thinking about the place of ethnic "minority" women in women-of-color feminisms, who were assimilated as groups (if not as individuals, given the particularities of phenotypic ascriptions, class immobilities, and linguistic, geographical, generational, and other factors) into whiteness sometime during the mid-twentieth century in the United States and Canada, there is often an assumption that assimilation constitutes privilege, that it is a volitional, unidirectional, permanent, and unproblematic transformation. This is naturalized with reference to dubious claims about the phenotypic proximity of ethnic whites to hegemonic whites—eliding the diversity of embodiments and reproducing a reifying realism about racialized perception. Moreover, Quintanales argues that "the 'social privileges' of lighter-than-black-ethnic-minority lesbians in this society are almost totally dependent on our denial of who we are, on our ethnic death" (1983, 153). While skin color "*may* confer on some ethnic minority women the option of being 'assimilated,' 'integrated' in mainstream American society," it comes at the price of "having to become ghost-like, identity-less, community-less, totally alienated" (154). She speaks eloquently of being torn between the "primary emergencies [of] race and culture" (154), of fearing that the expansion of the concept of racism—and of "women of color" as its subject—will mean its dilution, and particularly the displacement of historical experiences of enslavement, colonization, and imperialism as ontological anchors of the phenomenology of racial oppression (153). What is to be done with ethnic minority women who—at least according to late-twentieth- and early-twenty-first-century demographic taxonomies—are perceived as "white" and accorded at least some, if not all, of the privileges of whiteness, and may even be racists (153)?

The contradictions and ambivalences in my experiences of racialization and racism are in part a function of the fact that the process was neither instantaneous nor coherent. My experiences of racialization constitute a diachronic process that involved the imposition of institutionally racist ascriptions ("landed immigrant," "visible minority," "naturalized citizen," "nonresident alien"); it has occasioned intersubjective racializing encounters in different optic economies of "race"—for instance, in the sun-soaked ecology of the traditional territory of the Tongva and Chumash peoples, now colonized by the United States and renamed "Los Angeles," I am often "mistaken" for Latina. My racialization often makes me "visible but not legible" (Mendieta 2012, 152). This causes consternation in the subject of racialized perception whose intentionality is frustrated. Sometimes it has been Angla/white women who sought to fix my identity, conflating my "white privilege" with their own. Sometimes it has been women of color who have accused me of inauthenticity or pointed out the privilege which the "ability" to assimilate affords me. Usually, I tend to agree with both and only silently disagree. The idiosyncrasies of my experience hardly seem to matter in the grand scheme of a global system of white supremacy, in which my skin color and Canadian/European Union citizenships garner undeniable institutional privileges, and protect me from state violence and premature death. My body relatively easily crosses borders that render other people's crossings illicit, it enters spaces that are foreclosed to others, it is fed and sheltered and safe from mortars, land mines, drone missiles, stray and aimed bullets. My migratory travels were by airplane; not by boat, by dinghy, or on foot. I think about this as I cross the Aegean sea from an island in "Greek" territory to the mainland of the "Turkish" state; my identity card and a ticket bought with ten euro garners me safe passage over what has become a watery graveyard for thousands of migrants crossing in precarious vessels in the other direction. Given this necropolitical/biopolitical divide, any ambiguity seems superficial and the binarisms of racialization intractable.

In one of my classes I asked students to read Cherríe Moraga's 1979 essay "La Güera," and I was struck by how many of us identify with her words, how many of us seek a language to "understand the meaning of being and yet not being, of 'merging' and yet remaining utterly alone and in the margins of our society" (Quintanales 1983, 154). Moraga writes:

> In this country, lesbianism is a poverty—as is being brown, as is being a woman, as is being just plain poor. The danger lies in ranking the oppressions. *The danger lies in failing to acknowledge the specificity of the oppression.* The danger lies in attempting to deal with oppression purely from a theoretical base. Without an emotional, heartfelt grappling with the source of our own oppression, without naming the enemy within ourselves and outside of us, no authentic, nonhierarchical connection among oppressed groups can take place. (1983, 44–45)

Quintanales warns of a deeper problem of which the figure of the Greek woman is a symptom: "We are still seeing radical differences when they don't exist and not seeing them when they are critical" (1983, 154). Which differences matter, and which are immaterial?

I try to square my story with Moraga and Anzaldúa's insight that "visibility/invisibility as women of colour forms our radicalism" (1983, xxiv). In this book I discuss a position toward intersectionality that I have developed by reading and listening closely to "plurilogues"—to borrow Shireen Roshanravan's wonderful concept (2014)—staged within (queer) women-of-color feminisms. I understand "women of color" in the coalitional sense it gained in the U.S. context, as a political project, within which I have come to construct my own life trajectory, my affective, ideological, and political commitments, to try to fulfill my "responsibility to my roots" (Moraga 1983, 50), and to dream insurrectionary dreams for future generations. Moraga and Anzaldúa argue that to produce "theory in the flesh" we must struggle to "learn . . . how to live with . . . contradictions," embracing them as the "root of our radicalism" (1983, 5). I situate my scholarship in plurilogue with women-of-color feminisms, not because I want to territorialize or arrogate the work of those whose experiences I do not share, but because I want to contest the ease with which we deny our connections (Quintanales 1983, 156). I want to express my identity-loneliness, my lack of community, but also my gratitude to Black feminisms, which for over a decade have challenged and inspired me in ways that this book can only begin to express—this as an act of affirming our interconnectedness. I tell this story while fighting the voice in my head that sounds off rejection or ridicule. I humbly join my voice to those of others who have long suggested that social movements need to imagine identity and identification in radically different ways than those made hegemonic by nation-states, which continue to impose systems of racial classification (and to the extent that all maintain citizenship as a fundamental category of non/belonging, arguably *all* do, even if they disavow explicitly racialist terms). Can we reorient our perception so that lived understandings of identity, solidarity, and community are not totalized by demographic taxonomies of "race" and ethnicity, gender and gender identity, sexuality, nation, and religion? Can we tell stories about who and where we are that do justice and are accountable to the struggles of people who are not "us"? The argument I advance in this book does not claim originality or exactness—both arrogances of a colonial/positivist epistemic paradigm—but it is motivated by solidarity and seeks to contribute to our collective liberation; its condition of possibility is a sincere and profound desire to read and listen. Countering attempts to fix intersectionality to positivist, essentialist categories, to render it amenable to colonial state projects of differential inclusion, diversity management, and social control, in what follows I argue that "intersectionality" understood as categorial critique functions as a distal horizon, powerfully illuminating the urgent conceptual, political, ethical, and affective work to be done in the "here" and "now."

ACKNOWLEDGMENTS

I have been thinking about the issues that have found expression in this book for over a decade, since I first encountered the concept of intersectionality in a feminist philosophy course during my undergraduate years at the University of Alberta, and tried to square it with experiences of multiple marginalizations crosscut by privileges with which I was grappling. That course was taught by Cressida Heyes, who became my mentor and honors thesis supervisor and without whose encouragement I would not have thought it plausible that I pursue graduate studies. Dr. Heyes introduced me to feminist theory as a potentially socially transformative intellectual pursuit, and inspired me, as she did many of her other students before and since, to think wildly, argue sharply, write clearly, and teach kindly. My dissertation supervisor at McGill University, Alia Al-Saji, encouraged my diffuse interests while helping focus them into a thesis. As generous over the years with her friendship as with her patient guidance, Dr. Al-Saji expanded my intellectual horizons by introducing me to phenomenology—an orientation to philosophical thinking grounded in lived experience that forms the constitutive background of the analytical and hermeneutic arguments I attempt in these pages—and by encouraging me to recruit phenomenology toward race-critical ends; I am grateful for our marathon conversations, her sense of humor, and her ongoing support as I negotiate the vicissitudes of academic life. Marguerite Deslauriers and Hasana Sharp, my other two dissertation committee members, gave invaluable advice, posed difficult questions, and encouraged me to develop the project in its early phases with analytical acuity and hermeneutic rigor. I am thankful for the financial support I received during my doctoral studies from the Department of Philosophy, the Faculty of Arts, and the Social Sciences and Humanities Research Council of Canada. Subsequently, I developed earlier versions of certain chapters while a postdoctoral fellow at the Centre de recherche en éthique de l'Université de Montréal under the guidance of Daniel Marc Weinstock, and at the Institute for Gender, Race, Sexuality, and Social Justice of the University of British Columbia supervised by Becki Ross. My colleagues at California State University, Los Angeles, particularly Ann Garry—with whom I had so many productive exchanges about intersectionality and feminism—Talia Mae Bettcher, and Mohammed Abed (in Philosophy), and Benjamin Bateman, Molly Talcott, Dionne Espinoza, and Alejandra Marchevsky (in Women's, Gender, and Sexuality Studies), were wonderful interlocutors, inspiring educators, and supportive friends. The administrator of the Department of Philosophy, Donna Balderrama, infused our workplace with such unparalleled kindness and commitment that she redefined for me what can be humanly possible under such institutional constraints; not to mention that she saved me from certain disaster on too many occasions to count. I am grateful to the Center for Research on Genders and Sexualities at Cal State LA for awarding me a Faculty Research Fellowship, which enabled me to conduct research at San Francisco's Gay, Lesbian, Bisexual and Transgender Historical Society, and to archivists Rebekah Kim, Marjorie Bryer, and Alex Barrows for all their work keeping alive and ensuring our access to the historical memory of LGBTQI movements and communities in that city.

I drew insight and inspiration from the people positioned as my "students" at all of the institutions at which I have been so fortunate to teach; but I truly felt that at Cal State LA I was privileged to meet people who transformed me radically and confirmed all my secret hopes about humanity. I could write an entire book on this subject, about all the things that working with students at that beleaguered public institution taught me about our capacity to struggle, to connect, to create, and to learn together. Without wishing to diminish the collective process in which we were all together involved, I would like to express my gratitude specifically to certain "students"—scholars in their own right—who generously shared with me their ideas, their interpretations, and their questions in ways that have been deeply affecting. Imran Siddiqui's love of footnotes and scrupulously close readings easily outdoes my own; his generosity of spirit and intellect humbles me profoundly. I was inspired to research Somos Hermanas by Claudia Baltazar, who began working on her master's thesis focusing on the "third space" feminisms of women of color who had organized in the Bay Area; Claudia's tragic death interrupted that work and the life of a beautiful, brilliant person that I was honored to know, if all too briefly. I would also like to acknowledge the people who made up the Critical Race Feminisms seminar in spring of 2011, particularly Lisbeth Espinosa, who taught us all a great deal about the vital importance of honoring, integrating, and resisting on the basis of what she powerfully termed "the intersectionalities within"; Victor Morales, who is as resilient in his intellect as he is in his person; and Chogollah Maroufi, whose passion for learning is truly inspiring and is what I imagine makes him such an incredible teacher. The people who constituted my courses on gendered violence and who organized the public forums "Breaking the Chain of Gendered Violence through Education and Empowerment" (in 2010) and "What Is Done in the Dark Must Come to Light: Imagine an End to Gendered Violence" (in 2013) did no less than rock my world. I especially want to thank Bree Lacey, Brandon Edgar, Carlos Douglas, Christyne Taylor, Corinne Love, Diana Perez, Jillian Paul, Leonard López, Lucia Smith-Menzies, and Lysandro Valenzuela. I was honored to share safer space, mutual support, and lots of laughs with the people in The Queer Connection, for which student organization I served as faculty adviser; in every sense of these words: you know who you are. I am particularly grateful to the graduate students who did me the honor of asking me to serve as their master's thesis adviser, and whose work informed my own: Leonard López, who wrote powerfully about "prismatic identities" in his analysis of hate crimes law in relation to the coloniality of "intraracial" homophobic violence; Andres Garza, who pressed me to think phenomenologically about issues of epistemic injustice; and Anthony

Ristow, who got me thinking about the potentials and limitations of Foucault's thought for conceptualizing "racism" (this became the subject of a reading group we organized). I would also like to express my gratitude to those people in "my" classes who pushed my pedagogical limits, challenged my assumptions, and tested, frustrated, or aggrieved me—and perhaps whom I also tested, frustrated, or aggrieved—for engaging me in a sometimes uncomfortable process of dissensus, of conflict and, sometimes, but not always, of resolution with respect to the issues under discussion. Thank-you all for your patience with me as I was—and I hope I always will be—learning how to teach.

I am grateful to collaborators, editors, anonymous reviewers, conference organizers, and audiences who helped me develop, sharpen, and refine the arguments elaborated in the pages that follow. I would like to thank Jennifer Nash, whose work on intersectionality has inspired and challenged me; together we organized a panel at the National Women's Studies Association's "Difficult Dialogues" conference in 2009. Given that we had titled the panel "Beyond Intersectionality?" I think we were both more than a little apprehensive when we realized that Kimberlé Williams Crenshaw was in the room. I am "Beyond Grateful" to Professor Crenshaw for inviting me to present at UCLA's School of Law Critical Race Studies Symposium, "Intersectionality: Challenging Theory, Reframing Politics, Transforming Movements," in 2010, and for including my article in the special issue of *Signs* that she coedited with Sumi Cho and Leslie McCall. The special issue editors, together with Beth Ribet and *Signs* managing editor Miranda Outman-Kramer, were generous and rigorous with their critical advice, helping me develop the theoretical argument about intersectionality revealing identities as coalitions in relation to social-movement history. It has been a daunting honor to write about a living thinker as brilliant as Professor Crenshaw, whose work has inspired so many to challenge cognitive and affective habits, conceptual schemas, and political ideologies based on solipsism, domination, and exclusion. Encountering Carmen Vázquez, as well as the other activists who brought Somos Hermanas to life, in the archive and through their oral histories, writing, lectures, and interviews, renewed my optimism about what is possible when we collectively confront violence in our lives and enacted in our name in ways that acknowledge and respect the interdependence of personal and social transformation. I would like to thank Namita Goswami, Maeve O'Donovan, and Lisa Yount, editors of *Why Race and Gender Still Matter*, in which an earlier version of chapter 3 appears; Alia Al-Saji, who edited the Feminist Philosophy section of *Philosophy Compass* in which part of chapter 1 appears; Linda Martín Alcoff, Mickaella Perina, and Ofelia Schutte, who honored "Basements and Intersections" with the inaugural *Hypatia* Diversity Essay Prize and offered helpful suggestions for its improvement prior to its publication in that journal; Jen McWeeny, Shireen Roshanravan, and Pedro DiPietro, who helped me develop my reading of María Lugones's account of intersectionality and interlocking and intermeshed oppressions for their anthology *Speaking Face to Face/Hablando Cara a Cara*.

I am very thankful for the interest and faith that Alicia Christensen, acquisitions editor at University of Nebraska Press, showed in this project and for her support throughout the publication process, and to the staff in the Editorial, Design, and Production Department, particularly Assistant Manager Sabrina Stellrecht, as well as copy editor Jonathan Lawrence, for their meticulous and caring attention to the text. The anonymous reviewers who read the manuscript were generous with their criticism and immensely helpful in illuminating possible trajectories of revision; the series editors, Karen J. Leong and Andrea Smith, gave me latitude to choose which of these to pursue. Thanks to all of them, a collection of pages were alchemically transformed into a book.

These pages were written in many different places and owe their existence to many people who inspired, challenged, and cared for me as I wrote and rewrote them. In graduate school, I was surrounded by people whose intellectual curiosity and passions helped form my own: for this, and much more, I am grateful to Anna Feigenbaum, Elaine Brown, Tracey Nicholls, Florentien Verhage, Bryan Smyth, Mohamed Mehdi, Jasmine Rault, Megha Sehdev, Tamara Extian-Babiuk, Cynthia Reed, Spogmai Wassimi, Fatima Seedat, S. J. Brooks, Aziz Choudry, Jennifer Cuffe, and Allison Harrell. Thanks to Raph Beaulieu for needing no invitation to stop by; he was my always-welcome conduit to the outside world when I was in the thick of dissertation writing; and to Angel

Beyde for her supportive friendship during that harried time. Jackie Kingston-Campbell's frequent visits and letters and parcels from Novosibirsk taught me to embrace life as an adventure that knows no age. I am grateful to the people at the Simone de Beauvoir Institute, especially Trish Salah, Dolores Chew, Gada Mahrouse, Viviane Namaste, Candis Steenbergen, and Deb Lunny, and to the March 8 Committee of Women of Diverse Origins, who taught me so much about coalescing against the violences of racist heteropatriarchy. For their enduring friendships, I thank Ania Dymarz, David McVea, and Adair Rounthwaite. In Los Angeles, I was fortunate to be befriended by Ben Bateman, J. P. Drury, Mohamed Abed, Talia Bettcher, Susan Forrest, Molly Talcott, and Dana Collins. I will always feel profound gratitude to Riel Dupuis-Rossi for sharing part of the journey with me, for raising my consciousness and reminding me where I stand, and with whom, and to Vilma Rossi and Phill Dupuis for welcoming me into their families. Barbara Giuliani and Silvia Burzio made me feel benvenuta in Levà. In Mytilene, I shared rakomelo, practiced yoga, or talked gender politics with Vivi Papanikola, Vicky Bathrelou, Kiki Kourtoglou, and Ismini Gatou. In Lisbon, I was lucky for the supportive friendships of Lia Viola, Ilaria Bertazzi, and Elisa Scaraggi. For their filoxenia I thank Stella Chatzipantsiou in Thessaloniki, as well as Maroula Chatzipantsiou and Eleni Melitou in Palaiokomi. For so many rousing discussions, and so much good advice, I am grateful to my dear friend Litsa Chatzivasileiou. In the singular presence of Kaiti Nalmpanti I feel at home, time and time again; hers has been an embrace that helped me to gather the scattered fragments of a self. When I wandered, quite lost, into her city, Nayrouz Abu Hatoum opened her home to me, nourished me, let me work alongside her, and helped me celebrate as this book came to fruition. Eliza Kolovou has been there for me in the hardest moments, halving sorrows, and in the happiest, doubling joys. Fellow traveler Aila Spathopoulou gives me hope about matters small and large, teaching me to trust "the flow." Serdar Kandil's warmth, gentleness, and generosity won me over from the first moment. The indomitable Farha Najah Hussain teaches me about keeping my heart soft while taking strong stands; her love is a salve and a gift. I am lucky to be able to count on Natalie Kouri-Towe to help me gain perspective, often knowing me better than I know myself, lovingly setting me back on my path time and time again. Morfeas, Antartissa, and Juanita were tireless companions in the writing process; one could not hope for more affectionate collaborators. Effrosyni Dagdileli sustained and nourished me in all ways through the vagaries of writing; our constant conversation profoundly shaped me. Έφη, σε ευχαριστώ για τις μικρές ζεστές πέτρες από τις αγαπημένες σου παραλίες που έβαλες στην παλάμη μου και για όλες τις λέξεις που καταλάβαμε αντάμα. Κοντά σου έμαθα πως

η γλώσσα
που χρειάζομαι
να μιλήσω
είναι η ίδια
που χρησιμοποιώ
για να αγγίζω . . . (Moraga 1983, 149, my translation)

I owe everything to my parents, my first and best teachers, Margaret Ann Foley Carastathis and Dimitris Carastathis, for their love and support, since my very beginning. Principled and forgiving, generous and exacting, in their own ways, they raised me to honor the desire to be free; through the example of their own resilience they inspire me to find strength enough to keep trying. My grandfather Yiannis Carastathis, who passed away recently, always encouraged in me a love of learning, of languages, and of solitary walks. I felt closer to things faraway thanks to the late-night transatlantic phone calls from my late godmother, Yiorgia Atsa Iordanidou. I appreciate the gentle generosity of my aunt Joan Foley Chalmers, who offered her love and reassurance from afar. I am deeply indebted to my sister, Katerina Carastathis, for always having been there. This book is humbly dedicated to her, not least of all because she taught me to love books. It is also dedicated to the memory of my grandmother Katerina Atsa Karastathi, whose namesake my sister is, who died when I was a child but whose love I have carried with me, and has carried me, all these years. I think of her every time I wash dishes, hold a heavy wooden spoon in my hand, or smell flowers.

INTERSECTIONALITY

Introduction

How should we understand the concept of intersectionality given its ascendancy in feminist philosophy and in women's, gender, and sexuality studies as *the* way to theorize the synthesis, co-constitution, or interactivity of "race" and "gender"? As it has traveled from margin to center, "intersectionality" appears to have become a cliché, a commonplace, or a "buzzword" that garners widespread agreement that axes of oppression are not separable in our everyday experiences and therefore must be theorized together (K. Davis 2008). In a progressivist narrative, intersectionality is celebrated as a methodological triumph over "previous" essentialist and exclusionary approaches to theorizing identity and power relations; viewed as a research paradigm (Hancock 2007a, 2007b), it has even been characterized as the "most important contribution that women's studies has made so far" (McCall 2005, 1771), and is hailed as the inclusionary political orientation par excellence for the millennial generation (Hancock 2011). A quarter-century has elapsed since the term "intersectionality" was theorized by the Black feminist legal scholar Kimberlé Williams Crenshaw, who introduced the metaphor in 1989 and further elaborated the concept in 1991. One of the founders of Critical Race Theory in the U.S. legal academy, Crenshaw is the most widely cited (if rarely closely read) "originator" of intersectionality, although her work inherits a much longer history of Black feminist thought traced to the nineteenth century. In the intervening twenty-five years, it seems feminist theory has very much "settled down" with intersectionality. On the face of it this is a positive development, inasmuch as it demonstrates a consensus that homogenizing, essentialist, and exclusionary models of identity that falsely universalize relatively privileged experiences and identities to all "women," models that marginalize some (indeed, most) women while centering others, are unjust and inadequate to building truly emancipatory theories and political movements. But how does the prevailing conception of intersectionality, which (white-dominated) feminist theory has made very much its own, connect to Crenshaw's aims when she originally articulated the metaphor and developed the concept, or to the intellectual project of Black feminism? Although it is frequently characterized as "difficult work" (Nash 2010), intersectionality seems to have been "easily" appropriated by the white-dominated mainstream of feminist thought, even as Black feminism and women-of-color feminisms remain at the margins (or, are fetishized as tokens of "difference") and the social groups for which they advocate are systemically excluded from academic institutions. Nikol Alexander-Floyd diagnoses a "neocolonial," "post–black feminist approach . . . on intersectionality within the social sciences . . . that disappears or re-marginalizes black women" (2012, 9). All this raises the question, what is the relationship between intersectionality's "mainstreaming" (Dhamoon 2011) and the broader concerns of Black feminism, in which intersectionality is but one of a constellation of concepts, yet from which it seems to have become detached as the sole contribution this intellectual project has to offer?

These questions motivate my attempt in this book to examine the notion of intersectionality as a provisional concept and to explore how it may serve as a horizon of possibility for liberatory, coalitional feminist praxis in the embattled twenty-first century. Intersectionality faces a peculiar historical dilemma. On the one hand, the Anglo-American political mainstream declares that we find ourselves in a "postracial," "post-feminist," "postcolonial" era; identity-based claims are greeted with suspicion and groups seeking redress of historical injustice face public cynicism and fatigue. On the other hand, critical theories reveal not only that inequalities have not been attenuated, hierarchies have not been dismantled, and identities have not been dissipated into universal humanity; if anything, as global institutions adaptively reconfigure themselves in response to socially transformative movements, oppressive power relations have become increasingly mystified, inequalities seemingly more intractable, and institutions seemingly more difficult to transform. Moreover, an enduring obstacle to forming effective movements against oppressions is the fragmentation of identities and the divisions within and among communities of struggle—processes that are as much about violence, marginalization, and collusion with hegemonic power as they are about inadequate imaginations, flawed cognitive habits, and misplaced allegiances. Initially, intersectionality was explicitly aimed at contesting these representational, discursive, and intersubjective dynamics within antiracist and feminist movements seeking to transform social relations. Yet much of what Crenshaw's analysis revealed about identities, oppressions, and political struggle has been forgotten—some say systematically (Bilge 2013)—as intersectionality became mainstreamed as an institutionalized intellectual project. Although intersectionality has become an axiom of feminist theory and research and has been "institutionalized" (Nash 2008) in academic and, increasingly, in human-rights discourses and policy frameworks, flippant or vague references to "intersectionality" abound and can serve to obscure a profound critique of deeply entrenched cognitive habits that inform feminist and antiracist thinking about oppression and privilege. In other words, paradoxically, the success of intersectionality may mark its failure, the wide travel of the concept its shallow apprehension.

My aim in this book is neither to "settle" the various debates that "intersectionality" has generated nor to conclusively pronounce on its utility or inutility as a "grand theory" of oppression, discrimination, or identity (Cho, Crenshaw, and McCall 2013, 788–89). Instead, my point of departure is the observation that Crenshaw, Sumi Cho, and Leslie McCall make that "some of what circulates as critical debate about what intersectionality is or does reflects a lack of engagement with both originating and contemporary literatures on intersectionality" (788). I take up their call for "greater theoretical, methodological, substantive and political literacy" (792) and offer, in the chapters that follow, an engagement with Crenshaw's foundational texts, contextualized in the intellectual history which animates their framing of intersectionality as an analytic sensibility, a disposition, or a way of thinking. Indeed, I argue that intersectionality points to a way of thinking into which most of us have not yet become habituated. That is, I suggest intersectionality constitutes a profound challenge, as opposed to a determinate resolution of cognitive essentialism, binary categorization, and conceptual exclusion.

My intervention into the fraught field of "intersectionality studies" is twofold. On the one hand, I want to challenge the triumphal narrative of "political completion" (Wiegman 2012) that surrounds intersectionality as *the* way to theorize the relationship among systems of oppression. If intersectionality is bound to disappoint, as Robyn Wiegman argues (2012, 20), perhaps it is because the concept has been fundamentally misapprehended and tendentiously misappropriated. Detached from its political aims to redress Black women's invisibility in law and social-movement discourses, it has been harnessed to inverted representational objectives, namely, to signify mainstream feminism's arrival at a postracial moment. Intersectionality is routinely invoked as a corrective to exclusion within feminist theory and politics, whether it is espoused as the guarantor of ethico-political values, such as inclusion (Hancock 2011), or methodological values, such as complexity (McCall 2005). On the other hand, I argue that calls to go beyond intersectionality are premature. If, as I will try to show, intersectionality is a provisional concept, meant to get us to think about *how* we think, then the failure to confront it as such, and instead to deploy it as a theory of double or multiple oppression based on a positivist approach to categories (e.g., race, ethnicity, gender, gender identity, sexuality, disability, age, citizenship, etc.), means that the field of intersectionality studies is actually in its infancy (Collins 2009, vii)—neither at some impasse which signals its exhaustion nor at a mature phase which signals its completion. Accordingly, in seeking to "go beyond," the post-intersectional critique of intersectionality fails to fully confront the challenge to cognitive and perceptual habits that intersectionality advances. Intersectionality-as-challenge urges us to grapple with and overcome our entrenched perceptual-cognitive habits of essentialism, categorial purity, and segregation.

Taking a third way between complacency with intersectionality (as feminism's postracial *telos*) and its rejection in a premature attempt to "go beyond" intersectionality, I propose that immanent critiques of intersectionality (and of the field of "intersectionality studies") are crucial if we are to achieve analytic clarity, contextual rigor, and a politicized, historicized understanding of the trajectory of this concept. I argue that if intersectionality has been uprooted and transplanted in various sites, domains, and contexts, its roots in social-justice movements and critical intellectual projects—specifically, Black feminism—must be recovered, retraced, and embraced. Performing a close reading, in the chapters that follow I recover three overlooked yet crucial moments in Crenshaw's 1989 and 1991 essays: an overlooked metaphor that served as a companion metaphor to the now-famous intersection metaphor— that of the basement (1989, 151–52); an overlooked footnote in which Crenshaw makes it explicit that she intends "intersectionality" to serve as a provisional concept (1991, 1244–45n9); and an overlooked normative conclusion in which she argues that the implication of intersectionality for a theory and a politics of identity is that identities should be viewed as coalitions (1991, 1299). Finally, I synthesize my interpretation of intersectionality—as a provisional concept intimating the possibility of coalitional praxis—with decolonial feminism, which seeks to overcome the coloniality of heteropatriarchal gender: the violent historical enmeshing of binary gender in systems of capital, white supremacy, and empire (Lugones 2010, 747).

One of the implications of this heterodox reading of intersectionality is that it undermines the currently hegemonic view of the term as a synonym of double (or multiple) jeopardy. I argue against an understanding of intersectionality that, preserving the integrity of categories of "race," "gender," and other "axes" of oppression, conjoins them in order to "get at" the experiences of "multiply oppressed" groups. On this basis, I also contest the equation of "intersectionality" with the "race, gender, class (sexuality)" paradigm developed in sociology, psychology, and other empirical social sciences, which in my view is inherently additive even as it insists that "no simple mathematical relationship can capture the complexity of the interrelationships of these systems" (L. Weber 1998, 25; L. Weber 2010). While *stipulating* the simultaneous expression of "race, class, gender and sexuality . . . in every social situation," these categories are presupposed as analytically separable "systems of social hierarchies" (L. Weber 1998, 24). At first glance, the "crossroads" metaphor seems to support this kind of interpretation of intersectionality, as presupposing that "race" and "gender" constitute separate roads that meet at an intersection, which represents the social location of Black women (for instance) as the junction of "racial" and "gender" oppression. However, I argue against such a deployment of intersectionality, which assumes that the intersection of single-axis categories results in the representation of multiply oppressed groups (Lugones 2007). The categorial erasure and political exclusion of Black women from "women" and "Black people" is an intractable problem of representation which results from how the received categories have historically been produced and how they continue to be deployed. I disagree with theorists who argue that the intersection of categories changes their structure or content (see Garry 2012, 510). Intersectionality can make visible categorial exclusion, but it cannot remedy it at the level of representation; instead of complacency with received categories, it urges their reconceptualization—taking as the starting point for this process the social location of groups whose concrete, "simultaneous" experiences have been fragmented and distorted beyond recognition (CRC 1983; Lugones 2003; A. P. Harris 1990). Arguing against what has become the predominant usage of "intersectionality" may seem an exercise in futility; the reason for my insistence on this point is that I think the continued use of essentialist categories constructed through the privileging of the normative or prototypical members of groups reproduces (instead of contesting) this privilege at the prereflective, perceptual level (see Goff and Kahn 2013). Intersectionality was introduced as a politically engaged theoretical framework invested in sociolegal transformative praxis; its reduction to an additive conceptualization of oppression that reproduces exclusionary cognitive and perceptual habits thwarts its critical impetus. While it might be necessary to use existing categories in some instances, we should not harbor the illusion that their unadulterated junction constitutes "intersectionality."

In the later chapters of the book I emphasize how the political potential of intersectionality lies in our ability to reimagine our identities and our alignments in coalitional terms, revealing the inherent and potential impurity of categories by practicing their interconnectedness (see chapters 5 and 6). Intersectionality is often conflated with identity politics, in the sense that it is perceived as a narrow identitarianism that militates for the visibility of subjects caught in the intersection of race, gender, and other "axes" of oppression. (This assumes that intersectionality is an additive theory of double jeopardy, which, as I have already explained, I believe to be a misinterpretation.) The intersectional *critique* of identity politics—which reveals identity categories to be coalitions: internally heterogeneous, complex unities constituted by their internal differences and dissonances and by internal as well as external relations of power—has been overlooked by critics and post-intersectionality scholars who have misconstrued intersectionality as a naive form of identitarianism. Intersectionality is impelled by a politics of visibility for Black women; the implication of this liberatory politics—as the Combahee River Collective (CRC) articulated so powerfully in "A Black Feminist Statement"—is the "destruction of all the systems of oppression" (CRC 1983, 215). To understand why the liberation of Black women entails the liberation of all oppressed groups—why Black feminist politics are always already coalitional, even when they appear "separatist"—it is necessary to revisit the relationship of Crenshaw's intersection metaphor to the basement metaphor (see chapter 2). The CRC argues that Black (lesbian) women "might use our position at the bottom to make a clear leap into revolutionary action. If Black women were free it would mean that everyone else would have to be free since our freedom would necessitate the destruction of all the systems of oppression" (215). As Crenshaw's basement analogy shows, a symmetrical claim does not obtain with respect to an "identity politics" by and for relatively privileged members of oppressed groups, whose efforts to seek redress for the discrimination (only) they face within the parameters set by antidiscrimination discourses actually serve to reproduce social hierarchy, and specifically to condemn multiply oppressed groups to sociolegal invisibility, to relegate them to the "unprotected margins" of social life (Crenshaw 1989, 151–52; see chapters 2 and 4).

My perspective on intersectionality is an immanently critical one. To use the admittedly problematic metaphor of feminist "waves," intersectionality is a concept of undeniable importance in what are characterized as the "third" and "fourth" waves of feminism—although as we will see in chapter 1, its seeds were planted in the "first wave" and it put down roots in the "second" (see Thompson 2002). However, its easy appropriation means that often the aims of intersectionality are inverted, its theoretical content is oversimplified, and its political force is therefore effaced. This occurs in both critical and celebratory accounts, in which the metaphor is variously reduced to an additive junction of essentialist categories, upheld or dismissed as a naive form of identity politics, fetishized as *the* guarantor of political or theoretical inclusion, or aggrandized as a unified theory of "multiple oppressions." In my view, the transformative potential of intersectionality lies in its political and intellectual challenges to the normative segregation of social movements, liberatory discourses, cognitive matrices, and conceptual apparatuses. If those challenges have been systematically overlooked in the course of intersectionality's ascendancy, or conflated with the very different political norm of "inclusion," it is arguably within a "suspenseful" space carved by immanent critique—neither seeking to transcend intersectionality nor celebrating its "arrival"—that we can confront, tarry with, and understand its critical import, its theoretical significance, and its political potentialities. Paradoxically, if we are to advance the liberatory and transformative goals which initially motivated intersectionality, perhaps we need to suspend the assumption that the concept is itself the guarantor of these aims. One component of this project is to read intersectionality against the grain, contesting prevalent readings in what has come to be known as "intersectionality studies." This is not done merely out of a hermeneutic commitment to the "most accurate" reading, or to "police" or "discipline" the uses to which intersectionality is put, but rather in order to contribute to a collective process already under way of grappling with the concept's most generative interpretations (see May 2015).

I begin, in chapter 1, by offering a preliminary definition of "intersectionality" (drawn from Crenshaw's 1991 essay) and situating the concept in a trajectory of Black feminist thought that begins in the nineteenth century, tracing its relationship to antecedent concepts (double and triple jeopardy, interlocking oppressions) and contemporaneous concepts (multiple jeopardy, matrix of domination, etc.). I then examine intersectionality as a research paradigm that has crossed disciplinary boundaries and adduce four analytic benefits which its proponents claim it affords social theory: complexity, simultaneity, irreducibility, and inclusivity. Finally, I broach the fraught and complex question of identity in relation to intersectionality: If intersectionality is, in part, a framework for theorizing identity, should it be viewed as a general theory of identity, or as a theory of the identities of "multiply oppressed" groups, such as, prototypically, those of Black women? Can intersectionality account for the convergence of identity categories that confer privilege, and for those identities that are normatively "unmarked," such as those of white men?

In chapter 2, I recover an overlooked metaphor that, in Crenshaw's 1989 article "Demarginalizing the Intersection of Race and Sex: A Black Feminist Critique of Antidiscrimination Doctrine, Feminist Theory and Antiracist Politics," served as a companion metaphor to intersectionality: the basement metaphor. Largely forgotten in the "mainstreaming" of intersectionality, in addition to the now-famous intersection metaphor, Crenshaw offered the basement metaphor to show how—by privileging monistic, mutually exclusive, and analogically constituted categories of "race" and "sex" tethered, respectively, to masculinity and whiteness—antidiscrimination law functions to reproduce social hierarchy rather than to remedy it, systematically denying Black women plaintiffs legal redress. In this chapter I ask how we should interpret the widespread "forgetting" of the basement and the ascendancy of intersectionality. Why did the latter prove to be a more mobile traveling metaphor? I argue that the overlooking of the basement metaphor is symptomatic of the deracination of intersectionality from its origins in Black feminist thought, and that its effect has been to occlude Crenshaw's account of the sociolegal reproduction of hierarchical power. This theoretical argument is contextualized in a reading of recent antidiscrimination jurisprudence which reveals (contrary to what we might imagine or hope) that U.S. law entrenches, rather than alleviates, endemic discrimination, naturalizing systemic conditions of exploitation and oppression.

In chapter 3 my point of departure is an overlooked footnote in Crenshaw's 1991 article "Mapping the Margins: Intersectionality, Identity

Politics, and Violence against Women of Color," in which Crenshaw characterizes intersectionality as a "provisional concept." Elaborating an interpretation of intersectionality that sees it as anticipating or prefiguring the normative and theoretical goals that are often imputed to it, I argue that triumphal narrative of "political completion" (Wiegman 2012) that surrounds intersectionality—as *the* way to theorize the relationship among systems of oppression—helps to cement the impression of mainstream feminism's arrival at a postracial moment. First, I suggest we should approach intersectionality as a "provisional concept" that disorients entrenched cognitive habits. I draw on Sara Ahmed's (2006) work to suggest that disorientation is a vital, embodied experience that can not only reveal how we are presently normatively oriented but can also call into question or "queer" our normative orientations, leaving us productively unsure of how to move forward. We might contrast that productive uncertainty with the predominant view of intersectionality as "a kind of feminist truth, a proven account of how both identity and oppression are experienced" (Nash 2010). Finally, in this chapter I argue that we should exercise caution with respect to (postracial) discourses of "arrival" in which some deployments of intersectionality participate, as these seem to me to be motivated by a form of "aversive racism" within feminism (Son Hing et al. 2004), manifested in the simultaneous, nonperformative avowal and affective disavowal of antiracist and other anti-oppression politics.

In chapter 4, I discuss several critical arguments that have been advanced against or in relation to intersectionality, particularly in the last decade when the concept has increasingly come under scrutiny. On the one hand, the ascendancy of intersectionality was, from an early phase, marked by the relative absence of critique, which I suggest indicates a superficial engagement by scholars eager to embrace a concept that, once untethered from its origins and often emptied of its critical content, quickly began to circulate as a pliable "buzzword." On the other hand, some critiques that have, more recently, been articulated also fall prey to the tendency to oversimplify, misread, and reduce intersectionality to a shallow simile, overlooking its conceptual and political challenges to ways of thinking that are still prevalent and which critics often replicate even as they diagnose intersectionality's ostensible faults. Most critiques erroneously assume that intersectionality is, uncontroversially, a model of double or multiple jeopardy, amenable to positivist as well as postmodernist representational goals. In short, both critiques and approving deployments tend to overlook the critical significance of intersectionality, its provisional status, and its potential to destabilize essentialist cognitive habits. Given the shared premises of many critical and celebratory accounts, rather than simply dismissing critiques of intersectionality, in this chapter I read them as opportunities to consider the limitations of intersectionality's positivist deployments.

Following my assessment of these various critiques of the concept, in chapters 4 and 5, I continue my heterodox interpretation of intersectionality by examining its implications for theories of identity and for radical coalitional praxis. Although intersectionality has been overtly linked to coalition as a normative goal, few scholars have carefully examined Crenshaw's argument that an intersectional analysis ought to lead us to reconceptualize identities *as* coalitions (1991, 1299). Taking this overlooked normative conclusion as my point of departure, in this chapter I draw on social-movement history to explore the theoretical underpinnings and political implications of the claim that identity categories are potential coalitions, and trace the relationship of the concept of intersectionality to the concept of coalition in women-of-color feminisms. I suggest that reconceptualizing identities as coalitions enables us not only to form alliances across lines of experiential and political difference but also to constitute "coalitions of one" where one is aligned with all aspects of one's identity, particularly those that one has been encouraged to repress or deny. I argue that coalition should animate our understanding of intersectionality: conceptualizing intersectional identities in coalitional terms may help us avoid positivist and essentialist constructions of identity and subjectivity.

In chapter 6, I consider what it might mean to synthesize a robustly intersectional analytic sensibility with a decolonial politics. In Crenshaw's work and in the field of intersectionality studies, intersectionality lacks an explicit consideration of the coloniality of U.S. law and of the colonial and anticolonial dynamics in U.S. social movements. Yet a historicized understanding of oppressions requires an account of colonialism as an ongoing, diachronic process of long duration that haunts embodied identities, cognitive and perceptual habits, and human and nonhuman relationships. Using the architectural metaphor of "three pillars" upholding white supremacy, Andrea Smith has shown that coalitions among women of color and Indigenous women are imperiled by complicity in one another's marginalization, a phenomenon that is occluded by a singular, homogeneous conception of "racism" and a failure to view heteropatriarchy as crucial to its reproduction (2006, 2012). I juxtapose Smith's framework of "three pillars of white supremacy" and María Lugones's "modern/colonial gender system" with intersectionality to examine the points of convergence and divergence between these concepts. I also elaborate the reading of intersectionality, interlocking oppressions, and "intermeshed oppressions" advanced by Lugones (2003, 2007, 2010). Lugones argues that intersectionality—as a critique of colonial institutions, such as U.S. law, that embody the "logic of purity"—is compatible with but not identical to the coalitional, decolonial feminist project of overcoming the "coloniality of gender," that is, "racialized, capitalist gender oppression" (2010, 747). I suggest that in her decolonial feminism we can discern "post-post-intersectional" glimpses (Crenshaw 2014) that can help us to reanimate the interpretation of intersectionality I have been advancing in this book: as a struggle concept prefiguring the tasks ahead—including the formation of identities-as-coalitions that preserve multiplicity and heterogeneity—as opposed to a truth taken as axiomatic, signifying feminism's theoretical "completion."

We find ourselves at a juncture between skeptics who declare "intersectionality fatigue" and celebrants who declare "intersectionality's arrival." If we could articulate what is wrong with each of these positions, could we reinterpret intersectionality without taking for granted, as self-evident or as truism, the meaning of categorial "intersection" but rather using the intersection to reveal and contest categorial exclusions that are deeply entrenched in our perceptual, cognitive, and political lives? Animated by concerns stemming from women-of-color feminisms and decolonial feminisms, I problematize the institutionalization, mainstreaming, or neocolonization of intersectionality, tracing these developments to particular occlusions of Crenshaw's argument—provisionality (the footnote); hierarchy (the basement metaphor); coalitional identity (the normative conclusion)—that facilitated the deracination, detachment, and deployment of the concept in ways that may evacuate it of its political challenge and its political promise.

1

Intersectionality, Black Feminist Thought, and Women-of-Color Organizing

Although disembodied and depoliticized invocations of "intersectionality" abound, and some scholars pronounce favorably while others look skeptically on the "vagueness" or indeterminacy of the metaphor, it is at the outset important to recognize that the concept originates as a political intervention with determinate aims, inheriting a long history of struggle. The concept of intersectionality is fruitfully situated in a trajectory of Black feminist thought that begins in the nineteenth century, when African American women resisting the "whips and stings of prejudice, whether of colour or sex" articulated what it means to be confronted, as Anna Julia Cooper put it in 1892, by both "a woman question" and a "race problem" but to be constructed "as yet an unknown or unacknowledged factor in both" (Cooper [1892] 1998, 112; see Cooper [1930] 1998). Elise Johnson McDougald identifies in 1925 not only "the double task" that Black women confront but also the conflicts they face due to the divisions between "sex" and "race" in the emancipation struggle: "their feminist efforts are directed chiefly toward the realization of the equality of the races, the sex struggle assuming a subordinate place" (Johnson McDougald [1925] 1995, 82). Sojourner Truth's speech "Woman's Rights," delivered in 1851, disputes the prototypicality of white women's experiences in defining women's oppression:

> Look at my arm! I have ploughed, and planted, and gathered into barns, and no man could head me! And a'n't I a woman? I could work

as much and eat as much as a man—when I could get it—and bear de lash as well! And a'n't I a woman? I have borne thirteen chilern, and seen 'em mos' all sold off to slavery, and when I cried out with my mother's grief, none but Jesus heard me! And a'n't I a woman? (Truth [1851] 1995, 36)

Truth predicts that the movements for suffrage and abolition will have "white men . . . in a fix pretty soon" (36). However, the phenomenon that nearly a century and a half later Crenshaw will call "political intersectionality"—the segregation of feminist and antiracist agendas and the marginalization of women of color in both—will prove to militate against challenges to white male power and actually function to preserve white male privilege (see chapter 2).

Kathryn T. Gines traces what she terms "proto-intersectional" analyses operative in "early black feminism from the 1830s to the 1930s, long before we had the term intersectionality," citing Maria W. Stewart, Truth, Cooper, Ida B. Wells, McDougald, and Sadie Tanner Mosell Alexander as paradigmatic exponents of an engaged social analysis that, "through activist organizing and campaigning," challenged racism and sexism "not only as separate categories impacting identity and oppression, but also as systems of oppression that work together [and] mutually reinforce each other" (2014, 14, 24–25; Tong and Botts 2014, 216–17; see also Gines 2011). Eric S. McDuffie (2011) recovers the politically repressed history of what he calls "black left feminists" such as Claudia Jones, Louise Thompson Patterson, Beulah Richardson, and Esther Cooper Jackson, radicals whose grassroots activism, research, and analysis were vital not only to the rise of the Communist Party in Harlem and other Black communities in the mid-1930s but also to the formation of "collective identities" of struggle for African American women and of integrative paradigms for theorizing multiple oppressions that emerge in the 1970s and 1980s in Black feminist thought. Intersectionality originates in social-movement discourses that identified the manifold manifestations of oppression, discrimination, and violence that structure the conditions in which women of color live in the United States, Britain, and other white settler and imperial states. It is significant to retrace this history as an antidote to the appropriation and commodification of the intersection signifier, which, when emptied of its critical and subversive force, appears amenable to various neocolonial institutional projects of "diversity management" (Puar 2012, 53; Ahmed 2012). Properly recontextualized, intersectionality represents the condensation of social-movement and critical academic knowledges, motivated by insurrectionary intentions, transformative visions, and collective struggles.

In this chapter, focusing on its development in twentieth-century U.S. social-movement discourses, I discuss the relationship of intersectionality to antecedent concepts "double jeopardy," "triple jeopardy," and "interlocking oppressions" and its contemporaneous concepts ("multiple jeopardy" and "matrix of domination"). I then examine intersectionality as a research paradigm that has crossed disciplinary boundaries and adduce four analytic benefits that its proponents claim it affords social theory: complexity, simultaneity, irreducibility, and inclusivity. Finally, I broach the fraught and complex question of identity in relation to intersectionality: Is intersectionality a framework for theorizing identity, and if so, what "kind" of identity does it theorize?

ERASURE OF ORIGINS

By the mid-1980s, the language of "intersections"—if not the metaphor and concept of intersectionality as Crenshaw would, in a few years' time, elaborate them—had already been circulating in antiracist feminist thought. Antecedents of intersectionality include the notions of "double jeopardy" (Beal 1970a), "triple jeopardy" (TWWA c. 1970), "multiple jeopardy" (D. K. King 1988), and "interlocking oppressions" (CRC 1983). However, it is important to notice that these—as well as related concepts such as "interstices" (Spillers 1984) and "matrix of domination" (Collins 1990)—are all distinct concepts, each deserving of careful analysis. We sometimes encounter claims in the literature that one or another term is superior to and should be substituted for "intersectionality" (see, e.g., Razack 1998, 2005; Tong and Botts 2014, 248; see chapter 4). What happens even more often is that antecedent concepts are anachronistically conflated with intersectionality. In this respect, while it is of crucial importance to trace genealogies of intersectionality in historically previous intellectual and political movements, I tend to disagree that it is useful to characterize nineteenth-century Black feminism as "proto-intersectional," as Gines does (2014), or to retrospectively equate Black Communist theories of Black women's "superexploitation" under capitalism with intersectionality, as McDuffie does (2009, 2011). To do so is to flatten the contextual and denotative differences among distinct concepts, a move enabled by their connotative similarities. McDuffie argues that the erasure of "black left feminists" as a result of cold war political repression and their marginalization in histories of Black radicalism meant that some Black feminists organizing and writing in the 1970s—such as Frances Beal of the Third World Women's Alliance and Barbara Smith of the Combahee River Collective, who articulated conceptions of "double jeopardy" and "interlocking oppressions," respectively—were unaware of their "predecessors' work" and "had to reinvent the wheel" (2011, 209). Although McDuffie's meticulous history of Black Communist women's praxis guards against the false impression that Black feminism is a static, uniform body of thought, his use of "intersectionality" (understood as a theory of multi-axial oppression) as an analytic to trace its radical left genealogy risks positing that the concept has "always already" been there. His genealogical method raises an issue about the relationship of concepts to analysis: to say, for instance, that "early black feminists clearly understood the uniquely cruel, interlocking oppressions experienced by black women under capitalism," even though they "never used terms such as 'superexploitation,' 'triple oppression'" (2011, 48), or—for that matter—"intersectionality" is to assume the superfluousness of concepts, that is, to see them as "terms" that do not fundamentally alter, and reflect, the nature of the analysis being advanced.

Indeed, in the literature on intersectionality, Crenshaw is often said to have merely "coined" a term for a preexisting concept (see Collins 2011, 92). This is not only to diminish her philosophical creativity but also to elide intersectionality with an additive theory of "double jeopardy," or to a now accepted "truism" that racism and sexism "interact" in lived experience or are "mutually constitutive" at the level of social structure. In this way, Crenshaw is made to seem to be doing both less and more:

Intersectionality, Black Feminist Thought, and Women-of-Color Organizing less in that she is represented as merely "recycling" a preexisting concept (Nash 2008); more in that she is alleged to have constructed a positive theory of multiple oppressions. However, even on the latter view, despite their being given a now-obligatory citation, Crenshaw's texts are infrequently engaged deeply or closely (see Collins 2011, 92); even rarer is their careful juxtaposition with antecedent or contemporaneous texts. Rather than assume, as Nina Lykke suggests, that "the introduction of the concept of intersectionality . . . provided a name for a multiplicity of ongoing feminist debates" (2010, 78), a close engagement with the concept reveals its specific analytic and political functions, which cannot be assumed to preexist its elaboration or to be equivalent to other kinds of integrative theoretical frameworks. Thus, although Lykke offers a typology of "intersectional theories" that, in addition to those which "explicitly use the concept," includes what she calls "implicit feminist theorizings of intersectionality" and "feminist theorizings of intersectionality under other names," I suggest that intersectionality is not merely a nominal label for phenomena that may just as well be conceptualized "using other concepts and frames than intersectionality"; rather, intersectionality has a determinate extension, indexes a specific set of meanings, and is motivated by particular political and theoretical concerns (68).

Nikol Alexander-Floyd makes a useful distinction between intersectionality as an "ideograph" and intersectionality as an idea: "As an 'ideograph'"—an ideological paradigm signified by a single term—intersectionality "stands in for the broad body of scholarship that has sought to examine and redress the oppressive forces that have constrained the lives of black women in particular and women of color more generally" (2012, 4). As an idea, intersectionality constitutes "an analytically distinct concept" articulated in Crenshaw's work (4). Alexander-Floyd astutely points out that "these two dimensions" are frequently collapsed, and intersectionality is reduced to Crenshaw's definition in a way that decontextualizes and dehistoricizes her intervention in "the longstanding project of theorising by women of colour about identity from which [intersectionality] is derived," but without paying careful attention to the content of Crenshaw's argument either (4). Readings that "flatten" intersectionality (Michelle Fine quoted in Berger and Guidroz 2009,

70) by ignoring the structural sources of inequality while "just multiplying identity categories" (Crenshaw quoted in Berger and Guidroz 2009, 70) efface its liberatory aims (see chapter 2).

Jennifer Nash argues that intersectionality is used to mark the temporality of feminism, functioning paradoxically both as its "already-transcended past" and its "inevitable future" (2014b, 46). Although these invocations seem, at first glance, contradictory, they share a racialized ideology regarding the generative connection of Black women to intersectionality: "When intersectionality is imagined as feminism's future, intersectionality sheds black women in a postracial feminism that either presumes that black women need not be the center of intersectional work because intersectionality's virtue is complexity not identity politics *or* that intersectionality is an endlessly expansive analytic that can—and should—describe all subjects' experiences" (46). For Kathy Davis, the purported "vagueness" of intersectionality constitutes a theoretical strength: "Its lack of clear-cut definition or even specific parameters has enabled it to be drawn upon in nearly any context of inquiry" (2008, 77). Ange-Marie Hancock has argued that its association with women of color "obscure[s] the very richness of the content—the multivocality for which intersectionality is known": its methodological "prospects are far brighter" than the "inclusion-oriented content specialization for which intersectional scholarship is well known (2007a, 249–50). Yet for the "brighter prospects" of intersectionality to be realized, it must be severed from Black women's lives and bodies, which are overdetermined by their racialized gender as specific (as opposed to the "generic," "unmarked," "universal" categories of maleness and whiteness) and are only contingently the object of intersectional analyses. The easy appropriation of the model of intersectionality depends upon a "resubjugation of black women's knowledges" (Alexander-Floyd 2012, 11) even as the "complexity" that it ostensibly lends scholarship is based on a perception of Black women's identities as "complex" inasmuch as they are irreducible to categories of race (constructed through male solipsism) and gender (constructed through white solipsism). However, the fetishization of complexity—embodied in the call for "more intersections" (Nash 2014b, 46)—obscures the fact that "the issue is one of subjugation, not complexity" (Alexander-Floyd 2012, 11). Figured as feminism-future, the plea for proliferating intersectionality as feminist method par excellence (either by attending to previously ignored intersections of identity or by performing intersectional analyses in new empirical sites) is "underpinned by a belief that the analytic can radically transform" feminism and women's, gender, and sexuality studies (Nash 2014b, 46). However, in what is proclaimed as a post-identitarian theoretical moment, intersectionality is also increasingly cast as feminism-past by post-intersectionality scholars who view it as irredeemably and naively identitarian (46). "In both cases," argues Nash, "it is intersectionality's intimate engagement with black female flesh that is treated as suspect" (46). Both injunctions—to proliferate intersectionality and to relegate it to the past—treat the generative relation between Black feminism and intersectionality as contingent, accidental, and even compromising. If intersectionality is reduced to an identity claim, it is in part due to the fact that Black women's theorizing is constructed as a particularist narrative relevant only to their own "marked," specific, local experiences. Furthermore, the aspects of the concept of intersectionality as Crenshaw articulates it that appear to have had the most purchase are precisely those that reduce to white feminist concerns as they themselves understand and articulate them.

One paradoxical effect of intersectionality's discursive prevalence has been the reduction of the plural insights and analyses of Black feminisms and women-of-color feminisms to the status of critique of white feminism's exclusions (Roshanravan 2014; see, e.g., K. Davis 2008, 70; Zack 2007, 197). To the extent that intersectionality does function as such a critique, it might, paradoxically, be in part a consequence of abiding white solipsism that intersectionality has enjoyed this degree of "mainstream" success. As such, "intersectionality" is sometimes appropriated by white feminism as tokenized knowledge produced *by* feminists of color—but which is really *for* the moral enhancement of white feminism. Some instrumentalizing invocations of intersectionality—as way to "pay attention to difference"—are explicitly aimed at ensuring the relevance of academic feminist work, since, it is claimed, "at this particular juncture in gender studies, any scholar who neglects difference runs the risk of having her work viewed as theoretically misguided, politically irrelevant, or simply fantastical" (K. Davis 2008, 68; see also McWhorter 2004, 38–39). If a "theroretical division of labour between those of us who work on difference and those of us who don't" (Lugones 2003, 68) has becomes increasingly difficult to sustain within feminist scholarship, the question for the disengaged yet self-interested scholar becomes, "What can I gain from intersectionality?" (Hancock 2007a, 251; see Alexander-Floyd 2012, 15). In this vein, intersectionality sometimes becomes deployed by white feminists in service of overcoming what Lugones calls "the alleged problem of difference in their theorizing" (2003, 71): "Racist feminism does not see the violence done to women of color in denying that we are women or in requiring (the alternative is conceptually forced on us) that we assimilate if we are to be women at all" (70). This is conceived as a theoretical problem that requires a theoretical solution: "the attempted solutions to the 'problem of difference' try to rescue feminist theorising from . . . pitfalls that would render it false, trivial, weak, and so on" (72). Because it is assumed that the critique of "racist feminism" (Lorde 1984) "undermine[s] fundamentally the possibility of any theorizing to the extent that theorizing requires generalization. . . . [T]he focus of the solutions is on how to generalize without being guilty of false inclusion" (Lugones 2003, 70, 72; see A. P. Harris 1990). Lugones's parsing of "the problem of difference" helps to explain the popularity of intersectionality as a positivist theory of multi-axial oppressions, inasmuch as the addition of discrete categories of social analysis does nothing to displace the centrality to (white) feminist theorizing of a category of gender conceptualized through essentializing white (heterosexual, bourgeois, able-bodied, U.S. citizen, cisgender) women's experiences to those of all women (see A. P. Harris 1990; see chapter 3). Intersectionality is instrumentalized to advance white feminism's self-exoneration—effectively shutting down or defusing antiracist critique—and to secure its continued relevance in a shifting knowledge commodity market modulated by institutions' neoliberal absorption, containment, tokenization, and management of "diversity" (see Conclusion).

Perhaps the most egregious erasure of intersectionality's origins occurs when the concept is represented by white feminists as their own innovation, situated in a trajectory of white feminisms, rather than as an insight generated, and a theory elaborated, by Black feminists. To cite but one example, in their introduction to a recently published conference proceedings, editors Helma Lutz, Maria Teresa Herrera Vivar, and Linda Supik identify as the inaugural texts of intersectionality's "long history" (white) Marxist-feminist accounts of the relation between capitalism and patriarchy (they cite Michèle Barrett and Mary McIntosh's *The Anti-Social Family* (1982), "interventions from the perspective of (white) lesbian feminism . . . and publications on the connections between gender and disability" (Lutz, Herrera Vivar, and Supik 2011, 2). Here, a concept that, in part, performs a critique of white feminism is represented as the accomplishment of white feminism (20; see also Lykke 2011, 208; May 2015, 147). By flattening the difference between intersectional and other "integrative" approaches to feminist theory, which may well combine or synthesize previously discrete systems of oppression and exploitation (such as capitalism and patriarchy), intersectionality is rendered race-uncritical, effectively detached from Black and women-of-color feminisms—and more specifically from Crenshaw's work. Arguably, this appropriation is symptomatic of what Gail Lewis diagnoses as an "unconscious and unwitting disavowal and displacement . . . of the relevance and toxicity of race" to feminist discourse (2013, 870; see also Lewis 2009). In her "Postscript" to the volume edited by Lutz, Herrera Vivar, and Supik, Crenshaw expresses similar reservations about the uses to which "intersectionality" was put at this conference: "The debates seemed to be animated by propositions, expectations, and claims about intersectionality that were neither articulated nor fully attributed" (2011a, 221, see also 223). Not only is Black feminism erased as intersectionality's originating discourse, but women of color are erased from the socialist, lesbian, and anti-ableist discourses that are constructed as originary. In other words, Black feminisms are ideologically conflated with the race/gender dualism, which ostensibly expresses Black women's "intersectional" identity.

The retrospective gesture of erasure of the Black feminist genealogy of intersectionality—and the coalitional politics of women-of-color feminisms—are symptomatic of the "reinvention" of the concept "at the scene of the argument" to advance academic or institutional aims, deracinating it from "its origins in concrete campaigns for social justice" (Chun, Lipsitz, and Shin 2013, 920–21; see Tomlinson 2013). Moreover, the ideological construction of intersectionality as "feminist past" or "feminist future"—to borrow Nash's evocative terminology—means (mis)reading intersectionality as an epistemological guarantor of inclusion of women of color, as opposed to an index of exclusion, erasure, and marginalization. Whether it is cast as having already transcended exclusions, as having failed to resolve "the problem of difference," or as constituting the means to doing so in the imminent future, intersectionality is circulated in a moral economy as the currency of visibility for women of color; it has become a commodified signifier in a white-centered narrative of feminist progress through its appropriation and deracination, paradoxically contributing to the resubjugation of Black feminist knowledges (Alexander-Floyd 2012), the elision of women-of-color feminist movement history (Chun, Lipsitz, and Shin 2013), and the erasure of Black women's bodies (Nash 2014b). If this is true, the theoretical ascendancy of intersectionality should be read symptomatically as an indication of deep, unresolved problems of representation, power, and epistemic violence within feminist theory and politics, not celebrated as their transcendence.

RETRACING INTERSECTIONALITY'S ROOTS

When it is acknowledged, the contribution of Black and other women-of-color feminisms to white-dominated feminist theory is often seen to consist in integrating considerations of "race" into white solipsistic—but otherwise supposedly adequate—discourses about gender. On this reading, the "intersection" of "race" with "gender" cannot be anything but additive, since the constitution of the category "gender" through the exclusion of women of color is not interrogated. Intersectionality is represented as merely remedial to white feminists' ignorance of their own racial power and of their racial/class oppression of women of color. This is, in part, due to what Shireen Roshanravan describes as a "homogenizing tendency of superficial engagement that glosses Women of Color scholarship as a unified genre of thought defined solely in terms of its critique of feminism's racism" (2014, 41). Understood in these terms, women-of-color feminism cannot *but* have succeeded a prior, originary (if admittedly flawed) white feminism, which is dated to the nineteenth century. This temporal marginalization also results in a "whitewashing of second-wave feminism [that] has enabled the rise of a myth about all women of color being hostile to feminism, a myth that fails to explain the actual organizing done by feminists of color" (Roth 2004, 10). The erasure of women of color from feminism reproduces white hegemony (K. Springer 2005, 3). Kimberly Springer and Benita Roth have each argued for the parallel, synchronous development of white feminist and women-of-color feminist ideologies, activisms, and organizations (Springer 2005, 3; Roth 2004, 8). According to Roth's social-movement history, *Separate Roads to Feminism: Black, Chicana and White Feminist Movements in America's Second Wave*, "scholars have misunderstood the timing of feminist emergences" (2004, 8). White feminism has mistakenly been seen to originate first, with women-of-color feminisms emerging later "to add the factor of race/ethnicity to the feminist project" (8). However, this is inaccurate, since "there was roughly simultaneous emergence by 1968 of white and Black feminist groups. . . . Chicana feminists organized as early as 1969" (8).

Despite the notion often heard today that feminism was always a "white" movement deemed irrelevant by women of color, in the 1960s, Roth insists,

> many African American women activists and many Chicana activists became *feminists*, . . . espous[ing] a feminism that incorporated analyses of the consequences of mutually reinforcing oppressions of gender, race/ethnicity, and class (and, less frequently, sexual orientation), analyses which in turn influenced white feminists, such that feminists today acknowledge as axiomatic the necessity of recognizing multiple sources of domination in women's (and men's) lives. In short, in Black and Chicana feminisms of the second wave we find the roots of feminist insights about the *intersectionality* of inequalities in people's lives. (2004, 11, emphases in original; see also Burnham 2005, 24–25)

In *Living for the Revolution: Black Feminist Organizations, 1968–1980*, Springer characterizes Black feminist politics in autonomous organizations—such as the Third World Women's Alliance, the National Black Feminist Organization, the Combahee River Collective, the National Alliance of Black Feminists, and Black Women Organized for Action—as an "interstitial politics focused on articulating their race, gender, and class [and in some cases their sexual] identities as interconnected" (2005, 4, 5). "The interstitial politics formulated by black feminists stated that their socially constructed collective identity emerged from between that of 'blacks' and 'women'" (11), that is, "in the cracks" between two identity categories that left "black women with allegiances to black and women's rights 'feeling divided against ourselves'" (45, quoting Demita Frazier). Their participation in civil rights movements contributed to the "sparking of a black radical imagination," as a result of which "black feminists experienced increasing degrees of cognitive liberation, or awareness, first around racial issues and then gender oppression," which they "carried with them into the women's movement" (13). Black feminists formulated an interstitial politics in relation to discourses that, as they were "keenly aware," "did not include the simultaneous eradication of racism and sexism" (20–21). However, as Springer documents, Black feminist organizations in this period often struggled to "reconcile the heterogeneity of members' class and sexual orientation identities" through consciousness-raising, which "illuminated classism and homophobia as sites of struggle *within* black feminist organizations" and led to "schisms" that constituted causal factors in organizations' decline (17, emphasis in original; see chapter 5).

I now turn to a discussion of four precursor concepts to intersectionality: double jeopardy (Beal 1970a, 1970b), triple jeopardy (TWWA c. 1970), multiple jeopardy (D. K. King 1988), and interlocking oppressions (CRC 1983). Through a close reading, I want to challenge the assumption that these are interchangeable terms that refer, essentially, to "the same thing." This ostensibly shared referent is reduced to the lowest common denominator—that is, the barest description of elements they share in common: namely, the use of multiple categories of oppression and identity to describe, politicize, and struggle against the conditions facing Black women in the United States (although, it should be noted, they do not focus exclusively either on the United States or on Black women). This, in itself, was and remains an indisputably crucial task, since, as Beal wrote, "In attempting to analyse the situation of the Black woman in America, one crashes abruptly into a solid wall of grave misconceptions, outright distortions of fact, and defensive attitudes on the part of many" (1970b, 109). Indeed, the trajectory of intersectionality is beset with precisely such epistemic and affective obstacles as the earliest Black feminists describe in their statements. Accordingly, to Crenshaw's intersection metaphor and basement metaphor we might juxtapose Beal's metaphor of the "solid wall" that illustrates the institutionalized and habitual underpinnings of "hermeneutic marginalization and interpretative violence," productive of what Crenshaw more recently has articulated as an experience of "speaking into the void" (May 2014, 95; see Crenshaw 1991; see chapter 2).

DOUBLE JEOPARDY AND TRIPLE JEOPARDY

Beal's defining essay "Double Jeopardy: To Be Black and Female," which first circulated in a pamphlet, *Black Woman's Manifesto*, distributed by the Third World Women's Alliance in 1970, gives foundational importance to "the system of capitalism (and its after birth . . . racism)" for "reducing the black man in america to such abject oppression" and leaving "the black woman [with] no protector," subjecting "her" to sexual assault "by the white colonizer" and to "the worst kind of economic exploitation, having been forced to serve as the white woman's maid and wet nurse while her own children were, more often than not, starving and neglected" (Beal 1970a, 19, 22). Rejecting the twin "fallacies" of "black matriarchy" and "black patriarchy" as myth and as "counterrevolutionary," respectively, Beal advocates the "elimination of all kinds of oppression" (22–23). She argues that "capitalism finds it expedient to reduce women to a state of enslavement," to "systematically exploit" them as "a surplus labor supply" whose "superexploitation" is exacerbated through their exclusion from "racist and chauvinistic" unions (25); moreover, women's dehumanization gives "men a false feeling of superiority (at least in their own home or in their relationships with women)" that serves as "an escape valve for capitalism" (24). Beal addresses the "outright surgical genocide" of forced and coerced sterilization programs targeting "black women and men" not only within the territorial United States but also in clinics its government sponsors in "non-white countries" such as India and in U.S. colonies such as Puerto Rico, where "the salpingectomy has now become the commonest operation . . . so widespread that it is referred simply as 'la operación'" (26–27). Beal interprets forced sterilization, the unavailability of safe birth-control methods, and the criminalization of abortion as "symptoms" of a "repressive," "decadent society that jeopardizes the health of black women (and thereby the entire black race) in its attempts to control the very life processes of human beings" (29; see Beal 2005, 36).

Beal is unequivocal that Black women's struggle "for total emancipation" may have parallels with parts of white women's liberation movement—which she stresses "is far from being monolithic"—but "if the white groups do not realize" that women's emancipation requires "fighting capitalism and racism"—which, despite "the institutionalization" of "male chauvinism" in U.S. society, constitutes "the fundamental cause of the female condition"—then "we do not have common bonds" (1970a, 29–30). In other words, Beal insists on the primacy and foundational status of "a debilitating economic and social system" to Black women's oppression. She locates Black women—whom she describes as "slave[s] of a slave" (21–22)—at the bottom of a social hierarchy that can only be demolished with an eye to the bottom:

> The new world that we are struggling to create must destroy oppression of any type. The value of this new system will be determined by the status of those persons who are presently most oppressed— the low man on the totem pole [*sic*]. Unless women in any enslaved nation are completely liberated, the change cannot really be called a revolution. If the black woman has to retreat to the position she occupied before the armed struggle, they whole movement and the whole struggle will have retreated in terms of truly freeing a colonized population. (31)

During this period, Beal and her comrades were intensely engaged in research and activism against sterilization abuse—as we have seen, a central issue discussed in "Double Jeopardy: To Be Black and Female." The essay was intended for publication in Robin Morgan's collection *Sisterhood Is Powerful* (1970)—Beal explains that Morgan "wanted an essay on black women"—and also appeared in the same year in Toni Cade Bambara's anthology *The Black Woman* (Beal 2005, 37; see Roth 2004, 91–92). The concept of "double jeopardy" is not explicitly defined in Beal's essay, which was written in the context of consciousness-raising discussions in the Black Women's Liberation Committee (BWLC) of the Student Nonviolent Coordinating Committee (SNCC) in New York City in 1968 and 1969. With SNCC's demise, the BWLC was renamed the Black Women's Alliance (BWA) in 1969 and then, in 1970, renamed the Third World Women's Alliance (TWWA) to reflect the fact that non-African-identified Puerto Rican members had joined the organization. The TWWA became a site of coalitional activism between women of the two (overlapping) communities—Puerto Rican and African American—against reproductive oppression and state repression, and challenging male-dominated nationalist movements' attempts to control and exploit women's fertility and to subordinate them in revolutionary struggle (Beal 2005, 39–40; Burnham 2005, 20–21; see Nelson 2003, 59–60; Anderson-Bricker 1999). According to Linda Burnham, a member of the West Coast (San Francisco) chapter, the TWWA "grew out of a kind of dissatisfaction . . . amongst women in SNCC about the role of women" in that organization (2005, 19). As Burnham recalls, the TWWA became a multiethnic organization predominantly "made up of African American women, Asian women, and Latinas" and (at least) one Arab American member (19); in 1980 its West Coast chapter went through a transformation and became the Alliance against Women's Oppression, which included white women (23; see chapter 5).

At around the same time the BWA was renamed the TWWA, the concept of "double jeopardy" shifted to "triple jeopardy" to explicitly reference the triad of race, gender, and class (Beal 2005, 40). Indeed, the TWWA named its journal, published from 1971 to 1975, *Triple Jeopardy*, with the explanatory subtitle Racism, Imperialism, Sexism (TWWA c.

1970; Roth 2004, 11; Nelson 2003, 63; Aguilar 2012). Burnham reflects that "the intention of that newspaper was really to speak to the ways in which women of color experience the world, and speak to the issues that were not at that time being addressed by the white women's movement, or the mainstream women's movement" (2005, 20). Roth contends that the "TWWA established early the concept of Black feminist organizing as intersectional, with Black women constituting a 'vanguard center' whose liberation would mean the liberation of all" (2004, 91). This assessment converges with that of Beal herself, who, in an interview with Loretta Ross, reflects that the activists in the New York chapter of the TWWA challenged the "narrow perception" of a single-axis conception of feminism: "what we were trying to deal with was the integration of race, gender, class, in consciousness, and not like just put one above the other, because we didn't think it actually operated as one is more important than the other" (Beal 2005, 43). This integrative conception of how "oppression and exploitation . . . operate in the real world . . . came up in opposition to other kinds of ideological trends like Marxism or historical materialism," which insist on the foundational status of class exploitation (43). In this interview, Ross makes explicit the link between "double jeopardy" and "what Kimberly [*sic*] Crenshaw two decades later called intersectionality"; Beal replies: not "just her. It was that whole stream of white quote 'feminists.' Academicians is, I guess, the term we should use there" (44).

Although Beal seems to situate "double jeopardy" in tension with predecessor Marxist ideologies and successor "intersectional" frameworks, McDuffie's rich history of Black women's engagement in U.S. Communism illuminates some of the Marxist-Leninist influences on her thinking—even if Beal may not have been "initially aware" of them when writing her germinal essay (McDuffie 2011, 209). Specifically, Black women who agitated within the Communist left, such as Claudia Jones, who popularized the "superexploitation thesis" with respect to Black women's "location at the bottom of American society," viewed Black women domestic workers as "the vanguard of social change" 2011, 116). In her influential essay "An End to the Neglect of the Problems of the Negro Woman!" published in 1949 in the CPUSA's theoretical journal, *Political Affairs*, Jones argued that "Negro women—as workers, as Negroes, and as women—are the most oppressed stratum of the whole population" ([1949] 1995, 109). Jones revised the Marxist-Leninist concept of "superexploitation"—referencing "uniquely severe, persistent, and dehumanizing forms of capitalist exploitation" (McDuffie 2011, 8)—by linking it to Black women's role in reproduction. The occupational segregation of Black women in domestic service is "inherently connected" to "the special oppression [they] face" as Black people, as women, and as workers (Jones [1949] 1995, 111). The relegation of Black women to reproductive labor is justified by "the white chauvinist stereotype as to where [their] place should be," namely, the "stereotype of the Negro slave mother," "a traditional 'mammy' who puts the care of children and families of others above her own" (111). Thus, capitalist political economy structurally positions Black women in ways that coercively limit their own reproductive self-determination, while extracting maximal value from their reproductive and productive labor through their "complete exclusion from virtually all fields of work except the most menial and underpaid, namely, domestic service" (110). Jones argues that this process has, simultaneously, a racialized and gendered character: "The superexploitation of the Negro woman worker is thus revealed not only in that she receives, as woman, less than equal pay for equal work with men, but that the majority of Negro women get less than half the pay of white women" (110). As McDuffie parses it, Jones's view was that "triply exploited black women constituted" not only "the most exploited" group of workers but also "the most revolutionary segment of the U.S. working class, thereby challenging orthodox Marxist postulations that industrial (white male) workers represented the [revolutionary] vanguard" (2009, 34). Jones was inspired by the organizing efforts of the New York Domestic Workers Union, formed in 1936, but also echoed the analyses of three of her contemporaries: Esther Cooper Jackson, who authored the "most thorough study of black women household workers' unionizing during the Depression" (McDuffie 2009, 31) in the form of her master's thesis, "The Negro Woman Domestic Worker in Relation to Trade Unionism" in 1940 (Cooper Jackson [1940] 2015); Louise Thompson Patterson, who advanced an analysis of "triple exploitation" in her 1936 essay, "Toward a Brighter Dawn" (Thompson Patterson 2015); and Marvel Cooke, whose 1950 essay "The Bronx Slave Market," published in the NAACP journal, *The Crisis*, exposed "the race and class divisions between black and white women," constructed through white women's exploitation of Black women's domestic labor (see Cooke [1950] 2015; McDuffie 2009, 31, 34; McDuffie 2011, 170; L. Harris 2012). Eschewing universalizing accounts of gender, racial, or class unity, Jones invoked the concept of superexploitation to argue that "various other class fractions (including other exploited workers) benefit from" Black women's labor power and that their exclusion from trade unions and the existence of laws that limited their property rights and regulated their sexual, intimate, and reproductive lives politically and juridically normalized this superexploitation (Boyce Davies 2007, 43–44, 46; see Jones [1949] 1995, 110, 115, 116–17). Nevertheless, Jones emphasized a shared class interest, which "chauvinism on the part of progressive white women" prevented them from realizing: "this fight for equality of Negro women is in their own self-interest, inasmuch as the superexploitation and oppression of Negro women tends to depress the standards of all women" (116–17). Of special interest is Jones's construal of the relationship between struggles for racial, gender and economic justice:

> A developing consciousness on the woman question today . . . must not fail to recognize that the Negro question in the United States is *prior* to, and not equal to, the woman question; that only to the extent that we fight all chauvinist expressions and actions as regards the Negro people and fight for the full equality of the Negro people, can women as a whole advance their struggle for equal rights. For the progressive women's movement, the Negro woman, who combines in her status the worker, the Negro, and the woman, is the vital link to this heightened political consciousness. (120)

Because Jones was a leading theoretician in the CPUSA, her analysis "bore the stamp of Marxist-Leninist thinking" on the "woman question" and the "Negro question" (McDuffie 2011, 169), yet in Boyce

Davies's assessment it also "advanced Marxist-Leninist positions beyond their apparent limitations" (2007, 2). In the above passage, Jones can be read as subversively deploying a Marxist-Leninist conceptual arsenal (including such implied concepts as economism, vanguardism, basic versus epiphenomenal contradictions, and the prioritization of certain struggles over others) in order to claim for Black women their "rightful place in the Negro proletarian leadership of the national liberation movement," in the international socialist revolution, and in women's emancipation struggles (Jones [1949] 1995, 120). Disputing the conceptual segregation of the "questions" of racialized and gendered exploitation, Jones constructs Black women domestic workers as the definitive revolutionary subjects of the radical struggles of her era. Deploying Marxist-Leninist thinking against itself, she poses the rhetorical question exposing the marginalization of Black women within Communist left organizing: "Who, more than the Negro woman, the most exploited and oppressed, belongs in our Party?" (122). Written in a period of intense cold war repression following the Depression-era renewal but also the populist conservatization of the Communist Party, Jones's "An End to the Neglect of the Problems of the Negro Woman!" was highly influential within the CPUSA, which was developing radical theses reframing "Jim Crow and black suffering as forms of genocide" and acknowledging "the non-economic roots of 'male supremacy'" (McDuffie 2011, 164). After its publication, "articles about triply exploited African American women regularly appeared in party periodicals" (171). Yet Black women such as Jones, despite proving themselves "disciplined Communists," remained marginalized within the CPUSA, and as "outsiders within" they "grappled with sexism, racism, and sectarianism within the Communist Left" (218). Boyce Davies argues that Jones, whose numerous arrests, imprisonment, and eventual deportation to Britain in 1955, authorized by the Immigration Act of 1918, the Alien Registration Act of 1940, and the Internal Security Act of 1950 (enabling the state to deport foreign-born residents who were deemed "subversive"), was constructed materially and historically as an "outsider outside," "deported to another location conceptually and literally, outside the borders of U.S. thought" and territory (2007,

16). Moreover, "the erasure of black women's work and ideas . . . can be read as instances of the same superexploitation" that Jones so powerfully theorized (184).

Despite the attempted erasure of radical Black feminist thought through state repression and selective movement memory, intergenerational relationships among Black women organizers and intellectuals—such as the collaboration of Thompson Patterson with TWWA members Beal and Linda Burnham (McDuffie 2011, 199)—facilitated the survival and transmission of ideas across generational divides. At least three things seem important about Beal's and the TWWA's contribution to theorizing the relationship among what—much like the segregated constructs termed the "woman question" and the "Negro question"—were, in the late 1960s, considered distinct and discrete systems of oppression. First, it is notable that even though the assumption is that Beal's concept of "double jeopardy" refers to the two axes of race and gender—as stated in the subtitle, to being "Black and Female"—the essay seems to focus primarily on the relationship between class and race, constructing gender oppression as a third term symptomatic of a capitalist economic system whose "afterbirth" is racism. Therefore, I think it is erroneous to claim that only with the shift to "triple jeopardy" was the "additional" factor of class considered; it was central to Beal's theorization of Black women's oppression from the outset—perhaps so central, in fact, that she thought it superfluous to name it (see Boyce Davies 2007, 3). Here, we should consider the ideological context in which she was intervening (Burnham 2005, 23; see Aguilar 2012). The TWWA (and its predecessors, the BWA and the BWLC) "was strongly influenced by Marxism from its early days, from its origins . . . [and] also by national liberation movements, which were themselves influenced by Marxism and socialism" (Burnham 2005, 23; see Elbaum 2002). Even if, in hindsight, Beal interprets race, class, and gender as operative in a simultaneous, nonhierarchical relationship, perhaps due to the Marxist influences evident in "Double Jeopardy," in my view her account as she formulated it in 1970 is decidedly foundationalist and gives explanatory and causal priority to capitalism: specifically, to class exploitation, which has a determinate racial character. While she does not take recourse explicitly to an economistic base/superstructure model to characterize the relation of class to racial and gender oppression, Beal does construct racial capitalism as the "fundamental cause" of women's oppression and tends to relegate sexism to the (epiphenomenal) realm of ideology. Second, even though "triple jeopardy" makes the addition of class explicit to the race/gender dyad, even though it is not explicit in "double jeopardy" as a "third term," it is always already operative in, and indeed fundamental to, Beal's analysis; superexploitation under capitalism lends content to racial and gender oppressions facing Black women, and capitalism is constructed as the system that gives rise to the other two. In contrast to the "white women's liberation movement [which] is basically middle class," Black women's struggle as imagined by Beal departs from a lived experience of "extreme economic exploitation that most black women are subjected to day by day. . . . The economic and social realities of the black woman's life are the most crucial for us" (Beal 1970a, 30). Third, it is significant that Beal and the TWWA explicitly name systems— as opposed to "categories"—of oppression when conceptualizing the structural sources of Black women's oppression. While the notion of a "system" or "structure" admittedly contains a degree of abstraction, in this respect the reliance of many intersectional appeals on the still less tangible notion of "categories," or the geometrical notion of "axes," tends to obscure the genetic connection of experiences of oppression(s) to institutionalized power relations, and therefore equivocates with respect to a structural analysis.

If double jeopardy and triple jeopardy form part of the "prehistory" of intersectionality—and have their own prehistory in the concepts of triple and superexploitation—they are not, in my view, equivalent to or interchangeable with each other. In this respect I disagree with Roth's characterization that Beal's essay reflects an "intersectional stance" (2004, 91), even though it obviously does represent a significant and germinal effort to think integratively about multiple systems of oppression. The jeopardy model seems not to dispute the categorical distinctions among systems; rather, their fixity is assumed in the conjoining of categories of race, class, and gender. Such a contestation is, however, evident in the Combahee River Collective's intervention.

The Combahee River Collective emerged from the National Black Feminist Organization in the mid-1970s, and its groundbreaking statement was written collectively in 1977 by the "only three active members in the group" at the time: Barbara Smith, Beverly Smith, and Demita Frazier (B. Smith 2003, 69). The wide circulation of "A Black Feminist Statement"—first published in Zillah Eisenstein's book *Capitalist Patriarchy and the Case for Socialist Feminism*, circulated as a pamphlet, anthologized in *All the Women Are White, All the Blacks Are Men, but Some of Us Are Brave: Black Women's Studies* and in *This Bridge Called My Back: Writings by Radical Women of Color*, and included in Barbara Smith's own edited collection, *Home Girls* as well as in the journal *Off Our Backs*—is significant not only in the context of the later affirmation of intersectionality but also in terms of the knowledge production practices of U.S. women of color. Indeed, the circulation of the statement as a pamphlet gave Barbara Smith the impetus to publish the Kitchen Table: Women of Color Press Freedom Organizing Pamphlet Series (B. Smith 2003, 69). Notably, Smith characterizes 1977 as a "renaissance year" of Black feminism (69); it is not a coincidence that "A Black Feminist Statement"—with its decidedly integrative, transnational/internationalist vision—was published in the same year in which the coalitional term "women of color" becomes adopted at the International Women's Conference in Houston (75, 82; see Ross 2011; see chapter 5).

The concept of "interlocking systems of oppression" is invoked as the structural anchor of the experience of simultaneous oppressions and the target of integrated political struggle (CRC 1983, 210). In a sense, it mediates between what is essentially an additive metaphor of dual or triple oppressions and a *critique* of categories of oppression such that simultaneous experiences are fragmented in order to be (re)cognizable in hegemonic legal and social-movement discourses (see Dotson 2013). As I will argue, four crucial claims differentiate the CRC's conceptualization from the jeopardy model. First is the social ontological claim that "the major systems of oppression are interlocking" and that "the synthesis of these oppressions creates the conditions of our lives" (CRC

1983, 210). Second is the phenomenological claim that these "manifold" oppressions are experienced simultaneously by women of color, who are targeted by what are seen as multiple systems, and who lack any form of privilege (210, 214). Third is the identification of the praxical task of an "integrated analysis and practice" of struggle against "racial, sexual, heterosexual and class oppression" by and for Black (lesbian) women's liberation, which has never before been the priority of any "liberation" movement—in other words, the articulation of "identity politics" within a liberation framework (210, 213). Fourth is the introduction into the liberation imaginary of the need to transcend existing categories of oppression based on the synthetic, "simultaneous" experience of oppression "which is neither solely racial nor solely sexual" nor just the combination of the two categories, as these are defined on the basis of male and white normativity (213). It is significant that, in contrast to Beal's conceptualization of double jeopardy, which, at least as I interpret it, accords causal priority and therefore greater weight to racial capitalism than to sexual oppression, and to earlier Black left feminist articulations of "triple exploitation," the CRC argues that "sexual politics under patriarchy is as pervasive in Black women's lives as are the politics of class and race" (213). According to Barbara Ransby, this—among "the ideological tenets around which black feminists have organized"—is "perhaps [the] strongest . . . notion": that race, class, gender, and sexuality are "codependent variables that cannot readily be separated and ranked in scholarship, in political practice, or in lived experience" (2000, 1218). Ransby explicitly traces this integrative "spirit" to "the foundational vision outlined in 1977 . . . in the founding statement of the Combahee River Collective" (1219–20). Indeed, as Barbara Smith reflects in conversation with Beverly Smith a few years later, "we have defined as an important component of Black feminism" that "we don't have to rank or separate out [oppressions]. What we have to do is define the nature of the whole, of all the systems impinging on us" (B. Smith and Smith 1983, 116).

Furthermore, it is significant in terms of the subsequent development of women-of-color feminist organizing how, in contrast to the TWWA— which does not explicitly address heterosexism in its trinary systemic analysis and indeed "dealt badly with issues of sexuality . . . [and] was challenged [as an organization] around its homophobia" (Burnham 2005, 22; see chapter 5)—the CRC statement, written by a group of women of various sexual orientations and identifications, avows a collective political identity as "feminists and lesbians" (CRC 1983, 213). While these terms may have been conflated in the homophobic/heterosexist imaginary, claiming a Black lesbian/feminist identity "was a courageous and revolutionary move . . . in a social movement environment often divided by homophobia" (K. Springer 2005, 131). As Roth suggests, by explicitly naming "heterosexism as a key component of Black women's oppression"—even if a full analysis of heterosexism remained unelaborated (K. Springer 2005, 130–31)—the CRC ended "the relative silence in Black feminist theory over lesbianism" (Roth 2004, 11). The statement uses the term "heterosexual oppression" (the concepts "heterosexism" and "heteronormativity" become part of the lexicon later), and for "possibly the first time [readers] were forced to recognize *publicly* black lesbian existence, the daily oppression black lesbians face, and the considerable sexual diversity with black communities" (K. Springer 2005, 130). This contestation of heteronormativity and homophobia came with high personal and political costs, particularly for lesbian members (see B. Smith 2003); but it also "made it possible" for Black lesbians and lesbians of color to claim an integrated identity in the midst of divisive and fragmenting political ideologies: as Cheryl Clarke writes in the *Bridge* anthology, "to call my name out loud" (1983, 129).

The early 1980s in the United States were marked by the publication of several important texts—now canonical in women-of-color feminisms—in which the phenomena that "intersectionality" is now taken to name were elaborated. As Nira Yuval-Davis points out, the notion of multiple systems of oppression converging in the experiences of minoritized and racialized women was also explored in the early 1980s in the British context, notably by the Organization of Women of African and Asian Descent (OWAAD) and in the work of Floya Anthias and Yuval-Davis (who critiqued OWAAD's "additive approach"), in dialogue with the anti-violence organization Southall Black Sisters (see Anthias and Yuval-Davis 1983; Yuval-Davis 2011, 193; Patel 2000). The history of Black and women-of-color feminisms that this chapter constructs is admittedly U.S.-centric and incomplete. For instance, in Britain Black feminisms had a parallel, distinct trajectory (see *Feminist Review* issues 17 and 108; Amos et al. 1984; Gunaratnam 2014b; Mirza 1997; Gunaratnam 2014a), as they did in Canada (see Dua and Robertson 1999; Massaquoi and Wane 2007; Razack, Smith, and Thobani 2010. An account of the reciprocal influence of women-of-color feminisms developed in various geopolitical locations—in white settler states, imperial Western European countries, and colonized/postcolonial nations—unfortunately lies beyond the scope of this chapter.) In the United States, igniting the "eighties renaissance of writing by Black and other women of color" (B. Smith 1989, 11) were Cherríe Moraga and Gloria Anzaldúa's edited collection *This Bridge Called My Back: Writings by Radical Women of Color* (1981); Angela Davis's *Women, Race and Class* (1981); bell hooks's *Ain't I a Woman?* (1981); Gloria T. Hull, Patricia Bell Scott, and Barbara Smith's edited volume, *All the Women Are White, All the Blacks Are Men, but Some of Us Are Brave: Black Women's Studies* (1982); Barbara Smith's *Home Girls: A Black Feminist Anthology* (1983); and Audre Lorde's *Sister Outsider* (1984). The publication of these germinal texts would not have been possible had it not been for the formation of autonomous feminist presses, most notably Kitchen Table: Women of Color Press, founded in 1980 by Barbara Smith, Audre Lorde, Cherríe Moraga, and Hattie Gossett (see B. Smith 2003, 74; B. Smith 1989, 11). In "the era of the 'special issue'—the response of some white feminist journals . . . to increasing numbers of women of color raising the issue of racism in the women's movements," Kitchen Table Press "began because of our need for autonomy, our need to determine independently both the content and the conditions of our work and to control the words and images that were produced about us" (B. Smith 1989, 11). Smith explains:

We chose our name because the kitchen is the center of the home, the place where women in particular work and communicate with each other. We also wanted to convey the fact that we are a kitchen table, grassroots operation, begun and kept alive by women who cannot rely on inheritances or other benefits of class privilege to do the work we need to do. (1989, 11)

The texts named above also reflect the porous boundaries and cross-pollination of academic and social-movement knowledge production: the "border space between social movement and academic politics" in which the concept of intersectionality will, by the end of the decade, be articulated (Collins 2011, 92). Their conditions of possibility, their audience, and their goal are the political movements of Black women, Chicana and Latina women, and other women of color—many of whom were lesbian-identified—most of whom, in a literate culture adulating individual authors, remain anonymous.

BLACK FEMINISMS IN IVORY TOWERS

If Collins's assessment is accurate that "narratives of the emergence of intersectionality" ignore its aforementioned social-movement history, instead conflating its "point of origin" with the moment "when academics first noticed, named and legitimized this emerging field of study," then a significant task that lies before us is the construction of a political genealogy of intersectionality (2011, 92). Origin stories are ineluctably partial, interested narratives, and their erasures and elisions are at least of as much interest as the agents and motivations they foreground. For instance, Collins draws attention to the politics of citation with respect to Crenshaw's own work: as Collins points out, "stock stories of the emergence of intersectionality routinely claim that Kimberlé Crenshaw 'coined' the term intersectionality" in her article "Mapping the Margins: Intersectionality, Identity Politics, and Violence against Women of Color," published in the *Stanford Law Review* in 1991, whereas her earlier article "Demarginalizing the Intersection of Race and Sex: A Black Feminist Critique of Antidiscrimination Doctrine, Feminist Theory and Antiracist Politics," published two years earlier in the *University of Chicago Legal Forum*, "is not as widely cited" (Collins 2011, 92; see chapter 2). Later in this chapter we will examine how Crenshaw puts "intersectionality" to use in each article; first, I would like to juxtapose her account with contemporaneous Black feminist conceptualizations of categorial essentialism and multiplicity at the turn of the last decade of the twentieth century.

According to Collins, "in the 1990s, the intersectional political agenda of feminists of color—the need to simultaneously analyze and battle dominations of gender, class, race/ethnicity, and sexuality—migrated to the "mainstream" of feminist scholarship and activism" (2012, 14). While the "migration" thesis implies a territorial division between activism and scholarship, this border is more porous than the metaphor seems to allow: if anything, "migration" must be viewed as a reversible, circular, and not a unidirectional movement between clearly demarcated territories of "margin" versus "center," of activism versus scholarship. Indeed, although they occurred in the context of elite U.S. academic institutions, the interventions of Crenshaw and other Critical Race scholars in the legal academy constituted a form of radical, political contestation, an ideological struggle around the law as a legitimizing discourse of white-supremacist power (Crenshaw 2011b; see chapter 2). Crenshaw explicitly introduces the metaphor of intersectionality in a legal academic context as an inheritance of the history of women-of-color organizing. Moreover, it was her own "activist engagement [in anti-violence organizing] that brought me to this work" (Crenshaw quoted in Guidroz and Berger 2009, 65). However, in Collins's view, Crenshaw's intervention heralded an era of depoliticized intersectional scholarship. Collins writes:

> For me, the 1970s and 1980s were the heady days of intersectional scholarship . . . a time when the critical analytical lens of intersectionality was attuned to assessing significant social issues, thinking through the mechanisms of intersecting systems of power themselves, and/or trying to do something about social inequalities. Ironically some view Crenshaw's 1991 piece coining the term "intersectionality" as intersectionality's coming of age, yet this moment can also be interpreted as launching a decade where the initial vision of intersectionality became increasingly drowned out. (2009, ix)

Collins's critique of the depoliticization of intersectionality as a function of its institutionalization is well taken, but to conflate this process with Crenshaw's own intervention—which was explicitly politically motivated—seems problematic. It also obscures the fact that many activists who articulated precisely the integrative vision that led up to intersectionality—including CRC founding member, "A Black Feminist Statement" coauthor, and Kitchen Table publisher Barbara Smith—are or were also academics. In other words, the depolicitization thesis seems to rest, in certain renditions, on an *ad personam* authenticity claim about the author's identity, or on certain predetermined criteria for what constitutes political radicalism. Indeed, as an academic, Collins herself becomes a target of this kind of *ad personam* critique, advanced, for instance, by Delia Aguilar (2012), who charges Collins, King, and hooks with shifting the concept of interlocking oppressions from the "material anchor" of capitalism to "the realm of discourse," which, Aguilar contends, leads to the evacuation of its radical analysis.

With these caveats in mind, I would like to focus on four key texts which constitute key moments in the articulation of an integrative Black feminist theory within academic disciplinary contexts: Deborah King's "Multiple Jeopardy, Multiple Consciousness: The Context of a Black Feminist Ideology" (1988); Patricia Hill Collins's *Black Feminist Thought: Knowledge, Consciousness, and the Politics of Empowerment* (1990)—particularly chapter 11, in which she elaborates the concept of the "matrix of domination"; and Crenshaw's 1989 and 1991 articles. In chapter 3, I discuss a fifth crucial contemporaneous argument, elaborated by Angela Harris in "Race and Essentialism in Feminist Legal Theory," which powerfully articulates the erasures constitutive of "gender essentialism"—"the notion that a unitary, 'essential' women's experience can be isolated and described independently of race, class, sexual orientation, and other realities of experience" (1990, 585)—and its resistance through "multiple consciousness."

MULTIPLE JEOPARDY

King situates her concept of "multiple jeopardy" in a history of Black women's struggles against multiple subordinations, arguing that "the necessity of addressing all oppressions is one of the hallmarks of black feminist thought" (1988, 42–43). Whereas Black women articulated the interaction of racial and gender oppressions, white feminists drew on racial oppression analogically to convey "[white] women's subordinate status" (44). Given that movements for racial justice in the nineteenth and twentieth centuries served as "predecessors, catalysts, and proto-types for women's collective action," white feminists drew extensively on abolitionist and civil rights discourses to constitute a (white) feminist collective subject of resistance (44). However, race-sex analogies render Black women invisible; at the same time, King argues that analogies reveal that the categories of Blackness and femaleness are represented as generic, while in fact they are "intersectionally but invisibly" constructed as male and white (45; Carbado 2013, 826). Moreover, refuting the grounds for analogy, King argues that race-sex analogies assume that racial and gender oppression are formally similar—a presumption that the subsequent geometric language of "axes" takes to the limit—obfuscating their "profound substantive differences" (1988, 45).

King critiques Beal's concept of "double jeopardy" for "not conveying the dynamics of multiple forms of discrimination" and for being "overly simplistic in assuming that the relationships among the various discriminations are merely additive" (D. K. King 1988, 46–47). King interprets "double jeopardy" as describing "the dual discriminations of racism and sexism that subjugate black women," which "often entail . . . economic disadvantage," but takes Beal to task for failing to explicitly name class "as an autonomous source" of jeopardy (46). As I have argued, Beal explicitly discusses the foundational role of capitalism in constructing Black women as superexploited workers—finding it "expedient to reduce women to a state of enslavement" (Beal 1970b, 114)—and cites income statistics (115) which show that "black women have endured the very lowest of wages and very poorest of conditions of rural and urban poverty" (D. K. King 1988, 46). If Beal's term "double jeopardy" in combination with her subtitular focus on Black women fails to explicitly indicate capitalism and class, she can hardly be critiqued for ignoring class exploitation, employment discrimination, and poverty in her account. She cannot be more explicit that "the extreme economic exploitation that most Black women are subjected to day by day . . . is the factor that is most crucial for us" (Beal 1970b, 120). More convincing, however, is King's critique of Beal that double jeopardy and its successor concept, triple jeopardy, constitute essentially additive conceptions of oppression. She argues that in additive construals, the relationships among race, gender, and class "are interpreted as equivalent to the mathematical equation, racism plus sexism plus classism equals triple jeopardy. In this instance, each discrimination has a single, direct, and independent effect on status, wherein the relative contribution of each is readily apparent" (D. King 1988, 47). Moreover, King contends that the addition of discrete categories lends itself to "nonproductive" foundationalist claims that one factor is of greater importance than the other, but "such assertions ignore the fact that racism, sexism, and classism constitute three, interdependent control systems" (47).

However, it is not clear that King's own model of "multiple jeopardy" constitutes a substantive improvement over "double" and "triple jeopardy" in capturing the simultaneity and interdependence of oppressions. King contends that "the modifier 'multiple' refers not only to several, simultaneous oppressions but to the multiplicative relationships among them as well. In other words, the equivalent formulation is racism multiplied by sexism multiplied by classism" (1988, 47). Leaving aside the question of whether multiplication can be expressed as repeated addition (apparently sometimes, although not always), the more pressing issue seems to be whether or not the concept of multiple jeopardy might be just as dependent on the existence of independent variables or categorially distinct entities as the additive models that King critiques. Although King rejects foundationalist arguments that would give causal priority to one form of oppression over another, she supports a kind of contextual foundationalism, in which

> the importance of any one factor in explaining black women's circumstances . . . varies depending on the particular aspect of our lives under consideration and the reference groups to whom we are compared. In some cases, race may be the more significant predictor of black women's status; in others, gender or class may be more influential. (47, 48)

In other words, in King's "interactive model, the relative significance of race, sex, or class in determining the conditions of black women's lives is neither fixed nor absolute but, rather, is dependent on the socio-historical context and the social phenomenon under consideration" (49). But such contextual judgments would only be possible if the categories remain at least analytically distinct and appear to operate independently of one another. Moreover, even though King points out that heterosexism and homophobia constitute a fourth, untheorized source of jeopardy (citing Barbara Smith and Audre Lorde as exceptional in having addressed it), it drops out of the analysis in a subtractive way that reveals the essentially additive character of her model. Nevertheless, King's critique builds productively upon the jeopardy model inasmuch as it draws attention to the relationships *among* categories of oppression. The intended difference between "adding" and "multiplying" categories does not inhere in the categories themselves but in the relationships between the categories: how they have been constituted in relation to each other. This is perhaps most cogently articulated in her argument against the "'monist' approach of most liberation ideologies," which draws on Black women's "history of resistance to multiple jeopardies [which] is replete with the fierce tensions, untenable ultimatums, and bitter compromises between nationalism, feminism, and class politics" (51, 52). King argues that "to the extent that any politic is monistic, the actual victims of racism, sexism, or classism may be absent from, invisible within, or seen as antagonistic to that politic" (52). By contrast, "it is in confrontation with multiple jeopardy that black women define and sustain a multiple consciousness essential for our liberation, of which feminist consciousness is an integral part" (69). Black feminist ideology, for King, "would meld diverse ideologies, from race liberation, class liberation, and women's liberation" (71)—notably, gay and lesbian liberation ideologies are not included in this list—and has four features: it "declares the visibility of black women," "asserts our self-determination as essential," "fundamentally challenges the interstructure of the oppressions of racism, sexism, and classism both in the dominant society and within movements for liberation," and views "black women as powerful, independent subjects": as agents of political transformation and not as overdetermined victims of multiple oppressions (72).

This conception of Black women's agentic resistance also runs through Patricia Hill Collins's landmark text, *Black Feminist Thought: Knowledge, Consciousness, and the Politics of Empowerment*. Black feminism, according to Collins, represents "Black women as empowered individuals within multiple structures of oppression" (1990, 140). Black feminism has not only pluralized categories of oppression and terrains of resistance and asserted their interrelationship, "offering subordinate groups new knowledge about their own experiences"; Black feminist thought has also effected "a fundamental paradigmatic shift in how we think about oppression . . . revealing new ways of knowing that allow subordinate groups to define their own reality" (222). Although Collins makes a number of significant contributions to theorizing Black feminist politics of empowerment in this book—including the articulation of a collective Black women's standpoint (19–40) and the elaboration of an Afrocentric feminist epistemology (201–20)—in this section I focus more narrowly on the integrative model Collins proposes to visualize the relationship among multiple oppressions.

Collins's point of departure is the reconceptualization of race, class, and gender as "interlocking systems of oppression" (1990, 222). This inter-systemic theorization has two crucial effects: first, it transcends the analogical reasoning we saw being critiqued by King—or as Collins puts it, the descriptive enumeration of "similarities and differences" between forms of oppression; and second, by "focus[ing] greater attention on how they interconnect," it enables "the rethinking" of categories of analysis, oppression, and resistance (222). Crucial to the shift from methodological and political monisms to an integrative perspective is the location of Black women at the center of analysis (223). However, Collins emphasizes that the implications of a theoretical framework centered on Black women's experiences extend beyond their descriptive inclusion in established analytical models of racial, class, and gender oppressions to "an enhanced theoretical understanding" of how these constitute a single, unified, historically determinate system (225). She advocates the replacement of additive models of oppression, which assume a serial and cumulative effect of distinct systems, with an integrative both/and logic that can account for the varying, simultaneous degrees of "penalty and privilege in one historically created system" (225). If an individual can be "simultaneously oppressor and oppressed" based on multiple memberships in socially privileged and subordinated groups, that does not mean, however, that all forms of oppression are equivalent or "interchangeable," that they function in the same ways, that they are perceived in lived experience as the same, or that they can be resisted using the same strategies and tactics (225–26). Rather, they constitute different "dimensions" of the "social relations of domination" (226). Drawing on bell hooks and Johnella Butler, Collins conceptualizes social relations of domination as forming a "matrix" in which "race, class, and gender constitute axes of oppression that characterise Black women's experiences," while "other groups may encounter different dimensions of the matrix, such as sexual orientation, religion, and age" (226). For hooks, the shared "ideological ground" or "foundation" of these systems is a belief in hierarchy and domination (hooks quoted in Collins 1990, 226), while Butler emphasizes the importance of viewing the axes of race, class, and gender as nonhierarchical, in the sense that none has "primacy" over the others but instead all participate in a "matrix-like interaction" (Butler quoted in Collins 1990, 227).

Lending further concretion to the concept of the "matrix of domination," Collins traces how it is structured on several analytically distinct levels of social reality: the micro-level of personal biography or lived experience; the meso-level of social groups, communities, and cultures; and the macro-level of social institutions (227). Domination is experienced and resisted, but it is also reproduced at all three levels (228). Gaining an understanding of the relations among levels in reproducing the matrix of domination is important, since "domination operates not only by structuring power from the top down but by simultaneously annexing the power ... of those on the bottom for its own ends" (227–28). In this sense, the articulation of an African American women's standpoint by Black feminists constitutes a "conceptual tool ... to resist oppression" (228).

Collins argues that one way in which the matrix of domination goes uncontested is that particular axes of oppression are identified as opera-tive in a social group's collective experience, but at the same time, the axes that confer privilege to that group and which subordinate anoth-er group go unnoticed (1990, 229). The tendency is to relegate those axes on which a group is privileged to lesser theoretical and political importance than the ones on which the group is oppressed (229). Yet what "these approaches fail to recognize [is] that a matrix of domina-tion contains few pure victims or oppressors. Each individual derives varying amounts of penalty and privilege from the multiple systems of oppression which frame everyone's lives" (229). The both/and logic of an integrative approach to "the interlocking nature of oppressions" allows for a "broader focus" that "provides the conceptual space needed for each individual to see that she or he is *both* a member of multiple dominant groups *and* a member of multiple subordinate groups" (230). However, Collins insists that "race, gender, and class [are] the axes of investigation for African-American women" in a matrix-of-domination approach (230); so, the theoretical emphasis remains on how Black women occupy a systemic location of multiple, simultaneous oppres-sion. Moreover, this location yields a standpoint that is "a preferred stance from which to view the matrix of domination" as a whole—even if a Black women's standpoint constitutes "only one angle of vision," a "partial perspective," and a "situated knowledge" just as that of any oth-er group (234). In other words, Collins parts ways with the "vanguard center" construct of earlier Black feminist ideologies that we saw the TWWA and the CRC articulate, arguing that "no one group has a clear angle of vision" or "possesses the theory or methodology that allows it to discover the absolute 'truth'" (234; see Dotson 2014). Rejecting both positivism and relativism as epistemological approaches, Collins argues that Black feminist standpoint theory avows the partial, situat-ed, subjugated knowledges of African American women and advocates "larger epistemological dialogues concerning the nature of the matrix of domination" (1990, 236). Intergroup validation of the knowledge claims of groups based on distinctive standpoints—a kind of collec-tive intersubjective agreement—is the closest to "'objective' truths" that social theory can come (236). However, before such dialogues are possible—in which no one "need[s] to 'decenter' anyone in order to center someone else [but rather] one has only to constantly, appropriately, 'pivot the center'" (236, quoting Elsa Barkley Brown)—current epistemic injustices and power inequities between dominant and subordinated groups must be addressed (236). To desubjugate Black women's knowledges and to enable such horizontal dialogue between knowers in various social locations, a prior "decentering" of dominant groups who must relinquish epistemic privilege is necessary (237).

CRENSHAW'S METAPHOR AND CONCEPT OF INTERSECTIONALITY

Crenshaw expresses a similar relationship between "demarginalizing the intersection" and "decentering" the normative subjects whose experiences define the boundaries of categories of discrimination in law, in critical theories, and in social-movement discourses. In "Demarginalizing the Intersection of Race and Sex: A Black Feminist Critique of Antidiscrimination Doctrine, Feminist Theory and Antiracist Politics," the essay in which she introduces the intersection metaphor (discussed at greater length in chapter 2), Crenshaw demonstrates that "boundaries of sex and race discrimination doctrine are defined respectively by white women's and Black men's experiences" (1989, 143). Crenshaw's analysis of three discrimination suits brought against corporate employers by Black women plaintiffs demonstrates that antidiscrimination laws protect Black women only to the extent that their experiences of discrimination "coincide" with those of Black men or with those of white women (143). Placing Black women at the center of an analysis of U.S. antidiscrimination law—at the intersection of juridical categories of race and sex discrimination—reveals the inadequacy of doctrinal definitions of discrimination to capture and remedy Black women's concrete experiences of discrimination. In other words, the intersection of race and sex renders Black women's experiences invisible. In order to see this, Crenshaw invites readers to imagine that discrimination is traffic in a four-way intersection, "coming and going" in every direction (149). Cars traveling from any direction and sometimes from all four directions can collide in the intersection, causing an "accident." Analogously, if a Black woman is harmed because she is in an intersection, her injury could result from sex discrimination or race discrimination.... But it is not always easy to reconstruct an accident: Sometimes the skid marks and the injuries simply indicate that they occurred simultaneously, frustrating efforts to determine which driver caused the harm. (149)

Crenshaw shows how monistic definitions of discrimination, which define sex and race as mutually exclusive categories, render the simultaneous experience of gendered racism invisible and legal claims of "compound" discrimination inadmissible (149). These categories are constructed through the exclusion of Black women, whose experiences are seen as diverging from those white women and Black men who are imagined as the normative subjects of protected groups in antidiscrimination law (148). She argues that legal concepts of discrimination must be revised if they are to serve as remedies to historical and structural oppression. If discrimination is not reconceptualized in terms of the concrete experiences of Black women, the plaintiffs who are most likely to be recognized as victims of discrimination are those who actually experience the benefits of relatively—or, as we will see in chapter 2, of absolutely—privileged intersectional identities, that is, white women, Black men, and white men (140, 152). To the extent that antiracist, feminist, and legal discourses center implicitly on subjects whose racial oppression is inflected (and arguably mitigated) by gender privilege, or on subjects whose gender oppression is inflected (and arguably mitigated) by racial privilege, single-axis contestations of discrimination and oppression actually reproduce social hierarchies rather than undermining them (151–52). To illustrate this process, Crenshaw offers a second metaphor to her readers. She asks us to imagine people stuck in a basement in a multi-level structure representing social hierarchy; they are stacked, "feet standing on shoulders," so that some are supporting the weight of others whose heads "brush up against the ceiling" (151). There is a hatch in the ceiling through which only those who are at the very top can climb, thereby leaving the basement and entering the floor above (151–52). This hatch represents antidiscrimination law; only those who are disadvantaged by what the court cognizes as a singular factor of discrimination—who "but for" the ceiling would be on the floor above—or those whose experiences can be rendered recognizably similar to singularly burdened groups can climb through it (151–52). Those who face discrimination on the basis of what are conceived of as multiple distinct categories "are generally left" in the basement, precisely because the intersection of these categories is a location of social invisibility that is refused legal redress (151–52; see chapter 2).

In her more widely read—or at least more widely cited—essay, "Mapping the Margins: Intersectionality, Identity Politics, and Violence against Women of Color" (1991), Crenshaw builds on her metaphorical use of intersectionality, offering a threefold positive definition of the concept, the first aspect of which—structural intersectionality—is invoked most often in the operationalization of "intersectionality" in the literature. "Structural intersectionality" refers to "the ways in which the location of women of color at the intersection of race and gender makes our actual experience of domestic violence, rape, and remedial reform qualitatively different than that of white women" (1245). The second aspect, "political intersectionality," describes the fact that, historically, feminist and antiracist politics in the United States "have functioned in tandem to marginalize issues facing Black women" (1245). As Crenshaw puts it, "women of color are situated within at least two subordinated groups that frequently pursue conflicting political agendas" (1252). Neither agenda is constructed around the experiences, needs, or political visions of women of color; to the extent that antiracism reproduces patriarchy and feminism reproduces racism, women of color are asked to choose between two inadequate analyses, each of which "constitutes a denial of a fundamental dimension of our subordination" (1252). The third aspect, "representational intersectionality," concerns the production of images of women of color drawing on sexist and racist narrative tropes, as well as the ways that critiques of these representations marginalize or reproduce the objectification of women of color (1283). Crenshaw argues that in public and legal contestations over representations, discourses, and speech acts, "the rhetoric of antiracism provide[s] an occasion for racism" while "the rhetoric of antiracism provide[s] an occasion for defending . . . misogyny" (1292).

One question that arises as we read together these two landmark essays—which, it should be understood, represent only a small fraction of Crenshaw's broader intellectual production in Critical Race legal scholarship and Black feminist theory—is, What is the relationship between intersectionality as metaphor and intersectionality as defined in terms of structural location, political marginalization, and representational objectification? Are these two articulations and uses of intersectionality consistent, accordant, and therefore interchangeable? More specifically, is there a tension between Crenshaw's use of intersectionality as metaphor for Black women's sociolegal invisibility as a consequence of categorial exclusions, on the one hand, and her definition of intersectionality as a social location at the convergence of categories of race and gender, on the other? If, according to her earlier argument, "race" and "gender" render Black women's experiences invisible in courtrooms, in critical theories, and in political movements, can the deployment of these categories serve to illuminate "the actual experience" of women of color and their "qualitative differences" from those of white women? It is significant that even when defining the positive concept of "structural intersectionality" to "map" a "location that resists telling," its analytic force lies in tracing the categorial displacement of Black women's experiences, their difference from white women's, which overdetermines representations of gendered violence, policies and social practices concerned with its redress and elimination. It is also noteworthy that Crenshaw stresses that experiential differences are qualitative, not quantitative; it is not a question of women of color experiencing "more" violence or suffering "worse" oppression: the problem with such quantitative comparisons is that they take white women's gendered and racialized experiences as foundational, normative, and generalizable, while constructing the experiences of women of color variously as departing from or as culminating in the same logic of forms of violence that target white women, differing only in "magnitude" or "intensity": thus, as Angela Harris argues, "the word 'black,' applied to women, is an intensifier: if things are bad for everybody (meaning white women) then they're even worse for black women" (1990, 595–96).

However, even if, on an intersectional model, experiences are understood as qualitatively different, the location that structures them is nevertheless conceptualized in terms of extant essentialist categories that misrepresent women of color. This acknowledged tension appears internally to Crenshaw's 1991 essay, specifically in terms of the relationship between structural and political intersectionalities: to the extent that the specific, invisibly intersectional raced and gendered experiences of men of color determine the parameters of analyses of racial oppression and of antiracist strategies, and those of white women constitute the paradigm of gender oppression and the boundaries of "sisterhood," the problem inheres not only in the failure of both discourses to acknowledge "the 'additional' issue of race or of patriarchy, but that the discourses are often inadequate even to the discrete tasks of articulating the full dimensions of racism and sexism"—if we concede that these are, in fact, discrete tasks, which Crenshaw generally seems not to (1991, 1252; see chapter 3). In other words, the segregation of antiracist and antisexist discourses— effected through the simultaneous marginalization and continuous erasure of Black women in each "kind" of discourse—results in a distorted conception of "race" and "racism" and of "gender" and "misogyny." If this is true, then the abstract convergence of categories of "race" and "gender" to describe Black women's lived experiences reproduces their categorial invisibility. This may limit the utility of the concept of structural intersectionality—that aspect of Crenshaw's account which most closely resembles the additive jeopardy model—in decentering white- and male-privileged subgroups as the normative subjects of gendered and racial oppression and resistance. And yet, structural intersectionality is that aspect of Crenshaw's account which is most frequently taken up—whether explicitly invoked or not—in the burgeoning literature on intersectionality.

INTERSECTIONALITY AS A PARADIGM

Having traced—admittedly in a partial, schematic, interested, and inevitably incomplete way—intersectionality's conceptual roots in Black and women-of-color feminisms, and having briefly discussed Crenshaw's metaphorical and denotational uses of the concept (to which we will return again and again in the chapters to come), we are in a better position to assess the methodological merits imputed to intersectionality in the swelling field of "intersectionality studies." Indeed, in addition to the three senses of "intersectionality" that Crenshaw defines, the term is now used in the literature to refer to the theory or methodology used to identify and study these "real world" phenomena of structural, political, and representational intersectionality. The fact that "intersectionality" is used to refer both to material phenomena and to the analytic used to examine them sometimes results in apparently tautological statements—conflating the empirical "problem" with the analytic "solution"—in which "intersectionality" is "used to study intersectionality" (McCall 2005, 1772). As a methodology or heuristic, Collins (2003) notes, intersectionality can be used at the micro-, meso-, and macro-levels of social formations. Indeed, as Bonnie Thornton Dill and Ruth Enid Zambrana write, intersectionality reveals "the workings of power, which is understood as both pervasive and oppressive . . . at all levels of social relations" (2009, 11). Drawing on Collins's account of power in *Black Feminist Thought*, Dill and Zambrana argue that "intersectional analyses, as knowledge generated from and about oppressed groups, unveil . . . structural, disciplinary, hegemonic, and interpersonal dimensions of power and reveal how oppression is constructed and maintained through multiple aspects of identity" (2009, 7; Collins 1990).

In this section I focus on four main analytic benefits that are imputed to intersectionality as a research methodology or theoretical framework: simultaneity, complexity, irreducibility, and inclusivity. In contrast to unitary or additive approaches to theorizing oppression, which privilege a foundational category and either ignore or merely "add" others to it, intersectional approaches insist that multiple, co-constituting analytic categories are operative and equally salient in constructing institutionalized practices and lived experiences. For instance, Evelyn Simien argues that "in lived experience and political practice, certain identity categories overrule, capture, differentiate, and transgress others in the social, economic, and political structure of the United States. The theoretical demand is then to read these categories simultaneously" (2007, 270). Since, as Kathryn Russell points out, "a real-life person is not, for example, a woman on Monday, a member of the working class on Tuesday, and a woman of African descent on Wednesday," intersectionality responds to the "theoretical demand . . . to read these categories simultaneously" (2007, 47). There are at least two variations on the claim that intersectionality delivers simultaneity. The first is the phenomenological claim that intersectionality captures how oppressions are experienced simultaneously. The second is the ontological claim that intersectionality can theorize the convergence, co-constitution, imbrication, or interwovenness of systems of oppression. As we have seen, both claims have roots in predecessor concepts, particularly the concepts of interlocking systems of oppression, multiple jeopardy, and matrix of domination. Crenshaw's concept of structural intersectionality aims to render visible phenomenological experiences of people who face multiple forms of oppression without fragmenting those experiences through categorial exclusion (we will bracket, until chapter 3, the question of whether it actually claims to achieve this aim). The ontological anchor for experiences of multiple oppression and fragmented identity is the system of interlocking social structures. While these systems or axes are seen to mutually construct lived experiences at the individual and group levels and are given equal explanatory salience in intersectional approaches, by contrast, essentialist constructions of unitary categories "fragment" Black women's experiences and give primacy to one category of oppression over another, "as those who are 'only interested in race' and those who are 'only interested in gender' take the separate slices of our lives" (A. Harris 1990, 589).

The second purported theoretical benefit of intersectionality is that, unlike monistic approaches, it accounts for or captures experiential and structural complexity. Leslie McCall distinguishes between three kinds of complexity that intersectionality as a heuristic attempts to grasp, which corresponds to three approaches to "managing complexity" (2005, 1773). The intercategorical approach "focuses on the complexity of relationships among multiple social groups within and across analytical categories" (1786). The intracategorical approach examines complexity within a social group. Such groups, located "at neglected points of intersection" of axes of oppression, are studied through an intracategorical lens "in order to reveal the complexity of lived experience" of their members (1774). Finally, a third intersectional approach that McCall identifies is the anticategorical approach, "which is based on a methodology that deconstructs analytical categories. Social life is considered too irreducibly complex . . . to make fixed categories anything but simplifying social fictions" (1773). All three intersectional approaches agree that monistic, single-axis approaches fail to capture the complexity of social structures and subjective experiences. The claim is that monistic approaches to oppression are reductive: they reduce the "complex" experiences of "simultaneous" oppressions to simplistic unitary categories. This leads to the question, Is complexity inherent in experience, or does experience appear "complex" due to the reductive categories employed in its analysis? To the extent that the categorization of experience—using falsely universal and in fact exclusionary categories of "race," "gender," and other oppressions—is elided with experience itself, the imputation of complexity is never innocuous; indeed, it reflects the solipsism and exclusions involved in representing what are invisibly intersectional identities as "singular" and "simple." Alexander-Floyd is critical of the view that "complexity" is the criterion for assessing intersectionality's utility: "the issue is one of subjugation, not complexity" (2012, 11).

A corollary of the simultaneity and complexity benefits is the irreducibility benefit. Rather than reducing the phenomena of oppression to one foundational explanatory category (e.g., class) and ontologically privileging that category, intersectionality theorists argue that oppression is produced through the interaction of multiple, decentered, and mutually constitutive axes. This controverts orthodox Marxist approaches, for instance, which claim that class relations of exploitation—or the "economic base"—have causal and explanatory priority to gender and race, which are viewed as "epiphenomenal," immaterial, and divisive ideologies. For this reason, as we will see in chapter 4, it is perhaps unsurprising that Marxist feminists were among the first to critique intersectionality (even as Black Communist feminists are its unacknowledged historical precursors); those who advocate intersectionality's integration into a more "inclusionary" Marxist feminism tend to minimize or reject the irreducibility claim (see Gimenez 2001; Aguilar 2012; Brenner 2000;

S. Ferguson and McNally 2015). Yet irreducibility as an epistemic value refutes the primacy given by single-axis frameworks to one or the other form of oppression; a "hallmark" of intersectionality—as we have seen King argue of Black feminist thought more generally—is "the necessity of addressing all oppressions" simultaneously (1988, 43). The question arises, however, What is the relationship between the irreducibility and simultaneity of oppressions? A tension arises between, on the one hand, the claim that systems of oppressions are distinct and irreducible to each other, and on the other, the claim that oppressions are experienced simultaneously and are inseparable, which is not resolved by locating irreducibility at the analytic level and simultaneity at the phenomenological level. For instance, Sirma Bilge explains that numerous "authors emphasize the importance of 'maintaining analytical disassociations' between categories of difference . . . while still recognizing that 'in the real world, individual live these categories simultaneously'" (2010, 64). But it is precisely the material effects of the deployment of these analytically distinct categories in the lifeworlds of Black women and other women of color—in law, social movements, political discourses, and cultural narratives—that intersectionality and its precursors reveal and contest.

The last benefit attributed to intersectionality is inclusivity. The claim is that as a theoretical paradigm, intersectionality can act as a corrective against the white solipsism, heteronormativity, elitism, and ableism of dominant power and hegemonic feminist theory by making social locations and experiences visible that are occluded in essentialist and exclusionary constructions of the category "women" (see Spelman 1988). Ange-Marie Hancock argues that intersectional approaches are "inclusive and incisive" and foster "deep political solidarity" (2011, 183). Specifically, she promotes intersectionality as a solution to "the Oppression Olympics," a term introduced by Elizabeth Martínez to critique the "comparisons of suffering" between oppressed groups (Martínez quoted in Hancock 2011, 3; see Martínez 1993). This "race to the bottom," according to Hancock "prevent[s] recognition of common ground" and precludes "political solidarity" (2011, 3–4; see Fellows and Razack 1998). Inclusion as an analytic benefit corresponds to Crenshaw's analysis of political intersectionality, which reveals how transformative social movements have reproduced deeply ingrained cognitive and representational exclusions in the course of political practice. Here, the cognitive and conceptual dimensions of an inclusionary ethico-political praxis are emphasized: categories of oppression and identity have been structured and distinguished from one another through conceptual exclusions, prototypicality, and marginalization. However, as false universals, unitary categories are also constituted through false inclusion, tokenism, and appropriation; moreover, as a political norm it is not clear that inclusion always entails anti-subordination. One can be included in a category (e.g., as an outlier) or group (e.g., as a token), leaving the logic or terms through which it is constituted intact. The primacy, centrality, and hegemony of prototypical, normative, full, and proper members may go unchallenged, even as tokenized, minoritized, newcomer guests are admitted and accorded some "hospitality." In my view, while they represent well-intentioned efforts to tarry with integrative challenges to monistic thinking about groups, even "serial" (Young 1994) or "family relations" (Garry 2012) conceptions of social groups that nominally include diverse members (more so than do homogeneous Aristotelian categories) may reproduce relations of conceptual priority and derivativeness at the same time as they proffer inclusion—after all, isn't there someone always at the front and someone else at the back of the proverbial line? The point is that categories constructed prototypically do not evade the intersectional critique any more effectively than do categories constructed through necessary and sufficient conditions, precisely because intersectionality challenges the normative status accorded to those group members who are taken to be prototypical or whose experiences are taken to constitute the historical base of the category. In the absence of prototypical members, nominally included members are not taken to be representative of the category or of the other members who define it at its core, if not at its boundary limits.

I have raised some theoretical concerns about the plausibility of the analytic benefits imputed to intersectionality in theory. In research practice, according to empirical scholars, it is not clear how one ought to go about "researching" simultaneous oppressions without reducing them

Intersectionality, Black Feminist Thought, and Women-of-Color Organizing

to unitary categories or merely reverting to an additive model (Bowleg 2008; Belkhir and Barnett 2001). Through her qualitative and quantitative studies of stress and resilience among Black lesbians in the United States, Lisa Bowleg found that "it is virtually impossible, particularly in quantitative research, to ask questions about intersectionality that are not inherently additive" (2008, 314). Moreover, she concludes that "addition is often a critical step in preliminary analysis": she echoes Gloria Cuádraz and Lynnett Uttal's concession that "isolating" each category and its impact on the subject's experience is "an essential analytical step": hence, "the researcher must analyze each structural inequality separately, as well as simultaneously" (319; see Cuádraz and Uttal 1999). Similarly, Jean Ait Belkhir and Bernice McNair Barnett maintain that "despite the warning to scholars not to isolate race, class, or gender, this is a necessary step to understand the intersectionality in the end" (2001, 163–64). Intersectionality as a research method may capture the irreducibility of experience to any single category by using multiple categories of analysis, even if these are distinguished categorially from one another. Or, intersectionality may function less as a research method and more as a heuristic to interpret results of quantitative or qualitative research. In this sense, irreducibility, complexity, simultaneity, and inclusion may turn out to be methodological commitments on the part of the researcher more than they are aspects of the method reflected in the instruments chosen; "intersectionality" may be invoked to inform the analysis of data that may well have been collected or generated using monistic categories. However, as a methodological commitment in quantitative and qualitative research, irreducibility may displace simultaneity. Indeed, simultaneity—the nonfragmentation of a phenomenological experience—may be the most elusive of the purported analytic merits of intersectionality. At best, simultaneity seems to be a function of an integrative meta-analysis that synthesizes essentially additive data.

Bowleg's more recent research is more hopeful, suggesting an alternative way to empirically study intersectionality using qualitative methods. She advocates the "use of an interview guide approach to elicit narratives about intersectionality" (2013, 757). In her study involving Black gay and bisexual men, sample questions included:

"Let's suppose that someone dropped in from another planet and asked you to tell them about your life as a Black gay or bisexual man. What would you say?"; and "Some say they are Black first and gay or bisexual second. Others say that they are gay or bisexual first and then Black or male second. Then, there are others who say that they don't feel as if they can rank these identities. What about you?" (757)

By thematizing intersectionality—defined in this study as "The notion that multiple social identities interlock and are mutually constitutive" (757)—as a problematic to reflect on lived experiences, researchers elicit responses that "illustrate how the intersection of both advantaged and disadvantaged social identities undermine any idea that multiple identities could be additive" or singular (759). Indeed, Bowleg found that respondents "could not articulate what it was to be a man absent its intersection with race" (763); in other words, they could not inhabit an unmarked category of identity (maleness) that confers privilege, given the constitutive role of marked categories (homo- or bisexuality and Blackness) on the basis of which they experience oppression. Moreover, Bowleg's respondents who did rank their identities—for instance, emphasizing "I'm Black first"—seemed to her to be referencing "the consequence of power relations that shape the construction and salience of social identities":

> In asserting that they were "Black first," interviewees frequently referenced how racial micro aggressions and racial discrimination had fortified their view that race was their most salient identity. . . . [B]eing shunned by families, friends or coworkers [was given] as the key reason for not identifying as gay or bisexual, or doing so only within certain contexts. (764)

What is interesting about Bowleg's findings is that they situate narratives about the constitution of intersectional identities in the context of political intersectionality, that is, in the fragmenting effects of power relations both within and between social groups on multiply oppressed subjects' identities (see chapter 5). Significantly, in tracing the interlocking and mutual constitution of racialized, sexual, and gender identities, Bowleg's intersectional method relies on the unitary categories that were "emic" for her research participants (i.e., they have currency in the actual discourses with which Bowleg's respondents were likely to be familiar in their "everydayness"); however, her conclusions indicate the need to develop new terminology "that reflects men's intersectionality experiences in terms of race and gender" (765). In other words, while the interview guide approach uses emic categories, the normative conclusion of her research advocates the construction of etic categories, which, however, would more aptly express experiences of multiple oppressions. Bowleg suggests that while both men and women experience prejudice and discrimination based on gendered and racialized identities, "the absence of specific language to describe Black men's experiences at the intersection of race and gender is one factor that contributes to the invisibility of Black men's lives" in research and theory (765). As evinced by the interview questions quoted above, received language forces narratives of multiple oppression and identity into serial, ranked, marked, and unmarked categories, a constraint that respondents struggle to resist in narrativizing their experiences. In addition, despite the fact that Bowleg's research participants identify as gay and bisexual Black men, the category of sexuality drops out of Bowleg's normative conclusion, which appears to elide gay/bisexual and heterosexual Black masculinities in much the same way that hegemonic power relations, according to Bowleg's respondents, overdetermine Blackness and render disparaged sexualities invisible, inaudible, or inarticulable. Indeed, if we take seriously Crenshaw's argument about the determination of "race" and "gender" by "unarticulated baselines" of maleness and whiteness, we might conclude, as Devon Carbado does, that "Black male heterosexuality—unmarked in intersectional terms—often stands in for the race. It is the evidentiary body of racial injustice" (2013, 837). On the other hand, "Black women's gender diminishes their representational currency," and "a similar dynamic affects the racial standing of Black gay men" (837). Moreover, Bowleg's approach seems to assume that the intersection of race and gender lends Black women visibility— perhaps conflating their hypervisibility through objectification with the representation of their actual, subjective interests, experiences, and knowledges. Yet, Crenshaw's metaphor of intersectionality and the concepts of political and representational intersectionality reveal that Black women occupy a "location that resists telling" (Crenshaw 1991, 1242).

Even in sophisticated deployments of intersectionality as a qualitative (or quantitative) research paradigm, intersectionality often loses its critical provisionality with respect to existing single-axis frameworks. In chapter 3, I articulate the view that intersectionality is a "provisional concept" that has as its goal the development of an integrative methodology which would fuse what are now falsely separated, mutually exclusive categories of oppression and identity (Crenshaw 1991, 1244–45n9); however, as seems to be borne out by attempts to operationalize the framework in empirical research without reverting to the very categories it sets out to problematize, "intersectionality" does not seem to me to constitute, in itself, such a methodology.

INTERSECTIONAL IDENTITIES?

The dynamics of invisibility and visibility of embodied identities, subjectivities, and experiences are crucial and central to intersectionality as an intervention in categorial, essentialist thinking. If single-axis frameworks for conceptualizing oppression and resistance render Black women and other multiply oppressed groups invisible—if they refuse them representation as a group and refuse to see them representational power with respect to the groups to which they nominally belong—one question that arises is, What precisely does "intersectionality" make visible? Does it represent previously occluded experiences, or "intersectional identities"? Does it make visible the perceptual-cognitive and political mechanisms of exclusion and inclusion, which render some subgroups prototypical of, and others marginal to, group definition? In other words, is intersectionality a representationalist theory of identity that, acting as a corrective to the invisibility of multiply oppressed subjects within monistic politics, makes visible those who can now be declared to have "intersectional identities"? I return to these questions in later chapters, but for the moment I wish to interrogate the claim that intersectionality constitutes a representationalist theory of identity, and, supposing we grant that assumption for the moment, to examine various responses to the question, Which identities does intersectionality make visible?

There may be no straightforward answer to these questions, and there is certainly no agreement in the literature. One answer is that intersectionality advances a politics of visibility for Black women—to whose intellectual labor "intersectionality" owes its existence. As Julia Jordan-Zachery writes, "intersectionality articulates a politics of survival for black women" (2007, 256). As we have seen, the concept emerges from a tradition of Black women's resistance to subordination, exclusion, violence, and marginalization, both within a white-supremacist, heteropatriarchal, capitalist, colonial socioeconomy and within social movements contesting some aspects of hegemony and oppression while internally reproducing others. There are politically important grounds to insist upon intersectionality as a Black feminist politics of visibility, especially given the "post–black feminist turn" in intersectionality studies, and the concerns it should raise regarding the expansion or extension of intersectionality to other social identities—a move that seems to entail the intellectual and political disinheritance of Black feminists (Alexander-Floyd 2012). A politics of visibility can resist a "postracial feminist" deployment of intersectionality that "sheds black women," presuming that "black women need not be the center of intersectional work because intersectionality's virtue is complexity not identity politics *or* that intersectionality is an endlessly expansive analytic that can—and should—describe all subjects' experiences" (Nash 2014b, 46). Strong arguments have been advanced for the "decolonization" of intersectionality and its restoration to Black feminist thought (Floyd) and for the recasting of the master narrative about feminism's temporality, progress, and completion (Nash). But placing Black women at the center of intersectional work or restoring intersectionality to Black feminist thought does not necessarily entail that intersectionality is a representationalist theory of Black women's identity, even though it is commonly used as a shorthand for "Black women's identities" that function as the paradigm of multiply oppressed identities; neither does centering Black women's subjectivities entail the non-generalizability of intersectionality as a theory of identity (see McCall 2005, 1774; May

2015, 24). Still, it is not clear that intersectionality constitutes a "grand theory" of identity: Brittney Cooper suggests that the "most egregious" consequence of intersectionality's wide travel is "the tendency to treat intersectionality as a feminist account of identity, despite Crenshaw's (1991, 1244) very clear assertion that the framework did not constitute some 'new, totalizing theory of identity'" (B. Cooper 2015, 4). If Crenshaw invoked intersectionality as a metaphor to expose "fissures in identity politics" and the failures of representation that they occasion, "the theory has been accused of fomenting unhelpful and essentialist kinds of identifications" (4). Cooper joins María Lugones (whose reading of intersectionality we will more fully examine in chapter 6) in arguing against the view that intersectionality makes Black women's experiences visible: "Crenshaw's argument was that *failure* to begin with an intersectional frame would always result in insufficient attention to black women's experiences of subordination. She did not argue for the converse, namely, that intersectionality would fully and wholly account for the range or depth of black female experience" (4). Cooper draws on W. E. B. Du Bois's metaphor of "lifting the veil" to expose the racial "color line" that structures U.S. society: "while intersectionality should be credited with 'lifting the veil' . . . we should remain clear that the goal of intersectionality is not to provide an epistemological mechanism to bring communities from behind the veil into full legibility. It is rather to rend the veil" and to prevent its "reconstruction" (6).

Carbado argues against the conflation of intersectionality with "double jeopardy," or with a theory exclusively applicable to Black women's and other multiply oppressed identities, arguing that the framework should be used to theorize privileged identities—"men, masculinity, whiteness"—and expanded to include "sexual orientation [and other] social categories that are ostensibly beyond intersectionality's theoretical reach and normative concern" (2013, 817). He elaborates the concepts of "colorblind intersectionality" and "gender-blind intersectionality" to track "instances in which whiteness [or maleness, respectively] helps to produce and is part of a cognizable social category but is invisible/ unarticulated" (817). Indeed, these concepts highlight what Carbado characterizes as an "undertheorized dimension" of Crenshaw's original critique of how sociolegal, theoretical, and political rhetorics and logics produce "racialized modes of gender normativity" and gendered modes of racial normativity (817). That is, he reads Crenshaw as arguing that to the extent that white women's experiences define and are invoked as the "historical base" in discrimination suits (Crenshaw 1989, 149), "gender is invisibly but intersectionally constituted as white" and white women are accorded a "race-less [or race-neutral] status in . . . antidiscrimination laws" (Carbado 2013, 827). Carbado expands on Crenshaw's arguments to examine how in lesbian, gay, bisexual, and transgender social activism and legal advocacy, analogies between sexual identity and racial identity have functioned to secure "white homonormative investments" and reveal how, in the dominant imaginary, "whiteness anchors the intelligibility of gay identity, and Blackness is heterosexualized as a social category whose disadvantages and civil rights aspirations reside in the domain of history" (832; see Rosenblum 1994). In other words, Carbado focuses on how intersectionality may be used to reveal the inflections, mitigations, constructions, and elisions of privileged identities as these intersect "invisibly" with oppressed identities. His view is that "it is erroneous to conceptualize intersectionality as a theory whose exclusive focus is the intersection of race (read: nonwhite) and gender (read: nonmale)," since this "leaves colorblind intersectionality and gender-blind intersectionality unnamed and uninterrogated, further naturalizing white male heterosexuality as the normative baseline against which the rest of us are intersectionally differentiated" (2013, 841).

With respect to identity, one crucial problem that Crenshaw's intersectional critique reveals is that categories of oppression are defined in terms of "invisibly" intersectional experiences, namely, those of subgroups that are relatively privileged with respect to other members of the broader group, or, as Lugones puts it, of "transparent" group members (Lugones 2003, 140). In contrast to "thick" members, transparent members are those who perceive themselves as paradigmatic of the group, a perception that is generally confirmed and "becomes dominant or hegemonic in the group" (140). Transparent members arrogate representational and definitional power to determine who counts as a member of the group of which they become paradigmatic. In this way, thick members are continually made aware of their "otherness," of being outsiders within a group, and are relegated to the margins in intragroup contestations. Lugones argues that the false universalization of transparent members' interests as representative of the entire group marginalizes thick members through erasure. Their identities become fragmented, with the result that "thick members of several oppressed groups become composites of the transparent members of those groups" (140). There is an "invidious[ly] dialectic" relation between the fragmentation of individual and group identities: individual identities are fragmented because society is fragmented into homogenized groups that are constructed as pure of one another inasmuch as every group is structured through a normative affiliation to its transparent members. This structure of affiliation fragments persons who are torn in several different directions to separate groups; importantly, however, identification with other curdled, thick members (with whom one may or may not share certain group memberships) is foreclosed through this process of collective and individual identity formation. The exclusions of thick members—based on the logic of purity—"cross-fertilize" the disconnection of oppressions (141). As we will see in chapter 6, Lugones argues that this dialectic process of fragmentation at the individual and group levels results in the material phenomenon of interlocking oppressions and disjointed resistances; this occurs precisely because groups are imagined as the homogeneous, collective personifications of the identities of their normative, "transparent" members. To the extent that monistic oppressions are viewed as the reflections of the experiences of "transparent" subjects, their interlocking dissimulates the intermeshed oppressions based on the "prismatic identities" (López 2014) of "thick" subjects. Lugones reaches a very important normative conclusion about the politics of representation: unless we reconceptualize groups as "embracing a non-fragmented multiplicity," the representation of ostensible "group interests" will not actually benefit most group members, since these interests reflect only "transparent" members, whose very identities "embody the marginalization of thick members and contain their fragmentation" (2003, 141).

It is doubtful, moreover, whether the intersection of two categories defined through their prototypical, transparent members can yield a representation of thick members' identities or experiences (see chapter 3). For Black women, the intersection of two categories of identity ("race" and "gender") presupposes that one is oppressed as a "Black person" to the extent that one is not oppressed as a "woman," and vice versa. Therefore, conjoining the categories of "racial oppression" and "gender oppression"—to the extent that these are defined in terms of masculinity and whiteness—means that their intersection reveals the non-representation of Black women's identity. The conception of gender oppression is not "pure" of or "uncontaminated" by racial power but is inflected by racial privilege (and vice versa)—privilege that is rendered invisible in the false universalization of normative experience—making the categories "race" and "gender" seem mutually exclusive because racial and gendered oppressions are constructed as mutually exclusive. This is something to keep in mind as we explore further, in subsequent chapters, in what, precisely, the intersectional challenge to monistic thinking consists. We might contemplate the following paradox: on the one hand, as long as monistic categories of oppression (based on privilege) are preserved, their intersection cannot represent multiple, simultaneous oppression, since both categories (assuming two are intersected) are constructed precisely through the erasure of that experience. Yet, on the other hand, monistic categories are already invisibly intersectional, because they presuppose privilege on other axes. They are constituted through the analytic and political exclusion of social groups subordinated by what are viewed as "multiple" systems, whose identities remain fragmented and distorted through invisible lenses of privilege.

The aim of this chapter was to situate intersectionality in the intellectual legacy of Black feminisms and to trace its trajectory and relations to other struggle concepts developed in the context of political organizing by women of color. The mainstreaming of intersectionality has entailed its deracination and its depoliticization; emptied of its critical and subversive force, "intersectionality" is often called to do conceptual work that seems to invert the very aims of the theorists who inaugurated the concept and of the intellectual and political movements in which it germinated. I say this neither to "discipline" nor to "police" the "theoretical boundaries of intersectionality" (Carbado 2013, 841), nor to "dictatorially denote an extant definition of intersectionality," thereby foreclosing an "open dialogue" about the "proper conceptualization and application of the term" (Hancock and Yuval-Davis 2011, xii). It is, nevertheless, worth observing that in contrast to any number of other concepts, theories, or frameworks, arguments delimiting intersectionality's more or less defensible uses are now often derided as dogmatic, while reading practices that undermine its authorship seem to have become the norm. Are there different standards governing practices of citation when the authors in question do not occupy a privileged enunciatory location marked by whiteness and masculinity? Do the social-movement roots of intellectual projects such as Black feminism decisively undermine individuals' theoretical creativity, and render all attempts at conventional citation practice mere "creation story" (Grzanka 2014, xiv)? The project of historicizing intersectionality often appears to be shrouded in the same "vagueness" that other commentators purport is its strength; "no one can really say when the theory emerged. Some say the legal scholar Kimberlé Williams Crenshaw created it. Others locate it even further back, the Combahee River Collective Statement of 1977" (R. A. Ferguson 2012, 91; see also Grzanka 2014, xiv). Tracing intersectionality's intellectual and political history does not mean that its specific articulation in Crenshaw's work is interchangeable with the theoretical constructs that preceded or were contemporaneous with it. Such elisions may inadvertently license a superficial engagement with the generative intellectual work of women-of-color feminisms and the transformations and continuities among political contexts in which scholar-activists organize. Tracing intersectionality to its roots and gaining analytic clarity about its definition and its deployments in Crenshaw's work enable critical engagements with the concept, its past, and its future.

2

Basements and Intersections

If intersectionality has been appropriated without careful attention to its elaboration in the work of Kimberlé Williams Crenshaw, a close reading of her work—widely cited yet infrequently engaged—reveals that the intersection metaphor is called upon to do, at once, too much and too little theoretical work. In the wake of intersectionality's institutionalization, Crenshaw's substantive arguments have, too often, been superficially glossed, distorted, sloppily critiqued, or simply ignored. As intersectionality has traveled from its original context as a critical intervention in U.S. antidiscrimination law, it has crossed many disciplinary, methodological, and geographical boundaries. Although as a concept it originates as a critique of the tendency of law to ideologically obscure and materially reproduce oppression, in feminist theory "intersectionality" often stands in virtually, or metaphorically, as a synonym for oppression—to the extent that the term is commonly used without specifying what, precisely, is intersecting, or how. Kathy Davis argues that the "vagueness" of intersectionality partially explains its popularity and buzzword status (2008, 69). But is "intersectionality" vague, or is it appropriated without deep engagement with Crenshaw's work, and used in ways that distort and even invert the meaning of the concept?

Since Crenshaw's earliest invocation of the intersection metaphor in "Demarginalizing the Intersection of Race and Sex: A Black Feminist Critique of Antidiscrimination Doctrine, Feminist Theory and Antiracist Politics" (1989; hereafter "Demarginalizing"), "intersectionality" has, in the intervening two decades, become the predominant way in feminist theory to reference the relationship among multiple forms of oppression, discrimination, or identity. Yet it is striking that hardly any attention has been given to the other spatial metaphor in Crenshaw's early essay: the "basement" metaphor (1989, 149, 151–52). In this chapter I undertake a close reading of "Demarginalizing" to recover its companion metaphor, which has been largely forgotten in the "mainstreaming" of intersectionality in (white-dominated) feminist theory. In addition to the now-famous intersection metaphor, Crenshaw offers the basement metaphor to show how—by privileging monistic, mutually exclusive, and analogically constituted categories of "race" and "sex" tethered, respectively, to masculinity and whiteness—antidiscrimination law functions to reproduce social hierarchy rather than to remedy it, denying Black women plaintiffs legal redress. I argue that in leaving the basement behind, deployments of "intersectionality" that deracinate the concept from its origins in Black feminist thought also occlude Crenshaw's account of the sociolegal reproduction of hierarchical power. Significantly, this has been evinced not only in theory but also in the course of legal practice and jurisprudence. An analysis of how intersectionality has been deployed in U.S. antidiscrimination law demonstrates that the law insulates and reproduces white male privilege in the very gesture of extending redress for discrimination to multiply advantaged plaintiffs, while refusing it to multiply disadvantaged ones.

AN OVERLOOKED METAPHOR

Although Crenshaw's 1991 essay, "Mapping the Margins: Intersectionality, Identity Politics, and Violence against Women of Color" (hereafter "Mapping"), is more widely read and sometimes credited with introducing the concept of intersectionality, it was in her 1989 essay, "Demarginalizing," that she first issues the call for integrative analysis in antiracist feminist political and legal practice. Precisely because it represents hierarchy, it is remarkable that Crenshaw's basement metaphor has been overlooked in feminist theory. What is the relation of basements to intersections? What theoretical work is each metaphor doing in Crenshaw's account in "Demarginalizing"? Given the significance of both metaphors in Crenshaw's account, it is perhaps surprising how seldom discussions of intersectionality engage the basement metaphor. Of the two spatial metaphors she offers, why has the basement been relegated to obscurity? What happens to the metaphor of intersectionality if we detach it from the account of sociolegal hierarchy that the basement metaphor evokes? In leaving the basement behind, the intersection may have become a more mobile traveling metaphor, but at the risk of forgetting Crenshaw's crucial account of how relations of dominance and subordination are reproduced through the law and in political movements. My argument in this chapter proceeds as follows. First, I situate Crenshaw's argument in the broader intellectual context of race-critical feminist critiques of antidiscrimination law. Then, I perform a close reading of Crenshaw's "Demarginalizing" essay, which reveals that both spatial metaphors—the "basement" and the "intersection"—play an important role in her argument. I elaborate the implications of the disappearance of the basement, and coextensively, of a theory of hierarchical power from many "intersectional" accounts. Finally, I draw on Patricia Hill Collins (1998) and Katherine McKittrick's (2006) conceptualization of "flat geography" to suggest that, divorced from an account of hierarchy, deployments of "intersectionality" risk flattening power relations.

Some of the traction of the term "intersectionality" can surely be attributed to the antecedent concept of "interlocking systems of oppression," which, as we saw in the previous chapter, was defined in a movement context by the Combahee River Collective in "A Black Feminist Statement" as the structural anchor of the experience of simultaneous oppressions and as the target of integrated political struggle (CRC 1983, 210). Yet, although "interlocking systems" forms part of the intellectual, political, and existential history of Crenshaw's conceptualization of the intersection of categories of discrimination (1989) and of structural, political, and representational intersectionality (1991), these are all distinct concepts that deserve careful analysis and attentive operationalization. Juxtaposing Crenshaw's two metaphors with the CRC's account reveals something else: the notion that social power and hierarchy can be imagined spatially, represented in the vertical architecture connoted by the basement and its superincumbent floors, is expressed in the CRC's claim that "we might use our position at the bottom, however, to make a clear leap into revolutionary action. If Black women were free, it would mean that everyone else would have to be free since our freedom would necessitate the destruction of all the systems of oppression" (1983, 215). Here they draw explicitly on Michele Wallace, who observes that for "women who are Black who are feminists . . . there is not yet an environment in this society remotely congenial to our struggle"; "being on the bottom, we would have to do what no one else has done: we would have to fight the world" ([1975] 2000, 523, quoted in CRC 1983, 215). Significantly, fighting the world entails liberating the world: destroying all systems of oppression in a simultaneous, integrated struggle, radically transforming it through "identity politics"; for multiply oppressed groups working to end their own, "as opposed to . . . somebody else's oppression," the implications of self-emancipation are world-historical inasmuch as they require the dismantling of the entire interstructure of oppression (CRC 1983, 212). As we saw in chapter 1, the Combahee River Collective draws on the "vanguard center" politics of the Third World Women's Alliance—which, in turn, inherits this approach from Black Communist feminists such as Claudia Jones—who similarly argued that the liberation of Black women would entail the liberation of all other groups (Beal 1970a; Roth 2004, 91). The resonances to Marx and Engels's claim that "the proletariat, the lowest stratum of our present society, cannot stir, cannot raise itself up, without the whole superincumbent strata of . . . society being sprung up into the air" ([1848] 1996, 168) are likely not coincidental given the TWWA's Marxist leanings; just as Marx and Engels assigned a "world-historical role" to proletarians, capable of "abolishing their own previous mode of appropriation and thereby every other previous mode of appropriation" (168), so too, here, the CRC argues that Black women have a distinctive revolutionary task inasmuch as their self-emancipation will result in the emancipation of all other oppressed groups in the United States. Conceptualizing hierarchy in spatial, vertical, architectural terms thus has a long history, reflected, for instance, in the ethos of "lifting as we climb," adopted as the motto of the National Association of Colored Women founded at the turn of the twentieth century (Terrell 1898, 16; see Springer 1999, 2). These spatial conceptualizations of struggle are not—as intersectionality is often invoked today—mere or "empty" metaphors: as Ruth Wilson Gilmore and James A. Tyner have each argued, "a geographical imperative lies at the heart of every struggle for social justice" (Tyner 2007, 219; Gilmore 2002). Specifically, Black radicalism, Tyner proposes, "is about the remaking of spaces" (2007, 219). As we will see, members of the group situated at the bottom of the social hierarchy—whom Critical Race legal scholar Derrick Bell has evocatively imagined as "the faces at the bottom of the well" (1992)—are constructed as having the revolutionary potential through their self-liberation to liberate other oppressed groups (which other groups lack, because their "climbing" the social hierarchy, betraying an allegiance with those at the bottom, materially requires keeping hierarchy in place). The intellectual and political history of imagining "alternative geographies" (Tyner 2007, 218) arguably animates Crenshaw's invocation of the basement metaphor in "Demarginalizing."

CRITICAL RACE FEMINISM AND ANTIDISCRIMINATION LAW

One contribution of Critical Race Theory has been to expose how, in a post–civil rights era in which legal forms of oppression based on "race" and "sex" are supposed to have been eradicated, the law nevertheless reproduces oppressive social hierarchies. This belies, to quote Bell, a "commonly held view of racial advancement as a slow but steady surge forward" (1991, 597). Antidiscrimination law, in particular, helps cement a perception of the U.S. legal system as having reinvented itself on the way to creating a "postracial" society—while being one of the primary institutions reproducing whiteness as property. Cheryl Harris's (1993) groundbreaking analysis of whiteness as a form of property helps give content to the claim that white supremacy persists in a post–civil rights era where the ostensible deracialization of law has resulted in formal equality. After all, law protects property rights of all kinds, so the persistence of the valorization of whiteness through the legal right to exclude is not inconsistent with equality before the law understood as a civil right. As Harris explains, whiteness and property share a common premise a conceptual nucleus—of a right to exclude. This conceptual nucleus has proven to be a powerful center around which whiteness as property has taken shape. Following the period of slavery and conquest, white identity became the basis of racialized privilege that was ratified and legitimated in law as a type of status property. After legalized segregation was overturned, whiteness as property evolved into a more modern form through the law's ratification of the settled expectations of relative white privilege as a legitimate and natural baseline. (1993, 1714)

As we will see, recent decisions in antidiscrimination cases have upheld these "settled expectations" that naturalize white (male) privilege. Yet, along with affirmative action and the presidency of Barack Obama, antidiscrimination law is often held up as one sign that the "postracial moment" has already arrived. Warning more than twenty-five years ago against that misperception, Crenshaw argued that antidiscrimination law should not be viewed as "a permanent pronouncement of society's commitment to ending racial subordination" (1988, 1335). Rather, she characterizes antidiscrimination law as "an ongoing ideological struggle in which the occasional winners harness the moral, coercive, and consensual power of law"; consequently, "the victories it offers can be ephemeral and the risks of engagement substantial" (1335). In a recent article reflecting on twenty years of Critical Race Theory, she reiterates that "faith in formal equality's triumph over white supremacy was unwarranted; formal equality did little to disrupt ongoing patterns of institutional power and the reproduction of differential privileges and burdens across race" (2010, 1312). Here, Crenshaw diagnoses "the emergence of postracialism, a compelling ideological frame" that dehistoricizes race, relegates "racial justice discourse to the hinterlands of contemporary political thought," and announces the arrival of a "racially egalitarian America" (1313–14). Although "race remains available to mark non-white delinquency and to deploy disciplinary power to contain it," ideologically buttressing the criminalization, mass incarceration, and economic marginalization of non-white groups, the discourse of postracialism renders the "material consequences of racial exploitation and social violence" ideologically inaccessible (1327; see Haney López 2010).

In "Demarginalizing," Crenshaw performs an intersectional analysis of three cases that involve Black women plaintiffs alleging discrimination against their corporate employers. Crenshaw demonstrates that in U.S. courts, conceptual models of identity and discrimination—the mutually exclusive "protected" categories of "sex" and "race"—render legal redress impossible for Black women plaintiffs precisely because of their intersection. Black women were not viewed by the judges deciding these cases as "representatives" of either protected group to which they belong, Black people nor women, because their experiences diverge in gendered and racialized ways from those deemed the "historical base" (Crenshaw 1989, 148). When Black women are offered legal redress, it is on the condition that it is denied to other members of the group(s) whom they are taken not to represent. Relative privilege renders cognizable the discrimination claims on the basis of discrete categories advanced by white women and Black men (140). Moreover, white women and Black men emerge, in Crenshaw's argument, if not always as the direct beneficiaries of antidiscrimination laws and policies, as the imagined normative subjects of "protected" groups. By contrast, the intersection is a place of legal invisibility for Black women plaintiffs, who, by the positivist logic of representation underwriting antidiscrimination law, are denied legal redress. Precisely because of the "multidimensionality of Black women's experiences" of discrimination—which the law acknowledges only as compound, additive, or unitary—and the privileging of whiteness and maleness in defining "normative" experiences of discrimination, Black women find themselves excluded by design from protected classes, and also are generally denied redress as a distinct class.

Many people are astonished to hear the logic of the decisions Crenshaw cites, particularly the *DeGraffenreid* decision (which I discuss in detail in the next section). It contradicts the intuition that those who face the most egregious discrimination should justifiably receive the most extensive remedy. Accordingly, if Black women are the targets of compound discrimination, then it follows that multiple sources of discrimination would need to be addressed. But this reasoning presupposes a faith in the law that U.S. sociolegal history does not bear out. On the contrary, courts deciding discrimination claims exhibit pervasive bias against Black women plaintiffs, denying them redress for discrimination more frequently than any other group, including white men (Best et al. 2011). That the law has reconfigured itself against the potentially redemptive effects of legal reform and constitutional amendment is evinced in the role antidiscrimination doctrine plays in reproducing a class system articulating racial and gender hierarchies.

If, as Crenshaw argues, antidiscrimination law represents an ideological struggle, representation—in its political, legal, and perceptual-cognitive senses—plays a crucial role. The traffic in representations between white-supremacist and heteropatriarchal ideologies, democratic processes (such as state referenda that have repealed antidiscrimination and affirmative-action measures), and antiracist and feminist movements circulates in an economy that structures even habitual, prereflective perceptions of our gendered and racialized embodiments. The institutionalization of white patriarchal power through antidiscrimination law—notably, an important site of contestation of class relations—is evinced in the privileging of whiteness and masculinity even when these are not embodied in white male plaintiffs and especially when they are embodied in white male (corporate) defendants. If the failure of U.S. courts to redress discrimination against Black women by corporate employers is surprising, how can we reconcile the fact that white male plaintiffs, in whose favor courts have an existing presumption, more easily and more profitably win suits charging employment discrimination than do women and men of color and white women (Selmi 2001; Oppenheimer 2003; Best et al. 2011)?

Despite the endemic nature of gendered racism and other forms of discrimination in the workplace, Kevin Clermont and Stewart Schwab found that between 1979 and 2006 the plaintiff win rate for employment discrimination cases was 15 percent, as opposed to 51 percent for other cases (2009, 129–30). Revealing the asymmetry in resources between employees and employers, 42.76 percent of cases were appealed after the plaintiff (employee) won, whereas only 10.12 percent were when the defendant (employer) did—and employers won approximately 85 percent of the time (Clermont and Schwab 2004, 450). However, plaintiffs prove more successful when they mobilize social privilege in their discrimination claims: the economic staying power to pursue the litigation process through trial and appeals; the representational power to lay claim to protected groups or categories of proscribed discrimination; and the sociolegal power to compel courts to cognize and redress their experiences.

Consider *Rudebusch v. Arizona*, a successful Title VII discrimination claim filed by forty white male professors against their employer, Northern Arizona University (NAU). In 1995, after the implementation of a onetime equity pay raise, a class of NAU "female and non-minority male professors" sued the university's president, Eugene Hughes, for equal protection violations under §1981 and §1983 of Title 42 of the Civil Rights Act, which, intended to advance the Reconstruction Amendments to the U.S. Constitution, respectively prohibit intentional race discrimination in employment contracts and provide a remedy for the violation of federally protected rights (Rudebusch v. Hughes 2002). Less than a year later, class representative George Rudebusch and thirty-nine white male professors sued NAU under Title VII (Rudebusch v. Arizona 2007). In November 1996 the court consolidated the cases. It affirmed judgment in favor of the defendants in the class action, deeming Hughes "immune" from personal liability. But the Title VII action continued. The court found the equity pay raise violated the rights of white male faculty who had been ineligible for any increase. Although it denied the argument advanced by *Rudebusch* that the equity raise in itself "unnecessary trammeled" the rights of white male faculty members whose earnings were below average compared to their similarly gendered and racialized counterparts, the court nonetheless decided the equity pay raise went beyond "attaining a balance," raising some women's and non-white men's salaries above those of white male professors (Rudebusch v. Arizona 2007). It found that "the real question is not whether Rudebusch should have been brought up to the mean, but whether using the predicted salary of similarly situated white male faculty for the minority and female [salary] adjustments somehow overcompensated these minority and female faculty members" in a fashion that the court deemed "more than remedial" (Rudebusch v. Hughes 2002). In 2007, after ten years of litigation, the court awarded a settlement of almost $2 million. Of 261 plaintiffs alleging discrimination, forty obtained "relief" under Title VII, and all of them were white men. Moreover, the university had already "compensated" them for the equity raise, effectively reversing it.

Cheryl Harris's analysis of the contemporary manifestations of the legal protection and reproduction of property rights in whiteness focuses on affirmative action. Yet in the aftermath of the widespread repeal of affirmative-action measures, often by "democratic" processes such as state referenda in California and Washington, antidiscrimination law remains one of the legal spaces of contestation and reproduction of the sociolegal and economic capital of whiteness. As Harris writes, whiteness as property, in the postracial era, may have "taken on more subtle forms, but retains its core characteristic—the legal legitimation of expectations of power and control that enshrine the status quo as a neutral baseline, while masking the maintenance of white privilege and domination" (1993, 1715). In a more recent article, Harris and Kimberly West-Faulcon demonstrate how antidiscrimination law has been doctrinally reframed to focus on "disparate treatment of whites as the paradigmatic and ultimately preferred claim," a process they term "whitening discrimination" (2010, 81). They analyze the U.S. Supreme Court's decision in *Ricci et al. v. DeStefano et al.* (2009), a case brought by twenty firefighters (eighteen of whom were white and one Latino) successfully charging that the city of New Haven's decision not to certify the results of a promotional test that were skewed against Black and Latino firefighters (resulting in promotions only for whites) constituted racial discrimination (2010, 75; Ricci et al. v. DeStefano et al. 2009). Harris and West-Faulcon argue that "this doctrinal move has effectively constrained the operation of antidiscrimination law and remedies—indeed turning the remedies into racial injuries and further legitimizing a narrative in which whites are (or are at risk of being) repeatedly victimized because of their race" (2010, 82). As Crenshaw puts it, the "whitening" of the paradigmatic subject of antidiscrimination law reflects a "shifting signification of whiteness from a marker of racial privilege to racial victimization" whereby what is remedied is the "'diminished overrepresentation' of whites" in institutions and workplaces where they enjoyed dominance (2011b, 1335n250). Like affirmative action, which "was vacuumed out of its modest role as a facilitator of change, a corrector, a remover of obstacles, and . . . is now installed as the quintessential embodiment of the posse of ideas that it was designed to vanquish—discrimination, racial supremacy, segregation, and racial stereotyping" (Crenshaw 2007, 133), pay equity measures such as those contested by Rudebusch are constructed as illicit threats to naturalized white male entitlement. *Rudebusch v. Arizona* is an apposite illustration of the successful use of antidiscrimination law by white men to defeat measures that challenge racial-gendered hegemony by constructing as victims of discrimination those whose privilege to exclude is undermined by such measures. In other words, "whitened" antidiscrimination law is increasingly used to reproduce "societal discrimination for which there is no constitutional remedy," legally entrenching the racial (and gendered) privileges which material inequalities and oppressions produce (2011b, 1325).

REPRESENTATION AND INVISIBILITY

In "Demarginalizing," Crenshaw demonstrates that prevailing Title VII definitions of discrimination render Black women's experiences invisible to the courts and their claims of discrimination inadmissible. Claims combining race and sex discrimination frameworks are not cognizable under U.S. law (Carbado 2000). Crenshaw concludes that Black women's experiences of discrimination cannot be redressed by existing concepts: "problems of exclusion cannot be solved simply by including Black women within an already established analytical structure" that excludes them by design (1989, 140). The existing analytical structure—in law and political practice—is premised on the assumption that, as categories of discrimination and as corresponding aspects of identity, race and gender are discrete. To establish a prima facie case of discrimination, a plaintiff has to appeal to a protected factor (race or sex) in which to ground her claim of disparate treatment or impact. Even if, as some courts have allowed, multiple factors are named, this still presupposes a unitary conception of discrimination and identity.

Crenshaw shows that this unitary conception fails to account for Black women's lived experiences of discrimination. On the one hand, "Black women's experiences are broader than the general categories discrimination discourse provides" (1989, 149). Moreover, how these categories are interpreted and understood—their conceptual content—is based on the experiences of relatively privileged members of oppressed groups. Their specific experiences are falsely universalized to all members of those groups. As false universals, they render invisible the ways in which social privilege (conferred by race, gender, sexuality, national citizenship, and age, among others) mitigates or otherwise constructs experiences of oppression.

By now, intersectionality theory is widely accepted in feminist circles. It is widely conceded that we all have "intersectional" identities and that "how we experience discrimination," for those of us who do, "is shaped by the way in which our identities are compounded" (Carbado 2000, 2090). Despite this consensus, unitary categories of identity have not been supplanted and continue to be mobilized in essentialist terms, even when "intersected." Although white women's gendered experiences are still, arguably, seen as generalizable to all women, Black women's gendered experiences are not seen as representing those of all "women." This abiding asymmetry reveals that despite the theoretical ascendancy of intersectionality the representational claims that white women make on behalf of "women," whether in the course of feminist political practice or in courtrooms, are not available to Black women whose racialization is taken to preclude the generalizability of their experiences. Carbado discerns this logic in critiques of intersectionality which allege that "intersectionality is necessarily only and about Black women"; such critiques

> reflect . . . a similar representational problem: Black women cannot specifically name themselves in a theory (they are too similar to be different), nor can they function as the backdrop for the genesis and

articulation of a generalizable framework about power and marginalization (they are too different to be the same). (2013, 813)

Of course, white women's gendered experiences are no less racialized, and therefore no more generalizable than are Black women's; but this racialization is rendered invisible through the representational, territorializing claim to "women's" experiences that position white women as normative subjects of that category.

Black women remain "too similar to be different and too different to be the same": "'impossible subjects' of antidiscrimination law" (Carbado 2013, 813, quoting Mae Ngai). In the three cases that Crenshaw examines, Black women's representational claims—their claims to have faced workplace discrimination as Black women, as women, and as Black people—were dismissed by courts. In her analysis of *DeGraffenreid v. General Motors* (1976), *Moore v. Hughes Helicopter* (1983), and *Payne v. Travenol* (1982), Crenshaw demonstrates the following. In *DeGraffenreid*, the court refused to recognize the possibility of compound discrimination against Black women (1989, 148). Instead, it analyzed their claim using white women's experience as "the historical base" (148). As we will see below, this served to obscure the distinct forms and multidimensionality of discrimination that Black women experience (148). In *Moore*, the court decided that a Black woman plaintiff could not use evidence of discrimination against women to ground her discrimination claim, because "she had not claimed discrimination as a woman, but 'only' as a Black woman" (148). In this case, "the court would not entertain the notion that discrimination experienced by Black women is indeed sex discrimination," which the plaintiff could establish with reference to disparate impact statistics on women (148). Finally, in *Travenol*, the court concluded that Black women could not represent an entire class of Black people, due to presumed conflicts within that class along lines of gender. What this means is that if the court does allow Black women to use disparate impact statistics "indicating racially disparate treatment," as it did in *Travenol*, the remedy for discrimination determined by the court might not extend to Black men (148). In this case, antidiscrimination doctrine functioned as a "divide and conquer" strategy, presenting Black women with distinctive risks of engagement.

Crenshaw's analysis demonstrates that the law constructs Black women as representatives neither of a class subject to "sex" discrimination nor of one subject to "race" discrimination. This is important, because U.S. law considers that "discrimination proceeds from the identification of a class or category" (Crenshaw 1989, 150). Under Title VII, a finding of unlawful discrimination does not always require evidence of intent to discriminate; it can be based on descriptive statistical data showing disproportionate impact on a determinate group (Crenshaw 1989, 150n29; Carbado 2000, 2090). Sustaining the representational claim that one belongs to, and can stand in for, the group is crucial, since intent to discriminate and disproportionate impact are both measured with respect to a collectivized identity. In employment discrimination cases, the burden is on the plaintiff (the employee) to show that the defendant (the employer) has treated all individuals in the class in a similar way (Crenshaw 1989, 150). What the claimants must do, then, is to constitute themselves as representatives of an identifiable class and to demonstrate that all members of that class have faced similar discrimination.

Again and again, Black women were denied redress by the courts because the courts refused to view them as representatives of a class protected against discrimination. In the three cases Crenshaw considers, Black women's representational claims were dismissed using monistic concepts of discrimination, that is, discrimination based on sex and discrimination based on race (Crenshaw 1989). When race and sex intersect in Black women's legal claims, they render these claims inadmissible. Consider, for instance, the reply of the court to the plaintiffs in *DeGraffenreid*, a group of Black women who brought a complaint of compound discrimination against their employer, General Motors, alleging race and sex discrimination (Crenshaw 1989, 142). The plaintiffs were fired in a seniority-based layoff, which targeted Black women; seniority was based on prior discriminatory hiring, a fact that the court acknowledged but refused to redress, citing the lapse of the "time limitations" for employees to file a discrimination complaint with the Equal Employment Opportunity Commission (EEOC). Based on this, the court deemed that "the employer was free to consider that its earlier discrimination was lawful." White women and Black men had been hired earlier than Black women; their seniority, based on "legal" discrimination, protected them from dismissal. A prima facie case of discrimination under Title VII requires membership in a protected class, satisfactory job performance, adverse employment action, and different treatment from similarly situated employees outside the protected class. Yet Black women were denied redress in their compound claim of race and sex discrimination. This is how the court decided the case:

> The legislative history surrounding Title VII does not indicate that the goal of the statute was to create a new classification of "black women" who would have greater standing than, for example, a black male. The prospect of the creation of new classes of protected minorities, governed only by the mathematical principles of permutation and combination, clearly raises the prospect of opening the hackneyed Pandora's box. (DeGraffenreid v. General Motors 1976, 145; see Crenshaw 1989, 142)

Black women are not seen to constitute a class of "protected minorities," yet they are also denied redress as a "permutation" or "combination" of classes (of the class "Black people" and the class "women"). But this is problematic, since it is only to the extent that Black women's experiences are similar to those of Black men or white women—who are viewed as the prototypical members of their respective classes—that courts decide to extend them protection (Carbado 2000, 2090). Crenshaw writes, "boundaries of sex and race discrimination doctrine are defined respectively by white women's and Black men's experiences" (1989, 143). "Protection" is extended to Black women only to the extent that their experiences of discrimination "coincide" with those of Black men or with those of white women (143). To the extent that Black women's experiences do not coincide, their claims of race discrimination and sex discrimination cannot be evinced. Indeed, in *DeGraffenreid* the court reframed the plaintiff's compound discrimination claim as alleging separate claims of race discrimination and sex discrimination and then found evidence of neither (Carbado 2000, 2090). In refusing to treat the compound discrimination claim, the court constructed redress as a "super-remedy" that would ostensibly elevate Black women above Black men (and, by extension, above white women).

Yet why would considering Black women as a distinct protected class raise them above other classes? Would it not just place them at an equivalent standing? What seems to be presupposed in the court's remarks, and what it naturalizes with its finding, is Black women's structural positioning in racial and gendered hierarchies that privilege maleness and whiteness. If legislators did not intend that Title VII be used to protect Black women from discrimination against them as Black women, it was because they did not construct "discrimination" with Black women at the center of that legal concept (Crenshaw 1989; Carbado 2000). As Devon Carbado writes, the court's analysis in *DeGraffenreid* reveals that "Congress did not contemplate that black women could be discriminated against as black women" (2000, 2090), or we might add, that their superexploitation is naturalized so as to fall outside the legally cognizable boundaries of what constitutes "unlawful discrimination." What this means is that Black women's experiences of gendered racism are excluded not by accident, but by design. Black women are rendered unrepresentative, and therefore unrepresentable, by monistic concepts of discrimination that privilege masculinity and whiteness in their construction of protected classes.

"INTERSECTIONALITY" AND U.S. LAW

However, the *DeGraffenreid* standard has not gone entirely uncontested. But from an intersectional perspective, as I construe it, the alternative approaches presuppose problematic conceptions of discrimination. Yet some scholars, such as D. Aaron Lacy (2008), argue that successful "sex-plus" claims mean that courts have, at least to some extent, adopted an intersectional framework. In *Jefferies v. Harris County Community Action Association* (1980), a Black woman made a race- and sex-discrimination claim for first having been overlooked for a promotion, and then having been terminated in her position by her employer (Carbado 2000, 2090). The positions for which she applied were filled by Black men and non-Black women (of whom some were white and others were women of color). When a trial court dismissed her claim, she appealed, and the U.S. Court of Appeals for the Fifth Circuit agreed that the earlier court had failed to consider her claim of compound discrimination. In *Jefferies*, the court recognized that discrimination against Black women can exist "even in the absence of discrimination against black men or white women" (Jefferies v. Harris County Community Action Association; see Carbado 2000, 2091). In fact, the court stated that it is "'beyond belief' that Title VII would bar discrimination against women, or against blacks, but not against black [women]" (Bartlett and Harris 1998, 1068, quoting Jefferies v. Harris County Community Action Association). Departing from the *DeGraffenreid* standard, the court interpreted the "or" in the list of protected factors of discrimination as conjunctive, not disjunctive. That is, the court stated that Congress intended to prohibit discrimination based on any or all the listed characteristics: race, sex, national origin, and so on (Carbado 2000, 2091).

Although undermining the mutual exclusivity of protected grounds seems like a progressive judicial decision, it is important to note that what led to this finding was the "sex-plus" analysis earlier established by the U.S. Supreme Court in *Phillips v. Martin Marietta Corporation* (1971). It is significant that *Phillips* had been decided six years prior to *DeGraffenreid*, and nearly twenty years prior to the publication of Crenshaw's 1989 critique. This anachronism demonstrates that it is inaccurate to conflate "sex-plus" claims with Crenshaw's conception of intersectionality. In *Phillips*, the Supreme Court "held that the disparate treatment of a subclass of one sex can violate Title VII" (Carbado 2000, 2091). This decision was based on coupling a protected factor under Title VII (in this case, sex) with a nonprotected one (in this case, having preschool-age children). An employment policy that precluded women, but not men, with preschool-age children from holding certain positions violated Title VII. Extending "sex-plus" analysis to *Jefferies*, the U.S. Court of Appeals "characteriz[ed] her as a woman who, because of a secondary consideration, race, was treated differently" by her employer (Carbado 2000, 2091).

Indeed, in a footnote in "Demarginalizing," Crenshaw considers whether *Jefferies* is an exception to *DeGraffenreid* and argues that it affirms the racialized logic through which "sex discrimination" is territorialized by white women: "the very fact that Black women's claims are seen as aberrant suggests that sex discrimination doctrine is centered on the experiences of white women" (1989, 143n13). In a "sex-plus" claim, sex is given foundational status, to which is added "either an immutable characteristic or the exercise of a fundamental right" (Arnett v. Aspin 1994, 1241). As Carbado argues, there are three interrelated problems with "sex-plus" doctrine when applied to Black women's discrimination claims. First, it requires plaintiffs to argue that their race is subordinate or "secondary" to their gender in their experiences of discrimination (2000, 2091). Second, even though race is a protected classification under Title VII, "sex-plus" doctrine "equates race discrimination with other 'pluses' such as marital or familial status" (2091). Third, because plaintiffs can only add one "plus" to their sex-discrimination claim, the "sex-plus" doctrine "limits the number of characteristics a plaintiff can allege as contributing to her employer's discrimination" effectively to two (2091). Indeed, although courts have upheld the decision in *Jefferies* in the majority of cases, they have also upheld the "just pick two" rule concerning immutable, protected characteristics (Judge v. Marsh 1986; Levit 2002, 229).

Having fleshed out its implications, I take it that intersectionality theorists would scarcely agree that "sex-plus" represents the adoption by courts of an intersectional framework to cognize multiple, simultaneous, and nonhierarchical grounds. Indeed, "sex-plus" might be more accurately viewed as an additive framework, one that constructs a causal hierarchy among discrete protected factors and forms of discrimination. In this sense, the problem with extending "sex-plus" doctrine to an analysis of compound discrimination is that it misrepresents the relationship between "race" and "sex." "Sex-plus" doctrine is designed for identifying pretextual discrimination (i.e., where one kind of difference is used as a pretext to discriminate on the basis of another difference). But race is not just a pretext for gender discrimination. The doctrine implies that in adjudicating a Black woman's claim, "the plaintiff's racial identity [is] not itself important, but rather, that it was used as an excuse for 'sex' discrimination" (P. R. Smith 1991, 44–45). This obviates the profound effects of racism in Black women's lives. It also "conceptually implies that there is a raceless standardized group of women from whom Black women differ" and who are the normative civil rights subjects of "sex" as a protected category of identity (44–45). In other words, the "sex-plus" doctrine does not effectively redress the problems of representation facing Black women plaintiffs alleging discrimination. Black women's representational hold on "gender" and "race" remains tenuous, whereas their race-privileged and gender-privileged counterparts enjoy representational power. Neither are Black women seen as a "discrete and insular minority" (to use equal protection language); nor are they viewed as representatives of their "sex-class" or "race-class" in Title VII doctrine.

"Sex-plus" doctrine does not challenge the representational economy in which discrimination claims circulate. Contrary to Lacy's view, I argue we should not interpret it as an intersectional remedy. Lacy conflates "sex-plus" claims with "intersectional" ones; he concludes, "since *Jefferies*, courts have generally accepted intersectionality theory" (2008, 562). However, unlike Crenshaw's intersectional critique of categories of discrimination, "sex-plus" in no way transforms the operative categories, nor does it remove white women and Black men as the normative subjects of their respective protected classes. "Sex-plus" claims, furthermore, do not represent the simultaneity of, and nonhierarchy among, forms of discrimination, theoretical goals toward which intersectionality as an analytic sensibility aims.

However—evincing both the expansive influence of Crenshaw's argument and, paradoxically, the widespread inattention to it—in *Harrington v. Cleburne County Board of Education* (2001) the court made reference to "intersectionality," even obligating the plaintiff, Mary L. Harrington, to pursue an "intersectional" theory of discrimination to describe her claim. Harrington, an African American woman, sued a county school board in Alabama for violating the Equal Pay Act, the Equal Protection Clause, and Title VII, claiming she was paid less than whites and males in comparable positions, was given additional work, and received less compensatory leave time. While hers was a claim of "race and sex discrimination," the court, sua sponte (of its own accord), gave Harrington three options. First, she could limit her claim to one alleged basis of discrimination, either race or sex, abandoning the other. Second, she could divide her claim, alleging discrimination "either because she is black, or because she is female." Third, she could pursue an "intersectional theory" of discrimination, "that is, that the defendant treated her disparately because she belongs simultaneously to two or more protected classes" (Harrington v. Cleburne 2001). Interestingly, Harrington resisted the intersectional interpretation of her claim, unsuccessfully sought relief from the court's order, and continued to try to claim discrimination on "distinct grounds of race and sex discrimination theory, and not on the 'intersectionality theory' that she elected under duress because of the conditions imposed on the trial of claims based on distinct discriminatory motives" (Harrington v. Cleburne 2001). Rather than remedy political invisibility, in the courtroom "intersectionality" became a device through which the representational claims of still another Black woman plaintiff—whose case the court declared "a poster child for confusion in pleading"—were muted (Harrington v. Cleburne 2001).

Harrington may have tried to seek relief from the court's "intersectionality theory" because she was aware of how poorly "intersectional" claims fare in courts. Rachel Best and her collaborators (2011) quantitatively analyzed a representative sample of thirty-five years of federal employment discrimination claims. They found that not only are women of color "less likely to win their case than is any other demographic group," but "plaintiffs who make intersectional claims, alleging that they were discriminated against on more than one ascriptive characteristic, are only half as likely to win their cases" as plaintiffs who allege discrimination on a single protected ground—15 percent compared to 31 percent (2011, 2). If "intersectionality" as it is (mis)interpreted by courts can be shown to imperil rather than illuminate the discrimination claims advanced by "multiply disadvantaged" plaintiffs, what better evidence can be furnished for the claim that the law can adapt even to profound challenges to its analytical structure and its political legitimacy?

THE TWO METAPHORS

Legal categories of discrimination based on "race" and on "gender" fail to adequately represent the experiences of Black women. Not only as unitary categories, but even when intersected, they do not adequately represent their experiences. Although in many feminist deployments intersectionality is seen as the guarantor of an integrative analysis of race and gender, in Crenshaw's early account the intersection of race and gender categories reveals their inadequacy to account for and redress discrimination against Black women workers. To see this, Crenshaw asks us to

consider an analogy to traffic in an intersection, coming and going in all four directions. Discrimination, like traffic through an intersection, may flow in one direction, and it may flow in another. If an accident happens in an intersection, it can be caused by cars travelling from any number of directions and, sometimes, from all of them. Similarly, if a Black woman is harmed because she is in an intersection, her injury could result from sex discrimination or race discrimination. . . . But it is not always easy to reconstruct an accident: Sometimes the skid marks and the injuries simply indicate that they occurred simultaneously, frustrating efforts to determine which driver caused the harm. (1989, 149)

This metaphor—as nearly universal as traffic jams and gendered racism have become—nevertheless carries culturally specific resonances that are perhaps not appreciated everywhere (Lykke 2010, 71, 73–75). As we will explore further in chapter 4, many critiques of the intersection metaphor accuse it of being "too static," yet emphasize the *roads* (as opposed to the *traffic*) that "meet at an intersection, but . . . go in separate directions before and after this meeting" (Lykke 2010, 73). For instance, Dorthe Staunæs and Dorte Marie Søndegaard wonder whether it is possible to rely less on a "structuralist" approach and to "use the term *intersection* without thinking of crossroads but with focus on a place or space between sections (inter sections) which is productive of sociocultural phenomena. Twisting the concept in this way, one can inquire whether the intersection takes place between entities that are already fixed? Or is it the place that creates the entities?" (2011, 53.) Critiquing what they call the "classic intersectionality approach," Staunæs and Søndegaard propose a "Foucaultian take on power, coupled with the concept of intersectionality understood as a disorderly space of emergence" (53). Yet a more attentive reading of the passage reveals that the simile Crenshaw draws is between discrimination and *traffic* in an intersection: mobile, colliding, injurious. With U.S. litigation culture in the background, the allegorical quality of the metaphor is that the intersection functions as the site of an accident for which no driver—no form of discrimination—wants to take responsibility or claim fault.

"Race" and "sex," conceptualized in mutually exclusive terms and inflected by experiences of relative privilege, are not adequate to the simultaneity of experiences of what can only awkwardly be termed "compound discrimination"; rather, they fragment or even erase these multidimensional experiences. Categories of race and gender, whose imagined normative subjects draw on gendered or racial privilege, have been conceptualized to the exclusion of each other and through analogy. When intersected, they do not illuminate the causal history of Black women's oppression; as categories they are too narrow, precisely because they exclude each other. When Black women do seek legal redress using these categories, courts have devised any number of interpretations and arguments to reject their claims of discrimination.

The intersection metaphor speaks to the interplay between institutionalized gendered racism and its reproduction through antidiscrimination law and corporate power. The conceptual structure of categories of discrimination is such that when they intersect, they render experiences of compound, simultaneous discriminations invisible. But this is no accident. This is how law serves to reproduce deeply entrenched social hierarchies: by offering remedy for discrimination only where claims are nonintersectional, that is, where plaintiffs can demonstrate—through their hold on whiteness or maleness, or, indeed, both—that their experiences of discrimination are legible through one, and only one, category of discrimination. To show how such plaintiffs mobilize their relative privilege to ascend social hierarchies even as they reinscribe them, Crenshaw offers a second spatial metaphor.

Oppression is reproduced through antidiscrimination law; remedial strategies serve Black women plaintiffs only to the extent that they can be absorbed into protected social groups, which at the same time they are denied the ability to represent. This reproduces Black women's subordination in social hierarchies. Rather than remedying discrimination against Black women, antidiscrimination law actually reproduces it. The basement metaphor illustrates the crux of Crenshaw's argument about the sociolegal reproduction of gendered race/class hierarchies:

> Imagine a basement which contains all people who are disadvantaged on the basis of race, sex, class, sexual preference, age and/or physical ability. These people are stacked—feet standing on shoulders—with those on the bottom being disadvantaged by the full array of factors, up to the very top, where the heads of those disadvantaged by a singular factor brush up against the ceiling. Their ceiling is actually the floor above which only those who are not disadvantaged in any way reside. . . . [T]hose above the ceiling admit from the basement only those who can say that "but for" the ceiling, they too would be in the upper room. A hatch is developed through which those placed immediately below can crawl. Yet this hatch is generally available only to those who—due to the singularity of their burden and their otherwise privileged position relative to those below—are in the position to crawl through. Those who are multiply-burdened are generally left below unless they can somehow pull themselves into the groups that are permitted to squeeze through the hatch. As this analogy translates for Black women, the problem is that they can receive protection only to the extent that their experiences are recognizably similar to those whose experiences tend to be reflected in antidiscrimination doctrine. (1989, 151–52)

The "unprotected margin" of the basement is the intersection, a place of legal invisibility. Like the intersection, the basement is another spatial metaphor, but this one describes social hierarchy. Lines of power are imagined vertically rather than horizontally. As discussed earlier, in representing social hierarchy through a vertical structure, the basement metaphor evokes the CRC's claim that the liberation of Black women has the potential to uproot social hierarchy. Yet whereas the CRC sought a revolutionary strategy, calling for the "destruction of the political-economic systems of capitalism and imperialism as well as patriarchy" (CRC 1983, 213), the basement metaphor shows that strategies like anti-discrimination law function at best remedially, at worst to reproduce the existing hierarchy. Courts privilege those individuals who "but for" the ceiling would not be in the basement.

Indeed, as we have seen in the foregoing analysis of *Rudebusch*, those reasserting their entitlement to remain on the main floor, above the basement, have been even more successful. "Single-axis" challenges to discrimination mobilize sociolegal privilege, resulting in the reentrenchment of the established social hierarchy (Crenshaw 1989, 145; Rosenblum 1994). This is possible only if Black women and other multiply oppressed groups—on whose shoulders relatively privileged individuals stand to make these gains—continue to inhabit the basement. The existing social hierarchy is reproduced, not undermined, through some individuals' ascent. Moreover, white male privilege is naturalized in antidiscrimination law; the notion of "achieving a balance" literally preserves it.

Revealingly, Staunæs and Søndegaard do not consider Crenshaw's basement metaphor, even as they dismiss the utility of the "classic intersectionality approach" to studying "intersections which privilege corporate masculinity" (a variant on the dually privileged identities the commensurability of which with the intersectional model of identity I considered in chapter 1): "If we had applied the classic intersectionality approach in our research project on gender and management," they contend, "we would have retained the focus on the category of woman and on this group's difficult conditions, leaving unnoticed what was going on among the men above the glass ceiling" (2011, 52). Of course, "glass ceiling" is another architectural metaphor that reflects an analysis of hierarchical power bearing a striking resemblance to that suggested by the metaphor of a vertical edifice at the foundation of which is the basement. Significantly, the notion of the glass ceiling as an obstacle for women's corporate advancement addresses "but for" groups of workers. In their effort to revise what they call "classic intersectionality," these authors render invisible groups at the bottom of social hierarchies—for whom breaking the glass ceiling presupposes the arguably even less plausible task of leaving the basement—in the name of making visible white male corporate power.

Like the intersection metaphor, the basement metaphor is spatial, but I would suggest it is also temporal, representing a diachronic social process of gendered race/class formation. It exposes the ahistorical structure of juridical conceptions of discrimination, revealed in the intersection where responsibility for history, for the causality of the "accident" that injures a Black woman, is systematically refused. Eliding the historical origins and material character of the U.S. state and its institutions, as well as the system of property it defends, the law represents wrongful discrimination as a corruption of an otherwise fair or neutral process. "Wrongful" or "unlawful" discrimination in U.S. legal doctrine is a process-based conception, rather than a substantive one (Crenshaw 1989, 151). A process-based conception of discrimination assumes that, in the absence of wrongful discrimination, the hiring practices and relations of production in question are just. For instance, a "fair" process is corrupted when the employer bases a hiring decision on the applicant's gender or race, rather than the applicant's (gender- and race-neutral) qualifications. But the material conditions facing Black women plaintiffs in the cases Crenshaw examines were racial and gendered workplace segregation, endemic sexual harassment, and labor superexploitation. Yet the process-based notion of discrimination narrows the scope of antidiscrimination law such that it cannot provide restitution for the claimant's whole experience of discrimination over a lifetime, much less redress the oppression and exploitation of entire groups. Instead, discrimination claims most often focus narrowly on a single instance or act of discrimination, excised from history. Courts rarely accept claims of continuing violations, and have set a high evidentiary threshold for proving "systemic" and "serial" violations. Moreover, if an employee fails to bring a complaint to the EEOC in a stipulated time frame, the employer is allowed to view the discrimination as legal, as happened with regard to General Motors' discriminatory hiring practices in *DeGraffenreid*. Structural critiques of the exploitation of labor under capitalism as it articulates white supremacy and heteropatriarchy are inadmissible, even if structural oppression forms the institutional and political economic context for instances of discrimination or discriminatory acts. In other words, even though discrimination always occurs in a context of licit relations of oppression and exploitation, in order for a claim of unlawful discrimination to be advanced it must be abstracted from this context. Crenshaw concludes: "This process-based definition is not grounded in a bottom-up commitment to improve the substantive conditions [of life] for those who are victimized by an interplay of numerous factors of oppression" (1989, 151). In this way, antidiscrimination law mirrors the "focus on past discrimination" in affirmative action, which "locates the source of contemporary disparities in the past," not in a historicized sense but in requiring plaintiffs or aggrieved groups to "identify specific acts of past discrimination"; this forecloses the possibility of redress of phenomenologically broader, historically persistent, and overwhelmingly systemic forms of "societal discrimination, for which there is no constitutional remedy" (Crenshaw 2011, 1325). Although engaging with it may be unavoidable, the conceptual framework and institutional structure of antidiscrimination law presupposes and reproduces social hierarchy.

What does this analysis suggest for the potential of intersectionality? I argued in the previous chapter that we should recontextualize "intersectionality" in Crenshaw's work and in the intellectual tradition of Black feminism. This may limit its defensible uses and cause us to reject interpretations and critiques of intersectionality that fail to engage with the political, theoretical, and existential concerns by which intersectionality—understood as an integrative methodology or heuristic—was originally motivated. But, paradoxically, it may also broaden its uses, beyond the "narrow" interpretation of intersectionality that sees it as a non-generalizable theory because it presupposes an alignment of "Black women" with the specific and of "white women" with the generic. In other words, tracing the intersection metaphor back to Crenshaw's argument and relating it explicitly to the basement metaphor has the potential to disrupt what Carbado has called "colorblind intersectionality," which falsely "fram[es] intersectionality as only about women of color, . . . further naturalizing white male heterosexuality as the normative baseline against which the rest of us are intersectionally differentiated" (2013, 841). The basement metaphor reveals the complicity of single-axis conceptions of oppression and discrimination with the reproduction of white male sociolegal and economic power. That is not to say that intersectionality is best understood as a congruous framework to describe white male "identity," but rather that the two metaphors disclose the institutional, discursive, and conceptual functioning of gendered and racialized power. In this way, attention to the basement metaphor curbs the "colorblind" tendencies of a mainstreaming approach to intersectionality which seeks to secure its postracial arrival by reducing intersectionality to an inclusionary politics of diversity rather than to a coalitional politics of anti-subordination.

Moreover, as I will discuss in chapter 5, revisiting the two metaphors belies additive interpretations of "intersectionality" that take for granted the received categories of gender and race. Finally, my analysis reinvigorates Crenshaw's original conception of intersectionality as a provisional concept—which I elaborate in chapter 3. My reading suggests that Crenshaw did not initially propose intersectionality as a multi-axial theory of hierarchical power; yet this is precisely how intersectionality is invoked in feminist theory.

It is important to undertake close readings of Crenshaw's work when engaging with the concept of intersectionality, not only for the sake of textual accuracy, nor to fetishize a singular, transparent "truth" of the text. All readings—whether "close" or "casual"—are acts of interpretation, so that texts are invested with, and not just "mined" for, meaning by their readers. Yet my view is that texts are not infinitely flexible or passive with respect to the kinds of hermeneutic or analytic pressures we can exert on them, and interpretations can differ qualitatively with respect to their defensibility. Close readings are not necessarily uncritical or approbatory; in fact, in my opinion, close reading is vital to any convincing critique of a text. As a method, close reading does not operate on the level of assertion but rather performs interpretative arguments mobilizing textual (as well as contextual or subtextual) evidence. In other words, a close reading—as I would like to understand it—opens itself to a different interpretation as the very condition of its being performed. Of course, self-proclaimed "close readings" that aim to "terri-toritorialize" a text, foreclose "competing" interpretations, or snuff out criticism do circulate; as Nash argues of such reading practices—which she terms "intersectional originalism"—they "are not apolitical," and indeed, their claims to "'tell the truth' of intersectionality" should be approached critically (2015, 4, 16). In my view, we should be wary both of the "pretence" or "fantasy" of a "'pure' or 'true' intersectionality" (16) avowed by an "originalist" position, and of the many invocations of "intersectionality" that are entirely textually unmoored yet which nevertheless presume to impute meanings to the concept (or meta-phor) as it appears in specific texts. Therefore, I would argue against an interpretive strategy that ignores the "origins" of a concept both in relation to its author(s) and to the broader context of knowledge pro-duction and political contestation that informs it. Misapprehension, in this case, is not just about misattributing authors' intentions, or over-looking moments in a text; rather, it involves detaching the concept of intersectionality from its context in the existential conditions of Black women's lives and the theoretical concerns of Black feminist thought, and harnessing it to diametrically opposed representational purposes. In this connection, as we have already seen (chapter 1), it is important to underscore that "intersectionality" has a long history (Nash 2011a, 2011b; Dotson 2013); yet its historical antecedents are systematically overlooked, often by positioning white feminism as originary, and as emerging prior to women-of-color feminisms, or by interpreting a range of distinct concepts as semantically equivalent to each other.

It seems to me that the intersection metaphor alone cannot do all the representational and analytic work that "intersectionality" has been called on to do; nor does widespread reference to "intersections" in feminist theory necessarily indicate a robust theorization of interlocking systems of oppression. But, in fact, it seems that in Crenshaw's "Demar-ginalizing," the basement metaphor does some of this kind of work. It shows how antidiscrimination law reproduces an oppressive hierarchy. At the bottom of this hierarchy are Black women and other "multiply" oppressed groups who can stake claim neither to privileges stemming from whiteness nor to those stemming from maleness. The law defines discrimination in terms that allow only relatively privileged individuals, standing on the shoulders of people below, to climb out of the basement through a remedial "hatch"—mutually exclusive categories of "race" and "sex"—to the main floor above. The intersection metaphor indicates that those concepts are inadequate—if, in fact, the aim of the remedy is to eliminate social hierarchy. But we can as easily see this—that antidiscrimination law makes "winning and losing . . . part of the same deal" (Crenshaw 2011b, 1337)—by looking around at who is left in the basement, at whose faces remain "hidden at the bottom of the well."

"FLAT GEOGRAPHIES" OF POWER

Although metaphors are useful in discussions at a high level of abstraction to concretize complex concepts, they can nevertheless harbor certain risks. Peter Kwan argues that metaphors become dangerous when they "stand in for the concept itself" or for its careful, continued elaboration (2002, 328). When this happens, the metaphor is reified, increasingly taking the place of the phenomenon it seeks to explain. Standing in for an analysis of oppression, a spatial metaphor like intersectionality can paradoxically preclude an interrogation of its concrete manifestations. McKittrick and Clyde Woods observe an abundance of spatial metaphors in "analyses of black creative texts, yet they are often theorized as detached from concrete three-dimensional geographies" (2007, 7).

In this concluding section of the chapter I suggest that deployments of "intersectionality" that deracinate it from its origins in Black feminist thought, and specifically from Crenshaw's 1989 essay, "Demarginalizing," tend to flatten power relations rather than illuminate them. In this sense, it may be productive to read many "intersectional" accounts alongside McKittrick's project of reconceptualizing Black feminist geographies. McKittrick urges us to consider how the "spatial and bodily remnants of transatlantic slavery are unresolved . . . [and] recast as a geographic struggle" in Black feminist thought and movements (2006, 52). At the foundations of spatial organizations of hierarchies of racial power and knowledge are "patriarchal ways of seeing and white colonial desires for lands, free labor, and racial-sexual domination" (40). The dispossession of Black women's bodies through white-supremacist projects "rendered the black body a commodity, a site of embodied property"; this "territorialization" of the body—its "claiming," "ownership," and control by white power—transformed "ideas that justify bondage into corporeal evidence of racial difference" (44–45). Black women "have been relegated to the margins of knowledge and have therefore been *imagined* as outside the production of space" (54). As Radhika Mohanram argues, the "black body" has been "discursively incarcerated": naturalized simultaneously as immobile and "out of place," subjected to forced removal, dislocation, genocide, and functioning to construct the white settler as "mobile, free," a universal "subject who is able to take anyone's place" (1999, 15).

Violently situated at the margins of the human, Black women have reclaimed and theorized marginalization as "an experiential geography that highlights ideological confinement and the peripheral place of black gendered bodies" in white-supremacist and heteropatriarchal epistemologies and economies (McKittrick 2006, 55). For instance, in her germinal text *Feminist Theory from Margin to Center*, bell hooks argued that it is "essential for continued feminist struggle that black women recognize the special vantage point our marginality gives us and make use of this perspective to criticize the dominant racist, classist, sexist hegemony as well as to envision and create a counter-hegemony" (1984, 15). She famously urged Black feminism to transform marginality from "a site of deprivation" into "a site of radical possibility, a space of resistance" (1999, 149–50). Hooks insisted on the experiential sources of such a politics, and on the materiality of oppressions that it could potentially disrupt. In the wake of her influential writing, though, the margin seems to be invoked in feminist discourses as mere metaphor, "repetitively and sporadically called on to name difference" while erasing multiscalar processes of marginalization (McKittrick 2006, 57). As McKittrick argues, "all too often black women, or their experiences, or their ideas, are momentarily called on to raise some painful questions, or complicate an otherwise white space"; through such tokenistic interpellations of Black women and other marginalized groups, "the margin is emptied out, placeless, just theory, just language, and seemingly the *only* black feminist geography available in wider social theories" (57).

In this connection, McKittrick draws on the work of Patricia Hill Collins (1998a), who traces the history of the margin/center metaphor and finds a dramatic shift in its usage: originally, it referred to a political economic analysis of core/periphery relations. However, the margin/center metaphor became divorced from a conception of social hierarchy: if initially it functioned to decenter "hegemonic knowledge claims," through its repeated invocation "as yet another ahistorical, 'universal' construct . . . talk of tops and bottoms, long associated with hierarchy, was recast as flattened geographies of centers and margins" (Collins 1998a, 129). McKittrick elaborates: "Collins imagines the margins as flat precisely because she is frustrated with the theoretical inattentiveness to actual geographical displacements, those lived and living bodies that were/are fundamentally entwined with unequal multiscalar political and economic systems"; if the "margin is so consistently cast as metaphor [it] is precisely because it is actually inhabited by subaltern communities" (2006, 57–58). A "site of dispossession," the margin is not seen as "a legitimate area of deep social or geographic inquiry"; "it is an ungeographic space . . . all too often a fleeting academic utterance and easy to empty out, ignore, and add on in times of multicultural crises"; "it is an additive, metaphoric, inhuman stand-in for 'difference'" (58).

Might we discern a similar process through which intersectionality has become what Collins and McKittrick term a "flattened" or "flat" geography? Thrown around in a vague manner in too many discussions, the metaphor seems divorced from its origins in a critique of injurious hierarchies of sociolegal power and representational privilege. In one sense, the metaphor of intersectionality is designed to demonstrate how the intersection is juridically constructed as a flat, ahistorical space where collisions between categorically defined forms of discrimination occur (Crenshaw 1989, 149). The point is that the law is not interested in redressing power imbalances and transcending oppressive or exploitative social relations; it seeks to reproduce and legitimize them. The basement metaphor historicizes the intersectional injuries at the crossroads, illustrating how antidiscrimination law perpetuates social hierarchies: by locating Black women plaintiffs in an "unprotected margin" while naturalizing white male privilege, it extends "remedy" for discrimination occasionally to white women and Black men, most egregiously to white men, and to Black women only on condition that they can be absorbed into groups analogically defined through their exclusion. Yet in another sense, the theoretical work that intersectionality does to theorize how prevailing conceptualizations of oppression "fall flat," functioning to locate Black women in a space of juridical and political invisibility, itself is "flattened" through the empty invocation of intersectionality as an "ahistorical, 'universal' construct applied to all sorts of power relations" (Collins 1998a, 129).

For instance, it is often claimed that "we all have intersectional identities." Yet although it is important to deploy intersectionality as a heuristic to reveal how privilege structures monistic categories of identity, as the foregoing analysis of *Rudebusch*—symptomatic of the "whitening" of antidiscrimination law—reveals, the normative coextensiveness of masculinity and whiteness presents women of color with distinctive political and representational problems. I addressed this issue in chapter 1, where I examined the question of whether all identities are intersectional. There I suggested that since there are multiple ways to parse this claim, hinging on the particular conception of intersectionality that underlies it, it is perhaps not a fatal contradiction to agree and simultaneously to disagree with the notion that all identities are intersectional. In chapter 3, I will trace another modality of the flattening of intersectionality: its postracial use to signify the "arrival" of an inclusionary feminism that has transcended its legacies of exclusion and subordination.

Such a usage is arguably made possible by the systematic forgetting of the intersection's companion metaphor. In a recent essay, Crenshaw and her collaborators Sumi Cho and Leslie McCall clarify the intent of Crenshaw's early intervention in "Demarginalizing":

> The ends of problematizing the legal subject in class-action lawsuits ... were not limited to securing legal reforms that would grant greater inclusion to differently defined subjects, such as Black women. . . . Rather, understanding the trajectory of intersectionality as part of a larger critique of rights and legal institutions reveals how the intersectional lens looked beyond the more narrowly circumscribed demands

for inclusion within the logics of sameness and difference. Instead it addressed the larger ideological structures in which subjects, problems, and solutions were framed. (2013, 791)

Arguably, the basement metaphor represents—in vivid architectural terms—precisely those ideological structures which law as an institution that articulates white-supremacist, heteropatriarchal, and corporate power reproduces. Selective appropriation of the intersection metaphor, and forgetting of the basement metaphor, signals precisely the kind of commodification of Black feminist thought against which Collins and McKittrick warn (Collins 1998a, 58; McKittrick 2006, 59–61). To resist this, it is useful to remember that, in "Demarginalizing," the metaphor and the concept appear as a "radical critique of law premised in part on understanding how it reified and flattened power relationships into unidimensional notions of discrimination" (Cho, Crenshaw, and McCall 2013, 791). Intersecting the categories of race and sex shows that "Black women's experiences are broader than the general categories discrimination discourse provides" (Crenshaw 1989, 149). As I discuss in the next chapter, rather than supporting complacency with their continued use, Crenshaw invokes "intersectionality" as a "provisional concept" toward "a methodology that will ultimately disrupt the tendencies to see 'gender' and 'race' as exclusive or separable" (1991, 1244n9). Yet "intersectionality" is often invoked as a theory based on these same categories, which are stabilized and not disrupted in the process. Its normative upshot is reduced, at best, to a politics of "inclusion," or at worst, to "diversity management." This facilitates the impression that feminist theory— and the institutions in which it has come to enjoy some success—has arrived at some "postracial" moment, signified through vague appeals to "intersections" and secured through the forgetting of "basements."

3

Intersectionality as a Provisional Concept

In the previous chapter we saw that in Crenshaw's early work, intersectionality was one of two metaphors introduced to illustrate how law reproduces systems of domination, relegating Black women and other multiply oppressed groups to the "basement" of social hierarchy. The forgetting of the basement may coincide with the forgetting of those who are condemned to occupy it; the "flattening" of intersectionality may signal a depoliticizing shift in the mainstreaming of the concept. Drawing on Collins's and McKittrick's analyses of "flattened geographies," we began to trace how the concept's reduction to a metaphoric level of the "*language* of space" means that the "radical disruptions" of "white patriarchal space" (McKittrick 2006, 57) effected through Black feminist theoretical interventions and political struggles are increasingly stripped of their transformative power as they are absorbed into hegemonic feminisms. Thus, McKittrick's warning is well taken: "Black feminist theory, like other theories, can be erased because they are often relegated to the conceptual arena, rather than through the imbrication of material and metaphoric space; the margin can stand in for the black female body and the body itself is rendered conceptual rather than a site of humanness and struggle" (59–60). The trajectory of intersectionality evinces a parallel process: if intersectionality is often invoked as an objectifying proxy for Black women, it is just as often invoked as an empty space available for seizure by just about anyone. In a recent lecture, Crenshaw characterizes the current conjuncture in intersectionality studies as manifesting a "vexed contradiction": "although *intersectionality* was coined to counter the disembodiment of black women from law, the challenge today is to resist the disembodiment of black women from intersectionality itself" (Crenshaw 2014). This requires that we acknowledge and recognize that appeals to intersectionality might ideologically embody "precisely the politics that intersectionality had been mobilized to interrogate" (Crenshaw 2014; see Crenshaw 2015). If that is the case, the ascendancy or mainstreaming of the concept of intersectionality ought not be taken as a sign that the antiracist critique of feminism has "arrived," since not only some uses but the *predominant* usages of "intersectionality" seem to me to invert the theoretical aims of Crenshaw's intersection metaphor. Could "intersectionality" paradoxically function to impede the critical project that Crenshaw articulates in her 1989 and 1991 essays? Although "intersectionality" is celebrated within white-dominated feminism as a solution to exclusion within feminist theory and politics, I suggest we can, in part, attribute its mainstream success to an "aversive racism effect" within feminism, which seems all too eager to announce its arrival at a postracial, egalitarian destination. This aspirational, "postracial" intersectionality is reflected in the superficial engagement with Crenshaw's work in the past twenty-five years and with the broader intellectual production of contemporary and historical Black feminisms, notwithstanding the proliferation of "intersectional talk," that is, the "flattened" use of intersectionality to describe or denote converging categories of identity and oppression.

AN OVERLOOKED FOOTNOTE

In this chapter I continue a close reading of Crenshaw's germinal discussion of intersectionality, shifting my attention to her 1991 essay, "Mapping the Margins: Intersectionality, Identity Politics, and Violence against Women of Color," where in a footnote she explains in what spirit she proposes the concept of "intersectionality," or what the status of intersectionality is. If a metaphor as evocative as the basement can be overlooked and, indeed, forgotten in the process of institutionalizing intersectionality, a humble footnote has an even fainter hope of getting noticed. At the physical margins of a text, the footnote might seem like an aside or an afterthought, a detail of scarcely any importance. If it had been important, wouldn't the author have placed it in the main text? In normal-sized print? But reading footnotes can sometimes feel like accessing the nascent thoughts of a writer expressing intuitions or anticipating shifts that perhaps cannot be fully articulated, or indications of new directions prefigured through openings created by an argument. There is a sense in which footnotes mark that which just barely belongs, or that which is trying to make its way in. In legal academic writing, footnotes have a particular and often dual function: on the one hand, "to span the gaps," enabling the uninitiated or generalist reader to understand the argument in the main text; and on the other, appealing to a specialist audience, "to expand on the text's simpler point" (Magat 2010, 68). This illuminating note, which has been, like the basement, relegated to obscurity, likely falls in the category of "explanatory" or "discursive" (as opposed to "probative") footnotes, which can sometimes be "'empowered'" to constitute a "second text" (Magat 2010, 76, quoting John Ohle). If detractors warn readers to "keep your eye on the [main] text" and, lacking "a reason to travel below the line," not to "go there" (Magat 2010, 98), I would counter that it would be productive to dwell for a moment on this largely overlooked footnote, in which Crenshaw clarifies that she considers

> intersectionality a provisional concept linking contemporary politics with postmodern theory. In mapping the intersections of race and gender, the concept does engage dominant assumptions that race and gender are essentially separate categories. By tracing the categories to their intersections, I hope to suggest a methodology that will ultimately disrupt the tendencies to see race and gender as exclusive or separable. While the primary intersections that I explore here are between race and gender, the concept can and should be expanded by factoring in issues such as class, sexual orientation, age, and color. (1991, 1244–45n9)

Here, Crenshaw not only anticipates the criticism that intersectionality advances a dualistic account of race and gender which limits integrative accounts to considering merely two forms of oppression; more significantly for my present argument, she states that intersectionality represents a transitional concept which has as its ultimate goal the development of a methodology that would fuse what are now falsely separated as mutually exclusive categories. This suggests that intersectionality is not, itself, that methodology, but neither is it merely a buzzword. Both inflated and deflated appeals to intersectionality avoid contending with the critical task that intersectionality as an analytic sensibility identifies: the urgent need to construct new concepts to remedy epistemic and representational exclusions, to contest the discursive invisibility of Black women and other multiply oppressed groups situated at the intersection—the chasm—between mutually exclusive concepts of oppression, and to enable political coalitions which can overcome the fragmentation that characterizes extant and historical movements against oppression. On the one hand, inflated appeals to intersectionality suggest that the "intersectional turn" signifies the completion of these conceptual and political tasks. Intersectionality is celebrated as the remedy of, and as the only ethical stance toward, power relations within feminist theory and politics. On the other hand, deflated appeals negate the critical importance of intersectionality, skeptically demoting it to the status of buzzword, overhyped trend, or "mere" metaphor. Often, skeptical critics herald a "post-intersectional turn," a move that seems premature, to say the least. If the celebratory consensus around "intersectionality" is itself based on a superficial, disengaged deployment of the term, then what is needed is a reexamination or reinvigoration of intersectionality through a deeper, more robust engagement with the concept. What both inflationary and deflationary approaches fail to do is to critically contend with intersectionality, and with the theoretical texts and political movements in which it originated.

As Patricia Hill Collins observes, "Many approach intersectionality as if it is *already* defined and thus ignore the points of convergence and contradiction that characterize scholarship that claims to be informed by intersectionality" (2012, 21). Rather than assume that the celebratory consensus around "intersectionality" is based on a stable, positive definition, perhaps we should acknowledge the profound conflicts and contradictions that the consensus whitewashes, and instead view inter-sectionality as a provisional concept that anticipates, rather than arrives at, the normative or theoretical goals often imputed to it. The chapter proceeds as follows. First, examining Crenshaw's overlooked footnote, I will discuss the notion of a provisional concept and its critical import. What do we mean by a "provisional concept," and what function does it have? If intersectionality is a provisional concept, how, precisely does it intervene in the "settled expectations" affirming entrenched configura-tions and conceptualizations of "racial" and "gendered" power?

In a recent essay, Crenshaw distances her project from two interpre-tations of intersectionality: one which reads it as "a call for Black femi-nist particularity"; and another which takes it "simpl[y] illustrative of the incoherence of feminism per se" (2010, 152n3). Both interpretations assume that the central problem intersectionality addresses is that of essentialism. "Find[ing] neither interpretation compelling," Crenshaw clarifies that she has not "tended to frame [her] principle critiques in the language of 'anti-essentialism'"; rather, in her germinal work she called for "a more robust analysis of how difference makes a difference in marginalizing and sometimes erasing the consequences of a race-gender system for women of color" (152n3). Still, to the extent that difference and sameness are a central problematic of the debate around essentialism in feminism, it might be useful to consider how intersectionality as an analytic sensibility that reveals the dilemmas facing Black women (e.g., as plaintiffs asked either to force their broader experiences of discrimi-nation into the narrower, mutually exclusive categories of "gender" and "race" either by suppressing or exaggerating their difference from proto-typical subjects of groups) relates to Black feminist attempts to disrupt essentialist categorical thinking. To broach this question I will juxtapose Crenshaw's account with Angela Harris's contemporaneous critique of "gender essentialism." If intersectionality was not, by design, advanced as an anti-essentialist but rather as a critical realist (or "functional real-ist") project (Crenshaw 2010, 162), Crenshaw's efforts to problema-tize mutually exclusive categories of oppression and discrimination has interesting points of convergence with (and divergence from) Harris's account. Drawing on Sara Ahmed's phenomenological concept of disorientation, I will suggest that a provisional concept of intersectionality productively "disorients" habitual cognitive habits even as it advances "operational analyses" (Crenshaw 2010, 162) of exclusion, subordination, and marginalisation. Next, I attempt to show that many interpretations of intersectionality fail to engage with it substantively as a *critique* of dominant strategies of representation. This is significant because they interpret it, instead, as a positive representation of dually (or triply, or multiply) oppressed groups, such as women of color. Finally, I conclude the chapter by suggesting how we may engage with intersectionality as a point of departure, as opposed to the sign of arrival of feminist theory. Could at least some of the popularity of intersectionality be read through a white feminist desire to maintain racial innocence and assert feminism's arrival at a "postracial" moment? Vivian May has argued that "paradoxically, recognition [of intersectionality] can entail avoidance, even suppression, of black women's knowledge, even as it may seem to signal engagement" (2014, 94). I draw on the social psychological literature on nonracism and aversive racism to advance the argument that flippant, superficial, or obligatory references to "intersectionality" may be foreclosing the task of "demarginalizing the intersection."

PROVISIONALITY AND DISORIENTATION

I want to challenge the triumphal narrative of "political completion" that surrounds intersectionality as *the* way to theorize the relationship among systems of oppression. My aim is not to suggest that Crenshaw's account of intersectionality is wrong or unnecessary; on the contrary, the urgency of the tasks it identifies has been undermined through its misappropriation, namely, to cement the impression of mainstream feminism's arrival at a postracial moment. I argue that Crenshaw proposed intersectionality as a "provisional concept" that can help to disorient our entrenched, naturalized cognitive habits. The notion of a provisional concept reflects the intuition that in order to transform our thinking, let alone institutionalized practices, our current axiomatic assumptions, cognitive habits, and unreflective premises have to be at once engaged and disrupted. A provisional concept tentatively bridges the heuristic gap between present and future, between dominant ideologies and socially transformative justice claims, anticipating or pointing toward the transcendence of a way of thinking that maintains a hold over our imaginations, or which we are not capable of overcoming, yet which we can recognize as inadequate. As Crenshaw writes in another footnote, "there are significant political and conceptual obstacles to moving against structures of domination with an intersectional sensibility" (1991, 1243n4). For one, "prevailing structures of domination shape various discourses of resistance"; arguably, then, "people can only demand change in ways that reflect the logic of the institutions they are challenging. Demands for change that do not reflect . . . dominant ideology . . . will probably be ineffective" (1989, 1367n3).

The *Oxford English Dictionary* (OED) defines the adjective "provisional" as bearing "the nature of a temporary provision or arrangement; provided or adopted for the time being; supplying the place of something regular, permanent, or final." A provisional concept may be "accepted or used in default of something better"—in other words, "tentative[ly]." The OED offers two additional obscure yet, in this context, revealing meanings. Something provisional is "preparatory, preliminary"; it is "characterized by or exhibiting foresight." In this sense, a provisional concept is one "that provides for the future"; it is "provident; anticipatory." I suggest that rather than "settling down" with intersectionality, we should engage with its anticipatory promise. This approach toward intersectionality may enable us to reinvigorate our commitment to the theoretical and political aims that originally animated it.

Provisional concepts are communicatively advantageous, as they enable us to start or keep talking about something while undergoing the difficult and long social process of discursive and cognitive transformation. In other words, provisional concepts enable communication about a contested matter at the same time they signal the need to challenge our assumptions. Simply inventing inaccessible neologisms or acting as though we have a collective understanding that we actually do not may prove counterproductive. In connection to intersectionality, Ann Garry argues that "even if ordinary language is rightly considered conservative . . . in everyday speech it has a better chance of success than a theoretical approach that eschews our standard uses of . . . everyday concepts" (2012, 516). In this case, without recourse to the monistic and admittedly inadequate categories of race, class, gender, or sexuality, it "is more difficult to explain the ways in which oppressions intersect and to express or even locate our intersecting identities. . . . [A] little bit of stability in terminology, especially terminology that people already understand, can be valuable" to make oneself understood (516). Similarly, Mari Mikkola points out that "creating linguistic confusion between [feminist theorists] and ordinary speakers [is] unlikely to help in the task of challenging existing social conditions" (2009, 569). Yet she concedes that on at least some views of social transformation, "creating linguistic confusion [may be] a precursor to political action in that it challenges existing meanings of terms that are in some way insufficient or problematic" (570).

To the notion of confusion I prefer the notion of disorientation as elaborated by Sara Ahmed. Disorientation has a significant pedagogical function in Ahmed's view:

> In order to become orientated, . . . we must first experience disorientation. When we are oriented, we might not even notice that we are orientated: we might not even think "to think" about this point. When we experience disorientation, we might notice orientation as something we do not have. After all, concepts often reveal themselves as things to think 'with' when they fail to be translated into being or action. It is in this mode of disorientation that one might begin to wonder: . . . How do we know which way to turn to reach our destination? (2006, 6)

But disorientation is not merely a cognitive experience; it is a profoundly "vital," embodied experience that can unsettle expectations, shatter worldviews, or culminate in crisis (2006, 155), leaving us "unsure of how to go on" (Harbin 2012, 261). Nevertheless, considering the application of a phenomenology of "disorientation" to sexuality—given that sexual orientations are constructed as essences we purportedly "have," and some are normalized and exalted while others are pathologized and repressed—Ahmed proposes that rather than fleeing from disorientation to regain our "proper" orientation, we "not aim to overcome the disorientation of the queer moment, but instead inhabit [its] intensity" (2006, 107). I would like to suggest something similar—a queer approach, perhaps—with respect to intersectionality (see also Bilge 2012). What if intersectionality is meant to get us to thinking about how "we" think, as opposed to constituting an answer to a problem "we" already know and understand? What if it is meant to disorient "us," disrupting our cardinal certainty, as opposed to reifying the axes that would secure it? In this sense, reinvested with provisionality, intersectionality would "challenge . . . the pull of prevailing mindsets, in part by drawing from political expectations, lived experiences, and analytic positions not crafted solely within the bounds of dominant imaginaries" (May 2014, 96). Foreshadowing the argument I develop in chapter 5, we might consider Natalie Kouri-Towe's insights about how "queerness interrupts the nationalist and normative claims that solidarity movements are generally predicated upon; disrupting the normative claim of masculinist nationalism and challenging heteronormativity and reproductive futurities in anti-colonial movements" (2015, 74).

ESSENTIALISM AND INTERSECTIONAL DISEMPOWERMENT

Crenshaw states that her aim in "Mapping the Margins" is to "advance the telling" of the location occupied by women of color in hierarchies of power, which manifest insidiously in "the almost routine violence that shapes their lives" (1991, 1241–42). Indeed, "physical assault . . . is merely the most immediate manifestation of the subordination they experience" (1245). Yet rather than illuminating and addressing the matrix of institutional processes that construct violence against women of color, anti-violence rhetoric and intervention strategies have tended to aggravate violence and compound its structural causes. Crenshaw undertakes an anti-essentialist critique of the way in which the categories of "race" and "gender" are mobilized by anti-violence discourses in ways that marginalize women of color. In particular, Crenshaw demonstrates that prevailing constructions of identity "conflate . . . or ignore . . . intragroup differences." Antiracist and feminist political agendas centered on mutually exclusive oppressed identities result in "intersectional disempowerment" and a distorted, impoverished analysis of "racism and sexism":

> The need to split one's political energies between two . . . opposing groups is a dimension of intersectional disempowerment that men of color and white women seldom confront. Indeed, their specific raced *and* gendered experiences, although intersectional, often define as well as confine the interests of the entire group. For example—racism as experienced by people of color who are of a particular gender—male—tends to determine the parameters of antiracist strategies, just as sexism as experienced by women who are of a particular race—white—tends to ground the women's movement. The problem is not simply that both discourses fail women of color by not acknowledging the "additional" issue of race or of patriarchy but that the discourses are often inadequate even to the discrete tasks of articulating the full dimensions of racism and sexism. . . . [A]ntiracism and feminism are limited, even on their own terms. (1991, 1252)

Writing contemporaneously with Crenshaw, critical race legal scholar Angela Harris argued that essentialism is a deeply ingrained cognitive habit. Harris defines "gender essentialism" as "the notion that a unitary, 'essential' women's experience can be isolated and described independently of race, class, sexual orientation, and other realities of experience" (1990, 588). Essentialism results in additive accounts of oppression which impute a quantitative as opposed to qualitative difference among experiences of oppression: Black women are constructed as "white women with an additional burden" (592); consequently, "black women become white women only more so" (595). In other words, to a white-normative conception of "gender oppression" is added an ostensibly genderless but invisibly masculinized construct of "racial oppression," constructing 'the lives of people who experience multiple forms of oppression to addition problems: "racism + sexism = straight black women's experience" or "racism + sexism + homophobia = black lesbian experience" (588–89). Harris elaborates two characteristics of gender essentialism. First, gender essentialists marginalize racial oppression: "issues of race are bracketed as belonging to a separate and distinct discourse—a process which leaves black women's selves fragmented beyond recognition" (592). Second, essentialists center white women "as the epitome of Woman" (592); white women's *racialized* gendered experiences are constructed as normative, if not definitional of the essence of gender oppression. But to the extent that privilege renders racialization invisible, white women's gendered experiences are constructed as "race neutral." Resonating with the interrelated intersection and basement metaphors that, as we saw in the previous chapter, Crenshaw contemporaneously developed, Harris concludes that

> as long as feminists .. continue to search for gender and racial essences, black women will never be anything more than a crossroads between two kinds of domination, or at the bottom of a hierarchy of oppressions; we will always be required to choose pieces of ourselves to present as wholeness. . . . [B]lack women's experience will always be forcibly fragmented before being subjected to analysis, as those who are "only interested in race," and those who are "only interested in gender" take their separate slices of our lives. (589)

The intellectual convenience and emotional safety that essentialism represents for some (white) feminists nevertheless depends upon *silencing some voices in order to privilege others* (585, 589, 605–6). An anti-essentialist critique of essentialist constructions of categories of identity and oppression entails rendering visible—or audible—these acts and institutionalized practices of silencing, the cognitive habits that subtend them, and the intersubjective relations that they reproduce. Kristie Dotson argues that "to communicate we all need an audience willing and capable of hearing us. The extent to which entire populations of people can be denied this kind of linguistic reciprocation as a matter of course institutes epistemic violence" (2011, 238). Intersectionality as a provisional concept opens up the linguistic space for the kind of communicative exchange that is violently foreclosed by essentialist constructions of identities, oppression(s), and experiences and by the institutionalized production of ignorance about what are termed, presupposing essentialist logics that fragment concepts and discourses of oppression, "multiply oppressed" groups. Indeed, intersectionality has been the focal point or the catalyst for what have been termed "difficult dialogues" within women's, gender, and sexuality studies, as reflected in the eponymous title of a 2009 U.S. National Women's Studies Association conference on intersectionality. Yet as Nash argues, the danger is that "the fetishization of intersectionality's difficulty suggests that theorizing intersectionally will repair problems of feminist exclusivity" (2010).

Significantly, Harris eschews essentialism in all its forms, even as a counter-discursive strategy: "my aim is not to establish a new essentialism . . . based on the essential experience of black women"; yet to the extent that we need categories in order to cognize, she suggests "we make our categories explicitly tentative, relational and unstable" (1990, 586). This entails a shift from univocality toward multivocality in theory construction, premised on *multiple consciousness*, which Harris identifies as a "major contribution . . . that black women have to offer post-essentialist feminist theory" (608). As we saw in chapter 1, in another landmark essay, published a year before Crenshaw's, Deborah King theorizes the concept of multiple consciousness, arguing that "the necessity of addressing all oppressions is one of the hallmarks of black feminist thought" (1988, 43). A simultaneous struggle against all forms of oppression departs from the recognition that "to the extent that any politic is monistic, the actual victims of racism, sexism, or classism may be absent from, invisible within, or seen as antagonistic to that politic" (52). Essentialist constructions of operative categories render the actual experiences of people subjected to oppression invisible in, or irrelevant to, discourses of oppression that presuppose and falsely universalize hidden forms of privilege. By "demarginalizing" experiences of subjects who "do not have racial, sexual, heterosexual, or class privilege to rely upon," intersectionality—as a concept emerging from multiple consciousness at the interstices of monistic social movements—reveals essentialist, mutually exclusive categories of oppression as predicated on privilege (CRC 1983, 214).

Yet, arguably the dangers of essentialism are also evident in versions of intersectionality that reify categories of identity and install as their normative subjects prototypes of "multiple" (more often, of "dual") oppression. As we saw in chapter 1, Nash critiques the "use of black women as prototypical intersectional subjects" (2008, 4). Her objection is that "black women are treated as a unitary and monolithic entity" in intersectional scholarship, which relies upon the race-gender dualism; "differences between black women, including class and sexuality, are obscured in the service of presenting 'black women' as a category that opposes both 'whites' and 'black men'" (8).

While complexity is nearly universally imputed as one of the analytic benefits of intersectionality (see chapter 1), in my view, complexity is avoided in those operationalizations of intersectionality, which tend to reduce the concept to an additive model of oppression, emphasizing intergroup difference while occluding intragroup difference. Here, May's warning is well taken: "practitioners and critics alike may approach intersectionality as a form of binary thinking (not as a deep critique of this logic's harmful outcomes); disarticulate its interconnected precepts; interpret it via frameworks that buttress, rather than contest, normative/deviant binaries; or engage intersectionality in ways that rank identities and place forms of oppression in a hierarchy" (2015, 15). For instance, in chapter 1 we saw that some scholars advocate "separating out" analytic axes to "arrive" at intersectionality "in the end" (see May 2015, 159–68). This begs the question of whether such analytic categories are separable—which intersectionality as an analytic sensibility problematizes. Nira Yuval-Davis argues against the easy adoption of what according to McCall's taxonomy of intersectional approaches is termed an "intercategorical approach": "Unless it is complemented with an intra-categorical approach, [intersectionality] can be understood as an additive rather than a mutually constitutive [framework]" (2006, 7). Given the ubiquity of the trope of intersectionality that is a function of its "institutionalization" as an intellectual project (Nash 2008, 13), there has been a positivist uptake of the concept—especially in social science research—that seems to overlook entirely its critical (dis) orientation toward categories, and continues to deploy them as if they were unproblematic. Elizabeth Cole argues that a positivist approach to intersectionality "assumes the definition and operationalization of social/structural categories as independent variables," failing to "address the processes that create and maintain . . . the categories" (2008, 445). While intercategorical intersectionality—understood as an additive or "multiplicative" research paradigm—may well be *more* complex than other positivist methodologies that use singular and homogeneous categories of analysis, it nevertheless fails to tarry with the normative impetus of intersectionality as a *critique* of discrete, mutually exclusive, and analogically defined categories.

Indeed, there may be a fundamental incompatibility between intersectionality as a provisional concept and the positivist epistemology underlying many social scientific deployments of "intersectionality," a conflict that has not been theorized in the literature. After all, "intersectionality calls for an epistemological shift toward multiplicity, simultaneity, and 'both/and' thinking," which controvert positivist axiomata (May 2014, 99). May points out that as a "counter-hegemonic" concept "crafted 'interstitially'—in spaces between dominant frames—and fashioned within and across marginalized locations," intersectionality is incommensurate with positivist or "Enlightenment" epistemes, the ideological repositories of colonial capitalism "that helped forge the terms of subjection, hierarchy and categorization intersectionality seeks to transform" (99). (This is a point to which I return in chapter 6, when I consider how intersectionality may be synthesized with a decolonial analysis.) Moreover, from a robustly intersectional, post-positivist perspective, we might question the epistemic ideal of arrival at an empirically based, totalizing account of "social totality." Paul Cilliers argues that "if we acknowledge that the world in which we have to live is complex; we also have to acknowledge the limitations of our understanding of this world" (2005, 256). Indeed, "our knowledge of complex systems is always provisional" (259). The "easy" insertion of "intersectionality" in traditional quantitative and qualitative research methods which assume the operationalizability of received categories fails to tarry with its metatheoretical critique. Denise Najmanovich suggests that in the pursuit of complexity, what need to be invented are "new ways of figuration and new figures of thought" (2002, 91). However, as we saw in chapter 1, the challenge intersectionality poses is not necessarily best understood in terms of complexity, but rather in terms of anti-subordination, since it reveals how extant categories and hegemonic epistemological frames are saturated with, and reproduce, racialized and gendered relations of power. In a recent analysis of how mainstream antiracist and feminist rhetorical politics countering mass incarceration and interpersonal violence, Crenshaw writes that "the absences and collusions" of these discourses render the violence targeting girls and women of color in the criminal legal system "hidden in plain sight" (2012, 1434, 1435). But these "are not simply framing problems": "They point instead to political failures in the past that are continuously reproducing marginalities that extend into the future" (1434). The failures of antiracist and feminist discourses "to interrogate the dynamics of surveillance and punishment of poor women of colour" are not "mere oversights against which 'inclusion' is the remedy" but rather reveal how critical and liberatory movements can participate in and reproduce the constitutive logic of "the wider projects" (1450) and institutions of the state.

INTERSECTIONALITY AS A CRITIQUE OF REPRESENTATION

I have argued that we should approach intersectionality as a provisional concept that challenges prevailing ways of theorizing and resisting oppression, approaches that deploy categories based on discourses that silence and render invisible multiply marginalized groups, such as Black women. Yet in many accounts, intersectionality is reduced to an additive model based on the same categories it is critiquing. Arguably, then, there is an incompatibility between intersectionality as a provisional concept and the positivist epistemology underlying "additive" deployments of intersectionality, which often, as Harris has written, fragment experiences beyond recognition. As I will elaborate in the next chapter, a central problem with many positivist appropriations of intersectionality *and* critiques of these appropriations is that they fail to see intersectionality as a critique of representation, interpreting it as a straightforward "representationalist" politics. This is to assume that intersectionality represents a specific identity or identity-based political claim. On such a view, the "intersection of race and gender" would *represent* women of color. Yet this categorial intersection is a place of *invisibility*, not visibility; strictly speaking, in my view, the intersection reveals the institutionalized failure to hear Black women's representational claims, but it does not disclose the content of their experiences. Categories of race and gender oppressions *exclude* them by design. The intersection of these categories reveals the *failure* of representation. Intersectionality reveals the *absence* of concepts adequate to the lived experience of simultaneous oppression(s). As we will see in chapter 6, María Lugones writes that "the intersection misconstrues women of color"; it doesn't *represent* them (2007, 192–93).

While intersectionality reveals that it is imperative to transform our thinking so that categories of race and gender, which are falsely separated, become fused, in my view, intersectionality does not itself perform that fusion. Lugones's understanding of intersectionality as revealing that which is missing, and thereby illuminating the task ahead, is consistent with the interpretation I have been advancing of intersectionality as a provisional concept. Significantly, "we" *do not see* race and gender as "intermeshed or fused"; monistic constructions continue to have a stranglehold over our theoretical repertoire, and are even reflected in compound terms such as "gendered racism" or "racialized sexual violence." "Multiply oppressed groups"—a phrase that presupposes the fragmentation of our experiences even as it contests the conceptual exclusions responsible for it—are neither rendered visible nor represented by intersectionality. Rather, intersectionality reveals how prevailing constructs of oppression renders groups located at the intersection of oppressions invisible. What is made visible, perhaps, is invisibility. The cognitive task of constructing new concepts adequate to representing these marginalized experiences still lies before us. So too does the political task of articulating interconnections between struggles that are normally seen as unrelated, even conflicting, based on the self-representation of "multiply oppressed groups" whose claims have been epistemically silenced.

If we reinvigorate Crenshaw's conception of intersectionality as a provisional concept, it will be clear that it does not suffice to point to the convergence of monistic categories to demonstrate their mutual constitution. I therefore object to the view held by Floya Anthias (among many others) that it is important to "retain" the categories, since it not "possible to dispense" with them (2012, 13). Anthias believes the distinct categories track "autonomous or systemic features" that, when intersected, "produce . . . the derivative although specific saliency of intersectional or hybrid categories (such as ethnicised women)" (13). Therefore, she contends that we should

> interpret [the notion of the intersection] in a dialectical way rather than in a deconstructionist or reductionist way, therefore retaining the existence of categories themselves. . . . I do not think that it is possible to dispense with the social categories themselves, as they are a necessary component of analysis; they must therefore be specified before any intersectional analysis can take place. (13)

But the argument that the categories of race, gender, sexuality, and class are distinct from each other presupposes an analysis of systems of oppression which actually privileges the experiences of normative subjects unburdened by, and even benefiting from, oppression(s) on the other axes. In other words, the assumption that racial oppression is autonomous from gender oppression actually assumes a view of racial oppression inflected by gender privilege. For "ethnicised woman" to be a hybrid category, it is presupposed that one is oppressed as an "ethnicised person" to the extent that one is not oppressed as a "woman." So, in fact, our concept of racial oppression is not "pure" of gendered power; it is inflected by gender privilege. But privilege is rendered invisible in the false universalization of that normative experience, making the categories "race" and "gender" seem mutually exclusive because racial and gendered *oppressions* are constructed as mutually exclusive. In my view, Anthias's argument that we should retain the "autonomous" categories of "race" and "gender" misconstrues the intersectional challenge to monistic thinking. On the one hand, there is no such thing as an intersectional or hybrid category that can thematize multiple oppression so long as the monistic categories of oppression (based on privilege) are preserved; on the other, the monistic categories are, in a sense, *already hybrid* because they presuppose privilege on the other axes. Our accounts of the "simultaneous" experiences of oppression of social groups subordinated by what are viewed as "multiple" systems remain fragmented and distorted through invisible lenses of privilege. I believe this is what intersectionality as a provisional concept reveals.

NONRACISM, AVERSIVE RACISM, AND INTERSECTIONALITY

In an interview, Crenshaw reflects on the itinerary of the traveling concept of intersectionality: it has had "wide reach, but not [a] very deep" one; it is both "over- and underused; sometimes I can't even recognize it in the literature anymore" (quoted in Guidroz and Berger 2009, 76, 65). May observes that "rather than take up intersectionality's cognitive shift, it is folded into the already known, put outside the bounds of the logical, or characterized as passé" (2014, 106; see May 2015). I have argued that rather than take seriously the disorienting implications of engaging intersectionality as a provisional concept, the (white) mainstream of feminist scholarship has very much "settled down" with it, but with a version that is often hardly recognizable as such. My view is that as intersectionality has traveled from margin to center, it has become harnessed to different, and sometimes inverted, theoretical aims. In this section I explore whether the popularization of intersectionality may be read through a white feminist desire to construct a nonracist subjectivity. The *provisionality* of intersectionality—the work it indicates still remains to be done—has been all but forgotten when it is taken as the sign of feminism's arrival at a "postracial" moment.

In a curious twist of fate, intersectionality has come to play a role in the historical construction of white feminist moral identity, which, as Sarita Srivastava argues, "has been historically focused on benevolence and innocence" (2005, 33). Srivastava's research into emotionally resistant responses to antiracist interventions within Canadian feminist organizations indicates that "some of the deadlocks of antiracist efforts are linked to . . . preoccupations with morality and self" (31). Her research reveals that white feminists tend either "'not [to] see' racial inequality" or to "acknowledge racism as a concern 'out there' but [to] deny that they, their organizations, movements, or nations are implicated in racist practices" (40). As Srivastava discovered through her semi-structured interviews, challenges to white feminists' imagined nonracism "are often met with emotional resistance": with anger, tears, indignation and disbelief, summed up in the defensive question, "You're calling me a racist?" (42). But such defensive responses often serve to impede personal and organizational change: "The problem is that discussions about personnel, decision making, or programming become derailed by emotional protestations that one is not a racist and by efforts to take care of colleagues upset by antiracist challenges" (42). Srivastava concludes that "the struggle by some white feminists and feminist organizations to maintain an ethical nonracist feminist identity can . . . become an impediment to meaningful antiracist analysis and change" (40).

Figured as the corrective to feminism's theoretical and political exclusions, intersectionality is often used to defuse moral anxieties about racism and to project an ethical white feminist self. Alison Bailey points out that intersectionality prompts white feminists "to confront some very real fears about our authority and the fragility of the feminist canon we've struggled to create" (2010, 60). In this connection, it is significant that Kathy Davis attributes the success of intersectionality in part to the "implicit reassurance it provides that the focus on difference will not make feminist theory obsolete or superfluous" (2008, 72). We can read between the lines of Davis's assessment and add that intersectionality reassures *white feminists*, specifically, that they have not become obsolete or superfluous in what is heralded as a new feminist paradigm that decenters them and centers women of color. Paradoxically, intersectionality can impede profound engagement with racism, since attention to "intersections" can be paid without transforming power relations that structure practices of knowledge production. In this regard, May's analysis of "the unconscious workings of power in interpretive practices" is significant inasmuch as it reveals that "knowledge derived from and crafted in marginalized locations entails a double struggle: the struggle to articulate what cannot necessarily be told in conventional terms, and the struggle to be heard without being (mis)translated into normative logics that occlude the meanings at hand" (2014, 99).

How can "intersectionality talk" obscure, and even reproduce, intersectional disempowerment? The concept of "aversive racism" can help explain this paradox. Social psychologists developed the concept of aversive racism to describe (white, liberal) subjects who are motivated through the internalization of egalitarian values to appear nonracist. Yet aversive racists have also internalized systemic racism, which influences their implicit, unconscious, and automatic attitudes, of which they are typically unaware or unreflective (Son Hing et al. 2004, 275). The conflict between their explicit, conscious, and controlled attitudes and their prereflective ones results in what Leanne Son Hing and her collaborators call the "aversive racism effect" (275): aversive racists will discriminate only when they can find a "reasonable," putatively nonracist justification for doing so. When their discrimination is exposed as racism, aversive racists will resort to justificatory discourses to attempt to reestablish their racial innocence.

Can the mainstreaming of "intersectionality"—its "wide but not very deep reach"—be attributed to an "aversive racism effect" within white feminist scholarship? Could the reification of the concept as the guarantor of inclusion and diversity actually have served to impede meaningful engagement with intersectionality, and the Black feminist intellectual tradition from which it emerges (and women-of-color feminisms more generally)? Debjani Chakravarty and Elena Frank surveyed PhD dissertation abstracts written from 1995 to 2010 in U.S. women's, gender, and sexuality studies and found an "abundance of buzzwords" such as "intersectionality," which were, however, underdeveloped in the corresponding dissertations, a phenomenon they characterize as "a form of intellectual lipservice—promise without delivery" (2013, 70). Intersectionality is, as Bilge puts it, "'hailed' and 'failed' simultaneously" (2013, 407). Cited in order to signify inclusive politics, nonracist scholarship, or concession that "we need to talk about race" (among "other" axes of oppression), its invocation may have little to do with initiating antiracist (or, more generally, anti-oppressive) action. Further, if "intersectionality" is taken as the guarantor of an antiracist position, then such action (or further thought toward such action) may be deemed unnecessary. If "intersectionality" signals the arrival of feminism at a postracial *telos*, then antiracism becomes a redundant modifier of a triumphant feminism (as in the descriptor "antiracist feminist"). Moreover, a deracinated, power-evasive, disciplined form of "intersectionality" reassures white feminists in their positions of intellectual dominance within hegemonic feminism. As "buzzword," intersectionality seems to be the great leveler: Davis contends it promises "feminist scholars of all identities, theoretical perspectives, and political persuasions" that "they can have their cake and eat it, too" (2008, 72). But such reassurance seems premature, since privileged locations remain "discursively dangerous," as Linda Martín Alcoff has argued (1991–92, 7). Ethical and epistemological questions remain unresolved even as intersectionality might be taken by some to announce "open season" on "speaking about difference." Here, Martín Alcoff's warning is pertinent: "the impetus to always be the speaker ... must be seen for what it is: a desire for mastery and domination" (24). Intersectionality might appear to be an ethical way to "speak about difference," but as Martín Alcoff argues, "the problem with speaking for others exists in the very structure of discursive practice, no matter its content, and therefore it is this structure itself" that needs to be transformed (23). If intersectionality—evacuated of any provisionality—reassures white feminists that they have an unimpeachable position from which to speak, then we need to interrogate its adverse effects on generating antiracist (more generally, anti-oppressive) change.

A superficial deployment of the concept, which Bilge terms "ornamental intersectionality," can politically "undermine" and even "neutralize" its potential "for addressing interlocking power structures and developing an ethics of non-oppressive coalition-building" (2013, 408). Moreover, "ornamental intersectionality allows institutions and individuals to accumulate value through good public relations and 'rebranding' without the need to actually address the underlying structures that produce and sustain injustice" (408). In the neoliberal academic context, Bilge argues, intersectionality is (nonperformatively) deployed by "disciplinary feminism," which absorbs "counter-hegemonic fields of inquiry into an ever adaptive hegemony without altering its structure" (408–9). Annexed by disciplinary feminism and used to deflect precisely those marginalized subjects and knowledges that it seeks to render visible (as invisible) and audible (as muted), "intersectionality" becomes appropriated as the property of the white feminist theoretical mainstream, a process Bilge calls "the whitening of intersectionality" (412–13).

Robyn Wiegman characterizes intersectionality, without "exaggeration," as "*the* primary figure of political completion in U.S. identity knowledge domains" (2012, 240). This is a striking development for a term that was proposed, initially, as a provisional concept. I suggest that, paradoxically, taking intersectionality seriously may mean disrupting the facile consensus that has emerged around it and trying to radicalize its insights by reinvigorating its provisionality. As we will see in the next chapter, this is a different project than that advocated by those who claim to "go beyond intersectionality"; in my view, to make the "post-intersectional" move is to misunderstand the role of intersectionality in effecting the *conceptual transition* between essentialist, analytically discrete categories, on the one hand, and a (more) unified theory of oppression, on the other. The "post-intersectional" move is not only premature, since, "if anything, we are pre-intersectional"; in her conclusion of a recent lecture, Crenshaw expressed a "hope and an aspiration" for "a neo-intersectionality, a post-post-intersectionality, an erasure-of-the-'post'-intersectionality," which would enable us "to build more solid coalitions that reach across difference and reach across the globe" (2014).

If certainty about what "intersectionality" means reveals a failure to tarry with the concept in a substantive way, on the path to a "neo-intersectional" sensibility that embraces the political and cognitive tasks ahead, we face the dual task of disrupting the narratives of completion *and* of redundancy that surround intersectionality. In these first three chapters I have argued that a serious engagement would recognize that intersectionality—a concept with a long history—signals a point of departure, not the triumphant arrival of antiracist feminist theory; it constitutes part of a Black feminist intellectual tradition that is inadequately engaged when intersectionality comes to stand in metonymically for a multiplicity of heterogeneous and complex theories stemming from that tradition. In the next three chapters I discuss recent critiques of intersectionality, revisit an overlooked normative conclusion, and consider the possibility of a synthesis of intersectional and decolonial feminisms.

4

Critical Engagements with Intersectionality

If the 1990s and early 2000s were marked by an enthusiastic, if at times superficial uptake of the notion of "intersectionality"—marked by its widespread travel across various disciplinary and geopolitical borders but also by inattention to its origins, social-movement contexts, and political and theoretical implications—in more recent years the concept has come under criticism in feminist theory (see Garry 2012, 494–95). Indeed, May discerns a "mushrooming intersectionality critique industry," ranging from the "remedial" and even "quasi-Eugenic" (promising to "deracialize" intersectionality to "render it more robust and universally applicable") to calls for a "renaissance of gender-first or gender-universal approaches" (2015, 98, 101, 104). It is to a few of those critiques that I turn in this chapter. Synthesizing the literature, I group critiques into eight categories. The first four—each of which takes issue with some or all of the purported analytic merits of the intersectionality paradigm, which I discussed in chapter 1 (complexity, simultaneity, irreducibility, and inclusion)—are the Scalar Critique (intersectionality is too microscopic—or too macroscopic—and/or cannot account for all levels of social totality or the relationships among them); the Infinite Regress Critique (intersectionality could never account for the infinite differences that constitute social identities); the Mutual Exclusion Critique (intersectionality assumes a unitary model of identity or oppression, since the logical precondition of intersection is the mutual exclusion of the categories being intersected); and the Reinscription Critique (intersectionality reinscribes the epistemological and political problems it identifies; rather than overcoming them, it reifies them).

Four additional critiques I expose draw upon these foregoing four "ideal types" to advance a distinct, oppositional, or "frictional" intellectual project. First, the Marxist Critique contends that intersectionality lacks an explanatory theory of power, a problem that results from intersectionality's insistence on the irreducibility of racial, gender, and other oppressions to class exploitation (Gimenez 2001). Second, the New Materialist Critique claims that intersectionality is a form of representationalism, which stages an ontological dualism between (active) representation and (passive) represented and, having an inadequate theory of power to account for intersectional subjects' ambiguous agency, advances a defeatist theory of victimization (Geerts and van der Tuin 2013; Dolphijn and van der Tuin 2013). Third, the Assemblage Critique asserts that intersectionality presupposes the primacy of the (oppressed) subject and its investment or self-understanding in identitarian politics, taking as static entities (identities, axes of oppression) what are actually relations between and among human and nonhuman existents which are always already emerging, becoming, and transforming (Puar 2007, 2012). Finally, the Post-Intersectional Critique, largely articulated by scholars within the legal academy, alleges that intersectionality is too simplistic a theory or too crude a metaphor to account for the complex phenomenon of subordination, which can better be understood through alternative concepts such as "symbiosis," "interconnectivity," "cosynthesis," and "multidimensionality" (Ehrenreich 2002; Kwan 1997, 2000; Chang and Culp 2002; Hutchinson 1997, 2002; Valdes 1995).

The aforementioned critiques of intersectionality vary widely with respect to how convincing or plausible they are (which is, of course, a subjective judgment that depends on one's (pre)theoretical commitments), yet most (though not all) perhaps share one theoretical shortcoming: an oversimplification, reduction, or misreading of intersectionality which either sets up the concept as a straw figure that is easy to dismantle or tendentiously and sometimes inaccurately foregrounds one aspect of the metaphor or theory, occluding the others. As Carbado writes with respect to the critics of intersectionality he surveys in a recent article, they tend to "artificially circumscribe the theoretical reach of intersectionality as a predicate to staging their own intervention" (2013, 816). Moreover, none of the widely rehearsed critiques of intersectionality grant the concept provisionality with respect to the categories it critically engages; further, when they propose a new model of "synthesis or interaction of things that are otherwise apart," Carbado argues that "at the level of appellation, they are no more dynamic than intersectionality" (816). He explains this deficiency with respect to our "discursive limitations" undermining "our ability to capture the complex and reiterative processes of social categorisation"; he claims that "the strictures of language require us to invoke race, gender, sexual orientation, and other categories one discursive moment at a time" (816). If we were to engage intersectionality as a critique of unitary categories, instead of redeploying them under its mantle, we could transition from complacency to disorientation, deconstructing the false inclusions and exclusions that categorial essentialisms entail. But to the extent that intersectionality is regarded—both by its critics and its proponents—as a multiplicative theory concerned with intercategorical complexity (see McCall 2005), the discursive and representational limitations Carbado identifies are not likely to be overcome.

In adducing these critiques, I do not assume, as Barbara Tomlinson does in her recent rejoinder to "critics of intersectionality" (including this author), that their intent is always to undermine the project of critiquing subordination or even intersectionality as such (2013, 996). Indeed, I grant the possibility that Tomlinson appears to exclude, of immanent critiques, and indeed—to use Jennifer Nash's and Tricia Rose's formulation—of "loving critiques" (Nash 2014a, 8, 155n25; see Nash 2011b). Conversely, the apparent absence of critical engagement in celebratory invocations or operationalizations of intersectionality does not necessarily demonstrate any greater "fidelity" or attention to the concept, and may be just as (if not more) "careless"—to use Tomlinson's descriptor (2013, 996)—than are critical approaches. Hence, as May points out, the problem is not that intersectionality is being engaged critically, but rather "how intersectionality is read and portrayed," often in "violation" of intersectionality's basic premises (2015, 98). Rather than assuming that critics of intersectionality are always simply "wrong" about the positive views of intersectionality which their critiques address, I think there is something important to be learned about how intersectionality is predominantly mobilized by attending to this "mushrooming industry." Further, I do not emphasize (as Tomlinson does) the "rhetorical frameworks and tropes" of critical arguments; instead, I attempt to reconstruct their substantive objections to intersectionality.

THE SCALAR CRITIQUE

The first cluster of criticisms concern the scalar reach of intersectionality, that is, whether it is amenable to the study of micro-, meso-, and macro-levels of social reality. Particularly in its infancy, there was some debate even among proponents of intersectionality as to whether it functions as a micro-, meso-, or macro-level heuristic (or all three) (see Collins et al. 1995). It was in this context that some scholars first articulated a critique of intersectionality as being too limited to capture the various levels of social reality and the interactions among them. For instance, Martha Gimenez argues that intersectionality presupposes but does not theorize the relations of micro-level to macro-level phenomena. As a model of identity, she argues, structural intersectionality offers no resources to "link intersectionality to its macrolevel conditions of possibility, those 'interlocking' structures of oppression" (2001, 29). Taking the opposite view, Dorthe Staunæs interprets intersectionality as a macro-level theory, arguing that it does not illuminate how categories of gender and race function in the "lived experience of concrete subjects" and that the model needs to be supplemented with a theory of subjectification (2003, 101). Nevertheless, Staunæs states, intersectionality can be redeemed by relating it to "post-structuralist and social constructionist concepts of 'subjectivity,' 'subjectification,' 'subject position' and 'troublesome subject position'" (103). Elizabeth Butterfield is similarly optimistic about the political possibilities that intersectionality opens up, but she argues that "a new understanding of oppression will not be enough—we also need to formulate a new conception of the person" if we are to understand how oppressions intersect in the lived experience of concrete subjects (2003, 1).

One way that scalar critiques of intersectionality have manifested is through a distinction between the terms "interlocking oppressions" and "intersecting oppressions." In her earlier work, Collins distinguished between the terms "interlocking" and "intersectional," taking them to refer, respectively, to macro-level and micro-level phenomena:

> The notion of interlocking oppressions refers to macro level connections linking systems of oppression such as race, class, and gender. This is the model describing the social structures that create social positions. Second, the notion of intersectionality describes micro-level processes—namely, how each individual and group occupies a social position within interlocking structures of oppression described by the metaphor of intersectionality. Together they shape oppression. (Collins et al. 1995, 492)

However, Collins seems to discard this distinction in her later work, where she uses "intersectionality" to refer to all three analytic levels of social reality (1998b, 2003). Nevertheless, her distinction between interlocking oppressions and intersectionality proved influential inasmuch as some scholars drew on Collins to argue that the former concept is theoretically superior to the latter (Fellows and Razack 1998; Razack 1998, 2005; see also Tong and Botts 2014). For instance, Mary Louise Fellows and Sherene Razack claim that an "interlocking" approach theorizes "the relationships among hierarchical systems," whereas "intersectionality" merely stipulates or overlooks these relationships (1998, 335). They define "interlocking systems of oppression" as systems that "rely on one another in complex ways"; the examples they offer are capitalism, imperialism, and patriarchy, though from their discussion it becomes clear that this list is illustrative , not exhaustive (335). These systems of oppression come into being "in and through one another" and are sustained and supported by one another. Because systems "interlock" in "complex ways," Fellows and Razack observe that "it is ultimately futile to attempt to disrupt one system without simultaneously disrupting others" (335–36). In a monograph published the same year, Razack parses the difference between intersectional and interlocking approaches as one of analytic emphasis and theoretical acuity:

Analytical tools that consist of looking at how systems of oppression interlock differ in emphasis from those that stress intersectionality. Interlocking systems *need one another*, and in tracing the complex ways in which *they help to secure one another*, we learn how women are produced into positions that exist symbiotically but *hierarchically*. We begin to understand, for example, how domestic workers and professional women are produced so that neither exists without the other. First World policies of colonialism and neo-colonialism, which ultimately precipitated the debt crisis and the continuing impoverishment of the Third World and enabled the pursuit of middle-class respectability in the First World, were implemented in highly gendered ways. (1998, 13, emphasis added)

The implication is that intersectionality does not impute to systems the properties of mutual constitution, interdependence, and hierarchical organization. By contrast, Razack claims, an analysis of the way systems of oppression "interlock" illuminates the transnational matrix of power relations that produce subject-positions. For Razack, systems do not "merely" intersect, they interlock; the latter concept, for her, captures how their convergence brings into being new forms of oppression. For Razack the key difference seems to lie in the capacity of each heuristic to deal with phenomenological simultaneity and ontological mutual constitution of oppressions. In a more recent essay, she reiterates that she prefers

the word interlocking rather than intersecting to describe how the systems of oppression are connected. Intersecting remains a word that describes discrete systems whose paths cross. I suggest that the systems *are* each other and that they give content to each other. While one system (here it is white supremacy) provides the entry point for the discussion (language is after all successive), what is immediately evident as one pursues how white supremacy is embodied and enacted in the everyday is that individuals come to know themselves within masculinity and femininity. Put another way, the sense of self that is simultaneously required and produced by empire is a self that is experienced *in relation* to the subordinate other—a relationship that is deeply gendered and sexualized. An interlocking approach requires that we keep several balls in the air at once, striving to overcome the successive process forced upon us by language and focusing on the ways in which bodies express social hierarchies of power. (2005, 343)

Yet as we saw in chapter 1, simultaneity and irreducibility—"keeping several balls in the air at once"—are analytic benefits commonly imputed to intersectionality as well. Moreover, as Sirma Bilge has shown, some intersectional theorists claim mutual constitution as a premise of that approach as well, although views differ markedly on the ontological implications of that claim (2010, 63–65). For instance, Ann Garry argues that "the fact that [oppressions] are enmeshed in people's lives does not necessitate their antecedent conceptual fusion" (2012, 840). Nevertheless, as far as I am aware, Razack (1998, 2005) and Fellows and Razack (1998) do not offer arguments to support the distinction between interlocking and intersectional approaches; consequently, the distinction between "interlocking" and "intersecting" seems to be a matter of stipulation with little theoretical basis in the existing literature. Similarly, the disagreement about the heuristic emphasis of intersectionality on micro-, meso-, or macro-levels of social reality is not resolved with respect to concrete arguments that demonstrate why it functions better or worse at one level of explanation rather than another.

THE INFINITE REGRESS CRITIQUE

Addressing intersectionality's analytic promise to capture structural complexity without reducing or fragmenting simultaneous experiences of oppression(s), Alice Ludvig has argued that the fact that the social world is "insurmountably complex" raises serious problems for intersectionality (2006, 247). Ludvig contends that "the endlessness of differences seems to be a weak point in intersectional theory" (247). Here, perhaps Ludvig is drawing on Judith Butler's argument concerning "the illimitable process of signification itself," which defies attempts to "posit identity once and for all" (Butler 1999, 182–83). Butler (in)famously pillories "theories of feminist identity that elaborate predicates of color, sexuality, ethnicity, class, and able-bodiedness [which] invariably close with an embarrassed 'etc.' at the end of the list" (182). This "horizontal trajectory of adjectives" expresses the "striving" of these theories to "encompass a situated subject," while the "etc." reflects their "invariable failure" to "be complete" (182). Similarly, Wendy Brown contends that "the model of power developed to apprehend the making of a particular subject/ion will never accurately describe or trace the lines of a living subject," an intractable theoretical "paradox" that cannot be "resolved through greater levels of specificity," since "there are always significant elements of subjectivity and subjection [that] exceed the accounting offered by such lists" (1997, 94).

Ludvig's "infinite regress" objection also asks, On what basis can a judgment be made as to which categories are salient? For instance, she points out that in daily life it is often not possible to discern the specific category of prejudice at work in an experience of discrimination: "Subjectively, it is often not possible for a woman to decide whether she has been discriminated against just because of her gender or for another reason such as a foreign accent" (2006, 246). It is difficult to see why this even constitutes a criticism of intersectionality unless we assume the stability and adequacy of extant categories and believe that intersectionality claims an additive relationship obtains among them. In a similar vein as Ludvig's "insurmountable complexity" objection, Shuddhabrata Sengupta argues that the phenomenology of oppression ultimately defies its reduction to "axes," "structures," or even "systems"; he claims the "algebra of our world" is too irreducibly complex and contradictory, flouting even those theoretical approaches that aim to capture irreducibility (2006, 635). At the very least, Ludvig claims, intersectionality theorists are faced with a definitional problem: "Who defines when, where, which, and why particular differences are given recognition while others are not?" (2006, 247). Similarly, Kathryn Russell argues that we lack "arguments about when and where we can emphasize one factor over another" as well as "analyses about how gender, race, and class are connected" (2007, 35). She contends that "current scholarship seems to be caught in a bind between collapsing social categories together and separating them out in a list" (35).

That is not entirely an inaccurate assessment of the state of intersectionality scholarship. Yet precisely this quandary—whether to flatten or fragment social experiences of multiple oppressions—is anticipated in Crenshaw's germinal discussion of intersectionality (1989, 148–49). What this set of criticisms reveals is that the methodological and conceptual challenge that intersectionality presents to categorial essentialism has been sidestepped by much "intersectional" scholarly research, which assumes the stability and explanatory power of monistic categories even as it explores their permutations and combinations (see chapter 3). As we have seen, these categories have been defined with the experiences of relatively privileged subgroups as their "historical base" (148). The "bind" Russell identifies and the definitional problem Ludvig raises for intersectionality presuppose the adequacy of analytic distinctions between systems of oppression and aspects of identity, rather than problematizing those distinctions. The conflation of "complexity" and the "particular" with multiply oppressed groups (such as Ludvig's "women with a foreign accent"), and the corresponding conflation of "simplicity" and the "generic" with (relatively) privileged ones (such as women without an accent marked as foreign), reveals that a single-axis framework is assumed. In other words, the "infinite regress" objection seems to rely upon a positivist understanding of essentialist categories, rather than engaging intersectionality as a critique of such categories. One encounters such a deployment of categories even in that now-classic statement of post-identitarian, anti-foundationalist feminist theory:

> If one is a woman, surely that is not all one is; the term fails to be exhaustive, not because a pregendered "person" transcends the specific paraphernalia of gender, but because gender intersects with racial, class, ethnic, sexual, and regional modalities of discursively constituted identities. As a result, it becomes impossible to separate out "gender" from the political and cultural intersections in which it is invariably produced and maintained. (Butler 1999, 6)

Yet this statement performatively contradicts itself, showing no difficulty in deploying distinct discursive identity categories, at least analytically; indeed, the force of the claim that these categories intersect (thereby undermining the analytic separability or purity of "gender") seems to rest on the assumption of their prior mutual exclusivity.

THE MUTUAL EXCLUSION CRITIQUE

Indeed, still another ideal type of critique involves the relationship among categories that intersectionality theorists deploy. In skeletal terms, the argument is that the intersection of two categories logically presupposes that these categories are mutually exclusive. Of course, as we have seen in chapter 2, Crenshaw anticipates this critique, conceding that "the concept does engage dominant assumptions that race and gender are essentially separate categories"; yet she is explicit that the aim of "tracing the categories to their intersections" is "to suggest a methodology that will ultimately disrupt the tendencies to see race and gender as exclusive or separable" (1991, 1244–45n9). Indeed, the mutual exclusivity of emancipatory rhetorics is what Crenshaw's concept of political intersectionality contests:

> Feminist efforts to politicize experiences of women and antiracist efforts to politicize experiences of people of colour have frequently proceeded as though the issues and experiences they detail occur on mutually exclusive terrains. Although racism and sexism readily intersect in the lives of real people, they seldom do in feminist and antiracist practices. And so, when the practices expound identity as woman or person of color as an either/or proposition, they relegate the identity of women of color to a location that resists telling. (1991, 1242)

If mutual exclusion is, in part, what the intersectional critique of unitary categories problematizes, the most sophisticated versions of the "mutual exclusion" critique will be those which address interpretations of intersectionality that neglect to show how these categories are inadequate, interpretations that may even deploy them as if their analytic separability is phenomenologically legitimate.

To understand precisely in what the strongest versions of the "mutual exclusion" critique consist, it is useful to recall the distinction Leslie McCall makes in her widely referenced article, "The Complexity of

Intersectionality," between intercategorical, intracategorical and anti-categorical approaches to intersectionality research (2005; see chapter 1). As McCall parses this methodological distinction, if the *inter*categorical approach focuses on differences and relations among what are viewed as distinct social groups, requiring scholars to "provisionally adopt existing analytical categories," and the *intra*categorical approach focuses on differences and relations within social groups, only the *anti*-categorical approach deconstructs the received categories that construct social group memberships, viewing them as "simplifying social fictions that produce inequalities in the process of producing differences" (2005, 1773, 1774, 1776). McCall advocates for the intercategorical approach in her article, arguing that it is underrepresented in intersectionality research (1773). I would contend that most deployments of intersectionality operate with a degree of complacency about categorial distinctions and tend to naturalize demarcations between social groups. As we saw in the previous chapter, Nira Yuval-Davis critiques the intercategorical approach to intersectionality, arguing that "unless it is complemented with an intra-categorical approach, it can be understood as an additive rather than a mutually constitutive approach to the relationship between social categories" (2011, 7). According to Yuval-Davis, although social categories have distinct, irreducible "ontological bases," they are nevertheless "mutually constitutive in any concrete historical moment"; therefore, "simply assuming that any particular inter-categorical study would result in a full understanding of any particular social category in any particular social context, as McCall does, is also reductionist" (7–8). Instead, Yuval-Davis calls for "an intersectional approach which combines the sensitivity and dynamism of the intra-categorical approach with the more macro socio-economic perspective of the inter-categorical approach" (6). For Yuval-Davis, looking simultaneously between and within categories is a way out of what she identifies as a false dilemma which the distinction between inter- and intracategorical approaches raises. Moreover, Yuval-Davis's commitment to ontological pluralism undermines the forcefulness of her "mutual exclusivity" critique.

Yet research that assumes the stability, fixity, and homogeneity of social groups, social structures, and social identities can lapse into positivism, or into an additive model that combines monistic categories. Elizabeth Cole makes a compelling argument that a positivist, intercategorical approach to intersectionality, which "assumes the definition and operationalization of social/structural categories as independent variables," fails to "address the processes that create and maintain . . . the categories" (2008, 445). Cole points out that the positivist approach to intersectionality ignores the fact that Crenshaw identifies three ways in which Black women's experiences are (mis)represented by categories defined with white and male subjects as their historical base: their experiences can be similar to those of white women and/or Black men; they can be compounds of single-axis categories; or they can be broader than the categories—or their sum—allow (Cole 2009, 171; see Crenshaw 1989, 149). At issue are the "conceptual limitations of the single-issue analyses that intersectionality challenges. The point is that Black women can experience discrimination in any number of ways and that the contradiction arises from our assumptions that their claims of exclusion must be unidirectional" (Crenshaw 1989, 149). To see this, we must challenge the normative status of relatively privileged group members whose experiences become definitive of the group. Cole proposes that empirical researchers pose three questions to conceptualize "categories of identity, difference and disadvantage": "First, who is included within this category? Second, what role does inequality play? Third, what are the similarities?" (2009, 171). She continues:

> The first question involves attending to diversity within social categories to interrogate how the categories depend on one another for meaning. The second question conceptualizes social categories as connoting hierarchies of privilege and power that structure social and material life. The third question looks for commonalities cutting across categories often viewed as deeply different. (171).

Unlike McCall's schema, in which inter-, intra-, and anticategorical approaches are distinguished, Cole argues that these three questions are not mutually exclusive, but rather cumulative, that "each question builds on insights generated by the previous one" (2009, 171). Moreover,

Cole's questions ask us to do the opposite of what we are habituated into doing when confronted with categorial distinctions: to seek similarities across categories, and differences within them. In order to understand how, for instance, the category of gender is constructed through the exclusion of race—so that one is seen to be oppressed as a woman to the extent that one is not a person of color—one needs to simultaneously trace how difference is constituted, marginalized, disavowed, and hierarchized within a category, while commonalities between categories which reveal them not to be distinct but simultaneously operative in people's lives are systematically elided. Cole's insistence on tracing how categories are connotations of privilege and power is also tremendously methodologically important, yet it is rarely operationalized in the intersectionality literature. To say that categories are constructed prototypically around the experiences of normative subjects is to say that they are the sedimentations of operations of power and that their perceptual and cognitive use reproduces the systems of oppression that relegate certain subjects to the "basements" of social hierarchies, elevating others to the penthouse (see chapter 2). In my view, the continued, unreflective use of these categories naturalizes the very systems that intersectional scholars set out to contest, undermine, and transform.

In its strongest renditions, then, the "mutual exclusion" critique takes issue with a certain version of intersectionality that would reduce the construct to an additive or otherwise "interactive" model of jeopardy without problematizing the categories being deployed and addressing the relations of power in and through which they are constituted and reproduced. Another way to parse this critique is with respect to the normative claim of inclusiveness which is often attributed to intersectionality as a research paradigm and as a political sensibility. Can intersectionality deliver on the promise to transform feminist theory and politics by centering the experiences of multiply oppressed groups? Or does it participate in a "retrograde" form of identity politics which reproduces received notions of groups as separate and indeed constructs groups as ever smaller, more "specific," and less unifiable? Drawing on Crenshaw's largely overlooked discussion of identity-based politics (1991, 1299), Cole suggests that "although intersectionality may be misconstrued to suggest a politics of identity [of] vanishingly small constituencies, in fact the concept holds the promise of opening new avenues of cooperation" (2008, 447). By contrast, Naomi Zack is dubious that intersectionality can deliver on its inclusionary promise. Zack argues that while inter-sectionality may indeed overcome essentialist constructions of identity, "politically, it easily leads to a fragmentation of women that precludes common goals as well as basic empathy. The *de facto* racial segregation of both criticism and liberation along the lines of historical oppression sabotages present criticism and future liberation because women of color speak only to themselves" (2005, 7). She asserts that women of color are only heard in white feminist discourses "if they are willing to present themselves as representatives of this or that disadvantaged racial or ethnic group—they have lost the ability to speak to and be heard by white women as women"; she calls on feminist theory to go "beyond intersectionality" to achieve a truly "inclusive feminism" (78). Although Zack's incisive critique of the abiding racial politics of U.S. feminist dis-course is well taken, the tokenism she challenges hardly seems specific to, or inherent in, "intersectionality." Indeed, one of Crenshaw's aims in conceptualizing intersectionality was to reveal that positing white women's as the "standard sex discrimination claim" renders "claims that diverge from this standard" as "some sort of hybrid claim": precisely because Black women's experiences are "seen as hybrid," they are seen not to "represent those who may have 'pure' claims of sex discrimination" (1989, 146). When white women arrogate representational power in the ways that Zack and Crenshaw describe, contesting and redistributing that power is part of what intersectionality aims to do. To achieve this, I would suggest that what is required is a deconstruction and reconsti-tution of identity categories in ways that reveal groups' internal disso-nances as well as their interconnections with groups deemed separate from them (see chapter 5).

THE REINSCRIPTION CRITIQUE

The fourth cluster of criticisms of intersectionality concerns the concept's tendency to reinscribe at the level of identity the exclusions, marginaliza-tions, and false universalizations that it diagnoses at the level of political practice and perceptual-cognitive habit. It is a criticism that sometimes emerges from a post-identitarian sensibility which doubts the efficacy or legitimacy of identity-based claims in redressing oppressions that, in large part, constitute those identities. For instance, Lynne Huffer suggests that "the institutionalization of intersectionality as the *only* approach to gender and sexuality that takes difference seriously masks intersectionality's investment in a subject-making form of power-knowledge that runs the risk of perpetuating precisely the problems intersectionality had hoped to alleviate" (2013, 15). As we saw in chapter 3, Nash argues that the construction of "black women as prototypical intersectional subjects" whose "complex . . . experiences of marginality" are used to demonstrate the lacunae of single-axis theories of oppression has problematic effects: it tends to represent Black women as a "unitary and monolithic entity" and to elide differences such as sexuality and class "in the service of presenting 'black women' as a category that opposes both 'whites' and 'black men'" (2008, 4, 8–9). Here, Nash argues, in effect, that intersectionality reinscribes categorial homogeneity by relying on the same race/gender binary which it critiques to define the "intersectional" identities of Black women, eliding "the sheer diversity of actual experiences of women of colour" (9). Gender and race are constructed as "trans-historical constants that mark *all* black women in similar ways," regardless of the other dimensions of their social identities (7). While Nash acknowledges that Crenshaw does not intend to reduce intersectionality to a race-gender dualism, gesturing at the "need to account for multiple grounds of identity" (Crenshaw 1991, 1245), she argues that the (non)generalizability of intersectionality as a theory of identity—the possibility of extending intersectionality to various social identities— reveals its incapacity to theorize the relationship of oppression to privilege (Nash 2008, 11–12). That is, Nash's claim is that intersectionality flattens differences among Black women, and specifically that it obscures relations of oppression and privilege within the intersectional identity category, thereby reinscribing "dominant conceptions of black women as 'the mules of the world'" (Nash 2008, 12, quoting Hurston). Nash argues for a revived intersectionality that "abandon[s] its commitment to sameness" in order to approach "'black womanhood' as its own contested, messy terrain ... producing a potentially uncomfortable disunity that allows for a richer and more robust conception of identity" (12). Her critique does not amount to a call to multiply the intersections (from two to three or four categories of identity) but rather to consider how the process of intersectional identity construction replicates the essentialism of unitary models of identity (12).

The central issue in the "reinscription" critique concerns intersectionality's relationship to monistic categories of identity—its use of those categories even as it seeks to transcend them. To the extent that it traffics in unitary categories to articulate a marginalized location, intersectionality risks "conjur[ing] the very ontology that its exponents set out to undermine" (Carastathis 2008, 27). Evacuated of its provisionality, most deployments of intersectionality construct "race and gender as analytically separable" precisely by permanently "relegating Black women to their intersection"; this serves to perpetuates the unmarked racialization of the category "gender" (as white) and the unmarked gendering of the category of "race" (as male) (27). Intersectionality has evidently not displaced white women as the normative subjects of gender oppression, or Black men as the paradigmatic targets of racial oppression; it may even reinscribe their representational privilege to the extent that it is construed in a positivist fashion as a cumulative model of multiple jeopardy. If deployed in essentialist terms, the categories of race and gender are not changed by their intersection. The logical precondition for the possibility of their intersecting seems to be their purity of one another (as implied by the race/gender binary); however, it is more accurate to trace the condition of possibility of the intersection of race and gender to the respective prior gendering and racialization of these categories (28). This is revealed when one tests the hypothesis that intersectionality can be generalized as a theory of identity to relatively and multiply privileged subjects. For instance, the intersection of whiteness and maleness reveals that these categories "are already co-extensive or mutually implicated" (28). The redundancy of the intersectional analysis of ostensibly "unified" identities reveals that the categories of race and gender presuppose maleness and whiteness as their normative content—and Black men and white women as the normative targets of oppressions—are already invisibly intersectional, making their intersection at the structural location occupied by women of color a conceptually and politically productive impossibility. To the extent that intersectionality is evacuated of its provisionality and constructed as a representational concept adequate to the articulation of the experiences of women of color, the normative subjects of "race" and "gender" are not displaced from the center of these categories, even when intersected. The normative upshot is that intersectionality should be understood not as a model of identity but as a horizon of political contestation: if the problem of exclusion is a representational one—in its perceptual-cognitive, aesthetic, and political senses—it cannot be resolved at the level of identity, and hence "there is no sense in which individuals 'are' intersectional subjects" prior to or independently of their discursive assignment to the margins of categories of identity (29). Claiming intersectionality as an identity (which is how "structural intersectionality" has been widely interpreted and deployed) risks reifying "political intersectionality" at the level of identity "by discursively producing a political subject whose stable—if contested—identity is the sedimentation of . . . the failure of existing discourses to represent (in the descriptive and normative senses) the . . . experience[s] and interests of racialized women" (28–29).

Just as various exponents of the "mutual exclusion" critique aim not to "disprove" intersectionality but to reconstruct it in its strongest terms, so too, "expos[ing] the assumptions that underpin intersectionality" and which render it vulnerable to the "reinscription" critique examined here is motivated by commitments to anti-essentialism and anti-subordination (Nash 2008, 4; Carastathis 2008, 24, 29–31). The concern, then, is not, as Tomlinson contends, to make emancipatory claims "without referring to and using dominant discourses" (2013, 1009), but rather to reflect on the implications of remaining within the conceptual and political parameters that such discourses delineate. In this sense, I disagree with Tomlinson's claim that "working with and repeating hegemonic discourses is an inescapable feature of all oppositional arguments in a political world," even though I think she is absolutely correct that the enmeshedness of critique with its object is "not a problem singularly attached to the concept of intersectionality" (1009). However, to the extent that intersectionality is widely represented as a concept that has transcended, or is capable of transcending, the conceptual and political limitations of dominant discourses of identity and oppression, it is vulnerable to the "reinscription" critiques that I have exposited here. Moreover, Tomlinson's riposte to such critics of intersectionality overlooks not only the motivations and substantive claims of their arguments (focusing, instead, on the "rhetorics" that, on her reading, they employ) but also disregards the fact that (many, if not most) celebratory deployments of the concept do it a greater disservice than do (at least some) critiques. To claim that at the heart of intersectionality there is a constitutive tension concerning its relationship to unitary categories is actually to reveal it as a provisional concept (Crenshaw 1991, 1244–45n9) that crucially illuminates, but does not achieve, the transcendence of categorial essentialisms and political exclusions.

THE MARXIST CRITIQUE

As we saw in chapter 1, part of the inheritance of intersectionality is the articulation of a Black feminist socialist analysis that is embodied in the integrative concepts of "triple exploitation," "superexploitation," "double" and "triple jeopardy," and "interlocking systems of oppression," as well as in the activisms of Black left feminists, the Third World Women's Alliance, and the Combahee River Collective. Nevertheless, some of the earliest or the most trenchant critiques of intersectionality, specifically addressing its conceptualization of class in relation to other axes of oppression, have been articulated from a Marxist perspective without, however, addressing intersectionality's Marxian genealogy (Brenner 2000; Gimenez 2001; Aguilar 2012; Archer Mann 2013; S. Ferguson and McNally 2015; see also Gallot and Bilge 2012). Integrative approaches such as intersectionality challenge a number of precepts in doctrinaire Marxism, and they reveal (directly or indirectly) the "profound failure . . . in Marx's work . . . to comprehend patriarchal, racial, sexual and other forms of oppression that, along with class exploitation constitute the interlocking matrices of social relations" (Camfield 2014, 9). First, intersectional approaches assert the irreducibility and mutual constitution of systems of oppression, whereas orthodox Marxism considers racial and gender oppression as epiphenomena of causally basic class exploitation. Moreover, intersectionality emphasizes the simultaneity of oppressions and of resistances, while a dogmatic Marxism would tend to view antiracism and antisexism as divisive to working-class solidarity, and therefore as impediments to class struggle. If, for Marxists, racism and sexism constitute ideologies or forms of discrimination that are reflexes of contradictions between formal equality and material inequality inherent to liberal democracies, class is a function of a different and more fundamental order: that of capitalist exploitation. To the extent that intersectionality entails the leveling of hierarchies among categories of oppression, and remains, at the very least, agnostic about their relative salience in various contexts, the response from Marxist feminists, even those sympathetic to intersectionality, has largely been to reiterate the foundational status of class in relation to race, gender, and other axes (Gimenez 2001). Here I focus mainly on the critical argument advanced by Martha Gimenez, who addresses "race, gender, class" theorists and "intersectionality" theorists interchangeably.

Gimenez defends Marxist sociological approaches against the "ritual critique of Marx and Marxism," which diagnoses among their "alleged failures" "class reductionism" and an underdeveloped analysis of women's oppression (2001, 24). Although her main targets are scholars identified with the "race, gender, class" (RGC) approach, and indeed her essay is published in the journal *Race, Gender and Class*, to ground her arguments she principally cites Patricia Hill Collins (Collins et al. 1995), and she conflates RGC with intersectional and interlocking approaches. Gimenez identifies as RGC's "object of study" the "intersections of race, gender and class," which—following Collins's early macro- and micro-level distinction—are macrologically constituted in and through the interlocking of systems of racial, gender, and class oppression (2001, 26). Her argument against RGC/intersectional approaches is three-fold: first, it "erases the qualitative differences between class and other sources of inequality and oppression" (26); second, it implicitly entails structural determinism without adequately theorizing it—which, ironically she points out, is the same charge levied against orthodox Marxism (27); and third, it lacks a theory that would "link intersectionality to those macrolevel conditions of possibility, those 'interlocking' structures of oppression" (29).

First, rejecting the axiom of the nonhierarchy of oppressions, Gimenez asserts that class is not equivalent to race and gender, contending that "some power relations are more important and consequential than others" (2001, 31). There are two reasons given for why class is "qualitatively different from gender and race and cannot be considered just another system of oppression": first, "class relations . . . are of paramount importance for most people's economic survival is determined by them"; and second, class is not just "a site of exploitation" but also one at which "the potential agents of social change are forged" (31). While "racism and sexism are unremittingly bad," what uniquely "redeems" class is its "dialectical" potential to function as a revolutionary struggle identity (31). Gimenez acknowledges that class is not the only basis for constituting "resistance identities," but she does seem to assume that it is the only such identity inured from co-optation by hegemonic power (28). On the other hand, racial and gender identities may "emerge from the grassroots" but are vulnerable to being "harnessed by the state" and, in this way, are at risk of becoming "legitimating identities" (28). Yet it is not clear that class is differentiated from race and gender by these ascribed properties; or, if it is, this is only because class exploitation has been defined to the exclusion of racial and gender oppressions, and vice versa.

The second criticism of intersectionality concerns the "isomorphism" it posits between structural location and identity, which Gimenez claims is deterministic (2001, 27). Here, her objection is that just because an individual occupies an "objective location in the intersection of structures of inequality," this does not entail that the individual identifies with this location or with other groups situated there (28). This is the least developed of Gimenez's objections and the most difficult to motivate; it is unclear to me precisely why she thinks the "conflation" of objective location with identity is a problem for intersectionality, or why she does not grant the same dialecticity to racial and gender identities as she would to the concepts of class-in-itself and class-for-itself. Her point seems to be that "how 'intersectionality' is experienced . . . is itself thoroughly a political process" (28); but this is one of the central arguments

Crenshaw makes, and it constitutes the basis for Crenshaw's concept of "political intersectionality" (Crenshaw 1991).

Gimenez's third criticism, by contrast, is the most fully developed: in brief, she alleges that intersectionality is atheoretical insofar as it "cannot explain either the sources of inequalities or their reproduction over time" (2001, 29). According to Gimenez, intersectionality assumes but fails to theorize "the existence of a more fundamental or 'basic' structure of unequal power relations and privileges which underlie race, gender, and class" (29). Yet internal to Crenshaw's account is a complement to the intersection metaphor which illuminates the reproduction of hierarchy as it articulates sociolegal power (1989); this is the function of basement metaphor that we discussed in chapter 2. Gimenez charges that the RGC perspective lacks a substantive theory of race, gender, and class, and instead appeals to these as formal, ahistorical "taken for granted categories of analysis whose meaning apparently remains invariant in all theoretical frameworks and contexts" (2001, 29). To some extent, I am inclined to agree with Gimenez's assessment that a facile use of these categories prevails in intersectionality scholarship, where they often go undefined; indeed, their redefinition beyond the strictures of monistic theories is a process that has barely begun. But Gimenez's account offers little by way of advancing that project; although Gimenez defines class in classical Marxist terms as "exploitative relations between people mediated by their relations to the means of production" (24), she neither integrates white-supremacist and heteropatriarchal power into that conception of exploitation nor separately defines "racial" and "gender" oppressions. Rather, she contends that Marxism can come to the rescue of intersectionality from the impasse at which it finds itself if the latter rethinks the "postulated relationships between race, class, and gender" (30). Although she grants the "emancipatory" potential of the approach, it is not clear what, precisely, she thinks Marxism has to learn from intersectionality. Similarly, Sharon Smith (2013) argues that "intersectionality cannot *replace* Marxism—and Black feminists have never attempted to do so. Intersectionality is a concept for understanding oppression, not exploitation"; thus intersectionality cannot be anything more than "an additive to Marxist theory."

If Gimenez and other Marxist feminists have argued for a synthesis of intersectionality with Marxism (although in that unhappy marriage the former is clearly subordinate to the latter), feminists who identify as New Materialists critique intersectionality as a form of social constructionism for its commitment to "representationalism" (Geerts and van der Tuin 2013, 172; see Dolphjin and van der Tuin 2013). To be clear, New Materialist feminists distance themselves from Marxism notwithstanding the connotations that "materialism" carries (see Alaimo and Heckman 2008, 6n3). Departing from the observation that "language has been granted too much power" and that "matter" no longer "matters" (Barad 2003, 801), they critique the "linguistic turn" in feminist and gender theory, proposing "a new metaphysics" that restores "matter" to its "materiality" (see Jagger 2015, 321). According to Rosi Braidotti, New Materialism "emerges as a method, a conceptual frame and a political stand, which refuses the linguistic paradigm, stressing instead the concrete yet complex materiality of bodies immersed in social relations of power"; "the key concept in feminist materialism is the sexualized nature and the radical immanence of power relations and their effects upon the world" (Braidotti in Dolphjin and van der Tuin 2012, 21–22). New Materialists therefore reject the passive role to which "matter" is consigned in "representationalist" accounts, which privilege the discursive construction of materiality, eliding the "agentic" capacities of nonlinguistic entities; they affirm an "agential realist ontology" in contradistinction to what they take to be the antirealism in poststructuralist accounts (Judith Butler is the preeminent target) that emphasize the ineluctable linguistic mediation of materiality (Jagger 2015, 325; see Barad 2003). "Representationalism" is defined as "the belief in the ontological distinction between representations and that which they purport to represent; in particular, that which is represented is held to be independent of all practices of representing" (Barad 2003, 804). Representationalism effects a separation of "the world into the ontological disjoint domains of words and things" (811); it construes "matter as a passive blank slate awaiting the active inscription of culture" and views "the relation of materiality and discourse as one of absolute exteriority" (821n26). By contrast, an agential realist ontology to which New Materialists subscribe views matter as "a congealing of agency" in a process of "intra-active becoming" (822). The neologism "intra-action" indicates the epistemological and ontological inseparability of subjects and objects, relata that do not preexist relations but rather emerge through them (815).

From this theoretical paradigm, Rick Dolphijn and Iris van der Tuin advance a critique of intersectionality, constructing it as a form of "representationalism" (2013). They draw on Karen Barad's definition of "representationalism" to argue against what they characterize as "a Butlerian notion of intersectionality" (2013, 140). Here they echo Nina Lykke's misattribution of the intersectional paradigm to Butler, (inaccurately) stating that its emergence follows the 1990 publication of Butler's *Gender Trouble* (Lykke 2010, 2011; May 2015, 147): "the major voices of intersectional theory founded their distinctive framework on the same grounds as Butler and Butlerians, that is, by sticking to difference as a linguistic 'construction'" (Dolphijn and van der Tuin 2013, 133–34). The authors contend that intersectionality assumes a "duality between signification/representation (active) and materiality/reality (muted)" (134). Moreover, they assert that "what motivates intersectionality has always been part of the ["French"] concept of 'sexual difference,'" of which they cite Braidotti as an exemplar (136). They argue for a "rewrit[ing] [of] intersectionality according to [Barad's] agential realism, a concept close to Deleuze and Guattari's materialist notion of *agencements* (usually translated as 'assemblages')"—without acknowledging that precisely such a rewriting has already been attempted by Jasbir Puar (whose intervention we will discuss below) (138). But their interpretation of intersectionality reduces the concept to an additive positivism, according to which "it can be known, in advance, that only 'your' gender and 'your' ethnicity are at work" (139). "Replacing linguistics with ontology," they claim to excavate from "underneath a representationalist intersectional theory based on codification (an axiometric epistemology) . . . another intersectionality of becomings (a topological ontology) that had been there all along but that had been continuously overcoded" (140).

Dolphijn and van der Tuin's critique of intersectionality, which enables their New Materialist "rewriting," seems to rest chiefly on their assertion that intersectionality constitutes a form of representationalism. If representationalism is the belief in the distinction between a (linguistic) representation and the (matter) represented, gender representationalism would be the belief in a distinction between the concept "gender" and the materiality of lived gendered bodies. Intersectional representationalism, I take it, would be the belief in a distinction between the "intersection" of categories of race and gender and the lived experiences of gendered and racialized bodies. The central problem with their account is that Dolphijn and van der Tuin offer no arguments as to why intersectionality is a representationalism. Conflating intersectionality with an additive theory of double jeopardy, Dolphijn and van der Tuin overlook that the intersection is a place of invisibility which reveals that Black women's representational claims are undermined and confounded—in courtrooms and social movements—by mutually exclusive, single-axis conceptualizations of discrimination and oppression that exclude them by design. As I argued previously, the intersection of these categories reveals the *failure* of representation, the *absence* of concepts adequate to the lived experience of simultaneous oppression(s), and the *inadequacy* of both hegemonic and critical discourses to represent the material conditions of Black women's lives. If anything, intersectionality is a critique of hegemonic politics of representation and how these are reproduced in contestatory discourses such as antiracism and feminism.

Evelien Geerts and Iris van der Tuin advance a similar New Materialist critique of intersectionality. In an iteration of the "infinite regress" critique discussed above, they claim that the "intersectional model could lead to an endless proliferation of identities composed of ceaselessly intersecting categories"; "intersectionality's politics of representation leads to relativism," and it is therefore, according to the authors, defensible only on moral, and not on theoretical, grounds (2013, 172). The mainstreaming of intersectionality is explained with reference to its supposed allegiance to feminist standpoint theory (172) but is also credited to the "similarities between feminist postmodernism and intersectional theories," and specifically to Butler (174). The "blind spot" of intersectionality, they contend, is "representationalism," in whose "logic" "intersectional theory still . . . appears to fully embedded" (174). Specifically, the authors allege that intersectionality constructs "subjects such as Black women as being restricted by the hegemonic discourse, though they themselves claim to be able to see through it" (174). In addition to locating the scholar in an epistemically privileged, extra-discursive position, Geerts and van der Tuin accuse intersectionality of lacking "a profound analysis of power and its affected subjects" and of relying on "easy assumptions about the workings of power" that view it as a "purely restrictive force, leading to the under-theorization of the ambiguity of intersectional subjects' agency" (175). Here they draw on Wendy Brown's assessment of intersectionality (and of women-of-color feminist constructs more generally) as well as Puar's "assemblage critique" to argue that "intersectional analyses in general tend to be self-defeating since they cannot but analyze the intersectional subject in a split manner, falling back to the same bifurcated models they wish to criticize" (176; see W. Brown 1997; Puar 2007). This is a rendition of the "reinscription" critique, but one that seems disconnected from intersectionality as a body of knowledge originating in Black feminist thought. Indeed, the emphasis of intersectionality on making visible the invisibility of multiply oppressed groups such as Black women is taken to mean by Geerts and van der Tuin that "the experiences of oppressed subjects who are also partially privileged disappear, which turns inter-sectional theory into a rather defeatist theory of victimization" (2013, 175). If "intersectionality" is hardly recognizable in the two critiques I have surveyed, perhaps it is because of New Materialism's more gen-eral reading practices, which have been critiqued by Sara Ahmed as tendentious. Ahmed focuses on New Materialism's characterization of feminist theory as "anti-biological" inasmuch as it is committed to social constructionism (2008, 24). This "false and reductive history of feminist engagement with biology, science, and materialism shapes the contours" and invests with novelty a field that is "often represented as a gift to feminism in its refusal to be prohibited by feminism's prohi-bitions" (24). If Ahmed is correct that "such a gesture . . . become[s] foundational" (24) of New Materialism, we can discern similar moves in Dolphijn and van der Tuin's and Geerts and van der Tuin's respec-tive critiques and "rewritings" of intersectionality.

Perhaps the most influential critique of intersectionality has been articulated by Jasbir Puar, in two installments approximately five years apart: initially in her 2007 monograph *Terrorist Assemblages: Homonationalism in Queer Times*, and revised and elaborated in her 2012 article "I Would Rather Be a Cyborg Than a Goddess: Becoming-Intersectional in Assemblage Theory." Indeed, Patrick Grzanka characterizes Puar as one of "intersectionality's most committed critics" (2014, xvii). In *Terrorist Assemblages*, Puar practices an interpretative method comparable to an "intersectional" method described by Mari Matsuda as "asking the other question": "When I see something that looks racist, I ask: 'Where is the patriarchy in this?' When I see something that looks sexist, I ask, 'Where is the heterosexism in this?' When I see something that looks homophobic, I ask, 'Where are the class interests in this?'" (1991, 1189). As a point of entry into her project, Puar asks, "What is terrorist about the queer?" and, "the more salient and urgent question," in her view, "What is queer about the terrorist?" (2007, xxiii), in order to show how "queerness is always already installed in the project of naming of the terrorist" (xxiv). She introduces the concept of homonationalism (building on Lisa Duggan's "homonormativity"), which is framed by the biopolitical notions of "sexual exceptionalism," "regulatory queerness," and the "ascendancy of whiteness" in LGBTQI discourses, which "act as an interlocking nexus of power grids that map the various demarcations of race, gender, class, nation and religion that permeate constructions of terror and terrorist bodies" (xxiv). Sexual exceptionalism refers to the nationalist self-representation of the United States as inclusive and tolerant of sexual and gender minorities in contrast to what are constructed in its imaginary as "perverse, improperly hetero- and homo-Muslim sexualities" (xxiv). Regulatory queerness traces the projection of homophobia and transphobia onto minoritized Muslim populations by Western European states and LGBTQI nongovernmental organizations alike, which lead to calls to control, limit, or prevent the extension of residency and citizenship rights to Muslim migrants and communities (xxiv). The ascendancy of whiteness within "a global political economy of queer sexualities" is the controlling image of LGBTQI subjectivities which "coheres whiteness as a queer norm and straightness as a racial norm" (xxiv).

It is in this context that Puar at once acknowledges her "reliance upon" and appeals to "intersectional approaches," but she also concludes the argument in the book with a critique of the "limitations of feminist and queer (and queer of color) theories of intersectionality" (2007, 206). Through this critique she motivates the argument for a "queer" shift from intersectionality to assemblage (211)—although at times she also suggests that the concepts simply do different kinds of theoretical work and therefore "must remain as interlocutors in tension" (213). Her objection to intersectionality, which she interprets as a model of identity, is threefold. First, it assumes a metaphysics of presence and an "unrelenting epistemological will to truth" "stabilizing . . . identity across space and time" (215, 212). Second, the intersectional model "presumes that components—race, class, gender, sexuality, nation, age, religion—are separate analytics and can thus be disassembled" (212). These first two critiques are renditions of what I have characterized as the "reinscription" critique and the "mutual exclusion" critique. Her third objection, building on these two, is that intersectionality constitutes a "tool of diversity management and a mantra of liberal multiculturalism" and that it "colludes with the disciplinary apparatus of the state—census, demography, racial profiling, surveillance" in that it hems in and controls "difference," "encasing" it "within a structural container that simply wishes the messiness of identity into a formulaic grid" (212). Like the New Materialist critics surveyed above, inspired by Gilles Deleuze (from whom she draws the titular concept of "assemblage"), Puar contrasts intersectionality, which she constructs as a representationalism that "privileges naming, visuality, epistemology, representation and meaning," with assemblage, which, although "ontological," "tactile," and "affective," somehow escapes or explodes representation (215). Yet the claim that intersectionality attempts a representation of identity functions as an assumption, and it is not textually supported in Puar's argument. Indeed, Crenshaw's description of political intersectionality suggests that the intersection of categories of "race" and "gender" refuses visibility, knowability, naming, and representation to multiply oppressed subjects. What is made visible is their sociolegal erasure, and what is made present is their constitutive absence: "Black women are caught between ideological and political currents that combine first to create and then to bury Black women's experiences" (1989, 160). Indeed, intersectionality reveals that Black women's experiences are systemically rendered uncognizable and unrepresentable in oppositional discourses of political contestation and in hegemonic discourses of political legitimation. Moreover, constructing Black feminism as colluding with what is, in the final analysis, a white-supremacist, necropolitical (and not merely a "disciplinary") state apparatus, Puar fails to distinguish between generative Black feminist production and the appropriation and commodification of the products of that intellectual labor in the process of intersectionality's absorption by academics occupying discursively privileged enunciatory locations in elite private and state institutions.

In her article that responds to "anxieties" raised by her "apparent prescription to leave intersectionality behind (as if one could)," Puar elaborates on the politics of assemblages and revisits her critique of intersectionality (2012, 50). Here she performs a reading of Crenshaw's "formative" work, but not with the aim of "evaluating the limits and potentials of intersectionality for the sake of refining" it; rather, she proposes how intersectionality and assemblage "might be thought together" (51). Here she restates her objection to intersectionality as presupposing a metaphysics of presence and suggests that its theoretical sway is garnered by its commitment to "representational politics" (55). Puar glosses Crenshaw's intervention as an attempt to "rethink . . . identity politics from within" (51), but she moves quickly to discuss the "theory of intersectionality" in general terms (52). She does concede that "as a metaphor, intersectionality is a more porous paradigm than the standardization of method inherent to a discipline has allowed it to be" (59). To the "theory of intersectionality" she attributes the following two precepts. First, "all identities are lived and experienced as intersectional": "all subjects are intersectional whether or not they recognize themselves as such" (52). Second, she identifies as "'a key feature . . . decentering the normative subject of feminism'" (52, quoting Brah and Phoenix

2004). Not only has intersectionality failed to displace white women as normative subjects of feminist inquiry and politics, but given "the changed geopolitics of reception (one that purports to include rather than exclude difference)," intersectionality may even have become "an alibi for the re-centering of white liberal feminists" (53–54). Indeed, intersectionality produces women of color as the Other of feminism, still embedded in a gender foundationalism, due to its territorialization by white women (52). Puar is highly critical of attempts to situate intersectionality in a "discrete" genealogy of Black feminist thought, claiming that granting Black feminism generative status "might actually obfuscate" the variety of interpretations and deployments of intersectionality in Black and women-of-color feminisms (52). Tracing how intersectionality has traveled from the United States, where the concept arose from social-movement discourses, to western, central, and northern Europe, where the uptake of intersectionality is occurring in the insular and depoliticized space of the white-dominated academy, Puar observes that on both sides of the Atlantic," the language of intersectionality, its very invocation, it seems, largely substitutes for intersectional analysis itself" (53). While lucidly critical about the politics of race in European feminisms engaged with intersectionality, at another moment she chastises intersectional scholars for failing to "come into dialogue" with New Materialists (not exclusively, but largely developed in the Continental European context) who are "convinced of the nonrepresentational referent of 'matter itself,'" observing that "there has yet to be a serious interrogation of how these theories on matter and mattering might animate conceptualizations of intersectionality" (55–56). The weaknesses of New Materialism in theorizing racism, "race," and racialization are not addressed; neither is the insularity and detachment of this feminist theoretical school from social movements. Puar goes on to argue that it is not clear that the "categories privileged by intersectional analysis" can or should "traverse national and regional boundaries," since this travel may constitute still another instance of epistemological (re) colonization: to the extent that the "cherished categories" of intersectionality "are the products of modernist colonial agendas and regimes of epistemic violence," the global travel of intersectionality may signal

the imposition of "a Western/Euro-American epistemological formation through which the notion of discrete identity has emerged" (54;
see chapter 6). Yet New Materialism, which, in at least some instances
advocates a return to "biology" as the disparaged term of feminist social
constructionism (see Ahmed 2008), must also tarry with the modern/
colonial legacies of biological determinism in constituting scientific
racisms, rationalizing slavery economies, and perpetrating genocidal
reproductive politics, among other violences, epistemic and material,
that subtend Eurocolonial modernity.

The central criticism Puar develops against intersectionality concerns
its commitment to a metaphysics of presence, and specifically its failure
to engage critically with the normative construct of the subject, even as
it seeks recognition, representation, and redress for subjects in legal and
oppositional terms. Drawing a contentious distinction between disciplinary societies and control societies, she maps intersectionality—which,
she claims, asserts a liberal politics of inclusion to restore to visibility
excluded subjects through resignification and identity interpellation—
onto the former and assemblage onto the latter. In societies of control,
she claims, bodies are "modulate[d]" as "matter . . . through affective
capacities and tendencies"—except for those that continue to be subjected to disciplinary and punitive forms of power that may even culminate in premature death (2012, 63). Although Puar advocates a synthesis
of intersectionality and assemblage to theorize the "relations between
discipline and control" (63), the conceptual segregation of these forms
of power as targeting differentiated populations fails to contend seriously with the manner in which necropolitical and biopolitical regimes
actually articulate each other, and with the possibility that intersectionality actually has more to do with the way white-supremacist and heteropatriarchal power is reproduced than with the way Black women's
identities are constituted in this matrix.

Indeed, the basement metaphor illustrates how biopolitical power,
which confers recognition and exalts subjects whose identity claims
become legible through their hold on whiteness and masculinity, crucially depends upon and reproduces the necropolitical structure of the
basement. The image of bodies stacked on top of each other, feet stand-

ing on shoulders, evokes a horrific spatialized experience of captivity that resonates with the racialized violence of historical practices of slavery: like the physical entrapment of people abducted and forcibly transported on slave ships from west Africa over the Atlantic, the basement evokes "the topographies of cruelty" (Mbembe 2003, 40) that characterize transatlantic slavery and its aftermath in contemporary configurations of global white supremacy. Reading the basement metaphor through Achille Mbembe's analysis of the spatialization of necropower in early modern and late modern colonialism—a process Mbembe calls "territorialization" (Mbembe 2003, 25)—can guard against the "flattening" of Black feminist geographies through their incorporation in neoliberal imperatives of diversity management.

Puar continues her critique of intersectionality in a more recent piece, where her concern is how the "the intersectional subject gets tokenized or manipulated as a foil such that the presence of this subject actually then prohibits accountability toward broader alliances," in "a gestural intersectionality that can perform a citational practice of alliance without actually doing intersectional research or analyses" (2014, 78). Here she reiterates her construction of intersectionality as "isolating" categories of analysis as "separate and distinct conceptual entities" that only come to "intersect . . . at specific overlaps" (78). The problem with this rendition of the "mutual exclusivity" critique is not that her characterization of intersectionality does not obtain; it is that Puar fails to distinguish between the various deployments of intersectionality in order to motivate her claim of a difference in kind between intersectionality and assemblage, which a close reading of Crenshaw's texts makes it difficult to sustain. That is not to dismiss the critique Puar advances or to suggest that it is entirely without merit. On the contrary, I find Puar's interrogation of the travels and travails of a mainstreamed, whitewashed intersectionality suggestive and challenging as an opening to neo-intersectional engagements that restore its provisionality: thus it is worth dwelling on the following question that Puar poses: "What is a poststructuralist theory of intersectionality that might address liberal multicultural and 'postracial' discourses of inclusion that destabilise the [woman of color] as a mere enabling prosthetic to white feminists?" (2012, 54).

Like the "New Materialism" critique and the "assemblage" critique, the "post-intersectional" critique, advanced largely within the legal academy, draws on a critique of identity (which in some but not all cases is a post-identitarian critique) in order to argue for the supplanting of intersectionality with some other model or metaphor of categorial complexity. Post-intersectional critics proffer "new complexity theories" or "multidimensionality theories" which they argue transcend the conceptual limitations of the intersectionality model (Hutchinson 2002, 433; see Hutchinson 2001). They contend that "multidimensionality is a natural progression of the powerful analysis first deployed by intersectionality theorists" (2002, 439). These scholars generally acknowledge a theoretical debt to intersectionality, but they take themselves to be departing from it in a number of "substantive" ways (434). First, they introduce "sexual identity and heterosexism," a "serious interrogation" of which they argue is lacking in intersectional scholarship (434). Second, they assert the "universality of complex identity" and contest the claim, which they attribute to intersectionality, that only multiply oppressed groups occupy social locations at the intersections of axes of power (436). For instance, Nancy Ehrenreich introduces the concept of "hybrid intersectionality" to describe partially oppressed/partially privileged subjects (2002). This move, argues Darren Hutchinson, "places multidimensionality on a substantially different terrain than intersectionality, for it permits a more contextualized analysis of privilege and subordination" (2002, 436). The claim is that intersectional scholars' "singular focus on 'women of color'" disenables the "positional shift" from multiple oppression to multidimensionality as a general theorization of identity (437). Moreover, Hutchinson argues that multidimensionality gets beyond zero-sum constructions of oppression and privilege, enabling an examination of how Black heterosexual men (along with LGBTQI Black people) "have endured a history of 'sexualized racism'" that cannot be conceptualized if it is assumed that they enjoy privilege on the axes of maleness and heterosexuality (437). Conversely, by exposing the "hybrid intersectionality" of relatively privileged subgroups, multidimensionality precludes the self-representation of these groups as "uncomplicated and singular," or their disavowal of the way in which their experiences are inflected—in ways that benefit them and in ways that harm them—by multiple systems of oppression and privilege (438). A further claim is that multidimensionality moves from the level of identity to the systemic level to reveal how "systems of domination are mutually reinforcing" (438).

A focal point in the development of the post-intersectionality discourse within legal theory was the publication of Nancy Ehrenreich's 2002 article "Subordination and Symbiosis: Mechanisms of Mutual Support between Subordinating Systems," which argues that intersectional identitarians have stepped back from realizing the full implications of their analysis, namely, that it may be "impossible to eliminate one form of subordination without attacking the entire edifice of interlocking oppressions" (2002, 255). To move the analysis of subordination forward, Ehrenreich develops a "taxonomy" of mechanisms through which "interconnection" between systems is effected (256). In this analysis, she centers on "'singly burdened' individuals" who "simultaneously occupy positions of privilege and subordination, such as white women" (256). These groups face what she calls "hybrid intersectionality," an analysis of which reveals how systems of subordination sustain one another (257). Introducing the concept of "compensatory subordination," Ehrenreich challenges the assumption that "privilege" delivers an "unadulterated benefit" to singly burdened individuals and may instead act as a "double-edged sword," serving to "sustain and reinforce" their subordination (257). The metaphor of "symbiosis" is presented to illuminate the "mutually beneficial connection" among systems of subordination, and three mechanisms give content to this metaphor to show how these systems reinforce each other: first, the exclusion of certain members of groups in the construction of group interests; second, the exposure of vulnerable groups to subordination; and third, the obfuscation of the nature and sources of subordination (258).

Ehrenreich enumerates four objections to what she perceives as the "logical conclusions" of intersectional analyses, which "combine together to raise serious questions about the viability of identity theory" (2002, 271): first, the "zero sum problem: the apparent substantive conflict among the interests of different subgroups that seems to make it impossible to simultaneously further the interests of all"; second, the "infinite regress problem: the tendency of all identity groups to split into ever-smaller subgroups," until the only "coherent category" that remains is the individual; third, the "battle of oppressions problem"—"a rhetorical war over which group is worse off, which is most oppressed"—that results as a consequence of the first two problems; and finally, the "relativism problem" that arises concerning judgments about legitimacy claims to oppression if all subjects are simultaneously both "oppressor and oppressed" (267, 269). Indeed, Ehrenreich characterizes the "myth of equivalent oppressions" as "a harmful—although probably unintended—byproduct of intersectionality theory" (271).

Part of what Ehrenreich contests is the view that "women of color can represent white women," because the former experience a "pure" form of gender oppression uninflected by racial privilege (2002, 275). She attributes this claim to intersectionality, as well as the asymmetrical criticism that although white feminists have discursively arrogated this kind of representational power, their "hybrid" (as opposed to "pure") intersectional experiences are not universalizable to women of color (275). In this respect, Ehrenreich misses the asymmetry that obtains with respect to the "identity politics" of relatively privileged groups when compared to multiply oppressed groups. We saw in the earlier discussion of Crenshaw's basement analogy that efforts to redress a singular form of discrimination (inflected with and mobilizing privilege on other axes) actually serve to reproduce social hierarchy, while addressing multiple forms of discrimination simultaneously has the potential to uproot or dismantle the entire hierarchy (Crenshaw 1989, 151–52; CRC 1983; see chapter 2). This important asymmetry—rather than some territorial claim to a "pure" form of gender oppression—is what justifies, in part, the intersectional emphasis on women of color—in addition to, of course, the inherent value of eliminating discrimination against this multiply oppressed group whose interests, experiences, and liberation are marginalized within monistic social movements.

Instead, Ehrenreich centers—both in explicit, conscious ways and in ways perhaps less conscious—on the structural position of "hybrid" intersectional subjects, emphasizing how their failure to recognize how they are ultimately harmed by "divide-and-conquer tactics" serves to reinforce their own oppression (as well as reproduce that of others). For instance, Ehrenreich insists that we must focus on "the ways in which exclusion [of multiply oppressed subjects] works against the interests of the very group doing it, by reinforcing the very system it is trying to attack" (2002, 281). Yet ultimately, Ehrenreich claims, "the distinction between singly and doubly burdened individuals is admittedly artificial," since few people avoid experiencing "overlapping oppressions," and experiencing "privilege also (paradoxically) makes them vulnerable" (290). To the extent that Ehrenreich redefines privilege as a source of vulnerability to oppression, she constructs being oppressed on the basis of multiple identities and being oppressed on the basis of one as a distinction without a difference. The concept of "compensatory subordination" performs this maneuver in her argument.

Her first claim is that since privilege—and specifically the fear of losing it—can "deter resistance," those oppressed along one axis are less likely to challenge their subordination, despite the fact that the privilege they receive "usually makes it easier for them to resist their subordination" (2002, 291). As such, they can "come to accept their oppressed position along one axis in exchange for the privilege they experience along another" (291). While this may well be true, it is not clear that it serves to negate one's privilege to stay silent in the face of one's oppression; if it were the case that "acts of compensatory subordination actually exacerbate, rather than ameliorate, [one's] subordinated position" (293), would it be a hierarchy-climbing strategy on which many singly burdened individuals rely in a patterned way? Although, "in contending that privilege can harm the privileged," Ehrenreich disclaims the view that exercising privilege "somehow makes privilege less real," nevertheless she does insist that "compensatory subordination . . . is a trap . . . [that] harms the very individuals who are tempted to use it" (298); "the privilege individuals enjoy comes not just at the expense of another group, but at their own expense as well" (306). Part of the problem with the concept of compensatory subordination is that, as much as it critiques the zero-sum construction of privilege and oppression in intersectional approaches, it replicates precisely this quantitative relation, but simply reverses its logic: If intersectional analyses suggest that "hybrid" subjects are harmed by oppression and benefited by privilege, Ehrenreich responds that they are harmed by privilege to the extent that it coaxes them into acceding to their oppression. On an epistemological or motivational level, then, they may be worse off than multiply oppressed "pure" intersectional subjects who do not harbor illusions about their subordination and are in no position to calculate costs against benefits. But the deeper issue is that the notion of multidimensionality preserves precisely those categorial distinctions between forms of oppression that intersectionality reveals to depend on the experiences of privileged group members. In order to claim—of white women, for instance—that "both their subordination and their dominant status are effectuated by the same set of stereotypes," Ehrenreich preserves while combining monistic categories of race and class—which confer privileges—and a monistic category of gender—which locates them low in "a gender hierarchy among whites" (308). While claiming that "it is very difficult to distill out any essence of gendered experience from these racialized and sexualized particularities," her analysis does just that, mobilizing unitary categories to arrive at the appearance of paradox between "a racial hierarchy" in which white women, for instance, are "dominant" and "a gender hierarchy in which [they] are subordinated" (309). Her account is an additive model manqué, with the value added of motivating the apparently paradoxical claim that one's "subordination is inextricably bound to [one's] privilege" (309).

In itself, this insight is important, but in my opinion, it appears in more phenomenologically grounded terms elsewhere (e.g., Moraga 1983). The notion that "singly burdened individuals" feel "invested" in "the hierarchies that privilege them" (1983, 313) is precisely what is demonstrated by Crenshaw's account of the sociolegal reproduction of hierarchy through remedial measures such as antidiscrimination law (1989, 151–52). Indeed, it is not clear that the "symbiotic perspective" overcomes with any greater or lesser success the problems it has constructed for intersectionality (Ehrenreich 2002, 316–20). As Carbado argues, the problem with post-intersectional (among other) critiques of intersectionality is that they tend to "artificially circumscribe the theoretical reach of intersectionality as a predicate to staging their own intervention" (2013, 816). For instance, as Sumi Cho points out, it is not clear that intersectionality cannot be mobilized to account for what Ehrenreich terms "hybrid identities," since it performs a critique of how intra- and intergroup politics constitute identities and their normative subjects (2013, 398). Addressing Athena Mutua's "multidimensional" approach to masculinity, Cho questions whether "the problem with intersectionality is that it has become a 'pink ghetto,' overly populated by feminists (mostly of color)"; in seeking to go beyond it, Mutua's argument implicitly "relies upon a demographic analysis of intersectionality's end users" (399; see Mutua 2013). Perhaps something similar can be argued with respect to Ehrenreich's conceptualization of hybrid versus pure intersectionality and the host of metaphors and concepts she devises to address the former. Here, the demographic divergence is one of racialized identity—intersectionality is "for" women of color, while symbiosis is "for" white women—and the rhetorical strategy seems to be to "appeal to dominant groups' sense of self-interest" in order to form "coalition[s] . . . strong enough to carry the day" (2002, 324). If white women feel alienated by intersectionality, the concepts of compensatory subordination, hybrid intersectionality, and symbiosis can reassure them back into positions of (ostensibly self-defeating) dominance.

Ehrenreich's glib construal of coalition—as motivated by the self-interest of dominant groups—gives me an opening to foreshadow the argument of the following chapter, which concerns the relationship of intersectionality—as a critique of categories of identity—to coalitions. Chapters 5 and 6 illuminate the normative questions that intersectionality engenders as a critique of social movements and of the reproduction of hierarchies of power within them. In this way, we come full circle to the origins of intersectionality in organizing by women of color against the systems of oppression and the forms of power that pervade our lives. Only now we turn our gaze forward to consider how intersectionality as a provisional concept can materialize a coalitional horizon of struggle.

5

Identities as Coalitions

In this chapter I continue a close reading of one of Crenshaw's germinal essays, "Mapping the Margins: Intersectionality, Identity Politics, and Violence against Women of Color," in which she concludes that intersectional analysis of identity-based groups reveals them to be "in fact coalitions or at least potential coalitions waiting to be formed" (1991, 1299). For instance, Crenshaw writes, intersectionality "provides a basis for reconceptualizing race as a coalition between men and women of color" or as a "coalition of straight and gay people of color" (1299). Identity remains a useful basis for political organizing, as long as identity categories are conceptualized as coalitions (1299). Here, Crenshaw deliberately undermines the dichotomy between "identity politics" and "coalitional politics," whereby the former is viewed as a kind of separatism based on sameness while the latter depends on alliances built across differences. In fact, intersectionality reveals that this distinction between "identity" and "coalition" rests upon an exclusive focus on differences between groups, failing to consider differences within groups, which an intersectional critique of existing identity categories illuminates.

Although, as we have seen, intersectionality has achieved a kind of "buzzword" status (K. Davis 2008), the implications of this normative conclusion are rarely explored. In fact, one predominant critique of intersectionality doubts the efficacy of identity as a ground for political practice, contending that an intersectional conception of identity is divisive and could regress into a form of individualism. As we saw in chapter

4, certain critics argue that because intersectionality reveals intragroup difference it inevitably leads to divisions, rifts, and particularisms. On this view, the political implications of intersectionality are splitting apart or receding from "broader" collectivities in favor of narrow identity-based organizing—not unity across lines of difference. Alison Bailey terms this the "parsimony objection" to intersectionality and responds to one of its most sophisticated exponents, Naomi Zack, who critiques intersectionality on these grounds: "If intersectionality multiplies gender identities beyond necessity and if identity-based political movements follow in their ontological wake, then the feminist movement will be fragmented into 'segregated feminisms'" (Bailey 2009, 24; see Zack 2005, 71; see May 2015, 125–26). Intersectionality, on Zack's view, has the problematic ontological and political consequence of "multiplying axes of analysis and thus gender categories"; contra Zack, Bailey attempts to show that "intersectionality is not fragmenting" (2009, 21, 24) by invoking the distinction between "identity politics" and "coalition politics":

> Intersectionality is compatible with episodic segregation because it provides us with a conceptual vocabulary to start the difficult conversations required for successful coalition building. . . . If we understand building as a dynamic process requiring feminists to work across coalition and home spaces, and if we understand intersectionality as one way of bringing to the surface tensions between women that have prevented coalition building in the past, then intersectional tools can be understood as a necessary part of coalition building rather than as fragmenting. (2009, 25–26)

Yet Bailey preserves the distinction between identity-based and coalitional politics, viewing the latter intersectionally—as a space where heterogeneity and power relations produce "tensions" that must be addressed through "difficult conversations"; this account seems to naturalize identity groups as "homes," unadulterated by internal differences, and therefore to bypass the deeper challenge—and promise—intersectionality presents with respect to identity. Still, Bailey's response to the parsimony objection—the assumption that "in political contexts, intersectionality's speciation is seen to thwart collective action" (May 2015, 125)—is well taken: intersectionality *reveals* relations of subordination in homogenizing, falsely universal feminist politics; it does not *produce* this "fragmentation." Further, Elizabeth Cole furnishes an apt response to detractors who worry about "vanishingly small constituencies": conceiving of identities intersectionally, as coalitions, actually illuminates "new avenues of cooperation" (2008, 447). Intersectionality—as a critical project—reveals politicized identity categories to be held together variously by tacit, unspoken, deliberate, and explicit acts of alignment, solidarity, and exclusion, about which we must become more reflective and critical if mass organizing for social justice is to be more effectively pursued.

While many interpretations and deployments of intersectionality construe identity categories in essentialist terms, in this chapter I draw on social-movement history to argue that conceptualizing identities as coalitions—as internally heterogeneous, complex unities constituted by their internal differences and dissonances and by internal as well as external relations of power—enables us to form effective political alliances that cross existing identity categories and to pursue a liberatory politics of interconnection (Keating 2009; see Keating 2013). Conceptualizing identity coalitionally allows us to overcome some of the pitfalls of political alliances organized on the premise of homogeneous or essential identities. For one, the integration of all aspects of our individual identities is crucial to achieving the internal balance missing in one-dimensional political movements. Too often we are asked to subordinate one or more aspects of our identities to that which a monocular analysis privileges as significant. Audre Lorde writes:

> As a Black lesbian feminist, I find I am constantly encouraged to pluck out some one aspect of myself and present this as the meaningful whole, eclipsing or denying the other parts of self. But this is a destructive and fragmenting way to live. My fullest concentration of energy is available to me only when I integrate all the parts of who I am, openly . . . without the restrictions of externally imposed definition. Only then can I bring myself and my energies as a whole to the service of those struggles which I embrace as part of my living. (1984, 120–21)

When we give in to pressures to reduce the differences that constitute our identities, we are foreclosing a potential coalition with all those who share the repressed or excluded identities—not to mention betraying the possibility of a coalition among all parts of ourselves. Crenshaw's conceptualization of identities as "in fact coalitions" challenges us to "summon the courage" to contest exclusionary practices that marginalize some people while constructing other people as representative or prototypical of an entire group, community, or movement (1991, 1299).

Despite the power of Crenshaw's normative argument, "internal exclusions and marginalizations" continue to structure U.S. social movements, and even intersectional theorists tend to reify essentialized "group" identities "centered on the intersectional identities of a few" members (Crenshaw 1991, 1299; see Crenshaw 2015). Those who experience (what have been theorized as) multiple forms of oppression continue to face political intersectionality—the experience of being situated between two (or more) political movements claiming to represent them but pursuing mutually exclusive and often conflicting agendas that conspire to marginalize and fragment experiences of intermeshed oppressions (Crenshaw 1989, 160; 1991, 1251–52). Jennifer Jihye Chun, George Lipsitz, and Young Shin suggest that the creation of collective identities is always strategic, "partial, perspectival, and performative" and will "never encompass all dimensions of people's identities" (2013, 923). Still, the authors argue, "as an analytic tool, intersectionality can be used strategically to take inventory of differences, to identify potential contradictions, and to recognize split and conflicting identities not as obstacles to solidarity but as valuable evidence about problems unsolved and as new coalitions that need to be formed" (923).

If the coalitional promise of intersectionality remains largely unrealized, social-movement history arguably does furnish cases in which activists productively negotiated "the tension between assertions of multiple identity and the ongoing necessity of group politics" (Crenshaw 1991, 1296). What might we learn from revisiting their praxis, in which liberation is imagined in multiple registers, identities are conceptualized as plural, not singular, and movements are premised on finding the interconnections of struggles by forming relationships of accountability and compassion across lines of difference and dominance internal as well as external to "group" identities? And, considering present and future struggles, what political effects can centering the experiences and analyses of people who face multiple marginalizations have on the ways in which struggles and solidarities are envisioned? To address these questions, and to further concretize the reading of intersectionality in which I have been engaging, in this chapter I examine the role a coalitional conception of identity played in the solidarity activism of one U.S.-based organization, Somos Hermanas (We Are Sisters)—the solidarity project of the Alliance against Women's Oppression (AAWO), housed at the San Francisco Women's Building. AAWO was the organization that grew out of the dissolution of the Third World Women's Alliance, which, as we saw in chapter 1, conceptualized and struggled against the "Triple Jeopardy" of "Racism, Imperialism, [and] Sexism."[1] I then situate this activist intervention in relation to the contemporaneous intellectual production of women-of-color feminists, including Crenshaw, concerning the relationship of identities to coalitions, in order to tease out how conceiving identities coalitionally can help overcome social and subjective fragmentation. Lorde argued that overcoming fragmentation within transformative movements and at the level of identity requires a "redefining" of difference. If hegemonic ideology defines difference as a deviation from a "mythical norm," and white feminism construes it as an obstacle to a homogeneous and therefore politically efficacious "sisterhood," Lorde urges us to acknowledge "the creative function of difference in our lives" (1984, 111, 115–16). "Difference must not be merely tolerated, but seen as a fund of necessary polarities between which our creativity can spark like a dialectic," writes Lorde (111). When difference is not perceived through the prism of dominance, the interconnections among us can become the "groundwork for political action" (112).

SOMOS HERMANAS

On July 19, 1979, the Frente Sandinista de Liberación Nacional (FSLN; Sandinista National Liberation Front) formed a revolutionary government in Managua, Nicaragua, ending the forty-three-year U.S.-supported Somoza military dictatorship.[2] By contrast, in 1981, in the United States, after a decade of "economic restructuring . . . spurred by conservative renewal," the eligible electorate voted in Ronald Reagan, who, "within weeks of assuming the presidency," began his concerted attack on progressive and revolutionary nationalist movements and emerging states, and on internal colonies, racialized communities, poor people, women, and LGBT people within the territorial borders of the United States (Elbaum 2002, 40, 253–55). Within the United States, liberation movements had been subjected to infiltration and intense repression by counterintelligence programs for decades (James 1999, 111–13, 122; Dunbar-Ortiz 2005, 6). Roxanne Dunbar-Ortiz explains that the imprisonment and assassination of "consensus-building leaders" and the "discrediting and co-optation of activists" weakened these movements, as did their "failure to establish long-term, broad-based coalitions" (Dunbar-Ortiz 2005, 6). In November 1981, Reagan authorized the Central Intelligence Agency to spend $19.5 million to covertly organize, train, lead, and finance a counterrevolutionary army to remove the Sandinistas from power (Dunbar-Ortiz 2005, 117).[3] On December 21, 1981, the CIA launched the Contra War on Nicaragua and began a domestic propaganda campaign that, mirroring the military strategy, exploited divisions between Indigenous peoples (Miskitu, Sumu, and Rama, some of whom aligned themselves with the Somocista Contras) and Sandinista supporters (Dunbar-Ortiz 2005, 117–19). On December 19, 1983, the CIA staged an "exodus" of Miskitu to Honduras. According to Dunbar-Ortiz, the CIA, the Contras, and Christian missionaries had turned the Miskitu against the Sandinistas, who had made a major political and strategic error when their nationalism biased them against Indigenous peoples' claims to self-determination. The U.S. government exploited Indigenous insurgency by instigating what Dunbar-Ortiz describes as a "CIA-created Miskitu rebellion" and by running a publicly funded propaganda campaign within the United States alleging that the Sandinistas were guilty of atrocities against the Miskitu (129–31).[4] In this climate of intense repression and propaganda, the Sandinistas and the Asociación de Mujeres Nicaragüenses Luisa Amanda Espinosa (AMNLAE; Association of Nicaraguan Women Luisa Amanda Espinosa) were encouraging North Americans to travel to Nicaragua to make up their own minds about the revolution, while the United States was imposing an economic blockade and travel restrictions. According to Héctor Perla, "the FSLN leadership hoped that allowing U.S. citizens to witness firsthand the effects of U.S. policy on the average Nicaraguan would move them to return home to denounce its negative impact" (2009, 84). The FSLN believed that "U.S. working people can stop intervention" in Nicaragua, as Sergio Ramírez—elected vice-president of the Sandinista government in 1984—argued in a speech with that title in 1982 (Ramírez 1985). By 1986 more than one hundred thousand U.S. citizens had traveled to Nicaragua on solidarity delegations (Perla 2009, 84).

Reagan's reelection in 1984 coincided with the first Somos Hermanas delegation to Nicaragua, organized by AAWO at the invitation of AMNLAE.[5] Over the six years of its existence, Somos Hermanas grew to a national organization, with chapters in multiple U.S. cities, expanding its focus to El Salvador, Guatemala, and other Central American and Caribbean nations subject to U.S. imperialism (then, as now).[6] Somos Hermanas dissolved in 1990, and significantly, the archival materials reveal that the organization faltered as members experienced "the need to split [their] political energies" between multiple movements and organizing efforts to which they were committed—which Crenshaw characterizes as a form of "intersectional disempowerment" (Crenshaw 1991, 1252; see chapter 3).[7] In this sense, while I argue for the integrative effects of their organizing, it is worth noting the disintegrative influence of the broader social-movement context. A member of the first ten-day delegation (1984) and a national co-chair of Somos Hermanas (1984–90), Carmen Vázquez was also the founding director of the San Francisco Women's Building (1980–84) (Vázquez 2005). Her writing and oral history reveal the impact of Somos Hermanas on her life trajectory, suggesting that this organizing experience was a crucial factor in the integration of her multiple identities and political commitments (Vázquez 1991; 2005, 49). Vázquez's analysis of her experience offers evidence that conceptualizing identities in coalitional terms enables us to cross lines of difference in building alliances, which is crucial to any effective liberation movement. Conceiving of our identities as coalitions intimates an integrated practice of struggle. Yet no less significant a lesson to draw from Vázquez's activism and political thought is that political coalitions which attend to multiple forms of oppression help their members to integrate their identities as people— identities that through systemic oppression and monocular resistance movements have been fragmented, distorted, repressed, or negated. My analysis of Somos Hermanas draws on three main sources: Carmen Vázquez's oral history, produced through the Voices of Feminism Oral History Project; published works by Vázquez (1991, 1993, 1997, 2010); and archival research that I conducted in March and October 2011 at the Gay, Lesbian, Bisexual, and Transgender Historical Society Archive in San Francisco.[8]

The "national, multiracial" Somos Hermanas delegation that visited Sandinista Nicaragua in 1984 consisted of eighteen "Afro-American, Puerto Rican, Chicana, Peruvian, Asian, Arab and white women" from New York, Boston, Washington, DC, and the Bay Area, of whom eight were lesbian—at least two of them butch-identified—and ten were straight (Vázquez 2005, 49). Delegates included Loretta Ross, Marcie Gallo, Linda Burns, Roma Guy, Carmen Vázquez, Lucrecia Bermudez, and Nkenge Touré, and were members of various organizations, including the Black United Front, the International Council of African Women, Women for Women in Lebanon, the American Civil Liberties Union, KPFA Radio, and the Gay and Lesbian caucus of the Boston Rainbow Coalition (Vázquez 2005, 49–51; Hobson 2009, 233). Calling themselves a "veritable rainbow coalition," Somos Hermanas reported that the "multiracial composition [of the delegation] sometimes caused confusion [among Nicaraguans] because it did not jive with the image of the U.S. as a 'white nation'":

> In a working class district in Managua, mothers whose children had been killed by Somoza and by U.S.-backed contras embraced and greeted us as 'international mothers.' When we interrupted to explain that we all came from the U.S. and represented those sectors of women most oppressed by racism, sexism, and Reagan's budget cuts and war policies, one of the mothers broke into a smile, extended her arms and said, "Oh, how wonderful you have come!"[9]

Somos Hermanas

(We Are Sisters) Because...

FIG. 1. Somos Hermanas, *Somos Hermanas (We Are Sisters) Because* ... (pamphlet), n.d., Somos Hermanas archive, c. 1984–90, box 50/6, San Francisco Women's Building Records. Courtesy of the Gay, Lesbian, Bisexual, Transgender Historical Society.

That gesture of embrace would become the representative image of Somos Hermanas and its very definition of sisterhood: "Somos Hermanas means embracing our sisters in solidarity" (see fig. 1).

Emily Hobson argues that, significantly, who is embracing whom—Nicaragüense or Norteamericana—is left ambiguous in this image. Hobson interprets this ambiguity as "a strategy of representation" that "emphasized the shared context of transnational movement-building to foster egalitarian connections between women across the Americas" (2009, 87–88). Indeed, Somos Hermanas argued that "working in solidarity with our sisters in Central America means ... accepting with all our hearts and with the strength of our will that our sisters' struggle against U.S. intervention is one and the same as our own struggle for social justice in the U.S."[10] The notion of a mutual embrace could also be interpreted as referencing the historical trajectories of women of color living in North America by virtue of annexation, internal colonialism, diaspora, and coerced or enslaved migration. Could Vázquez, whose emigration at the age of five from Puerto Rico to New York City—"a place I thought was the moon [but turned out to be] the harshness and poverty of the Lower East Side, Harlem, Welfare and the Projects" (1993, 218)—have experienced the delegation to Nicaragua as a kind of diasporic return? Vázquez recounts that "it was just phenomenal to be in an environment like that and to be embraced by [Nicaraguan women]. And it was interesting to me because they embraced us as allies, you know, as American allies, as women" (2005, 49). She describes it as "truly a journey of magic": "It was the first time in my life I'd been to a socialist country, to a country in Latin America other than Puerto Rico. It was an opportunity to bring my passion for solidarity with other Latina women, my lesbian self, and my anti-racist self together" (1991, 54).

Specifically, Vázquez recounts how, through her participation in the solidarity delegation, she had an "invaluable experience in how I could be Latina, lesbian and able to challenge the assumptions of heterosexism within the context of my own culture" (1991, 54). One night the Somos Hermanas delegation was invited to an evening of dancing with another delegation, of Cuban musicians, "all men" (54). "The men were asking the women to dance and a great time was had by all except that the lesbians were none too thrilled by this arrangement. In deference to our hosts, we said nothing, but in the midst of that silence my friend Lucrecia Bermudez strode across the patio and very formally asked 'Bailemos?'—'Shall we dance?' We did. Not a minute into our dance, a Cuban gentleman took it upon himself to correct the situation" (54). But Lucrecia held Carmen "firmly" and "told the young man no, thank you": "The silence had been broken," Vázquez reflects, while "our dignity remained intact" (54). Their dance was a "small act of cultural militancy [that] shattered the heterosexual premise that a woman will always prefer a man"—"a simple act made possible by our respect for our culture and our political unity with the Nicaraguans" (54). Vázquez reflects that it was a "simultaneous embrace [of] the rituals of dance that we know in our blood" and an occasion to "learn from the rhythms, myths, traditions and values of my people about who I am [as a Puertoriqueña butch lesbian]" (54). Lucrecia's invitation—"*Bailemos?*"—occasioned another embrace, in which she held Carmen firmly, "as a whole human being, not fragments of one" (54).

Could the iconic embrace that became the symbol of Somos Hermanas represent the desire for wholeness of women of color who belong to diasporas and internal colonies structurally positioned at the margins of white/Anglo-dominated U.S. society and—as lesbians—survive at the margins of their own communities as well? "On a political level," Vázquez states, "it was just a huge leap for me, that integration of all of those things" (2005, 49). Vázquez was inspired by the political and social revolution undertaken by Nicaraguans, by the role of women in that revolution, and by the support she found in Bermudez and others to be "be visible and without apology."[11] A proud Puertoriqueña lesbian in the solidarity delegation, Vázquez returned to the United States with "the humility to understand that my place in the struggle for liberation is one of many and that my struggles as a lesbian are no more and no less an institutional reality than are my struggles against racism and economic injustice" (1991, 54). Nkenge Touré, another member of the Somos Hermanas delegation, shared how inspired she felt: "I have wanted all my life to go to a place to actually see and be part of a people who are struggling to build a new society. My heart is very full."[12]

When they returned from Nicaragua, Somos Hermanas delegates began planning a West Coast regional network to support the work of AMNLAE. The Somos Hermanas Network was launched at a conference on "Women in Central America" that was held around International Women's Day (March 8–10, 1985) at Mission High School in San Francisco and was attended by five hundred women. Seventy-five women of various ages, the majority Chicana and Latina women living in the Bay Area, became core members of Somos Hermanas (Hobson 2009, 284). Later in the year, organizers convened on the East Coast, and by 1986 Somos Hermanas had formed local chapters in Boston, New York, Louisville, Fresno, Santa Cruz, and Watsonville in addition to the original

Bay Area chapter housed in San Francisco's Women's Building. Some of the organizers in these chapters were members of the second Somos Hermanas delegation to Nicaragua, in 1986. National co-chairs Vázquez and Diane Jones returned one more time in 1987.[13] Somos Hermanas identified themselves as "a national, multiracial organization of women, lesbian and straight, who are committed to organizing ourselves and others to promote peace and stop U.S. intervention in Central America and the Caribbean." Many members were active in feminist movements; lesbian and gay rights movements; Black, Puerto Rican, and Chicano liberation movements; communities of faith; and trade unions. They had organized to defend affirmative action and to oppose Klan activity; they were peace movement activists; solidarity activists with Asian and African anticolonial struggles; members of Jesse Jackson's Rainbow Coalition; immigration and refugee rights organizers; and Socialist Party members (Vázquez 2005).[14]

Emphasizing their "diverse experiences," the group declared, "Somos Hermanas with the women of Central America because we share the burdens of militarism and war, of poverty, sexism and racism. . . . Somos Hermanas because we oppose racism and see it as a pillar of U.S. militarism." Members of Somos Hermanas conceptualized their solidarity with Nicaraguan women as stemming from their analysis that "building the bonds of sisterhood . . . demands a clear understanding of how U.S. military and economic policies directly contribute to the impoverishment of women in Central America and women in the United States, particularly women of color."[15] In other words, they mobilized on the basis of what Cathy Cohen has termed a "shared marginal relationship to dominant power" (1997, 458). It is important to note that the activists who organized as Somos Hermanas were voicing their solidarity from the margins—or as Himani Bannerji puts it, "the colonial heart"—of the liberal democratic white settler state (2000, 75). In this respect, placing Somos Hermanas in the context of lesbian, feminist, antiracist, and anti-imperialist movements reveals that while the group's members acted as bridges between these disparate agendas and diverse communities—"taking the goals, objectives, resources, and projects of the Somos Hermanas Network into the circles of people whose lives we already touch"—they remained at the margins of social-movement histories. Yet from their marginal social location within "the belly of the beast," Somos Hermanas extended their embrace across national borders that had cut across their own lives.[16]

Situating Somos Hermanas in the political geography of San Francisco's Mission District in the 1980s, prior to its gentrification, reveals the intersection of multiple social movements, diasporas, and communities (Allison and Vázquez 2007, 2; Dunbar-Ortiz 2005, 42–43; Hobson 2009, 292). By the 1970s more than fifty thousand Nicaraguan immigrants—some of whom were political exiles who had fled the Somoza dictatorship in the 1930s—and their descendants lived in San Francisco, many of them residing in the Mission District, which became an epicenter of the U.S.-Nicaragua solidarity movement and a recruitment ground for the FSLN (Dunbar-Ortiz 2005, 42–43).

Perla argues that the "roots of what came to be called the Nicaragua solidarity movement lie in the political activism of Central American activists in the United States," specifically, Nicaraguan immigrant organizers who had fled the repressive Somoza regime (2009, 83). Nicaraguan exiles began to mobilize in response to the December 1972 earthquake in Managua and organized to "protest against the corruption and brutality of the Somoza regime, and to oppose U.S. support of the dictatorship" (83). Perla identifies as the earliest such organization the Comité Cívico Latinoamericano Pro-Nicaragua en los Estados Unidos, which was formed in San Francisco, where it founded the Mission Cultural Center for Latino Arts, which functioned "a counterpublic space for the Nicaragua solidarity movement" (83). The exiles' movement and the appeals for international solidarity on the part of the Sandinistas and Nicaraguan civilians mobilized North Americans; by 1986, eighty thousand U.S. citizens had signed a "Pledge of Resistance" to "protest legally or through civil disobedience in the event of a major U.S. escalation in Central America" (92). Several organizations "shipped large quantities of direct assistance and sent large numbers of U.S. volunteers to Nicaragua" in an effort to "offset the costs of the Contra War" (91). Between 1985 and 1987 the organization Quest for Peace raised over $127 million in humanitarian assistance from U.S. residents, the same amount approved by Congress in August 1985 and October 1986 to fund the Contras. Perla characterizes the Nicaragua solidarity movement as a "transnational grassroots movement for social justice [in which] activists in North and Latin America cooperat[ed] to achieve a shared objective" (94). This transnational solidarity activism prevented the Reagan administration from "escalat[ing] its war on Nicaragua or [from using] the vastly more powerful weapons and resources at its disposal" (94). U.S.-based activists pressured Congress to "cut off Contra aid," after which Reagan continued to fund his administration's interventionist policy illegally, "a move that nearly brought about Reagan's impeachment" (94). Reagan failed in his goal of restoring the Somocistas to power, as the Contras were never successful in overthrowing the FSLN, which was voted out of power in 1990 through "the very same democratic process that it had inaugurated" (95).

Perla's analysis controverts a common conception of U.S.–Central America solidarity movements which assumes that activists are privileged, white citizens moved by altruistic or moral reasons to support "a distant struggle that [does] not directly affect them" (2009, 95). This casting eclipses the agency of diasporic Latinoamericana/os in initiating the movement, and of people of color within the United States who organized in multiracial coalitions against war and imperialist intervention. White-dominated U.S.–Central America solidarity organizations predicated their conception of solidarity—as witnessing, international accompaniment, and citizen lobbying of the U.S. government to change its foreign policy—on U.S. citizen privilege (C. Weber 2006; see Mahrouse 2014). In contrast, organizations whose bases were made up of diasporic communities and, more generally, people of color relied on different strategies, emphasized person-to-person connections, and—I would suggest—advanced a coalitional conception of identity.

What is significant, for my purposes, is how Somos Hermanas bridged disparate movements by drawing on a coalitional conception of their identities. This bridging work consisted of integrated struggle against interlocking systems of oppression, which they conceptualized in transnational terms. Moreover, as the Somos Hermanas archive reveals, in their organizing they "had to deal with the racism, homophobia, anti-communism and sexism of some of the other solidarity organizations."[17] Distinguishing itself from "other Central American Solidarity Groups," Somos Hermanas overtly supported women's revolutionary struggle in Central America and advanced an interlocking analysis "consciously making the connections between the U.S. military budget and role in Central America and poverty and deterioration of social services, housing, medical care, employment and education in the U.S." in addition to the "concurrent increase in racism, sexism, and gay-bashing, all of which disproportionately affect poor people and women and especially women of color."[18] While Somos Hermanas has been rendered invisible in social-movement histories, the archive attests to the vibrancy of their organizing. Through delegations to Nicaragua and El Salvador, demonstrations, conference organizing, report writing, film screenings, popular education, material aid campaigns, dances, and house meetings, Somos Hermanas contributed to a transnational social movement that engaged and transformed diasporic, ethnic, sexual, and gender identities.

Unlike many other transnational solidarity movements, which construct a moral foundation for activism that privileges the agency of global North citizens, Somos Hermanas envisioned solidarity with Nicaraguan women as having an objective basis in the domestic and international effects of the Reagan administration's policies, and as benefiting women of color in the United States as much as Nicaraguan women. Somos Hermanas explicitly addressed women lacking social privilege within U.S. territorial borders. They argued that as people of color and poor women in the United States, they had no choice but to oppose U.S. intervention in Central America: "It is integral to our common struggles for liberation. . . . Just as the U.S. has a 'special interest' in maintaining the domination of Central America, we have a 'special interest' in supporting the self-determination of our Central American sisters. The bonds of our sisterhood compel us to cry out and actively join our sisters in opposing our common oppressor." Sharing an oppressor, for Somos Hermanas, meant sharing a struggle: "Our sisters' struggle against U.S. intervention is one and the same as own struggle for social justice in the U.S."[19] This perception was not, it seems, one-sided, as claims of sisterhood have often been—delusions of privilege. The secretary of international relations of AMNLAE, Ivon Siu, told the Somos Herma-nas delegation in 1984:

> We see you as our sisters. You are aware of our difficulties and share similar experiences. You are fighting against racism and women's oppression. Our struggles have many points in common so that we may be straightforward in discussing our situation. Our problems are those of underdevelopment and a dependent economy. . . . We were subjected to population control, forced sterilization and high infant mortality, with many of our children dying from malnutrition and infections. Most of our population is between 14 and 25 years old. Under Somoza it was a crime to be young and many died as a result of political repression.[20]

To say that our oppressor and our struggle is the same is not to say that we share the same experience as one another. The rhetoric of "global sis-terhood" has rightly come under criticism for its tendency to elide "the diversity of women's agency in favor of a universalized Western model of women's liberation" (Grewal and Kaplan 1994, 17). Yet Somos Herma-nas forged its conception of sisterhood and transnational solidarity in an analysis of what Inderpal Grewal and Caren Kaplan have called "scattered hegemonies such as global economic structures, patriarchal nationalisms, 'authentic' forms of tradition, [and] local structures of domination" (17). In this respect, Somos Hermanas embodied Chandra Mohanty's insight that "sisterhood cannot be assumed on the basis of gender; it must be forged in concrete historical and political praxis" (1988, 67).

Uncovering the work of Somos Hermanas—one of the long-standing sponsored projects of the San Francisco Women's Building—is signifi-cant in terms of U.S. feminist history as well. Vázquez, a leader in both organizations, reflects that the "Women's Building was the reason for Somos Hermanas" (2005, 47). In the 1980s and 1990s the San Francisco Women's Building became "a critical site for the development of the women's movement in San Francisco that had a strong foundation in a progressive race-class analysis" (48). That achievement resulted from a "major, major, major power struggle" by lesbians of color who made up the majority of the Women's Building staff, while white women dominated the owning organization, the Women's Centers, which had purchased the building in 1979 (48). The workers at the Women's Building pushed for a merger with the Women's Centers, which eliminated the hierarchy, diversified the leadership, and put women-of-color staff members onto the board of their own organization. After the merger, the leadership of the Women's Building had a mandated representation (75 percent) of women of color (Vázquez 2005, 48; Hobson 2009, 90).

Lesbians of color who were active in projects housed at the Women's Building countered the white dominance of gay liberation and lesbian feminist movements in San Francisco.[21] In her white-focused history of gay and lesbian organizing in San Francisco, Elizabeth Armstrong analyzes neither the Women's Building nor Somos Hermanas, though she mentions lesbians of color forming multiracial coalitions to pursue multi-issue social-justice agendas in the 1980s and 1990s (2002, 152). In the 1970s and 1980s the Women's Building sponsored projects that included the Women's Prison Coalition (1976–78), Rosie Jimenez Coalition (1982), Women of All Red Nations (1983–88), Somos Hermanas (1984–90), Remember Our Sisters Inside (1985–89), and Mujeres Unidas y Activas (1989–present).[22]

As an organizing space for Somos Hermanas, the Women's Building also differed from earlier women-of-color organizations in the Bay Area in the predominance of out lesbians in its leadership and membership (K. Springer 2005, 130–38). Ten years earlier, the West Coast chapter of the TWWA (predecessor to the AAWO, which initiated the Somos Hermanas delegation) had excluded, and may even have expelled, its lesbian members (131; see chapter 1). While the West Coast branch of the TWWA had been a multiracial coalition of women of color, the AAWO decided to allow white women to join but maintained a majority women-of-color membership until its dissolution in 1990.[23] Vázquez explains that since "very few" straight women worked regularly at the Women's Building in the 1980s, the main tensions and conflicts were about racism, not homophobia: "I don't really recall that there was a whole lot of tension between lesbians and straight women. The tensions were between white women and women of color" (2005, 48). Yet racism and classism were often expressed through the regulation of gender identity. Vázquez states that class- and racially inflected tensions emerged at the Women's Building from the hostility of middle-class white lesbian activists toward butches working in the building, who were women of color (42, 45). For working-class women of color, butch/femme was "just how lesbians were," says Vázquez (2010, 6). Vázquez recalls that some women of color broke with this pattern; they were middle-class Argentine and Peruvian lesbian feminists who "had their own ... unique styles ... but they also were not hostile towards a gender expression that was different" (2005, 45). She recounts that "to actually present as butch was not a happy thing in San Francisco"; white lesbian feminists frequently charged her with "emulating the patriarchy, being a man" (42). "In order to survive in that context, I changed," she states, approaching in her gender presentation the "androgynous" norms of white lesbian feminism (42).

Engaging in solidarity activism with Somos Hermanas enabled Vázquez to integrate multiple identities, finding, perhaps, a home for all aspects of her self in this coalition. Being embraced by others enables one to embrace parts of oneself that have been derided, denied, and diminished. When asked by Kelly Anderson about the impact of the 1984 delegation on her life, Vázquez recounts that it

> integrated all of [her identities] in a living, joyful, experience. And you know, and that was about being in a country that had had a successful revolution, where women were leaders. I mean, Comandante Dora Maria Tellez—oh, my God. She did not come out to us as a lesbian, but several of the women came out after the meeting wanting her baby, I'll tell you that. (Vázquez 2005, 49)

Téllez, known as "Comandante Dos," was a commander in the FSLN (Randall 1994, 230; 1995, 40–54). In 1979 she led "her mostly female high command" in taking control over Léon from Somoza's National Guard, a crucial battle in establishing the revolutionary government. As minister of public health, she spearheaded Nicaragua's HIV/AIDS strategy and worked to legitimize lesbian, gay, and transgender struggles both within the FSLN and in the broader society (Randall 1992, 178n5).[24]

It is beyond the scope of this chapter to assess the complex gender, racial, sexual, and colonial dynamics of the Sandinista Revolution or of its aftermath (see AMNLAE 1983; Stoltz Chinchilla 1990; Randall 1992, 1993, 1994, 1995; Figueroa 1996; Bayard de Volo 2001, 2012; Isbester 2001; Babb 2003; Kampwirth 2004; and Dunbar-Ortiz 2005). Lorraine Bayard de Volo argues that the Sandinistas interpellated women "primarily as mothers," which was "often an empowering experience that also reshaped social views on women's place in politics"; yet it was to "deferential and self-abnegating" political activity that women were recruited under the maternal mantle (Bayard de Volo 2001, 4). The Nicaraguan mothers who embraced Somos Hermanas delegates may have been members of Mothers of Heroes and Martyrs, an organization with which Somos Hermanas was in communication. Vázquez remembers having "had long conversations" with some of the women from AMNLAE "about being a lesbian and what it meant. . . . [W]e were having those discussions, but we were having them in a context of deep respect and you know, lots of rum and dancing, and so that made it easier, for sure" (2005, 49). Nicaraguan lesbian feminists have critiqued AMNLAE's lesbophobic and antifeminist tendencies (Randall 1992, 67, 77; 1995, 918; Arauz 1994, 276–77). Yet Margaret Randall notes the "reciprocal influence" of U.S. and Nicaraguan lesbian and gay movements in the context of transnational solidarity (1992, 70). The organized LGBT movement in Nicaragua is said to have emerged in 1985 (Randall 1993, 911; see also Babb 2003). Rita Arauz, a Nicaraguan who was "an open lesbian feminist" living in San Francisco's Mission District when she was recruited by the FSLN in 1976, recounts that "it was within the homosexual community that I began to organize a movement of solidarity with the Sandinistas in the war against Somoza" (1994, 268). Arauz's organization, GALA—Gay Latino Alliance—marched in solidarity with the Nicaraguan Revolution at the first national lesbian and gay March on Washington in October 1979 (268).

The Somos Hermanas delegation, the dance with Lucrecia, the encounter with the masculine-of-center Comandante Téllez, and meeting women engaged in a successful social revolution gave Vázquez the means to integrate all aspects of her identity and to celebrate her culture and masculine gender presentation (Vázquez 2005, 2010). She relates that embracing her butch identity "was made possible by the many women of color who claimed identity within a liberation framework" (2010, 6). Though not exclusively a lesbian-of-color organization, Somos Hermanas was at the forefront of the project of integrating struggles that were falsely separated in people's minds by virtue of the scattered hegemonies of heteronormativity and nationalism, and it contributed not only to lesbian visibility but to articulating the connections among race, class, gender, and sexuality to enable alliances that can (and did) challenge imperialist power (Vázquez 2005, 90).

There are many lessons to be drawn from Somos Hermanas by scholars of social-movement history and by coalitionally minded activists. For my purposes, one central lesson is that understanding one's identity as a coalition enables one to cross naturalized boundaries imposed by systems of oppression, for instance, national borders. This is crucial if we are to bridge what Vázquez calls "the silos of identity that our movements have become" (2010, 1). More generally, the Hermanas' analyses and identifications enabled a form of transnational solidarity activism that departs in crucial ways from models that have rightly been critiqued by antiracist feminists for reproducing hegemonic power relations (Mahrouse 2008, 2014). Situating Somos Hermanas in its historical moment enables us to recast the dominant narratives of U.S.-based feminist, LGBT, and solidarity movements, a narrative that obscures the political agency of women of color, "depicting them as the rank and file in coalitions rather than the impetus behind [them]" (James 1999, 168; see also Thompson 2002).

Ideally, integration occurs not only at the level of the political movement but at the very personal level of one's own embodied identity. To the extent that their identities are constructed by oppression and by resistance, members of multiply oppressed groups face the existential challenge of constructing internal as well as external bridges. Bringing together the aspects of one's identity that have been falsely separated (both in the institutions of dominant society and in single-issue political movements) amounts to forming a coalition of one, in which one is aligned with all parts of oneself, especially those that one is taught to deny, repress, or even annihilate. Coalitions of one are strategies of survival for those who are regarded by their "natural" communities as outsiders, traitors, and fakers. Yet they can function as a microscale version of political coalitions, which have also been theorized as emerging out of necessity. Vázquez "believe[s] in coalitions" because "my survival is dependent on my ability to close the gaps between the different worlds that converge in me, and on my ability to cross over from my queer world or my Puerto Rican world or my women's world and build alliances. It is only on the strength of those alliances that I can be whole—a Puerto Rican lesbian living in a straight, sexist, and racist world" (1993, 221).

INTERSECTIONALITY AND COALITIONS

Vázquez's construal of the relation of coalitions to her survival as a multiply oppressed person illustrates how conceptualizing identity in single-axis terms actually serves to reinscribe the oppressions one incurs, through the false dichotomies that structure these liberatory movements. As we have seen, Crenshaw's reconceptualization of identities as coalitions troubles a commonplace dichotomy between coalitional and identity-based groups. Coalitions are usually contrasted with identity-based groups in the following way: identity-based groups are spaces of similarity, seclusion, and safety, whereas coalitions are spaces of difference, confrontation, and risk (Reagon 1983). On this view, coalitions are born of necessity, not in order to fulfill needs of recognition, belonging, solidarity, or inclusion (Matsuda 1991, 1190): we seek those things from identity groups where others "like us" invite us in, share and affirm our experience, and offer their analyses, insights, coping strategies, and support. Yet Bernice Johnson Reagon's argument that feminists should pursue coalitional rather than separatist politics rests on the astute and painful observation that separatism on the basis of identity almost always excludes some people who nevertheless identify, say, as women or as lesbians (1983, 349). And so, for many people, identity-based groups are not experienced as "homes" but as "barred rooms," another metaphor Reagon uses to describe them (346–47). Deliberately disrupting the dichotomy between "home" and "coalition," Crenshaw invites us to think about how we might form coalitions "in the name of [those] parts of us that are not at home" (1991, 1299). In this section of the chapter I parse some of the theoretical implications of Crenshaw's largely overlooked normative conclusion.

There are at least two interpretations of the claim that intersectionality should lead us to think of identity categories as "in fact coalitions" or as "potential coalitions." The first interpretation is that this is an ontological claim about the nature of identity—about what identities are. The second interpretation is that this is a political claim about the possibilities of organizing across differences, even across identity categories. The two interpretations bring to mind the analytic distinction Leslie McCall makes between "intracategorical" and "intercategorical" intersectional approaches (2005, 1773, 1787; see chapter 4). Conceptualizing identity categories as "in fact" coalitions, I want to suggest, enables us to focus simultaneously on intragroup and intergroup differences. The second interpretation—that an intersectional analysis should lead us to form coalitions with other groups—assumes that intercategorical distinctions constitute coalitions. But if identity categories *are* coalitions—constituted by internal differences as much as by commonalities—then this changes how we think about the political task of coalitional organizing. The emphasis shifts from forming coalitions across group differences to recognizing that groups are already internally heterogeneous. The experiences of their members—including those people exiled, unrecognized, tokenized, or denied visibility within a group—are discontinuous, differentiated, sometimes even in conflict with one another. That is not to say that members of a social group have nothing in common. Nor is it to say that groups dissolve under the intersectional lens into individuals whose experiences are entirely idiosyncratic; as Patricia Hill Collins has evocatively expressed, every group occupies a location of "heterogeneous commonality" (2003, 221). I would suggest that identity groups are productively conceptualized as coalitions by virtue of their internal heterogeneity and the tacit or explicit creative acts through which they are organized and represented as unified. Models of coalitions that presuppose the fixity of coalescing groups—and the homogeneity of collective identities—elide intragroup differences, a danger to which intersectionality as a critique of categories alerts us. But such models also naturalize politicized identities, constructing the boundaries between groups as pre-given and obscuring their genealogies.

Yet identities are also potential coalitions, in the sense that when viewed intersectionally they illuminate interconnections and interrelations, as well as grounds for solidarity, that reach across and reveal differences within categories of identity. But our common experiences are a "bond, not a political roadmap," as Vázquez has written (1993, 222). Reflecting on the U.S. LGBT movement, Vázquez observes:

> Our ability to work effectively in political coalition with those who share with us the assaults by the right wing has been hampered both by the single lens focus on oppression based on sexual orientation and by the misguided notion that we can address racism and sexism within our own movement through consciousness raising without a political agenda that specifically addresses racism, sexism and economic injustice. (223)

Our ability to align and coalesce with people "outside" our movement who do not identify with its superordinate sexual and gender identities—yet to whom "the majority of us are connected ... by blood, by class, and by spirit"—is contingent on recognizing, celebrating, and organizing meaningfully on the basis of the intersections within (Vázquez 1997, 133). For this to happen, "the dialogue we must engage in" has to be "about the truth of who we are, the whole truth" (133).

Yet perhaps because the dominant understanding of intersectionality is relatively uncritical regarding the use of extant categories, with some important exceptions, not many theorists who invoke intersectionality have interpreted identities as coalitions, nor have many pursued coalition as a challenge to single-axis conceptions of identity (important exceptions inform my discussion: Matsuda 1991; Martínez 1993; Cohen 1997; A. Y. Davis and Martínez 1998; Lugones 2003; Cole 2008; Cole and Luna 2010). Indeed, the contrast generally drawn between identity and coalition renders less visible the differences within, that is, the intersections that internally constitute any social group. Moreover, Cole argues that the categorical approach to intersectionality in empirical research "assumes the definition and operationalization of social/structural categories as independent variables," without "address[ing] the processes that create and maintain . . . the categories" (2008, 445). In this sense, some deployments of intersectionality reproduce what AnaLouise Keating calls "status quo stories about identity," which prevent us from honing our perception to produce analyses and politics of "interconnection" (2009). Status quo stories about racial identity "reinforce the belief in permanent, separate racial categories," while status quo stories about gender identity naturalize heteronormative constructions of binary gender categories (Keating 1995, 902). María Lugones argues that "the fragmentation of perception disempowers our resistance by making deep coalitions logically impossible as it undermines the very possibility of fashioning larger and complex resistant collective subjectivities" (2003, 160). A "lack of fluency in resistant logics" results in closed boundaries, in communities modeled on nations, in authenticity and legitimacy tests for membership (159–62). If some people have the "marks of solid identity" and they become arbiters of inclusion in "homeplaces," in communities constructed as nations, others do not and are "exiled," rendered invisible, turned into "imaginary beings" (151–52). Furthermore, categorical approaches to intersectionality tend to assume that "forming political alliances . . . within populations deemed socially similar is a straightforward matter" (Cole 2008, 446). Yet, as Angela Harris argues, the construction of identity categories is always a creative (as opposed to a merely descriptive) act (1990, 613). Cole argues that conceptualizing identities as coalitions allows us to "trouble the ideal of 'natural' affinity groups" (2008, 446). What is crucial about Crenshaw's coalitional conceptualization of identity is that it brings to our attention the fact that "any attempt to mobilize identity is a negotiation [of the] various political interests, conflicting though they may be, that exist within an identity category" (Crenshaw 1995, 12).

Arguably, members of multiply oppressed groups positioned between movements that refuse to view identities as in fact coalitional, and struggles as optimally interconnected, are in a unique position to express and communicate these existing and potential interconnections. Differences within us can enable radical alliances among us (Barvosa-Carter

1999). The experience of conflicting commitments to political movements can illuminate a "practice of integrated struggle," which Cheryl Clarke identifies as "a core principle of black feminism—what we now call intersectionality" (2010, 781).

At stake in this normative argument about identities as coalitions are at least two competing ways of thinking about intersectionality and categories of identity that, in my view, differ vastly in their political and theoretical implications and their political ramifications. The first is the dominant, "categorial" interpretation and deployment of intersectionality, which takes intersectionality as consisting of merging, compounding, adding, joining, or uniting discrete, mutually exclusive, and stable categories of identity (race and gender, paradigmatically) that (on this view) correspond to analytically and/or ontologically discrete—if intersecting—systems of power. I contend that institutionalized forms of "intersectionality," which tend to interpret the concept in a categorial way, can function as an alibi for, and even as an impediment to, coalitional praxis, enabling a postracial discourse of feminism's arrival, and evading (even while appearing to "name") issues of racist, heteronormative, transphobic, ableist, and class (among other) forms of subordination. Indeed, as I argued in chapter 3, some white feminist deployments of intersectionality seem to have more to do with the desire to project an innocent, nonracist feminist moral self than with actually transforming relations of power that structure feminist knowledge production and political agendas. As a descriptive positivism, the normative implications of intersectionality are reduced to a politics of inclusion, which leaves white dominance in and over feminism undisturbed. By shifting the political emphasis of women-of-color feminisms from coalition to inclusion, white hegemony and property (expressed in the power to include or exclude) in feminism is reproduced. Moreover, as we saw in chapter 1, inclusion is posited as the resolution of what Lugones has called the "problem of 'difference'" within white feminist theory: "intersectionality" functions to rescue feminist theory from its theoretical weaknesses, and the focus becomes how to keep on generalizing within established analytical frames (2003, 72–74). As Shireen Roshanravan argues, the inattention to women-of-color feminisms is partly "enacted in contemporary feminism [by] responding to 'the problem of difference' with a politics of inclusion that changes the content but not the terms of feminist engagement"; "such a politics of inclusion does not address women of colour as knowing subjects but as demographic representations of a superficial diversity" (2014, 57). Inclusion of "difference" inevitably lapses into tokenism; I would suggest that this is the political consequence of "intersectionality" widely understood as a methodology that does not require that we revise precisely those categorial divisions it was, I have argued, innovated to critique.

On the other hand, exploring Crenshaw's largely ignored claims about identity categories as coalitions allows us to envision a counterhegemonic interpretation of intersectionality. Intersectionality, in Crenshaw's account (1989), reveals the inadequacy of categories of discrimination—as well as of struggle—constructed using the logics of mutual exclusion and prototypicality that abstract the experiences of relatively privileged members of oppressed groups and, falsely universalizing them, render them representative of all members of the groups in question. For women of color, queer people of color, and other multiply oppressed groups, conceptualizing identity groups as "in fact" coalitions shifts our attention to the "intersectionalities within"—the multiplicity and contradictions of our identities politicized by social movements that have failed to grasp the social totality and lived experiences of multiple oppressions in a nonfragmented way (Espinosa 2011).

In this respect, it is important to historicize the concept of coalition as it is theorized by women-of-color feminists, who, as Roshanravan (2014) argues, have articulated diverse motivations, orientations, and strategies for coalescing (and not coalescing). Indeed, the political identity (as opposed to the demographic descriptor) "women of color" incarnates a coalitional consciousness, manifested in the "bridging" work of integrating disparate struggles against interlocking systems of oppression (Moraga and Anzaldúa 1983; CRC 1983). "Women of color" has also functioned as a potential—and at times a powerfully real—coalition in the United States. While that term might be used in a nominal, demographic, and therefore colonial sense, its politicized meaning—for instance, the meaning that Combahee River Collective members and

Bridge theorists gave it—was a coalitional one. This was a "differentiated notion of coalition" which recognizes that women of color have varying (and even opposed) experiences of racialization (Hong 2005, xxvii–xxviii; see R. A. Ferguson and Hong 2011). Through coalitional political movements, women of color were actively "constructed as a new social/political subject" whose experience was acknowledged to be heterogeneous and whose political strivings were to enact solidarity (A. Y. Davis and Martínez 1998, 300). Through "coming together," women from various racialized ethnic groups came to recognize that gendered racism does not operate in a singular, internally consistent way. Rather, as J. Kehaulani Kauanui argues, "multiple racializing logics and trajectories were formed along the forceful lines of white property interests" (Kauanui 2008a, 30; see A. Smith 2006, 2012). In U.S. society, processes of differential racialization, structured and institutionalized through laws of hypodescent (the so-called "one-drop rule" determinant of Black identity) and hyperdescent (determinant of Indigenous identity), and segregation and selective assimilation, mean that women of color and Indigenous women often have contradictory experiences of gendered racism (Kauanui 2008a, 25; see A. Smith 2006, 2012; see chapter 6). Yet as Moraga and Anzaldúa put it in their introduction to the *Bridge* anthology, coming to consciousness of such "contradictions" constituted "the root of our radicalism" (1983, 5).

Barbara Smith and Loretta Ross reflect on the adoption by Black feminists of the coalitional identity "women of color" at the International Women's Conference in Houston in 1977, and by Kitchen Table Press at its founding meeting in 1980 (B. Smith 2003, 74–76, 82): "We made a decision from day one," Smith reflects, "that we would be a press for all women of color," which was particularly important "given that most of us were indeed of African heritage" (75). Ross (2011) traces the history of "women of color" to the 1977 Houston Conference, which a group of Black feminists from Washington, DC, attended in order to articulate "A Black Women's Agenda" to a white-dominated leadership that had devoted to "minority" women's issues a mere three pages in its two-hundred-page analysis. When they arrived in Houston, other groups of racially oppressed women wanted to sign onto, and join their own analyses to the Black feminist "Agenda"; in the context of those negotiations, the term "women of color" was devised to represent this coalitional formation. Ross emphasizes that "they didn't see it as a biological designation . . . it is a solidarity definition; a commitment to work in collaboration with other oppressed women of color who have been minoritized" (2011).

With this rich history of coalitional resistance as the backdrop, numerous scholars and activists have suggested that women of color are potentially ideal coalitional subjects in virtue of facing multiple simultaneous oppressions as well as multiple exclusions from social movements (Parker 1991; Hurtado 1996; Cole and Luna 2010). Yet Edwina Barvosa-Carter suggests that "modernity has made multiple identity a real and necessary aspect of life for everyone living in modern conditions" (1999, 112). Barvosa-Carter traces multiple identity (as a condition of possibility of multiple consciousness) to "modern conditions" of war; colonization and decolonization processes; "natural" disasters caused by climate change; dispossession and economic exploitation that "have displaced millions of people around the globe," resulting in "cultural intermixture" which in turn "generates multiple identity" (112). Characterized by "multiplicity, contradiction, mutual conditioning, situationality, and relationality," multiple identity is a departure from identity as something "singular, stable, and definitive" (113, 111). Barvosa-Carter argues that "multiple identities can connect people to a number of social groups and communities that can, in turn, potentially become politicized and mobilized in order to achieve particular social justice goals" (123). While multiple identity is not a guarantor of coalitional cohesion, as "difference within us" it is "one psychosocial factor that can aid in the formation of diverse coalitions" (124).

If identities are always already multiple rather than singular, identity politics needs to pursue multiple political goals, goals around which multiple overlapping groups might coalesce. Yet coalitions are often viewed as temporary, exigent forms of political organizing that are built around shared issues rather than shared identities or even shared ideologies. For instance, Elizabeth Martínez, in a conversation with Angela Davis about coalitions, states that "coalitions, networks, alliances, should never make the mistake of demanding ideological unity. They can expect unity around an issue" (A. Y. Davis and Martínez 1998, 301). It has even been argued that coalitions pose an "identity threat" to individual constituents, because they require them to compromise the distinctiveness of their "own" group (González et al. 2008, 96). This antagonistic relationship between identity-based and coalitional organizing is highlighted by Richard Delgado, who claims that coalitions compel "the oppressed [to] come to identify with their oppressors" in which gains made by oppressed groups are limited to those which happen to converge with the interests of dominant groups (quoted in James 1999, 168). Delgado continues:

> Gains are ephemeral if one wins them by forming coalitions with individuals who really do not have your interests at heart. It's not just that the larger, more diverse group will forget you and your special needs. It's worse than that. You'll forget who you are. And if you don't, you may still end up demonized, blamed for sabotaging the revolution when it inevitably and ineluctably fails. (quoted in James 1999, 168)

But is this not precisely what the intersectional critique of unitary identity categories reveals about identity-based groups? That prototypical or normative group members fail to endorse the issues and invalidate the experiences of marginal members whose invisibility secures the illusion of group unity and identity? To assume the homogeneity of received identity categories is to ignore the force of the intersectional critique and to continue to presuppose that members of constituted identity groups share the same, undifferentiated experiences and have equal representational capital to define group-wide agendas and to be heard in making demands. Arguably, this forgetting of the intersectional critique of identity politics enables Delgado to claim that "little is gained from coalition; working in concert may even diminish efficiency because it takes time to . . . become familiar with each other" (2003, 876). His choice of example is indicative: "Blacks might need to learn Spanish, while Latinos might need to adjust to Black ways of speaking, relating, and doing business" (876). Yet "Black" and "Latina/o" are, in fact, themselves pan-ethnic, multilingual, and pan-national coalitional identities, differentiated internally by gender identity, sexuality, age, generation, dis/ability, religion, class, and citizenship status.

While intersectionality usefully deconstructs the false dichotomy between identity and coalition, it should not lead us to romanticize the latter; indeed, pessimism about the efficacy of coalitions is echoed by women of color and Indigenous women who have learned from experience that "when we try to work in coalition with the mainstream, the mainstream benefits, and we don't" (Ross quoted in Cole 2008, 449; see Trask 1991; see Matsuda 1991; see chapter 6). Skeptical or cautious accounts of coalitions, particularly those based in actual experiences of betrayals of solidarity and accountability in the course of political organizing across lines of difference and dominance, must be seriously considered. However, I would suggest that it is not difference as such that undermines identities-as-coalitions; rather, it is relations of dominance that place limits on identification and solidarity under prevailing conditions of white supremacy and settler colonialism as it articulates heteropatriarchal power (see chapter 6). Moreover, these relations of dominance cannot be mapped entirely onto coalitions, since this is to occlude intragroup heterogeneity and to overstate intergroup heterogeneity. For instance, this obviates the experiences of women and queer people within nationalist political movements that claim to represent them but in fact render them subordinate to patriarchal leaderships. Grievances and "horizontal" oppressions exist within, across, and between organized ethnic and pan-ethnic groups and white settlers, along lines of gender/gender identity, sexuality, citizenship status, national origin, disability, class, or religion. Indeed, as we have seen, the contrast drawn between identity and coalition renders less visible the "differences within" and exaggerates the "differences between," eliding the intersections that constitute any social group. In this way, contrasting coalitions to identity-based organizing promotes a homogenized conception of groups that intersectionality reveals to be illicit and untenable.

Intersectionality reveals that identities *already* are coalitions. In her conclusion that launched our discussion in this chapter, Crenshaw writes that the category of race should be seen as a coalition among racialized men and women and/or among queer and straight people of color. What could this mean? To unpack the claim, we might refer to Lugones's distinction between groups perceived through oppressive vision and groups perceived through resistant vision (2003, 151). While groups are formed through operations of power, identities are also configured around communities of resistance. In another article, Crenshaw points to the process through which Black identity was transformed during the civil rights movement from a marker of exclusion to a "basis for public power and political action" (1995, 8). "What was a marker for subordination—identity—is now a source of connection and political empowerment," she writes (8). Contrary to their representation as static, immutable, essential, and even biologically determined markers of difference, identities are reconfigured and resignified in and through political engagement. Therefore, "any attempt to mobilize identity is a negotiation, a discussion among those in identity groups to put forth an agenda that fully recognizes the various political interests, conflicting though they may be, that exist within an identity category" (12). For this reason, Davis has problematized nationalism as the "paradigm for our community-building processes" (A. Y. Davis and Martínez 1998, 299), while Sumi Cho has demonstrated how the rhetoric of "family" serves to cement white women's heterormative identification with white men—who, under racially segregated kinship relations, are constructed as their (actual or imagined) husbands, sons, or fathers—and simultaneously to naturalize their disidentification with, and oppression of, women of color (2002, 408–13). In their modern/colonial renditions, "family" and "nation" function as regulatory norms that naturalize the unity they seek to forge (see chapter 6).

As we have seen, coalitions have been conceptualized by some women-of-color feminists as politically exigent given the configuration of hegemonic power. As Reagon puts it, You don't go into coalition because you just *like it*. The only reason you would consider teaming up with someone who could possibly kill you, is because that's the only way you can figure you can stay alive" (1983, 343–44). Mari Matsuda maps the coalition/identity distinction onto another set of distinctions between risk and safety, necessity and desire. She states that "coalitions are formed out of necessity" by "individuals from divergent social backgrounds and positions coming together to work toward a common goal" (1991, 1190, 1183). For Matsuda, as for Reagon, there are benefits to coalescing that outweigh the discomfort and difficulty of organizing politically with others who are "not like you" (Reagon 1983, 346). Coalescing across lines of subordination and privilege is necessary at this historical moment, since "no subordinated group is strong enough to fight the power alone" (Matsuda 1991, 1190). As Elizabeth Martínez puts it, "We have to fight together because there is a common enemy" (A. Y. Davis and Martínez 1998, 297). Women-of-color feminists thus affirm an integrative tradition of struggle that views coalitions as "necessary because of complex interlocking structures of oppression and privilege" (CRC 1983; Cole and Luna 2010, 75). Furthermore, Matsuda argues that "working in coalition forces us to look for both the obvious and the non-obvious relationships of domination" between nominal and prominent members of groups (1991, 1189; see Cohen 1997). When we are trapped in single-axis political agendas or mired in the specificities of our own experiences of oppression (and those of people "like us"), coalitions enable us to "ask the other question" about the nexus of power relations that any transformative project needs to understand and attack (Matsuda 1991, 1189). Yet identities-as-coalitions reveal that "the power," the "common enemy," and even "the Man" is not just external to oppressed groups but that relations of domination express themselves horizontally, quickly reconfiguring internal hierarchies and producing internalized oppressions. Moreover, intersectionality can encourage us to bring our critical gaze inward, intimating how forming coalitions of one is an act of resistance against the normative internalization of political fragmentation by multiply oppressed subjects.

Vázquez tells us that "the liberated body must live through many identities and in many movements" (2010). The integration of intersectional identities that are disparaged, denied visibility, and marginalized within identity-based politics is crucially interconnected with the collective ability to integrate struggles against simultaneous oppression(s). Perhaps we can be most fully ourselves in relation to others in movements that advance coalitional conceptions of identity and that articulate the connections between what have been theorized as discrete systems of oppression. The archive of Somos Hermanas reveals that we can do politics in ways that allow the possibilities of coalition and solidarity to construct our identities as much as those relations of domination against which we struggle.

5. Alliance against Women's Oppression and Somos Hermanas, newsletter, Fall 1984, Somos Hermanas archive, c. 1984–90, box 50/11.

6. Somos Hermanas, "Who We Are," organizational pamphlet (c. 1985), Somos Hermanas archive, c. 1984–90, box 50/6.

7. "Letter to CarEth Foundation," 1989, Somos Hermanas archive, c. 1984–90, box 50/14.

8. Archived materials pertaining to Somos Hermanas span boxes 50/6 to 50/15 and 35/1 and 35/2 of the San Francisco Women's Building Records, 1972–2001, housed in the Gay, Lesbian, Bisexual, Transgender Historical Society Archive in San Francisco; at that archive I also consulted box 34/9 (Carmen Vázquez's speeches) and boxes 34/12 and 34/16 (AAWO). I was interested in internal organizing documents such as meeting minutes, letters, etc., as well as public documents such as pamphlets, posters, speeches, and publications that revealed how the organizers in Somos Hermanas conceptualized and mobilized their identities.

9. Alliance against Women's Oppression and Somos Hermanas, "Defending the Country, Proud to Be Women, Conquering the Future," newsletter, Fall 1984, 1, Somos Hermanas archive, c. 1984–90, box 50/11.

10. "Proposal for a West Coast Regional Network" (c. 1985), 2, Somos Hermanas archive, c. 1984–90, box 50/6.

11. Women made up 30 percent of the FSLN's combatants and held important military, political, and social leadership positions (e.g., Dora María Téllez, Gladys Baez, Nora Astorga, Doris Tijerino, etc.). Yet the revolutionary discourse mobilized women in gendered and sexist ways (Figueroa 1996; Bayard de Volo 2012). Some commentators argue that progress occurred only when women's and feminist concerns converged with the nationalist interests of the male FSLN leadership (Randall 1992; Bayard de Volo 2012).

12. Touré quoted in newsletter, Fall 1984, 1, Somos Hermanas archive, c. 1984–90, box 50/11.

13. "Somos Hermanas 1987 Assessment" (c. 1988), 1, Somos Hermanas archive, c. 1984–90, box 50/8.

14. See also "Who We Are" (endnote 6).

15. "Proposal for a West Coast Regional Network," 1.

16. "Proposal for a West Coast Regional Network," 2.

17. "Somos Hermanas 1987 Assessment," 1.

18. "Somos Hermanas Needs You" (c. 1989), Somos Hermanas archive, c. 1984–90, box 50/11.

19. Proposal for a West Coast Regional Network," 2.

20. Ivon Siu quoted in newsletter, Fall 1984, 2. Somos Hermanas archive, c. 1984–90, box 50/11.

21. "Recruitment Plan for Somos Hermanas" (n.d.), Somos Hermanas archive, c. 1984–90, box 50/7.

22. Women's Prison Coalition, box 52/14; Rosie Jimenez Coalition, box 49/11; Women of All Red Nations (WARN), box 51/21; Remember Our Sisters Inside (ROSI), box 49/10; and Mujeres Unidas, box 60/4; all in San Francisco Women's Building/Women's Centers.

23. Both the TWWA and the AAWO were affiliated with the communist organization Line of March. AAWO members went on to form the Oakland-based nonprofit organization Women of Color Resource Center (D. Brown and Sánchez 1994; Elbaum 2002, 82, 274; K. Springer 2005, 131; Hobson 2009, 282–83).

24. Despite the FSLN's electoral defeat, she was reelected in 1990. Now a historian, Téllez was denied a visa by the U.S. government in 2005 after being invited to take up a position at Harvard (Campbell 2005; see also B. Springer 2011).

6

Intersectionality and Decolonial Feminism

This book has focused closely on the concept of intersectionality, insisting on the specificity of the history of its articulation while suggesting the breadth of its potential to undo positivist, essentialist, and segregationist habits of thought. But the institutionalization of intersectionality as a subfield of women's, gender, and sexuality studies or even as an axiom of feminist knowledge production has not occurred in a vacuum, nor is it the only instance of the subsumption of knowledges generated by women-of-color feminists into the mainstream of white-dominated feminist scholarship. Similar stories can be and are told about other subfields of the interdiscipline, which would seem to respond to what white feminists have constructed as "the problem of 'difference'" (Lugones 2003), and whose ascendancy is marked and marred by the token inclusion and simultaneously the segregation of minoritized women in the discrete "subfields" of intersectional, transnational, and Indigenous/Native feminisms. Indeed, the identity-based specialization of labor that these divisions imply has implications for their deployment in institutional projects of diversity management and the training of "difference" into colonial demographic categories, which women-of-color and Indigenous scholars are then called upon to naturalize with their embodiments (Falcón and Nash 2015). Sylvanna Falcón and Jennifer Nash observe how in U.S. women's, gender, and sexuality studies, transnationalism and intersectionality are "pitted against each other" as intellectual projects competing for scarce resources (2015, 4); recently, transnationalism has been deployed alongside post-identity critiques of intersectionality that construct U.S. Black women as domestic, immobile, specific, parochial, and "the subject of women's studies past" (3). Falcón and Nash astutely argue that the "demise" of the descriptor "third world feminism" (see chapter 1)—which, "even as it produced certain kinds of elisions, necessarily underscored continuities between projects that we might now call 'intersectional' and 'transnational'" (4)—enables a rigid "separation of intersectionality and transnationalism, a division which pits U.S. black women against other women of color" (5). Not only does this false distinction between transnational and Black/intersectional feminisms conceal the coalitional identities that women of color created under the banner of transnational and third world feminisms across territorial borders (see chapter 5); it also naturalizes the coloniality of the United States and other white settler state formations, reifying its imperial claim to territorial sovereignty while eliding the ongoing colonialisms it perpetrates against Indigenous, Hawaiian, Puerto Rican, African diasporic, Chicana/o, and other internally colonized groups. The coloniality of this methodological nationalism is evident in the conflict it produces between "U.S. nationals"—whose relationship to the state, its institutions, and the dominant society is elided— and "aliens"—who are urged from above and below to disidentify with "domestic" Black and other internally colonized communities. We would do well to consider, in addition to the segregation of intersectional from transnational feminisms (as Falcón and Nash urge), their division from a third term, Indigenous feminisms. In this way we can begin to challenge the "vanishing" of Indigenous women within women's, gender, and sexuality studies: the "present absence" of Native peoples "in the U.S. colonial imagination," a violently produced "'absence' that reinforces at every turn the conviction . . . that the conquest of Native lands is justified" (A. Smith 2003, 72). It is worth considering to what extent the genocidal demographic projects of the U.S. state have affected the relatively lesser visibility of Indigenous feminism in white-dominated academic institutions, and, conversely, to what extent Indigenous feminisms have resisted assimilative and appropriative commodification in and through (not) becoming objects of disciplinary knowledge. For instance, Audra Simpson and Eve Tuck and K. Wayne Yang have each argued for methodologies of "refusal," to resist the "settler territorialization of Indigenous/Native/community knowledge, and to *expand* the space for other forms of knowledge, for other thought-worlds to live," outside of colonial academic institutions (Tuck and Yang 2014, 817; Simpson 2007, 2014). Refusal is both an epistemological and a political stance for Simpson, who analyzes its relationship to sovereignty for Indigenous nations as a decolonial alternative to the "presumed 'good' of multicultural politics": recognition (2014, 11).

In this chapter, by way of resisting the disciplinary segregation of minoritized, women-of-color, Black, and Indigenous feminisms—which dissimulates as to the political geography of imperial and neocolonial relations that a decolonial perspective can reveal as cross-cutting reified national boundaries—I consider to what extent intersectionality is compatible with the project of a decolonial feminism. My aim is neither to equate intersectionality and decolonial feminism nor to adjoin or append the latter to the former. Rather, I hope to explore what kinds of theoretical and political work a decolonial-intersectional feminist coalition can do. First, I consider the compatibilities and tensions between decolonial/Native feminist theories and intersectionality, as it has been articulated by Crenshaw, as it has been taken up within the white-dominated interdiscipline of women's, gender, and sexuality studies, and as it has been interpreted in the previous chapters: as a radically provisional critique of categories which reveals them to be constituted as much by internal as by external relations of power. Second, I trace what a decolonial "border thinking" about intersectionality might constitute, drawing on the work of Gloria Anzaldúa, Walter Mignolo, and AnaLouise Keating. Then, I turn to a consideration of Andrea Smith's argument about the possibilities and limitations of coalitions among various racially oppressed groups of women of color within the colonial territorial borders of the United States in order to examine the implications for intersectionality of an internally plural conceptualization of "race," racialization, racism, and racial violence. Finally, I perform a reading of María Lugones's work, by which I have been deeply inspired, that synthesizes Lugones's heterodox reading of intersectionality with a decolonial feminism that seeks to animate coalitions against multiple oppressions constituted and fractured in and through the coloniality of power. In closing, I consider recent arguments about the easy appropriation of the concept of "decolonization" in (settler-dominated) social-justice discourses and about the tensions that emerge in attempts to "decolonize" (non-Indigenous) antiracist and feminist politics.

DECOLONIAL CHALLENGES TO HEGEMONIC FEMINISM

Kanien'kehá:ka feminist activist Ellen Gabriel argues that "modern feminism and the fight for women's equality owes its birth to Indigenous women" (2011, 183). Yet the relation of hegemonic feminism, which participates in and thus reproduces settler colonialism in its appeals to state power as the guarantor of formal equality, and Indigenous women's struggles for self-determination in and against the "atmosphere of violence" produced by the inextricable systems of heteropatriarchy and colonialism is historically fraught, to say the least (Monture-Angus 1995, 170). Broaching this conflict as it manifests in contemporary academic feminism, Maile Arvin, Eve Tuck, and Angie Morrill (2013) offer a typology of five decolonial challenges that Native feminist theories pose to white-dominated feminist discourses within gender, sexuality, and women's studies that I would like to juxtapose here with the reception, limitations, and promise of intersectionality. The first challenge is to "problematize settler colonialism and its intersections" with heteropatriarchy and heteropaternalism (2013, 14). Rather than representing white settler colonialism as it articulates heteropatriarchal power as an "event" most often located in the historical past, they argue it must be acknowledged as a "structure": "a persistent social and political formation" that continues to be reproduced and "to shape the everyday lives of Indigenous and non-Indigenous peoples" (27). Not dissimilarly, as we have seen, the non-representable injury that occurs at an intersection of categories of discrimination is misrepresented as an "event" in (colonial) antidiscrimination law and jurisprudence, eliding the historical and structural dimensions of oppression—including its licit forms—in redressing only those "instances" of discrimination that are rendered intelligible within the dictates of the law (see chapter 2). The authors' first challenge coincides with intersectionality to the extent that feminist scholars are urged to attend to the articulation of heteropatriarchy with a system of knowledge and a structure of power that is persistently disavowed or repressed in the constitution of an epistemology of ignorance around the coloniality of the United States and other settler societies. But this should not be interpreted as a call to consider colonialism as still another axis of oppression in addition to those already under intersectionality's purview; an additive approach to intersectionality that would "run . . . a 'colonialism road' through the intersection will not correct [the] oversight" of the ways in which colonial oppressions manifest in Indigenous peoples' lives (Bailey 2009, 68). Rather, Arvin, Tuck, and Morrill urge us to engage in an analysis of the coloniality of power—"a persistently violent domination that marks the flesh," to quote Lugones's evocative definition—and survives formal decolonization processes (where those have indeed occurred, decidedly not in white settler states)—in constituting what Lugones calls the "modern/colonial gender system" (2007, 188). In other words, the first challenge does not amount to a call to multiply intersections, but rather to give content to the attributed relation of "mutual constitution" among extant unitary categories (202). According to Lugones, whose heterodox reading of intersectionality we will examine closely below, "it is only the logic of the mutuality of construction that yields the inseparability of race and gender" (208n15).

The second challenge posed by Native feminist theories to the "whitestream" of the interdiscipline is to "refuse erasure but do more than include" Native feminisms and Native women. They argue that "the project of inclusion can serve to control and absorb dissent rather than allow institutions like feminism and the nation-state be radically transformed" (Arvin, Tuck, and Morrill 2013, 17). This assessment seems to have been borne out in the ascendancy of intersectionality over the past quarter-century. If intersectionality has been depoliticized in part through the misrepresentation of its anti-subordination claims (at the sociolegal as well as the perceptual-cognitive levels) as pleas for inclusion of "different" women in existing categories and frameworks, Native feminist theories can coalesce with a neo-intersectional approach around a refusal of erasure while rejecting inclusion and multicultural management (17). Inclusion is "central" to the reproduction of hierarchical power (17). While "inclusion" is superficially propounded to be the antidote to "exclusion," Crenshaw explicitly states that "problems of exclusion cannot be solved by simply including Black women within an already established analytical structure"; intersectional critique urges us to rethink the "entire framework" through which Black women's experiences of discrimination are cognized, narrated, and redressed (1989, 140). Arvin, Tuck, and Morrill urge us not to view Native feminism as "an identity label" which from a "non-Native perspective" can construct Native feminist theories as "merely a specialized subset of whitestream feminism" within "the seemingly neutral field of feminism as a whole" (2013, 17). Reducing women-of-color and Indigenous feminisms to "subfields," "mere identity politics," or even (as we saw in chapter 4) "representationalisms" means failing to engage with their theoretical analyses of systems of power, which implicate all subjects and social groups. While an approach that aims at inclusion would leave settler-accommodating accounts of, for instance, U.S. society and U.S. law intact, Arvin, Tuck, and Morrill advocate a confrontation with the radical incommensurability of settler and Indigenous feminisms. Moreover, as will be discussed below drawing on Andrea Smith's germane conceptualization of the "Three Pillars of White Supremacy," constructing these as narrow, discrete identity-based discourses means failing to see the interconnections among plural and sometimes contradictory manifestations of racism as it articulates heteropatriarchal power (A. Smith 2006, 2012).

This brings us to the third challenge that Arvin, Tuck and Morrill identify: they call on feminists to "craft alliances that directly address differences" (2013, 20). "Native feminisms are not meant to be easily consumable"; they explicitly challenge both the "missionary zeal" of white feminisms, which heteropaternalistically construct Indigenous women whom they Other into the objects of their rescue efforts, and the appropriation of indigeneity at a moment when the commodification of Native cultures and knowledges is on the rise (21–22). For instance, Hawaiian nationalist and feminist scholar Haunani-Kay Trask observes the impediments to coalitions with haole (white settlers) whose general ignorance . . . about where they are geopolitically (on stolen Hawaiian land, not off the coast of Santa Barbara on a tiny vacation spot) and who they are (foreigners) creates deep-seated tensions in a coalition with Hawaiians. This, along with our historic situation of oppression, places us in a position where forming common ground with non-Natives, especially haole, means that we must suppress our true sentiments, that is, our cultural and political nationalism, in order to make coalitions work. Real organizing of Hawaiians, then, takes place among Hawaiians, not in coalitions. (1991, 1209)

Given the studied ignorance of non-Natives about "where and who they are" and their recalcitrant opposition to Hawaiian sovereignty, Trask suggests that Hawaiians have found it necessary to pursue a strategy of organizational separatism, coalescing "rarely" with haole and "only for struggles . . . of short duration" (1210). From a Hawaiian perspective, haole—who have sought positions of political and economic dominance in Hawai'i through militarism and tourism—have simply not proven themselves to be trustworthy allies. The bottom line of coalitional organizing, Trask observes, is always a function of power: "As far as the haole were concerned, the coalition was to concentrate on non-Hawaiian issues," premised on "loving American ways of life" that are anathema to Hawaiians, rather than respecting and restoring Hawaiian sovereignty (1209). Trask's account shows that lacking a "nuanced understanding" of their social location and a reflective process of identity formation, settlers cannot "nurture" a coalitional identity with Hawaiians (Cole and Luna 2010, 81). A coalitional identity in this sense would be premised on a shared commitment to decolonization—with asymmetrical implications for Hawaiians and haole—that preserves differences, rather than seeking to assimilate Hawaiians to hegemonic U.S. values, ideologies, and political-economic formations. Trask's observations concern the barriers posed to forming and sustaining genuine, decolonial coalitions that preserve differences while undermining relations of domination. These barriers are erected by white settlers who arrogate definitional and representational power while cultivating epistemologies of ignorance about the nature, implications, and consequences of their participation in colonialism. Trask expresses skepticism concerning the political utility and feasibility of coalitions given how deeply entrenched among haole is the denial and disavowal of colonialism and how enthusiastically they participate in its continuation. It is precisely these commitments, alignments, and identifications (with a colonial state, or the lifeways, ideologies, and values of a society whose dominance that state secures) that need to be interrogated if non-Indigenous people are to become allies in coalitions with Indigenous people, in which "differences are respected and issues of land and tribal belonging are not erased in order to create solidarity" (Arvin, Tuck, and Morrill 2013, 19). This view of the relationship between difference and solidarity is shared by the intersectional conception of coalition as we explored it in the previous chapter. By contrast, the suppression of difference as a creative force (see Lorde 1984) underwrites the predominant understanding of coalitions as organized around homogeneity, expressed in partial structural similarities, fleeting ideological convergences, or contingently shared agendas between what are seen as two or more different but internally homogeneous groups that enter into a "risky" or "cynical" alliance. Difference is generally seen as threatening coalitions, while intersectionality reveals it as the condition of possibility—acknowledged or unacknowledged—of any collective political act, including mobilizations of identity that appear to congeal around sameness. Trask's analysis reveals that the true threat to alliances across lines of power is not difference but rather the reproduction of relations of domination within a coalition. On a certain reading (which I advanced in chapter 5), intersectionality suggests that such dynamics also occur in "identity-based" organizing, and even at the micro-level of multiple identity, in which aspects of one's identity that have been falsely represented as separate and distinct are hierarchized in order to resolve internal dissonances that result from political failures to build bridges across segregated, mutually exclusive political struggles.

The fourth and fifth challenges that Arvin, Tuck, and Morrill identify are of an epistemological order: to "recognize Indigenous ways of knowing" (2013, 21) and to "question academic participation in Indigenous dispossession" (25). Specifically, the authors identify three areas in which Indigenous knowledges are suppressed, even by otherwise critical gender, sexuality, and women's studies scholars, in favor of colonial understandings: land, sovereignty, and futurity/decolonization (21–24). White-dominated feminist discourses are called upon to "recognize the persistence of Indigenous concepts and epistemologies" that undermine the totalizing definitions imposed by settler colonial institutions and ideologies. Indeed, what is required is not just a simple acknowledgment of competing worldviews and theories, but "revising conventional concepts of sovereignty, decolonization, and social change" from ones based on colonial relations of property, patriarchy, and the naturalization of the nation-state to those with "Indigenous peoples at the center" (24). They draw on Andrea Smith to argue that "one of the most radical and necessary moves toward decolonization requires imagining and enacting a future for Indigenous peoples—a future based on terms of their own making" (24; see A. Smith 2010). Non-Indigenous feminists are invited to engage Indigenous epistemologies in a non-appropriative way and simultaneously to examine how "the discursive and material practices" of academic feminism "participate in the dispossession of Indigenous peoples' lands, livelihoods and futures, and then to divest from these practices" (Arvin, Tuck, and Morrill 2013, 25). In this connection, the authors reiterate that it is not a matter of including "Native feminist theories as a specialized subfield" but rather of a realignment "toward dismantling not just heteropatriarchy, but also the settler colonial nation-states that heteropatriarchy upholds" (28).

These epistemological challenges raise the following question for intersectional scholars to consider: What is the relationship of intersectionality to the institutions and hegemonic discourses of settler colonial nation-states—specifically to U.S. law, in relation to which the metaphor was first developed? As we saw in chapter 4, Puar charges intersectionality with failing to tarry with the history of colonial violence underlying the categories of race and gender (among others), which, she contends, are uncritically redeployed by intersectional scholars (2012, 54). Indeed, she charges intersectionality, as a "tool of diversity management," with "collud[ing] with the disciplinary apparatuses of the state—census, demography, racial profiling, surveillance" (2007, 212). However, this critique risks eliding significant differences among deployments of intersectionality and decontextualizes the concept from its trajectory of insurrectionary Black feminist thought. Intersectionality as a critique of legal discourse intervenes in the inherently colonial institution of U.S. law, revealing that even those aspects of law that are represented as redressing injustices tend to reproduce precisely the hierarchies and relations of power on which they depend (see chapter 2). Hence I think it is a mistake to elide the critical apparatus with the terrain it engages, reducing it to "a left-liberal law reform project . . . aimed at making liberal legal rights frameworks a bit better at accounting for [multiple discriminations]" (Bhandar 2013). Charging intersectionality as such of complicity with an irredeemably antiblack, misogynist, colonial state depends upon a forgetting of its roots in what Joy James terms "revolutionary black feminisms" (as opposed to "black bourgeois feminism," with which intersectionality is often conflated) (1999, 182). This framing of intersectionality fails to consider how "Black feminist liberation ideology challenges state power by addressing class exploitation, racism, nationalism, and sexual violence with critiques of and activist confrontations with corporate-state policies" (83). In this way, the critique of antidiscrimination law that intersectionality effects is forgotten, while Black feminisms are homogenized as petitioning for "civil rights" and thereby legitimizing the existence of the settler colonial/imperialist state. Even if Crenshaw does not explicitly thematize the coloniality of law in her 1989 and 1991 articles, I would suggest that her intersectional intervention reveals the traffic between institutionalized power and struggle identities in ways that enable us to question how colonial hegemony inflects our ideals of and aspirations for justice. In other words, intersectionality has the potential to address the coloniality of categories that are still widely employed in social-justice projects, which cannot itself be equated with "decolonizing" these movements but seems to be a necessary condition for moving in a decolonial direction.

Intersectionality must be contextualized in the broader effort of Critical Race Theory to demonstrate that the "failure of legal reform" and its discursive "rationalization" were grounded in a "claim to rationality itself," that is, how heteropatriarchal white supremacy is inscribed in the construct of "the rule of law" and how this construct "rationalize[s] existing racial power" (Crenshaw 2011b, 1308–9). Rather than conflating Critical Race Theory—and intersectionality as one of its central conceptual offerings—with reformism because it tarries with the inherently conservative and indeed oppressive institution of (settler colonial) law, Crenshaw argues that Critical Race Theory exploited "law's apparent intimacy with the prevailing racial order" to stage "an intellectual sit-in" (1310).

Nevertheless, Rita Kaur Dhamoon's assessment that "settler colonialism remains under-theorized within mainstream and even women of color feminisms"—and specifically, we might add, within intersectional scholarship—is well taken (2015, 31). Still, Dhamoon is hopeful that intersectionality "can be deployed to illuminate" the forms and processes of settler colonial power, thereby enabling "a more complex conception" of this multidimensional structure (33). However, a deployment of intersectionality that would be compatible with decolonial politics would have to go "beyond narrow forms of identity and left-liberal discourse," in which it is, currently, too often mired (33). It remains to be seen, writes Dhamoon, whether "the gender-race-class mantra will be displaced to account for colonialism 'in the margins'" (33), that is, to examine the ways in which racialized and minoritized groups are complicit in settler coloniality both in virtue of their structural positioning on unceded, arrogated Indigenous territories and in and through their appeals to colonial state power to recognize or legitimate their justice claims.

BORDER THINKING ABOUT INTERSECTIONALITY

If it is a misrepresentation to reduce intersectionality to its postracial deployments in the service of neutralizing liberatory discourses and "managing diversity," at the same time, we must consider how calls to "go beyond" intersectionality also circulate and gain currency in the very same knowledge economy structured by colonial institutions. In this context, the appeal to original conceptual innovations that ostensibly transcend the limitations of previous concepts can embody "a missionary zeal" of "penetrating the frontier" of knowledge (Wendy Rose quoted in Arvin, Tuck, and Morrill 2013, 20; see Conclusion). As Mignolo warns, the notion of "originality" is "part and parcel of the modern control of subjectivity" (2009, 4). According to Mignolo, decolonial thought requires precisely the opposite movement: the tracing of embodied histories of resistance to the epistemic violences of Western European/colonial formations. Mignolo identifies the task of decolonial thinking as the "unveiling of epistemic silences of Western epistemology and affirming the epistemic rights of the racially devalued" (4). In order to challenge the hegemony of colonial epistemic regimes, he observes, "it is not enough to change the content of the conversation"—a kind of interlocutory politics of inclusion—but rather, "it is of the essence to change the *terms* of the conversation" (4). I have suggested (chapter 3) that is precisely this perceptual-cognitive shift in our ways of thinking about oppression and resistance that intersectionality, as a provisional concept, calls upon us collectively to attempt to effect. If this is true, construals of intersectionality as an inclusionary epistemology, research method, or politics fail to tarry with its fundamentally disorienting, subversive, and insurrectionary epistemic character.

In this regard, we might consider AnaLouise Keating's critique of a now-dominant deployment of intersectionality as reinforcing rather than deconstructing "status-quo thinking" about identity, difference, and social transformation (2013, 37). Keating defines "status-quo stories" as those which comprise "worldviews that normalize and naturalize the existing social system," preventing us from "imagining the possibility of change"; they "both rely on and reinforce a separatist framework and a metaphysics of negative difference" (35). In short, "status-quo stories are divisive, teaching us to break the world into parts and label each piece"; through their continual reiteration, "these labels solidify, and we read them as neutral descriptions about reality" (35). For Keating, three characteristics of (mis)deployments of intersectionality render it amenable to "reinforc[ing] our status-quo stories": first, its tendency to signal rather than enacting what she calls an "inclusionary, deeply multicultural approach" (we might pause to consider, here, given the foregoing discussion of the pitfalls of "multicultural" politics of "inclusion," whether this is, indeed, the most productive construal of what a decolonial intersectional approach can offer); second, a superficial engagement through which intersectionality is "used to mark difference yet recenter gender"; and third, the reduction of intersectionality to an "acknowledgement of difference without thorough exploration of these differences" (37). In these respects, intersectionality is evacuated of normative force—that is, of its coalitional power—in that it is constructed as a mere "labelling process" through which no attempt is made to "generate commonalities" between people positioned on obverse sides of institutionalized lines of dominance (37). Hence, argues Keating, "the differences function like walls, not thresholds" (37). Here I am reminded of Frances Beal's metaphor of the "solid wall" that Black women encounter when attempting to decenter the normative subjects of monistic politics (see chapter 1). In contrast, Keating advocates what she terms "threshold theorizing," a mode of reflection and praxical engagement that is inspired by Anzaldúan insights and therefore has much in common with what Mignolo calls "border thinking" (10–11). Thresholds are "transitional, in-between spaces," and "threshold theories" are those that "facilitate and enact movements 'betwixt and between' divergent worlds" and "established categories"; they are "frictional, containing partial assertions and not-quite-this-but-not-quite-that perspectives"; they are characterized by an "oscillating ambivalence" that makes them "complex, contradictory, and multiplicitous"; they "offer no final destination, no permanent fixed truths"—but, precisely for these reasons, they "enable us to redefine and reconcile conflicts and fragmentation" (11).

Can a neo-intersectional approach productively converse with a decolonial epistemology, activating a productive disorientation to hegemonic modern/colonial habits of thought and, indeed, leading us down a wayward path as opposed to the trajectory of institutional "success" that has been paved for it? Can a neo-intersectional sensibility help us to undertake an epistemic mutiny against institutionalized or "ornamental" iterations of the term that announce the completion of a putatively postracial feminism? Can intersectionality coalesce with decolonial feminism in order to address and redress the deep structures and continually unfolding historical processes that constitute settler colonialism?

Mignolo characterizes the decolonial thinker as "engag[ing] in epistemic disobedience"—a precondition to undertaking "civil disobedience" (2009, 15). Significantly, the aims of a decolonial intervention in hegemonic epistemological formations are not narrowly "academic" in nature: the call is not for "the 'transformation of the disciplines'" (20). Is it, then, precisely this claim—that intersectionality's central achievement has been to transform the academic (inter)discipline of women's, gender, and sexuality studies—that a decolonial approach to intersectionality should begin by critically interrogating? How might we cast the trajectory of intersectionality beyond the colonial-capitalist terms of success and failure in order to enliven its deeper promise for conceptual, discursive, and social transformation? Rather than assert that intersectionality is inherently complicit with or inherently trans-gressive of the coloniality of power and its epistemic manifestations, I would like to propose that we undertake a decolonial "border thinking" about intersectionality—one that explores how the provisional deploy-ment of the concept can help undermine the racial and gender politics of the "hubris of the zero point" (Santiago Castro-Gómez quoted in Mignolo 2009, 2; see Mignolo and Tlostanova 2006, 206). In other words, intersectionality can reveal how the mapping of the world from an ostensibly "detached, neutral point of observation" (Mignolo 2009, 2)—as, for instance, is claimed by legal discourse or, indeed, by certain white feminisms—is, in actuality, inflected by and suffused with racial and gendered power. Furthermore, attempts at challenging this hege-mony that rely upon the normative invisibility of unmarked embodi-ments of privilege reproduce the very "colonial matrix of power" which constructs the variable "loci of enunciation" (2–3) that are disavowed in attempts to speak in falsely universal terms as/for oppressed groups. Intersectionality as a making-visible of the relations of epistemic and representational power in and through which certain subjects can come to territorialize liberation discourses and through which these territori-alizations are naturalized or go widely uncontested remains a necessary and incomplete intervention in a social imaginary structured by binary, monistic, essentialist—in a word, modern/colonial—categorial think-ing. Significantly, the coloniality of these representational dynamics are not unique to "remedial" strategies that assent to the parameters set by colonial institutions, such as law; they are also in evidence in "revolu-tionary" liberation struggles waged on the backs of nominal members of groups whose political claims are denied, aspects of whose identities are disavowed, whose contributions to collective struggle are minimized, and whose resistances and aspirations for justice within their "own" communities are, sometimes violently, negated. Intersectionality potentially reveals continuities in the ways that identity is (or is not) mobilized in various resistant discourses, demonstrating that paternalism, white solipsism, heteronormativity, misogyny, and other manifestations of the coloniality of power pervade and undermine cultures of resistance. Moreover, given what Kristie Dotson (2014) calls the "multistability" of oppression, tensions and contradictions can emerge internal to what is perceived as a single category of oppression (e.g., "racial" oppression) or an intersection of categories of identity (e.g., "women of color"), which, to the extent that they go unacknowledged, can undermine the liberation efforts of always already coalitional groups. As we will discuss below, drawing on Andrea Smith's (2006) analysis of the three pillars of white supremacy as they articulate heteropatriarchy, liberatory coalitions must address—to invoke Dotson's evocative formulation—the "open range of 'topographic' possibilities" of which oppression "admits" (2014, 51), that is, the multiple manifestations and understandings of oppression that prevail even within what is seen as a single social group.

Coalitions that activate the intersectional insight that identities are plural, heterogeneous, and sometimes contradictory militate against the fixing, reification, and naturalization of borders as the framework of intelligibility of subjects, communities, families, and nations and the relations of affinity or conflict among and between them. As we saw in the previous chapter, coalitional identities refuse the logic of patriarchal nationalism, crossing borders both external and internalized that construct our subjectivities in a bordered and indeed fortressed world. Intersectionality understood as a critique of exclusionary categories of identity can lead to an experience of interconnectedness and also of self-integration that competing notions of identity politics foreclose, particularly for those deemed outsiders, traitors, or fakers by their "natural" communities—in other words, for those subjects whose ascribed inauthenticity functions as the guarantor of the cohesion of the group identity. Among multiply oppressed people, it is not only a shared relationship to hegemonic power that motivates coalition; it is a shared relationship to *oppositional* power—that is, to monistic political movements. As Keisha Lindsay (2009) argues, what binds multiply oppressed people together is not a shared identity per se but a shared negotiation of monistic identity politics. Mignolo contrasts "a politics of identity" with "identity politics," arguing that "the former is open to whomever wants to join while the latter tends to be bounded by the definition of a single identity" (2009, 14). Singular identities, rallying around concepts like "family," "nation," and "home," function as norms that naturalize the unity they seek to forge. Politicized identities revealed as coalitions, by contrast, transparently represent the acts of "coming together" from "different perspectives" to "develop purpose that has meaning for all members" (Parker 1991, 1194). As Sharon Parker puts it, "unity is not achieved through homogeneity, but by bringing heterogeneous elements into a whole" (1195). While the relationships bounded by "family" and "nation" normatively extend to those represented as "the same" as oneself—a sameness territorialized in terms of property, descent, inheritance, and ownership—coalitions require a different affective topography and a resistant ontology of interconnection: feeling and materializing a diffuse, promiscuous solidarity with people whom norms of belonging consign to the exterior of one's bounded realm of affective concern, or with those denied visibility within it (see Cole and Luna 2010, 82; Keating 2013). If we have been educated into thinking of "community" in racist, colonial, and heteropatriarchal terms of "family" and "nation"—which are naturalized as entitlements and/or responsibilities for racially privileged groups, while kinship and reproductive self-determination are denied to racially oppressed groups— reconceptualizing identity, kinship, and belonging as collective, creative acts of coalition has the potential to liberate our imaginations and our relationships from the strangleholds of hierarchy and domination, on both sides of the colonial fracture. As we will see below, Lugones argues that "the fragmentation of perception disempowers our resistance by making deep coalitions logically impossible as it undermines the very possibility of fashioning larger and complex resistant collective subjectivities" (2003, 160). That is, fragmented perception forecloses the creation of communities of resistance through more complex ways of seeing than the logic of oppression allows. By contrast, "coalition is always the horizon that rearranges both our possibilities and the conditions of those possibilities" (ix).

Coalitions, in this horizonal sense, constitute borderlands of identity, to evoke the concept that Gloria Anzaldúa so powerfully develops in her work. For Anzaldúa, "life in the borderlands" is experienced as an "intimate terrorism," in which alienation from all cultures to which one does and does not belong traps one "between *los intersticios*, the spaces between the different worlds [one] inhabits" (Anzaldúa 1999, 42). But it also generates resistance: "And if going home is denied me then I will have to stand and claim my space, making a new culture—*una cultura mestiza*—with my own lumber, my own bricks and mortar and my own feminist architecture" (44). Indoctrinated into heteropatriarchy at pain of exile, Anzaldúa affirms, "I *made the choice to be queer*" (41). Violated and betrayed by her own people as a "dark-skinned woman," *la prieta* has been "silenced, gagged, caged, bound into servitude with marriage . . . sterilized and castrated in the twentieth century. For 300 years she has been a slave, a force of cheap labor, colonized by the Spaniard, the Anglo, by her own people" (44). The borderlands are not romanticized even as they offer the conditions of possibility for a liberatory shift in consciousness: "*La mestiza* constantly has to shift out of habitual formations," and specifically "from convergent thinking," a Western, positivist analytic mode, to "divergent thinking . . . toward a more whole perspective, one that includes rather than excludes" (101). Significantly, Anzaldúa argues that mestiza consciousness "copes by developing a tolerance for contradictions, a tolerance for ambiguity" and makes creative use of the ambivalence born of a "plural personality" that "sustain[s] contradictions" (101). The dualisms that entrap mestiza consciousness are transcended by "healing the split that originates at the very foundation of our lives, our culture, our languages, our thoughts" (102). This is neither easy nor automatic but requires a "massive uprooting of dualistic thinking in the individual and collective consciousness" (102). "Su cuerpo es una bocacalle," declares Anzaldúa ("your body is an intersection"): "*La mestiza* has gone from being the sacrificial goat to becoming the officiating priestess at the crossroads" (102). The "encrucijada" ("crossroads") is a violent, fraught, but also generative topography. "To survive the Borderlands / you must live *sin fronteras* / be a crossroads" (217).

To *be* an intersection between two categories that are hegemonically kept apart is to constitute "the battleground / where enemies are kin to each other; / you are at home, a stranger," writes Anzaldúa in her evocative poem, "To live in the Borderlands means you" (1999, 216). Rather that resolving this "deadly" tension, Anzaldúa argues for sustaining or "bridging" the contradiction in an embodied, militant, subversive, healing, integrative way. Dwelling in borderlands, engaging in border thinking, is an "anti-imperial response . . . to the colonial difference" that constitutes the geographic, political, subjective, cultural, and epistemic divides that make up the modern/colonial world (Mignolo and Tlostanova 2009, 208). Border thinking resists the "zero point epistemology" that rationalizes Western European imperial power (210), and it does so in part by shifting from abstract, disembodied "theological and egological" rationality to an epistemology based on what Mignolo and Tlostanova call "geo- and body-politics" (210). Decolonial thought embraces the double consciousness that border dwelling generates (211; see Du Bois 1961). The point of approaching intersectionality, then, as conducive to "border" or "threshold" thinking about identity and oppression is not to merely deconstruct categories, thinking that in this way they will simply disappear, but to inhabit them coalitionally as one does the borderlands.

The tensions and contradictions that monistic thinking produces are not resolved by intersecting categories, but they are revealed as such. Roderick Ferguson's (2012) discussion of how we might productively "read" intersectionality is germane in this connection. Ferguson argues that intersectionality is "naturalized as the sign of discreteness," whether by a positivist, celebratory deployment which reads intersectionality as "a stable and discrete object that is ready for measurement and data extraction," or, equally, by a critical interpretation which reads intersectionality as replicating discreteness and seeks to identify a theory that will better, more accurately, and with greater certainty and exactness capture multiplicity (93). The latter approach errs, argues Ferguson, insofar as it attempts to resolve a material problem at the level of language: "the problem of discreteness or essentialism" cannot be "circumvent[ed] . . . in language through neologisms" (94). Indeed, "to make a new word is to run the risk of forgetting the problem or believing it solved" (Gayatri Chakravorty Spivak quoted in Ferguson 2012, 94). Ferguson advocates a deconstructive reading practice that places the concept of intersectionality "under erasure" in order to "consciously analyse [the] artifice" of categorial analytical exactness (95). Rather than fixing intersectionality as a hermeneutic positivism, albeit one deploying multiple categories of analysis, Ferguson urges that we approach it as "a writerly text" that has a plurality of meanings and facilitates generative thinking rather than offering a singular meaning (96). This can enable a direct confrontation with the very ideology of discreteness itself, and the material conditions that subtend it, allowing "the emergence of new kinds of political and intellectual subjects" (96). A border thinking about intersectionality can facilitate ways to reconceive identity, subjectivity, collectivity, and (non)belonging that resist the coloniality of power as it constructs categorial, dichotomous, hierarchical logic and as it naturalizes borders that render some crossings illicit while serving as an alibi for violent territorializations.

THE PILLARS OF WHITE SUPREMACY AND THE COLONIALITY OF GENDER

María Lugones, whose theory of intersecting, interlocking, and intermeshed oppressions we will discuss in the next section, argues that the coloniality of power produces multiple genders on either side of the colonial divide (see Lugones 2007, 2010). A similar claim is advanced by Andrea Smith (2006, 2012), who discerns multiple and sometimes contradictory logics subtending white supremacy, resulting in differential processes of racialization and variable forms of racism targeting groups of women of color. White supremacy is not "enacted in a singular fashion; rather, white supremacy is constituted by separate and distinct, but still interrelated logics" (2012, 67; see also 2006, 67). Smith argues that the primary "pillars" of white supremacy are three and that they correspond to, or act as, "anchors" for three political-economic systems: slavery/antiblack racism, "which anchors capitalism"; genocide, "which anchors colonialism"; and orientalism, "which anchors war" (2012, 68). She uses the language of intersectionality to characterize the "intersecting" relationships among these white-supremacist logics. Her normative goal is to motivate an insurrectionary, anticolonial, antiracist coalitional politics that addresses "the intersections of settler colonialism *and* white supremacy simultaneously" (88). She contrasts this "intersectional" approach to the assumption prevalent in ethnic studies scholarship and women-of-color feminist organizing alike, that "communities of color share overlapping experiences that they can compare and organize around" (67). This presumes that white supremacy functions through a singular and coherent logic in constructing, targeting, and oppressing various racialized groups. The model of "shared victimhood" fails to capture the ways in which "we not only are victims of white supremacy but are complicit in it as well. . . . What keeps us trapped within our particular pillars of white supremacy is that we are seduced with the prospect of participating in the other pillars" (70). This recognition is crucial if "strategic alliances" are to be forged "based on where we are situated within the larger political economy"; moreover, coalitions cannot only address racial oppression: they must also address complicity (70). One implication of Smith's pillars argument is that what are conventionally understood as ethno-racial groups (an understanding that follows closely the demographic taxonomies of the racial/colonial state) may be "destabilized" by a focus on distinct and intersecting logics of white supremacy (70). She draws on Dylan Rodriguez to argue that "rather than organize around categories based on presumed cultural similarities or geographical proximities, we might organize around the differential impacts of white supremacist logics" (70). To develop a sufficiently complex analysis of white-supremacist/settler colonial power as it articulates heteropatriarchy, we must inhabit sites of resistance based not solely on similarities but also on divergences, contradictions, tensions, and complicities, through a negotiation of which we can broaden our struggles (see Cohen 1997, 483). This is not a claim for recognition or visibility but rather an argument for understanding, in terms more complex than perhaps the language of "identity" allows, how we are differentially positioned with respect to systems of power that are normatively not thought together.

However, Smith discerns in "the move to 'postidentity,'" which privileges hybridity and mixture and refuses binary logic, an unwitting appropriation of "colonized indigenous peoples as foils for the emergence of postcolonial, postmodern, diasporic, and queer subjects" (2010, 63). If Native studies is to "intersect" with queer-of-color theory, borderlands theory, and decolonial feminist critique, what is needed is an "identity plus politics": "a politic that marks all identities and their relationship to the fields of power in which they are imbricated" (63). Indeed, whereas the theories explored in the foregoing discussion "tend to be critical of binaries," Smith argues that "it is important not to have a binary analysis of binaries" (57). Indeed, "a binary analysis of the colonizer and colonized can sometimes be helpful in highlighting the current conditions of settler colonialism that continue to exist today both in the United States and in the rest of the world" (58). She suggests that "the presumption that binarism is bad and hybridity good often works against indigenous interests," often relying—as she charges Anzaldúa of doing—on a "mixed" or "hybrid" subject who is "positioned against the Native foil": "a rigid, unambiguous Indian [that] becomes juxtaposed unfavorably with the mestiza who 'can't hold concepts or ideas in rigid boundaries'" (57). This relegates Indigenous peoples to a "primitive past," constructing their identities as "premodern precursor" to mestiza identity (57). Abstracted from the settler colonial context, a "valorization of mixedness" fails to recognize how colonial law uses the genocidal logic of hyperdescent to undermine claims to Indigenous identity, citizenship, and sovereignty precisely through an equation of mixedness to inauthenticity and assimilation. The point is not, I take it, to reify the binaries that operate in settler colonial law and ideology, but rather to reveal their material operation. This supports Ferguson's (2012) claim that the stranglehold that ideologies of discreteness have over us cannot be undone at the level of language. Conceptual transformations require material transformations—not as temporally prior preconditions but as co-constitutive, multidimensional struggles. Smith's arguments in favor of reconceptualizing the structural bases of white supremacy are therefore articulated in a movement context, calling for and participating in the formation of coalitions that address the "intersections" of multiple manifestations of institutionalized, structural, systemic racisms as they articulate heteropatriarchy in ways that do not "fall back on the presumptiveness of the white-supremacist, settler state" (2012, 88). "When we no longer have to carry the burden of political and cultural purity," writes Smith, "we can be more flexible and creative in engaging multiple strategies and creating a plethora of alliances that can enable us to use the logics of settler colonialism against itself" (2010, 58).

Although Smith's insistence on the plurality of the logics of racism is astute, her analysis of the relation between white supremacy and heteropatriarchy—which tends to view the latter as a singular, homogeneous form of power—could fruitfully be complemented by Lugones's conceptualization of the modern/colonial gender system, which I believe is consistent with Smith's insight, articulated throughout her work, that the colonial imposition of heteropatriarchy on Indigenous societies not structured hierarchically served to naturalize colonial and racial hierarchies (Smith 2005, 17-18; 2006, 72; 2010, 62). Smith and Lugones offer analyses that give content to the mutual constitution claim that circulates in intersectional scholarship with respect to the relationships among what are viewed as discrete "axes" of oppression. Moreover, their conceptualizations illuminate new logics through which to problematize discreteness as a presupposition of mutual constitution on the way toward a synthetic analysis that overcomes the fragmentation of representation that intersectionality reveals.

Lugones traces the "congealing" of the modern/colonial gender system "as Europe advanced its colonial project" arguing that compulsory, violently enforced, and "consistently perverse" heterosexuality was as formative of imperial power as imperial power was of it (2007, 187, 202). Emerging during the Spanish and Portuguese colonization of the Americas in the fifteenth century, it "created different arrangements for colonized males and females than for white bourgeois colonizers" that, Lugones argues, persist into the colonial present (186). Compulsory heterosexuality engenders a division of labor that "permeates racialized patriarchal control over production, including knowledge production" (206). In some cases, the colonial gender system created categories of gender where none previously existed, as Oyèrónkẹ́ Oyěwùmí (1997) has argued with respect to Yoruba society in what is now Nigeria. In other cases, European sex/gender constructs interacted in complicated ways with "local" or "indigenous" patriarchies. In all cases, gender relations were fundamentally transformed through the violent introduction of a colonial gender system that regulated the racialization of gender, creating multiple genders on the "light and dark sides" of racial binaries (Lugones 2007). Heterosexualism and its attendant gender hierarchies became powerful metaphors for racialized relations of rule, as in the mid-nineteenth-century trope of the "Family of Man" (McClintock 1995, 357–58).

The modern/colonial gender system has "light" and "dark" sides that install differential gender norms for "white" colonizers and racialized colonized people: the "light side" constructs hegemonic gender relations between white, bourgeois women and men; it constitutes the hegemonic meaning of these gender categories (Lugones 2007, 206). "The dark side of the gender system was and is thoroughly violent," writes Lugones (202). It involved the "reduction [of nonwhite people] to animality, to forced sex with white colonizers, to such deep labor exploitation that often people died working" (206). Lugones's analysis of the "dark side" of the modern/colonial gender system illuminates the economic function of gender, that is, its role in colonial dispossession, appropriation, and superexploitation of labor. Linking the appropriation and violation of bodies to that of land, Smith argues that "the project of colonial sexual violence establishes the ideology that Native bodies are inherently violable—and by extension, that Native lands are also inherently violable" (2005, 12). The two senses of "conquest"— territorial and sexual—are imbricated and historically inextricable, constructing the heteropatriarchal foundation of white-supremacist, settler colonial power. Notably, in an early article Smith critiques Crenshaw's intersectional analysis of violence against women of color (Crenshaw 1991), arguing that Crenshaw "falls short of describing how a politics of intersectionality might fundamentally shift how we analyze sexual/domestic violence" (A. Smith 2003, 71). Smith argues that to the extent that sexual violence is instrumental to colonization, "then entire communities of color" are its targets (71). Yet she agrees with Crenshaw's emphasis on the qualitative difference between racialized experiences of gendered violence and those experiences of gendered violence inflected and perhaps mitigated by racial privilege, a function of the inseparability of colonial, racial, and gender oppression (72).

DECOLONIAL INTERSECTIONALITY?

Reading the founding texts of intersectionality scholarship "against the grain" of the dominant interpretation—which arguably participates in the "categorial, dichotomous, hierarchical logic . . . central to modern, colonial, capitalist thinking about gender, race, and sexuality" (Lugones 2010, 742)—Lugones's explicit critique of the prevailing understanding of intersectionality is that it reproduces the "categorial separation" of categories based on the invisibility of women of color (2007, 192–93). Rather than making visible the experiences of women of color—as has been widely imputed to intersectionality—the intersection of these categories reveals the failure of representation, the absence of concepts adequate to the lived experience of simultaneous oppression(s). Lugones writes:

> Intersectionality reveals *what is not seen* when categories such as gender and race are conceptualized as separate from each other. . . . [T]he logic of categorial separation distorts what exists at the intersection, such as violence against women of color. . . . So, once intersectionality shows us what is missing, we have ahead of us the task of reconceptualizing the logic of the intersection so as to avoid separability. It is only when we perceive gender and race as intermeshed or fused that we actually see women of color. (2007, 192–93)

While this may be read simply as a critique of intersectionality, I think it is more productive to view it as a heterodox interpretation that delimits the scope and intent of the concept to reveal the theoretical and politi-

cal work that still lies ahead. I would suggest that this is not inconsistent with Crenshaw's own characterization of the provisionality of
intersectionality in her early work. The hermeneutic question here is
whether intersectionality constitutes a representational theory of identity (as the dominant interpretation assumes), or whether it can be
understood more fruitfully as a critique of representations that rely
upon extant categorial axes of oppression. Elaborating the latter interpretation, Lugones argues:

> Modernity organizes the world ontologically in terms of atomic,
> homogeneous, separable categories. Contemporary women of color
> and third-world women's critique of feminist universalism centers
> the claim that the intersection of race, class, sexuality, and gender
> exceeds the categories of modernity. If *woman* and *black* are terms
> for homogeneous, atomic, separable categories, then their intersec-
> tion shows us the absence of black women rather than their pres-
> ence. (2010, 742)

The intersection of monistic categories reveals that they render multiplicity invisible. Insofar as it preserves these categories, intersectionality
does not transcend modern/colonial cognitive limitations, although
it anticipates and illuminates the task of conceptual transformation
and "impure resistance." Intersectionality reveals that insofar as we are
trained into perceiving and thinking through the logic of purity, we are
not habituated into seeing race and gender as "intermeshed or fused";
to the extent that multiple oppressions are understood through "pure"
concepts and resisted through interventions that "contest univocally
along one axis of domination" (Lugones 2003, 222), social movements
contribute to at least as much as they combat social fragmentation. If "the
internalization of domination" produces a "dichotomizing imagination"
that entraps us in "the need to control," by contrast, "impure" perception "disrupt[s] dichotomies in resistance to domination" (196). Impure
resistance is curdled, coalitional resistance based on the understanding
that "identifications have to be forged rather than found as natural or
inevitable" (198). For "curdled beings," thick members of fragmented

groups, vulnerable to the logic of purity and "susceptible to transparency," it is particularly important to stop "see[ing] split-separation from other curdled beings as sensical in our resistance to oppression" (143). "The fragmentation of perception disempowers our resistance by making deep coalitions logically impossible," writes Lugones (160), but "coalition is always the horizon that rearranges both our possibilities and the conditions of those possibilities" (ix).

Lugones proposes a distinction between intermeshed and interlocking oppressions that corresponds to the ontological difference between multiplicity and fragmentation in her account. She argues (particularly in her later work) that the concept of interlocking oppressions—an antecedent concept to "intersectionality" introduced (at least in print) by the Combahee River Collective in "*A Black Feminist Statement*" (CRC 1983)—disguises multiplicity and fragments oppressed groups and individuals (Lugones 2003, 223–24). However, this does not mean that "interlocking oppressions" is a "bad concept": Lugones clarifies that it is "not merely an ideological mechanism, but the training of human beings into homogeneous fragments" (224). At the second level of her analysis, then, Lugones argues that "interlocking oppressions" and "intermeshed oppressions" function jointly, creating "a conceptual maze that is very difficult to navigate" (224). Intermeshed oppressions are misrepresented as interlocking, both by systems of domination and by social movements that "contest univocally along one axis of domination" (222); "everywhere we turn we find the interlocking of oppressions disabling us from perceiving and resisting oppressions as intermeshed" (224), mystifying the fact that oppressed people's lives and struggles are interconnected. Finally, Lugones offers a "theory of resistance to both the interlocking of oppressions and to intermeshed oppressions" (208). This theory of resistance activates "a spatial politics that emphasizes difference," one that does not "mythify territorial enclosures and purities of peoples, languages, traditions," but instead negotiates "intersections where subaltern sense is fashioned in the tense and where ongoing crossings between multiple resistant worlds of sense are sometimes tentatively, sometimes powerfully enacted" (220).

What is interesting in Lugones's interpretation of the "intersection" metaphor is that it seems to me to restore it to its original meaning in Crenshaw's 1989 essay, liberating it from the significations that "intersectionality" has subsequently acquired. For one, the intersection is read as a space of violent reduction, of invisibility, and of desubjectification. Further, as I will argue in what follows, Lugones rejects a positivist, "identitarian" deployment of "intersectionality" that reifies axes of identity and, by implication, constructs the intersection as the site of a politics of location for multiply oppressed subjects, so that Black women, for instance, are purported to have "intersectional identities" made visible by an intersectional politics. By contrast, Lugones argues that their intersection does not *represent* women of color; rather, given the logic of purity informing the categorial construction of axes of "race" and "gender," the intersection functions as an index of their *invisibility* (2007, 193). Importantly, she concludes, "once intersectionality shows us what is missing, we have ahead of us the task of reconceptualizing the logic of the intersection," to "perceive gender and race as intermeshed or fused [so] that we actually see women of color" (193). Intersectionality is not the theoretical solution to intermeshed and interlocking oppressions, or, as it is hegemonically re-presented, the arrival of an "inclusive" feminism; rather, in "showing us what is missing" it constitutes the point of departure for a liberatory, coalitional project of "decolonizing gender" (Lugones 2007, 2010).

According to Lugones, "the interlocking of oppressions is a central feature of the process of social fragmentation, [which] requires not just shards or fragments of the social, but that each fragment be unified, fixed, atomistic, hard-edged, internally homogeneous, bounded, repellent of other equally bounded and homogeneous shards" (2003, 232n1). Intermeshed oppressions are represented as interlocking, but "representation" is not merely an ideological process: intermeshed oppressions are socially, discursively constructed—by systems of dominance and by single-axis social movements—as separable, distinct phenomena, affecting discrete groups with divergent political agendas. In other words, the interlocking of oppressions obscures the simultaneity of experiences of multiple, intermeshed oppressions and dissimulates the necessity of contesting and resisting multiple oppressions simultaneously. As Lugones writes in "Tactical Strategies of the Streetwalker/Estrategias Tácticas de la Callejera," where she more fully develops the distinction between intermeshed and interlocking oppressions,

> oppressions interlock when the social mechanisms of oppression fragment the oppressed both as individuals and collectivities. Social fragmentation in its individual and collective inhabitations is the accomplishment of the interlocking of oppressions. Interlocking is conceptually possible only if oppressions are understood as separable, as discrete, pure. Intermeshed oppressions cannot be cogently understood as fragmenting subjects either as individuals or as collectivities. Thus, the interlocking of oppressions is a mechanism of control, reduction, immobilization, disconnection that goes beyond intermeshed oppressions. It is not merely an ideological mechanism, but the categorial training of human beings into homogeneous fragments is grounded in a categorial mind frame. Interlocking is possible only if the inseparability of [intermeshed] oppressions is disguised. (2003, 223–24)

Lugones's point is not just the semantic objection to the prefix "inter-" in "interlocking," which, as Marilyn Frye apparently insisted to Lugones, implies "two entirely discrete things . . . that articulate with each other" (Lugones 2003, 146n1) but whose articulation "does not alter the monadic nature of the things interlocked" (231–32n1). After all, Lugones concedes that "intermeshed"—which shares the same prefix—implies "still too much separability" (231–32n1). By offering "intermeshed oppressions" as a new term, Lugones is not trying to "one-up" the existing concept of "interlocking oppressions" and the theorists who invoke them. On the contrary, in an earlier essay she describes her reluctance "to give up the term because it is used by other women of color theorists who write in a liberatory vein about enmeshed oppressions" (146n1). Although in her earlier work she is searching for "better images" to render the simultaneity of multiple oppressions (146n1), as her thought progresses, I think she diagnoses different political conditions requiring different conceptualizations and resistances, to be signified by different terms. It is not just that "intermeshed oppressions" is a better concept for the same phenomenon that "interlocking oppressions" names; rather, "intermeshed oppressions" signifies an ontological, existential, and social condition of multiplicity that has been discursively and materially obscured through a systematic process of social fragmentation, through the interlocking of oppressions.

In her essay "Toward a Decolonial Feminism," Lugones articulates a methodological shift from "women of color feminisms" to a "decolonial feminism" (2010, 746). She conceptualizes the modern/colonial gender system as a "resistant response to the coloniality of gender" but offers it as a problem that is "being set up rather than answered" (746). Decolonial feminism is defined here as "the possibility of overcoming the coloniality of gender," that is, "racialized, capitalist gender oppression" (747). It is a "movement toward coalition that impels us to know each other as selves that are thick, in relation, in alternative socialites, and grounded in tense, creative inhabitations of the colonial difference" (748). This possibility is intimated in the anti-, pre-, and postcolonial cosmologies, ontologies, epistemologies, and histories of resistance that inform decoloniality (749, 753).

If women-of-color feminisms have (rightly or wrongly) become synonymous with an identitarian project of intersectionality, decolonial feminism unravels the historical production of racialized gendered identities, synthesizing an intersectional awareness of multiplicity that the modern/colonial logic of purity renders invisible through categorial fragmentation with a theorization of the coloniality of power (Lugones 2007, 188–89). Intersectionality, writes Lugones, remains useful "when showing the failures of institutions" to address "discrimination or oppression against women of color" (2010, 757n9). But the emphasis of a decolonial feminism shifts from explicating the logic of domination to perceiving both oppression ("the coloniality of gender") and resistance ("the colonial difference at the fractured locus") that women of color, Indigenous women "fluent in native cultures," and women in colonized groups embody (758n9). In this respect, decolonial feminism radicalizes the generativeness of resistant perception, knowledge, and affect: it moves beyond critique to construct "a different logic"; for even when we "unravel . . . the logic of the oppressor's gaze . . . [and] discover its irrationality we are not on our way towards a resistant subjectivity" (Lugones 2003, 156). Challenging race-gender binarisms, categorial positivisms, and colonial logics, decolonial feminism calls upon us to "intervene at the level of meaning" (3).

Yet, Lugones advises us not to "think what [we] cannot practice," but rather to "live differently in the present, to think and act against the grain of oppression" (2003, 5). This requires that we historicize our epistemic and enunciatory locations, our perceptual and cognitive schemas, and our affective and political commitments. It requires that we attempt a decolonial shift from received, hegemonic ways of thinking and living to resistant ways. How each of us does this depends on tarrying with the questions of "who and where we are," which imply differential responsibilities and relations based on this structural positioning along colonial divides. Intersectionality can reveal the problem of colonial thinking as it structures our perceptual-cognitive experience, the extent to which it has become habitual and goes unquestioned—even at the very same time as it is pronounced as having been transcended. As an analytic sensibility, or a critical (dis)orientation toward categorial hegemony, intersectionality can illuminate the need to resist fragmentation and domination at the level of critical discourses, political movements, and embodied identities. Honing our resistant perception against our being "torture[d] . . . into simple fragmented identities" opens up a space for "rearranging one's own identity, for making the complexity of one's own subjectivity explicit, for articulating it, for making it public" (Lugones 1998, 50–52). Intermeshed oppressions, violently forged through a modern/colonial gender system, are interlocked through categorial and social fragmentation, a process that the multiply oppressed, curdled being concretely "comes to understand through a jarring vivid awareness of being broken into fragments" (Lugones 2003, 231). For Lugones, lived experience also discloses "that the encasing by particular oppressive systems of meaning is a process one can either consciously and critically resist with uncertainty," through a collective, decolonial feminist coalitional praxis, "or [one] to which one can passively abandon oneself," dwelling invisibly in a deadly intersection (231).

In this chapter I have pursued the question of the relationship between intersectionality and decolonial feminism. Can a synthesis between a provisional concept of intersectionality and a decolonial feminist praxis serve the political project of decolonization? Such an argument must be attentive to the pitfalls, evasions, and depoliticizations of "decolonization," arguably inherent in the enunciatory location—in my case, that of an immigrant to, and naturalized citizen of, a white settler state—from which it is articulated. Specifically, I am wary of appropriative appeals to "decolonization" that increasingly seem to circulate in "critical" settler academic discourses (including feminism) without fundamentally altering non-Indigenous relationships to land, sovereignty, and power. Thus, in concluding the above discussion prefiguring a "decolonial intersectionality," I would like to avoid closure by reflecting on the ongoing debate about "decolonizing antiracism" and other critical social-justice projects, and specifically, the apparent ease with which, in recent years, the concept of "decolonization" is appropriated, often in ways that distort its actual meaning or evade its political implications for non-Indigenous groups, settlers and immigrants (see Lawrence and Dua 2005; Sharma and Wright 2008–9; Phung 2011; Sehdev 2011; Jafri 2012; Tuck and Yang 2012; Dhamoon 2015). Indeed, it is worth noting that "intersectionality" and "decolonization" circulate in not dissimilar ways in the settler academy, and are often invoked as an alibi, ostensibly to guarantee the ethical or political commitments underpinning intellectual projects, or the "inclusiveness" of curricula, academic disciplines, and institutions. In fact, such appeals avoid tarrying both with the militancy of the concepts they invoke—the normative claims they imply—and with non-Indigenous people's complicity with colonial power. Specifically, facile appeals to "decolonization" seem to evade the question of land, and the genocidal violence against Indigenous people that maintaining colonial state control over Indigenous land bases entails. Tuck and Yang observe "with growing apprehension" a metaphorical use of "decolonization" as a synonym for a range of social-justice projects, a use that serves to "domesticate" the concept (2012, 3). Being "grafted" onto or "subsumed" under existing critical frameworks is, they argue, "just another form of settler appropriation" (3):

> Decolonization as metaphor allows people to equivocate . . . because it turns decolonization into an empty signifier to be filled by any track towards liberation. In reality, however, the tracks walk all over land/people in settler contexts. . . . [I]n our view, decolonization in the settler context must involve the repatriation of land simultaneous to the recognition of how land and relations to land have always already been differently understood and enacted; that is, *all* of the land, and not just symbolically. This is precisely why decolonization is necessarily unsettling; especially across lines of solidarity. . . . Settler colonialism and its decolonization implicates and unsettles everyone. (2012, 7)

Tuck and Yang identify several "settler moves to innocence" through which the unsettling implications of decolonization are evaded as the concept is "absorbed" into settler colonial discourses (even emancipatory or transformative ones). I would like to focus here on two that seem to be particularly important for the present argument: "colonial equivocation" and "conscientization" (4). The first refers to "the homogenizing of various experiences of oppression as colonization," or "all struggles against imperialism as 'decolonizing,'" a move that, the authors argue, "creates a convenient ambiguity between decolonization and social justice work, especially among people of color, queer people, and other groups minoritized by the settler state" (17). If it is true in some sense that "we are all colonized," this claim is nevertheless "deliberately embracive and vague" and enabling of the "inference: 'None of us are settlers'" (17). Arguing for the historical salience and contemporary relevance of a tripartite structure of power that locates Indigenous people—"those who have creation stories, not colonization stories about how we/they came to be in a particular place"—in a non-constitutive relation to settlers and descendants of enslaved people, Tuck and Yang probe how social-justice efforts may be "invested" in settler colonialism even if they are antiracist or contest white supremacy (17–18). For instance, as Lisa Kahaleole Hall has argued, "The logics of some forms of antiracist struggles paradoxically can undermine group identities by advocating for a form of social justice based on the equal treatment of individuals," resulting in the "vanishing" of Indigenous peoples from antiracist politics (as well as from feminist theory) (2008, 277). Hence, Tuck and Yang argue, "Vocalizing a 'multicultural' approach to oppressions, or remaining silent on settler colonialism while talking about colonialisms, or tacking on a gesture towards Indigenous people without addressing Indigenous sovereignty or rights, or forwarding a thesis on decolonization without regard to unsettling/deoccupying land, are equivocations" (2012, 18).

Relatedly, a second move to settler innocence Tuck and Yang describe is "conscientization," which involves focusing on "decolonizing the mind, or the cultivation of critical consciousness, as though it were the sole activity of decolonization" and a proxy for "the more uncomfortable task of relinquishing stolen land" (2012, 19). The critical reader of the literature on intersectionality may notice a similar set of evasions and equivocations with respect to its uptake. Thus, Vivian May's titular emphasis on "Unsettling Dominant Imaginaries" by "Pursuing Intersectionality" resonates here (2015). Indeed, May argues that, by resisting the "erasure or forgetting that progress narratives tend to encourage," intersectionality can "rupture stories about the nation's evolution and to unsettle its setter logics in great part because [its] both/and approach is amenable to 'apposition,'" which she describes as "a flexible and destabilizing interpretative method capable of reading time periods and multiple identities concurrently, in syntactical relation" (2015, 57). If this, most promising version of intersectionality embodies a decolonial orientation, in a not too dissimilar way to "decolonization," "intersectionality" is often used to defuse rather than to enact challenges to the prevailing material and ideological colonial, white, supremacist, heteropatriarchal orders.

Still, likely to resist such comparisons, Tuck and Yang call for "an ethic of incommensurability" infusing decolonial approaches to solidarity and coalition. They suggest that "decolonization offers a different perspective to human and civil rights approaches to justice, an unsettling one, rather than a complementary one. Decolonization is not an 'and.' It is an elsewhere" (2012, 36). If this is true, then an attempt to "merge" an intersectional analytic sensibility with a decolonial politics could be still another evasion of the difficult realizations that the latter entails. But what if an intersectional sensibility could enable us to realize precisely the praxical orientation to solidarity between groups situated in diametrically opposed yet structurally intertwined ways that Tuck and Yang identify? What if it enables us to grasp and embody the conditions of possibility for "solidarity . . . in what is incommensurable rather than [in] what is common" (28)? As Andrea Smith and J. Kehaulani Kauanui suggest, decolonization projects are falsely separated from efforts to realize gender justice (A. Smith and Kauanui 2008, 247; Kauanui 2008b, 285–86; see also Ramirez 2008, 305). Consequently, "this lack of an intersectional perspective prevents us from ascertaining how colonialism is itself a gendered process" (A. Smith and Kauanui 2008, 247). That is, an intersectional sensibility can help to illuminate the non-metaphorical gendered relationship between the dispossession of land, of bodies, and of knowledges, and turn our attention to the "dangerous intersections" (A. Smith 2005, 1) that constitute the modern/colonial gender system. This system implicates us all in divergent, contradictory, but radically interdependent ways and, if viewed intersectionally, intimates the possibilities for inhabiting our struggle identities in coalitional ways. Moreover, if engaged in a politics of refusal—as opposed to a politics of recognition or representation that inadvertently reproduce settler colonial logics of visibility, knowability, and management—an intersectional sensibility could enable the construction of "mass movements" through the "coalition-building" that "broad-based" efforts to dismantle interlocking systems of power would seem to necessitate (Simpson and Smith 2014, 10; A. Smith 2008, 315). If we grapple with intersectionality as a provisional concept that enables us to live our struggle identities in a radically different way, eschewing the categorial, representational, and political violence in and through which they have been forged to fragment, marginalize, and silence some subjects while exalting and empowering others, can we envision, on the horizon, an intersectional politics of coalition which intimates the decolonial "elsewheres" that all of us—on all sides of colonial divides—urgently need to imagine?

Conclusion

Intersectionality has gained a nearly axiomatic status in feminist theory and women's, gender, and sexuality studies. It has been described variously as "the most significant contribution" of the interdiscipline (McCall 2005, 1771); as a "buzzword," the purported "vagueness" of which may hold the secret to its "success" (K. Davis 2008, 69); and as "*the* primary figure of political completion in U.S. identity knowledge domains" (Wiegman 2012, 240). Yet this success story is tempered by critiques of its "mainstreaming" (Dhamoon 2011), its "institutionalization" (Nash 2008, 2014b), its "depoliticization" (Bilge 2013; Collins 2009), and its "colonization" by post–Black feminist deployments (Alexander-Floyd 2012), giving us grounds to question whether nothing fails like success. After all, claims of the "self-evidence" of intersectionality as quintessential feminist method paradoxically coexist with "scholarship that presumes gender" as the "foundational" category of analysis (Puar 2012, 53). At the same time, however, it is doubtful to what extent attempts to "go beyond" intersectionality are apposite; given the knowledge economy in which they circulate, post-intersectionality has been charged with "epistemic distortion," "hermeneutic violence and interpretative marginalization" (May 2014, 94–95). As we have seen, theorists who propose "alternative" frameworks often construct intersectionality as a straw figure in order to render more impactful their own intervention (Carbado 2013, 816).

Sirma Bilge diagnoses the ascendancy of this interdisciplinary subfield within "disciplinary academic feminism" as a function of neoliberal power relations structuring knowledge production; she argues that intersectionality, a "sought-after signifier" of "diversity," has been depoliticized or repoliticized in the service of hegemonic institutional aims (2013, 407–8). As a result, intersectionality is "hailed and failed simultaneously" (407). On the other hand, the purported obsolescence of intersectionality, from my point of view, distorts the extent to which the work intersectionality—if a personification might momentarily be permitted—calls us to do remains largely unfinished. Moreover, the "easy" appropriation of intersectionality has contributed to the misperception that by merely "hailing" intersectionality, certain epistemological, methodological, and political commitments are secured. In the context of academic knowledge production, "hailing" intersectionality is often manifested in the form of throwaway citations or disembodied quotations to Crenshaw's work. If Crenshaw is now routinely cited as the originator of the concept, in earlier reception this was not always the case; acknowledgment of authorship is hedged with minimizing descriptors, such as dismissive claims that she has merely "coined" a term for a preexisting concept (see chapter 1).

Yet, on the other hand, Jennifer Nash has argued that we should treat celebratory calls for "more intersectionality" with "suspicion" and "analytic skepticism": "While the interdisciplinary push towards intersectionality has led to rich scholarship on identity and power, it has also produced an uncritical notion of intersectionality as a theoretical constant rather than as a dynamic theoretical innovation within a terrain of struggle" (2010). Emphasizing the provisionality of the concept, immanent critique of intersectionality supports attempts to reinfuse intersectionality with dynamicity, instability, and critical momentum. By contrast, the post-intersectional move often makes a critical error: it reduces "intersectionality" to the predominant, positivist interpretation of the concept, failing to tarry with its profound critique of categorial essentialism. Given that "intersectionality" has come to mean many different things and even to signify contradictory epistemological and political projects, these various significations must be untangled, subterraneous theoretical contestations excavated, and their divergent implications for political practice carefully considered.

If a number of criticisms of the dominant deployment of intersectionality are well taken, I suggest we should have concerns about the status of such criticisms given that they circulate in a neoliberal/settler colonial economy of academic knowledge production that values originality, commodifies innovation, and rewards the often premature declaration of paradigm shifts, particularly when performed by elite theorists who wield epistemic and discursive power. Arguably, intersectionality—originating in "marginal" knowledges produced through women-of-color feminist movements—was transformed into hegemonic knowledge through not dissimilar discursive means that certain "post-intersectional" critics now seek to deploy, and, in some cases, from comparable epistemic/academic locations. Within women's, gender, and sexuality studies in particular, a special premium attaches to a form of radicalism that, operating primarily through critique, figures itself as "transcendent" of the real or imagined conceptual limitations plaguing its predecessor or "competing" frameworks. In its deconstructive and in its prescriptive moments, "transcendent radicalism" diagnoses theoretical or political shortcomings in competing theories that it supersedes or to which it is immune. Placing the theorist temporally beyond the "past" or "present" of feminist theory (Nash 2014b), or spatially at the margins of the mainstream theoretical terrain, is, paradoxically, how the "outradicalizing" move gains its mainstream credibility: after all, the self-image of the interdiscipline of women's, gender, and sexuality studies is predicated, at least in part, on fostering counterhegemonic, marginal, heterogeneous knowledge production. The moral dimension of "transcendent radicalism" is that, in the "race to outradicalize," the theorist aspires to a position of innocence (Fellows and Razack 1998), untainted by, or immune to, the limitations of concepts, frameworks, or theories now deemed irredeemably "problematic." But to position one's own "competing" theory as "pioneering" or to locate it at the "frontier" of knowledge is to reproduce the values of a colonial epistemology while reaping the benefits of a neoliberal capitalist knowledge economy.

Evacuating the concept of intersectionality of its provisionality, commodifying it as a guarantor of superficially espoused ethical, political, and epistemological commitments, and detaching it from the account of hierarchy and subordination that it originally articulated has made the metaphor more mobile while "flattening" its geography of power (see chapters 2 and 3). Intersectionality has been rewritten as amenable to positivist epistemologies that actually serve to legitimate a colonial history of racial gendered violence; its commodification is symptomatic of the broader neoliberal economy in which academic knowledge is produced and circulates, and of abiding anxieties about the "problem of difference" specific to the interdiscipline of women's, gender, and sexuality studies, which gives special inflections to the risks and rewards of "radical critique," "subaltern knowledge production," and "counterhegemonic" theory. Both positivist appropriations of intersectionality—which detach the concept from Black feminism in order to afford it mainstream palatability—and post-intersectional critiques—which construct "intersectionality" as either implicated too much or too little in the "specificity" and "difference" of Black women's subjectivities and experiences—rely on a commodity model of knowledge production that fetishizes "difference," evades accountability, inflates originality, and promotes capitalist competition as an implicit (if explicitly disavowed) value of feminist knowledge production in neoliberal times.

My reading of Crenshaw's foundational essays, in which she elaborates intersectionality as a metaphor and defines it as a provisional concept, suggests that the construction of certain identities or experiences as "intersectional" elides the deeper critique of categorial thinking and representational territorializations that we are enjoined to undertake. At the same time, people increasingly invoke the notion of intersectionality in order to narrate their own lived experiences and to generate collective understandings of processes of exclusion and marginalization within oppressed communities and resistant collectivities. Naming oneself an intersectional feminist or speaking from an avowed intersection of identity categories are ways that indeed may make legible in the present context a critical relation to exclusionary discourses such as white solipsistic feminisms and heteronormative, patriarchal nationalisms. The critique of intersectional identity I present here should not be read as militating against a "groundswell" of such self-identifications (Okolosie 2014, 92). Rather, I suggest we engage the emergence of intersectional identity—

like that of any identity—as a discursive event, and trace the processes by which it is embraced, ascribed, and resisted (Scott 1991, 792–93). Invoking Gayatri Chakravorty Spivak, Joan Scott has argued in favor of

> "mak[ing] visible the assignment of subject-positions," not in the sense of capturing the reality of the objects seen, but of trying to understand the operations of the complex and changing discursive processes by which identities are ascribed, resisted, or embraced, and which processes themselves are unremarked and indeed achieve their effect because they are not noticed. To do this a change of object seems required, one that that takes the emergence of concepts and identities as historical events in need of explanation. This does not mean that one dismisses the effects of such concepts and identities.... It does mean assuming that the appearance of a new identity is not inevitable or determined, not something that was always there simply waiting to be expressed, not something that will always exist in the form it was given in a particular movement or a particular historical moment. (1991, 792)

Just as María Lugones was reluctant to give up a concept (interlocking systems of oppression) "because it is used by other women of color theorists" engaged in a politics of identity within a liberation framework (2003, 146n1), and instead tried to understand what its scope and extension might be, we might justifiably be reluctant to relinquish intersectionality because of the company the concept keeps and the work it enables us to do under prevailing discursive conditions in which, admittedly, emancipatory rhetorics generally remain beholden to monistic concepts of oppression and identity (see May 2015, 108–9). To be clear, I have not advocated giving intersectionality up, or giving up on intersectionality: rather, I would agree that "intersectionality can't wait" (Crenshaw 2015) and am suggesting that we engage it more deeply, not as an epistemological or ethical guarantor, but as a profoundly destabilizing, productively disorienting, provisional concept that disaggregates false unities, undermines false universalisms, and unsettles false entitlements. The argument I have advanced I think makes sense in a particular context (of women's, gender, and sexuality studies in the United States and Canada), and its terms may not be translatable in all the contexts to which the concept of intersectionality has traveled. For instance, Lola Okolosie observes that if it has an "accepted academic currency and weight" in the U.S. context, that is decidedly "not the case in Britain," where its viability and validity is widely and sometimes acrimoniously debated (2014, 91). Gail Lewis, as well as Umut Erel and her collaborators Jin Haritaworn, Encarnación Gutiérrez Rodríguez, and Christian Klesse, trace the displacements of "race" in the travel of intersectionality to *rasse*-uncritical academic contexts in Germany and elsewhere in central and northern Europe, whereby lived experiences of gendered racism have been made marginal to theoretical, abstract, depoliticized discussions on the procedural or conceptual merits of intersectionality (Lewis 2013; Erel et al. 2008, 272). Vrushali Patil argues that intersectionality is "shaped by geographies of colonial modernity" and is domesticated by a methodologically nationalist U.S.- and Western-centric frame; "the focus of intersectional analyses in general continues to be on the putative West," ignoring "cross border dynamics" (2013, 853–54). It would be erroneous to generalize the conditions underwriting intersectionality's institutionalization in the United States to the various contexts to which it has—or has not—traveled.

In "Intersectionality: Mapping the Movements of a Theory," their introduction to a special issue of the *Du Bois Review*, Devon Carbado, Kimberlé Crenshaw, Vickie Mays, and Barbara Tomlinson emphasize the provisionality of intersectionality, its inexhaustibility, and its incompleteness (2013, 304). If intersectionality cannot be contained, anthropomorphized, and reduced to a set of interests, or ever completed, its potential lies in its ability to reveal and transform relations of power, as these constitute the categories basic to our thinking, the conditions that structure our lives, and the identifications that enable our resistances. Intersectionality, as Crenshaw intended it, "is a concept animated by the imperative of social change" (Carbado et al. 2013, 312). It is up to us to reinvent intersectionality in ways that challenge its appropriation by institutionalized mandates of diversity management, commodification, and epistemic totalization—inhabiting the coalitions it engenders—as the horizon of our collective praxis.

Horizons—which often come to our attention at sunrise and at sunset—can signify the limits of our perception and hence the limits of our world. Always in the distance, they nevertheless beckon us to cross them. As both limit and threshold, horizons appear out of reach; yet, in phenomenological terms, horizons constitute the background against which our immediate experience comes into relief, gains meaning, and is illuminated. The horizon may seem singular from a fixed perspective: viewed in the distance from the shore over a sea or ocean, it may appear as a single, unbroken line fixed in space and time. But as it is approached by a moving body, it shifts, eludes, always keeping its distance. What might it mean to think of a concept like intersectionality as a horizon: as the farthest place we can see from where we are presently standing, but that frustrates our attempts at measurement, resists being totalized by our gaze, and, in fact, brings into our awareness the limits of our perceptual reach? Temporally, the horizon can signify futurity, but it can also be viewed posteriorly (as when it is reflected in a rear-view mirror of a car moving in the opposite direction), bringing us into a relationship with history that enables us to see how the past "bear[s] on the present and the future" (Muñoz 2009, 27). In bearing on the present, "the past does things"; it does not remain "static and fixed" (28). Constituting us in relation to past and future—always behind us and always before us—the horizon also intimates what José Esteban Muñoz has called "the hollow nature of the present," a present that "is not enough" (21, 27). Urging us to resist an anti-utopian turn in queer theory, Muñoz asks us to "insist on a queer futurity because the present is so poisonous and insolvent" (30). In fact, on his view, "we are not quite queer yet":

Queerness, what we will really know as queerness, does not yet exist. I suggest that holding queerness in a sort of ontologically humble state, under a conceptual grid in which we do not claim to always already know queerness in the world, potentially staves off the ossifying effects of neoliberal ideology and the degradation of politics. (22)

The "ontological humility" that queerness represents for Muñoz may also guide a "queer" approach to intersectionality as a radically disorienting, provisional concept illuminating decolonial struggles for social justice (see chapters 3 and 6). Approaching intersectionality horizonally means restoring to it the provisionality of knowledge produced through contestations of the poisonous conditions structuring the present; it also means refusing the closure of "intersectionality" by positivisms that would only be satiated by epistemic totalization. If the horizon has been conflated with the cardinal directions imposed by the modern/colonial spatio-cultural mapping of the world, its violent bisection into "East" and "West," "North" and "South," it can also radically disrupt the perceptual hold such a worldview has on our lived experiences. The horizon is not a knowable "straight line" or a "self-naturalizing temporality" (Muñoz 2009, 25); to approach it as such is to lull oneself into the false comfort of cardinal certainty and to willfully ignore the violences of "zero-point" epistemologies. If the "hubris of the zero point" is to imagine oneself as occupying a non-place, inhabiting a "detached and neutral point of observation" from which "the knowing subject maps the world" (Mignolo 2009, 2), the horizon intrudes into this conceit by locating us in an embodied here and now. Seen queerly, the horizon can inspire and humble us; it will generously nourish our struggles for an "elsewhere" and an "otherwise," but it will always disappoint a desire for mastery. The horizon exceeds our reach, it interrupts our gaze, but it also plentifully welcomes our strivings. The "horizonal temporality of queerness" discloses "a path and a movement to a greater openness to the world" (Muñoz 2009, 25). The horizon is not beholden to us, but we are beholden to it. It calls on us at once to be humble and hopeful, both here and there, then and now, to remember and to imagine: it helps us make sense of, delight in, and mourn beginnings and endings and especially live utterly the twilight moments in between.

REFERENCES

Aguilar, Delia. 2012. "Tracing the Roots of Intersectionality." *Monthly Review Zine*, April 12. http://mrzine.monthlyreview.org/2012/aguilar120412.html.

Ahmed, Sara. 2006. *Queer Phenomenology: Orientations, Objects, Others*. Durham: Duke University Press.

———. 2008. "Some Preliminary Remarks on the Founding Gestures of the 'New Materialism,'" *European Journal of Women's Studies* 15 (1): 23–39.

———. 2012. *On Being Included: Racism and Diversity in Institutional Life*. Durham: Duke University Press.

Alaimo, Stacy, and Susan Heckman. 2008. *Material Feminisms*. Bloomington: Indiana University Press.

Alexander-Floyd, Nikol G. 2012. "Disappearing Acts: Reclaiming Intersectionality in the Social Sciences in a Post-Black Feminist Era." *Feminist Formations* 24 (1): 1–25.

Allison, Dorothy, and Carmen Vázquez. 2007. Interview by Kelly Anderson. Transcript of video recording, November 19. Voices of Feminism Oral History Project, Sophia Smith Collection, Smith College, Northampton MA.

AMNLAE (Asociación de Mujeres Nicaragüenses Luisa Amanda Espinosa). 1983. "Women in Nicaragua: How We Are Organized." In *Third World—Second Sex: Women's Struggles and National Liberation*, edited by Miranda Davies, 164–72. London: Zed.

Amos, Valerie, Gail Lewis, Amina Mama, and Pratibha Parmar, eds. 1984. *Feminist Review* 17: "Many Voices, One Chant: Black Feminist Perspectives."

Anderson-Bricker, Kristin. 1999. "'Triple Jeopardy': Black Women and the Growth of Feminist Consciousness in SNCC, 1964–1975." In *Still Lifting, Still Climbing: Contemporary African American Women's Activism*, edited by Kimberly Springer, 49–69. New York: New York University Press.

Anthias, Floya. 2012. "Intersectional What? Social Divisions, Intersectionality and Levels of Analysis." *Ethnicities* 13 (1): 3–19.

Anthias, Floya, and Nira Yuval-Davis. 1983. "Contextualizing Feminism: Gender, Ethnic and Class Divisions." *Feminist Review* 15:62–75.

Anzaldúa, Gloria. 1999. *Borderlands/La Frontera: The New Mestiza*. 2nd ed. San Francisco: Aunt Lute. First published 1987.

Arauz, Rita. 1994. "Coming Out as a Lesbian Is What Brought Me to Social Consciousness." In *Sandino's Daughters Revisited: Feminism in Nicaragua*, edited by Margaret Randall, 265–85. New Brunswick NJ: Rutgers University Press.

Archer Mann, Susan. 2013. "Third Wave Feminism's Unhappy Marriage of Poststructuralism and Intersectionality Theory." *Journal of Feminist Scholarship* 4:54–73.

Armstrong, Elizabeth A. 2002. *Forging Gay Identities: Organizing Sexuality in San Francisco, 1950–1994*. Chicago: University of Chicago Press.

Arnett v. Aspin. 1994. 846 F. Supp. 1234. 1994 U.S. Dist. LEXIS 3973 (U.S.D.C., 1994). http://www.lexisnexis.com/us/lnacademic.

Arvin, Maile, Eve Tuck, and Angie Morrill. 2013. "Decolonizing Feminism: Challenging Connections between Settler Colonialism and Heteropatriarchy." *Feminist Formations* 25 (1): 8–34.

Babb, Florence E. 2003. "Out in Nicaragua: Local and Transnational Desires after the Revolution." *Cultural Anthropology* 18 (3): 304–28.

Bailey, Alison. 2009. "On Intersectionality, Empathy and Feminist Solidarity: A Reply to Naomi Zack." *Journal for Peace and Justice Studies* 19 (1): 14–36.

———. 2010. "On Intersectionality and the Whiteness of Feminist Philosophy." In *The Center Will Not Hold: White Women Philosophers on the Whiteness of Philosophy*, edited by George Yancy, 51–70. Lanham MD: Lexington Books.

Bannerji, Himani. 2000. "Geography Lessons." In *The Dark Side of the Nation: Essays on Multiculturalism, Nationalism and Gender*, 63–86. Toronto: Canadian Scholars' Press.

Barad, Karen. 2003. "Posthumanist Performativity: Toward an Understanding of How Matter Comes to Matter." *Signs: Journal of Women in Culture and Society* 28 (3): 801–30.

Barrett, Michèle, and Mary McIntosh. 1982. *The Anti-Social Family*. London: Verso.

Bartlett, Katherine, and Angela Harris. 1998. *Gender and the Law: Theory, Doctrine, Commentary*. 2nd ed. New York: Aspen Law and Business.

Barvosa-Carter, Edwina. 1999. "Multiple Identity and Coalition-Building: How Identity Differences within Us Enable Radical Alliances among Us." *Contemporary Justice Review* 2 (2): 111–26.

Bayard de Volo, Lorraine. 2001. *Mothers of Heroes and Martyrs: Gender Identity Politics in Nicaragua, 1979–1999*. Baltimore: Johns Hopkins University Press.

———. 2012. "A Revolution in the Binary? Gender and the Oxymoron of Revolutionary War in Cuba and Nicaragua." *Signs: Journal of Women in Culture and Society* 37 (2): 413–39.

Beal, Frances. 1970a. "Double Jeopardy: To Be Black and Female." In *Black Woman's Manifesto*, 19–34. Pamphlet. New York: Third World Women's Alliance.

———. 1970b. "Double Jeopardy: To Be Black and Female." In *The Black Woman: An Anthology*, edited by Toni Cade Bambara, 109–22. New York: Washington Square Press.

———. 2005. Interview by Loretta Ross. Transcript of video recording, March 18. Voices of Feminism Oral History Project, Sophia Smith Collection, Smith College, Northampton MA.

Belkhir, Jean Ait, and Bernice McNair Barnett. 2001. "Race, Gender and Class Intersectionality." *Race, Gender and Class* 8 (3): 157–74.

Bell, Derrick. 1991. "Foreword: The Final Civil Rights Act." *California Law Review* 79:597–611.

———. 1992. *Faces at the Bottom of the Well: The Permanence of Racism*. New York: Basic Books.

Berger, Michelle T., and Kathryn Guidroz, eds. 2009. *The Intersectional Approach: Transforming the Academy through Race, Class and Gender*. Chapel Hill: University of North Carolina Press.

Best, Rachel, Lauren B. Adelman, Linda Hamilton Krieger, and Scott Eliason. 2011. "Multiple Disadvantages: An Empirical Test of Intersectionality Theory in EEO Litigation." *Law and Society Review* 45 (4): 991–1025.

Bhandar, Brenna. 2013. "On Race, Gender, Class, and Intersectionality." *The North Star*, 25 June 25. http://www.thenorthstar.info/?p=9065.

Bilge, Sirma. 2010. "Recent Feminist Outlooks on Intersectionality." *Diogenes* 225:58–72.

———. 2012. "Developing Intersectional Solidarities: A Plea for Queer Intersectionality." In *Beyond the Queer Alphabet: Conversations on Gender, Sexuality and Intersectionality*, edited by Malinda Smith and Fatima Jaffer, 19–23. Ottawa: Canadian Federation for the Humanities and Social Sciences.

———. 2013. "Intersectionality Undone: Saving Intersectionality from Intersectionality Studies." *Du Bois Review* 10 (2): 405–24.

Bowleg, Lisa. 2008. "When Black + Lesbian + Woman ≠ Black Lesbian Woman: The Methodological Challenges of Qualitative and Quantitative Intersectionality Research." *Sex Roles* 59 (5–6): 312–25.

———. 2013. "'Once You've Blended the Cake, You Can't Take the Parts Back to the Main Ingredients': Black Gay and Bisexual Men's Descriptions and Experiences of Intersectionality." *Sex Roles* 68 (11/12): 754–67.

Boyce Davies, Carole. 2007. *Left of Karl Marx: The Political Life of Black Communist Claudia Jones.* Durham: Duke University Press.

Brah, Avtar, and Ann Phoenix. 2004. "Ain't I a Woman? Revisiting Intersectionality." *Journal of International Women's Studies* 5 (3): 75–86.

Brenner, Johanna. 2000. "Intersections, Locations, and Capitalist Class Relations: Intersectionality from a Marxist Perspective." In *Women and the Politics of Class*, 293–324. New York: Monthly Review Press, 293–324.

Brown, Damita, and Kim Sánchez. 1994. "Transforming Organizing Strategies for the Nineties: The Women of Color Resource Center." *Inscriptions* 7. http://ccs.ihr.ucsc.edu/inscriptions/volume-7/damita-brown-kim-sanchez.

Brown, Wendy. 1997. "The Impossibility of Women's Studies." *differences: a journal of women's studies* 9 (3): 79–101.

Burnham, Linda. 2005. Interview by Loretta Ross. Transcript of video recording, March 18. Voices of Feminism Oral History Project, Sophia Smith Collection, Smith College, Northampton MA.

Butler, Judith. 1999. *Gender Trouble: Feminism and the Subversion of Identity.* New York: Routledge. First published in 1990.

Butterfield, Elizabeth. 2003."Intersectionality: New Directions for a Theory of Identity." *International Studies in Philosophy* 35 (1): 1–12.

Camfield, David. 2014. "Theoretical Foundations of an Anti-Racist Queer Feminist Historical Materialism." February 17. *Critical Sociology* 0896920513507790.

Campbell, Duncan. 2005. "US Bars Nicaragua Heroine as 'Terrorist.'" *The Guardian*, March 4. http://www.guardian.co.uk/world/2005/mar/04/highereducation.usa?INTCMP=SRCH.

Carastathis, Anna. 2008. "The Invisibility of Privilege: A Critique of Intersectional Models of Identity." *Les Ateliers de l'Éthique/The Ethics Forum* 3 (2): 23–38.

Carbado, Devon M. 2000. "Race and Sex in Antidiscrimination Law." In *Encyclopedia of the American Constitution*, edited by Leonard Williams Levy and Kenneth L. Karst, 2089–93. 2nd ed. New York: Macmillan.

———. 2013. "Colorblind Intersectionality." *Signs: Journal of Women in Culture and Society* 38 (4): 811–45.

Carbado, Devon, Kimberlé Williams Crenshaw, Vickie M. Mays, and Barbara Tomlinson. 2013. "Intersectionality: Mapping the Movements of a Theory." *Du Bois Review* 10 (2): 303–12.

Chakravarty, Debjani, and Elena Frank. 2013. "Abstracting Academic Feminist Aspirations: What Do Doctoral Dissertation Abstracts (1995–2010) Say about an Emergent Interdisciplinary Field?" *Feminist Formations* 25 (3): 57–78.

Chang, Robert S., and Jerome McCristal Culp Jr. 2002. "After Intersectionality." *UMKC Law Review* 71:485–91.

Cho, Sumi. 2002. "Understanding White Women's Ambivalence towards Affirmative Action: Theorizing Political Accountability in Coalitions." *UMKC Law Review* 71:399–418.

———. 2013. "Post-Intersectionality: The Curious Reception of Intersectionality in Legal Scholarship." *Du Bois Review* 10 (2): 385–404.

Cho, Sumi, Kimberlé Williams Crenshaw, and Leslie McCall. 2013. "Toward a Field of Intersectionality Studies: Theory, Applications and Praxis." *Signs: Journal of Women in Culture and Society* 38 (4): 785–810.

Chun, Jennifer Jihye, George Lipsitz, and Young Shin. 2013. "Intersectionality as a Social Movement Strategy: Asian Immigrant Women Advocates." *Signs: Journal of Women in Culture and Society* 38 (4): 917–40.

Cilliers, Paul. 2005. "Complexity, Deconstruction and Relativism." *Theory, Culture and Society* 22 (5): 255–67.

Clarke, Cheryl. 1983. "Lesbianism: An Act of Resistance." In *This Bridge Called My Back: Writings by Radical Women of Color*, edited by Cherríe Moraga and Gloria Anzaldùa, 128–37. 2nd ed. New York: Kitchen Table: Women of Color Press.

———. 2010. "*But Some of Us Are Brave* and the Transformation of the Academy: Transformation?" *Signs: Journal of Women in Culture and Society* 35 (4): 779–88.

Clermont, Kevin M., and Stewart J. Schwab. 2004. "How Employment Discrimination Plaintiffs Fare in Federal Court." *Journal of Empirical Legal Studies* 1 (2): 429–58.

———. 2009. "Employment Discrimination Plaintiffs in Federal Court: From Bad to Worse?" *Harvard Law and Policy Review* 3 (1): 103–32.

Cohen, Cathy J. 1997. "Punks, Bulldaggers, and Welfare Queens: The Radical Potential of Queer Politics?" *GLQ* 3 (4): 437–65.

Cole, Elizabeth R. 2008. "Coalitions as a Model for Intersectionality: From Practice to Theory." *Sex Roles* 59 (5–6): 443–53.

———. 2009. "Intersectionality and Research in Psychology." *American Psychologist* 64 (3): 170–80.

Cole, Elizabeth R., and Zakiya T. Luna. 2010. "Making Coalitions Work: Solidarity across Difference within U.S. Feminism." *Feminist Studies* 36 (1): 71–98.

Collins, Patricia Hill. 1990. *Black Feminist Thought: Knowledge, Consciousness, and the Politics of Empowerment.* London: Routledge.

———. 1998a. *Fighting Words: Black Women and the Search for Justice.* Minneapolis: University of Minnesota Press.

———. 1998b. "It's All in the Family: Intersections of Gender, Race and Nation." *Hypatia* 13 (3): 62–82.

———. 2003. "Some Group Matters: Intersectionality, Situated Standpoints, and Black Feminist Thought." In *A Companion to African–American Philosophy*, edited by Tommy L. Lott and John P. Pittman, 205–29. Oxford: Blackwell.

———. 2009. "Foreword: Emerging Intersections: Building Knowledge and Transforming Institutions." In *Emerging Intersections: Race, Class, and Gender in Theory, Policy and Practice*, edited by Bonnie Thornton Dill and Ruth Enid Zambrana, vii–xiv. New Brunswick NJ: Rutgers University Press.

———. 2011. "Piecing Together a Genealogical Puzzle: Intersectionality and American Pragmatism." *European Journal of Pragmatism and American Philosophy* 3 (2): 88–112.

———. 2012. "Looking Back, Moving Ahead: Scholarship in Service to Social Justice." *Gender and Society* 26 (1): 14–22.

Collins, Patricia Hill, Lionel A. Maldonado, Dana Y. Takagi, Barrie Thorne, Lynn Weber, and Howard Winant. 1995. "Symposium on West and Fernmaker's 'Doing Difference.'" *Gender and Society* 9 (4): 491–513.

Cooke, Marvel. (1950) 2015. "The Bronx Slave Market." *Viewpoint Magazine* 5. October 31. https://viewpointmag.com/2015/10/31/the-bronx-slave-market-1950.

Cooper, Anna Julia. (1892) 1998. "The Status of Women in America." In *The Voice of Anna Julia Cooper: Including a Voice from the South and Other Important Essays, Papers, and Letters,* edited by Charles Lamert and Esme Bhan, 109–20. Lanham MD: Rowman and Littlefield.

———. (1930) 1998. "My Racial Philosophy." In *The Voice of Anna Julia Cooper: Including a Voice from the South and Other Important Essays, Papers, and Letters*, edited by Charles Lamert and Esme Bhan, 236–37. Lanham MD: Rowman and Littlefield.

Cooper, Brittney. 2015. "Intersectionality." In *The Oxford Handbook of Feminist Theory*, edited by Lisa Disch and Mary Hawkesworth. Online publication date August. Last accessed September 1, 2015. DOI: 10.1093/oxfordhb/9780199328581.013.20.

Cooper Jackson, Esther. (1940) 2015. "The Negro Woman Domestic Worker in Relation to Trade Unionism." *Viewpoint Magazine* 5. October 31. https://

viewpointmag.com/2015/10/31/the-negro-woman-domestic-worker-in
-relation-to-trade-unionism-1940.

CRC (Combahee River Collective). 1983. "A Black Feminist Statement" [first
published in 1977]. In *This Bridge Called My Back: Writings by Radical
Women of Color*, edited by Cherríe Moraga and Gloria Anzaldúa, 210–18.
2nd ed. New York: Kitchen Table: Women of Color Press.

Crenshaw, Kimberlé Williams. 1988. "Race, Reform, and Retrenchment: Transformation and Legitimation in Antidiscrimination Law." *Harvard Law
Review* 101 (7): 1331–87.

———. 1989. "Demarginalizing the Intersection of Race and Sex: A Black Feminist Critique of Antidiscrimination Doctrine, Feminist Theory and Antiracist Politics." *University of Chicago Legal Forum* 140:139–67.

———. 1991. "Mapping the Margins: Intersectionality, Identity Politics, and
Violence against Women of Color." *Stanford Law Review* 43 (6): 1241–99.

———. 1995. "The Identity Factor in Multiculturalism." *Liberal Education* 81
(4): 6–12.

———. 2007. "Framing Affirmative Action." *Michigan Law Review* 105 (First
Impressions 10): 123–33.

———. 2010. "Close Encounters of Three Kinds: On Teaching Dominance
Feminism and Intersectionality." *Tulsa Law Review* 46 (1): 151–89.

———. 2011a. "Postscript." In *Framing Intersectionality: Debates on a Multifaceted Concept in Gender Studies*, edited by Helma Lutz, Maria Teresa Herrera
Vivar, and Linda Supik, 221–34. Abingdon: Ashgate.

———. 2011b. "Twenty Years of Critical Race Theory: Looking Back to Move
Forward." *Connecticut Law Review* 43 (5): 1253–1352.

———. 2012. "From Private Violence to Mass Incarceration: Thinking Intersectionally About Women, Race, and Social Control." *UCLA Law Review* 59:
1418–72.

———. 2014. "Justice Rising: Moving Intersectionally in the Age of Post-
Everything." Paper delivered at the London School of Economics, March 26.
http://www.lse.ac.uk/newsAndMedia/videoAndAudio/channels/public
LecturesAndEvents/player.aspx?id=2360.

———. 2015. "Why Intersectionality Can't Wait." *Washington Post*, September
24. https://www.washingtonpost.com/news/in-theory/wp/2015/09/24
/why-intersectionality-cant-wait.

Cuádraz, Gloria Holguin, and Lynnett Uttal. 1999. "Intersectionality and In-
depth Interviews: Methodological Strategies for Analyzing Race, Class, and
Gender." *Race, Gender and Class* 6 (3): 156–86.

Davis, Angela Y. 1981. *Women, Race and Class*. New York: Random House.

Davis, Angela Y., and Elizabeth Martínez. 1998. "Coalition Building among People of Color: A Discussion." In *The Angela Y. Davis Reader*, edited by Joy James, 297–306. Malden MA: Blackwell.

Davis, Kathy. 2008. "Intersectionality as Buzzword: A Sociology of Science Perspective on What Makes a Feminist Theory Successful." *Feminist Theory* 9 (1): 67–85.

DeGraffenreid v. General Motors. 1976. 413 F.Supp. 142 (E.D. Mo. 1976).

Delgado, Richard. 2003. "Linking Arms: Recent Books on Interracial Coalition as an Avenue of Social Reform." *Cornell Law Review* 88:855–84.

Dhamoon, Rita Kaur. 2011. "Considerations on Mainstreaming Intersectionality." *Political Research Quarterly* 64 (1): 230–43.

———. 2015. "A Feminist Approach to Decolonizing Anti-Racism: Rethinking Transnationalism, Intersectionality, and Settler Colonialism." *Feral Feminisms* 4:20–37.

Dill, Bonnie Thornton, and Ruth Enid Zambrana. 2009. "Critical Thinking about Inequality: An Emerging Lens." *Emerging Intersections: Race, Class, and Gender in Theory, Policy and Practice*, edited by Bonnie Thornton Dill and Ruth Enid Zambrana, 1–21. New Brunswick NJ: Rutgers University Press.

Dolphijn, Rick, and Iris van der Tuin. 2012. *New Materialism: Interviews and Cartographies*. Ann Arbor: Open Humanities Press.

———. 2013. "A Thousand Tiny Intersections: Linguisticism, Feminism, Racism and Deleuzian Becomings." In *Deleuze and Race*, edited by Arun Saldanha and J. M. Adams, 128–43. Edinburgh: Edinburgh University Press.

Dotson, Kristie. 2011. "Tracking Epistemic Violence, Tracking Practices of Silencing." *Hypatia: A Journal of Feminist Philosophy* 26 (2): 236–57.

———. 2013. "Knowing in Space: Three Lessons from Black Women's Social Theory." *Labrys: Études Féministes/Estudos Feministas* 23. http://www.labrys .net.br/labrys23/filosofia/kristieok.htm.

———. 2014. "Making Sense: The Multistability of Oppression and the Importance of Intersectionality." In *Why Race and Gender Still Matter: An Intersectional Approach*, edited by Namita Goswami, Maeve O'Donovan, and Lisa Yount, 43–58. London: Pickering & Chatto.

Dua, Enakshi, and Angela Robertson. 1999. *Scratching the Surface: Canadian, Anti-Racist, Feminist Thought*. Toronto: Women's Press.

Du Bois, William Edward Burghardt. 1961. *The Souls of Black Folk*. New York: Fawcett World Library. First published in 1903.

Dunbar-Ortiz, Roxanne. 2005. *Blood on the Border: A Memoir of the Contra War*. Cambridge MA: South End Press.

Ehrenreich, Nancy. 2002. "Subordination and Symbiosis: Mechanisms of Mutual Support between Subordinating Systems." *UMKC Law Review* 71:251–324.

Eisenstein, Zillah R. 1978. *Capitalist Patriarchy and the Case for Socialist Feminism*. New York: Monthly Review Press.

Elbaum, Max. 2002. *Revolution in the Air: Sixties Radicals Turn to Lenin, Mao and Che*. London: Verso.

Erel, Umut, Jin Haritaworn, Encarnación Gutiérrez Rodríguez, and Christian Klesse. 2008. "On the Depoliticization of Intersectionality Talk: Conceptualizing Multiple Oppressions in Sexuality Studies." In *Out of Place: Interrogating Silences in Queerness/Raciality*, edited by Adi Kuntsman and Miyake Esperanza, 265–92. New York: Raw Nerve Books.

Espinosa, Lisbeth. 2011. Personal communication with the author. Los Angeles, May 31.

Falcón, Sylvanna M., and Jennifer C. Nash. 2015. "Shifting Analytics and Linking Theories: A Conversation about the 'Meaning-Making' of Intersectionality and Transnationalism." *Women's Studies International Forum* 50:1–10.

Fellows, Mary Louise, and Sherene Razack. 1998. "The Race to Innocence: Confronting Hierarchical Relations among Women." *Journal of Gender, Race, and Justice* 1:335–52.

Ferguson, Roderick A. 2012. "Reading Intersectionality." *Transcripts* 2:91–98.

Ferguson, Roderick A., and Grace Kyungwon Hong, eds. 2011. *Strange Affinities: The Gender and Sexual Politics of Comparative Racialization*. Durham: Duke University Press.

Ferguson, Susan, and David McNally. 2015. "Social Reproduction beyond Intersectionality: An Interview." *Viewpoint Magazine* 5. October 31. https://viewpointmag.com/2015/10/31/social-reproduction-beyond-intersectionality-an-interview-with-sue-ferguson-and-david-mcnally.

Figueroa, Evelyn. 1996. "Disarming Nicaraguan Women: The Other Counterrevolution." *Columbia Journal of Gender and Law* 6 (1): 273–321.

Gabriel, Ellen. 2011. "Aboriginal Women's Movement: A Quest for Self-Determination." *Aboriginal Policy Studies* 1 (1): 183–88.

Gallot, Fanny, and Sirma Bilge. 2012. "Enjeux et défis de l'intersectionnalité: Entretien avec Sirma Bilge" [Issues and challenges of intersectionality: Interview with Sirma Bilge] *Contretemps*, April 30. http://www.contretemps.eu/interventions/enjeux-défis-intersectionnalité-entretien-sirma-bilge.

Garry, Ann. 2012. "Who Is Included? Intersectionality, Metaphors, and the Multiplicity of Gender." In *Out from the Shadows: Analytical Feminist Contributions to Traditional Philosophy*, edited by Sharon Crasnow and Anita Superson, 493–530. New York: Oxford University Press.

Geerts, Evelien, and Iris van der Tuin. 2013. "From Intersectionality to Interference: Feminist Onto-Epistemological Reflections on the Politics of Representation." *Women's Studies International Forum* 41 (3): 171–78.

Gilmore, Ruth Wilson. 2002. "Fatal Couplings of Power and Difference: Notes on Racism and Geography." *Professional Geographer* 54 (1): 15–24.

Gimenez, Martha. 2001. "Marxism and Class, Gender, and Race: Rethinking the Trilogy." *Race, Gender and Class* 8 (2): 23–33.

Gines, Kathryn T. 2011. "Black Feminism and Intersectional Analyses: A Defense of Intersectionality." *Philosophy Today* Issue Supplement 55:275–84.

——. 2014. "Race Women, Race Men and Early Expressions of Proto-Intersectionality." In *Why Race and Gender Still Matter: An Intersectional Approach*, edited by Namita Goswami, Maeve O'Donovan, and Lisa Yount, 13–26. London: Pickering & Chatto.

Goff, Phillip Atiba, and Kimberly Barsamian Kahn. 2013. "How Psychological Science Impedes Intersectional Thinking." *Du Bois Review* 10 (2): 365–84.

González, Roberto, Jorge Manzi, José L. Saiz, Marilynn Brewer, Pablo de Tezanos-Pinto, David Torres, María Teresa Aravena, and Nerea Aldunate. 2008. "Interparty Attitudes in Chile: Coalitions as Superordinate Social Identities." *Political Psychology* 29 (1): 93–118.

Grewal, Inderpal, and Caren Kaplan, eds. 1994. *Scattered Hegemonies: Postmodernity and Transnational Feminist Practices*. Minneapolis: University of Minnesota Press.

Grzanka, Patrick R., ed. 2014. *Intersectionality: A Foundations and Frontiers Reader*. Boulder: Westview Press.

Gunaratnam, Yasmin, ed. 2014a. *Complicit No More*. London: Media Diversified.

——, ed. 2014b. *Feminist Review* 108: "Black British Feminisms."

Guy-Sheftall, Beverly, ed. 1995. *Words of Fire: An Anthology of African-American Feminist Thought*. New York: The New Press.

Hall, Lisa Kahaleole. 2008. "Strategies of Erasure: U.S. Colonialism and Native Hawaiian Feminism." *American Quarterly* 60 (2): 273–80.

Hancock, Ange-Marie. 2007a. "Intersectionality as a Normative and Empirical Paradigm." *Politics and Gender* 3 (2): 248–54.

——. 2007b. "When Multiplication Doesn't Equal Quick Addition: Examining Intersectionality as a Research Paradigm." *Perspectives on Politics* 5 (1): 63–79.

——. 2011. *Solidarity Politics for Millennials: A Guide to Ending the Oppression Olympics*. New York: Palgrave Macmillan.

Hancock, Ange-Marie, and Nira Yuval-Davis. 2011. "Series Introduction: The Politics of Intersectionality." In *Solidarity Politics for Millennials: A Guide* to *Ending the Oppression Olympics*, by Ange-Marie Hancock, xi–xxii. New York: Palgrave Macmillan.

Haney-López, Ian. 2010. "Is the 'Post' in Post-Racial the 'Blind' in Colorblind?" *Cardozo Law Review* 32 (3): 807–31.

Harbin, Amy. 2012. "Bodily Disorientation and Moral Change." *Hypatia* 27 (2): 261–80.

Harrington v. Cleburne County Board of Education. 2001. 251 F.3d 935. 2001 U.S. App. LEXIS 10488 (11th Cir. 2001). http://www.lexisnexis.com/us/lnacademic.

Harris, Angela P. 1990. "Race and Essentialism in Feminist Legal Theory." *Stanford Law Review* 42 (3): 581–616.

Harris, Cheryl. 1993. "Whiteness as Property." *Harvard Law Review* 106 (8): 1707–91.

Harris, Cheryl, and Kimberly West-Faulcon. 2010. "Reading Ricci: Whitening Discrimination, Racing Test Fairness." *UCLA Law Review* 58:73–165.

Harris, Lashawn. 2012. "Marvel Cooke: Investigative Journalist, Communist, and Black Radical Subject." *Journal for the Study of Radicalism* 6 (2): 91–126.

Hobson, Emily. 2009. "Imagining Alliances: Queer Anti-imperialism and Race in California, 1966–1989." PhD diss., University of Southern California.

Hong, Grace Kyungwon. 2005. *The Ruptures of American Capital*. Minneapolis: University of Minnesota Press.

hooks, bell. 1981. *Ain't I a Woman? Black Women and Feminism*. Boston: South End Press.

———. 1984. *Feminist Theory from Margin to Center*. Boston: South End Press.

———. 1999. *Yearning: Race, Gender and Cultural Politics*. Boston: South End Press. First published 1990.

Huffer, Lynn. 2013. *Are the Lips a Grave? A Queer Feminist on the Ethics of Sex*. New York: Columbia University Press.

Hull, Gloria, Patricia Scott, and Barbara Smith, eds. 1982. *All the Women Are White, All the Blacks Are Men, But Some of Us Are Brave: Black Women's Studies*. New York: The Feminist Press.

Hurtado, Aida. 1996. *The Color of Privilege: Three Blasphemies on Race and Feminism*. Ann Arbor: University of Michigan Press.

Hutchinson, Darren Lenard. 1997. "Out Yet Unseen: A Racial Critique of Gay and Lesbian Legal Theory and Political Discourse." *Connecticut Law Review* 29:561–645.

———. 2001. "Identity Crisis: Intersectionality, Multidimensionality, and the Development of an Adequate Theory of Subordination." *Michigan Journal of Race and Law* 6:285–317.

———. 2002. "New Complexity Theories: From Theoretical Innovation to Doctrinal Reform." *UMKC Law Review* 71:431–45.

Isbester, Katherine. 2001. *Still Fighting: The Nicaraguan Women's Movement, 1977–2000*. Pittsburgh: University of Pittsburgh Press.

Jafri, Beenash. 2012. "Privilege vs. Complicity: People of Colour and Settler Colonialism." Equity Matters, Federation of Humanities and Social Sciences, March 21. http://www.ideas-idees.ca/blog/privilege-vs-complicity -people-colour-and-settler-colonialism.

Jagger, Gill. 2015. "The New Materialism and Sexual Difference." *Signs: Journal of Women in Culture and Society* 40 (2): 321–42.

James, Joy. 1999. *Shadowboxing: Representations of Black Feminist Politics*. New York: Palgrave.

Jefferies v. Harris County Community Action Association. 1980. 615 F.2d. 1025. 1980 5th Cir. U.S.A. Federal Court of Appeals. http://openjurist.org/615 /f2d/1025.

Jones, Claudia. (1949) 1995. "An End to the Neglect of the Problems of the Negro Woman!" In *Words of Fire: An Anthology of African-American Feminist Thought*, edited by Beverly Guy-Sheftall, 107–23. New York: The New Press.

Jordan-Zachery, Julia. 2007. "Am I a Black Woman or a Woman Who Is Black? A Few Thoughts on the Meaning of Intersectionality." *Politics and Gender* 3 (2): 254–64.

Judge v. Marsh. 1986. 649 F. Supp.770 (D.D.C. 1986). http://www.lexisnexis .com/us/lnacademic.

Kampwirth, Karen. 2004. *Feminism and the Legacy of Revolution: Nicaragua, El Salvador, Chiapas*. Athens: Ohio University Press.

Kauanui, J. Kehaulani. 2008a. *Hawaiian Blood: Colonialism and the Politics of Sovereignty and Indigeneity*. Durham: Duke University Press.

———. 2008b. "Native Hawaiian Decolonization and the Politics of Gender." *American Quarterly* 60 (2): 281–87.

Keating, AnaLouise. 1995. "Interrogating 'Whiteness,' (De)Constructing 'Race.'" *College English* 57 (8): 901–18.

———. 2009. "Recognizing Each Other: Toward a Politics of Interconnect- edness." Paper presented at the National Women's Studies Association Conference—"Difficult Dialogues," Atlanta, November 14.

———. 2013. *Transformation Now! Toward a Post-Oppositional Politics of Change*. Chicago: University of Illinois Press.

King, Deborah K. 1988. "Multiple Jeopardy, Multiple Consciousness: The Con- text of a Black Feminist Ideology." *Signs: Journal of Women in Culture and Society* 14 (1): 42–72.

King, Thomas. 2003. *The Truth about Stories: A Native Narrative*. Montreal: McGill University. Canadian Broadcasting Corporation Massey Lectures. http://www.cbc.ca/radio/ideas/the-2003-cbc-massey-lectures-the-truth -about-stories-a-native-narrative-1.2946870.

Kouri-Towe, Natalie. 2015. "Solidarity at Risk: The Politics of Attachment in Transnational Queer Palestine Solidarity and Anti-Pinkwashing Activism." Ph.D. diss., University of Toronto.

Kwan, Peter. 1997. "Intersections of Race, Ethnicity, Class, Gender and Sexual Orientation: Jeffrey Dahmer and the Cosynthesis of Categories." *Hastings Law Journal* 48:1257–64.

———. 2000. "Complicity and Complexity: Cosynthesis and Praxis." *DePaul Law Review* 49:673–87.

———. 2002. "The Metaphysics of Metaphors: Symbiosis and the Quest for Meaning." *UMKC Law Review* 71:325–30.

Lacy, D. Aaron. 2008. "The Most Endangered Title VII Plaintiff? Exponential Discrimination against Black Males." *University of Nebraska Law Review* 86 (3): 552–94.

Lawrence, Bonita, and Enakshi Dua. 2005. "Decolonizing Antiracism." *Social Justice* 32 (4): 120–43.

Levit, Nancy. 2002. "Introduction: Theorizing the Connections among Systems of Subordination." *UMKC Law Review* 71:227–49.

Lewis, Gail. 2009. "Celebrating Intersectionality? Debates on a Multifaceted Concept in Gender Studies: Themes from a Conference." *European Journal of Women's Studies* 16 (3): 203–10.

———. 2013. "Unsafe Travel: Experiencing Intersectionality and Feminist Displacements." *Signs: Journal of Women in Culture and Society* 38 (4): 869–916.

Lindsay, Keisha. 2009. "Black Women, Intersectionality, and Identity Politics." Paper presented at the National Women's Studies Association Conference— "Difficult Dialogues," Atlanta, November 13.

López, Leonard Paul. 2014. "Chicano *Mens*: Hate Crime, Coloniality, and the Critique of Rights." Master's thesis, California State University, Los Angeles.

Lorde, Audre. 1984. *Sister Outsider: Essays and Speeches*. Freedom: Crossing Press.

Ludvig, Alice. 2006. "Differences between Women? Intersecting Voices in a Female Narrative." *European Journal of Women's Studies* 13 (3): 245–58.

Lugones, María. 1998. "Motion, Stasis and Resistance to Interlocked Oppressions." In *Making Worlds: Gender, Metaphor, Materiality*, edited by Susan Hardy Aiken, 49–52. Tucson: University of Arizona Press.

———. 2003. *Pilgrimages/Peregrinajes: Theorizing Coalition against Multiple Oppressions*. Lanham MD: Rowman and Littlefield.

———. 2007. "Heterosexualism and the Modern/Colonial Gender System." *Hypatia* 22 (1): 186–209.

———. 2010. "Toward a Decolonial Feminism." *Hypatia* 25 (4): 742–59.

Lutz, Helma, Maria Teresa Herrera Vivar, and Linda Supik, eds. 2011. *Framing Intersectionality: Debates on a Multifaceted Concept in Gender Studies*. Abingdon: Ashgate,

Lykke, Nina. 2010. *Feminist Studies: A Guide to Intersectional Theory, Methodology and Writing*. New York: Routledge.

———. 2011. "Intersectional Analysis: Black Box or Useful Critical Feminist Thinking Technology?" In *Framing Intersectionality: Debates on a Multifaceted Concept in Gender Studies*, edited by Helma Lutz, Maria Teresa Herrera Vivar, and Linda Supik, 207–20. Abingdon: Ashgate.

Magat, Joan Ames. 2010. "Bottomheavy: Legal Footnotes." *Journal of Legal Education* 60 (1): 65–105.

Mahrouse, Gada. 2008. "Race-Conscious Transnational Activists with Cameras." *International Journal of Cultural Studies* 11 (1): 87–105.

———. 2014. *Conflicted Commitments: Race, Privilege and Power in Solidarity Activism*. Montreal: McGill-Queens University Press.

Martín Alcoff, Linda. 1991–92. "The Problem of Speaking for Others." *Cultural Critique* 20:5–32.

Martínez, Elizabeth. 1993. "Beyond Black/White: The Racisms of Our Times." *Social Justice* 20 (1–2): 22–34.

Marx, Karl, and Friedrich Engels. (1848) 1996. *The Communist Manifesto*. In *Karl Marx: Selected Writings*, edited by Lawrence Simon, 157–86. Indianapolis: Hackett.

Massaquoi, Notisha, and Njoki Nathani Wane, eds. 2007. *Theorizing Empowerment: Canadian Perspectives on Black Feminist Thought*. Toronto: Inanna.

Matsuda, Mari. 1991. "Beside My Sister, Facing the Enemy: Legal Theory Out of Coalition." *Stanford Law Review* 43 (6): 1183–92.

May, Vivian M. 2014. "Speaking into the Void: Intersectionality Critiques and Epistemic Backlash." *Hypatia* 29 (1): 94–112.

———. 2015. *Pursuing Intersectionality, Unsettling Dominant Imaginaries*. New York: Routledge.

Mbembe, Achille. 2003. "Necropolitics." Translated by Libby Meintjes. *Public Culture* 15 (1): 11–40.

McCall, Leslie. 2005. "The Complexity of Intersectionality." *Signs: Journal of Women in Culture and Society* 30 (3): 1771–1800.

McClintock, Anne. 1995. *Imperial Leather: Race, Gender and Sexuality in Colonial Conquest*. New York: Routledge.

McDougald, Elise Johnson. (1925) 1997. "The Double Task: The Struggle of Women for Sex and Race Emancipation." In *Words of Fire: An Anthology of African-American Feminist Thought*, edited by Beverly Guy-Sheftall, 79–83. New York: The New Press.

McDuffie, Eric S. 2009. "'No Small Amount of Change Could Do': Esther Cooper Jackson and the Making of a Black Feminist Left." In *Want to Start a Revolution? Radical Women in the Black Freedom Struggle*, edited by Dayo Gore, Jeanne Theoharis, and Komozi Woodard, 25–46. New York: New York University Press.

———. 2011. *Sojourning for Freedom: Black Women, American Communism and the Making of Black Left Feminism*. Durham: Duke University Press.

McKittrick, Katherine. 2006. *Demonic Grounds: Black Women and the Cartographies of Struggle*. Minneapolis: University of Minnesota Press.

McKittrick, Katherine, and Clyde Woods. 2007. *Black Geographies and the Politics of Space*. Toronto: Between the Lines.

McWhorter, Ladelle. 2004. "Sex, Race, and Biopower: A Foucauldian Genealogy." *Hypatia* 19 (3): 38–62.

Mendieta, Eduardo. 2012. "Migrant, Migra, Mongrel: The Latin American Dishwasher, Busboy, and Colored/Ethnic/Diversity (Philosophy) Hire." In *Reframing the Practice of Philosophy: Bodies of Color, Bodies of Knowledge*, edited by George Yancy, 147–66. Albany: State University of New York Press.

Mignolo, Walter D. 2009. "Epistemic Disobedience, Independent Thought and De-Colonial Freedom." *Theory, Culture and Society* 26 (7–8): 1–23.

Mignolo, Walter D., and Madina V. Tlostanova. 2006. "Theorizing from the Borders: Shifting to Geo- and Body-Politics of Knowledge." *European Journal of Social Theory* 9 (2): 205–21.

Mikkola, Mari. 2009. "Gender Concepts and Intuitions." *Canadian Journal of Philosophy* 39 (4): 559–83.

Mirza, Heidi Safia, ed. 1997. *Black British Feminism: A Reader*. New York: Routledge.

Mohanram, Radhika. 1999. *Black Body: Women, Colonialism and Space*. Minneapolis: University of Minnesota Press.

Mohanty, Chandra Talpade. 1988. "Under Western Eyes: Feminist Scholarship and Colonial Discourses." *Feminist Review* 30:61–88.

Monture-Angus, Patricia. 1995. *Thunder in My Soul: A Mohawk Woman Speaks*. Halifax: Fernwood.

Moore v. Hughes Helicopters. 1983. 708 F.2d 475. 1983 9th Cir. U.S. Court of
Appeals. http://openjurist.org/708/f2d/475.

Moraga, Cherríe. 1983. *Loving in the War Years/Lo Que Nunca Pasó Por Sus
Labios*. Boston: South End Press.

Moraga, Cherríe, and Gloria Anzaldúa, eds. 1983. *This Bridge Called My Back:
Writings by Radical Women of Color*. 2nd ed. New York: Kitchen Table:
Women of Color Press. First published 1981.

Muñoz, José Esteban. 2009. "Queerness as Horizon: Utopian Hermeneutics
in the Face of Gay Pragmatism." In *Cruising Utopia: The Then and There of
Queer Futurity*, 19–32. New York: New York University Press.

Mutua, Athena. 2013. "Multidimensionality Is to Masculinities What Intersectionality Is to Feminism." *Nevada Law Journal* 13:341–67.

Najmanovich, Denise. 2002. "From Paradigms to Figures of Thought." *Emergence* 4 (1–2): 85–93.

Nash, Jennifer C. 2008. "Re-thinking Intersectionality." *Feminist Review* 89:1–15.

———. 2010. "On Difficulty: Intersectionality as Feminist Labor." *The Scholar
and Feminist Online* 8 (3). http://sfonline.barnard.edu/polyphonic/nash
_01.htm.

———. 2011a. "Home Truths on Intersectionality." *Yale Journal of Law and
Feminism* 23:445–70.

———. 2011b. "Practicing Love: Black Feminism, Love-Politics and Post-
Intersectionality." *Meridians* 11 (2): 1–24.

———. 2014a. *The Black Body in Ecstacy: Reading Race, Reading Pornography*.
Durham: Duke University Press.

———. 2014b. "Institutionalizing the Margins." *Social Text* 32 (1): 45–65.

———. 2015. "Feminist Originalism: Intersectionality and the Politics of Reading." *Feminist Theory*. December 24. 10.1177/1464700115620864.

Nelson, Jennifer. 2003. *Women of Color and the Reproductive Rights Movement*.
New York: New York University Press.

Okolosie, Lola. 2014. "Beyond 'Talking' and 'Owning' Intersectionality." *Feminist Review* 108:90–96.

Oppenheimer, David Benjamin. 2003. "Verdicts Matter: An Empirical Study of
California Employment Discrimination and Wrongful Discharge Jury Ver-
dicts Reveals Low Success Rate for Women and Minorities." *UC Davis Law
Review* 37:511–66.

Oyěwùmí, Oyèrónkẹ́. 1997. *The Invention of Women: Making an African Sense
of Western Gender Discourses*. Minneapolis: University of Minnesota Press.

Parker, Sharon. 1991. "Understanding Coalition." *Stanford Law Review* 43 (6):
1193–96.

Patel, Pragna. 2000. "Southall Black Sisters: Domestic Violence Campaigns and Alliances across the Divisions of Race, Gender, and Class." In *Home Truths about Domestic Violence: Feminist Influences on Policy and Practice—A Reader*, edited by Jalna Hanmer and Catherine Itzin, 167–84. London: Routledge.

Patil, Vrushali. 2013. "From Patriarchy to Intersectionality: A Transnational Feminist Assessment of How Far We've Really Come." *Signs: Journal of Women in Culture and Society* 38 (4): 847–69.

Payne v. Travenol. 1982. 673 F.2d 798. 1982 5th Cir. U.S. Court of Appeals. http://openjurist.org/673/f2d/798.

Perla, Héctor, Jr. 2009. "Heirs of Sandino: The Nicaraguan Revolution and the U.S.-Nicaragua Solidarity Movement." *Latin American Perspectives* 36 (6): 80–100.

Phung, Malissa. 2011. "Are People of Colour Settlers Too?" In *Cultivating Canada: Reconciliation Through the Lens of Cultural Diversity*, edited by Ashok Mathur, Jonathan Dewar, and Mike DeGagné, 289–98. Ottawa: Aboriginal Healing Foundation.

Puar, Jasbir K. 2007. *Terrorist Assemblages: Homonationalism in Queer Times.* Durham: Duke University Press.

———. 2012. "'I Would Rather Be a Cyborg Than a Goddess': Becoming-Intersectional in Assemblage Theory." *PhiloSOPHIA: A Journal of Continental Feminism* 2 (1): 49–66.

———. 2014. "Disability." *TSQ: Transgender Studies Quarterly* 1 (1–2): 77–81.

Quintanales, Mirtha. 1983. "I Paid Very Hard for My Immigrant Ignorance." In *This Bridge Called My Back: Writings by Radical Women of Color*, edited by Cherríe Moraga and Gloria Anzaldúa, 150–56. 2nd ed. New York: Kitchen Table: Women of Color Press.

Ramirez, Renya K. 2008. "Learning across Differences: Native and Ethnic Studies Feminisms." *American Quarterly* 60 (2): 303–7.

Ramírez, Sergio. 1985. "U.S. Working People Can Stop Intervention in Central America" [speech delivered on March 4, 1982]. In *Nicaragua, the Sandinista People's Revolution: Speeches by Sandinista Leaders*, edited by Bruce Marcus, 1–7. New York: Pathfinder.

Randall, Margaret. 1992. *Gathering Rage: The Failure of 20th Century Revolutions to Develop a Feminist Agenda.* New York: Monthly Review Press.

———. 1993. "To Change Our Own Reality and the World: A Conversation with Lesbians in Nicaragua." *Signs* 18 (4): 907–24.

———. 1994. *Sandino's Daughters Revisited: Feminism in Nicaragua.* New Brunswick NJ: Rutgers University Press.

———. 1995. *Sandino's Daughters: Testimonies of Nicaraguan Women in Struggle*. Rev. ed. New Brunswick NJ: Rutgers University Press.

Ransby, Barbara. 2000. "Black Feminism at Twenty-One: Reflections on the Evolution of a National Community." *Signs: Journal of Women in Culture and Society* 25 (4): 1214–21.

Razack, Sherene. 1998. *Looking White People in the Eye: Gender, Race and Culture in Courtrooms and Classrooms*. Toronto: University of Toronto Press.

———. 2005. "How Is White Supremacy Embodied? Sexualized Racial Violence at Abu Ghraib." *Canadian Journal of Women and the Law* 17 (2): 341–63.

Razack, Sherene, Malinda Smith, and Sunera Thobani. 2010. *States of Race: Critical Race Feminism for the 21st Century*. Toronto: Between the Lines.

Reagon, Bernice Johnson. 1983. "Coalition Politics: Turning the Century." In *Homegirls: A Black Feminist Anthology*, edited by Barbara Smith, 343–55. New York: Kitchen Table: Women of Color Press.

Ricci et al. v. DeStefano et al. 2009. U.S.S.C. 07-1428. http://www.justice.gov/sites/default/files/crt/legacy/2010/12/28/ricci_sctdec.pdf.

Rosenblum, Darren. 1994. "Queer Intersectionality and the Failure of Recent Lesbian and Gay Victories." *Law and Sexuality* 4:83–122.

Roshanravan, Shireen. 2014. "Motivating Coalition: Women of Color and Epistemic Disobedience." *Hypatia* 29 (1): 41–58.

Ross, Loretta. 2011. "The Origin of the Phrase 'Women of Color.'" Western States Center Reproductive Justice Training. Portland, January 28. https://youtu.be/82vl34mi4Iw.

Roth, Benita. 2004. *Separate Roads to Feminism: Black, Chicana, and White Feminist Movements in America's Second Wave*. Oxford: Cambridge University Press.

Rudebusch v. Arizona. 2007. U.S. Dist. LEXIS 70690 (D. Ariz., 2007). http://www.lexisnexis.com/us/lnacademic.

Rudebusch v. Hughes. 2002. 313 F.3d 506. 2002. U.S. App. LEXIS 24713 (9th Cir. Ariz., 2002). http://www.lexisnexis.com/us/lnacademic.

Russell, Kathryn. 2007. "Feminist Dialectics and Marxist Theory." *Radical Philosophy Review* 10 (1): 33–54.

Scott, Joan W. 1991. "The Evidence of Experience." *Critical Inquiry* 17 (4): 773–97.

Sehdev, Robinder Kaur. 2011. "People of Colour in Treaty." In *Cultivating Canada: Reconciliation through the Lens of Cultural Diversity*, edited by Ashok Mathur, Jonathan Dewar, and Mike DeGagné, 263–74. Ottawa: Aboriginal Healing Foundation.

Selmi, Michael. 2001. "Why Are Employment Discrimination Cases So Hard to Win?" *Louisiana Law Review* 61 (3): 555–76.

Sengupta, Shuddhabrata. 2006. "I/Me/Mine—Intersectional Identities as Negotiated Minefields." *Signs: Journal of Women in Culture and Society* 31 (3): 629–39.

Sharma, Nandita, and Cynthia Wright. 2008–9. "Decolonizing Resistance, Challenging Colonial States." *Social Justice* 35 (3): 120–38.

Simien, Evelyn M. 2007. "Doing Intersectionality Research: From Conceptual Issues to Practical Examples." *Politics and Gender* 3 (2): 264–71.

Simpson, Audra. 2007. "On Ethnographic Refusal: Indigeneity, 'Voice' and Colonial Citizenship." *Junctures* 9:67–80.

———. 2014. *Mohawk Interruptus: Political Life across the Borders of Settler States*. Durham: Duke University Press.

Simpson, Audra, and Andrea Smith, eds. 2014. *Theorizing Native Studies*. Durham: Duke University Press.

Smith, Andrea. 2003. "Not an Indian Tradition: The Sexual Colonization of Native Peoples." *Hypatia* 18 (2): 70–85.

———. 2005. *Conquest: Sexual Violence and American Indian Genocide*. Boston: South End Press.

———. 2006. "Heteropatriarchy and the Three Pillars of White Supremacy: Rethinking Women of Color Organizing." In *Color of Violence: The Incite Anthology*, edited by Incite! Women of Color against Violence, 66–73. Cambridge MA: South End Press.

———. 2008. "American Studies without America: Native Feminisms and the Nation-State." *American Quarterly* 60 (2): 309–15.

———. 2010. "Queer Theory and Native Studies: The Heteronormativity of Settler Colonialism." *GLQ: A Journal of Gay and Lesbian Studies* 16 (1–2): 42–68.

———. 2012. "Indigeneity, Settler Colonialism, White Supremacy." In *Racial Formation in the Twenty-First Century*, edited by Daniel Martínez HoSang, Oneka LaBennett and Laura Pulido, 66–90. Berkeley: University of California Press.

Smith, Andrea, and J. Kehaulani Kauanui. 2008. "Native Feminisms Engage American Studies." *American Quarterly* 60 (2): 241–49.

Smith, Barbara, ed. 1983. *Home Girls: A Black Feminist Anthology*. New Brunswick NJ: Rutgers University Press.

———. 1989. "A Press of Our Own: Kitchen Table: Women of Color Press." *Frontiers: A Journal of Women's Studies* 10 (3): 11–13.

———. 2003. Interview by Loretta Ross. Transcript of video recording, May

7–8. Voices of Feminism Oral History Project, Sophia Smith Collection, Smith College, Northampton MA.

Smith, Barbara, and Beverly Smith. 1983. "Across the Kitchen Table: A Sister-to-Sister Dialogue." In *This Bridge Called My Back: Writings by Radical Women of Color*, edited by Cherríe Moraga and Gloria Anzaldùa, 113–27. 2nd ed. New York: Kitchen Table: Women of Color Press.

Smith, Peggy R. 1991. "Separate Identities: Black Women, Work, and Title VII." *Harvard Women's Law Journal* 14:21–76.

Smith, Sharon. 2013. "Black Feminism and Intersectionality." *International Socialist Review* 91. http://isreview.org/issue/91/black-feminism-and-intersectionality.

Son Hing, Leanne S., Greg A. Chung-Yan, Robert Grunfeld, Lori K. Robichaud, and Mark P. Zanna. 2004. "Exploring the Discrepancy between Implicit and Explicit Prejudice: A Test of Aversive Racism Theory." In *Social Motivation: Conscious and Unconscious Processes*, edited by J. P. Forgas, K. D. Williams, S. M. Laham, 274–93. Oxford: Cambridge University Press.

Spelman, Elizabeth V. 1988. *Inessential Woman: Problems of Exclusion in Feminist Thought*. Boston: Beacon.

Spillers, Hortense. 1984. "Interstices: A Small Drama of Words." In *Pleasure and Danger: Exploring Female Sexuality*, edited by Carole Vance, 73–100. Boston: Routledge and Kegan Paul.

Springer, Brandon. 2011. "A Revolution within a Revolution: Queering Sandinismo in Nicaragua." *University of Colorado Boulder Honors Journal*. https://issuu.com/cuhonorsjournal/docs/honorsjournal2011.

Springer, Kimberly, ed. 1999. *Still Lifting, Still Climbing: African American Women's Contemporary Activism*. New York: New York University Press.

———. 2005. *Living for the Revolution: Black Feminist Organizations, 1968–1980*. Durham: Duke University Press.

Srivastava, Sarita. 2005. "'You're Calling Me a Racist?' The Moral and Emotional Regulation of Antiracism and Feminism." *Signs: Journal of Women in Culture and Society* 31 (1): 29–62.

Staunæs, Dorthe. 2003. "Where Have All the Subjects Gone? Bringing Together the Concepts of Intersectionality and Subjectification." *Nora* 11 (2): 101–10.

Staunæs, Dorthe, and Dorte Marie Søndegaard. 2011. "Intersectionality: A Theoretical Adjustment." In *Theories and Methodologies in Postgraduate Feminist Research: Researching Differently*, edited by Rosemarie Buikema, Gabriele Griffin, and Nina Lykke, 45–59. New York: Routledge.

Stoltz Chinchilla, Norma. 1990. "Revolutionary Popular Feminism in Nicaragua: Articulating Class, Gender, and National Sovereignty." *Gender and Society* 4 (3): 370–97.

Terrell, Mary Church. 1898. "Progress of Colored Women: An Address Delivered before the National American Women's Suffrage Association." February 18. Washington DC: Smith Brothers Printers. In *From Slavery to Freedom: The African-American Pamphlet Collection, 1824–1909.* http://tinyurl.com/ChurchTerrell.

Thompson, Becky. 2002. "Multiracial Feminism: Recasting the Chronology of Second Wave Feminism." *Feminist Studies* 28 (2): 337–60.

Thompson Patterson, Louise. 2015. "Toward a Brighter Dawn." *Viewpoint Magazine* 5. October 31. https://viewpointmag.com/2015/10/31/toward-a-brighter-dawn-1936. First published 1936.

Tomlinson, Barbara. 2013. "To Tell The Truth and Not Get Trapped: Desire, Distance, and Intersectionality at the Scene of the Argument." *Signs: A Journal of Women in Culture and Society* 38 (4): 993–1018.

Tong, Rosemarie, and Tina Fernandes Botts. 2014. "Women of Color Feminisms." In *Feminist Thought: A More Comprehensive Introduction*, by Rosemary Tong, 211–54. 4th ed. Boulder: Westview Press.

Trask, Haunani-Kay. 1991. "Coalition-Building between Natives and Non-Natives." *Stanford Law Review* 43:1197–1213.

Truth, Sojourner. (1851) 1995. "Woman's Rights." In *Words of Fire: An Anthology of African-American Feminist Thought*, edited by Beverly Guy-Sheftall, 36–37. New York: The New Press.

Tuck, Eve, and K. Wayne Yang. 2012. "Decolonization Is Not a Metaphor." *Decolonization: Indigeneity, Education and Society* 1 (1): 1–40.

———. 2014. "Unbecoming Claims: Pedagogies of Refusal in Qualitative Research." *Qualitative Inquiry* 20 (6): 811–18.

TWWA (Third World Women's Alliance). c. 1970. *Triple Jeopardy: Racism, Imperialism, Sexism.* Third World Women's Alliance Records, 1971–1980. Sophia Smith Collection, Smith College, Northampton MA.

Tyner, James A. 2007. "Urban Revolutions and the Spaces of Black Radicalism." In *Black Cartographies and the Politics of Space*, edited by Katherine McKittrick and Clyde Woods, 218–32. Toronto: Between the Lines.

Valdes, Francisco. 1995. "Sex and Race in Queer Legal Culture: Ruminations on Identities and Inter-connectivities." *Southern California Review of Law and Women's Studies* 5 (25): 57–66.

Vázquez, Carmen. 1991. "Bursting the Lavender Bubble." *Out/Look* 609:53–55.

———. 1993. "The Land That Never Has Been Yet: Dreams of a Gay Latina in the United States." In *The Third Pink Book: A Global View of Lesbian and Gay Liberation and Oppression*, edited by Aart Hendriks, Rob Tielman, and Evert van der Veen, 217–24. Buffalo NY: Prometheus.

————. 1997. "Spirit and Passion." In *Queerly Classed: Gay Men and Lesbians Write about Class*, edited by Susan Raffo, 121–34. Boston: South End Press.

————. 2005. Interview by Kelly Anderson. Transcript of video recording, May 12 and 13 and August 25. Voices of Feminism Oral History Project, Sophia Smith Collection, Smith College, Northampton MA.

————. 2010. Keynote Address. Butch Voices LA Conference, October 10, West Hollywood CA. http://bvla2010.com/keynote-award-speeches-2. Last accessed January 10, 2013.

Wallace, Michele. (1975) 2000. "Anger in Isolation: A Black Feminist's Search for Sisterhood." *Village Voice*, July 28, 6–7. Reprinted in *Let Nobody Turn Us Around: Voices of Resistance, Reform, and Renewal: An African American Anthology*, edited by Manning Marable and Leith Mullings, 520–23. New York: Rowman and Littlefield.

Weber, Clare. 2006. *Visions of Solidarity: U.S. Peace Activists in Nicaragua from War to Women's Activism and Globalization*. Lanham MD: Lexington.

Weber, Lynn. 1998. "A Conceptual Framework for Understanding Race, Class, Gender and Sexuality." *Psychology of Women Quarterly* 22:13–32.

————. 2010. *Understanding Race, Class, Gender, and Sexuality: A Conceptual Framework*. Oxford: Oxford University Press.

Wiegman, Robyn. 2012. *Object Lessons*. Durham: Duke University Press.

Young, Iris Marion. 1994. "Gender as Seriality: Thinking about Women as a Social Collective." *Signs: Journal of Women in Culture and Society* 19 (3): 713–38.

Yuval-Davis, Nira. 2006. "Intersectionality and Feminist Politics." *European Journal of Women's Studies* 13 (3): 193–209.

————. 2011. *Politics of Belonging: Intersectional Contestations*. London: Sage.

Zack, Naomi. 2005. *Inclusive Feminism: A Third Wave Theory of Women's Commonality*. Lanham MD: Rowman and Littlefield.

————. 2007. "Can Third-Wave Feminism Be Inclusive? Intersectionality, its Problems and New Directions." In *The Blackwell Guide to Feminist Philosophy*, edited by Linda Martín Alcoff and Eva Feder Kittay, 193–207. Malden MA: Blackwell.

INDEX

mestiza consciousness, 215

methodological nationalism, 200

micro-, meso-, macrolevels, 128–31, 156, 206

Mignolo, Walter, 201, 209–10, 211, 214

Mikkola, Mari, 110

Mission Cultural Center for Latino Arts, 175

modern/colonial gender system, 12, 220–22, 232

Mohanram, Radhika, 98

Mohanty, Chandra, 178

monistic categories of oppression/discrimination, 67, 82, 84, 118, 119, 136, 145, 158, 214, 223

Moore v. Hughes Helicopter (*Moore*), 81

Moraga, Cherríe, ix, xv, 39, 189

Morgan, Robin, 29

Morrill, Angie, 202

Mosell-Alexander, Sadie Tanner, 16

Mothers of Heroes and Martyrs, 181

Mujeres Unidas y Activas, 179

multidimensionality, 75, 81, 90, 126, 156–61, 209. *See also* multiplicity

multiple consciousness, 42, 45, 114, 190

multiple genders, 164, 217, 221

multiple identity, 166, 190, 206

multiple oppressions, 6, 8, 16, 19, 45, 46, 61, 133, 188, 202, 223, 225, 226

multiplicity, 75, 81, 90, 116, 119, 217, 223

multistability of oppression, 213

Mutua, Athena, 161

mutual constitution, 1, 9, 16, 18, 54, 55, 56, 60–61, 70, 115, 118, 129–30, 130–31, 135, 142, 203, 219–20

mutual exclusion. *See* exclusion

mutual exclusion critique, 125, 134–38, 151, 155

mythical norm, 167

myth of equivalent oppressions, 158

Najmanovich, Denise, 116

Nash, Jennifer C., 20, 63, 96, 127, 139, 199–200, 234

National Alliance of Black Feminists, 26

National Association for the Advancement of Colored People, 32

National Association of Colored Women (NACW), 72–73

National Black Feminist Organization, 26, 36

National Women's Studies Association (NWSA), 114

Native feminisms. *See* Indigenous feminism

necropolitics, 152, 154

Negro question, the, 32

New Materialism, 126, 146–49, 153–54

new materialist critique, 146–49

New York Domestic Workers' Union, 31

Okolosie, Lola, 236

one-drop rule, 89

Oppression Olympics, 158

Organization of Women of African and Asian Descent, 38

origin stories, 40, 153

Oyěwùmí, Oyèrónkẹ́, 221

Pandora's box metaphor, 83

Parker, Sharon, 214

parsimony objection, 164

Patil, Vrushali, 238

Payne v. Travenol (*Travenol*), 81

Perla, Héctor, 169, 175, 176

To order or obtain more information on these or other University of Nebraska Press titles, visit nebraskapress.unl.edu.

CPSIA information can be obtained
at www.ICGtesting.com
Printed in the USA
LVHW04*1451290418
575303LV00005B/56/P

9 780803 285552

Sowing the Seeds of Change

CHINESE STUDENTS,
JAPANESE TEACHERS,
1895–1905

*Studies of the East Asian Institute,
Columbia University*

The East Asian Institute is Columbia University's center for research, publication, and teaching on modern East Asia. The Studies of the East Asian Institute were inaugurated in 1962 to bring to a wider public the results of significant new research on Japan, China, and Korea.

PAULA HARRELL

Sowing the Seeds of Change

CHINESE STUDENTS,
JAPANESE TEACHERS,
1895–1905

Stanford University Press 1992
Stanford, California

Stanford University Press
Stanford, California
© 1992 by the Board of Trustees of the
Leland Stanford Junior University

Printed in the United States of America

CIP data appear at the end of the book

To Edgar with love

Acknowledgments

This book has taken shape over years of research and reflection in China, Japan, and Washington, D.C.—and in more unlikely places, like Thailand and Jordan. I owe a debt of gratitude on this long road traveled to a great many friends for the constancy of their kind interest and gentle inquiries about current progress. As both friend and mentor, I would like especially to thank Dr. C. Martin Wilbur who encouraged me through the years to pursue my fascination with the Sino-Japanese encounter and the student experience in Meiji Japan. My thanks go also to Joshua Fogel, Andrew Nathan, and Morris Rossabi for their very helpful comments and advice at various stages of finalizing the work; to Barbara Mnookin for her keen editorial eye; and to Frank Shulman for tracing my whereabouts to keep me informed of new developments in the field. Research for the book was carried out primarily at the Hibiya Library, Tōyō Bunko, and Diet Library in Tokyo and at the Library of Congress in Washington, D.C. I am grateful to the staffs of these institutions for their generous help in locating source materials. Chu Mi Wiens of the Library of Congress, the late Shumpei Okamoto, friend from Columbia days, and Eiji Seki, now Japan's ambassador to Hungary, very kindly checked most of my translations from Chinese and Japanese. In the final summing up, I am most deeply grateful to my husband, Edgar, and to my three sons, Erik, Philip, and Matthew, for their constant good cheer and unwavering optimism that the last page would finally be written.

Contents

Photograph section follows p. 144

Sowing the Seeds of Change

CHINESE STUDENTS,
JAPANESE TEACHERS,
1895–1905

Introduction

ON A SPRING DAY IN 1896, thirteen young Chinese arrived in Tokyo without fanfare or publicity at the start of an experiment. They were the first Chinese sent to Japan as students under a new bilateral arrangement, pioneers in what was to become a full-fledged overseas study program designed to revitalize China with lessons from the Meiji development experience. One can picture the new arrivals, excited yet apprehensive as they stepped down from the train at Shimbashi Station, searching amid the crowd of kimonos, school uniforms, and business suits for the official welcoming party from the Chinese legation. In this first view of Tokyo, vibrant, easily blending old and new, they could sense the success of Meiji Japan. Yet other, conflicting emotions must have intruded as well: the Asian faces they saw were at once the pesky "dwarf people" of common parlance and the victors over China in the short and humiliating Sino-Japanese War brought to a final settlement only the year before.

One can imagine, too, that the thirteen Chinese, with their traditional queues and long gowns, were themselves the object of curious stares as they stood in the crowd at Shimbashi waiting for trunks to be unloaded and transportation to be arranged to legation quarters. For four of the new arrivals, being the object of curiosity and, worse still, the butt of jokes of children on the street, became unbearable after a few weeks, harder to stomach even than the steady diet of Japanese food. Utterly homesick, the four abandoned the program and returned to China for good. For the rest, a special course of studies was arranged by the principal of the Tokyo Higher Normal School, Kanō Jigorō. A hardy seven pursued the course to completion, receiving diplomas from their proud mentor at the end of the 1899 school year. A contemporary photograph shows three of the successful candidates in pale scholars' gowns standing behind three seated Japanese teachers, the handsome, mustachioed Kanō commanding the scene from the center.

By the time these first overseas students, or *liu hsueh-sheng* (*ryū-gakusei* in Japanese), had completed their course in 1899, another 100 Chinese students were enrolled in Japanese schools. The figure for 1902 stood at 400–500; for 1903 it was 1,000. By 1905–6, a year after the Russo-Japanese War, between 8,000 and 9,000 Chinese were studying in Tokyo; in fact, some estimates suggest as many as 20,000.[1] Over five years, what had started as a government-sanctioned overseas study program, modest in size, had mush-roomed into a large-scale and largely unregulated migration of students abroad, the first such phenomenon anywhere in the world. Not only was it a large group; it was an increasingly rebellious group, prone to the anti-dynastic dissidence that eventually led to revolution in 1911. How this happened, how thousands of overseas students became alienated from the Ch'ing state, cutting ties to tradition along with their queues, is the subject of the study to follow.

The process of alienation from central authority, while appearing in acute form in the case of China's youth, was part of a larger trend toward the diversification of society and consequent adjustment of central/local power relationships occurring throughout the last century of Ch'ing rule. Unraveling the complex of forces driving this slow transformation of traditional structures and social groupings—the increase in commercial activity, explosive population growth, and, prodded by the Western capitalist advance, the expansion of trade, communications, and modern industry—lies beyond the scope of this introductory discussion. What is essential here, anticipating points to come, is simply to delineate the changes themselves, particularly in the closing decades of the nineteenth century, for it was only in the context of a changing China that the role of youth took on pivotal importance.

The most immediate signs of change late in the century were in the material, physical world: more telegraph lines and steamships, the growth of cities, an increase in traded goods, and the appearance of small manufacturing industries, processing plants, and credit and banking offices. Research is just beginning on the various provincial economies, particularly on patterns of economic growth in China's interior provinces. But certainly along the coast, there is evidence that a burst of commercial activity beginning in the 1870's had a transforming effect on society as a whole, creating new career opportunities, increasing geographical and occupational mobility, and blurring traditional class distinctions. The old, separate categories of "gentry" and "merchants" gave way in common usage to the composite "gentry-merchants" (*shen-shang*); as time went on, "gentry-merchant-reformers" might have been a more apt term. By whatever label, this was a new social elite, still prizing rank and privilege within the traditional power structure, yet actively engaged in the modernizing sector as well, and possessing a political independence born of economic self-sufficiency and a mastery of new skills and information. Out of this stratum emerged a new-style community leader, the "elite manager," who assumed public management functions at the local level—establishing and directing educational, welfare, and public works organizations, for example— often bypassing centrally appointed county officials and their staffs of local-hires.[2]

As these new, unofficial organizations chipped away at the center's traditional control network, an expanding press in the hands of certain elite activists undercut central authority in another way, inviting public appraisal of Peking's competence in national decision making. Both developments were a measure of the growing incapacity of the Manchu court and central bureaucracy either to restrict or to tap the potential of the newly invigorated local elites. Power was slipping from Manchu hands. The enormous pressures of internal rebellion and foreign intrusion, bringing fiscal burdens and problems of control that would have strained the most effective government, overwhelmed a group too ingrown, corrupt, and backward-looking to be capable of consistent leadership. The center's reliance on provincial military forces during and after the Taiping upheaval in the mid-nineteenth century established a pattern of dependence difficult to reverse. Provincial, not central, authorities thereafter took the initiative in planning and implementing modernization programs. Governors-general like Chang Chih-tung, Liu K'un-i, and Yuan Shih-k'ai, commanding strategic provinces in the south and northeast, held a preponderance of power, garnering support from local elites in their own provinces on the one hand and, on the other, pushing reform on the center. For all their political assertiveness vis-à-vis the Court and metropolitan officialdom, however, these provincial leaders still saw it in their interests to maintain an effectively functioning central structure. When the Court in a last-ditch recentralizing bid endorsed the set of far-reaching administrative reforms known as the New Policies (*hsin-cheng*) in 1901, Chang and his colleagues took a lead role in directing the new program, hoping to perpetuate their own power within a modified imperial system.[3]

The institutional consequences of the power shifts and associated economic and social changes highlighted above were modest, certainly before 1905 and even after. Both provincial bureaucrats and local elites were reluctant to cut their ties with the basic imperial model, the old familiar edifice of monarchy, bureaucracy, and legitimating ideology that guarded a highly consensual society against dreaded chaos. Accepting the status quo institutionally was made easier by the fact that operationally the state was becoming less directly intrusive at lower levels, leaving room for maneuver outside the system: in 1900, China's population of 400 million, about 100 million more than in 1800, was governed by a regular civil service whose numbers had remained fixed at no more than 40,000. Lacking the means to finance the expansion of local bureaucracies, the government tolerated the growth of informal subadministrations to handle the extra workload locally. At the same time, the civil service recruitment system continued to issue qualifying degrees, either through examination or through sale, forcing the swelling ranks of would-be officials into jobs outside the state sector.

While the imperial idea remained intact for the moment, there was a pervasive change in perspective within the new social elite that suggested less certainty about its long-term prospects. It is difficult to define precisely the facets of this changed perspective, but certainly included were a new openness, a new focus on national goals, a general acceptance of the need to modernize, a hint that reform outside tradition was worth considering. Even the central authority, operating more collegially than in the past, showed greater tolerance for competing views (couched in the proper *ch'ing-i*, "pure discussion" or "disinterested opinion," format), while the local press boldly demanded more competent leadership and wider consultations in policy formation.[4]

The decision of China's top leadership to send students to Japan in the years after the Sino-Japanese War was reflective of this new reformist perspective. For the first time, "opening to the outside world," to use the current formulation, was endorsed as part of national policy. In the 1890's, just as in the 1980's, the shift away from a traditional policy of self-reliance toward a more active strategy of learning from abroad was precipitated by national crisis—in the 1890's, defeat by the Japanese, in the 1980's, a stagnating economy. In both cases, international comparisons, the apparent success of the West and Japan in achieving their wealth and power goals, fueled arguments for a more pragmatic approach to borrowing from the outside. Chang Chih-tung popularized "what works" in his *t'i-yung* slogan of the 1890's (*Chung-hsueh wei t'i, Hsi-hsueh wei yung* or "Chinese learning for the essential principles, Western learning for practical applications"), just as Deng Xiao-ping did in the 1980's with *pai-hei mao* (*Pu kuan pai mao hei mao, chih yao chua chu lao shu shih hao mao* or "It doesn't matter if a cat is black or white as long as it catches mice").

Support for greater pragmatism and new openness was in no way intended to signal more freedom of thought or political pluralism. Chinese initiators of programs of study abroad and outside assistance had in mind controlled reform in a controlled society. The objective, ultimately, was to strengthen the state by modernizing its underpinnings—the economy, the military, the school system. Students sent overseas were to contribute to this process by selectively introducing foreign technology and ideas. As we will see in the chapters to follow, how to stay master of the ship, how to keep reform from spilling over into the political sphere, was a nagging worry for those powerful provincial governors like Chang Chih-tung who were the promoters of the reform enterprise, and certainly for the Manchu hard-liners at the center. It was precisely on the issue of power-sharing that Chang and others in China's top leadership group came to differ with members of the new elites—bankers, businessmen, educators, and intellectuals—and their offspring, the younger generation of students, whose commitment to the imperial system was the least firm of all.

Recent scholarship has contributed greatly to our understanding of the dynamics of late Ch'ing politics, particularly of the role played by provincial leaders, nongovernmental elites, and new political thinkers. Less attention has been paid to the "twenty-something" generation, a group caught up in the foreign crises of the 1890's, less inclined than their elders to look to the past for solutions to present problems, less fearful of chaos. The focus of the present book is on one of this generation's most politically active elements, the Chinese students in Japan. It is the thesis of the study that these overseas students, themselves a product of a changing society, greatly accelerated the pace of change. For the first time, thousands of young Chinese had the direct experience of living in a country more advanced than their own; they went to Japan looking for solutions to China's backwardness and came away literate in political alternatives. They were willing to say and do what thousands more within their own elite circles were only thinking. There was a tremendous multiplier effect to student dissidence, in part because theirs was simply a bolder articulation of oppositionist sentiments that had already taken hold among Chinese elites, in part because, in reinserting themselves into Chinese society, they tended to join the modernizing sector—new schools, new armies, new agencies—where they had greater independence of action.

Of course, this is all with the benefit of hindsight. In the late 1890's, when decisions were being made on overseas study, there were few patterns to look to and certainly no precedent to suggest that those entrusted with the mission of strengthening China might undermine the regime in power. To the contrary, the prime example in the minds of the Chinese leaders, Meiji Japan, suggested a positive outcome, that youth trained abroad could contribute to planned reform in a law-and-order society. As we will see in Chapters 1 and 2, Japan's success in creating a strong, unified state made a profound impression on Chinese Japan-watchers after the Sino-Japanese War. This, and the fact that Japan had made enough progress in building national power to qualify as a competitor with the West in the Pacific, accounted in part for the "learn from Japan—or, more accurately, "learn about the West through Japan"—focus of China's initial opening to the outside world. Other factors had to do with cost effectiveness. Study in Japan meant lower transportation and living costs than study in Western countries; language and cultural affinities offered the possibility of learning more, faster.

But it was not simply a case of China's awakening to the multiple benefits of studying the Meiji model. Japan was pushing the idea. The thrust of Meiji foreign policy was the expansion of Japanese interests on the Asian mainland. Japanese businessmen, teachers, military advisers, energized by "Asia for the Asians" and "common culture" themes, made their way to China with the full backing of their own government, and, uncharacteristic as it seemed, at the request of the Chinese. Study in Japan for Chinese fit in with this new vision of Sino-Japanese cooperation. It was, to use current terminology, a single element in Japan's development assistance package for China, one that offered mutual benefits: for Chinese, the chance to learn the techniques of modernization, for Japanese, the prospect of exerting influence on those intended to be China's future leaders. To both sides, training Chinese with Japanese help and thereby contributing to a strengthened China, seemed to hold promise of developing a counterforce against the bogey that faced them both—the threatening presence of the West in East Asia.

The restructuring of the Sino-Japanese relationship in a world dominated by the Western powers is another dimension of the present study. It is a field inadequately explored by Western scholars, despite the richness of materials and the continuing centrality of the relationship, political, economic, and cultural, to the balance of power in East Asia and the Pacific.[5] Sending students to Japan was an indicator of the new level of contacts that began in the 1880's and became more important in the postwar decade, when an increasingly pragmatic China and a Japan with a growing sense of mission saw their interests coincide. The study-in-Japan program, in other words, was a product not only of a changing China but of a changing Sino-Japanese relationship. In the sudden bloom of good relations, a brief interlude between two wars, thousands of Chinese youth had their eyes opened to the outside world through the filter of the Meiji experiment. This put a peculiar stamp on the attitudes they developed toward Western ideologies and institutions, toward Great Power politics, and, for better or for worse, toward Japan itself.

As 1905 drew to a close, it became clear that, in terms of the political goals set out by the original planners, the study-in-Japan program was a dismal failure. The Ch'ing structure, far from being revitalized by the program, was weakening under pressures exerted in part by its products. And Sino-Japanese bonds, far from being strengthened, were rapidly deteriorating. The overseas study experience had produced thousands of disaffected youth, core members of China's first truly national revolutionary organization, the T'ung-meng Hui (Alliance Society), which was founded in August, and instigators of an anti-Japanese protest of unprecedented size and scope in December. From this point on, China's domestic politics entered a more turbulent period.

The story of the students, how their experience in Japan transformed their outlook on the world, how it politicized them, is the heart of the present work. There are certain pitfalls, of course, in trying to illuminate the life of "the students" rather than focusing on the experiences of one of them. Ever present is the danger of attributing to the group as a whole the views of its more articulate members. Furthermore, the student group in Japan was large (perhaps 10,000 in the peak year 1905–6), removed enough in time to preclude the use of interview techniques and other sophisticated methods of data gathering, and made up of individuals differing markedly from each other in age and origins, not to speak of personality.

In an effort to present as complete a picture as possible, the present work examines the student group from several vantage points. Chapter 3 provides a bird's-eye view. It uses available data to analyze such factors as the students' socioeconomic background, age composition, and enrollment patterns. The chapter then shifts to the psychological dimension, examining the individual experience of the Chinese student in Japan and his interaction with the Japanese. Having established some sort of profile of the typical *liu hsueh-sheng*, Chapters 4–8 focus on the overseas students in action—organizing, writing, striking, demonstrating. Chapter 4 is a transition piece, a catchall of "firsts"—the first student organizations, the first translation ventures, the first foray into radical politics. Chapters 5–8 then proceed to detailed case studies of student protest movements and involvement in revolutionary ventures. This was the period, 1902–5, when student numbers increased twentyfold and Japan, for many, became less a place of study than a base for political intrigue. With Chapter 9, the spotlight moves from what the students were doing to what they were saying, to an analysis of their intellectual concerns and political tendencies as revealed in the pages of the student magazines published in Japan beginning in 1903. The Epilogue offers some reflections on the broad significance of the study-in-Japan program, and of study abroad generally for the 1911 Revolution and for China's latest phase of reform.

Several factors fed the political activism that became characteristic of the Chinese students in Japan. One was the simple fact of being away from China, less constrained by traditional codes of behavior and able to observe from a distance China's political leadership and manner of interaction with the international community. What the students saw was a China on the downturn economically and militarily, rent internally by the Boxer atrocities, pressured from the outside by Russia and Japan in the northeast and France in the south. Their initial discontent with the weakness of China's response turned to frustration with China's policy makers and, finally, when it became clear that the student voice would not be heard, with the policy-making system itself. The anti-Manchuism that the students came to espouse was not so much a matter of ethnic bias as one of simple anti-authoritarianism. It was directed not only against the Manchus but against powerful Chinese figures like Chang Chih-tung who were connected with the Manchu establishment—the very men, ironically, who stepped up government-financed support for study in Japan in the post-Boxer years.

A second and related factor in the student turn to activism was watching Japan on the rise. A mere ten years after its triumph over China in 1895, Japan ranked as an ally of Britain, victor over Russia, and defender of its own sphere of influence on the China mainland. There was a curious duality in the Chinese view of Japan as success followed success. On the one hand, Chinese were admiring, even proud, that an Asian nation could make the grade; on the other, they were suspicious of Japanese intentions toward China and resentful of anything that smacked of arrogance.

In an odd juxtaposition, the most pro-Japanese Chinese of the decade included not only pragmatic upholders of the Ch'ing state like Chang Chih-tung but also Sun Yat-sen, China's most prominent anti-Ch'ing revolutionary. The former were after Japanese technology; the latter sought Japanese backing for anti-Ch'ing resistance. Sun went far beyond Chang and others in emphasizing the positive, "common culture" aspects of the Sino-Japanese relationship. In fact, so much has been written about Sun, who lived in Japan off and on after 1895, that the pan-Asianist dream he shared with his Japanese friends has been seen as enjoying wider currency in Chinese thinking than was actually the case. An analysis of the student encounter with Japan and the Japanese shows, on the contrary, a steady rise in both anti-Japanese sentiments and the willingness to express them.

At the heart of the matter is the fact that Sun's Japanese contacts differed markedly in kind and extent from those of the students. Apart from some prominent Japanese politicians who showed a tolerant interest in Sun—as in the reform advocate K'ang Yu-wei and others—as a possible influential force in Chinese politics, Sun had personal friends among Japanese, right-wing activists totally committed to him and their joint cause of promoting revolution in China. He was treated as a respected equal. He was not, as the students were, forced to deal on an everyday basis with a general public that tended to look down on Chinese, nor did he face, as they did, an array of Japanese authority figures—teachers, school administrators, public officials. Students clashed with Japanese at all levels, increasingly so as Japan's drive to consolidate power in Korea and Manchuria seemed to make mockery of "common culture" ties. The majority of students came away from their Japan experience with a strongly anti-Japanese and, more generally, anti-imperialist bias, and this was an important ingredient of modern Chinese nationalism. But even here there was a paradox: for a generation trying to establish China's place in the world, imperialism, defined in Social Darwinist terms as the ultimate in national power, was not only something to resist but something to strive for.

A third factor that turned Chinese students in the direction of oppositional politics was the Meiji intellectual environment. For all of its emphasis on orthodoxy in nationalist thought, Meiji Japan was—at least relative to Ch'ing China—a hothouse of competing ideas. Caught up in this environment, students became more cosmopolitan in outlook, interested in different political systems and views, and increasingly inclined to question traditional beliefs. They were China's new liberals. Believers in freedom of expression, they were among the first in modern China to use the press as a tool to inform, to popularize anti-authoritarian views, and to convince the public of the need for national unity to survive in a world of competing powers. Nationalism was the topic given most coverage in the pages of the student magazines, particularly theories of national power from the Social Darwinist lexicon.

By 1905 and the end of the first phase of the *liu hsueh-sheng* story, Chang and others in the Ch'ing regime were poised to "deepen the reforms," to use the current phrase. But it was the old problem of too little, too late. The opposition had been radicalized. In ever-larger numbers, the educated elite, many of them young graduates of Japanese schools or products of the new schools in China, demanded immediate and thoroughgoing political reform: namely, sharing power through representative institutions. Some believed this could be achieved through change from within, incorporating the Manchus into some kind of constitutional monarchy. Others, student members of Sun's T'ung-meng Hui among them, felt that ridding China of Ch'ing rulership altogether was the necessary precondition for broadening popular participation in China's political life and putting China on a fast track to modernization. The year 1911 saw the ouster of the Ch'ing but left unresolved other issues raised by turn-of-the-century dissidents: how to institutionalize political pluralism, establish a feasible alternative to reform from above, and, as the ultimate goal, catch up economically with Japan and the West.

ONE

Origins of the
Study-in-Japan Program

I N THE 1870's, a study-in-Japan program for Chinese would have been unthinkable. China and Japan had no formal diplomatic relations until 1871, and it took another six years for an exchange of permanent overseas missions. In any case, Japan was then too technologically backward itself to play the role of teacher. Logically enough, it was to the West that China turned to get its initial, firsthand look at the outside world.

In 1871, the very year Chinese and Japanese were hammering out the details of their commercial accord, a Chinese Yale graduate, Yung Wing, was putting the finishing touches on a project to finance a U.S. education for some 120 Chinese youths, mostly poor boys from Canton. It was a sound project educationally; with the joint support of Yale College faculty and the Connecticut Board of Education, the youngsters spent five years or more living with American families and attending secondary schools in small towns in the Connecticut River Valley. But the project was discontinued after 1881 amid criticism from conservatives at home that it was too costly and had produced an Americanized product, poorly prepared in his own language and culture. A second effort, actually a series of arrangements, directed primarily to training Foochow arsenal personnel in military industries in England and France, suffered from chronic underfunding and was eventually suspended in the mid-1880's.[1] All together, whatever potential there might have been to expand study abroad in this period was lost in problems of financing, cultural distance, and the lack of full government-to-government support. In short, it was an idea before its time.

By contrast, the study-in-Japan program as it took shape after the

Sino-Japanese War was very much an official, bilateral arrangement, grounded in mutual policy interests reinforced by affinities of language and culture. On the China side, the decision to send students to Japan was not a sudden inspiration, a knee-jerk reaction to military defeat. It was part of a growing consensus among China's top leaders, beginning in the 1880's, that nationwide reform of the educational system was key to the success of the country's modernization efforts. It also reflected a new appreciation, again developing over time, of Japan's potential role in helping China modernize. Likewise, the Japanese postwar decision to accommodate Chinese students was not a sudden, magnanimous gesture by a victorious nation. It grew out of a belief, increasingly popular among Japanese from the 1880's on, that Japan had a special role to play in China's political and economic life.

The purpose of this chapter is to examine how Japan's assistance policy to China, which included study in Japan, evolved out of changing perceptions on both sides of the goals of a modern Sino-Japanese relationship. The emphasis is on doers rather than thinkers, on those grappling with current realities as opposed to classical abstractions. It is not always possible, of course, to make such a neat distinction, nor should it be thought that dealing with one another was the only, or even the central, concern of most Chinese and Japanese of the period, whether of activist or intellectual bent.

Quite to the contrary, perhaps the most striking feature of the Sino-Japanese relationship was the extent to which it was a by-product of a more urgent concern with Western inroads in the region. *Seiryoku tōzen*, "Western power advancing eastward," as the Japanese termed the mid-nineteenth-century explosion of Western power into the Pacific, jolted China and Japan with the realities of superior military and economic power and a cultural alternative dominated by themes of progress and survival of the fittest. From that point on, the compelling issue for both countries was how to reconcile modern technological civilization—which came in Western guise—with traditional cultural values and political norms. Fear of the Western advance, rather than purely bilateral issues, defined both Japanese initiatives (beginning in the 1860's) to establish treaty ties with China and the Chinese response to those initiatives. From Japan's standpoint, closer relations with its East Asian neighbor appeared a potential way to build a line of defense against Western encroachment. In China, the Western menace fueled arguments both for and against opening up to Japan. The ultimate decision to yield to Japanese insistence was based on the "better the devil you know" argument—that it was wiser to deal with Japan as it was in 1870 than to risk dealing with a future Japan fortified by Western alliances and Western technology.

A second feature of the Sino-Japanese relationship was the very newness of it. When China and Japan signed their commercial accord in 1871, it was after two centuries of no official contacts and only limited trade, a curious period of nonrelations prompted by Ch'ing China's preoccupation with consolidating power on the mainland and Tokugawa isolationism.[2] People-to-people contacts were rare during this period: a few Ming loyalists who took refuge in Japan following the Manchu takeover, the occasional Japanese monk given permission to visit temples of renown in China, Chinese traders calling in at Nagasaki, and Japanese seamen shipwrecked on the China coast. Evidence suggests that the Tokugawa, at least, relied heavily on these informal—and in the last case, illiterate—sources for an update on their not-too-distant neighbor, this in itself apt testimony to the remoteness of the relationship.[3] An important consequence of this hiatus was that Chinese and Japanese of the 1870's and even of the late 1890's, when the first Chinese students began trickling into Japan, knew little about each other's contemporary society. The fact that four of the first thirteen students headed home after only a few weeks suggests how lacking in knowledge both they and their sponsors were about the realities of life in Meiji Japan.

Still, the Sino-Japanese relationship had a unique psychological/ historical dimension that helped bridge the knowledge gap: the consciousness of shared traditions—Chinese traditions—stretching into the distant past. Even during the Tokugawa, a voluminous flow of Chinese books into Japan via Nagasaki ensured a continued discourse on things Chinese. It was not an uncritical view on Japan's part. This is not the place for a discussion of the *kokugaku* (national learning) versus *kangaku* (Chinese learning) controversy that enlivened Japanese intellectual circles in the eighteenth and early nineteenth centuries except to note, first, that it led to a revision in thinking about the validity of Chinese systems in the Japanese setting, and second, that it had ceased to be a burning issue by midcentury.[4] At this point, that is, familiarity with Chinese history and Chinese classical writings was, like schooling in Greek and Latin for Westerners, simply the hallmark of the well-educated man. It did not imply or require admiration of contemporary China. It was a commitment not to nation, but to culture, or, more precisely, to what was perceived as universal culture.

Even this began to erode in the Meiji years as it became increasingly clear that by modern measures of worth—wealth and power—Japan was the preeminent state in Asia. By the end of the century, common culture themes much touted by Japanese pan-Asianists and their few Chinese sympathizers were as much the product of political expediency—history reactivated in the service of modern political goals—as a reflection of a genuine belief in a shared cultural legacy as a legitimate basis for détente.

Chinese Perspectives on Japan

During the first twenty years of modern Sino-Japanese relations, when the major foreign policy concern was Western encroachment, relatively few Chinese found compelling reason to think about Japan. China's window on Japan was provided mainly by diplomats assigned to the Tokyo legation, a total of around 100 in the period from 1877 to 1894. Many found time outside their official duties for scholarly pursuits, producing works of high quality on Japanese culture, history, and contemporary society aimed to counter Chinese stereotypes about Japan. Still, the total output was small in the prewar period. Only about thirty research works and travel accounts on Japan were published between 1868 and 1894, compared with some 300 in the period 1895–1911.[5]

Though foreign service was not the most sought-after career path for Chinese bureaucrats, Tokyo in the early days attracted a number of promising young scholar-officials. Ho Ju-chang, China's first minister to Japan, was a thirty-nine-year-old *chin-shih* (metropolitan graduate) who later, just before the Sino-French War, became manager of the Foochow shipyard. Ho compiled a record of his mission, offering details of his trip, describing his quest for a suitable rental to house the legation, and listing Japan's central government offices and regional political divisions. He had little to say about the Japanese beyond such prosaic utterances as "Japanese men are rude; the women refined. They are a short people." But perhaps we can forgive him this superficial account, knowing that the pressing question of the disposition of the Ryukyu Islands, coupled with the minutiae of getting the legation operational, took his time and attentions elsewhere.[6]

It was Ho Ju-chang's hand-picked secretary of legation, Huang Tsun-hsien, who epitomized the best of the scholar-diplomats of the period. Huang, who was thirty and a recent *chü-jen* (provincial graduate) when he accompanied Ho to Japan in 1877, developed contacts with many influential Japanese intellectuals and politicians during his five years there.[7] "Developed contacts" perhaps has too modern a ring to it, the busy diplomat exploiting sources of information. In Huang's case, and for others to follow, "getting to know the Japanese" was only partly to function better on the job. It was also for literary reasons—to exchange poetry with appreciative Japanese intellectuals. For all the Europeanization of Japanese society in the early Meiji years, there were still many Japanese whose education in the Chinese Classics and poetic predilections made them eager Sinophiles.[8]

Poetry was not simply composed and exchanged. It was collected and published. Huang Tsun-hsien's first anthology, *Miscellaneous Poems on Japan* (Jih-pen tsa-shih shih), appeared in 1879. A kind of lyric accompaniment to a forty-volume research work he was in the process of writing, *Treatises on Japan* (Jih-pen-kuo chih; 1887), the poetry collection was evidently intended to entertain Chinese readers as it informed them about life in Japan. Huang, like most of his colleagues, did not understand Japanese and had to rely on the editorial comments and "written conversations" of Japanese friends in producing his final copy.[9]

Another man in Ho Ju-chang's Tokyo entourage who was actively involved in Japanese intellectual circles and knew the language well was a staffer named Wang Chih-pen. Wang was unusual in his evident contentment with Japanese life. After serving as tour guide for prominent China scholar Oka Senjin on his trip to China in 1884, Wang returned to Japan and spent the rest of his life there, roving the country and teaching Chinese composition at various private, clan-sponsored academies.[10]

Chinese diplomats assigned to cities other than Tokyo pursued the same literary interests. For example, a staff member named Huang Ch'ao-tseng, sent first (1881) to Kobe and then, two years later, to Yokohama, put together three informal collections of poetry during his tenure. In 1884, on orders from the new minister to Japan, Li Shu-ch'ang, Huang made an eight-month tour of Japan for purposes of compiling an anthology of Japanese poems. Ninety-six writers contributed to the resulting collection.[11]

Yao Wen-tung was another of Li Shu-ch'ang's staff members whose official duties were apparently no impediment to an active literary life. The thirty-year-old Yao arrived in Japan in 1882 and remained there until 1888, through the tour of Li's interim replacement Hsü Ch'eng-tsu. His poetic talents earned him the admiration of his Japanese literary friends and the sobriquet "our literary eminence." Yao's departure on home leave in 1885 was the occasion for a series of farewell banquets, culminating in a send-off feast in which his admirers dished up forty-one poems and five essays as the literary course. These were published a few years later, in 1889, in a volume commemorating the sixtieth birthday of Yao's mother. All together, twenty-two titles have been located under Yao's name, either works written by him on Japan or compilations by Japanese in his honor.

Yao's purpose in writing and publishing was not, as one might expect, to inform a Chinese readership about a literary tradition alien to their own—that is, a native Japanese literary output—but to introduce works composed by Japanese in *kanbun* (Chinese composition). For Yao, an appreciation of Chinese language and literature, symbol of Japan's ancient cultural debt, was a fitting basis for cementing modern Sino-Japanese ties.[12]

Yao's Japanese contacts over a six-year period were from all evidence extensive, warm, and genuine. Like so many of his colleagues, he obviously appreciated, even treasured, friendships with educated ("cultured") Japanese who themselves prized their sophistication in Chinese learning. Yet it was an oddly limited relationship in which what the Chinese found to respect in Japanese culture was only their own reflection: Japanese calligraphic and belletristic attainments in a Chinese medium. Other aspects of Japanese culture were viewed with a critical eye as being either inferior derivatives of things Chinese, unfortunate imitations of Western ways, or simply Japanese barbarisms.

Typical of Chinese commentary on Japan's native tradition and behavior is the diatribe of an anonymous Chinese author, writing in 1885. He objects to the custom of men and women bathing together, to the use of the solar calendar, and to the frivolity of the Japanese marriage ceremony. He accuses Japanese of being at once narrow-minded and promiscuous, even incestuous, in allowing certain family relationships (a widow marrying her brother-in-law, for example) not sanctioned by the Chinese Classics. He faults the Japanese government for its lack of principle, for slavishly studying the West, for interfering with private enterprise, and for its aggressive policy toward the Ryukyus and Taiwan. In fact, the author can find only two good things to say about Japan, which he mentions at the outset, oddly juxtaposed: Japanese prohibitions on opium and Christianity; and the convenience of Kobe's overpasses and two-laned bridges.[13]

Given this kind of prejudice, seeing that a Chinese import had been made over into something equal to—though different from—

the original came as a shock to many Chinese visitors. This was nowhere more evident than in their frustrated attempts to read street signs written in "Chinese" characters. How were they to know that the characters *yu tzu*, which might mean "your son" in Chinese, meant "egg" (*tamago*) in Japanese, or that tempura, a three-character word with the Chinese equivalents "heaven," "wife," and "net" referred to a Japanese version of fritters.

One topic that thoroughly roused anti-Japanese feelings was Japan's East Asia policy. Yao Wen-tung, for example, in an article he wrote in 1882 at the time of the crisis over Korea, argued that Japan was becoming ever-more arrogant and, like an overindulged child, must be chastised. The specifics of how to deal with Japan militarily he outlined in a work entitled *Japan's Geography and Military Might* (Jih-pen ti-li ping-yao), published by the Tsungli Yamen (China's Foreign Affairs Agency) in 1884.[14] The consensus of Chinese Japan-watchers was that while Japan presented a genuine threat, it was a threat China could contain. In the words of one legation staff member writing in 1887:

Taking the long view of the Asian scene, all things considered, it is a good thing that China and Japan are making contacts. However, if Japan steps up actions of cunning and guile, China, rich in resources and land area, is quite capable of either attacking Japan or defending itself. There is nothing essentially frightening about Japan.[15]

To Yao, too, it seemed that China had little to fear. According to him, China had taken the lead in the East Asian arms race, thanks to more than ten years of research, expenditures of millions, and the efforts of hundreds of talented people that had gone into turning out Western-standard weaponry. "It goes without saying that our armaments are superior to Japan's."[16] Such assessments seem astonishing, to say the least, considering what was to come a few years later, but the Chinese were not alone in their rosy view; many contemporary Western observers also thought that China had the military edge over Japan.[17]

Still, a few prewar Chinese commentators were free of the cultural blinders that caused so many of their colleagues to see nothing positive about Japan except its appreciation of Chinese belles lettres. Apart from the aforementioned Huang Tsun-hsien, Wang T'ao, a scholar-journalist who made a four-month visit to Japan in 1879, and Cheng Kuan-ying, a Shanghai businessman, were particularly influential in introducing the educated public in China to Meiji Japan's multifaceted approach to modernization. They were among the handful who early on saw in the Japanese modernizing experiment, in the attempt to adopt and acculturate Western technology and institutions, a possible model for China to follow.

In his seminal work *Treatises on Japan*, Huang wrote of the sweeping institutional changes then (1877) in progress:

After the Restoration, Japan copied the West in everything; systems of taxes, conscription, laws, schools, and the like were established. Only the creation of a national assembly, regarded with great importance in the various Western countries, is lagging behind. The reasons cited for this are a difference in national polity [*kuo-t'i*] or the fact that the people are backward.[18]

Huang was a keen observer of Japan's popular rights movement, which was at its most turbulent stage in the years he was with the legation. Whatever the outcome, he noted pointedly, the Japanese government had acknowledged the people's right both to discuss and to establish a new political system.

Turning to the Japanese economy, Huang described how the Meiji government through direct management and subsidies had played the leading role in stimulating growth in the manufacturing and transport sectors. He wrote admiringly of the government's drive to acquire new products and advanced technology from abroad. Japan had sent official missions to several foreign countries, he noted, to investigate agricultural techniques and new manufactures. Acting on their recommendations, the government purchased foreign agricultural products on a selective basis—sheep from North China, horses from New York, grapes, cotton, and tobacco from Europe— in an effort to introduce new farm enterprises into Japan. Along with this, schools were set up to instruct the citizenry in such areas as farm management and business techniques. As incentives to boost production, the government established competitive exhibitions of agricultural products, awarding a series of prizes in the Emperor's name.[19]

Discussions of Meiji modernization invariably settled on a comparison of China's performance with Japan's, using the West as the yardstick of success. Wang T'ao, for example, explained Japan's ability to command a measure of respect from Westerners this way:

It is because the Japanese strive for mastery over the entire range of Western methods [*hsi-fa*]. They have not yet been able to deprive the West of its foothold in their country, but they have adopted the West's strength and have shown a marked ability, in so doing, to rely on their own efforts [*neng tzu wei chih*].[20]

Huang echoed this view, pointing out, further, that while Japan was actively absorbing Western culture and while Western nations themselves continued to rapidly advance in wealth, power, and scientific achievement, Chinese persisted in sneering at all foreigners as barbarians. It was this "stupid self-deception" (*wu-chih yü-mei*), he said, that was at the root of China's weakness.[21] The same self-critical tone was found in Cheng's *Warnings to a Prosperous Age* (Sheng-shih wei-yen; 1892). How shameful, he wrote, that the largest country in Asia finds itself surpassed by a small country like Japan. Or again, "Our population and land area are ten times those of Japan, yet we don't have half the number of trained people or schools offering a Western curriculum as Japan."[22]

Such self-criticism could not erase an attitude of condescension. Beware of exaggerating Japan's achievements, warned Wang T'ao. Japan was "outwardly strong but rotten at the core."[23] In an 1888 commentary, K'ang Yu-wei, a major reform figure of the postwar period, expressed the prevailing view:

Japan is a small island, disadvantaged in terms of natural resources. [Yet] in recent years, its leadership has effected reforms and instituted political change. Within ten years, many old patterns have been abolished and the groundwork laid to initiate [new programs]. [Japan has] pacified the Ryukyus in the south and developed the Ainu in the north. The great European nations cast a sidelong glance [at Japan], yet dare not pry. Now, given China's large land area, abundance of natural resources, sizable population, traditions of able kingship, model of governmental organization finely honed by a succession of philosophers, unified mode of thinking, and, capping all this, the benevolent virtues of the Empress Dowager and the Emperor, what weakness is there that could hold [China] back?[24]

Japanese Asia Activists

Though the desire to understand, emulate, and "catch up" with the West was a driving force throughout the Meiji period, there were lingering doubts about the compatibility of Western-style modernity and Japanese-ness. While Chinese held fast to their cultural superiority, Japanese were faced with choosing between two universal cultures—Western and Chinese—each with origins outside a purely native tradition. Accepting the Western alternative, as most Japanese did in the early Meiji years (our Sinophiles friendly with Chinese legation staff were a small, if prominent, minority) seemed to necessitate rejecting the Chinese. The most clearly articulated version of this view was the *datsu-A* or "escape from Asia" proposition put forth by the educator-philosopher Fukuzawa Yukichi: that culturally and politically Japan should dissolve ties with countries like China and Korea on the grounds that they were backward. For "if we keep bad company," Fukuzawa warned, "we cannot avoid a bad name."[25]

Implicit in the *datsu-A* message was that Japan stood unique among Asian nations in having the potential to pattern its growth after the Western model. In stressing Japan's uniqueness, *datsu-A* supporters shared something fundamental with their ideological opponents, a small but growing group of young intellectuals and publicists active from the 1880's on who decried what they perceived as Japan's overindulgence in Westernization. For these anti-Westernizers, Japan was unique not because it stood apart from the rest of Asia in its potential for emulating the West, but precisely because it was Asian and could offer a development model different from, yet as good as, that of Western nations. This was the message of those who in the 1880's and 1890's sought to revive public interest in Japan's Chinese/Asian origins, celebrating the "Mongolian civilization" that had developed along the Yellow River as equal in maturity and sophistication to Western civilization.[26]

In part because cultural choice was forced on the Japanese, in part because from the early Meiji years Japan's national security was linked to mainland concerns, what to do about Asia became a burning ideological issue in prewar Japan in a way not duplicated in China. Though still a minority, the Japanese who gave priority to China/Asia concerns formed a larger, more diverse group than those on the China side who focused on Japan. Japan had its share of China-watchers, to be sure, diplomats stationed on the mainland responsible for sending a flow of official information to Tokyo. But unique to the Japanese side were two additional and eventually overlapping categories of people concerned about Asia: participants in special interest organizations (*yūshi*) and superpatriots (*shishi*). The difference between them was more a matter of style than conviction, the part-timer with other professional credentials and concerns versus the full-time activist. In the first category were political party stalwarts, members of the House of Peers, top Meiji government officials, and journalist-intellectuals. The second consisted of a hodgepodge of soldiers of fortune, business-promoters, crusaders, and hustlers. Both *yūshi* and *shishi* were in agreement in their concern over the excessive Westernization of Japan and their commitment to Asian solidarity in the face of the Western advance. China, within the context of national security and economic development objectives, represented opportunity.

The earliest effort to promote improved Sino-Japanese relations and draw attention to Asian issues was a small, officially sanctioned Sino-Japanese friendship society called the Kō-A Kai (Revive Asia Society), set up in Tokyo in 1880. Funded in part by the Emperor, the Kō-A Kai counted in its membership the Chinese minister to Japan Ho Ju-chang and a number of prominent Japanese, including Count Nagaoka Moriyoshi of the House of Peers and Yanagihara Zenkō, the leading negotiator during the 1871 Sino-Japanese treaty talks. The militant *kō-A shugi* (revive Asia-ism) of some of the members offended others, and the name was changed to the more neutral-sounding Ajia Kyōkai (Asia Association) in 1883.[27]

In 1890, *yūshi* and *shishi* joined hands and founded the Tōhō-kyōkai (Oriental Association). Initiated by a few old China hands with military and business connections, the group was dedicated to overcoming the information gap on Asia—"Although we have people who are familiar with things from the faraway West, there are none with a thorough knowledge of conditions in the various Asian countries nearby"—thereby encouraging Japanese trade and settlement within the region. The new organization drew considerable support. Around 300 people had joined by the summer of 1891; on the eve of the Sino-Japanese War the membership was almost 1,000.[28] It was a diverse group. Liberal and conservative politicians, many Western-educated, joined with journalists, adventure-seekers and entrepreneurs. At least two young members were soon to rise to national position—the association's vice-president, Prince Konoe Atsumaro, German-educated representative of the old nobility, who was a member and later (in 1896 at the age of 33) president of the House of Peers, and Komura Jutarō, a graduate of Harvard Law School, who served as foreign minister during the Russo-Japanese War.[29] The leader of the Liberal Party, Ōkuma Shigenobu, was a Tō-hōkyōkai member, as was his colleague Inukai Ki. Other prominent members were the journalist Kuga Katsunan, the Liberal Party radical Ōi Kentarō, Arao Kiyoshi, promoter of expanded Sino-Japanese trade, and Tōyama Mitsuru, doyen of Japan's ultranationalist movement. The fact that over the next decades these people, diverse in background, united in commitment, continued to interact in similar Asia groups lent consistency to Japan's outlook on the rest of Asia.

While Kō-A Kai and Tōhōkyōkai members were working to convince the home audience of the primacy of Asian relationships, other Japanese of the *shishi* variety, seeking a more direct involvement, made their way to China for purposes of research, trade, and adventure. Before 1896, these missionaries for a Japan-led Asian front were few in number, though in the recounting of individual exploits they have often taken on larger-than-life proportions. What led them to China in the first place were not only special feelings for China and strong views on the importance of Japan's Asia ties, but accidents of circumstance and personal idiosyncrasies. The career of Kishida Ginkō (1833–1905), pioneer promoter of expanded Sino-Japanese trade, is illustrative. Kishida was a self-made man, a risk-taker with an unerring eye for the profitable venture. After years of leading a catch-as-catch-can existence as a fugitive from Tokugawa justice, Kishida started on the road to success in the mid-1860's, when he became an assistant to J. C. Hepburn in Hepburn's dictionary compilation project. Kishida made his first trip to China in 1866 to arrange for the publication of the later renowned Japanese-English dictionary. The next years were spent developing new enterprises—the first regular shipping business between Tokyo and Yokohama, Japan's first ice plant—with a stint as a journalist, before he launched, in 1877, the business that was to make him his fortune, a pharmaceutical outlet in the Ginza with the intriguing name Hall of Pleasurable Delights. The following year, Kishida broke into the China market with the establishment of a branch pharmacy in Shanghai. Over the next decade, Kishida became something of a local institution in Shanghai, a natural goodwill ambassador talking up the prospects of expanded Sino-Japanese commercial ties and a sponsor of Japanese newly arrived in China.[30]

In 1886, Kishida was visited at his Shanghai store by Arao Kiyoshi, who was in China for the first time on an army intelligence mission. Though it was by all accounts a happy meeting of the minds, Arao was a very different sort from Kishida, ever the "economic animal" bent on turning a profit. A recent graduate of Officers Training School, Arao was cut out of the samurai mold, disciplined, arrogant, and a thorough Japanist. For him, trade promotion was but a means to the end of expanding Japanese power and influence on the mainland. As one story, probably apocryphal but in character, has it, on being asked why he had applied for a China assignment when most of his colleagues were trying hard to avoid it, Arao answered: "I go to China to conquer China. After taking charge there, I will introduce better government and on the basis of this, hope to revitalize Asia."[31] As a first step in this grand design, Arao opened a pharmacy in Hankow as a base for exploring the Chinese interior and issuing anti-Russian propaganda.

Among the thirty or so young Japanese gathered around Arao in the late 1880's are names that crop up again in the next two decades of China ventures: Nezu Hajime, Takahashi Ken, Munekata Kotarō, Nakanishi Masaki, Ide Saburō, Tanabe Yasunosuke. Dressed in Chinese garb, most of them fluent in Chinese, they trekked into the hinterlands gathering information about local products, geography, and customs. In the pages of the Kokuryūkai and Tō-A Dōbunkai collections, stories abound about these men and their daring, discipline, and self-sacrifice. At a practical level, the marketing and intelligence operations of Arao and his comrades were financed from profits of Kishida-style pharmacies newly opened in Peking, Chungking, Changsha, Tientsin, and Foochow.[32]

After three years' experience in China, Arao decided the time was ripe to expand Japan's commercial activities by establishing a Sino-Japanese trade association with offices in twenty-five port cities. His bid for Japanese official and public backing for this project drew admiring comments and words of approval. Translating this into financial support, however, proved a daunting task at a time when official attention was focused on major domestic issues. A much-reduced version of Arao's original design, called the Nisshin Bōeki Kenkyūjo (Sino-Japanese Trade and Research Center), struggled along as a business school–trade outlet in Shanghai from 1890 to 1894, when the outbreak of the Sino-Japanese War ended the venture.[33]

Postwar China: Reform and Reaction

War forced the leaders of both countries to take stock, to clarify their purposes and perspectives. China's quick and crushing defeat not by a Western power but by an Asian neighbor undermined Chinese notions of superiority and discredited the single-sector, "damage-limiting" approach to modernization. For China, rethinking modernization as a total national process and structuring policies accordingly became a matter of survival. For Japan, the war marked an advantageous new turn in international relations. Victory confirmed the correctness of its modernizing path. Its self-image improved, as did its rating in the eyes of Westerners and other Asians. This new national confidence fueled discussion on the need for a better-defined Asia strategy, including a policy of assistance to progressive forces in China. It was here, in the matter of reform in China, that both sides perceived their interests to be served, and it was here that both—China warily, Japan with zeal—moved forward to test the waters of cooperation.

The general population of China was unaffected by the course of the war or the implications of the defeat. It had been a limited war, confined to sporadic military engagements in faraway Korea and China's northeast, involving few civilian casualties and causing no large-scale devastation of town and countryside. In the absence of communications between policy makers and the people, the average Chinese peasant either knew nothing at all about the conflict with Japan or assumed a Chinese victory.

But for the informed, China's loss of territory, finances, and face came as a shock. Shimonoseki produced a policy crisis among intellectually and politically articulate elements both inside and outside the government. Despite the government's repeated and long-standing declarations of the intent to "self-strengthen" the nation, such modernization programs as existed before the war were the result of the personal initiatives of certain energetic governors— Chang Chih-tung, Li Hung-chang, Liu K'un-i—and thus were at best regional in scope. After the war, the leadership as a whole showed an increased willingness to deal with underlying problems rather than warding off immediate crises, and to move from local activities to developing a national and multisector strategy for reform and modernization. There was no unanimity of view, however, on how much of the Chinese system was to be included in this overall design for change. At issue, in particular, was whether the modification of political institutions was a necessary precondition for modernization to "take" in other spheres of Chinese life.

The politics of reform centering on this issue and its denouement in 1898 have been much studied and need not be replayed here.[34] What is important to note is simply the extent to which postwar reformist thinking began to crystallize around two basic positions, each of which was self-consciously outward-looking. One was Chang Chih-tung's approach, *t'i-yung* (the Chinese essence–Western practice amalgam) in service of authoritarian reform.[35] The other was that of K'ang Yu-wei, who saw institutional changes as the only way to "catch up" in a world of the wealthy and powerful.[36]

In time, these positions and their partisans became irreconcilable. But in the years immediately following the war, when the issue of China's future course first became the subject of national debate, Chang and his colleagues lent a sympathetic ear to the younger politicians ranged around K'ang Yu-wei. To K'ang, who had talked reform with Chang as early as 1886, Chang in particular provided an inspiring model of the innovative governor-general vigorously implementing development projects in provinces under his jurisdiction. And Chang, for his part, was no doubt gratified to note the increasing enthusiasm among younger scholar-officials for the "self-strengthening" activities he had long held important. When K'ang Yu-wei organized his Ch'iang-hsueh Hui (Strengthening Through Study Society, known by foreigners as the Reform Club) a few months after the treaty with Japan was concluded in April 1895, Chang's name was on the roster of forty-three members, along with such other top officials as Liu K'un-i and Yuan Shih-k'ai. Chang contributed funds to the society, as he did to the subsequently formed Shanghai Ch'iang-hsueh Hui, though for political reasons he declined to join that group. Chang's caution was well advised. Within six months of their founding, the Peking and Shanghai reformist groups and their affiliated magazines were banned at the behest of the conservative court faction. But the tide could not be stemmed. The fate of the Peking and Shanghai study societies notwithstanding, at least sixty-three similar groups sprouted up in the years 1896–98, including Shanghai counterparts of groups set up in Tokyo, the Hsing-ya Hui (Kō-A Kai) and its successor, the Ya-hsi-ya Hsieh-hui (Ajia Kyōkai).[37]

Out of this groundswell of support for reform among elites at all levels grew a new interest in learning from the outside world, including Japan. Before the war, when self-strengthening advocates looked to the West and Western technology, K'ang Yu-wei had been one of the few voices urging his government to consider the Meiji experience in formulating its own modernization programs. In the mid-1880's, as a concrete step in this direction, he proposed translating into Chinese current Japanese materials, many of them originally in Western languages. Neither K'ang's general advice nor his project received official support, in part because K'ang himself was a relative unknown, in part because the authorities were still unpersuaded of Japan's economic and military edge over China. After the war, in the atmosphere of gloom over China's demonstrated weakness, K'ang's arguments got a more sympathetic hearing among senior officials and from the young Kuang-hsü Emperor. As a newly appointed official (with the Board of Works beginning in 1895), K'ang directed to the Emperor's attention a stream of briefing papers on reform, citing the Japanese example not only as a model to follow but as proof that an Asian nation could make the grade. In a document of 1897, K'ang fueled his arguments with references to both the Meiji reforms and the Russian reform program under Peter the Great:

Originally, [Japan and Russia], like China today, were vunerable [to foreign intrusions]. Now, [however], they differ from us in being successful and strong. Japan is close to us geographically; in political forms and customs we are alike. [In reforming its government], Japan achieved rapid results, instituting measures in systematic fashion. It would be easy for us to adopt this [model] for our own use.[38]

Another of K'ang's documents, *An Account of Japan's Political Reforms* (Jih-pen pien-cheng k'ao), was forwarded to the Emperor through the Tsungli Yamen in 1898. Here K'ang sharpened the contrast with Japan:

Japan initially had the same conservative, antiforeign spirit as China. Its feudal *bakufu* system, which the rulers sought to perpetuate, differed from ours and was even more of an impediment to reform. And yet [Japan's] success has been rapid due to the fact that from the beginning of the reform period a purposeful policy was defined and various operating principles agreed upon. If we examine the Restoration from the start, we see that a great many new measures [were enacted]. The following were the most important: (1) the determination of a national policy [announced in] solemn covenant between the Emperor and his officials, (2) the establishment of an evaluative mechanism for the purpose of recruiting talented men, and (3) the creation of an office to draft regulations and the establishment of a constitution.[39]

As K'ang shaped an agenda for radical reform, Chang Chih-tung articulated the gradualist position in a series of essays entitled *Exhortation to Study* (Ch'üan-hsueh p'ien). Completed about two months before the K'ang-inspired reform movement in the summer of 1898, the work received Court approval for wide distribution among provincial officials. The appeal of *Exhortation to Study* lay in its attempt to strike a balance between social and political conservatism—it strongly endorsed strengthening the established order—and a liberal approach to problems of industrial and educational development. The concept itself was vintage Chang. In education, for example, he had for years supported the development of modern schools offering a combined curriculum of Western scientific studies and Chinese humanities courses in place of the exclusively classical program of the traditional academies (*shu-yuan*). What was new was the emphasis on national planning: in education, Chang called for establishing a national system of modern schools and to this end, proposed developing a training-abroad program and revising the civil service examination. *Exhortation to Study* provided the first justification of study in Japan within the larger context of a total reform of the educational system.[40]

Citing the advantages of firsthand observation over mere book knowledge, Chang pointed to the careers of the Japanese leaders Itō Hirobumi and Yamagata Aritomo and the importance of their overseas study experience to their service in government. The reasons Chang cited for his choice of Japan over Western countries as the location for a government-sponsored study-abroad program were all eminently practical: geographical proximity would allow a low-cost program relatively easy to supervise; language similarity would mean that students could absorb new material with greater ease and speed; and the relative compatibility of Chinese and Japanese social customs would allow students to gain twice as much in half the time as they would from study in Western countries.[41]

By the spring of 1898, Chang's position on Japan as a training resource, and more broadly, as a development model had gained wide currency. It was just at this time that the Tsungli Yamen, with the encouragement of the Japanese minister to China, issued a document stipulating that the Northern and Southern Commissioners, provincial governors, and the Tsungli Yamen language school might nominate students for study in Japan.[42] Moreover, however much the group in power in the Hundred Days from June to September differed from Chang and his supporters on the direction and pace of political reform, in education they were in complete agreement on the potential value of the Japan connection. In his series of decrees on educational reform, K'ang Yu-wei highlighted Japan's experience in promoting popular education and in building a new leadership group through training abroad. He argued that it was Japan's strategy of making a modern education accessible to the entire population, not the superiority of military weaponry pure and simple, that accounted for the Japanese victory in the war of 1894–95. K'ang proposed that China adopt the Japanese public school model, with its primary, middle, and special schools, and again made a case for translating books from Japanese. Indulging in a bit of optimism, he remarked that while it had taken Western nations some 300 years to rise to wealth and power, and Japan thirty, China with its enormous land and human resources could reach those heights in a mere three if the talents of its people were released through education.[43]

K'ang's remark typifies the attitude of Chinese leaders toward Japan in the postwar years. Expressions of respect for Japanese achievements were qualified by assertions that China had the potential to achieve more, faster. It was not any peculiarly Japanese quality that accounted for Japan's success, but merely that the reformist impulse, present also in Chinese tradition, had taken hold earlier there. This sensitivity about China's status relative to Japan went along with an underlying distrust of Japanese intentions in seeking closer ties with China. We must recall that the K'ang Yu-wei of 1898 who urged fellow reformers to adopt Japanese models was the same K'ang who two years earlier, at the end of the war, raised a petition calling for a resumption of hostilities with Japan. Chang Chih-tung, increasingly receptive to postwar Japanese offers of educational assistance, remained cautious and aloof in his personal dealings with Japanese emissaries.[44] China's postwar tilt toward Japan, in other words, had nothing to do with feelings of East Asian affinity; it was a simple question of self-interest, a desire to use Japan for quick access to Western technology and as a likely ally in checking the Russian military buildup on China's northern borders.[45]

The seizure of power by the Empress Dowager and the conservative faction in the fall of 1898 slowed the momentum on study in Japan. K'ang Yu-wei, key proponent of the program, was now out of the picture, lucky to escape with his life to a safe haven in Tokyo. Japan, the host country, was in the delicate position of having provided a place of exile for K'ang and his protégé, Liang Ch'i-ch'ao. Chang Chih-tung, too, was tainted by his past associations with the ousted reformers; his pro-Japanese leanings in the years the reform movement was gathering strength did him no good, either. Study in Japan was a less-inviting prospect for all concerned; student numbers remained at no more than 100 for the next two years.

The Manchu hard-liners' return to power had more serious consequences than closing the door to the outside world. It meant support in high places for the Boxer movement, a peasant-based rampage of antiforeignism that had its climax in the siege of the Western legations in Peking in the summer of 1900. What is important to our story of the study-in-Japan program is that Chang Chih-tung, Liu-K'un-i, Yuan Shih-k'ai, and other regional leaders formed an independent moderating bloc, which prevented the spread of Boxer influence south, urged restraint on Peking, and kept diplomatic channels open for eventual settlement of the crisis. Theirs was then the task of designing a new reform program to signal to the Powers the Dowager's good faith in pursuing an acceptable modernizing course. From Chang's perspective, the centerpiece of what became known as the New Policies was the series of documents on educational reform he drafted jointly with Liu K'un-i in 1901. These represented the culmination of Chang's lifetime of activities in educational development. They authorized the establishment of a nationwide system of modern schools, initiated changes in the civil service examination system, and endorsed study in Japan for the same reasons of practicality he had outlined earlier in his *Exhortation to Study*: cost effectiveness and similarities in language and culture. Training

young people in Japan was seen as a quick and efficient way to introduce new skills in general and, in particular, to supply teachers for
the expanding network of modern schools in China. The 1901 documents went several steps further than the *Exhortation* proposal in
permitting students to study abroad at their own expense and encouraging bureaucrats and school administrators to go to Japan on
study missions.[46]

Postwar Japan: Lending a Helping Hand to China

If the war plunged China into a crisis of self-doubt, in Japan it produced an upsurge in public confidence: it was possible, after all, to
be modern, powerful, and Japanese. Concrete gains from the Treaty
of Shimonoseki—the acquisition of Taiwan, an indemnity from
China, the confirmation of Korea's sovereignty—inspired visions of
a Japanese leadership role in Asia that even foreign interference in
the peace terms (forcing Japan to retrocede the Liaotung peninsula) could not dispel. Japan, in the public eye, was ready to *datsu-
A,* "escape from Asia," and play the part of a Western power in the
scramble for concessions on the Asian mainland.

After 1895, articles on imperialism as an inevitable and even laud-
able path to follow appeared with increasing frequency in the Japanese press. "What is there to mourn over in the survival of the fittest, in the replacing of the bad by something good?" asked one
Japanese writer. "If imperialism forced reform on those who would
not otherwise adopt it, where is the harm?"[47] Moral considerations
aside, economic and demographic factors were cited as well: "Is it
to be supposed for a moment . . . that Japan can keep out of the
current that is sweeping everything before it? Does any sane person
suppose that these islands will suffice to maintain the population
that they will contain in another few decades? And if our people fail
to find sustenance here, what other course is open to them but to
spread themselves out over the world as the chief Western races have
done?"[48]

Postwar advocates of a stronger regional role for Japan took as a
basic premise the need to follow the Western lead in a world where
only the fittest survived. They also argued that in the inevitable
competition with the West, Japan had a special advantage in Asia.
"Asia is Asia's Asia," wrote Konoe Atsumaro. "Asian problems must
unquestionably be solved by Asians. Although the Ch'ing state has
markedly declined, the fault lies in its politics, not with the Chinese
people. Once there is better leadership, joint action to preserve

Asia's integrity [*tōyō hozen*] will follow; it will not be at all difficult." Politically, Asia for the Asians meant a Japan-led Asian bloc allied against the West. Morally, it was Japan's answer to the "white man's burden," the civilizing mission Westerners cited to justify imperialist actions abroad.[49]

Reflecting Japan's more assertive mood toward Asia, new China/ Asia associations were formed. Most were—like the Tō-A Kai (East Asia Society), established in 1897—research and information services after the fashion of the still active Tōhōkyōkai and Ajia Kyōkai. Only the Dōbunkai (Common Culture Society), set up in the summer of 1898, took an action-oriented approach, seeking to establish links between Tokyo-based research groups and Japanese businesses, schools, and newspapers operating in China.[50] To those involved in the proliferating number of China groups, it soon became apparent that a consolidation of scarce resources and energies would better serve the goal of promoting expanded Japanese interests on the mainland. The prospect of financial aid from the Foreign Ministry's "secret fund," monies channeled to groups supporting Japan's regional interests, was an added incentive for them to coordinate their activities.[51] It was this kind of thinking that led to the formation of the Tō-A Dōbunkai (East Asia Common Culture Society; TDK) in November 1898.[52]

The TDK members were of diverse background and political bent. Many were in the *yūshi* category, people like the first president, Konoe Atsumaro, young, Western-educated, profoundly concerned about Japan's role in Asia, and in responsible government posts that necessarily involved them in international issues.[53] Others were old China hands like Munekata Kotarō, daring *shishi* followers of the late Arao Kiyoshi. Gathering together these China experts and enthusiasts,[54] the TDK developed a sound organizational and financial base. Like other prominent Asia groups of the day, notably the later renowned Kokuryūkai, the TDK was at once a government-subsidized intelligence operation and a kind of Asia lobby prodding the government to adopt a more forceful and coherent regional policy. Reflecting the prevailing view of the leadership and public alike in the postwar years, the society's inaugural statement cited cultural affinities and historical ties to justify a Japanese special relationship with China:

Relations between Japan and China have long endured. There is cultural understanding; moral precepts are similar. In terms of emotions, [the relationship] is [as close as] that between elder and younger brother; from the standpoint of power, the two nations are interdependent. Formal intercourse continued unchanged from of old because it proceeded from the justice of natural laws and the rightness of human principles. How different this is from the World Powers, hastily making détentes, [then] vying with and destroying each other. Who could have foreseen that a few years ago the brothers, not counting their blessings, would quarrel among themselves. And the Powers have used this situation to their advantage, thus making that state of affairs increasingly difficult. Alas, is it not imperative at present that we forget our mistakes, abandon hostility, and resist insults coming from abroad? At this juncture, the [Japanese and Chinese] governments, prizing justice and propriety, must increasingly strengthen bilateral relations. Below the governmental level, businessmen and the general public, in trust and concern for mutual benefit, must continuously improve neighborly goodwill.[55]

The TDK was immediately put to the test of defining its special relationship with China over the issue of the ousted reformers K'ang Yu-wei and Liang Ch'i-ch'ao, who sought asylum in Japan. The situation with K'ang was particularly touchy. Official support for him in the form of permanent asylum could only cause problems with the reinstalled conservative government. But denying him even temporary asylum would send the wrong signals to China's progressives, many of whom had pro-Japanese leanings. In handling this risky business, the TDK, with Konoe as leading player, acted as the government's agent, receiving the exiled politician, then quietly arranging for his departure for Canada.

K'ang and Konoe met for the first time on November 11, 1898, about a month after K'ang's arrival in Japan. As recorded by Konoe, the conversation was a verbal tug-of-war, with K'ang trying to wrest a commitment of aid from Konoe, and Konoe seeking to pull the discussion back to more general professions of support for strengthened bilateral ties. Asians must solve Asian problems, Konoe insisted. What were K'ang's views on the possibility of Japan and China enforcing an Asian Monroe Doctrine? K'ang wasted little time in reply but turned with zest to the specifics of the China scene: "The Emperor's thinking is, furthermore, that there is no other [possible course of action] but simply to appeal to Japan for aid."[56] However noncommittal Konoe was on the aid question, it was quite clear that K'ang's continued presence in Japan was an impediment to improved relations with the Ch'ing government. In a conversation with Liang Ch'i-ch'ao in January 1899, Konoe gently remarked that the interests of Sino-Japanese relations would be better served if K'ang would leave Japan for Europe or North America. This was finally accomplished in March 1899.[57]

Later, in November, when Konoe made a visit to China, it was

Liang's turn to come under fire. Governor-general Chang Chih-tung, in a meeting with Konoe, conveyed the government's wish that Liang be deported from Japan. In this case, Konoe balked, claiming that Liang was not a threat and, furthermore, that his ouster would do little to curb the activities of the large group of reformist sympathizers in Japan. Having made the gesture in K'ang's case, the Japanese government was clearly unwilling to go any further in damaging potentially useful ties with the Chinese reformist party.[58]

A revealing sidelight on the range of Japanese contacts with Chinese political activists in the postwar years is the TDK connection—however tenuous—with Sun Yat-sen's revolutionary party. When Konoe arrived in China on his 1899 visit, he was approached for interviews not only by the K'ang/Liang people, but also by Sun's supporters. As TDK head and a guest on Chinese soil, he explained, he could grant his time to neither, invoking the TDK principle of neutrality in matters of Chinese internal politics. Yet Konoe seemed well apprised of Sun's activities and aware of his potential. On Chang Chih-tung's reaction to Sun, Konoe recorded in his diary: "When I asked 'What about Sun Yat-sen,' he dismissed Sun as a petty thief, not worth bothering about. But he did not seem to be aware of the fact that, more than the K'ang/Liang group, Sun's party (the so-called revolutionary party) is on the rampage in Kwangtung and, in extreme cases, as far as Hunan and Hupei."[59] Though there is no evidence that Konoe himself had any direct dealings with Sun, he was in regular contact with Inukai Ki, a fellow TDK member who was one of Sun's chief backers, and he also knew Miyazaki Torazō, perhaps Sun's staunchest Japanese follower.[60]

Although the Japanese government continued to monitor the movements of the K'ang/Liang and Sun forces through the network of contacts built up over the years among Asia activists, after 1899 it increasingly gave the weight of its support to progressive regional leaders like Chang Chih-tung, Liu K'un-i, and Yuan Shih-kai. The TDK was at the forefront of promoting such a policy. During the Boxer disturbances, TDK people in and out of South China on intelligence-gathering missions sought to persuade both their Chinese contacts and their colleagues in the Japanese government of the wisdom of a Japanese-backed league of southern governors.[61] As the Powers (now for the first time including Japan) marched into Peking to break the back of the Boxers, support for the progressive wing of Ch'ing officialdom appeared to be the only hope for restoring stability. Sympathy for radical fringe groups like Sun's revolutionary party continued to exist among certain Japanese, but financial and material support was no longer forthcoming.[62]

In helping progressive forces fashion a modernized China, Japanese identified a special role for themselves in educational development. Common culture would facilitate the transfer of advanced knowledge in the physical and social sciences and in educational methods and systems. Japanese interests in China—always the ultimate objective—would expand as the influence of new Meiji culture touched the lives of the next generation of Chinese leaders. On the China side, officials like Chang Chih-tung could not have agreed more that improvements in education were critical to China's rapid modernization. When Konoe proposed to Chang in 1899 three areas where Japan could be of assistance in educational development—training Chinese students in Japan, sending Japanese teachers to China, and inviting Chinese educators to survey Japan's school system—Chang expressed delighted approval.[63]

Study in Japan for Chinese, in other words, was not an isolated project but part of a large-scale, multifaceted program of Japanese aid to China's education. Efforts in this direction began even before the Boxer uprising, with the TDK taking a lead role. Immediately after its formation in late 1898, the TDK began extending subsidies to existing Japanese-managed schools for Chinese in China. TDK members also got Liu K'un-i's approval to set up a school in Nanking to train not only Chinese but future Japanese China experts.[64] In Japan, the TDK established a preparatory school for Chinese and Korean students called the Tōkyō Dōbun Shoin. Opening its doors in January 1902, it was designed to provide newly arrived students with courses in the Japanese language and general studies before moving them on to more specialized work in regular schools.[65]

The Tōkyō Dōbun Shoin was by no means alone in its effort to provide a special preparatory course for the increasing flow of Chinese students to Japan. Some dozen schools and programs specially designed for Chinese students were set up in the years after 1898, some of them privately operated, others managed by well-established universities and academies.[66] One of the earliest schools to organize a Chinese student division was the Seijō School (Seijō Gakkō), a preparatory school for the Army Officers School (Rikugun Shikan Gakkō). In April 1899, Colonel Fukushima Yasumasa of the General Staff and later Seijō's director, was sent to China for talks with Liu K'un-i and Chang Chih-tung. Fukushima stressed the need for Sino-Japanese cooperation to counter the Western threat to East

Asia; he cited, in particular, mounting pressure from Russia as the Trans-Siberian Railway neared completion. To a receptive Liu and Chang, Fukushima offered Japanese assistance in strengthening China's army, including an invitation to Chinese military students to study in Japan. Chang immediately sent over four youths to enter Seijō; this group was soon followed by about thirty others, some dispatched by Chang and Liu and some sent under the auspices of Governor-general Ts'en Ch'un-hsuan of Szechuan and Governor-general Yuan Shih-k'ai of Chihli. The first graduating class in the summer of 1900 numbered forty-five.[67] At the time of the "Seijō Incident" in the fall of 1902 (see Chapter 5) there were a recorded 186 Chinese students enrolled at the school.

Other early schools for Chinese in Japan originated with the efforts of K'ang Yu-wei and Liang Ch'i-ch'ao to provide better schooling for the overseas Chinese community in Yokohama. Their Yokohama Ta-t'ung School, set up in 1897, was the model for a counterpart school in Tokyo, the Tokyo Ta-t'ung School, founded by Kashiwabara Buntarō in 1898. In 1901, Kashiwabara and Inukai Ki reorganized this venture into the East Asian Commercial School (Tō-A Shōgyō Gakkō), with a reported enrollment of around 130. Overseas Chinese, along with such Japanese notables as Count Ōkuma and Prince Konoe, were the school's principal backers.[68]

A larger-scale effort, which also evolved with input from both Chinese and Japanese, was the Kōbun Institute (Kōbun Gakuin), established in January 1902. Its founder was Kanō Jigorō, the same Kanō who, as principal of the Higher Normal School (Kōtō Shihan Gakkō) in 1896, had been entrusted with the education of the first thirteen Chinese students sent to Japan. That initial encounter had produced seven graduates in the spring of 1899 trained in the Japanese language and general studies, including history, science, and mathematics, and, more important, conscious of the extent to which their outlook had changed. "If we compare our thinking with three years ago, we are really different people," declared Chi I-hui in his valedictory speech of 1899.[69]

Despite a few successes, what was most apparent to Japanese educators was how poorly prepared most young Chinese were for study in Japan. In designing the Kōbun program, Kanō took pains to accommodate their—and China's—special requirements. A three-month trip to China in mid-1902, financed by the Japanese Foreign Office, gave Kanō a chance to examine firsthand Chinese educational facilities and to exchange views with such officials as Chang Chih-tung and Liu K'un-i and their advisers. The trip was an intensive one, taking him to Peking, Tientsin, and major cities in Hunan, Hupei, Anhui, Kiangsu, and Chekiang for a heavy schedule of meetings and banquets. Kanō played the role of foreign expert, answering questions on curriculum development, textbook acquisition, higher education, and the teaching of ethics, *kanbun*, and judo. He argued strongly on a number of occasions for long-term training and higher-level specialized education to supplement the short-term intensive courses favored by his Chinese hosts.[70] Kōbun attracted large numbers of students. By 1904, it had added five classroom buildings to the original facility to handle increasing enrollments. Between 1902 and 1906, 1,959 Chinese graduated from the institute.[71]

The second element of the Japanese aid-to-education program—encouraging Chinese authorities to hire Japanese teachers and educational advisers—was pursued with equal vigor. According to Sanetō, in 1905–6, about 460 Japanese were teaching in Chinese schools; for 1909, he gives a figure of 311 (out of a total foreign teaching community in China of 356). Japanese Foreign Office surveys do not include 1905 and show 424 education and training advisers for 1909 and 125 "other advisers and technicians."[72] Whatever the precise number of Japanese teachers in China, certainly their impact on student-age Chinese was great. In January 1905, *Chūō Kōron* estimated that some 30,000 Chinese youths were currently receiving a Japanese-style education either in Japan or under Japanese tutelage in China.[73]

Occasionally, Japanese were responsible for the overall design and staffing of schools for Chinese in China. More often a school established by Chinese would hire one or two Japanese teachers, or a province a single educational adviser. For example, a TDK report dated November 1899 lists a total of six Japanese teachers at three different Wuhan schools; and a 1902 newspaper account names Watanabe Ryōsei, former head of the Tokyo Music School, as educational adviser to Yuan Shih-k'ai, a Mr. Tono as Chang Chih-tung's adviser, and a Mr. Morimoto slated to serve the Szechuan governor in that capacity.[74] Many teachers and experts were people of considerable reputation in Japan. Hattori Unokichi, teacher at the Higher Normal School and Tokyo University, became head of the Teacher Training Division at Peking University under the new dean, Wu Julun.[75] Professor Iwaya of Kyoto University was hired by the Chinese government as a legal adviser to help compile a new legal code.[76]

The TDK was involved in some of the arrangements to send teachers to China. In mid-January 1903, for example, Chang Chih-tung requested the society's assistance in hiring Japanese as staff members for the newly constructed San-chiang Normal School. By the end of the month, through the good offices of Nezu Hajime, former principal of a Japanese-sponsored school in China, eleven persons had been selected for three-year tours, at salaries ranging from 200 yen to 400 yen a month.[77] Nezu himself, after a trip to China the year before, had given an optimistic picture of Japanese influence on educational development, particularly in the districts under Chang's jurisdiction. The Japanese language had joined English as part of the basic school curriculum throughout South China, he reported, and Chang was currently employing Japanese instructors along with Germans to staff his military academies; both German and Japanese officers were involved as well in training Chang's regular troops.[78] Count Nagaoka reported a similar use of Japanese instructors and methods after his talks with Liu K'un-i in January 1902. He concluded that the current trend throughout South China was to rely on Japan for advice.[79]

The educational adviser and teacher often played a pivotal role in the development of new schools in China. The career of Nakajima Saishi, who worked in China in this capacity for over a decade, illustrates the influence that could be exerted in a receptive environment. Nakajima's association with China began in 1891, when he went there as a student of Buddhism. After seven years of study and travel throughout the country, he got a job teaching Japanese at an academy in Chihli province run by the prominent Chinese educator Wu Ju-lun. Very likely it was under Wu's influence that Nakajima returned to Japan in 1899 to take up the cause of training Chinese students. Early 1901 saw him back in Peking, probably funded by the TDK, as an adviser on school development projects.[80]

In discussions with Li Hung-chang in March 1901, Nakajima proposed that China hire Japanese teachers as part of a large-scale program to build up a system of primary, secondary, and normal schools throughout the country. The advantage of using Japanese teachers, he told Li, was that they had thoroughly digested European and American culture and at the same time shared much with Chinese in terms of racial characteristics, culture, and written language. Stressing the practical, Nakajima noted that food, clothing, and housing were enough alike in the two countries that Japanese teachers would require lower salaries than Western ones. Though Li Hung-chang did not disagree here, he expressed grave doubts about Japan's ultimate intentions in promoting such a scheme. Surely the Japanese government meant to interfere in China in the manner of the other Powers? Nakajima cautioned Li not to confuse political party pronouncements with Japanese government policy. He assured Li that a commitment to China's integrity and a stern posture toward Russia accurately reflected Japanese policy.

Nakajima's long-term plan was to place at least one Japanese teacher in every existing school at the prefectural and district levels—a total of some 2,000 schools. In view of provincial funding constraints, he proposed a first-phase program to develop 185 prefectural-level normal schools into model institutions training elementary teachers. The question of the Japanese teachers' salaries was a point of contention between Li and Nakajima. Li found the proposed salary of 100–150 yen a month too high; Nakajima protested that it was quite reasonable, considering that those selected would be conversant in both Chinese and Western studies.[81]

Two weeks after the interview with Li Hung-chang, Nakajima opened a secondary school in Peking called the East Asian Culture Academy (Tōbun Gakusha). Reportedly subsidized by both Li and Yuan Shih-k'ai, it was the first Japanese-run school in the capital. Wu Ju-lun served as adviser. The school sparked an immediate interest among Chinese youth. An entering class of sixty at the time school opened increased to 180 a week after classes began. The curriculum offered both traditional Chinese studies and Japanese language study. Nakajima taught in both divisions and took on odd jobs as well in order to raise funds for school materials. Once enrollment reached 280, Nakajima hired six Japanese teachers. The final 1901 figure for entering students was 801. The following year, new students numbered 331; thereafter enrollment leveled off to around 150 a year until the school closed in 1906.[82]

Early in 1902, Nakajima had a series of interviews with Governor-general Yuan Shih-k'ai on the subject of using Japanese assistance in developing schools in Paoting prefecture. Yuan invited Nakajima himself to play a role in Paoting educational affairs, but he declined, reluctant to take his energies away from the Tōbun Gakusha project. However, over the next few years, he arranged for Tōbun Gakusha faculty and graduates to fill posts in the new Paoting school system as it took shape under Yuan's direction. Between 1902 and 1903, five schools were established: a police school, a normal school, an agricultural school, an army officers school, and a secondary school. At least half the teachers at these schools were Japanese. The normal school alone employed ten under the direction of Watanabe Ryōsei, who served as head of faculty while continuing in his role as Chihli's educational affairs adviser.[83]

The development of the agricultural school shows how receptive

Chinese officials could be to outside advice. Nakajima proposed that Yuan organize basic agricultural courses for rural youth designed to serve also as a vehicle for informing farm families generally about up-to-date agricultural technology. With Yuan's approval, Nakajima proceeded to hire some teachers from his Tōbun Gakusha to staff the school; others were engaged in Japan when he, in the role of translator, accompanied Wu Ju-lun on a trip there in July 1902.[84] To complete arrangements for the school, Yuan sent a study mission headed by Huang Ching to Japan in 1902. There, Huang and his group of five spent two and a half months (July 25–October 7) studying Japanese agricultural methods. In addition to collecting material for several accounts of his trip, Huang arranged to hire three Japanese instructors and purchased sample farm implements. The school began operating on his return.[85]

After the Boxer disturbances, several Sino-Japanese educational projects were implemented by the Japanese military contingent stationed in Peking as part of the allied peacekeeping force. To improve China's security capability, the Japanese began to recruit and train a Chinese police force. One of the top Manchu officials, Prince Ch'ing, was so impressed with the results that he formally entrusted the education of Chinese police officers to the police section of the Japanese army. The result was the establishment of the Police Affairs School (Ching-wu Hsueh-hsiao). The school, which stayed open after the departure of the occupying forces in June 1901, operated with a 10,000 yuan monthly subsidy from the Ch'ing government and was managed by Kawashima Naniwa, a Japanese adviser supplied by the military. He had three Japanese and several Chinese instructors working under his direction. The student body numbered around 300. In 1902, the school selected twenty high-ranking officers for further training in Japan. In 1906, under pressure from nationalistic Chinese youth, the arrangement between Kawashima and Prince Ch'ing was canceled, and the police school was put under Chinese management. However, Kawashima, along with several of the Japanese staff, stayed on until 1911. Reportedly, some 3,000 youths graduated from the school during the period 1901–6 and took up assignments with police forces in Peking and other cities.[86]

These instances of Japanese assistance to China only scratch the surface of the programs launched in the postwar years. From the Japanese standpoint, cultural and humanitarian aid—promoting educational exchanges, developing China's school system, and two areas we have not touched on, expanding the number of newspapers in China and improving medical care—were viewed as ways to

strengthen the Sino-Japanese relationship and thus Japan's own security. In the final analysis, the late Meiji attempt to "open up"
China, to bring it the fruits of the "civilized" world, was strikingly
similar to the Western approach to China in the same decades. If the
sum total of these efforts strikes us as expansionist, aggressive, and
occasionally condescending, they must be balanced against a great
many instances of individual idealism and dedication. The Christian missionary found his match in the evangelist of "Asia-first-
ism"; the one no less than the other pursued both national goals
and transcendental values—whether to the glory of God or to the
glory of the Japanese Emperor—but the recipient country was supposed to benefit as well. China, under the tutelage of Westerners or
Japanese, was meant to progress to a state of modernism and
strengthened national life.

Of course, the Japanese had something special to offer, an ingredient psychologically appealing to the Chinese. This was the vision
of "yellow" unity against the "whites." On this basis, in the period
before 1905, when Japan was only an aspiring imperialist, many
Chinese could accept their neighbors as members of the same team;
and more, as demonstrating that it was possible to be both Asian
and modern.

It is essential to bear in mind that if Japan's objectives were essentially shaped by self-interest, some of the means it used to achieve
those objectives—teacher-student exchange, aid to education—coincided neatly with China's own aspirations and goals. Japanese advice and advisers were sought after, not imposed. The Chinese
wanted to learn "modernization" in the quickest, most efficient way
possible with the least expenditure of scarce funds. In this sense,
China's study-in-Japan program nicely "fit the bill," just as, in the
same way, it seemed perfectly consistent with current Japanese desires to play a leading role in directing China's future course. The
Konoes and Nakajimas were well in tune with the Chang Chih-
tungs and Yuan Shih-k'ais. What no one took adequately into account in all this were the Chinese students themselves, what their
own aspirations might be in a changing order. As we will see, increasingly after 1900, Chinese youth selected out as targets of attack
both their Japanese hosts and their Chinese sponsors.

TWO

Study Tours for Chinese Officials

O F ALL THE intended consequences of China's new receptivity to Japanese assistance, educational reform was the most profound and lasting. By 1910, China's educational system was, in structure and objectives, far less elitist, far more supportive of mass education, than ten or fifteen years earlier. Such a transformation was not accomplished at a single stroke. It was the result of an interactive process involving a number of internal decisions and outside influences, a process, also, of domestic consensus building on the priorities of modernization.

The decisions on education issued between 1901 and 1905 moved from statement of principle to blueprint for action, step by step dismantling the civil service examination system and, in a sense, giving central government sanction to changes that were already under way—notably the school development projects—at the provincial and local levels. Daunting as the task of instituting reforms throughout China was, given the inadequacy of central and local financing, lack of trained teachers, and reluctance in some quarters to part with old ways, it was clear after 1905 in what direction China was moving: toward a system of primary, middle, and higher schools modeled after Japan's.[1] A decisive factor in this reform process is what we would now put under the heading of technical assistance and study tours. This was a two-way street, involving not only Japanese teachers and advisers working in China (as described in Chapter 1) but also Chinese officials, educators, and businessmen going to Japan for a firsthand look at education and the modernizing sector generally.

The study tour, in which an officially sponsored delegation was sent overseas for a month or more expressly to investigate particular institutions and methods, was a postwar phenomenon. Sanetō, in his lifetime of research on Sino-Japanese relations, located 117 published accounts of Chinese missions to Japan dating from 1898 to 1906; 105 of these appeared between 1901 and 1906.[2] In sponsoring overseas visits, top officials like Chang Chih-tung and Yuan Shih-k'ai were both encouraging and capitalizing on intensified interest in reform among China's elites at all levels during this period. The various briefings and trip reports that resulted provided them a useful guide on the specifics of Japan's modernization programs and, in particular, a Chinese perspective on those programs. The fact that the reports were published and very likely widely distributed among officials involved in education also helped build a consensus for the changes Chang and others were trying to implement. An important consequence of this "opening to Japan" was that this program, unlike the one that sent Chinese youths to study in the United States in the 1870's, grew out of a fully supportive environment at home.

The typical study tour consisted of a leader and an accompanying staff of five to ten people. If the 117 extant accounts are taken as the total for the 1898–1906 period—and there were probably more trips—as many as 1,000 Chinese professionals of various kinds paid short-term visits to Japan in this period. An analysis of twenty of the trip reports shows the authors to be generally well educated. This is reflected primarily in the style and organization of the written accounts. In only a few cases is the exact degree status known: Wu Ju-lun, for example, had a *chin-shih* degree, as did at least two others (Lin Ping-chang and Chang Chien); and two men (Chou Hsueh-hsi and Yao Hsi-kuang) had *chü-jen* degrees. On the other side, at least one official visitor, Lo Chen-yü, was an examination failure.[3] Diversity was the rule in the professions represented by the mission leaders, though it is probably safe to say that all were active in the modernizing sector. Some of them were prominent figures— the dean of Peking University Wu Ju-lun; the industrialist Chang Chien; the Manchu prince Tsai Chen; Director of the Imperial Bank of China Liu Hsueh-hsün; and the legal expert Tai Hung-tz'e (whose account is a record of his trip as a member of the 1905 constitutional commission). Others were of more modest background, such as Huang Ching, an agricultural expert hired by Yuan Shih-k'ai; Hu Yü-chin, a teacher; and Li Tsung-t'ang, who played the role of troubleshooter in the student protests of 1902 and 1903. Very likely Li, and others too, were better known figures in their day. Li, for example, made nine trips to Japan, dispatched variously from Anhui and Kiangsu.

Most of the study tours were financed by provincial authorities. Out of our sample of twenty, Yuan Shih-k'ai was responsible for seven, all of which were sent specifically to gather technical information useful to his program of economic and educational development. Chang Chih-tung sent out at least two people to study the Japanese school system: Lo Chen-yü, acting as consultant in agriculture and education, who made a trip in 1901, and Mu Ch'üan-sun, who made his in 1903.[4] The Tsungli Yamen in 1899 financed the tour of the banker Liu Hsueh-hsün; he was charged with preparing a report on industry and commerce for that office, as well as briefing Chang Chih-tung and Li Hung-chang on his return.

In other instances, the trip originated in a Japanese invitation, though how it was financed is not clear. Lin Ping-chang, for example, was asked to attend the 1903 Osaka Exhibition by an unidentified Japanese connected with that event. One of his duties while there was to hire a Japanese teacher for a Foochow school. Chang Chien was also invited by the Japanese to see the exhibition.[5] Occasionally, a man applied to provincial authorities on his own initiative and got permission to go to Japan. Some ambitious officials were probably responding to Chang Chih-tung's proviso in the 1901 documents on educational reform that promotions in office be linked to periodic study trips abroad. The author of one account explains in his preface that in the fall of 1905 certain local leaders in Kiangsu offered to finance the costs of sending selected gentry to Japan to study educational affairs; but since his own interests lay in commercial and industrial affairs, he had applied to the provincial governor to make the trip using his own funds.[6]

The objective of the study tours was much the same. With the exception of Li Tsung-t'ang, who was sent to Japan on two occasions for the specific purpose of investigating student disturbances, Chinese visitors directed their attention to two key areas, education and economic development. This choice reflected Ch'ing policy priorities. It also indicated what the host government thought was important for China, for the programming for the visits was done from the Japan side. Each Chinese official traveler was put into contact with essentially the same people: government officials, especially those from the Foreign Office and Education Ministry; educators and school principals; Sino-Japanese friendship groups; and bankers and businessmen.

The educator who was on virtually everyone's program was Kanō

Jigorō, principal of the Higher Normal School. Kanō was actively involved with China's educational development from the time he was asked (by Education Minister Saionji Kimmochi) to manage the first Chinese student program in 1896. He talked with scores of Chinese officials on his subsequent trip to China in the summer of 1902.[7] Thus it was that our Chinese visitors trooped to the Higher Normal School to hear Kanō lecture on the system, methods, and philosophy of Meiji education. Another key educator on the circuit was Shimoda Utako, principal of the Women's Practical Arts School and an outspoken feminist. Shimoda was an extremely energetic personality, described as a thoroughgoing Asia-firster who believed that Japan should take the lead in China's educational development. She took her cause of education for Chinese women to the highest levels, drawing the attention even of the Empress Dowager in Peking.[8] Of course, Chinese study tour members met with many lesser names in education as well, school principals from the elementary through the postsecondary level.

Count Nagaoka Moriyoshi of the TDK had a central role in hosting these visitors. He was involved in making arrangements for tours of educational institutions, assigning interpreters, and introducing mission members to Japanese officials. The TDK as an organization also held welcome meetings for certain of the Chinese guests. Wu Ju-lun, the dean of Peking University, was one so honored. Konoe, Nagaoka, and the venerable Kishida Ginkō attended the fete given Wu on his 1903 visit. Wu's case is a particularly interesting one in terms of contacts. By all accounts, his visit generated a great deal of enthusiasm among Japanese educators and Asia lobbyists, as well as the press, which gave complete coverage to all of his meetings and discussions. He had appointments with the education minister and the president of Tokyo University, invitations from educational associations such as the Educational Affairs Research Society, and meetings with such China interest groups as the Tōhōkyōkai, an organization listed as the Tōyō Club, and the Kokuryūkai. Accompanying Wu on his rounds, as interpreter and guide, was Nakajima Saishi, educational adviser to Yuan Shih-k'ai in the Paoting model school project.[9]

Businessmen gave an equally cordial welcome to Chinese counterparts sent to observe Japan's commercial and industrial progress. Liu Hsueh-hsün, from the Imperial Bank of China (established in 1896), and Chou Hsueh-hsi, economic consultant to Yuan Shih-k'ai, met with Mitsui representatives, bank directors, and appropriate officials in the various ministries. Liu, in particular, was accorded VIP

treatment. He was personally escorted on his tours of Mitsui operations by the Japanese consul in Shanghai, and had appointments
with Foreign Minister Aoki, the minister of justice, and two senior
government advisers, Itō Hirobumi and Yamagata Aritomo.

As all this suggests, the Chinese observers' contacts with Japanese were limited to the educated elite. No one was talking to the
man on the street, though as we will see, observations were made
about ordinary Japanese as a group lumped together. Moreover, with
the sole exception of Chang Chien, who ventured out to Hokkaido
to observe agricultural development, the visitors focused their time
and attention on major cities—Kobe, Osaka, Kyoto, and especially
Tokyo and environs. The typical program concentrated on visits to
schools of all levels and specializations, with additional time spent
on tours of prisons, police stations, factories, banks, and, in 1903,
the Osaka Exhibition.

The visitors' observations, put to paper, followed a pattern of description, comparison, and prescription. In all sectors in the postwar
period, the Japanese development experience was viewed as a model
for China to follow. Chinese visitors, though not totally uncritical,
were definitely admiring of Japanese achievements. Japan, said one
visitor writing at the end of 1899, stood out as the only nation in
Asia making progress.[10] Echoing these sentiments, a writer in 1903
attributed the success of Japan's *fu-ch'iang* (fu-kuo ch'iang-ping;
wealthy country, strong army) policy to a planning capability that
was lacking in his own country.[11]

Summing up the pragmatic approach most Chinese took toward
the policy of learning from Japan, Chang Chien in his mission report
recounts a conversation he overheard between two Chinese students. One, resentful of Japanese condescension, deplored the fact
that because of financial constraints, Chinese were forced to learn
secondhand from Japan rather than directly from the West. Why, he
asked, should Chinese youth suffer the arrogance of the Japanese?
His companion took a more practical view of things. If study in
Western countries was not feasible on a large scale, the only way to
achieve China's long-term modernization goals was to stick it out
in Japan. Chinese, in other words, must be willing to humble themselves now before their Japanese teachers in order to shape a future
of national wealth and power.

Education for National Unity

Chinese visitors routinely were given an initial briefing on the Japanese educational system by someone in the Education Ministry or

by a leading school administrator, often the China expert Kanō Jigorō. Chinese rapporteurs duly recorded this information in detail, offering their readers organizational charts of the school system and sample curricula, along with descriptions of the administrative and planning functions of the Education Ministry and central government as a whole. In his briefings, Kanō, in particular, did not confine himself to the Japanese educational scene, but commented freely on educational development in China. He sought to impress on his guests the urgency of making elementary education universal in China and the concomitant need for expanded teacher training. To cap his argument in favor of mass education, he used the West as a base of comparison, pointing out that the primary aim of education in Europe and the United States was to produce a populace possessed of commonsense knowledge, not simply a scholarly elite.[12]

The fact that Japan had adopted a mass-education approach is precisely what struck Chinese visitors most forcibly. As one observed: "Primary education is national, universal education without distinction between rich and poor, clever and simple. Everyone is ordered to school; no one lacks this daily necessity of life."[13] Another, writing in the same vein, noted: "Nationwide, rich and poor, male and female, must enter regular elementary school at age seven. Otherwise, parents are punished by a fine."[14] Mu Ch'üan-sun, who visited the Girls Higher Normal School in Hongo ward on his 1903 trip, noted that in the kindergarten attached to the school, half the 170 pupils were children of wealthy families and paid school fees and the others were non-fee-paying children of the poor.[15]

But what impressed visitors even more than the acceptance of the principle that the poor must be educated at public expense was the approach to schooling for the handicapped. Almost without exception, Chinese were given a tour of the Tokyo School for the Blind and Dumb. Most visitors recorded in detail the functioning of the school—unique teaching methods, daily schedules, size of enrollment, and facilities. Ch'ang Po-wen, for example, reported that the school had more than eighty blind students of both sexes and more than 220 with hearing defects. A staff and faculty of twenty-eight handled the program for these handicapped children at an annual expense of 16,000 yen. After explaining the use of a modified Braille system for teaching the blind to read, Ch'ang took note of the appropriateness of the school slogan, "The nation wastes no talent." Admirable as he found the humanitarianism of aiding the handicapped, what impressed him the most was the value the Japanese placed on each individual as a potential producing member of society. "The universality of education in Japan is attested to by the fact that even the blind and dumb, the rejects, are not abandoned. With this approach how can education not but 'raise the country.'" [16]

The relationship between the educational system in Japan and "raising the country," or national progress, was of key interest to Chinese visitors. Particularly intriguing to them was the fact that building national consciousness was an explicit goal of Meiji education. As Kanō explained to one visitor, the Imperial Rescript on Education (1890) was intended to aid in the process of creating national spirit. Moreover, the rescript was not a vague abstraction but was brought to life in the classroom through various practices and organizational techniques promoted by the Education Ministry.[17] Ethics (te-yü), visitors were told, was chief among the "three yü's" at the core of Japanese education, the others being physical education (t' i-yü) and mental training (chih-yü).[18] By ethics was meant cultivating loyalty to the Emperor and love of country from the earliest school days, through such daily activities as having the children sing patriotic songs, bow before the portrait of the Emperor, and parade through the school grounds with Japanese flags in hand. Ch'ang Po-wen was told by his Japanese hosts: "True loyalty to the ruler and love of country must be fostered by the elementary and middle schools. Of the courses offered, the most important is ethics." Escorted into the civics classroom where a graduation ceremony was in progress, Ch'ang observed: "Teachers and pupils were all gathered together. By classes they filed forward, solemnly and in orderly fashion singing the national anthem to the accompaniment of musical instruments. Afterwards they paid their respects, bowing several times, to the portrait of the Emperor displayed on the wall." [19]

Nearly every Chinese visitor recounted in similarly glowing terms the well-orchestrated behavior of Japanese schoolchildren. Even the youngest showed unusual discipline and responsiveness to instructions from teachers. After visiting a Japanese kindergarten, Lin Ping-chang remarked that the teaching of four- to six-year-olds was so effective that "in their conduct and behavior, the pupils without exception conformed to established norms." [20] Hu Yü-chin described a scene he witnessed on an elementary school playground:

A woman teacher was leading a [group of] forty to fifty new entrants, aged six and above, to view a demonstration [of calisthenics]. They all were excited and wanted to follow suit. When one segment [of an exercise drill] was over, the little ones all applauded. Subsequently, they too joined in the exercises. From beginning to end, they were the picture of uniformity and discipline. What is remarkable is that at the outset there were all together between three and four hundred students on the playing fields. Some were playing games, others were tugging at the teachers' clothes, still others formed circles or stood holding hands. The teachers gaily joined in with these activities. When the whistle blew, each individual returned to his line. Talking subsided, and there was silence. Once the drill was over, [the youngsters] resumed their games as before. Subsequently, an organ was played, and every student returned to his classroom, marching in time to the organ music. It was absolutely beautiful![21]

The visitors were interested in how the national unity message was conveyed in the regular curriculum as well. History courses, they observed, were a particularly useful vehicle for emphasizing Japan's unique features, thus stimulating national consciousness.[22] Wu Ju-lun passed on to readers the advice he received from Japanese colleagues on how to use the classroom situation to develop patriotism: emphasize the teaching of national history, display political maps, particularly highlighting territories seized by foreign powers, and strive for language unification.[23] Hu Yü-chin reported seeing classroom display maps with Taiwan and Fukien ports colored similarly, as if all were under Japanese administration. Nor need loyalty-building be confined to the classroom. As Kanō Jigorō explained to Hu, plays, songs, newspapers, and short stories might also be employed as educational devices to stimulate patriotic spirit among the public generally.[24]

Chinese visitors were careful to point out that the nationalism fostered through the school system was based on the principle of preserving what was essentially Japanese. The Europeanization that prevailed in the first decades after the Meiji Restoration had been supplanted by a blend of East and West:

Japan, in the thirty years since the Restoration, has imitated the Western example in every way. But in this country, the old-style manners are still observed. Moreover, there has been specially established in the schools a course called "principles of preserving the national essence." China's new educators take pains to discredit the old way of life. Even when it comes to [such things as] diet and everyday activities, there is nothing that they do not want to change.[25]

On the same theme, Hu Yü-chin criticized the Chinese students in Japan who, he said, arrived with only superficial knowledge of Chinese learning and then proceeded to get drunk on Western ways, entirely rejecting their heritage. "They do not realize that Japan has a Japanese national essence and China a Chinese national essence."[26]

There seemed to be general agreement in mission reports that the

Chinese system ought to be overhauled on the Japanese model. This was explicitly stated by a number of visitors. Wang Ching-hsi capped his description of a completely state-financed elementary school in one of Tokyo's poorer districts with the comment: "Our country, introducing a new school system in a period of financial stringency, particularly ought to take this [school] as a model."[27] Hu Yü-chin, reporting on the practice of using student teachers in demonstration kindergartens attached to teacher training institutes, observed: "What a good method that is! The student teachers get field experience, and the kindergarten teachers themselves need not overwork."[28] Hu and others also commented favorably on the system of requiring teacher-graduates to teach for five years in public schools as repayment for a government-financed college education. Finally, in outlining the range of schools available in Japan, including vocational schools, schools for the handicapped, and reformatories, Ch'ang Po-wen commented: "This model is extensive and, furthermore, ought to be extremely useful to us."[29]

Educational Practice

Chinese observers were clearly impressed by three aspects of Meiji education: that it was universal, that it promoted social-intellectual conformity, and, above all, that it helped indoctrinate the populace with loyalty to throne and country. In short, observers were struck by the possibilities of creating a "new people," enlightened and patriotic, through a centrally planned and administered educational policy.

Equally interesting to the visiting Chinese was how policy was implemented, how the school system was actually set up and managed. Perhaps the most sophisticated observer of the Japanese educational scene was the veteran educator Wu Ju-lun, who had been appointed dean of Peking University in early 1902. It was to prepare for his new duties that Wu was sent to Japan by Superintendent of Educational Affairs Chang Po-hsi. His was a broad mandate: to look into educational facilities for women as well as men, the education of the poor, and vocational education for the lower classes, with a view to formulating reform policies for China.[30] As mentioned earlier, his visit stirred much excitement in the Japanese press, which followed his every move and utterance, recording verbatim conversations between him and such leading educators as Kanō Jigorō. Wu explored every aspect of educational development. On a visit to Kyoto University, for example, he inquired about textbooks and teaching materials, the annual budget, the relationship between the university and middle schools, and employment prospects for graduates.[31] In a meeting with Professor Inoue Tetsujirō of Tokyo University, Wu focused on the problems faced by early Meiji leaders in trying to set up an educational system for Japan. How were school districts determined, Wu wanted to know, and what happened in regions where people were too poor to pay school taxes?[32]

In this same interview with Inoue, Wu brought up a question he posed again and again during his Japan stay: "Virtually all past generations of Japanese were educationally grounded in Chinese learning. More recent scholars have thrown it out in favor of Western culture. In terms of ultimate talent, which generation, past or present, represents the superior product?"[33] Inoue, avoiding a direct answer, questioned Wu's basic premise that the West had supplanted the East in Japanese pedagogy. While conceding that Japan's elementary- and middle-school curricula closely followed the European and American pattern, he argued that Japan had been selective about what it had adopted from the West, and that the result was an amalgam of Eastern and Western thinking. Wu himself could appreciate the selective approach. Even as he probed into every facet of education in Japan, he forcefully maintained that not all of what he saw was applicable to the Chinese setting.

Other visitors shared Wu's interest in exploring Eastern and Western models of educational development. Wang Ching-hsi, speaking to a Japanese educator on the subject of current Chinese educational policy, stated that the goals were to make primary education universal and in the process to fashion a curriculum in technical training.[34] On the question of selecting the new or Western learning versus the old or Eastern version, Wang asserted that the choice must be guided by practicality:

The world is in controversy over the relative value of new learning, old learning, Eastern learning, Western learning. There are conflicting sets of priorities and, in the confusion, no common ground can be reached. In my humble opinion, no matter whether [what is learned] is new or old, Eastern or Western, still, the first order of priority is that it can be put to practical use.[35]

On this theme of adopting "what works," many Chinese visitors applauded Kanō's statement that courses in Japanese schools were designed with an eye to their relevancy to Japan's present problems and current needs.

Visitors were impressed with the variety of training programs offered by Japanese schools to meet the demands of a modernizing society for new skills. As Chu Shou commented:

In terms of the names used for [the different levels of] schools, China and Japan are in accord. Yet the reality behind the names is utterly unalike. Chinese schools are set up solely [for instruction] in classical subjects. In the case of Japan, what is taught has been extended to military subjects and trade, to the arts, agriculture, music, sewing, teaching the blind to read, the deaf to speak, dance, physical education. Schools have been established in every field.[36]

The emphasis put on physical education intrigued the Chinese, and they looked to its immediate practical value. Kanō Jigorō the judo enthusiast was an active supporter of sports and exercise programs. It was because Japanese were so short, one Chinese visitor observed, that they turned to physical education as a means to "improve the race."[37]

The Japanese emphasis on training technicians, military experts, and agricultural specialists was of special interest, too. Chang Chien wrote in 1903 that it was essential to encourage Chinese students to enroll in technical and agricultural studies. He felt that though there had been a perceptible shift in this direction, too many still chose politics and law with an eye to an official career.[38] Chang departed from the standard format on his Japan trip. He ventured out of Tokyo to visit textile factories and went as far as Hokkaido to examine rural reclamation and development projects. He visited an agricultural school near Osaka to get a firsthand view of an animal husbandry program and to see Japan's system of agricultural experiment stations in operation. What was particularly noteworthy to Chang about the school itself was that after completing the agricultural course, students did not go on to a higher level but instead returned to their native areas to put what they had learned into practice.[39]

Chinese visitors were keenly interested in Japanese teaching methods, which emphasized active participation in the learning process over rote memorization. On a visit to the Tokyo Higher Commercial School, Ting Yuan-fang noted that in learning the rudiments of international finance, students would take on certain roles in the business world. Student A would be the banker, B a Chinese merchant, C a British merchant, D a Korean merchant, and E a wholesale dealer. From week to week students would exchange roles and accounts would be settled monthly.[40] Hu Yü-chin, in his account of primary-school programs, observed that the complex drills practiced by the youngsters as part of their music and physical education courses served to instill habits of discipline. He made note also of children at play, building bridges and houses out of blocks: "What better way to develop intellectual capabilities than through these so-called kindergarten toys."[41]

Student participation in activities of the "real world" was epitomized in an approach to learning new to Chinese—the work-study program. Ting Yuan-fang noted that among the things students could learn at the Tokyo Higher Industrial School were paper manufacture, electrical engineering, and the preparation of seaweed products. He seemed impressed that half the students' time was spent in classroom training and the other half in productive labor.[42] Other kinds of innovative techniques also struck the visitors as promising for China: the use of student-teachers, demonstration schools, and the single-grade system, in which a teacher was responsible for only one grade or course, as against the multigrade system, in which a teacher taught the first four grades and a variety of subjects.[43]

School facilities—plant and equipment—were described in considerable detail by Chinese visitors. In a tour of Kanō Jigorō's Higher Normal School, Hu pointed out in admiring tones the size of the institution. There were sixty classrooms, in addition to workshops, a library, an auditorium seating 400–500 people, a dining hall and dormitories. On a visit to Tokyo University's science laboratories, Hu, obviously impressed, offered a precise description of the available equipment, which included devices to measure light and sound, an X-ray machine, and a seismograph said to be Japanese-made.[44] Libraries were another learning resource Hu and others took pains to describe. The Tokyo University library, Hu reported, contained over 170,000 volumes in Chinese and Japanese plus 140,000 in English and other European languages.[45] The visitors perceived that it was not only the extent of the available facilities that made the Japanese school system an effective instrument for development, but the careful thought that had gone into their design: "The excellence of the Japanese school system derives from its practical concerns such as the fact that classrooms in middle and elementary schools are designed in accordance with standards of hygiene and lighting, not with an eye to elegance."[46]

Japanese Society

Education was the key area of interest for most Chinese visitors to Japan after 1898; specifically, how the Japanese school system produced literate, loyal, and technically competent citizens. But in the course of their two- to three-month stays, they naturally observed and absorbed much about other aspects of Japanese society. Even Chinese educators were routinely given tours of factories, prisons, and police stations, and, less often, of farming areas.

Chang Chien gave particular attention to the problems of rural development. In a conversation with Kanō Jigorō, he explained that he wanted to visit town and village schools, not just those in the city. He wanted to see schools financed by local people hard pressed for funds, not just those subsidized by the government. Chang described in his journal farming techniques he observed on a train ride to Aomori. While in Aomori, he paid visits to agricultural schools and a land-development company. When told by a company representative that 90 percent of Hokkaido's land area had yet to be opened up, he was inspired to wax enthusiastic about the region's potential for future growth.[47]

Chang Chien and other Chinese observers took special note of the agricultural research and extension services then operating in Japan. Some forty experiment stations had been set up throughout the country, staffed with researchers who were mostly recent graduates of agricultural schools.[48] This system of linking research directly with farming, Wang Ching-hsi informed his readers, had resulted in a manyfold increase in farm production.[49] Particularly in the area of sericulture, Chinese observers were impressed with the experiments aimed at eliminating silkworm diseases and developing improved varieties of mulberry leaves and methods of preparing the cocoon. China could surely revive its declining share of the silk industry, they concluded, if attention was similarly given to research and development.[50]

One of the few Chinese officials sent to Japan before 1905 for the express purpose of looking into Japan's economic development was Chou Hsueh-hsi, whose later entrepreneurial activities included founding the well-known Chi Hsin Cement Company. When Chou was dispatched to Japan by his employer, Yuan Shih-k'ai, in the spring of 1903, he was at the start of his successful career, and no doubt his sixty-day study tour served to shape his convictions about the steps China should take to ensure industrial-commercial progress. Chou's Japanese hosts escorted him around a fast-paced tour of banks, government financial agencies (the Finance Ministry and the Bureau of the Mint), Mitsui Bussan, printing presses, schools, a copper-smelting factory, and a glass plant. Chou was led to conclude, with some slight exaggeration: "In Japan at present there is not a person who does not demand foreign goods, and there is not a single foreign product that is not copied by Japanese manufacturers. That is how a petty, little country is able to stand up in an era when the great powers are engaged in commercial war."[51]

In a document recorded at the end of his diary, Chou elaborated on this theme and offered several recommendations to the Chinese government:

Japan's three most notable reform programs are in military training, educational development, and manufacture. [Since] the military aspect depends solely on total national strength, it need not be discussed. Schools and factories, managed by the people themselves, have suddenly multiplied more than tenfold within the last ten-odd years. The speed of progress surpasses anything yet seen in the world. At present, throughout the country, virtually everybody is attending school. Nearly every foreign product in daily use is found also in Japanese manufacture. Recently, moreover, [Japan] is shipping these manufactured commodities to Europe and America as part of its struggle for economic rights.[52]

The Chinese government, too, Chou continued, had begun to understand the urgency of establishing a nationwide school system and promoting the manufacturing sector. But, to date, successful implementation of programs in these areas had been hampered by difficulties of financing. How was it, he asked, that Japan's development had moved forward apace while China lagged behind? He dismissed national character as a fundamental factor in the difference: pre-Meiji Japanese were, if anything, more provincial-minded and resistant to change than their Chinese neighbors. The answer, to his mind, lay most of all in geography. Thanks to a relatively small land area, Japan was quickly able to establish a transportation and communications network, thereby fostering national unity and paving the way for the introduction of other modern technologies and institutions. The Chinese government, by contrast, was saddled with the task of administering a domain so vast and varied that there were sometimes marked differences in language and custom from one village to the next, not to say between regions and provinces. In these circumstances even the best-conceived programs were likely to founder in the early stages.

Chang Chien and Chou Hsueh-hsi typified most Chinese official visitors in focusing their attention above all on institutional arrangements—how ministries, banks, and educational institutions functioned to promote modernization—and on the nationalistic drive displayed by the leadership and general populace alike. In their reports, at any rate, less space was given over to assessments of Japan's total economic output and level of technology. In describing a visit to a factory, for instance, they would typically dwell more on the management aspects than on the types of machinery used in the manufacturing process. Comments on advanced technology tended to be casual observations of travelers taken with this or that device. One might have expected relatively sophisticated observers, recording their impressions of Tokyo in their diaries, to offer a comprehensive look at citywide or national transportation and communications systems, yet most devoted more space to describing the Ueno Zoo, an apparent "must" on the list of tourist attractions. Only a few seemed aware of the broader implications of the modern devices they found so intriguing. Hu Yü-chin, writing in 1904, described a shadowgraph showing scenes from the Russo-Japanese War and remarked with enthusiasm on the educational potential of the moving picture. At Tokyo University, he carefully itemized the equipment available in the science laboratory. He also reported to his readers that the telephone, just coming into general use, linked up some 15,000 establishments in Tokyo.[53] Wang Ching-hsi commented that telephones were everywhere in Tokyo, allowing people to discuss important matters without leaving their quarters.[54]

Not everyone was willing to credit Japan with the new technology in evidence there. When a visitor from Kiangsu inspected Japan's machinery exhibit at the Osaka Exhibition, he observed with a sneer that but for copying Western machines, Japan would have only rickshaws and milkwagons to display.[55] This jibe captures the general feeling of most visitors from China: that in the modern world, like it or not, the term civilization connoted technological rather than belletristic sophistication; and that the level of technology Japan displayed was not so much a product of its own creative impulse as a result of successful borrowing. In part, this attitude reflected a habitual reluctance to admit Japanese superiority. It also implied an acceptance of the notion that institutional strengthening was fundamental to getting the modernization process moving effectively. Once the framework was established, borrowing technology posed no insurmountable problem. This was the kind of advice Chinese visitors were getting from their Japanese hosts. Chou Hsueh-hsi, viewing China's sadly small entry in the Osaka Exhibition's machinery section, recorded Finance Minister Matsukata Masayoshi's comment that if China could get its financial house in order, it would be the strongest nation in the world.[56]

A Japanese institution universally praised by Chinese observers was the legal system. Hu Yü-chin told his readers that the police force, which got its start in 1872, now (1904) had 30,000 men nationwide manning some 10,000 police boxes. The fire-fighting section of the force, he reported, originally bought all of its equipment from Western countries, but since Japan had begun to manufacture its own equipment, more and more of the purchases were Japanese-made. So effective had the police force become, "it compares favorably with [police systems] in Europe and America and has won praise from Westerners."[57] Hu proposed that the Chinese government ought to establish a nationwide police force of its own. (This was probably intended to give a nod of approval to the work of the Peking Police Affairs School, set up with Ch'ing government funds and Japanese advice following the Boxer disturbances.)

Japanese prisons provided a stark contrast to those in China of the day. What touring visitors noted particularly was the emphasis on humane treatment and the concern for rehabilitation. Prisons were "Western-style," they reported, with clean, adequate-sized rooms for comfortable, communal living. Cells were equipped with reading materials, running water, and electric lights, commented one Chinese writer, something even schools in China lacked. Prison doctors made periodic checkups of the inmates. The sick were isolated and given separate bathing areas. To ensure a certain dietary standard, prison food was tested by the staff before being fed to inmates. Of course, prisoners not obeying regulations were put into solitary confinement on short food rations. But cruel and unusual punishments, the Japanese guides explained, went out with the Tokugawa era. In the case of the death penalty, beheading had been outlawed, leaving death by firing squad or hanging as the supposedly more civilized alternatives.[58]

Education was a key part of the prison program. In the first place, prison wardens and guards themselves were required to have a middle-school education. As for prisoners, classroom instruction was provided for youths sixteen and under, and books were available to all. In addition, prison workshops provided opportunities for on-the-job training in metalworking, carpentry, bean curd making, and the like. Thus criminals, in the same way as the mentally and physically handicapped, were encouraged to join the Japanese labor force. Hu, after a tour of a Japanese prison, had this to say about its Chinese counterpart:

We cannot hide the fact that, as frequently testified to in press translations, Europeans and Americans cast a critical eye on Chinese prison abuses. Recently, in Tokyo, I have had occasion to talk with a number of officials who, likewise, often censure our penal system. This also cannot be concealed. To discuss the situation candidly: not only are the official regulations confusing, those [responsible for] implementing them connive with each other [to thwart the system]. A major legal case may drag on for years without a decision being reached. In a minor case, the sentiments of a single responsible official determine whether [punishment] is light or severe. Under such conditions, [even] before sentencing, [a person on trial] may be physically punished to extract a confession. Once a person is imprisoned, there are instances where the jailer, administering his own brand of justice, flogs the prisoner. At the very worst, innocent people, who have become implicated in a crime, have wasted away and died in prison before their cases are settled. Those who are fortunate enough to get out of prison not only lack the wherewithal to launch themselves on a new road, but also have not received the skills training to enable them to make a livelihood. As a result, they inevitably once again fall afoul of the law. This [state of affairs] cannot be concealed; everybody knows it.[59]

Hu offered his readers a careful description of the Japanese court system. Courts at local levels were combined with higher courts of appeal after the model of the German legal system. By contrast, in China, the district magistrate was ultimately responsible for all lawsuits arising in his area of jurisdiction. Since the population in that area might be as many as 250,000 people, and the magistrate had other duties to perform, the judicial process rarely provided a full and just review of any case. Hu proposed that China adopt a variant of the Japanese system, with a series of lower courts in administrative divisions below the district level and courts of appeal at higher levels. "I know that sooner or later we must institute such a system. This includes devising a less severe penal code, which will make it possible both to protect people's lives and to recover extraterritorial rights."[60] Lin Ping-chang, on a visit to a Tokyo local court, was given a briefing on how the judicial system in Japan developed first on the French and then on the German model. Lin was particularly impressed with the length and comprehensiveness of the judicial process. All facts were investigated and reported in great detail; witnesses might be retained for long periods to offer testimony; retrial was possible, as well as referral to higher courts, as measures to guard against corruption. Yet, concluded Lin, with all this, legal scholars in Japan still viewed the system as inadequate and in need of revision.[61]

In assessing the Japanese experience, Chinese visitors highlighted several political lessons. They pointed to Japan's effective leadership. Young, talented bureaucrats in the early Meiji years had made some sound decisions about achieving national unity as a base for

the drive for modernization. Such steps helped close the gap between leaders and ordinary folk, and increased popular enlightenment and receptiveness to change.[62] Leadership at the local level
also drew the attention of Chinese visitors. By contrast to China,
noted one observer, where there tended to be discord between local
gentry and officials on the one hand and gentry and the local populace on the other, in Japan "each town and village has established a
town office where public affairs at the local level are handled by a
town head in an orderly display of self-government."[63] Echoing current sentiments on the much-discussed topic of self-government in
China, he recommended that China adopt a system of routinely fill-
ing local offices with local people, gentry or elders, who would feel
committed to serve in their native area and would enjoy the trust of
their constituents.[64]

Central planning was another fact of Japanese political life that
Chinese pointed to with approbation. Japan's commercial-industrial
successes and rapid progress toward *fukoku* (rich country) status
were the result of the planning mentality in force since the Restoration, declared Chou Hsueh-hsi. "China, with its extensive land
area and large population yet increasingly beset by poverty and
weakness, should take a lesson from this."[65] Planning in education
had led to successes there too: a remarkable rise in general literacy,
an increase in the technically skilled, and, particularly noteworthy
to Chinese observers, the creation of a populace willing to make a
commitment to nation. Key to the effective implementation of
plans, some visitors realized, was an effective communications system. In Japan, Chou pointed out, "no village or city is without the
telegraph and telephone."[66]

Chinese observers were clearly impressed with the public welfare
aspects of Japanese governmental activity. Educating the handicapped, rehabilitating lawbreakers, and providing health facilities
for factory workers were not public policy matters in China.[67] Of
course, pure humanitarianism was less the goal for Japanese leaders
than harnessing the potential of each and every citizen for the common national good. Yet it was precisely this overall objective of education in nationalism, with its observable success in creating a national consensus, that caught the visitors' attention.

In striking contrast to pre-1895 descriptions of Japanese as eager
"comers" but somewhat lacking in moral fiber, our Chinese visitors
had words of praise for the Japanese character. Chu Shou, visiting
Tokyo at the end of 1898, wrote admiringly of the Japanese people's
drive and dedication:

Just a month has passed since I arrived in Japan. I have seen many four-year-old boys and girls in school. I have seen [Japanese] officials, businessmen, and ordinary folk, down to servants and workmen, without exception, reading newspapers and books in their spare time. Alas. How can we speak in the same breath of China's [old-style] classical learning?[68]

In the same vein, Hu Yü-chin commented: "Japanese diligence [*yung-hsin*] is precisely what our nation ought to emulate."[69] Hu, writing in 1904 during the initial phase of the Russo-Japanese conflict, predicted a Japanese victory. Still other Chinese observers put great emphasis on the exemplary public behavior of the Japanese. For example, Ho Pin-sheng, in his description of the crowds gathered at Tokyo's Hibiya Park in 1906 to welcome a member of the British royal family, noted the orderliness of the gathering, a decorum that he attributed to both a finely developed sense of public spirit and the effective functioning of the Japanese police force. Ho went on to contrast these police officers with their Chinese counterparts, whom he indicted as untrustworthy, illiterate, susceptible to bribery, and on the whole, more likely to aid and abet crime than to deter it.[70]

Japan, in the view of our Chinese official travelers, offered a model for an improved Chinese future. Their reasoning echoed that of observers a generation earlier minus the strong undertone of anti-Japanese feeling: if little Japan could attain power and prestige in the eyes of the world, huge China could do it faster and better. But interest in Japan's modernizing sector did not necessarily translate into optimism about prospects for a close Sino-Japanese political partnership. Only the rare visitor made reference to pan-Asianist themes:

China and Japan have the same culture and race—a brotherly relationship. Even though Japan recently has concluded an alliance with Britain, I fear she cannot fully depend on it. Those who are not the same kind generally in the end become alienated. . . . I deeply hope that China will gradually self-strengthen in order to jointly resist the eastward advance of Western strength [*ou-li tung-chien*].[71]

On balance, Chinese study tour participants were representative of the new local elites. They were products of a traditional education, yet they were innovative, open-minded, engaged. For these people, most of them a rung or two below the Chang Chih-tungs on the official ladder, what we today would call development problems—institutional change, economic growth, social betterment—were the top priorities. Japan, for them, was an acceptable development model, especially in the field of education and training, the cornerstone of all programs of change. Given the consistency of this kind of thinking among our sample group of travelers, it is safe to conclude that China's study-in-Japan program, though articulated best by Chang Chih-tung and others, enjoyed wide support among the current generation of middle-level leaders. Furthermore, as we will see more clearly in the chapters to follow, what this generation hoped for from their overseas students was not so far from the students' own expectations of their future role.

Most of the Chinese visitors were in contact with the Chinese student community in Tokyo. Hu Yü-chin mentions appointments at the Chinese Student Union and the Kiangsu Provincial Society office.[72] Huang Ching also paid a visit to the Student Union. He named several students (including Chang Tsung-hsiang and Ts'ao Ju-lin, whom we will meet later) and apparently consulted with them on the purchase of agricultural equipment for Yuan Shih-k'ai's new training center.[73] Chang Chien, in his account of his 1903 tour, wrote approvingly of the fact that increasing numbers of Chinese students were enrolling in programs of technical training so crucial to China's future needs.[74]

In the course of their regular tours of schools, most visitors made note of the number of Chinese students enrolled. Chou Hsueh-hsi, for instance, remarked that 170 Chinese were attending the military preparatory school, Seijō Gakkō, adding that they were taught in classrooms separate from the Japanese students.[75] Wang Ching-hsi was closely involved with the student group. He escorted to Japan twenty-three students scheduled to enroll at the Kōbun Institute. On their arrival at Shimbashi Station, he and his charges were met by a student welcoming party. A few days later, Wang was the honored guest at a meeting of fifty to sixty Chihli students. Asked for comments, he spoke of the key role of education in the process of national development:

National prosperity is based on education. Chinese civilization has been developing for over 4,000 years. In both its spiritual and its physical aspects, it is brilliant and unsurpassed. But what is appropriate depends on the period. [If] in praising the past, one depreciates the present, or in pursuing the results, forgets the causes, one loses the best of both. At present, the intellectual approach of a single nation is inadequate to face this age of acute struggle. We must take as our approach cosmopolitan learning; then we will be able to stand imposingly on our own. In establishing schools we are still currently at the germination stage. It is not that it is difficult to find excellent seeds, just that it is not easy to cultivate them. You, gentlemen, have braved a lengthy journey across the sea to pursue your studies. Stimulated by a foreign environment, inevitably your patriotism will increase a hundredfold. Once you have completed your studies and returned to China, you will sow and cultivate, stimulate and nourish. Your responsibility cannot be relegated to others. But watch carefully what you plant; do not let weeds run rampant through the new sprouts. Harvest time is not far off.[76]

THREE

The Student Encounter
with Japan

C HANG CHIH-TUNG AND OTHER progressive officials of his generation clearly thought it possible to control the process of change they were initiating. They were confident that they could maintain the allegiance of the newly trained returned students by absorbing them into a modified version of the dynastic system. They hoped, not unrealistically, that the Chinese might, like the Japanese before them, use new technology, new national consciousness, and new institutional ideas to forge national strength under imperial sanction. What they tended to gloss over were some of the essential differences between the Japanese political and social system and their own: the greater homogeneity of Japanese society; Japan's more explicit structure of political loyalties; the revolutionary character of what was styled the Meiji Restoration; and the fact that the Meiji Emperor, the connecting link to the creation myth itself, had both religious and temporal claims to legitimacy, whereas his counterpart in China represented an alien minority group (the Manchus), whose right to rule was increasingly being challenged by "pure" ethnic Chinese.

In time, as we know now, the progressives' hopes were dashed. Chinese students came to oppose not only the Manchus, but those like Chang himself whose fortunes were tied to the Manchu state. The specifics of how this happened and what it meant to China's political life and relations with Japan form the story of succeeding chapters. This chapter provides a profile of the student group in Japan as background to that story. It surveys the students as a group in terms of age, fields of study, family history, motives for choosing to go abroad, and the like. A central source for this survey is a 1903 roster of 663 Chinese students, listing (for most) their ages, provincial origin, arrival date in Japan, school affiliation, and scholarship or nonscholarship status. The discussion then turns to examine the experience of the individual student—what motivated him to go to Japan, and how he interacted with Japan and the Japanese.

Educational and Family Background

The term "student" as it applied to the *liu hsueh-sheng* covered a broad range of ages and backgrounds. Reporting on the expected predominance of the over-thirty generation in a group of new arrivals in 1901, the *Japan Weekly Mail* commented: "It is said that 400 Chinese students are about to come to Japan. They are called 'students' but many are already office-holders who will study methods of discharging the functions with which they are entrusted."[1] The reality was that of those actually in Japan in 1902–3, about 67 percent were aged seventeen to twenty-five, and most of the rest (20 percent) in their late twenties. Only 8 percent were thirty or over, and 5 percent were under seventeen, including some youngsters of six and seven.[2] Such an age structure suggests that the majority of the students were mature and approached their Japan experience equipped with the standard Chinese classical education. But, it also suggests that relatively few could have been officeholders—the 8 percent in their thirties at most. The average age of those attaining even the qualifying or bachelor's (*sheng-yuan* or *hsiu-ts'ai*) degree in China was about twenty-five, and though that degree certainly conferred a certain prestige on the holder, particularly in rural areas, appointment to office was reserved for those who went on to success in the higher examinations and were thus likely to be well over twenty-five.[3]

The *liu hsueh-sheng* represented the new generation, most of them born in the late 1870's and 1880's. They were, in a metaphoric sense, the children of the study tour participants described in Chapter 2 and shared with them the ready pursuit of "learning from the outside." The very notion of "overseas student" reflected the increase in social mobility at the turn of the century, the uncertainty about civil service career prospects, and the consequent search for new skills and job opportunities in the modernizing sector.

There was no standard résumé among the students. Some had already achieved success in the examinations. Chang Tsung-hsiang, for example, a Chekiang native, passed the first government examinations for the bachelor's degree (*hsiu-ts'ai*) in 1895, when he was only eighteen, then went to Japan two years later on scholarship to enroll in the law program at Tokyo Imperial University.[4] Hu Yuan-t'an, born into a Hunan family of noted scholars, likewise had obtained his bachelor's degree before going to Japan in 1902 to study at the Kōbun Institute as a scholarship student.[5] Other degree holders went as self-supporting students. Tung Hung-wei had achieved the master's or provincial graduate degree (*chü-jen*) equivalent before going to Japan for a period of self-financed study at Waseda University.[6] Lin Ch'ang-min, whose father was a Hanlin scholar (the best of the metropolitan or doctoral degreeholders), obtained the bachelor's degree in 1897, then later decided to study in Japan. Lin graduated from Waseda with honors in political economy in 1909.[7]

Other students were from scholar-official families, but, for one reason or another, either rejected the examination route completely or abandoned it midway. Chang Chi (1882–1947), a well-known Kuomintang figure, grew up in a scholarly environment in Hupei but chose to enroll as a self-supporting student at Waseda University at age nineteen rather than take the civil service examinations. China's great literary figure Lu Hsün (pen name of Chou Shu-jen) could count both minor officials and businessmen among his Chekiang relatives. But with his father terminally ill and his grandfather implicated in a bribery scandal, the family fell on hard times, and young Lu chose modern technical studies over the long, uncertain course to success in the civil service. He first enrolled in the Kiangnan Naval Academy (Nanking), then transferred to the Mining and Railroad School (Nanking), from which he was graduated in 1901. In the spring of 1902, Lu was sent to Japan on a Nanyang scholarship to study medicine. There he ultimately abandoned medical studies for a career in literature.[8] Hu Han-min, a close associate of Sun Yat-sen's and a prominent figure in Republican China, belonged to a poor but well-educated category of overseas students. Hu lost both parents—his father was a legal secretary—at an early age and was left to support numerous siblings. Somehow Hu managed to study for and pass the provincial examination for the *chü-jen* degree in 1901; a year later, he was sent to Japan on scholarship by the Kwangtung governor.[9]

There is evidence—again from a few individual cases—of other than scholar-official families sending their sons to Japan. Wu Yü-chang, later a leading member of the Chinese Communist Party, was from a low-income family in Szechuan. Chang Shih-chao came from a Hunan farming family.[10] Tsou Jung's (see Chapter 7) father was a merchant in Szechuan, who gave his son a sound education in the Classics but could not persuade him to take the civil service examinations. Feng Tzu-yu, well-known chronicler of the revolutionary period, was born in Japan, the son of a Chinese merchant in Yokohama.[11]

Many other students, whose family backgrounds are unknown, were, like Chang, Tsou, and Feng, young and in Japan on their own or family funds. Twenty percent of the students identified by age on the 1903 roster were under twenty, and almost all of these youths (90 percent) were self-supporting. For example, Chou Hung-yeh, a native of Hunan, arrived in Japan in 1899 at age seventeen to enroll as a self-supporting student at Waseda University.[12] Yin Yüan-i from Hupei was eighteen when he entered the Kōbun Institute in 1901 on his own funds.[13] Again, Li Wen-fan, a Kwangtung native, began his training in Japan in 1900 as an eighteen-year-old self-supporting student, eventually winning a degree from Hōsei University.[14] While some of these teenagers were remarkably well qualified by classical standards—Wu Lu-chen reportedly had won his *chü-jen* degree at the tender age of sixteen before embarking on study in Japan[15]— most were probably not. This is a point of some significance since they would not have had the sense of commitment to the Ch'ing system fostered by years of struggling to become civil servants.

Still, judging from their placement level in Japanese schools, the majority of Chinese students in Japan in 1902–3, if not showing the precocity of Wu Lu-chen, were at least adequately trained in China's literary tradition before going overseas to study. The Chinese government intervened on this point in 1902, issuing a regulation requiring students desirous of pursuing study in Japan to have first completed middle-school-level training in China. But there was an occasional slipup. A student diarist writing in 1905 cited the case of one "student" who could not even read primary-level characters on his arrival. After a special preparatory course he was able to compose essays. According to the diarist, this case illustrated at one and the same time, the effectiveness of Meiji educational methods and the inattentiveness of Chinese officials to the quality of youth they were selecting for overseas study.[16] "Quality," of course, is a relative term. Chinese students, whatever the depth of their classical training, were woefully unprepared in science and mathematics. Once in Japan, even the most senior people were assigned to grade-school-level math classes, there to learn the basics of addition, subtraction, multiplication, division, and fractions.[17]

Given the close correlation between education and socioeconomic status in late imperial China, it seems safe to conclude from the sample that the 660 students in Japan in 1903 were representative of the roughly 1 percent (4,000,000) of China's population classified as classically educated, wealthy, and privileged.[18] Just how privileged, how economically self-sufficient, is more difficult to say. The fact that study in Japan was more affordable than study in the West obviously opened up the opportunity for overseas study to a wider group economically, though often at considerable sacrifice.[19] Wu Yü-chang records the difficulties he and other aspiring overseas students had in raising funds for the Japan trip. Ts'ao Ju-lin describes how his family found it necessary to sell a plot of land to finance his study in Japan.[20]

That young people had more options and were taking advantage of them is suggested by the fact that 60 percent of all students in Japan in 1903 were there on their own funds, including half of those in the 17–25 age bracket (and as noted, a full 90 percent of those in the under-20 group). The central government had paved the way by explicitly sanctioning self-financed overseas study, seeing in it a means of acquiring new talent without any drain on the treasury. The same concern for central finances led the government to spread the burden of supporting the 40 percent who were on scholarship: their sponsors included province and county governments, as well as factories, businesses, and merchants' associations.[21] The diversity of funding sources, both state and private, highlights the degree of public support for "opening to the outside world." Study abroad, in other words, seemed to serve the interests of many segments of the social elite at the turn of the century.

For reasons having to do with cost, the Chinese student group in Japan was probably less homogeneous than the groups that went to the West. As an observer writing in 1908 remarked, "Living in Tokyo is four times cheaper than in any European or American country, and, but for this cheapness, 1000's of students would never have been able to leave their native land."[22]

Motivations

"Thousands of students" was no exaggeration. Over a remarkably short span of years—1900–1905—the number of Chinese going overseas for study mushroomed, and the composition changed to include more short-term students, nearly all of whom were self-supporting. Three factors were involved in the upsurge in numbers. One was explicit central government support for study abroad as part of the post-Boxer reform program (Chapter 1). A second factor was the decision to phase out the thousand-year-old civil service examination system. This was accomplished over a four-year period through a series of measures designed at once to modify the style and content of the examination and reduce the number of exam-takers. Beginning in 1901, the old "eight-legged essay" format was abolished and allowance was made for new perspectives in answering test questions. The following topic from a 1902 provincial examination shows the attempt to blend the traditional and the modern:

When Japan renovated her style of Government what things were of prime importance and what things have proved to be of good effect? In regard to her altering everything to Western ways, those who know say that it cannot but be that Japan has exceeded what she ought to have done. Yet, what things can be taken from the midst of the others and shown to be wrong? To-day are there methods of mending and saving [China]? Follow the subject into all its branches and subdivisions; say with minute accuracy what things are a mirror for China to use.[23]

"Foreign" subjects were also introduced into the test format, including a special economics section in 1903.

A second aspect of this phasing-out process saw traditional degrees awarded for a modern as well as the traditional education. For example, a document prepared by Chang Chih-tung in 1904 stipulated that students completing their studies in Japan would be evaluated before leaving Tokyo by the Chinese minister and the general supervisor of students, and then, on their return to China, further examined by an imperial commissioner. A student would be awarded a Chinese degree based on the level and type of school attended in Japan and on his final marks and the degree or diploma received. Basic guidelines for equivalent degrees were precisely outlined: honors graduates of a Japanese government high school were eligible for the *chü-jen* degree, graduates of Japanese government universities were eligible for the *chin-shih* degree, and so on. As more and more people attained degree status through a modern schooling, the government increasingly reduced the numbers allowed to sit for the now-modified civil service examination.[24] By the time the official examination was formally terminated in 1905, a new system of evaluation and testing was well in place. Reportedly, between 1906 and 1911, some 1,388 returned students were awarded degrees after passing the revised examination; 90 percent of them had studied in Japan. Again, of the 255 higher degree (*chin-shih* and *chü-jen*) recipients listed in the *China Yearbook* of 1912, 95 percent had been trained in Japan.[25]

Phasing out the examination system had profound social implications. It meant that the route to power and prestige now lay in the new learning and degrees from foreign institutions. As the prestige value of foreign study increased, study in Japan became a particularly attractive option, since it was a financial possibility for many.

The third factor that contributed to the growing numbers of students in Japan had to do not with Chinese domestic policy but with the rising fortunes of the host country, Japan. Referring to Japan's acknowledged prestige in the post-Boxer years, the *Japan Weekly Mail* observed in 1901: "The Yangtze Viceroys are evidently looking towards Japan with constantly increasing interest as the country upon whose doings they are to model their own measures of progress."[26] Japan's victory in the Russo-Japanese War demonstrated the success of its modernization program and gave force to its claims to imperialist power. That Japan, an Asian nation, had bested a modern Western power drew respect from European observers and admiration from Chinese and other Asians. Learning from Japan made sense.

For many young Chinese, particularly in the early years of the program, the decision to study in Japan was guided by considerations of career advancement pure and simple. Ts'ao Ju-lin, for example, had Japan study recommended to him by Chang Tsung-hsiang and others who had been there and had spoken of Japan as a progressive country that treated foreign students well and provided a low-cost, modern education.[27] Arriving in Japan in 1900, Ts'ao spent four years there as a self-supporting student, studying first at Waseda, then pursuing a law program at the Tokyo Law Academy. Law degree in hand, he returned to China, where he won the *chin-shih* degree and a civil service post for his performance on the government's first special examination for returned students in 1905.

Of those sent to Japan on scholarship, a number shared Ts'ao's motives of career advancement. Chang Tsung-hsiang, mentioned above, passed the preliminary examination for the *hsiu-ts'ai* degree in 1895, then three years later accepted a Nanyang scholarship for study in Japan. Returning to China with an LL.B., he, like Ts'ao, was awarded the *chin-shih* degree in the 1905 examination; this won him a post in the law revision office.[28]

In the case of other scholarship students, motivations for Japan study appeared to shift midstream. Shen Hsiang-yün, Hu Han-min, Ch'in Yü-liu, and Ch'en T'ien-hua, to give but a few examples, were selected as scholarship recipients by their respective governors or governors-general.[29] Shen was handpicked by Chang Chih-tung himself on the basis of his outstanding school record. Yet, while in Japan, all four turned into outspoken critics of Ch'ing officialdom, including especially Governor-general Chang. Tracing this story more fully in these and other cases is the substance of succeeding chapters. Suffice it to say here that a capacity for good scholarship often went hand in hand with an independence of spirit nurtured and given an outlet in the Japanese environment.

Clearly, some students who accepted scholarships were thinking beyond career advancement in the usual sense, though at the outset their goals were ill-defined. The lure of Japan, from accounts provided by brothers and friends, was that it represented modernity, strength, new ideas, opportunities for freedom of expression. To Lu Hsün, for example, Japan study was to compensate for what he knew to be the inadequate technical training he had received at the Nanking naval school.

Of course we all looked forward to graduation. But when the time came, we felt rather let down. We had climbed the flagpole several times, but needless to say were not half qualified to be sailors; we had attended lectures for several years and been down the pits several times, but could we mine gold, silver, copper, iron or lead? The fact was, we had no such faith ourselves, for this was not as simple as writing an essay "On the Need to Have Effective Tools to Do Good Work." . . . Only one course was left to us: to go abroad.[30]

In Wu Yü-chang's case, an uncertain career path led to the decision to pursue study in Japan. He portrays himself in the years after 1898 caught between a growing fascination with the "new learning" and a reluctance to abandon the standard route to career advancement via the civil service examinations. Failure in the first examination series was the turning point. Fearful of failing again, Wu decided to sample a modern education at a school in Szechuan run by a returned student from Japan. When this proved unsatisfactory, he joined forces with his elder brother and friends in plans to go to Japan as self-supporting students. In the Japan venture, Wu faced two obstacles: first, he had a wife and children to support, and second, he and his comrades lacked adequate funds. He resolved the first problem with apparent ease by convincing himself of the necessity of sacrifice for the larger good; the second problem was overcome by a series of efforts, including the sale of a piece of land, that got the group first to Shanghai, then on to Japan.[31]

Wu's experience was the fairly common one of an ambitious youth, attracted to the new learning or new politics, whose interest in going to Japan was heightened by enthusiastic reports of relatives and friends who had studied there. It was becoming "the thing to do." Beyond this, many young Chinese felt it their patriotic duty to study abroad: to "save the nation" required new skills. A number of those who enrolled in Japanese military schools were so motivated.[32]

Contact with Japanese working in China was obviously a deciding factor for some young people. Chang Chi, for example, made the trip to Tokyo in 1899 in the company of Nakajima Saishi, educational adviser to Yuan Shih-k'ai. Tsou Jung (whose tragic career we will come to in due course) was influenced in his decision to study abroad by Japanese he met in Chungking. Many Japanese were teaching in China at the time. Many others, like Kanō and Shimoda, visited China to advise the leadership on educational development in general and, specifically, to recruit students.

Increasingly after 1900 a compelling reason for going to Japan was to escape arrest and imprisonment by the Ch'ing authorities. The patriotism that motivated some was, for others, becoming anti-Ch'ing. Sung Chiao-jen fled to Japan in 1904 to avoid interrogation for his part in an uprising in Changsha.[33] When, in 1904, Chang Shih-chao found himself a prime suspect in an assassination plot, he, too, wisely decided to try the life of an overseas student. Impressed with Japan's successes in modernizing, he remained in Tokyo as a student until 1908, when he went off to Scotland to continue his studies in political economy.

Enrollment and Fields of Study

According to the 1903 roster, more than 60 percent of the Chinese students were enrolled in the various senior secondary schools and programs set up specially to cater to their educational needs: the Kōbun Institute, the Seijō School (Chinese students division), the Tokyo Dōbun Academy, and the Seika School. Another 15 percent were pursuing a higher education, half at Tokyo Imperial and Waseda universities and half in various professional schools. Except for a few students studying at vocational schools, the rest were enrolled in preparatory schools, presumably, judging by their ages, with the aim of entering higher institutions of learning.

The vast majority of the students were enrolled in liberal arts, teacher training, and military studies, with only a handful pursuing science and technology majors. To some extent, this reflected the interest of officials like Chang Chih-tung, who wanted trained people to fill slots in the new schools and new army units. Another, practical reason for the heavy concentration on the humanities was simply that, given the low level of science and mathematics training in China, most students were unprepared to study anything else.

Liberal arts and teacher training programs between them absorbed about 40 percent of the 1903 group. The Kōbun Institute set the standard here, with several curriculum choices designed by Kanō Jigorō following his extensive conversations with Chang Chih-tung in 1902. The regular program was a three-year course running forty-three weeks a year, with thirty-three hours of class a week. The first year focused heavily on Japanese-language study, supplemented by a few introductory hours in history, mathematics, ethics, and physical education. In the second year, the student plunged into a full schedule of courses, including, in addition to a continuation of first-year subjects, geometry, algebra, chemistry, drawing, and (as an elective) English. Third-year students had the option of following a science and math stream, with courses in ethics, Japanese, geometry, algebra, trigonometry, chemistry, zoology, botany, drawing, English, and physical education, or a humanities stream that substituted history courses for chemistry, algebra, and geometry. Judging from the number of subjects covered and the number of hours spent on each subject (e.g., five hours of geometry every third week), the Kōbun program provided more of a survey of various fields than study in depth.

Kōbun also offered short-term options in teacher training, police studies, science, and music, with program length varying between six months and a year and a half. The intensive courses were taught using interpreters. There was considerable debate among both Chinese and Japanese educators on the merits of long-term versus short-term training. Waseda University held out for the standard curriculum, but a number of other institutions, including Hōsei University, designed intensive courses for Chinese. Kanō Jigorō believed there was a place for both.[34]

Thirty percent of the group were cadets at Seijō, in service in training units, or enrolled in the Kōbun Institute's police studies course. Seijō, which began its program for Chinese in 1898 with the admission of four students from Chekiang, was particularly well reputed among Chinese. Its Chinese student division had expanded significantly after the Boxer uprising as pressures grew to develop a modern Chinese army. By 1903, it had already turned out 106 Chinese graduates.[35] But it was not until 1904 that sending batches of Chinese youth to Japan for military study was endorsed as national policy.[36] In the spring of that year, on the recommendation of the Chinese minister to Japan, Yang Shu, the Bureau of Military Training announced a new program to send 100 students to Japan annually for a four-year course of military studies. Each province was assigned a quota and required to supply half the funding, the other half to be provided by the bureau. In making this a full scholarship program, the intent was to close out military studies as an option for the self-supporting student. Self-supporting students already enrolled in military studies in Japan were allowed to continue as long as their academic performance and conduct were satisfactory.[37]

The standard military studies route took students first through the preparatory course at Seijō or its successor school, Shinbu Gakkō, then to practical training in an army unit, followed by a period of higher-level study at the Army Officers School (Rikugun Shikan Gakkō). Only the unusual few gained entrance to the Military Staff College. Between 1898 and 1907, 499 Chinese had completed both the Shinbu course and practical training. At the close of that decade, seventy-five were still in training, and 255 had entered Army Officers School. The fact that in 1932 half the members of the Nationalist Government's military commission were Japan-trained illustrates something of the impact this program had on a generation of Chinese military.[38]

The remaining 30 percent of the 1903 group consisted mostly of either college-level students studying law, science, engineering, business, agriculture, and medicine or students in unspecified preparatory programs, presumably involving a large measure of language training in Japanese—about 40 to 45 percent, respectively. A few students (the remaining 15 percent) were enrolled in primary schools, vocational courses, or English language programs.

It is difficult to generalize about the Chinese students' length of stay in Japan. A list of ninety-seven graduates from 1898 to 1902 appended to the 1903 roster shows forty-four as 1902 graduates of three- or four-year military-related programs (including six trained in Tokyo and Osaka munitions factories), forty-six as graduates of one- to six-month teachers training courses offered by the Kōbun Institute, and the other seven as products of four-year language and special studies programs. In the next few years, particularly with the influx of students after the Russo-Japanese War and the expansion of programs to accommodate them, the Chinese student population floating in and out of short-term courses, often of doubtful quality, grew substantially. According to a Chinese Education Ministry report of 1907, when some 7,000 Chinese students were in Japan, 60 percent were enrolled in short-term courses, 30 percent were taking the general course, 5–6 percent were withdrawing before completion, 3–4 percent were in higher specialized schools, and a mere 1 percent were attending university.[39]

A breakdown of enrollments by the student's home province is confirming evidence of the considerable social mobility at the turn of the century. In early 1902, according to the *Japan Weekly Mail*, twelve of the eighteen provinces were represented. Kiangsu and Chekiang headed the list with forty-five and forty-two students, respectively.[40] By 1903, every province except Kansu had at least one native son in Japan. Again, the coastal provinces were best represented. Kiangsu and Chekiang alone accounted for more than a third of the total on the 1903 roster, with 129 and 110 students, respectively.

Examining provinces grouped by governor-generalships, we find that the Liang-Kiang provinces (Kiangsu, Anhui, Kiangsi) topped the list, with a combined total of 187 students, followed by the Min-Che group (Fukien, Chekiang) with 158, and the Hu-Kuang provinces (Hupei, Hunan) with 135. The Liang-Kiang figure is to be expected: Liu K'un-i and Chang Chih-tung, planners of the study-abroad program, were the incumbent governors-general in the 1900–1903 period; their successor, Wei Kuang-t'ao, was also known for his modernizing zeal. The Min-Che provinces were under the leadership of Hsü Ying-kuei from 1898 to 1903; Hsü was the architect of a policy to introduce Western military technology and training methods into the two provinces. Tuan-fang occupied the Hupei-Hunan governor-general's post between 1902 and 1904. Though Tuan was held in low esteem by radical students, he was involved in the typical range of reformist activities, including the promotion of modern industries and schools. Chihli also supported a sizable number of students in Japan—forty-two in 1903. Here, too, the number correlates with the man in the governor's seat. Chihli, which because of its strategic importance rated a governor-general of its own, was headed by Yuan Shih-k'ai for the period 1901–7; we have already touched more than once on Yuan's interest in educational reform.[41] Finally, it is worth noting that there were only twenty-three Manchus (about 3 percent of the total) on the 1903 list, most from the various banner armies.

The pattern of provincial representation of students was fairly consistent. A *Japan Weekly Mail* article of January 1904, which reported the Chinese student total at somewhere between 1,200 and 1,400, again showed the southern and coastal provinces supplying the greatest number of students. A March 1906 *North China Herald* article offered a percentage breakdown by province based on a total of 8,620 students. The southern/coastal preponderance still held true, but Szechuan—a western province—now had a large contingent of students in Japan. The figures were Hunan, 17 percent; Hupei, Kiangsu, and Szechuan, about 13 percent each; Chekiang, Chihli, and Kwangtung about 7 percent each; and the remaining 23 percent "fairly evenly distributed" among the other provinces.[42]

Entirely underrepresented among the Chinese overseas students were women. Only eleven are recorded on the 1903 roster, ten (half of them under the age of fifteen) registered at the Imperial Women's Association, and one at the Japan Women's College. At the turn of the century, Japanese women, not Chinese, were at the forefront of female progress in Asia, particularly in the area of education. Having gained the right to an education as part of the Meiji reforms, certain Japanese women, notably Shimoda Utako, founder of the Women's Practical Arts School and dean of the Peeresses' College, were eager to see Chinese women follow the same path. By 1902, Shimoda had seven Chinese women under her wing at the Practical Arts School. Two persevered through the two-year course, graduating in July 1904. In that same year, Hunan province sent twenty women to Japan for intensive courses in teacher training and industrial arts. It was an interesting group of women, all "from good families" but of a wide range of ages (fourteen to fifty-three). In 1907, Fengtien dispatched twenty-one women to enroll in the Practical Arts School, and Kiangsi sent ten. The number of Chinese women students in Japan in that year edged up to about 100, a significant rise but still a mere 1 percent of the entire student group. Only ninety-eight women graduated from their various programs between 1904 and 1920. The women seemed to have made up in energy what they lacked in numbers. Theirs was one of the first major efforts to publicize the cause of women's rights in China.[43]

Guidance and Counseling

Many prospective students, we can be sure, tried to learn all they could about the study-in-Japan programs. Some had little more to go on than the casual counseling of friends recently returned home. Lu Hsün illustrates what the quality of much of this freely given advice was:

The authorities approved of study abroad, and agreed to send five students to Japan. But one of these five did not go, because his grandmother wept as if it would kill her. That left just four of us. Japan was very different from

China; how should we prepare ourselves? A student who had graduated a year ahead of us had been to Japan; he should know something of conditions there. When we went to ask his advice he told us earnestly: "Japanese socks are absolutely unwearable, so take plenty of Chinese socks. And I don't think bank-notes are any good; better change all the money you take into their silver yen." The four of us all agreed. I don't know about the others, but I changed all my money in Shanghai into Japanese silver yen, and I took with me ten pairs of Chinese socks, white cloth socks. And later? Later we had to wear uniforms and leather shoes, so those cloth Chinese socks proved completely useless. And as they had long given up using silver coins of the one-yen denomination in Japan, I changed mine at a loss into half-yen coins and bank-notes.[44]

But most students probably got their information through the written word, since the press routinely covered the overseas study programs. Liang Ch'i-ch'ao's Yokohama-based publications, *Public Opinion* (Ch'ing-i pao) and *New People's Miscellany* (Hsin-min ts'ung-pao), told their large Chinese readership a lot about Meiji Japan and the activities of the Chinese students there. The Shanghai-based daily *Su pao* printed a regular column on overseas student affairs. The Chinese students in Japan themselves published ten magazines in the years 1900 to 1904, which were widely distributed in China.[45] In addition to providing readers with information on what the students were doing and learning, many of these publications projected an anti-Manchu image, an added note of excitement, no doubt, for many youth considering a study tour in Japan. At a more functional level, there were several handbooks available in the early 1900's specifically designed to introduce prospective students to the Japanese school system and prepare them for life in Japan.[46] These give a fascinating view of what it was like to be a Chinese student in Japan at the turn of the century.

Ts'ao Ju-lin, in his autobiography, mentions the usefulness of a handbook prepared by Chang Tsung-hsiang in 1901. Entitled *Guide to Study in Japan* (Jih-pen yu-hsueh chih-nan), the work provided a full introduction to the academic scene, along with information on travel expenses to Japan, options in student housing, and the cost of miscellaneous items like clothing and public baths.[47] Another widely used guide was the *Handbook for Students Abroad* (Liu hsueh-sheng chien).[48] This work, published by the Tokyo-based Chinese Student Union in 1906, was broader in scope than the earlier *Guide to Study*, a veritable "everything you want to know about a study tour to Japan." It was an odd compendium of often seemingly irrelevant information—instructions on how to swim, for example—combined with useful suggestions on effective study techniques, all interlaced with exhortations to be determined, diligent, and personally clean.

Both handbooks offered prefatory essays stressing the importance of study abroad to China's future. The one in the earlier work echoed arguments used by Chang Chih-tung and others: that study abroad had given a demonstrable boost to Japan's development and could do the same for China; that, as a relatively advanced nation, Japan had a role to play as a conduit of Western technology; and that study in Japan was China's most cost-effective option. The author struck a new note in raising the question of the marketability of the new skills to be acquired in Japan, suggesting that in the current period of change, the mere availability of such skills would create a demand for them.

Written after the Russo-Japanese War, when Chinese students were flooding Japan, the 1906 handbook's introductory message did not seek so much to justify and promote study abroad as to explain the phenomenon taking place. It was a political message, quite in contrast to the 1901 essay. The outflow of youth, we are told, was symptomatic of political instability at home, China's precarious position internationally, the corruption of Chinese society, and the failure of Chinese scholarship to measure up in the modern world. The last weakness was identified as the primary constraint on China's growth and development. Whereas in China the goal of scholarship was to perpetuate a body of knowledge from the past, for the rest of the world scholarship was directed to a struggle for the most advanced science and technology. "Where knowledge is abundant, both the individual and the nation reap the benefit." Study abroad, readers were told, would help a generation of China's youth develop new perspectives on learning as a tool for national survival. Having declared themselves in favor of a modern, utilitarian approach to education, the authors were traditionalist enough to cite the importance of personal virtues in the pursuit of study abroad: a determined spirit, they argued, with supporting phrases from classical Chinese thinkers, was the key to all learning.[49]

A major function of the student handbooks was to guide prospective students through the Meiji educational system. Both works emphasized that, with the array of options before them, students would be well advised to have their goals clearly in mind before selecting a school or study program. Indeed, for many students, making this choice must have been an overwhelming experience. China at the time could boast only a veneer of modern schools on a foundation of private family/clan academies, all basic preparatory institutions that in curriculum, method, and objective had remained unchanged for centuries. In Japan, the student newly arrived faced a complex system of both private and state-supported schools where one proceeded by levels—primary, secondary, and higher—and different types of training—general academic, vocational, technical, military, professional. While the student could expect some assistance from the Chinese legation, there were no student placement services or guidance counselors to ease his way into the appropriate Japanese school. Both handbooks provided detailed diagrams of the Meiji school system, with accompanying text on the length of various programs, entrance requirements, and current level of tuition and fees. Particular attention was given to schools most often attended by Chinese: schools offering a general or liberal arts program like the Dōbun Academy, the Kōbun Institute, and the Seijō School, and specialized or professional schools in law, economics, literature, commerce, agriculture, science, and medicine. Chang Tsung-hsiang in his *Guide to Study in Japan* provided sample curricula for middle schools, college preparatory courses, and advanced study programs. The advanced programs, he warned, were only appropriate for mature, senior people prepared to pursue a single aspect of a discipline—constitutional law within the law program, for example. Chang encouraged all students to take full advantage of their stay in Japan by devoting the summer vacation months to intensive study.[50]

The 1906 work, as might be expected, had more of a "hands-on" feel to it. In a long section on study methods, readers were lectured on the importance of motivation in successful learning, on the necessity of studying when rested and alert, preferably in the morning, and on how to get the best return on their efforts to study in a foreign language by selecting in the first place well-written, well-organized reading materials. Students were advised on how to deal with the large volume of reading they were expected to cover in a Japanese school program: the memorization-recitation method used in studying the Chinese Classics was not feasible, the authors warned; one must read for key ideas and be prepared to take notes in outline format. The section on notetaking techniques ended with a long discourse on how one committed to memory essential ideas extracted from a large body of material.[51]

In its concern for all manner of adjustment problems, the *Handbook for Students Abroad* provided a lengthy section on the Japanese language. There were lists of Japanese simplified characters, of characters in current Japanese usage not found in Chinese, of characters slightly altered in the Japanese written version, and of the

Japanese names for the root portions of the characters or "radicals," as they are known. *Kana,* the Japanese phonetic system, was also explained.[52] One has only to recall the bewilderment of Chinese visitors of the 1880's at some of the Tokyo street signs to gauge the importance for the new student of this information on written language.

Both guides devoted considerable space to the matter of school fees and living expenses. We noted earlier that for many students study in Japan represented a financial sacrifice. The *Handbook for Students Abroad* warned that expenses were "an important consideration," varying as they did in accordance with price fluctuations and type of school.[53] School fees centered on an entrance examination charge and tuition expenses. The former ranged from one to five yen for public schools and one to two yen for private institutions. Monthly tuition ran from one to two and a half yen for public and one to two yen for private schools with the school year calculated as ten months.

In the case of board and room, the other major expense, students had three basic options. The most reasonable choice was the school dormitory, at a cost of about five to seven yen a month. In addition to being the cheapest living arrangement, Chang Tsung-hsiang noted, the dormitory had the advantage of providing a better regulated environment. On the minus side was the "inconvenience" of having to live together with Japanese students. Living in a boarding house meant greater freedom, but lodgings alone could cost from two to six yen a month, and board ranged from a low of five yen to ten yen for a first-class establishment. A third option was to rent a house, which several students might do together for a fee of ten to twelve yen a month, exclusive, of course, of expenses for food. Chang mentioned still another possibility, living with a Japanese family, but this was not usually workable, he pointed out, because upper- and middle-class families tended to have no interest in hosting a Chinese student, and lower-class families lacked the room.

Several categories of miscellaneous expenses filled out the financial picture for the student. Books and school supplies came to about three yen a month. Such items as haircuts, newspapers, public baths, school uniforms, and entertainment accounted for another three yen monthly. Student expenses obviously varied considerably, depending on the particular student, but a conservative estimate for the 1901 school year would put the total at about 150–200 yen. By 1906, the figure had risen to 250–300 yen. Y. C. Wang gives us a useful comparative look at how Chinese students fared in the

United States and Japan, not much later, in 1909–10. In that period, the Chinese government gave scholarship students in Japan a yearly stipend of 450 yen, those in the United States the equivalent of 1,110 yen ($960).[54] Study in the United States was thus about two and a half times as expensive as study in Japan.

The 1906 handbook included a fascinating section entitled "Japan for Students in Straitened Circumstances." Youths from poor families were told that if they were intent on study abroad and did not fear a hard day's work, Tokyo was the place for them. In this city of a million and a half people, thousands of jobs were available. "If you don't begrudge hard work, you will be able to find a job to maintain yourself. Compare this with existing in your home village, where advancement is not possible. There is all the difference in the world."[55] The authors suggested possible jobs and probable monthly earnings: delivering newspapers for six to seven yen; selling newspapers for a likely profit of ten yen; delivering milk; working as a scribe; pulling a rickshaw. The job of rickshaw driver, students were cautioned, was the hardest work of all; one must be prepared "to sacrifice everything to achieve your goal."[56] Unfortunately, there are no data available to indicate how many students took this advice and joined the Japanese labor force.

To the Chinese student, Tokyo offered a dazzling new array of choices. As the *Handbook for Students Abroad* put it:

Tokyo is the capital city of the whole of Japan. All kinds of facilities are available there. It truly is a mecca of learning and a center for schools. . . . But [Tokyo] also teems with dangerous lures and a host of temptations, so that only those students who are set in their ambitions and of strong character will not go astray and fall into evil ways. Thus the student in Japan must be able to single-mindedly pursue his goals, not be swayed by outside influences, and not [behave in such a way as] to be laughed at by his [fellow] villagers.[57]

To Chiang Monlin, whose brief trip to Japan was followed by study in the United States, impressions of Tokyo were bound up with sensitivities about being Chinese:

I visited the exposition in Ueno Park dozens of times and was impressed with the industrial development of Japan. In a war museum where prizes of war were shown I was very much ashamed to see the Chinese flags, uniforms, and weapons seized in the Sino-Japanese War and I tried vainly to dodge the eyes that stared at me. In the evening the park was illuminated with thousands of electric lights and the happy populace of Tokyo paraded on the grounds with myriad lanterns in their hands, shouting Banzai! . . . The general impression I had of Japan was very favorable. The whole country was a garden. The people were well dressed, their cities clean. They were perhaps inwardly conceited, but courteous to strangers. Compulsory education made the general level of the people much higher than in China, and this was perhaps the secret of Japan's becoming a world power. These were the impressions I carried home after a month's stay.[58]

Whether because urban development was not a topic of particular interest to the unsophisticated Chinese students or because comparisons with Chinese cities provided too painful a contrast, it is rare to find them giving as full a description of Tokyo as the one offered by Ts'ao Ju-lin:

The banks and business establishments located just outside the Imperial city are all large, multistoried buildings. From this area, the Ginza, to Ueno, Tokyo is at its noisiest and most bustling. One still uses the old horse and carriage routes to go back and forth. Principal means of transportation are the rickshaw and the trolley. Very few notables use carriages; they also ride rickshaws. Rickshaws operate with two people, one pulling, one pushing, and attain considerable speed. Major thoroughfares are paved with gravel; tarred roads are a rarity. Residences are located on side streets, which, like the alleys in North China, become impassable when it rains. All residential structures are Japanese-style. Mansions, also of Japanese design, boast elegant gardens. In the Ginza area, one occasionally sees shops that combine Japanese and Western styles, but these are a rarity. Parks are everywhere, built up simply upon the natural geographic features of the area and furnished with tea houses where strollers might rest and children play. The Ueno and Asakusa parks are relatively large. Ueno offers a zoo, a library, a museum, botanical gardens, and a fish preserve. . . . Asakusa Park is just a carnival and amusement area traversed by people from all walks of life.[59]

For lack of much of a written record in this department, one is left to wonder whether Chinese youths arriving in Tokyo from their capital city shared anything of the reaction of Valentine Chirol, a British correspondent, who wrote in 1895:

After Peking the streets of the Japanese capital seemed to be incredibly well kept, and almost equally incredible was its intricate network of telephone and telegraph wires, and at night the great arc lights, which, however, barely dimmed the twinkling of the ubiquitous little Japanese lanterns. Great modern blocks of Government buildings and, in the suburbs, large factories and tall chimneys afforded abundant if sometimes unsightly evidence of the growth of modern utilitarianism, but the mysterious shrines of Shiba and Asakusa, surrounded by parks and gardens thrown open to all comers, had not lost their hold upon the imagination of a poetic people.[60]

Very likely most of the students bound for Japan had gotten a taste of modern city life from Shanghai, their point of departure. Chirol made no attempt to mask his own prejudices:

To realise fully the abomination of a Chinese town, one must pass straight out of the cleanliness and symmetry of the foreign settlements in Shanghai, into the filth and stench and chaos of the native city. They are divided only by a broad thoroughfare and a deep archway under the ruinous walls of the Chinese city. On the one side, under a peculiar but eminently practical form of municipal self-government, has risen within the last four decades a busy, thriving, well-drained, well-ordered, well-lighted city, with an excellent supply of water, with spacious promenades, with handsome well-kept streets, with commodious houses and fine public buildings, with immense warehouses and business premises, and along the whole river-side, a succession of magnificent quays and commodious docks, fitted in fact with all the modern appliances, which have enabled it to become one of the greatest shipping centres of the world, and the greatest emporium of trade in the Far East. On the other side, under the blight of Mandarin misrule, the ancient native city is slowly rotting away in the decrepitude and sloth of its palsied old age.[61]

Attitudes of Visitors and Hosts

In fact, it was mostly Western observers like Chirol who measured the comparative progress of the two countries in terms of miles of railroad track and telegraph lines, sanitation, electrification, and the like. When Chinese spoke of Japan's remarkable progress since the Meiji Restoration, they more often than not skipped the specifics of technological/economic advance and turned to the key political result of that progress, namely, that Japan now could hold its own among the Powers, and to the vehicle for Japan's success, its system of universal education. Ts'ao Ju-lin, for example, reflecting on his student days, wrote admiringly of the widespread availability of schooling in Japan that already by the turn of the century had produced a remarkably high literacy rate. One even found rickshaw drivers reading in their spare time, Ts'ao noted. He added that not only were Japanese at all levels able to read, but with many newspapers available, and journalism held in high prestige, "ordinary people, even women, were informed about world affairs."[62]

In his commentary on the school system, Ts'ao drew particular attention to Tokyo's military schools and the stiff entrance examinations for foreign students. Wu Yü-chang offered an interesting firsthand view of Seijō School, which had about 180 Chinese enrolled by early 1903. Seijō enjoyed the reputation of providing first-rate instruction and a highly disciplined existence. Students were housed on campus and only allowed off the premises on Sundays and two afternoons during the week. Demanding class work presumably occupied the on-campus hours. For Wu, an absorbing interest in mathematics was reinforced by the excellent instruction at Seijō. Writing from the vantage point of old age, he conveys a wholly positive view of his Seijō experience.

It is not surprising, however, to find Chinese students speaking admiringly of the high quality of education in Japan. As mentioned earlier, the breadth and modernity of curricula, the comprehensiveness of the system, were in great contrast to the on-the-whole halting efforts to introduce new schooling in China. Nor should we wonder at expressions of admiration for the spirit of patriotism evident in Japan. This phenomenon always brought comment from outsiders, from Western journalists to Chinese diplomats. Ts'ao Ju-lin saw evidence of that patriotism in the preference among Japanese to buy domestic goods over those of foreign manufacture. Another student, writing in 1905, attributed the failure of Chinese student marriages to Japanese women to the wives' ardent patriotism; loyalty to nation somehow interfered with loyalty to spouse, thus leading to conjugal disharmony.[63]

In describing the setting in which students found themselves and their perceptions of it, we are skirting around a question with a contemporary ring to it—the social adaptability of the Chinese student. To begin with, we must note that the problem of how the foreign student adjusted to his host country was not of focal interest to either Chinese or Japanese of the day. Quite to the contrary, it was thought better that Chinese not intermingle with Japanese. In the example from the student handbook cited above, the necessity of close contact with Japanese students was pointed out as the drawback in dormitory living. Sanetō notes that the 1905 diarist "So Kau-mon," in his account of six months in Japan, does not mention a single Japanese friend.[64]

But is it so puzzling, really, that there was no attempt by the authorities—on either side—to encourage interaction between the Chinese and Japanese students? We are dealing, after all, with the first systematic large-scale study-abroad program. The concept of intercultural understanding was not built into the program. More important, from the China side, the objective was not to learn about Japan but to learn about the West through Japan. Those like Chou Tso-jen who approached Japan with the artist's eye and came away admiring the Japanese aesthetic sense were rare indeed.[65]

Likewise, from the Japanese side, the emphasis was on supervising the Chinese student and ensuring the quality of the education he received, not on helping him fit into his new environment. For this, he was left to his own devices, and to such counseling as was provided by the student handbooks and the Chinese legation.

For many Chinese students, adjusting to Japan was difficult at best. For a starter, the food, dress, and customs were all markedly different from what they were used to. It is hardly any wonder that

Chinese women, required to arise at 5:30 A.M. to sweep classrooms on unsteady bound feet, had second thoughts about study in Japan, particularly when their morning rice was too sticky for them to eat.[66] Even harder to deal with was the attitude of many Japanese toward their Chinese visitors. As we have seen, the Japanese image of Chinese underwent a profound shift in the aftermath of the Sino-Japanese War. Chinese, respected and revered for centuries as the very authors of civilization, were now depicted in the popular press as objects of derision, as antediluvian in a modern world of technological advance. Ordinary Japanese—that is, the majority of urbanites (Tokyoites) from small shopkeepers to rickshaw drivers to student-age youths, who, in particular, were more excited by the banzais of victory than the intellectual glories of a Chinese past—were clearly patronizing if not contemptuous of the Chinese students with "their long queues coiled on top of their heads upraising the crowns of their student caps to look like Mt. Fuji."[67] There are numerous recorded instances of Japanese children dogging the heels of Chinese students, pointing at their queues and shouting out ethnic slurs.[68]

Lu Hsün recounts an episode of more restrained but no less discriminatory treatment at the hands of his fellow students at the Sendai Medical College, where he was the only Chinese enrolled. When final marks were posted for the first year, and Lu Hsün was listed among those receiving a passing grade, a group of his classmates issued a protest letter, accusing him of getting the test questions beforehand from the instructor. As Lu noted sarcastically: "China is a weak country, therefore the Chinese must be an inferior people, and for a Chinese to get more than sixty marks could not be due simply to his own efforts."[69] The final humiliation for Lu Hsün occurred when he attended a magic lantern show just after the Russo-Japanese War and had to endure the cheering of his classmates as slides flashed by of Chinese spies for the Russians being executed by Japanese soldiers. This incident had a devastating effect on the would-be doctor. He left Sendai soon after and abandoned medicine for literature.[70] For the Chinese student generally, the knowledge that he was looked down on by his Japanese hosts produced at once feelings of self-doubt and resentment. This psychological state lent emotional vigor to the student protest movements we will examine in subsequent chapters.

Certain students were concerned about improving the Chinese image abroad. The student-produced 1906 handbook, with its potpourri of homilies, advice, and information, gave special emphasis to tips on behavior and personal habits, likely a response to complaints from Japanese. Cleanliness was a key item: dormitory rooms must be kept clean and tidy, and clothing laundered often. Students were even given guidance on how to bathe Japanese-style. A section on health urged students to get adequate sleep, follow a balanced diet, and maintain a regimen of exercise. A list of do's and don't's circulating among students in 1906 was even more explicit. In addition to emphasizing sanitation (students must keep their clothing and lodgings clean, wash thoroughly before entering the Japanese bath, and avoid spitting and urinating in inappropriate places), it decreed the "rules" of proper public behavior: when walking on crowded streets, one must stay on the right-hand side; when meeting a friend on the street, one must refrain from greeting him in a loud voice; on a crowded streetcar, one must offer one's seat to old people, children, and women; at night, one must converse in a low voice out of consideration for those who retire early. Other admonitions related to current Japanese practice: before entering a Japanese house, one must exchange shoes for slippers; one must not ask people their ages; when served a plate of cakes, one should use chopsticks to transfer a piece into one's left hand rather than putting it directly into the mouth. Certain bits of advice are such obvious common courtesies as to cause us to wonder if some of the Chinese students were completely lacking in social graces. For example, students were reminded to close doors when entering or leaving someone's house and if left alone inside, to refrain from snooping around or rummaging through the host's personal belongings.[71]

This document gives us some clues to the everyday lives of students, particularly their interaction with the Japanese. Judging from the advice given, it seems that much of Chinese student behavior was offensive to the Japanese public. Perhaps the most interesting aspect of this 1906 catalogue of do's and don't's is that it reflects a new concern on the part of Chinese for their image abroad, an uncomfortable awareness that they, of all people, might be regarded as lacking in civility and good manners even by the Japanese. What a turnabout, this feeling of inferiority! What a contrast to the confidence with which Chinese had gone to Japan a mere twenty years before, when they could count on being received with honor and respect!

By the time these tips on manners were written, there were an estimated 8,600 Chinese students in Tokyo, and their conduct was a problem. There exists a novel from this period (1907), a lengthy piece entitled *An Unofficial History of Study in Japan* (Liu-tung wai-shih), which, for all its obvious attempt to titillate the senses, nevertheless offers interesting sidelights on the everyday lives of Chinese students. For one thing, and this was probably most typical of the student enrolled in short-term intensive courses, study was by no means the central activity in the daily existence of the novel's characters. In one scene, a student is described as forgetting the day of the week, so seldom did he attend class. In another, the author describes wild gambling parties among students, remarking that certain scholarship students would no sooner receive their stipends than they would fritter away the money in games of chance.[72]

The *Unofficial History*'s story line turns on a series of incidents involving different students in the pursuit of Japanese women. To give but one variation on this underlying theme, a student named Chou becomes infatuated with a schoolgirl he has caught sight of on her daily route past his lodgings. In what seems a bold move, he sends her a letter expressing his eagerness to meet her in person. The girl's response is an immediate visit to Chou's room. The young man's reaction to her evident interest is a marriage proposal, including an offer to draw up a contract agreeing to pay an appropriate sum to the girl's guardian. Chou finalized this liaison in only four days, the author tells us, not because of his unusual charm but because the schoolgirl was in fact a prostitute on the prowl for Chinese students. She had originally solicited in the Waseda University area, but after being picked up by the police, she had moved to Kanda, where the competition was so fierce, she had enrolled in a girls' school so as to improve her image—and her chances. Chou was no innocent victim, however. From his immediate offer of payment, the author explains, the girl knew he was an old hand in prostitute quarters.[73]

How many liaisons of this kind existed is impossible to document, but there is evidence that it was not uncommon. "So Kaumon," for example, in his 1905–6 account, describes how "free marriages" between Chinese students and Japanese women were often formalized in a brief ceremony, with a teacher officiating and fellow students as witnesses.[74] In most cases, the Japanese involved were of lower-class origin, and the "marriages" lasted only through the student's stay in Japan. Many students had wives waiting for them back in China. A more lasting example from this period is the marriage of Lu Hsün's brother, Chou Tso-jen, to a Japanese girl who had been a maid at the brothers' lodging house during their student days. Whether it was her origin or some other point of friction, Lu Hsün's relationship with his Japanese sister-in-law was never a friendly one.[75] From our standpoint of trying to understand the students' interaction with Japanese, the evidence of these international marriages suggests a problem area. On the one hand, it was one of the few situations where students were in friendly contact with ordinary Japanese. Yet the fact that liaisons with foreigners were frowned on at any social level meant that Chinese students as a whole were regarded with suspicion by the more respectable among the lower- to middle-class citizenry.

If students received a welcoming gesture at all it was from upper-class, educated Japanese, the Kanō Jigorōs, Konoes, and Count Nagaokas, precisely the group described in Chapter 1 as the backbone of the China Lobby of the day. Ts'ao Ju-lin in his memoirs spoke of the contrast in attitude between the children on the street with their taunts and mocking laughter and the school instructors who sought to inspire Chinese students to work hard by pointing out their potential role in strengthening Sino-Japanese friendship. Not that such encouragement was necessarily politically motivated. Often it sprang simply from a feeling of genuine sympathy for the lonely, confused overseas student.

Perhaps the best-known example of a close teacher-student relationship involved Lu Hsün and his anatomy teacher at Sendai. In a short story entitled "Mr. Fujino," Lu Hsün describes his teacher as a gentle, kindly soul who, out of concern that his Chinese pupil was handicapped by an inadequate understanding of Japanese, took it on himself to correct all of Lu's class notes on a daily basis. As Lu prepared to leave Sendai and medical study, a saddened Fujino presented him with a farewell photograph, which, according to the story, the author treasured for the rest of his life. Since Fujino seems to have recalled his association with Lu Hsün with considerably more detachment than that expressed by his famous pupil,[76] one wonders how much of the closeness must be attributed to the demands of drama. Even so, judging from the following assessment, respect and affection surely existed:

But somehow or other I still remember him from time to time, for of all those whom I consider as my teachers he is the one to whom I feel most grateful and who gave me the most encouragement. And I often think: the keen faith he had in me and his indefatigable help were in a limited sense for China, for he wanted China to have modern medical science; but in a larger sense they were for science, for he wanted modern medical knowledge to spread to China. In my eyes he is a great man, and I feel this in my heart, though his name is not known to many people.[77]

Ts'ao Ju-lin's contact with Japanese, though matter-of-factly recorded, was far closer than this. After staying for a time in a regular lodging house, Ts'ao was invited by the family of the prominent journalist Nakae Chōmin to board with them. He remained there for three years. Nakae himself had died shortly before Ts'ao joined the family, but Nakae's widow kindly recounted for the young Chinese her husband's experiences during his student days in France. Judging by the length of his stay, Ts'ao's relationship with the family was a happy one. Ts'ao mentions how solicitous and sensitive to his feelings the Nakaes were—often fixing him special Western dishes, for example, so convinced were they that he would dislike the Japanese fare.[78]

But such instances of special kindness appear to have been rare and confined to those upper-class, educated Japanese who were proponents of China's study-in-Japan program from the first. Generally, in their everyday dealings with Japanese, the Chinese students met with an attitude of indifference and even hostility. This mixed reception is much like what greets many foreign students studying in a small college town in the United States today: a supportive school atmosphere but suspicion and unfriendliness from the local townspeople. A major difference, of course, is that nowadays students from abroad are encouraged to intermingle with Americans of all kinds— learning about the United States is considered part of their educational experience—and foreign student advisers and other school staff attempt to ease the newcomers through any social problems they might have. That there was no guidance-and-counseling mechanism at all for our Chinese students is hardly surprising, but the lack of one had important implications. First, it meant that hundreds of young Chinese left Japan after several years' study without having developed any conscious understanding of or sympathy for the Japanese people and their culture. From the standpoint of the Japanese China activists, this represented a missed opportunity, since it was precisely the creation of a special relationship that they were hoping for when they broadcast slogans of the *dōbun* (common culture) variety. Quite to the contrary, as we will see in subsequent chapters, the students' feelings of alienation from the Japanese easily slipped into resentment and hostility toward Japan and suspicions of the motives of the Japanese government in hosting foreign students.

Second, excluded as they were from most social relationships with Japanese, Chinese students tended to form close-knit groups among themselves. Students from one province mingled with those from other areas, and a great deal of out-of-school time was spent in intense discussions of the China problem. For all the rules and regulations of Meiji society, foreign students were free to form discussion groups and to dip into a wide variety of Japanese newspapers, magazines, and translated books. Both worked to give them a whole new perspective on what it was to be Chinese. In our attempt to analyze student attitudes and activities, we must stop from time to time to remind ourselves of how vastly different Ch'ing China and Meiji Japan were—the one intellectually conservative, politically repressive, laboring under immense economic problems; the other vibrant with new ideas, enjoying relative freedom of the press, fast growing economically and militarily, looked on as an equal, or almost an equal, by the Powers. Moreover, not only was a Chinese student thrust into this relatively liberal environment, he was freed from the restrictions of his own, as any student away from home would be. Expectations of parents, the watchful eye of family and clan, social taboos, codes of conduct so strictly defined in the Chinese context, were a week's travel away. It is small wonder that a few students ran to excesses in their pursuit of pleasure while a still greater number indulged themselves in talk and more talk about their own and China's future.

FOUR

The Beginnings of Student Activism

C HINESE STUDENTS and turn-of-the-century Tokyo had all the makings of political drama. The typical student was in his early twenties, rather well educated, a product of the privileged class, yet likely as not from a family whose fortunes were on the downturn. His motives for going abroad to study included personal advancement, but also a vague yearning to contribute to a strengthened China. Impressionable, interested in politics, and inclined toward a nonconformist outlook, the young Chinese newly arrived in Tokyo found a new taste of personal freedom in an environment alive with ideas and "isms" from the outside world. Opinions on the China problem, the merits of imperialism, the relative virtues of Japan and the West, and other issues of the day, bruited about in the Japanese press, soon became the stuff of lively debate and argument for Chinese students meeting in small groups after school hours.

As students in an overseas setting, they were able to do what they could not do openly at home: organize. And organize they did, a whole range of extracurricular activities in translation, journalism, and politics, to the point where one wonders how some of the busiest youths found any time at all for the more prosaic demands of homework and study. But "extracurricular" does not really convey the whole story. For most students were living examples of the principle of putting knowledge to work, of integrating study with real life. Thus, they learned Japanese, then translated. They learned about alternative political systems, then wrote articles to inform others. It was an intense, committed group of young people, engaged in the issue of reform in China and intrigued with the role they might play in influencing public opinion.

This chapter focuses on the start-up of student organizations and magazines in the years 1900–1903 and the early rumblings of anti-Ch'ing dissent. The picture that emerges is one of diversity, of scattered energies. Groups were formed, then split. Publications appeared, then went out of business. And certainly student involvement in direct action against the Ch'ing regime tended to be fleeting and small-scale. One might be tempted to dismiss these modest, often transitory, activities with a summary word or two, were it not that so many were "firsts" in the history of modern Chinese journalism, the translating of foreign works, and student political activism. Not only that, the existence of a student community with a nexus of organizations was itself something new. Here students got practice in public speaking, political debate, and organizational techniques, experience that increasingly came into play in the issue-oriented student protests that began in mid-1902.

Students as Translators

In late 1900, fourteen Chinese students in Tokyo established the Translation Society (I-shu Hui-pien She), a group dedicated to translating articles and books from Japanese into Chinese.[1] The society was short-lived, its total output modest. Yet the appearance of this group of student translators, the first of its kind, signaled the new Chinese receptivity to ideas from outside and triggered a burst of translation activity by Chinese on a scale previously unmatched.

Before 1900, both Chinese translators and works translated from Japanese were rare items on China's literary scene. It was Westerners, typically Protestant missionaries fluent in Chinese, who were the chief contributors to a growing body of translated works, most originally in English, French, or German. True, some were concerned only with turning out the Bible and a variety of simple tracts aimed at converting the masses. But others sought to win the hearts and minds of China's educated elite by offering up the fruits of the Western enlightenment. Timothy Richard, for example, director of the Society for the Diffusion of Christian and General Knowledge in the 1890's, promoted the publication of a variety of translated works in the sciences and humanities. His own translation of Robert Mackenzie's *History of the Nineteenth Century* became a bestseller when it was issued at the time of the Sino-Japanese War.

The Chinese government itself was supportive of translation ventures as early as the 1860's, when it established the T'ung-wen kuan, popularly known as the Interpreters College, and the Translation Bureau attached to the Kiangnan Arsenal. Westerners held key positions in both: an American missionary, W. A. P. Martin, was president of the T'ung-wen kuan, and an Englishman, John Fryer, was the chief translator for the Kiangnan Translation Bureau. Fryer himself was responsible for two-thirds of the 170 translations of Western scientific articles and manuals the bureau issued in its thirty years of operation.[2]

Many of these translations were reprinted within a few years in Japan, where, among the educated, Chinese functioned as a second language. Martin's translation of Henry Wheaton's *Principles of International Law*, published in Peking in 1864, was issued in Japan the following year. Some works, like Martin's, were simply reprinted. Others, like William Muirhead's *Complete Geography*, which was published in Shanghai in 1854, were brought out with notations (*kunten*) added to indicate Japanese word order, then, several years later, translated into Japanese.[3]

By the 1890's, there appeared two notable exceptions to the pattern of Westerners directing the translation of works from European languages into Chinese. One was the literary figure Lin Shu (1852–1924), ever remembered for creating classical Chinese versions of 150 works of Western literature. Lin was not, properly speaking, a translator, since he did not work from the original materials but based his books on Chinese colloquial renditions supplied to him orally by others. Yen Fu (1854–1921), then, was really the first Chinese literatus to make the translation of Western works a systematic and lifelong concern. In the decade 1899–1908, Yen Fu produced his most important translations, replete with commentaries and interpretive essays—of Thomas H. Huxley, J. S. Mill, Montesquieu, and Adam Smith.[4]

As for books translated from the Japanese, there was very little to choose from before the Sino-Japanese War. As mentioned in Chapter 1, members of the Chinese diplomatic mission to Tokyo issued several works on Japan in the late 1880's that were compiled and translated from various Japanese sources. But aside from these few items, the literary output of the mission staff centered on straight reporting on Japan or poetry written in Chinese for a well-educated Japanese audience.

After the war, as Chinese attitudes toward Japan began to shift, there was an upsurge of interest in translating works from Japanese. Proposals to that effect were heard from a number of senior political figures, including K'ang Yu-wei, Liang Ch'i-ch'ao, and Chang Chih-tung. All subscribed to the thesis that because of similarities in written language, China could learn more expeditiously about Western development through Japanese translations than by embarking on the tedious course of translating numerous volumes directly from European languages.[5] After ten years of trying, K'ang Yu-wei managed to get enough financial backing to establish a translation bureau in Shanghai in 1896. The following year, he published a list of 7,750 Japanese books in sixteen categories that he recommended for translation into Chinese. Slightly less than half were Japanese translations of Western works; the others were original works by Japanese writers, many of them dealing with Japan rather than the United States or Europe. This ratio, as much as anything else, indicates K'ang's abiding interest in Meiji Japan as a development model for China.[6]

How many works K'ang's translation bureau actually produced is unclear. It is easier to document the efforts of Japanese translators, who likewise increased their output in the years after the Sino-Japanese War. There were a number of variations on the theme of rendering Japanese titles into Chinese. The earliest method was not, properly speaking, "translation" at all. It was simply taking books originally written for Japanese audiences in *kanbun*, classical Chinese punctuated for Japanese, and reprinting them, minus the notations, for Chinese readers. In this category were Okamoto Kambo's *Historical Record of Nations* (Wan-kuo shih-chi) in ten volumes, first published in 1878, then reprinted in China in 1895, and *Translations of American Annals* (Fan-i Mei-li-chien chih), itself a translation from English into *kanbun*, reissued for Chinese readers in 1895. The Japanese also turned out works written in the first instance for Chinese readers, many with titles like *New Topographical Records of China, Japan and Korea* (Hsin-chuan Tung-ya san-kuo ti-chih), *A New Ethic for Asian Unity* (Ta-tung ho-pang hsin-i), and *The Fortunes of the Orient* (T'ai-tung hsiu-ch'i), suggesting their mission of trumpeting the East Asian soldiarity theme.[7]

Japanese translators joined the staffs of some of China's earliest periodicals. Kojō Teikichi (who later became well known as a professor at Tōyō and Keiō universities) managed the Japanese section of Liang Ch'i-ch'ao's magazine *Current Affairs* (Shih-wu pao), which dated back to 1896. Kojō is credited with translating a book on Japanese school regulations and another volume, originally in Japanese, on the industry and commerce of China. Both were published by

Current Affairs. Another Japanese scholar, Fujita Toyohachi, a teacher at a Shanghai school, was involved in a translation project sponsored by the magazine *Agricultural Studies Report* (Nung-hsueh ts'ung-shu), which first appeared in 1897. In the next few years, Fujita and a Japanese colleague reportedly assisted in the publication of 315 Chinese versions of Japanese treatises on agriculture. Over half (fourteen of twenty-seven) of the translations listed in the one surviving issue of *Agricultural Studies* were turned out by Japanese translators. Clearly at this stage much of the work being done to make Japanese publications available to Chinese readers was the work of Japanese themselves.[8]

Access to outside ideas, particularly those coming the Japanese route, was precisely the stuff of the study-in-Japan program as it took shape in the mind of Chang Chih-tung. By 1898 Chang, unresponsive in the 1880's to K'ang's proposed translation bureau, had come around to his views, and for the same reasons of practicality: that given the similarity of written Chinese and Japanese, it made more sense for Chinese to translate or retranslate from Japanese than to take the time to learn European languages.[9] Translations would serve a twofold purpose: to introduce Western ideas; and to publicize the Meiji model of development, itself testimony to Asian success in adopting Western technology and institutions. Each and every student sent off to Japan was intended to be the facilitator of this process of translation in the broadest sense. Small wonder, then, that the Chinese students in Japan early on set their hands to the task.

When the Translation Society was founded in 1900, the Japan study-abroad program had been in operation for four years. People like Chi I-hui, who had gone to Japan with the first batch of thirteen students in 1896, had by now developed the requisite language skills to take on translation projects as an extracurricular pursuit.[10] The appearance of the society meant that at last Chinese themselves were independently selecting and translating books and articles from Japanese.

The society put out the first issue of its literary organ, *Translation Journal* (I-shu hui-pien), in December 1900. It contained ten translated extracts, four from Japanese works and the others from American, French, and German writers. Among them were Rousseau's *Social Contract*, Johann Kaspar Bluntschli's *A General Discussion of Public Law*, and *Contemporary Political History* by Ariga Nagao.[11] An interesting sidelight is that Ariga's extract, continued in the second issue of the *Journal*, marks an early reference in Chinese to both Marx and Ferdinand Lassalle, identifying them as founders of divergent schools of socialism. The translator felt impelled to define socialism for his readers:

Deploring the inequalities between rich and poor in which the laborer exists under the oppressive system of the capitalist group, certain Western scholars have evolved a theory advocating equal distribution of wealth and a guaranteed livelihood to all people. They call it socialism. By "social" is meant planning for the whole society and not just for one individual or a single family. The well-field system in China of ancient times is simply what is now termed socialism.[12]

Journal staffers somehow also found the time to translate entire books. A list of full translations in the second issue offers fourteen Western and eight Japanese titles. Since most of the Western works had already appeared in Japanese versions, it is reasonable to assume that the majority were retranslations rather than direct translations.

Included in the eight original Japanese works were two by Fukuzawa Yukichi—*A General Outline of Civilization* and *Comments on Current Affairs*—and a compilation of the lectures of Katō Hiroyuki. Both of these men were members of the famed Meirokusha set up in 1873 as a scholarly discussion group devoted to popularizing the new theories from the West. The younger generation of Japanese scholars versed in Western thought was represented as well: Ariga Nagao's elaborate study of the formation of a nation-state, *A Study of National Law*, was one of the listed translations. Another was *A Discussion of International Relations*, by Kuga Katsunan, a strong supporter of expanding Japan's role as an East Asian regional power.

Society staff also undertook to translate more purely educational materials. The society in its own name handled translations of university-level lectures. A separate group called the Educational Textbook Translation Bureau was formed in mid-1902 from among society staff members to concentrate on producing middle-school texts for Chinese readers.[13] There are hints as well of other small-scale translation efforts, some similarly offshoots of the Translation Society operation. For example, Editor Chi I-hui simultaneously directed a Shanghai outlet called the Students Abroad Publishing House.[14] Other evidence points to joint Japanese and Chinese translation endeavors. To cite one instance, Shanghai's Commercial Press, established in 1897, made an arrangement with a Japanese firm in 1902 to handle the translation and publication of original Japanese-language materials.

As time went on, new student groups were formed on the model of the Translation Society, most notably the Hunan Translation Society, organized in late 1902 and responsible for a magazine entitled *Translations by [Hunan] Students Abroad* (Yu-hsueh i-pien). Unlike the *Translation Journal*, with its emphasis on scholarly works in history and political science, this publication featured translations from the Japanese press and current magazines, often on topics related to Western political history. The first issue, for example, offered such titles as "A History of Nineteenth-Century Scholarship" (from *Taiyōhō*) and "The Struggle in the Pacific" (from *Nihon Shimbun*). Liang Ch'i-ch'ao, himself a key figure in transmitting Japanese works to a Chinese readership,[15] followed with interest the progress of the student translation projects. He accorded the Hunan magazine moderate praise, saying that it generally provided accurate and readable translations from the Japanese original texts. He was more laudatory about the *Translation Journal*, pronouncing its output superbly done and a major contribution to national knowledge.[16] Years later, summing up the period, Liang noted that no sooner was a new book published in Japan than several translations appeared, to the point that it became customary to announce projected translations in magazines so as to avoid duplication.[17]

Thanks to this hunger to learn and transmit new ideas, within a matter of years the Chinese reading public was getting a large dose of the modern world through Japanese eyes. A compilation covering the years 1902–4 lists 533 available titles; 321, or about 60 percent, were original Japanese works; and most of the others were retranslated from the Japanese.[18] At the high point of translations from Japanese in 1903, 187 books were rendered into Chinese, more than the Kiangnan Arsenal's Translation Bureau had turned out in thirty years. Another point of comparison is that the arsenal's translations were almost entirely scientific and technical treatises, whereas those selected by the students showed a heavy bias in favor of the humanities, especially law and political science, history, pedagogy, geography and philosophy.

Early Ventures into Radical Politics

Student involvement in the summer of 1900 in a plot to oust the Empress Dowager set off alarm bells among Chinese officials and polarized the small student group in Japan into what contemporary sources referred to as "progressive and moderate cliques." The plot itself was an ill-fated effort to organize a coalition of dissidents, including the K'ang/Liang clique, Sun Yat-sen, the secret societies, and the overseas students, for the purpose of putting the Kuang-hsü

Emperor in power as the head of a constitutional monarchy. Action was to start with an uprising in Hankow and other cities in the Yangtze Valley. Masterminding this scheme was a Hunanese named T'ang Ts'ai-ch'ang, a close associate of one of the reformers who had been executed for his part in the 1898 Reform Movement.[19]

T'ang made a trip to Japan in the spring of 1899 for talks with the various Tokyo-based Chinese groups. For all his efforts, he failed to extract more than an expression of moral support from Sun and a promise of financial assistance from K'ang. He fared slightly better in his contacts with students. As many as fifteen decided to join the rebel cause and prepared to return to Shanghai with T'ang at the end of 1899.[20] Eventually, T'ang's plan was uncovered, and the whole enterprise came to naught.

But what had a lasting effect was the painful realization on the part of the Ch'ing authorities that some of the overseas students represented a danger to the regime. Worse still, these were young people on government scholarship, some of them Chang Chih-tung's own protégés. As the *North China Herald* put it with a note of sarcasm: "A large number of them are Chang Chih-tung's own pupils, whom he sent to Japan to be educated, when he was full of reform himself, and they apparently have been weak enough to believe that the Viceroy was in earnest when he wrote his recent pro-reform treatise."[21] At least four *liu hsueh-sheng* were executed for their part in the abortive uprising, along with their leader, T'ang Ts'ai-ch'ang.[22]

Nothing from this point on could allay Chang Chih-tung's fear that the whole community of Chinese students in Japan was being contaminated with ideas from the K'ang/Liang camp. At this time, it should be noted, not only for Chang but for Ch'ing officialdom in general, K'ang and Liang, not Sun Yat-sen, were the chief bogeys of radicalism. They were better known than Sun, and their movement had scholarly underpinnings that made it more appealing to the broad reform constituency and therefore more of a threat to old-style progressives like Chang. Furthermore, even later, after Sun had achieved some notoriety, the three were lumped together as "radicals," with no fine distinctions made between reformist and revolutionary positions.[23]

Chang's anxiety in the aftermath of Tang's abortive Hankow uprising that the students might be "radicalized" by the outlawed reformers prompted a series of cables to the Chinese minister to Japan, Li Sheng-to, and to the Hupei supervisor of students. On October 1, 1900, Chang informed Minister Li that he had been told of a student social club called the Promote Determination Society (Li-chih Hui) with connections to K'ang Yu-wei and Liang Ch'i-ch'ao. According to his informant, the society, which had held only occasional meetings when it was first organized, was now meeting almost daily for discussion, speechmaking, and the formulation of ill-advised platforms. This sounded too much to Chang Chih-tung like another uprising in the making.[24]

The same day Chang sent a cable to the Hupei supervisor instructing him to warn students about the dangers of associating with the likes of K'ang Yu-wei and T'ang Ts'ai-ch'ang. He should also try to disabuse the students of any notion they might have that T'ang was a martyred patriot. After all, asked Chang, in any nation of the world would talk of assassinating officials and seizing control of cities earn the speaker anything less than the death penalty?[25] Chang fired off a second cable to the supervisor on October 9, urging him once again to caution students about contacts with the K'ang/Liang camp.[26]

These cables were preliminary to a formal statement on the Hankow affair and student involvement in it issued from the office of Governor-general Chang one month later. This document, "A Warning Statement to the Shanghai National Assembly and the Students Abroad,"[27] was not only forwarded to Minister Li Sheng-to on November 5, but also sent to other Chinese diplomatic representatives abroad and to provincial officials. It provided a detailed official version of the Hankow plot: the buildup of T'ang Ts'ai-ch'ang's Shanghai group, the roles of K'ang and Liang, the reputedly broad membership base recruited from the secret societies, and the principles outlined by the rebels. Only in the last few pages did Chang directly admonish the students abroad, and here not by threat of reprisal but by painting the dire consequences to China of their involvement with the K'ang group. If students abroad spread extremist views, flouted their obligations to the Throne and the government, and supported rebellion, he wrote, their foreign hosts would grow wary, withholding both respect and aid to China. Ultimately, foreign nations would take China's internal disunity as a signal to "slice the melon." China would be destroyed as a nation, its people becoming—in Chang's image—like the Jews, despised wanderers in the world. It was precisely to prevent such a national disaster, Chang argued, that students were being sent abroad at government expense. Educated youth were critical to a China of the future, free of corruption in government and rising from weakness to world power status.[28]

Some Chinese students in Tokyo took exception to Chang Chih-tung's interpretation of the Hankow events. Shen Hsiang-yün, who, ironically enough, had been handpicked for study in Japan by Chang himself, drafted a counter statement. In it, he described the execution of T'ang Ts'ai-ch'ang and two of his student supporters, adding an epitaph for Chang Chih-tung: "He sought to avoid being ridiculed as an official of a nation destroyed; yet he will bear the shameful reputation of having executed scholars."[29] Chang avoided a direct rebuttal. Instead, he requested students at three Hupei schools to compose essays refuting Shen's views. One of these, a piece claiming that revolution would mean the ruin of China, was given Chang's nod of approval. Copies were printed and distributed among the student group in Japan. Shen's comment on this new challenge was that 260 years of Manchu misrule had already brought China to ruin.

The post-Hankow atmosphere of growing alienation between officialdom and certain students abroad served to further etch out what Feng Tzu-yu, a student in Japan at the time, terms moderate and progressive factions within the Chinese student community.[30] Those on the moderate side often acted as guides and interpreters for visiting government officials. Their interest in staying in official good graces was reinforced, Feng points out, by the 1901 changes in the civil service examination system that opened up bureaucratic posts to qualified graduates of Japanese schools. For such attention to official career, the moderates were labeled opportunists and "running dogs" of officialdom by the minority progressives.[31]

The growing difference in views meant that tempers ran high at student discussion meetings. Ts'ao Ju-lin gives a personal account of an acrimonious exchange at an evening of debate sponsored by the Promote Determination Society. Ts'ao spoke in support of constitutional monarchy. His position was that the Manchus, as one of the ethnic minority groups in China, should be accorded a role in the future body politic—that of supplying the figurehead monarchs. Real power would be vested in various representative institutions as provided for in a constitution. Ts'ao felt that China's political structure needed to be rebuilt but saw no reason to discard the foundation. In his view, revolution—a complete destruction of structure and foundation—would only bring killing and bloodshed to a people already burdened with poverty. Chang Chi, spokesman for the progressives, rose in protest after Ts'ao's oration. He disputed the assertion that the Manchus were in any way Chinese—"How can the descendants of our Yellow Emperor be classed with these Tartar slaves?"—and argued that whatever the destruction accompanying revolution, it was preferable to the hardships now endured by the Chinese people. These were evidently passionately held positions: this particular debate ended in a fist fight between the two featured speakers.[32]

The Promote Determination Society continued to sponsor political meetings until at least March 1903, when the twenty-two-year-old daughter of K'ang Yu-Wei was the invited speaker. To an audience of a hundred, she spoke in support of the *pao-huang* ("protect the Emperor") principle, cautioning students about the dangers of revolution.[33] It was a message that fell on receptive ears, since by this time there were only moderates left in the group. The radical element, growing more vocal in the post-Hankow atmosphere, split off in the winter of 1902 to form the Youth Society (Ch'ing-nien Hui), which, according to founding member Feng Tzu-yu, was the earliest revolutionary organization among the Chinese students in Japan. Most of the thirty-odd members were Waseda University students representing a number of different provinces. Little is known about the Youth Society's goals. A charter drawn up for the group was reportedly lost in 1904.[34]

Apart from the clandestine activities implied in Feng Tzu-yu's account, the Youth Society was involved in that favorite pastime of most of the Chinese students, translation. A number of translations were advertised under the society's label, the first being a retranslation from the Japanese of *A History of the French Revolution*.[35] The Youth Society also organized political meetings. The same Miss K'ang who spoke before the Promote Determination Society addressed a far larger audience—reportedly 1,000 Chinese and Japanese students—at one of its gatherings. Her speech, delivered, oddly enough, in English (one must assume that there were interpreters present or that a prepared text was handed out), was essentially a plea for joint action by Chinese reformers and such Japanese China-experts as Prince Konoe to plan for a strengthened China. On this occasion, Miss K'ang was harsh in her judgment of Ch'ing politicians, characterizing the Court of Peking as the enemy of all Chinese women and singling out for special censure the Court favorite Jung-lu.[36]

The Chinese Student Union

The functions of social club, political discussion group, and translation and publishing center were combined in a single organization established in early 1902, the Chinese Student Union (Chung-kuo

Liu-hsueh-sheng Hui-kuan). Like the Promote Determination Society, the union was designed as a nonpartisan, multiregional group. The Chinese minister to Japan, Ts'ai Chün, who attended the formative meeting held on New Year's Day 1902, greeted the new group with enthusiasm. The existence of this kind of group, he said approvingly, would make it easier for Chinese studying in Japan to bear separation from their homeland. Hence they would work more effectively to attain what in his mind was the ultimate goal, that of "repaying the nation" through public service. Minister Ts'ai was named honorary head of the new union, with the Hupei supervisor as his deputy.[37]

The New Year's meeting was a unique moment of good feeling between the minister and the overseas students. Controversy soon developed over the name of the organization: was it to be *Chung-kuo* Liu-hsueh-sheng Hui-kuan, with the stress on China as a modern nation, or *Ch'ing-kuo* Liu-hsueh-sheng Hui-kuan, where respect was paid to the Ch'ing dynasty? Minister Ts'ai, as a principal contributor to union funds—other contributions came from student members—pressured certain students into endorsing "Ch'ing-kuo." Later on, other students insisted they were "men of China," not "men of the 'Ch'ing dynasty,'" and so used the prefix "Chung-kuo." As a result, the union is referred to by both names in accounts of the period, depending on the viewpoint of the writer.[38]

Membership in the union was open to all Chinese students in Japan. At the start, there were 278 members. Within five months, the number almost trebled.[39] Actually, these figures reflect not only the popularity of the new organization, but also the sharp rise in the number of Chinese students in Japan in this five-month period. Twelve executive secretaries, selected by the total membership, managed the union's activities. Many were concurrently officers in the Translation Society.[40] The leadership included both moderates like Chang Tsung-hsiang and Ts'ao Ju-lin and progressives. Chang Chi reportedly became an executive secretary in 1904, when he fled to Japan after being implicated in the attempted assassination of a provincial governor.[41]

From the outset, the Student Union served as a guidance center to handle inquiries from students in China about study in Japan and to orient the ever-increasing number of arriving students. In an announcement appearing in the *Translation Journal*, prospective students were told to write a letter to the union's main office should they wish to be met by an executive secretary at either Yokohama or Shimbashi. Students were also referred to union representatives in Kobe, Shanghai, and Tientsin should they require direction from those points. New arrivals were encouraged to participate in union activities. A popular offering was an introductory language course in Japanese held in classrooms on the second floor of the two-story union building in Kanda. On the first floor were a bank, a bookstore, an auditorium for general meetings, and a reception hall used for entertaining visiting Ch'ing officials and other high-level guests.[42]

In what was probably a revenue-earning activity, the union early on became involved in the publication and sale of student magazines and monographs. Already by June 1902, the *Translation Journal* listed the Student Union as its distributor.[43] As time went on, the union expanded its publishing operations, handling individual works as well as the output of small translation and research societies and, starting in early 1903, printing the magazines of the Hunan, Hupei, and Kiangsu student societies.[44]

The Student Union was central to the lives of all Chinese students in providing a gathering place, a common meeting ground for the discussion of current political issues. As we will see, it figured in every student protest from 1902 on. It was the place for thrashing out issues and settling disputes. But the union did not at any point take an unequivocal anti-government stance as an organization; the presence of a number of political viewpoints among members, with the majority leaning in the constitutionalist direction,[45] made it impossible to do so. Nevertheless, in the eyes of Ch'ing officials, who read subversion in any expression of political opinion, the union was as suspect an organization as the earlier Promote Determination Society. A directive on educational matters issued by the Chinese government in 1903 called for a careful watch on its activities: "If the union deals in matters that are disruptive of law and harmful to public security, matters that are not its concern, the Minister and Supervisor ought to communicate this to the appropriate Japanese office, which will conduct investigations and impose control measures in the hope of stopping evil practices."[46]

Provincial Societies

Starting in mid-1902, some of the provinces with larger representations of students in Japan—Hunan, Hupei, Chekiang, and Kiangsu—established their own student associations. Seeking out the company of fellow provincials who shared customs, perspectives, and tastes in food was natural enough. But there was another reason for provincial groupings, eminently practical, and this had to do with ease of verbal communication. Given differences in dialect (really language) in spoken Chinese, a student from Hunan could scarcely understand one from Shanghai, an impediment to comfortable discussion and debate. By 1905, at the high point of student numbers in Japan, virtually every province had its own student association. These competed for the students' time and allegiance with the Student Union, various school clubs, and political groups, all of which were trans-provincial organizations.

Communication was what the provincial societies were all about. They were committed to research, disseminating knowledge, and creating public opinion. The larger societies—those of Hupei, Chekiang, and Kiangsu—published thick monthly magazines. While promoting provincial loyalty was the immediate aim of all this effort, the long-term objective was to build national unity. Love of province, in the words of the Hupei Society organizers, was the first step in love of country.[47]

The Hupei, Chekiang, and Kiangsu groups had elaborate organizational structures, essentially similar, which provided a model for the T'ung-meng Hui two years later.[48] There must have been a job for every society member. Hupei operations centered on departments of journalism, editing, education, and intelligence-gathering; the Chekiang bylaws provided specifically for the publication of a monthly magazine and research into Chekiang affairs; and the Kiangsu group's organizational chart showed a department of economic enterprise, along with departments of education, intelligence-gathering, and publication.

The plan for intelligence work shows an unprecedented interest in Chinese life at the grass-roots level. The Kiangsu Society, for example, outlined an ambitious scheme to assign student researchers to each prefecture (*fu*) and county (*hsien*) in the province. Their job was to prepare maps of local areas and studies of everyday life, covering everything from farming practices and trade to class relationships and religion. Since the researchers were based in Japan, they were charged with recruiting friends or relatives at home to do the actual information-gathering. Offices were to be set up in designated places in Kiangsu for receiving data and forwarding them to Japan.

The Chekiang Society's intelligence department described a similar system of Tokyo researchers with China-based stand-ins operating through general and branch transmission offices in the province.[49] The Hupei Society, without spelling out how the data it wanted were to be gathered, specified eleven research topics, some of which would have given any researcher pause. "Nationality" or "race" (*min-tsu*) was one suggested topic. The reason for pursuing this subject, the student magazine explained in an editorial note, was that while the world powers had advanced already from nationalism to imperialism, China was still in its infancy in developing nationalistic thinking.[50]

Whether these information-gathering schemes involved anything other than pure research—planning for local uprisings, for example—is far from clear. It is also unclear how productive the departments were, beyond the fact that a number of reports and appended maps appearing in the student magazines are credited specifically to them.

The provincial societies' executive branches consisted of the heads of the various departments, two or three general affairs officers (*shu-wu*), a secretary (*shu-chi*), and an accountant (*k'uai-chi*). The Hupei charter also provided for a president (*tsung-li*). Under the Kiangsu charter, the top executive was a business manager (*shih-wu-chang*), and provision was also made for an inspector (*chien-ch'a-yuan*), whose functions were disciplinary, and for an unspecified number of representatives. All officers were to be elected by majority vote of the membership for six-month terms. General meetings were scheduled several times annually, with executive sessions conducting business in the interim. Special meetings might be called at the discretion of the executive branch. The general membership of each provincial society consisted essentially of the Chinese students in Japan, though the Chekiang charter opened membership as well to Chinese officials and gentry residing in Japan, and the Hupei bylaws stipulated that "sympathetic comrades" at home might join the Tokyo-based society.

The Rise of an Opposition Press

Intoxicated with the power of the printed word, the chance to inform and influence an increasingly literate Chinese public, the energetic students who organized the Hupei, Chekiang, and Kiangsu societies immediately turned their enthusiasms to producing monthly magazines: *Hupei Students Circle* (Hupei hsueh-sheng chieh), *Tide of Chekiang* (Che-chiang ch'ao), and *Kiangsu* (Chiang-su).[51] The freedom to do this, to issue to the people at large written commentary not only highly critical of government policy but heaping abuse on the top leadership, was a complete novelty for turn-of-the-century China.

Periodicals aimed at shaping public opinion had in fact been in circulation in China only since the Sino-Japanese War.[52] The earliest of these were products of the various reform clubs, efforts that the regime alternatively countenanced and suppressed in the years 1896–98, depending on how critical they ventured to be about its current policies. Well-known examples are the Peking Development Studies Society's *Chinese and Foreign Report* (Chung-wai kung-pao) and the *Development Studies Journal* (Ch'iang-hsueh pao), put out by the society's Shanghai branch. Another well-known propaganda piece of the reformist party was *Current Affairs* (Shih-wu pao), started in 1896 in Shanghai. This paper was largely financed by contributions from Governor-general Chang Chih-tung. When Chang sought to moderate what he viewed as rampant radicalism in the paper's discussions, he precipitated the resignation of its young editor, Liang Ch'i-ch'ao.[53]

Consistent use of the press as an anti-government propaganda instrument was initially by the hand of Liang in the period after the reform movement was crushed and he was an exile in Japan. Liang's first publication, the triweekly magazine *Public Opinion* (Ch'ing-i pao), made its debut on December 23, 1898, just six months after the coup d'état that put the conservatives back in power in China. Financing was provided by members of the overseas Chinese community in Yokohama, key backers of K'ang and Liang and their Protect the Emperor Party (Pao-huang Hui). *Public Opinion* broadcast the message of constitutional monarchy, popular rights, and Sino-Japanese friendship. It was a popular magazine. At 3,000–4,000 copies an issue, each running to about forty pages, it had the largest circulation of any Chinese journal of the day. Sales representatives were maintained at home and abroad: Shanghai, Tientsin, Peking, Hankow, Hong Kong, Australia, and the United States. But it enjoyed only a brief success. A government import ban cut the circulation, and the magazine was forced to close on December 21, 1901, after publishing 100 issues.[54]

Undeterred, in early February 1902, Liang started another reform party organ, also out of Japan, called *New People's Miscellany* (Hsin-min ts'ung-pao). Ch'ing officials took a more permissive stance on the sale of this magazine, which adopted a relatively moderate tone toward the Empress Dowager and her Court favorites. From an initial 2,000 copies, the circulation rose rapidly, to 5,000 in August and 9,000 by early 1903. The message of the *New People's Miscellany* was that the Chinese people needed to be informed and educated— to become, in effect, "new people," responsible citizens—before political reform was possible. Education was the critical issue, Liang told his readers, but since nationalism (*kuo-chia chu-i*) was the cry of the day, the magazine would also devote space to political discussion. *New People's Miscellany* continued for six years, for a total of ninety-six issues.[55]

Even before Liang Ch'i-ch'ao's prolific pen contributed reformism to an opposition press, more radical political views had been finding their way into print by one means or another. The first magazine openly calling for revolution was the *China Daily* (Chung-kuo jih-pao), established in Hong Kong in 1899, with financing from Sun Yat-sen and some of his merchant friends. *Su pao* (which figures large in a later chapter) had been founded earlier but did not explode with anti-government attacks until the spring of 1903. In Japan, a handful of radical students produced two short-lived papers, *Enlightenment Journal* (K'ai-chih lu) and *The Chinese National* (Kuo-min pao), launched in 1899 and 1901, respectively.

Enlightenment Journal, first issued in the winter of 1899, was the brainchild of Feng Tzu-yu, whose father, a Yokohama merchant, was helping to finance both the *China Daily* and Liang's *Public Opinion*. Feng the younger's magazine assailed both the Manchus and the foreign powers in China. In an article entitled "The Boxers and Their Contribution to China," for example, the magazine praised the Boxers for initiating active resistance to foreign encroachment but lamented their lack of attention to Manchu misrule: "Our people constantly speak of the shame of being slaves of the foreigners, yet they are not aware of the humiliation of being enslaved by the Manchus. They constantly speak of ousting the foreign races, yet do not know enough to resist the alien Manchu race."[56]

Planning the first issue of *Enlightenment Journal* at a time when Liang Ch'i-ch'ao was on a trip to Hawaii, the enterprising young editors got permission to use *Public Opinion's* printing and distributing facilities. This arrangement continued until the spring of 1901, when the acting management of *Public Opinion*, alarmed at the popularity of the fledgling journal, withdrew the privilege. *Enlightenment Journal* was forced to close.[57] Its place was immediately filled in June 1901 by *The Chinese National*, which was founded by Shen Hsiang-yün, Chi I-hui, Chang Chi, and others who had been involved in the Hankow uprising. Sun Yat-sen initially provided funds for the journal's publication, but his contributions were somehow inadequate or discontinued, for after eight months and four issues, it shut down.[58]

The provincial magazines, when their time came (February 1903 for *Hupei Students Circle* and *Tide of Chekiang* and April 1903 for

Kiangsu), had the advantage of broad backing from the large and growing group of Chinese students in Japan. There is little doubt that they attracted a large readership early on. In fact, *Hupei Students Circle* announced in its September 1903 issue that the magazine had been printing upwards of 7,000 copies for several months. This figure puts it well ahead of *Public Opinion* (average circulation, 3,000–4,000) and not far behind *New People's Miscellany* (9,000–10,000). The Hupei monthly was bound to have reached a far greater audience than it claimed, though, since there was much sharing of dissident literature.[59] The distribution of the student magazines was evidently well thought through, with arrangements made with numerous bookstores in China and overseas—thirty-five distributors was the high point for *Hupei Students Circle*, seventy-three for *Tide of Chekiang*, and forty-six for *Kiangsu*. Advertisements in the Kiangsu and Hupei magazines specifically mention discounts for volume sales.

The Ch'ing government was not pleased. On December 30, 1902, before the first issue of *Hupei Students Circle* had even reached the bookstores, Chang Chih-tung sent a cable to Minister Ts'ai Chün in Tokyo registering his strong disapproval: the students should be spending their stay in Japan solely in study and translation; they had no business issuing a publication given to rash comments on Ch'ing politics. Chang demanded an end to the venture; he punctuated his order with a threat to cut off the scholarship funds of any student failing to comply.[60] He later sent a cable directly to the Hupei group, ordering three of the magazine's editors to return to China. His order was ignored.[61]

Some months later, the central government prepared a policy statement applicable to all three provincial magazines: "We find that last winter the Chinese students in Japan established periodicals that are being distributed everywhere. In these periodicals are found editorial discussions; though such discussions enlighten the people, they often contain absurd, biased phrases."[62]

Lest such language corrupt young pupils, any students found buying, reading, or distributing the Tokyo magazines faced immediate expulsion from school. School officials who were lax about banning the magazines would be asked to resign.

The government's crackdown, combined with escalating costs of publication, helped bring the magazines to an abrupt halt after a year or less of publication. *Hupei Students Circle*, the first to appear, was the first to leave; its final issue was dated September–October 1903. *Tide of Chekiang* held on another month, putting out its tenth issue in November–December. *Kiangsu* maintained operations until June 1904. The return to China of some of the original staff for political reasons or simply because their schooling was finished probably contributed to the magazines' shutdown. In what turned out to be its last issue, *Hupei Students Circle* begged readers to bear with publication delays: most of its reporters were going home for the months of summer vacation.[63]

To get ahead of our story a bit, the demise of the three provincial publications resulted in a temporary lull in student polemical writing. It was a full year before the next student magazine, *Twentieth-Century China* (Erh-shih shih-chi chih Chih-na), made its debut under the guidance of Sung Chiao-jen and Chang Chi. Banned by the Japanese government almost immediately because of its anti-Japanese tone,[64] the magazine was subsequently taken over by the T'ung-meng Hui as its literary organ and reissued under the name *People's Magazine* (Min pao). The year 1906 saw seven new magazines established by Chinese students in Japan; the following year nearly twenty appeared. This proliferation of publications led one contemporary observer to conclude: "nowhere is it easier to start a magazine than among the Chinese students in Japan. Two or three promoters, a special meeting, a few speeches, and a general subscription are all that is necessary. Contributors are volunteered, editors are elected, and both are gratis."[65]

FIVE

The Seijō School Incident, 1902

IN 1902, the Chinese students in Japan began to emerge as an independent political force. There had been intimations of this in the previous two or three years: political debates held in various student clubs, student connections with the Hankow plotters, a fleeting voice of dissent in student publications. But though the Ch'ing government viewed with alarm the least suggestion of student involvement in politics, such dissidence as existed had been small-scale, impermanent, and, in most cases, confined to the level of general intellectual debate over national issues. Only in the Hankow affair had some few students shown themselves to be vulnerable to appeals from the outlawed forces of reform.

By contrast, in 1902 the Chinese students in Japan began to organize their ever-increasing numbers for the purpose of registering dissent over a specific issue. For the Chinese student, taking on the role of political agitator was something new. To be sure, he had the *ch'ing-i* precedent to draw on, but this involved mainly mature scholars, often officials of some importance, including well-known censors, not generally those of his generation. Not only that, though *ch'ing-i* advocates were increasingly active, openly critical, and concerned with contemporary issues from the 1870's on, they were political insiders. No one was attacking the imperial system itself, only certain policies, people, and practices that were preventing the system from operating as it ideally should.[1]

The Chinese students in Japan represented the political outsiders, frustrated members of the new social elites, who wanted a political voice yet lacked even the *ch'ing-i* channel for expressing their views.

Finding alternatives was a trial-and-error process in an environment in which there was no state-sanctioned right to public dissent and in which such tactics of protest as sit-ins, boycotts, and propaganda were largely untested. We must also bear in mind that though the Chinese students in Japan had formed organizations—the Chinese Student Union, provincial societies, translation groups—from the start, none of these groups operated under a clear-cut political ideology that would incline members to seek out opportunities for protest. Students, in other words, did not mount protests in the express hope of dramatizing a doctrinal point or showing up the system as corrupt and unjust. Instead, something of the reverse took place. Protests tended to be sparked off more or less spontaneously by a specific grievance; and in the course of these actions, students refined their thinking on a range of issues and formulated a set of political ideals.

Numerous incidents took place in the years between 1902 and 1905 in which students adopted an independent, critical posture, but three in particular were sizable and serious enough to excite our interest now and certainly to cause concern among senior officials at the time: the Seijō School incident of 1902, a clash between Chinese students and the Chinese minister to Japan over the question of admission to the military preparatory school; the student anti-Russia campaign of 1903, which was sparked off by Russian aggression in Manchuria; and the Education Ministry incident of 1905, in which students protested against a set of regulations issued by the Japanese government.

The chapters to follow devote considerable space to recounting the course of each of these protest movements, beginning with the first. Only such complete accounts adequately reveal the process whereby actions taken initially by a few students rapidly took on the proportions of an independent student movement. Furthermore, these student protests merit our close attention as a measure of how turbulent and unstable Chinese society was after the turn of the century. In the student disturbances are reflected both the sharp cleavage that developed in these years between the reform-minded and the Ch'ing establishment and the parallel development of radicalism within the ranks of the reform-minded. In neither case, of course, did this involve a sudden, dramatic break; it was a matter, rather, of a steady erosion of relationships. As we will see, the increasing numbers of malcontents among the Chinese students were never entirely out of touch with more conservative elements within the gentry, the merchants, and even Ch'ing officialdom. Theirs was not a class war, one socioeconomic group pitted against another, but a political-cultural animus directed with increasing single-mindedness at the Manchu autocracy and its long-time supporters. Tracing the twists and turns of events and relationships enables us to comprehend something of the reality and complexity of the Chinese condition. It helps us begin to understand the profound humiliation felt by educated Chinese at their nation's weakness vis-à-vis the Powers, their shifting perceptions of where solutions lay, and their rising expectations in both the political and the economic sphere leading eventually to revolution in 1911. In the student political experience, in other words, lies part of the explanation of how a national consensus finally developed in opposition to Ch'ing rule.

Seeds of Conflict

Early 1902 witnessed a widening breach between Chinese officialdom and the Chinese student group in Japan. On the official side, the attitude was one of wariness. The rise in numbers of Chinese students in Japan—and notably of those not on government scholarship—brought with it the problem of controls. Already in June 1899, Minister Ts'ai Chün's predecessor, Li Sheng-to, had requested the appointment of a general supervisor of students to take charge of the sixty or more Chinese students then in Japan. Though these students were officially the responsibility of the Chinese legation, with so many now coming in, Li argued, overburdened consular officials could not adequately supervise their education.[2] Of even greater moment than the rise in numbers was the fact that certain students were showing radical tendencies. As we have seen, even Chang Chih-tung, the inspiration behind sending students to Japan, was haunted by visions of student involvement in a second Hankow.

Tensions between students and the Manchu establishment heightened under Li Sheng-to's successor. Neither Ts'ai Chün's qualifications nor his personality endeared him to the student group. A native of Kiangsi, Ts'ai was reputed to be one of the wealthiest of Chinese officials. His career in government service had flourished under the patronage of the Court favorite Jung-lu.[3] Positions in the London and Madrid legations were followed by a top-level appointment in Shanghai. His career was not without blemish. At the time he was named minister to Japan (summer 1901), rumors circulated about his unscrupulous business dealings during his tenure in Shanghai three years before.[4] Once in Japan, Ts'ai's relations with the student community reached a peak of cordiality at the opening ceremony of the Chinese Student Union and deteriorated rapidly thereafter. He is described by a contemporary student, Ts'ao Ju-lin, as being ignorant, wily, stubborn, and conceited.[5]

The first note of open hostility between Ts'ai Chün and the Chinese students was sounded over the so-called "secret dispatch affair." On March 28, 1902, the Tokyo morning papers featured the text of a purportedly confidential communique Ts'ai sent to the Chinese Foreign Ministry on February 8 recommending that the study-in-Japan program be terminated.[6] Since the document was highly impolitic in its references to Japan's China policy, it became a focal point of discussion in the Japanese press.

Liang Ch'i-ch'ao's *New People's Miscellany* printed the entire text based on the Japanese version. According to that version, Ts'ai's document was an attack on the embryonic dissident movement represented by the K'ang/Liang group. To sap this movement of its strength, the document argued, required a two-pronged offensive. Every effort should be made at one and the same time to undermine the K'ang/Liang influence among Chinese merchants, thereby depriving the movement of its financial backing, and to rid the student community of K'ang/Liang inspired notions of freedom, popular sovereignty, and revolution.

But not only were K'ang Yu-wei and Liang Ch'i-ch'ao brought under attack. The Japanese government, too, was implicated for its role in harboring such rebels. Moreover, certain Japanese were said to be secretly inciting the students to mount a rebellion in China. Ts'ai allegedly reported: "I fear that in the future the numbers will be on the increase. It will not be a homogeneous group; there will be an upsurge in radicalism. The Japanese stand to gain by a rebellion in China."[7] In any case, Japan, with all its moral and political decay, was having a corrupting effect on the Chinese student. They paid no heed to official directives and lacked both filiality and knowledge of the Classics. In short, since the study-in-Japan program, far from creating a youthful base of support for the Ch'ing government, was contributing to the growth of dissent, it ought, very simply, to be abandoned.[8]

Controversy arose at once over the authenticity of this text. *New People's Miscellany* accepted it as a likely product of Ts'ai Chün's pen. So did most of the Japanese press. A Japanese Foreign Office report stating that a communique from Ts'ai on the student problem was sent to the Chinese Foreign Ministry and then forwarded directly to the Commissioner of Southern Ports, Liu K'un-i, coupled with a rumor of a rivalry between Ts'ai Chün and one of Liu's top aides, led Japanese newspapers to conclude that the printed version was the genuine article, leaked to the press from Liu's office to ruin Ts'ai's standing.[9] Other sources judged the text to be a forgery. On the afternoon of March 28, the president of the TDK, Prince Konoe, paid a visit to the Chinese legation, where he was given an explanation of the matter directly from Minister Ts'ai.[10] Ts'ai's words apparently left Konoe fully convinced that the dispatch calling for a halt in the study-abroad program was a fabrication. The English-language paper, the *Japan Weekly Mail*, agreed: "It is now clearly established, according to good authority, that the secret dispatch recently attributed to His Excellency Mr. Ts'ai was the outcome of a political intrigue." No particulars were given regarding the "good authority" or the "political intrigue."[11]

When all was said and done, it was clear that Ts'ai had sent some sort of dispatch to his government urging added controls on the student group in Japan. A memorandum from the Chinese Foreign Ministry to Ts'ai dated May 19, 1902, opens with a reference to his communique on the student question, subsequently transmitted in a confidential document to the Liang-Kiang and Hu-Kuang governors-general. According to the Foreign Ministry, the document was "leaked" to the press, where it appeared in distorted form. This prompted a visit to the Foreign Ministry from the Japanese minister to China, Uchida Yasuya, who was assured that the actual document contained no remarks critical of the Japanese, that Ts'ai had merely indicated the need to enforce certain standards of conduct on the students under his charge.[12] Ts'ai Chün himself confirmed this version of the affair in a press interview in Tokyo. He admitted sending a communique to the Foreign Ministry warning Chinese authorities to exercise caution in the selection of students for Japan, but denied writing the document printed in the Japanese papers.[13]

Nevertheless, Ts'ai took a beating in the Japanese press for his supposed insults to Japan.[14] Even the *Japan Weekly Mail*, one of the few newspapers that accepted the published text as a forgery, commented that Ts'ai was "ill-advised" to have left the Japanese press account so long uncontradicted: "It is now only too probable that his opportunities for usefulness in this country have been curtailed."[15] The *Asahi Shimbun* correspondent in Peking reported that Ts'ai had sent in his resignation, a report that was subsequently denied by the minister himself.[16] As for the original subjects of the affair, the Chinese students, they managed on the whole to hold their deep resentment of Ts'ai's proposal in check until the following summer, when they openly clashed with him over another issue.

With emotions still running high over the secret-dispatch affair, another event occurred that contributed to the developing atmosphere of confrontation between the Chinese minister and the students. In April 1902, with Chang Ping-lin as the mastermind, Feng Tzu-yu, Chou Hung-yeh, Wang Chia-chü, Ch'eng Chia-sheng, and others arranged to hold an anti-Manchu rally.[17] It was scheduled for April 26, the date of the death of the last Ming emperor and was styled as "a meeting to commemorate the conquest of China." History was to be the vehicle to arouse support for a revolution in China—a racial revolution that, in Chang's terms, would rid China of Manchu injustice and restore the Han Chinese to a position of rightful power.[18]

Chinese students and merchants were informed of the meeting. Liang Ch'i-ch'ao and Sun Yat-sen, who were residing in Yokohama at the time, both expressed support. The Chinese minister soon learned of plans for the rally, and at his request, it was banned by the Japanese police.[19] Later, at a small meeting held in Yokohama, Chang Ping-lin read the manifesto he had composed for the Ueno rally.[20]

In response to this anti-Manchu incident, Minister Ts'ai—this time in a publicly verified report—advised his government of the necessity of carefully screening prospective candidates for the study-in-Japan program.[21] Commissioner of Southern Ports Liu K'un-i also sent a warning message to the Chinese government. In a communique to the Chinese Foreign Ministry on May 11, Liu cited a telegram he had received from General Fukushima Yasumasa reporting that Chinese political exiles in Japan were seeking to stir up anti-Manchu sentiment among the Chinese students there. Fukushima assured Liu that Japanese authorities were taking all necessary steps to suppress such activity.[22]

Direct Confrontation

Mounting tensions between the Chinese minister and the Chinese student community over the secret-dispatch affair and the suppression of the anti-Manchu rally soon erupted in an open clash in the much-publicized Seijō School incident. At issue was Ts'ai's reluctance to grant recommendations to nine self-supporting students seeking admission to the Seijō School, Japan's premier military preparatory school. It was a matter that was particularly ripe for dispute because of the ambiguity of the regulations for Chinese students entering Japanese schools.

Those regulations, laid down by both governments, point once again to the question of supervising the ever-increasing number of Chinese students in Japan. From the Chinese side, the main problem was the self-supporting student. The scholarship student, selected by his provincial governor, put under the charge of the Chinese minister, and dependent financially on official funds, was given considerable leeway to "study any branch of Western science or art best suited to [his] abilities and tastes."[23] In their joint communique to the Throne in 1901, Liu K'un-i and Chang Chih-tung had simply urged that all provinces send students abroad on scholarship, especially to Japan, to pursue military and liberal arts courses and such specialities as agriculture, engineering, and business. No mention was made of special requirements for school admission. As we have seen, self-supporting students were also urged to go abroad for study: they promised to add to the nation's pool of skills without any strain on the government budget.[24] However, to keep its hand in, the government subjected those students to certain requirements. These were set out by Liu K'un-i in a report on the dispatch of Kiangnan-sponsored students to Japan: "In the case of a self-supporting student going abroad, he must first be guaranteed by his clansmen; then he must be examined by the provincial judge and thereupon given a recommendation."[25] Ts'ai Chün was to cite this document as the Seijō incident unfolded.

On the Japanese side, the admissions requirements tended to be more formally set out than this, at least for state schools. On July 4, 1900, the Japanese Education Ministry issued a ruling on foreign students entering schools under its supervision. The first clause made their enrollment conditional on a written guarantee from their minister or consul to Japan. Subsequent clauses dealt with presenting the letter of guarantee to school heads and other admission procedures.[26] No distinction was made between self-supporting and scholarship students.

This ruling, which seems clear enough, was referred to in Chang Tsung-hsiang's 1901 *Guide to Study in Japan*. The problem was that the *Guide* went on to distinguish between state schools—those under the Education Ministry—and private schools. True, in the case of state schools, students must have a reference from the Chinese minister or consul, as the Ministry of Education ruling stated. But for entrance to private schools, according to the *Guide*, a reference from any reputable person, either Chinese or Japanese would do.[27] The nine students seeking admission to the Seijō School in the spring of 1902 very likely took their lead from the *Guide*.

To add to the confusion, there was some question whether Seijō was a state or a private school. Some contemporary sources, such as *New People's Miscellany*, considered it a state school, and as such, open only to foreigners who had a letter of recommendation from their diplomatic representatives.[28] Prince Tsai Chen, charged with investigating the Seijō incident, agreed, noting that up till now all Chinese students, whether self-supporting or scholarship, had had the necessary documentation.[29] A *Japan Weekly Mail* article hedged on the matter, first implying that Seijō was a public school where a recommendation must be presented, then referring to it as a private institution.[30] It seems that Seijō was, in fact, a state school, but as preparatory to the Army Officers School, it was administered by the General Staff Office, not the Education Ministry.[31]

Seijō had admitted its first Chinese students, four in number, in 1898. All four had been sent by Chang Chih-tung after Fukushima Yasumasa of the General Staff had urged on him and other high officials the benefits of study in Japan.[32] In January 1899, Commissioner of Southern Ports Liu K'un-i, Szechuan governor Ts'en Ch'un-hsuan, and Chihli governor-general Yuan Shih-k'ai all followed suit. For the benefit of foreigners, Seijō supplemented its regular military preparatory course with a program in Japanese-language study. The school was noted for its strict discipline and excellent instruction. There, in two and a half years of rigorous study, a Chinese student might complete the equivalent of five years of Japanese middle school.[33] In July 1900, the first class of Chinese students—forty-five all told—graduated from Seijō. All of them entered the Army Officers School. The next class, of thirty, graduated in March 1902 and went on to the Officers School or joined Japanese military units.[34]

On June 12, 1902, a contingent of fifty-two Chinese students arrived in Japan. Twenty-one were scholarship students, including eight young women (half of whom intended to enroll at the Peeresses' College and the others to enter elementary school).[35] The remaining thirty-one were self-supporting students, probably for the most part Nanyang Academy dropouts.[36] The guidance counselor for these self-supporting students was Wu Chih-hui, a *chü-jen* degreeholder from Kiangsu who had studied in Japan in 1901.[37] Nine of them, from Kiangsu, Kiangsi, and Chekiang, applied to Minister Ts'ai for certification to enroll in the Seijō School. When no reply was forthcoming, Wu Chih-hui drafted a long petition to Ts'ai. He reminded the minister that a character reference for one of the nine signed by five enrolled Chinese students was already on record at the legation. On July 13, Wu discussed the matter with Wu Ju-lun, dean of Peking University, then in Japan on an official study tour. In apparent sympathy with the substance of Wu Chih-hui's letter, Wu Ju-lun consented to convey it to Ts'ai Chün.

On July 18, Wu Ju-lun informed anxious students that the minister would accept the document signed by the five students as a bona-fide reference for the one applicant. In anticipation of success, the other students set about getting personal references. Some twenty persons, including Chang Tsung-hsiang, author of the *Guide* and a student in Japan since early 1899, acted as guarantors. The completed documents were submitted through Wu Ju-lun.

When by July 25 there was still no order from the legation certifying admission for the nine applicants, Wu Chih-hui again appealed to Wu Ju-lun. The dean responded by sending a letter to Minister Ts'ai that same day, stating that the nine references had been properly filed. Reminding the minister that he (Ts'ai) had agreed to recommend that the applicants be admitted before summer vacation, so they could join the Seijō summer program, Wu pointed out that the school would recess for vacation on July 27. It was thus urgent that the minister personally issue certification notes that very day, the 25th.[38]

The answer to this appeal was unexpected. On the evening of July 27, Wu Ju-lun passed on to Wu Chih-hui a copy of a Japanese General Staff Office memorandum replying to a communique from Ts'ai:

We acknowledge your recent communique on the matter of Chang Tsung-hsiang and other Chinese students now in Tokyo recommending nine self-supporting students from Kiangsu, Chekiang, and Kiangsi who wish to enter the course of study at Seijō Gakkō. However, in the past only those who had a recommendation from you were allowed to enter. Your present communication is something of a departure from precedent. Hence, we request that you personally issue notes of certification. . . . Further, Seijō is currently on summer vacation. Please wait until classes begin the first part of September. At present, it is not convenient to allow entrance.[39]

The students were dumbfounded. It was not clear to them why the minister had referred the matter of certification to the General Staff. Nor did they understand why, if he had somehow felt it necessary to consult the Japanese military, he had not clearly endorsed the nine. What was obvious was only that there was no longer hope of gaining entrance to Seijō in time for the summer program.

A confrontation between the Chinese students and Minister Ts'ai was unavoidable. Ts'ai was later to claim that the students concerned about Seijō admission acted precipitously, hurrying over to the legation before he had had time to follow up on the General Staff's request.[40] Prince Tsai Chen, in his report to the Ch'ing government, stated that because of the large number of applicants involved, the minister felt it imperative to consult with Japanese authorities before making a decision. And since Chief of Staff Fukushima was on holiday, the minister was unable to take immediate action on the matter.[41]

According to *New People's Miscellany*, the students no sooner got the news than they suspected bad faith on the part of both Ts'ai Chün and Wu Ju-lun. The only course that appeared reasonable to them was to confront the two men in person and demand an explanation. On the following day, July 28, a delegation of twenty-six students sought to question Wu Ju-lun about the minister's position. Wu proved uncommunicative, asserting only that he was not qualified to speak for the minister. Greatly agitated, the twenty-six then converged on the legation, insisting on a meeting with Ts'ai. Legation officials and Japanese representatives called in from the General Staff Office and Foreign Office urged the youths to be patient, however long it might take the minister to resolve the admissions problem. The students refused to leave.[42]

After eight hours, Ts'ai Chün capitulated. With Wu Chih-hui as spokesman, the students were allowed in his presence to state their case: since the use of students as guarantors was unacceptable to the General Staff, they were petitioning the minister to certify the applicants himself in accordance with past practice. Ts'ai Chün responded with two objections. In the first place, unlike previous applicants, the nine students had failed to produce letters of reference from their provincial governors or local officials, and his own hands were tied because he had received instructions from the Chinese government to the effect that self-supporting students were no longer to receive recommendations. All he was empowered to do, then, was to forward the student guarantees to the General Staff with a note of explanation. As his second argument, Ts'ai maintained that the General Staff had, in fact, refused admission to the nine in its reply to him. Since this was at distinct odds with the students' understanding of the General Staff's memorandum, Wu Chih-hui pursued the matter further. It came out that an error in terminology in the General Staff communication accounted for the minister's assertion. Instead of using the term "tsu-sung" for "recommend," as was appropriate between offices of equal rank, the staff had asked the minister to personally "pao-sung" the students, a term with the same meaning but used to describe the action to be taken by someone of inferior rank. Seeing this, Ts'ai Chün had been highly insulted and let the matter drop, choosing to construe the use of an improper term for "recommend" into a refusal to grant admission.[43]

Presuming that the General Staff's position had now been clarified—that there was no obstacle to admission save the minister's endorsement of the nine applicants—the students sought to persuade Ts'ai to issue the required recommendations. To this end, Wu Chih-hui, again speaking for the group, launched into an oration on the merits of allowing self-supporting students to pursue military studies. First, with China in financial crisis, yet in urgent need of skills acquired abroad, the government should give every encouragement to youths willing to pay their own way for foreign study. Second, China's primary national need was to develop a military establishment and a system of military education. Military study for the self-supporting student thus appeared as a happy solution to a variety of problems. Certain that the Chinese minister would support what was in the national good, Wu explained, the applicants had decided to take their appeal for recommendations directly to him.[44]

Growing bolder, Wu Chih-hui went so far as to advise Ts'ai on the discharge of his office. Even if the General Staff had demurred in the matter of admissions, it was the minister's duty to press the students' cause. He must exercise his prerogative as a representative of Chinese nationals in dealings with the Japanese, just as he ought to show an independent spirit in assisting his own government to shape foreign policy. "You must be a critical Minister [vis-à-vis the Court]. We wish to be critical students in regard to you. . . . We hope that you and Wu Ju-lun will be able to rid yourselves of bureaucratic indifference."[45]

Wu Chih-hui managed one final verbal parry before he was cut off in his discourse on study abroad. His point of departure was the secret-dispatch affair, undoubtedly an unwelcome subject for Minister Ts'ai. He recounted Yuan Shih-kai's comments on the affair, which had appeared recently in Shanghai papers. While Yuan had dismissed the communique as a forgery, he had gone on to outline his own rather liberal views on study abroad. He was not unduly worried about students being imbued with notions of freedom and equality, he said. Such notions were, after all, at the foundation of European nationhood and, if applied carefully, could foster China's national growth as well. Obviously, Wu intended Yuan's comments as an odious contrast to Ts'ai Chün's own conservative approach to study abroad.

At this point, Wu Ju-lun and the Foreign Office's representative, Kobayashi, interrupted Wu, cautioning him against further digressions. Undaunted, Wu presented three student demands related to the specific issue of Seijō admission: "(1) Hereafter, if students desirous of entering Seijō School have the guarantee of five reliable enrolled students, the Minister must automatically give his recommendation; (2) if, after the students have been certified, the Japanese government opposes admission without good cause, the Minister must fight for permission for the students to enter; and (3) if his struggle yields no positive results, the Minister must force the issue by threatening to resign." Not surprisingly, Kobayashi commented that the students were speaking with considerable presumption in referring to the minister's resignation. Wu Chih-hui countered with the remark that in the case of Chinese officials, it was necessary to speak in extremes to get even a modicum of constructive action. At this, Minister Ts'ai angrily left the room.[46]

Even with this apparent break in negotiations, the students refused to leave the legation. Kobayashi and Wu Ju-lun went off to consult with Ts'ai Chün in private and returned to announce that the three student demands would be met. Wu Chih-hui, exacting as before, asked if the concession represented the position of Kobayashi or that of the minister. Kobayashi was forced to admit that the minister had agreed to only the first two demands; he, Kobayashi, was acceding to the third in the name of the minister; that is, if the minister showed any reluctance to resign as stipulated, Kobayashi himself would request his resignation.[47] This was not acceptable to the students. For Japan to interfere in such matters was an insult to China's national integrity.

The meeting had come to a complete impasse. The students steadfastly refused to leave the legation until the minister himself acceded to all three student demands. But Wu Ju-lun and Kobayashi could make no headway in their attempt to intercede for the students with the minister. At last, the Japanese police were called in. Little resistance was offered as thirty or forty policemen ushered the students out of the legation. Wu Chih-hui and Sun K'uei-chün— who had made at least one outspoken remark in the course of the meeting—were taken to police headquarters for questioning.[48]

The following day, July 29, about fifty students gathered at the legation to protest the action of the night before and to demand another hearing with the minister. Twenty were arrested, questioned, and released. The protest was renewed on July 30, despite Minister Ts'ai's issuance of a formal statement warning against dissident activities.[49] This time, an estimated 260 students assembled to endorse a cable to be sent to the Chinese Foreign Ministry:[50]

Minister Ts'ai has disobeyed imperial orders in repeatedly refusing to certify the students abroad. Yesterday, certain students went to the legation to entreat the Minister again and again to issue recommendations. Far from doing so, the Minister ordered the police to enter the legation and arrest the students. This truly represents a loss of national sovereignty and an insult to the scholar class. We humbly beg [Foreign Minister] Prince Kung to memorialize on our behalf that Minister Ts'ai be recalled. We eagerly await your order.[51]

Ts'ai countered with his own version of the events of the past few days:

Nine students expelled from the Nanyang Academy came to Japan as self-supporting students. Before their requests for recommendations to enter military studies could be handled, they took it upon themselves to band together and arrange for a group of students to come to the legation on successive days. Day and night, they created disturbances, battering at the gates and breaking windows with flagrant rudeness. Fortunately, the Japanese police seized and subdued them.[52]

On August 5, without prior warning, Wu Chih-hui and Sun K'uei-chün were taken into police custody and read their deportation orders. A student petition to the Ministry of Internal Affairs and Wu's dramatic suicide attempt were to no avail. The two were summarily expelled the following day with a one-way ticket to China.[53]

Before the Japanese police intervened, the student protest centered on the specific issue of school admission. But once the police forcibly removed students from the legation, the character of the protest changed: the Seijō affair became tied to broader political concerns. The grievance now turned on the violation of China's national sovereignty; and the chief culprit here was not so much Japan as Minister Ts'ai and through him the whole of Chinese officialdom:

Ts'ai Chün is a small-scale model of the entire government bureaucracy.... The present government's capacity to rule was completely dissipated long ago. Still, it has something to rely on as a protective shield. What does it rely on? Foreigners. If the people in word or deed do something displeasing to the government, it hands over ultimate authority to foreigners, who cut down the people as subhumans.[54]

If anything the students became more vociferous after Wu and Sun were deported, seizing on the theme of the abdication of sovereign rights with a vengeance. Meetings at the Student Union in Kanda produced a resolution calling for acts of protest against Minister Ts'ai's surrender of authority to the Japanese. Students at the Kōbun Institute boycotted classes.[55] A group of about 100 students from other schools declared their intention to return to China in protest.[56] Apparently, for many this was not a wholehearted commitment. Hu Han-min, a student who did carry through his declared resolve to leave Japan, expressed disappointment at the hesitancy of some of his comrades when it came time to depart.[57]

Still other students continued to bombard Minister Ts'ai with protest letters, determined to extract a satisfactory explanation regarding Seijō admission procedures, Wu and Sun's deportation, and Japanese police intervention. A student sit-in at the legation on August 16 again resulted in the forcible removal and arrest of students. On this occasion, Ch'in Yü-liu acted as spokesman:

> If the Minister decides that he is unwilling to recommend [the nine], there is no harm done in treating the matter as finished. But the matter of the deportation of Wu and Sun is a grave insult to our national polity and a great loss of national sovereignty. The Minister is an official of China; the students are the Chinese people. If the Minister can protest and does not, he is neglecting his responsibility. If the students can make requests and do not, they are derelict in their duty. . . . The [students'] present request to see the Minister is quite distinct from the request of Wu and Sun. They came on behalf of the students [desirous of] entering school. We come to struggle for the recovery of national rights.[58]

The Search for a Solution

In the week following this incident, Student Union leaders worked to reach a settlement of the Seijō affair through the good offices of two TDK representatives. On August 27, the union issued a letter outlining a new admission policy, presumably sanctioned by the Japanese government. The first clause proposed the appointment of a general supervisor of students at the discretion of the Chinese government. Japan, it was stated, would offer no objection to such an appointment. Clause 2 stipulated that Chinese students seeking admission to schools under Education Ministry control must have recommendations from one of three private schools: the Tokyo Dōbun Academy, the Kōbun Institute, or the Seika School. To qualify for a recommendation, students must have been enrolled in one of the three schools at least six months or be guaranteed by two enrolled Chinese students, and pay a deposit fee. Clause 3—the one most pertinent to the Seijō affair—stated that the students currently seeking to enter school might renew their appeal after the return of General Fukushima.[59]

The issuance of these guidelines created a split in student ranks. In an unsigned letter to *New People's Miscellany*, certain students raised objections to the union-sponsored agreement. First, they took exception to the fact that the two Japanese intermediaries were TDK members and thus, in their view, not qualified to represent the Japanese government. Nor, on the Chinese side, was the whole Chinese student body consulted at any point. The settlement was in effect the private production of the TDK representatives and the Student Union officers. Second, they objected to the mention of the Japanese government's concurrence in the proposal for a supervisor. It was offensive to defer to foreigners in any way when the appointment was a purely Chinese matter. Third, the terms of clause 2 left the Chinese student group in a worse position than before the Seijō affair. Students had been allowed to enter Japanese state and private schools of their own selection; and whether self-supporting or on scholarship, they were given recommendations by the minister as required. As matters stood now, the nine applicants to the Seijō military course had still not gained admission, and students planning to enroll in liberal arts courses had the added burden of securing a recommendation from one of three designated schools. In addition, the proviso that qualified students must have been in school in Japan for six months and must pay a deposit fee discriminated against the self-supporting student already pressed for money and time. Finally, clause 3 was merely a delaying tactic. It seemed unreasonable that negotiations over Seijō admission could not be conducted with the acting chief of staff in General Fukushima's absence.[60]

The Chinese authorities, meanwhile, decided to look into the matter themselves. In August, the Liang-Kiang governor-general commissioned Li Tsung-t'ang to investigate the Seijō affair. Based on talks with Japanese officials and students, Li drew up a report that in substance paralleled the more detailed account given in *New People's Miscellany*.[61] On September 1, Prince Tsai Chen, representing the Chinese Foreign Ministry, arrived in Japan to make a further investigation.[62] Prince Tsai held extensive talks with Japan's Foreign Minister, Baron Komura. He also spent considerable time trying to mend fences with the Chinese student community. In a meeting with about 400 Chinese students at the union, he praised the students for their patriotism and perseverance and went so far as to speak of a coming reform era when there would be better communications between rulers and ruled. Following Prince Tsai's speech, a Tokyo University student made an appeal on behalf of the self-supporting students, asking the prince to present their case to the Throne with a request that a special office be created to handle the affairs of the Chinese students in Japan.[63]

Prince Tsai's report on the Seijō affair, filed with the Chinese Foreign Ministry on September 22, reflected both his student contacts and his talks with Baron Komura. It was an evenhanded account, emphasizing the element of misunderstanding or lack of real communication between Ts'ai Chün and the students. The students, he said, fully expected that Ts'ai would comply with their request for certification, simply because he had done so in the case of those Chinese students—including self-supporting—already enrolled at Seijō. Consequently, when no word was immediately forthcoming from Ts'ai, they interpreted it as a refusal and went to the legation to protest. Ts'ai Chün, on his part, thinking that there were too many applicants involved, felt obliged to refer the matter directly to the General Staff Office. Since that had not been the past practice, the Staff Office had requested Ts'ai's endorsement of the applicants. Ts'ai, wishing to discuss the matter further with Chief of Staff Fukushima, opted to delay action until Fukushima's return from a summer holiday.[64]

Based on his discussions with Komura, Prince Tsai proposed the appointment of a general supervisor of students, whose initial task would be to work with the Japanese government in clarifying its educational policy toward the Chinese students. Chinese Foreign Ministry officials, as well as Japan's representative in China, Minister Uchida, supported this proposal.[65] So did Minister Ts'ai Chün in Tokyo. In a memorandum to the Throne of September 25, 1902, Ts'ai requested that a recognized scholar be appointed to oversee student affairs. Ts'ai avoided mention of the Seijō affair, simply pointing to the need for a special office now that student numbers were on the rise—swelling to more than 600 in the past eight months. With changes in the examination system, this trend was likely to continue as students clamored for specialized Western studies. Only the creation of a special supervisory office would ensure daily official contact with the student group.[66]

By imperial decree of October 21, 1902, Wang Ta-hsieh, second secretary in the Foreign Ministry, was appointed general supervisor of the Chinese students in Japan.[67] As his first order of business, he was to work with Japan's Education Ministry, Foreign Office, and General Staff Office on draft regulations for the Chinese students in Japan.[68] Before leaving for Japan on December 21, Wang Ta-hsieh consulted with Governor-general Chang Chih-tung and Governor En-shou of Kiangsu on the education of students abroad. He arrived in Japan on January 3, 1903, and was presented with all student records by Minister Ts'ai, who then arranged for him to meet with Foreign Minister Komura.[69] According to Wang's own records, he had frequent visits from students soon after his arrival. This is borne out by student accounts, which portray Wang as accessible and willing to listen to the students' opinions. Apparently, Wang clashed with Minister Ts'ai over how to handle the students and asked to be recalled. At the end of 1903, he was made senior adviser to the Foreign Ministry, and in 1905, he became chief secretary of the Chinese legation in Washington.[70]

Minister Ts'ai's standing suffered as a result of the Seijō affair. It was, in fact, a memorandum from an imperial censor criticizing his handling of the student disturbances that had prompted the Ch'ing government to commission Prince Tsai Chen to investigate the matter.[71] According to the *North China Herald*, the censor was especially upset at Ts'ai Chün's calling in the Japanese police.[72] In another report, the *Herald* alleged that an imperial message had been dispatched directly to Ts'ai censuring him for his conduct.[73] Rumors circulated within months of the affair that Ts'ai was under pressure to resign.[74] In fact, he was not relieved of his post until early October 1903, when he handed over the seals of office to Yang Shu.[75]

The students came in for their share of blame. The same Foreign Ministry telegram to Prince Tsai that charged him to look into Ts'ai Chün's conduct recommended stern punishment for troublemaking students as well. When Governor-general Chang Chih-tung heard of the affair, he sent off a telegram to the Hupei supervisor in Japan instructing him to warn Hupei students not to get involved.[76] Somewhat surprisingly, the nine students whose applications to Seijō had touched off the incident were admitted to the school in January 1903.[77]

Minister Ts'ai's reaction to the affair was to attempt to clarify and tighten controls on new arrivals. On October 10, 1902, he sent a set of draft regulations to the Foreign Ministry, the thrust of which was to free the minister from responsibility over student affairs.

Most of Minister Ts'ai's proposals were directed to the self-supporting students. To begin with, a student wishing to come to Japan on his own should be required to have a recommendation from local officials, this to be granted only after careful investigation of his character and academic qualifications. If the student wished to enter the military course at Seijō School, this must be explicitly stated on his recommendation. The minister, by Ts'ai's design, was to act only as a rubber stamp, issuing admission papers to those presenting the proper recommendations. During their stay in Japan, self-supporting students should be under the charge of the provincial supervisors of scholarship students or under a special supervisor. Any instances of rebellious conduct reported by the school director to the student supervisors and to the legation should result in expulsion and deportation. Although Ts'ai Chün provided that self-supporting graduates of notable achievement be recognized on a par with graduates on scholarship, his bitterness toward the privately funded student was evident. In clause 9, he proposed that should any self-supporting student die in Japan, arrangements for transporting the body home would be in the hands of the supervisor, and the costs must be met by the student's own funds or, if inadequate, by contributions from other self-supporting students.[78]

The minister also recommended that, assuming there was to be a general supervisor, the appointee should consult with him and Japanese authorities on taking office and then submit a proposal of his own to the Foreign Ministry.[79] There is no evidence that Wang Ta-hsieh ever produced such a document during his short tenure in Japan.

Some of the ambiguity surrounding admission requirements was resolved in October 1903, with the issuance of several sets of regulations governing study abroad drawn up by Chang Chih-tung in consultation with Japanese Minister Uchida. Here it was clearly stated that all Chinese students—whether scholarship or self-supporting—desirous of entering either state or private schools in Japan must have a recommendation from the Chinese minister to Japan or from the general supervisor of students. One of the key aims of the regulations was to put the students on notice that failure to toe the line would have serious consequences. Unacceptable behavior, in Chang's terms, was behavior "disruptive of law and harmful to public security"—what he clearly meant by this was involvement in politics. The penalties were expulsion from school and deportation from Japan. Despite Ts'ai Chün's attempt to dissociate his office from the supervision of students, China's minister to Japan, along with the general supervisor, was given ultimate authority in cases of student misconduct.[80]

The first definitive statement on Chinese students in military studies in Japan appeared in a set of sixteen regulations issued by China's Military Training Office in May–June 1904. This document stated that since military education was a national need, it should be pursued exclusively by the scholarship student. Self-supporting students already enrolled in military studies in Japan were to be asked about their future intentions and, if allowed to continue the course, transferred to the books as scholarship students.[81] This attempt to keep self-supporting students from pursuing a military program in Japan was not wholly effective. Sometime in 1903 or 1904, under the guiding hand of the Tokyo University law professor and China interventionist Terao Tōru, the Tōhin School (Tōhin Gakudō) was established as a private venture specifically to accommodate such students.[82]

Ch'ing officials were not being unduly alarmist in tightening controls over students, for the Seijō disturbances had indeed given impetus to the growing dissident movement. On August 22, 1902, before attempts to effect a compromise between the students and Minister Ts'ai began, a sympathy meeting attended by over 200 youths was held at Chang's Gardens in Shanghai. Though much publicity was given to the meeting itself, a proposal for going on to organize as the "Association to Assist Students in Pursuing their Studies in Eastern Asia" apparently came to nothing.[83]

To more lasting effect was the appearance at the end of 1902 of two radical groups with ties to the Seijō activists. One, in China, came into being as a direct result of student action at Nanyang Academy on November 16, 1902, when 145 students withdrew in protest against a ban on the possession of *New People's Miscellany* and books on the "new learning."[84] A small group of these students, after consulting with Ts'ai Yuan-p'ei, Chang Ping-lin, and the key Seijō activist Wu Chih-hui, set up a group called the Patriotic School in Shanghai. They were joined by dropouts from the Nanking Military School. The daily news sheet *Su pao* was adopted as the group's literary organ. In Japan, the Seijō incident acted as a stimulus to the formation of an avowedly revolutionary group, the Youth Society.

The Seijō disturbances signaled a deepening alienation between Chinese officialdom and the student group in Japan. Yet at this stage it was by no means a simple polarity, for various shades of political belief were represented within both groups. On the student side, the words and deeds of Wu Chih-hui and Ch'in Yü-liu put them on the radical end of the political spectrum, at some considerable distance from the relatively moderate position taken by the Student Union leaders, who sought to reach a compromise. In terms of numbers, fewer than 10 percent of the total student group participated in the legation sit-ins, though over 40 percent were involved in sending the protest cable to the Foreign Ministry. Of the officials involved in the Seijō affair, Prince Tsai and Wu Ju-lun were obviously sympathetic to the students' cause. Minister Ts'ai Chün, bungling, uncompromising, and conservative, shared with such notables as Chang Chih-tung and Li Sheng-to a growing distrust of the increasingly numerous and independent youth under his charge. In the final analysis, a desire to assert his authority was probably his chief motive for hedging in the matter of issuing recommendations. And, fair or not, it was Minister Ts'ai who, in the minds of the students, appeared as the archetype of the establishment bureaucrat, quite willing, as his use of the Japanese police showed, to betray China to the Foreign Powers.

SIX

The Rise of
Anti-Imperialism, 1903

THE YEAR 1903 witnessed a series of student protests against the Foreign Powers for interfering in China's affairs and against the Manchu government for failing to supply strong leadership in a time of crisis. As in the case of the Seijō disturbance, it was often a minor matter like school admissions procedures that roused students' anger. However, in the atmosphere of growing distrust between the students and the authorities—both Chinese and Japanese—whatever the initial point of dispute, it invariably escalated into a clash over issues of national sovereignty, domestic leadership, and the right to dissent.

Protests Against Japan and France

One of the most curious of the 1903 disputes erupted over the Japanese government's arrangements for the Chinese display booth at the Osaka Exhibition. Student sensitivities were aroused by announcements appearing in two Japanese newspapers on March 8, 1903, that the Races of Man Pavilion would consist of displays of the aborigines of Hokkaido (the Ainu) and Taiwan, and of the peoples of the Ryukyus, Korea, China, India, and Java. Emphasis was to be on physical types, standard of living, and premodern customs.[1] The Chinese exhibit was to include twenty-one Chinese women with bound feet, one smoking opium.[2] Chinese students at once objected both to China's being grouped with these other Asian peoples and to the selection of its most unfortunate characteristics for display purposes. Student Union leaders drafted a public letter of protest, notable as much for its tone of condescension toward other Asians as for its indignation over the alleged discrimination against the Chinese people:

The map of our nation has not yet changed its configuration; the people of our nation are not yet termed chattel. But for all this, when we are classed with India, it amounts to regarding us as slaves. When we are ranked with Korea, it signifies that we are considered menials. In the same way, exhibiting Chinese people with those of Java and with the Ainu clearly indicates that we are held to be savages.[3]

China was treated with contempt by the Japanese and other foreigners, the writers explained, because its people lacked national pride, the element that above all would decide the outcome of the current struggle for mastery among peoples of the world. The blame for this lack of pride fell squarely on the shoulders of high-ranking Chinese officials, who allowed all manner of anti-Chinese incidents to go unchallenged.

A draft of the letter was sent to a Chinese merchant in Osaka, who enlisted the support of his fellow merchants in registering a protest against the objectionable display. The union further appealed by public letter to Prince Tsai Chen, at that time the imperial commissioner to the exhibition, and to officials and merchants in China, calling for a boycott of the exhibition on the grounds of discrimination. The Japanese government finally yielded to student pressure. Exhibition officials were ordered not to hire Chinese nationals to perform in the Races of Man Pavilion.[4]

But the matter did not end there. After the pavilion opened, it was discovered that one of the employees wore Chinese dress and had bound feet. The Japanese claimed she was from Taiwan. Chinese student observers said she was Hunanese. Appeals to the Chinese consul at Kobe and to Minister Ts'ai for an investigation of the matter were ignored. Hunan students then held a club meeting to discuss possible action. If on investigation the employee turned out to be Hunanese, they would withdraw from school and return to China in protest. Waseda University student Chou Hung-yeh, chosen as their representative, made the trip to Osaka, questioned the girl, and decided that she was not Hunanese after all. As concrete proof for his fellow provincials, Chou extracted from Japanese authorities a formal affidavit stating that the employee was a Taiwan resident. In the course of lengthy conversations with exhibition officials—before securing the affidavit—Chou articulated the real issue behind the Hunan group's seemingly exaggerated concern about the origins of one pavilion employee: it was the fact that China, by being included in the Races of Man Pavilion at all, was being relegated to an inferior position relative to Japan.[5]

As student grievances over the Races of Man Pavilion were being settled, a further dispute arose. On March 11, Ch'in Yü-liu and other students made a trip to Osaka to visit the exhibition. They soon became embroiled in arguments with exhibition officials over the inclusion of Fukien native products in the Taiwan display. Once again, a seemingly trivial matter was elevated to an issue of national concern: the linking of Fukien and Taiwan was taken as symbolic evidence of Japan's intentions to include Fukien in a Taiwan-based sphere of influence. "Although our nation is weak, Fukien is definitely still our territory. That the Japanese go so far as to rank it with Taiwan is a grave insult."[6] But not only were the Japanese criticized; Chinese officials also came under fire for remaining silent when informed of such insults. "Those in authority are supposed to safeguard the provinces. Yet in a perpetual stupor, they hand over all provincial rights in a neat package to foreigners."[7]

Ch'in sent an urgent telegram to fellow students in Tokyo requesting them to assign several students fluent in Japanese to take charge of the Osaka situation. A bid for support was also made to the Chinese consul in Kobe and to Minister Ts'ai. Ch'in made it clear, however, that if Chinese officials refused to cooperate, the students would handle the matter on their own. He further threatened that if the Japanese authorities failed to comply with the student demand to move the Fukien display, the students would move it themselves. As it turned out, the students were left more or less to their own devices. The Kobe consul, reluctant to take any initiative in the matter, merely sent a report to Ts'ai Chün. Ts'ai, meeting with student representatives in Tokyo, acknowledged the need for an investigation on the grounds that the Fukien goods were lacking the necessary import documents, but beyond this he was content to have the students take charge. Negotiations between students and various exhibition officials were protracted. In the student accounts, these minor officials appeared unwilling to act on their own authority, fearful lest any changes be made through other than proper channels. Eventually, the students won their point. The Fukien goods were moved to the Szechuan booth.[8]

This furor had not died down before another broke out when word reached the students in April of French intervention in Kwangsi province. As reported in the foreign press, the governor of Kwangsi, Wang Chih-ch'un, was on the point of accepting French offers of military aid to help crush local insurgents in return for railroad and mining concessions.[9] At a meeting at the Student Union in Tokyo on April 24, union officers and representatives of the provincial societies decided to send telegrams of protest to the central government, to the Liang-Kuang governor-general, and to the Szechuan governor, demanding that the French offer be rejected, and Wang recalled. A slightly different text was sent to the Shanghai Education Association, along with a request for cooperation in the protest. On April 25, the union convened a general meeting on the issue at Kanda's Kinki Hall. About 500 attended. The only action taken at this meeting was a decision to send a follow-up letter to the government elaborating on the telegrams.[10]

Parallel protests were arranged by students and merchants in Shanghai. On April 22, about fifty Shanghai merchants originally from the two Kwang provinces drafted telegrams to four prominent officials—all Kwangsi natives—asking them to support a policy of opposing any expansion of French interests. They also decided to organize a general protest meeting of Kwangsi-Kwangtung natives residing in Shanghai. A circular was issued the morning of April 25, announcing that a meeting would be held that afternoon at Chang's Gardens and citing action taken by the Tokyo Chinese students. Reportedly, 500 persons attended the Shanghai meeting. The *North China Herald* commented: "It is a pity such short notice was given of the mass meeting. . . . Otherwise there would have been ten times the number present."[11]

On the question of Wang's ouster, many in the Chinese government were inclined to agree with the protesters—but only because of his failure to crush the rebellion. As early as February, the Grand Council had the question of Wang's removal from office under consideration.[12] In March, some thirty censors and officials denounced Wang to the Throne for arrogance and gross incompetence. But for the intervention of his powerful patron Jung-lu, Wang might have faced immediate impeachment.[13] As it happened, no charges were brought until September, when Wang was ordered to Peking for trial and punishment for allowing his troops to pillage. Whether the student- and merchant-led protests were a factor in Wang's final indictment is not clear, but the *North China Herald* was impressed with the public outcry over the issue: "That the Chinese, of their own initiative, should convene public meetings to discuss political questions is an indication of a trend of thought which marks a new departure."[14]

The Student Anti-Russia Movement

Japanese effrontery and French meddling were mere sideshows compared with the issue of Russia's continued occupation of Manchuria. Russian troops had crossed into Manchuria at the time of the Boxer uprising as part of the allied military offensive against Peking. Though Russia claimed this was a temporary measure, it made no move to withdraw its troops. China was in difficult straits. Trying to force Russia's hand just as peace talks convened could result in harsher settlement terms, particularly since the position of the other Powers was an unknown.

That consideration led Li Hung-chang, China's chief negotiator with the Russians, to adopt a conciliatory approach. This put him at odds with an anti-Russia faction within the Chinese government, whose principal spokesmen were the powerful Governors-general Liu K'un-i and Chang Chih-tung. Fearing that concessions to Russia would trigger similar demands from the other Powers, they favored joining Japan and Britain in a bloc against Russia. The Ch'ing Court, indecisive, sought to get the best of both worlds, entrusting to Li the responsibility of negotiations with Russia while still keeping channels open to the views of Chang and Liu. Li, at the time of his death in November 1901, was in the process of working out a "private" agreement between China and Russia that would have sanctioned a position of Russian special privilege in Manchuria. When the ministers of Japan, the United States, and Britain were informed—through a Chinese government source—of the terms of the supposedly "private" draft, they issued notes of protest to Saint Petersburg. These were seconded by anti-Russian memorandums to the Throne from Liu and Chang. In the face of multiple pressures, Russia withdrew the draft agreement.[15]

The Russian drive for power in Manchuria was further blunted by a growing spirit of cooperation between Japan and Britain, which was ultimately formally sealed by the Anglo-Japanese Alliance of January 1902. Given Russia's clear threat to its own East Asia interests, Japan would likely have looked favorably on a joint agreement with Britain at any point after the Sino-Japanese War. Britain's perception of the wisdom of such cooperation came later, in the summer of 1901, in response to Russia's troop movements in Manchuria and the nagging fear that Russian financial overtures to Japan might result in improved ties.[16] The alliance acted as a momentary check on Russian expansion in Asia. On April 8, 1902, Russia signed an agreement with China providing for a phased evacuation of Russian troops from Manchuria.

The April 8 treaty stipulated the withdrawal of Russian troops in a three-stage process at six-month intervals.[17] In October 1902, Russia withdrew from the areas designated in the treaty as agreed. But as the deadline for the second stage, April 8, 1903, came and went, no apparent preparations were being made for a withdrawal. Instead, according to press reports, troops were simply being transferred from Chinese cities to Russian barracks along the Chinese Eastern Railway.[18] Some newspapers claimed an actual buildup of Russian military forces, reflecting Japanese fears that, under cover of withdrawal, the Russians were transporting more and more troops east along the Trans-Siberian Railroad.[19] Furthermore, Russia allegedly was taking steps to control mining interests in Manchuria, to place Russian administrators in Manchuria's three major cities, and to take over customs operations.[20] Newspapers began forecasting war between Russia and Japan, whose own aspirations in the Korea-Manchuria area were being threatened. The Japanese press was at a pitch of excitement. The public was offered complete coverage, both firsthand reportage and editorial comment, on the Manchurian crisis.[21] Leading politicians and intellectuals formed the Taigaikō Dōshikai (Comrades' Society for a Strong Foreign Policy) to whip up public support for forcibly ousting the Russians from Manchuria. Speaking at the group's formative meeting on April 18, 1903, a Tokyo University professor argued that the only course open to Japan was all-out war, and that the Japanese had to acquire Manchuria as an outlet for their excess population.[22]

The intense anti-Russian feeling gripping Japanese academic and press circles in the spring of 1903 had a profound effect on the Chinese student community in Tokyo. The student magazines devoted much space to detailed accounts of Russian troop movements and broad surveys of Russian foreign policy aims. Both the informative material and the bias that animated it were derived from the Japanese press. We may speculate, knowing something of their pattern of reaction, that the Chinese students organized discussion meetings among themselves or attended meetings held by their Japanese counterparts over the Manchurian question. But it was not until late April that they launched a public protest, the result of two specific incidents: a statement on Manchuria made by the Russian chargé d'affaires in Peking, and the Russians' issuance of what came to be known as the "Seven Demands."

On April 28, 1903, *Tokyo Jiji Shimbun* put out an extra edition to report an exclusive interview with the Russian chargé in Peking, C. V. Planson. Planson, in a moment of candor, told his interviewer that Russia was totally opposed to extending the open-door policy to Manchuria. His argument was that Russia's high level of investment in the region entitled it to special rights and concessions. But what distressed Chinese student readers of the article even more than claims to a Russian sphere of influence was Planson's statement of Russia's ultimate objective in the region: "Present Russian policy calls for positive action to secure the Three Eastern Provinces and return them to the map of Russia."[23] Intensifying the alarm caused by Planson's rash words was the disclosure the same day of a set of demands transmitted in a secret Russian communique to the Chinese government on April 18.[24]

The thrust of the Seven Demands was to make the recognition of Russian special interests in Manchuria a precondition for the withdrawal of troops in accordance with the treaty concluded the year before. It was stipulated, for example, that apart from the city of Yingk'ou (at the top of the Liaotung Peninsula), the Chinese government must not open commercial ports, and that the Yingk'ou customs superintendent must be a Russian national. Once the demands were made public, Britain, the United States, and Japan sent notes of protest to the Russian government. With this backing, China refused to translate the demands into treaty form, asserting that no meaningful arrangements for Manchuria could be made until after Russia withdrew its troops.[25] Russia, though it denied at one point that the demands had ever been issued, continued to press for their acceptance, all the while maintaining the occupation of Manchuria.[26]

Reports of Planson's statement and the Seven Demands, translated in the student magazines from the Japanese accounts, provoked an immediate and energetic response. On April 29, the day after the reports appeared, around fifty students attended an early morning meeting arranged by Student Union leaders and representatives of the Youth Society and provincial clubs.[27] The student magazines provide detailed coverage of this and subsequent meetings in all their emotional intensity. Many of the students' statements sound remarkably like the dramatic—almost desperate—professions of patriotism characterizing the Chinese student outcry in

June 1989. In the initial, public phase of the anti-Russia movement, the students saw themselves as the most patriotic of all Chinese, as a kind of pressure group urging their government to take a tough stance against the Russians, including the use of military force if need be. They wanted, at this stage, to get a hearing for their views. It was only when faced with a clearly negative response from key decision makers that the mood turned anti-Ch'ing.

Principal spokesmen at the April 29 meeting were T'ang Erh-ho and Niu Yung-chien. T'ang had arrived in Japan in 1902 from his native Chekiang to attend the preparatory military school, Seijō Gakkō.[28] Niu, a native of Kiangsu, had been a student in Japan for the first time in 1898. He returned to China in 1900, then retraced his steps to Japan when put under surveillance for revolutionary activities.[29] T'ang's initial reaction to the Seven Demands was to propose that telegrams be sent to the Commissioners of the Northern and Southern Ports urging them to support a war policy. Niu, however, was scornful of the petition approach; it had proved entirely ineffective, he claimed, citing the recent case of telegrams sent to protest French interference in Kwangsi Province.[30] "Chinese patriots shed bitter tears, yet do no more than talk. They are not themselves able to manage things and simply look to others for solutions. Having others manage our difficulties while we discuss the aftermath is not the way to be a citizen."[31] Students must substitute action for words, Niu argued, must organize a volunteer unit prepared to join a Chinese force against the Russians. Only after this positive step was taken would it be meaningful to send telegrams to the two commissioners. "Then the world will realize that those in our student group who do not fear death represent the first cry in an awakening shout of the entire nation."[32]

Niu proposed that the Student Union call a meeting of the entire Chinese student group for the purpose of organizing an anti-Russia volunteer unit under union sponsorship. Union officers Chang Tsung-hsiang and Ts'ao Ju-lin wanted no part of this bid for their group's endorsement. In their view—and their forecast proved correct—such a makeshift "army," far from helping to check the Russian advance in Manchuria, would succeed only in arousing the suspicions of the Ch'ing government. Niu then turned to two members of the Youth Society, Yeh Lan and Ch'in Yü-liu, who gave him their enthusiastic support. But since their small, professedly radical group had attracted few members thus far, they concluded that the cause of heightening nationalist spirit would be better served by creating a new group committed to a specific position—resistance to Russia. The two agreed to act as the founding members of what was to be called the Resist-Russia Volunteer Corps (Chü-O I-yung-tui). Niu immediately drafted a circular hastily calling students to a general meeting that afternoon at Kinki Hall in Kanda.[33]

Despite the short notice, some 500 students attended the Kinki Hall meeting. It was a five-hour session, mostly devoted to speeches given by thirteen students. T'ang Erh-ho, who by now had clearly had second thoughts about the volunteer army, chaired the meeting and delivered the key address.[34] He offered a gloomy prognosis: in the current confrontation with Russia, China was doomed to either defeat in battle, should it choose to open hostilities with Russia, or to humiliation, should it choose to avoid war by capitulating to Russia's demands. Once Manchuria was lost, foreign flags would soon be raised over the eighteen provinces of China proper. At that point, it would be too late to marshal China's forces on a national scale for a fight to the death. "Is not today the finest opportunity for our great people to shed blood?"[35] While China was still a sovereign nation, then, it should declare war on Russia and sacrifice Chinese lives for the defense of Manchuria. In such case, T'ang argued, even if China's ultimate fate was annihilation, later generations would remember it for its dead heroes.

Students must make the initial commitment to patriotic action, T'ang declared. No longer could they afford to shirk responsibility with the excuse that they lacked the necessary credentials to deal with national crises:

It is said that the best course is to finish our studies, return home, and then deal with the problem. But if we wait until then, China will already have been destroyed for several decades [sic]. . . . Surprisingly, there are many among the student group who do not share these views. Therefore, I feel that those who are not afraid to die, who are willing to sacrifice their lives for China, should sign up at once to form a corps and prepare for immediate departure to join the army in the North.

It was not that the students themselves represented any kind of significant fighting force, T'ang said in response to a question from the floor:

We simply have been aroused by the great principles of nationhood and have sworn to give our lives to ignite the determined spirit of our people. Should China fall, we few students would be of no more significance than one hair on nine oxen. In view of this, when the people of our nation learn of our action, they will be moved to tears.

The primary function of the student volunteer unit, in T'ang's view, was one of moral suasion.

T'ang was further questioned about the assumptions underlying his call for volunteers to join a national military effort: that China's government was, in the first place, in a position to support a war policy, and, second, that Yuan Shih-k'ai would see fit to select students for military appointment. T'ang's reply in each case indicated a belief that Chinese authorities would respond favorably to student anti-Russia action. He cited current reports indicating that the government had rejected Russia's demands. In his view, this implied that the government had adopted a hard-line policy that included war as a contingency. As for Yuan Shih-k'ai, T'ang saw no problem. Yuan was in the process of recruiting troops. Why should he have any reservations about accepting student volunteers?

Following T'ang's speech, which, in grandiose fashion, even outlined plans to form a headquarters staff for the new "army," students were invited to come forward to enlist. T'ang, as chairman, urged them to air their differing views before signing and cautioned them especially to consider the consequences of joining the corps. "This is a death roster. Take care." At this point, few were willing to make the commitment. By April 30, only thirty students had signed up for the corps (compared with some fifty agreeing to join the headquarters staff).[36]

To publicize their anti-Russia position with a view to winning a broader base of support, students sent off thirty telegrams the next day, to Yuan Shih-k'ai and to the members of the two Shanghai activist groups, the Education Association and the Patriotic School. The texts of all these telegrams were similar: a statement of the urgency of the current crisis, followed by a plea for cooperation in the resistance effort set in motion by the students in Tokyo.[37]

In Shanghai, the message from Tokyo was read to a gathering of some 1,200 merchants, gentry, and students at Chang's Gardens.[38] This was another in the series of Shanghai meetings held in the spring of 1903 to protest the French in Kwangsi and the Russians in Manchuria. Already on April 27, shortly after the Seven Demands were presented to the Ch'ing government, Shanghai students and teachers had organized a meeting to discuss the Manchurian problem. Two protest telegrams were drafted at that time, one to the Chinese Foreign Ministry, the other to the Foreign Offices of all the Powers except Russia. Chinese Foreign Ministry officials were warned to expect a loss of independence, foreign intrusions, and internal dissension if the Russian demands were accepted. The Foreign Offices of the Powers were told that concession would set off a Boxer-like wave of anti-foreignism. In this heated atmosphere, it is hardly surprising that the students' telegram was greeted with demonstrations of support. Contemporary accounts report that after it was read the entire Shanghai assemblage stood in silent salute, a gesture of respect for the patriotism of the Chinese youths in Tokyo.[39] Then, over 100 members of the Patriotic School enlisted in a Shanghai Resist-Russia Volunteer Corps. A reply telegram was sent to the Tokyo activists informing them that some Shanghai students planned to come to Japan to help coordinate Shanghai-Tokyo anti-Russia activities.[40]

Meanwhile, Peking University students had taken action of their own, asking education authorities to convey to the Throne their opposition to the Seven Demands. Their request was turned down, with the reminder that discussing national policy was not within the competence of the student community, a comment that later provoked angry reaction among students in Tokyo.[41] Peking students also sent a telegram to their Tokyo comrades pressing for action in the current crisis. A reply telegram informed them that a volunteer unit had already been set up in Tokyo.[42]

As promised, the students in Japan sent a long follow-up letter to Yuan Shih-k'ai, outlining their position.[43] The opening sentence condemned Russia for violating the Treaty of 1902 by making troop withdrawal conditional on new demands, demands that "deprive us of our sovereignty, insult our national policy, treat our government as a puppet, and hold our people in utter contempt."[44] Russia's action was just the latest in a series of foreign intrusions since 1895, in which each country sought to exceed the gains of the others. In the current crisis, France and Russia were partners in aggression, France aggravating rebel disturbances in the South so as to snatch the Kwangtung-Kwangsi area, while Russia prepared to rob China of territory in the North. Meanwhile, whether from ignorance or fear, the Chinese government and the Chinese people remained entirely inert in the face of crisis:

China is about to become a battleground of the foreign powers, and we on our part are resigned and vacillating. . . . The most tormenting of disasters is before our very eyes, yet for an illusory peace of the moment we will trust our luck that others will take pity on us. Even the most stupid and shameless person in the world would realize that this could not be.[45]

A few days after the Volunteer Corps was formally established in Tokyo, the major provincial societies—those of Fukien, Kiangsu,

Hupei, Hunan, Chekiang, Yunnan, Kweichou, and Kwangtung—held meetings to review how things were progressing. According to accounts in the student magazines, enthusiasm was running high, and the new military unit was roundly endorsed by everyone. No doubt the young journalists chose to reproduce the most emotional scenes to arouse the sympathy of readers. A fourteen-year-old student from Fukien, for example, wrought up over the issue of the Seven Demands, reportedly rushed to the front of the meeting room to sign the roster of volunteers. Struggling with classmates who sought to restrain him because of his youth, he cried out, "I am going to die for my country. What if I die young?" As he signed his name, one of his friends tearfully begged him not to seek a martyr's death and offered to march north in his stead.[46]

A sidelight on the emotional temper of the students in Japan is provided by the activities of a curious little group called the Mutual Love Society (Kung-ai Hui). This "society," formed on May 4 after the Volunteer Corps was formally launched, was composed of some ten or so Chinese women students in Tokyo. These early women's liberationists set out their ambitious goal in the opening lines of their charter: "This Society takes as its aim the salvation of 200 million Chinese women. We wish to restore to them their inherent rights and to imbue them with national consciousness, allowing them to fulfill their natural duty as women citizens."[47] At a special meeting over the Manchurian crisis, the society members announced that, consistent with their principles concerning the political role of women, they, too, must take responsibility and assist in the effort begun by male students. They thereupon joined the Japanese Red Cross Society with the intention of volunteering as nurses in military action against the Russians.[48]

Evidently, to some students "Volunteer Corps" was not sufficiently military sounding for at a general meeting on May 2, the name was changed to "Student Army." This small "army"—of 121 students, according to a list in the May 18 issue of *Su pao*—was divided into three units, each consisting of four sections. Lan T'ien-wei, a Hupei scholarship student attending the Army Officers School, was made commanding officer.[49] The army "headquarters," consisting of five sections—propaganda, management, accounting, secretarial, and advisory—was under the supervision of an administrative chief.[50] Feng Tzu-yu identifies twenty-nine students as members of the headquarters staff. Thus around 150—army volunteers plus headquarters personnel—of the 800 Chinese students in Tokyo at the time were active participants in the anti-Russia effort.

On May 5, a schedule of events was issued, and on May 6, the Student Army held its first military drill.[51]

It was also the last drill—at least publicly announced. Sometime between May 4 and May 7, the Japanese Foreign Office warned the general supervisor of Chinese students, Wang Ta-hsieh, that the Student Army represented an embarrassment to the conduct of Japan's foreign relations.[52] If the students wished to protest Russian aggression, that was outside the Japanese government's control, Wang was told, but under no circumstances could the government allow Chinese students to carry out military training exercises on Japanese soil.[53] On May 7, the students received an order from Wang to discontinue operations. Student leaders agreed to disband the army, but resolved to form a "military affairs discussion society" in its place. They stressed that the new group would retain the spirit, if not the organizational form, of the old.[54]

The Association for National Military Education

The successor group, called the Association for National Military Education (Chün-kuo-min Chiao-yü Hui), was established on May 11. Most members of the army apparently shifted their allegiance to the new organization, since the two groups had roughly the same number of members.[55] But this was more than a simple name change. In the first place, the association tried to broaden its base by holding out honorary membership to provincial officials and merchants who contributed time or money. Moreover, the association was much less sanguine than its predecessor about the possibility of influencing Ch'ing foreign policy and about the likelihood of getting any measure of central government support for its anti-Russia efforts.

Evidence of this shift in mood is found in an appeal for financial aid published in *Kiangsu* and *Su pao*. Directed explicitly to the gentry and merchant readers of those journals, it began with a statement of Russian atrocities, went on to say that China would be forced into a war in Manchuria even against its will, and concluded with a request for donations to support student soldiers. The students were ready to rush into danger, to bear the horrors of war even to the point of sacrificing their lives, all to show the world that China, too, had patriots. But now, as the time for departure approached, there was an urgent need for outside funding: "Should the merchants and gentry at home and abroad hear about [our cause] and sympathize with it, should they awaken to the danger to themselves and their families, and if they try to understand the anguish [behind] our prayers for death [on the battlefield], then they will unstintingly lend us a helping hand and make good any shortfalls."[56]

Still, the students decided to carry through with a direct appeal to the one top official who had appeared sympathetic to them in the past—Chihli governor-general and Commissioner of Northern Ports Yuan Shih-k'ai. One of the association's first acts was to send a delegation of two, Niu Yung-chien and T'ang Erh-ho, to confer with Yuan. At a farewell gathering for Niu and T'ang on May 13, Yeh Lan emphasized that the two were not acting in the name of the association members alone but represented the loyal, dare-to-die spirits among China's entire population. Association members were urged to keep up their own level of patriotic consciousness in Niu's and T'ang's absence. "If we slacken in spirit, if we are not diligent in drill practice, we fail these two gentlemen, Niu and T'ang, and our 400 million people. If the hundred of us for one hour of the day forget our nation, forget our humiliation, forget danger and death, we are forsaking Niu and T'ang and our 400 million people."[57]

In his speech, Yeh conveyed the acute sense of crisis that had characterized the mood of the anti-Russia movement from the very beginning: "China's fate hinges on the fate of Manchuria, and Manchuria's existence depends on whether we fight or not." With this as their send-off message, Niu and T'ang departed from Yokohama aboard the *Hakuai-maru* on May 14.[58] Their mission was a fiasco. While rumors circulated about their execution in Tientsin,[59] the truth of the matter was much less dramatic: repeated attempts to see Yuan had gotten them no further than the gate of his office compound. Officials encountered along the way refused to take the mission seriously, advising the young men to attend to their studies and leave national affairs to experts.

Thoroughly disappointed, Niu and T'ang returned to Tokyo, only to be taken to task by *Su pao* for their lack of persistence in trying to see Yuan and for assuming that lobbying in official circles was feasible in the first place.[60] Their comrades were, on the whole, much more charitable. At a July 5 welcome home meeting, association members claimed that the mission had afforded them new insight into how the bureaucracy operated; for that alone, the two ought to be given a special citation in recognition of their services. This proposal was adopted over mild protests from Niu and T'ang that the honor was unmerited.[61]

The real importance of this July 5 meeting lay elsewhere: in a revision of the association charter that was to turn the group into an anti-government organization. This action climaxed a shift in thinking during May and June as the Ch'ing government clarified its position on student involvement in resistance to Russia. That position was mild enough in the beginning. For example, shortly after the association was formed, Supervisor Wang Ta-hsieh passed on to student leaders a telegram from Education Minister Chang Po-hsi, in which he emphasized that the government was determined to reject Russia's demands in any event and advised students to keep to their studies and not meddle in foreign policy. Prince Tsai Chen said much the same thing in a letter of May 18 responding to student requests for his support.[62] It was the line the two student representatives, Niu and T'ang, would be given as they sought in vain to get a hearing in Tientsin. Still, an article in the *North China Herald* in mid-May suggests an element of confusion among Ch'ing authorities about how to interpret the student anti-Russia movement. "It is now reported from Peking that these protests and patriotic offers of the young Chinese students of both sexes in Japan created quite a flutter of excitement and astonishment amongst the old fogies at the head of affairs in Peking."[63]

Events of late May were to change official reaction from exhortations to study to threats of arrest and punishment. The official alarm was sounded when an association member reported on the sly to Minister Ts'ai that the group's ultimate objective was to promote revolution.[64] Based on this report, Ts'ai sent a telegram to Tuan-fang, the acting Hu-Kuang governor-general, to the effect that the association was using the slogan "resist-Russia" as a cover for revolutionary operations. Tuan-fang was clearly concerned, particularly in the face of persistent rumors that recent returnees from Japan were responsible for the current student unrest in China. On May 27,[65] he sent a telegram to the governors of coastal provinces warning them that certain returned students were intent on joining with rebel elements in China to create disturbances in the Yangtze Valley. He urged them to exercise the utmost stringency in dealing with student subversives.[66] The *North China Herald* interpreted the action as an attempt to smother all dissent: the governor-general had "sent instructions to all the Taotais and prefects under his jurisdiction in Hupeh to put a stop to all manner of free speech and discussion of Government affairs amongst the people."[67]

In conjunction with Tuan's order, the central government purportedly issued an edict ordering the arrest and execution of returned students suspected of revolutionary leanings.[68] When the edict was printed in the June 5 issue of *Su pao*, the government angrily accused the magazine of fabricating the document. The paper's editors maintained that it was authentic, that they had obtained a copy from the office of the Liang-Kiang governor-general.[69] Whether authentic or not, other official communications of May and June confirm that the pronouncement captured something of the mood of certain government authorities toward the Chinese students in Japan. Moreover, it took on a kind of reality in the sense that it markedly affected student feelings about the Ch'ing government. A dynamic example of this is an article written by Chang Chi that appeared in *Su pao* on June 10. Using the edict as his starting point, Chang leveled his first attack against those students who had sought government support for anti-Russia operations. "Your ideals are high. Why suddenly today do you act in contradiction to these ideals, seeking to resist Russia on behalf of the Manchus, begging for pity from the Manchu government, wishing to be the vanguard of an army, willing to be lackeys?"[70] Such appeals to the Manchus, said Chang, had appeared in early association statements and accounted for the dispatch of special representatives to the North. In response, the government had denounced the students for rebelling against the Throne and ordered their summary execution. The students should have expected this, said Chang, for attempting, as Han Chinese, to deal with these "Manchu thieves."

The remainder of the article was a scathing attack on the Manchus. It took as its point of departure the edict's assertion that since the nation had supported scholars for some 200 years, it was something less than grateful on their part not to return the favor. In fact, Chang insisted, the Han Chinese had only suffered at the hands of the Manchu rulers. Citing examples from the sack of Yangchow to the present surrender of rights and territory to the Powers, he charged that the race-conscious Manchus were intent on maintaining themselves as a people even at the expense of the Han. In conclusion, Chang made clear his own order of priority in dealing with China's enemies, domestic and foreign: "Be not concerned with the success or failure of your enterprise, but keep in your heart the spirit of vengeance. Do not consider the external threat, but take as your task expelling the Manchus."[71]

From the available evidence, then, the meeting of July 5, 1903, represents a turning point in the students' aims and tactics. Hitherto, the association differed little from its predecessor, the Volunteer Corps or Student Army. Now, by the actions of a core group of association members, it was transformed into a secret, radical organization.[72] To that group, the series of events in the past two months—Chinese minister Ts'ai Chün's warning to Tuan-fang about student revolutionary aims, the alleged edict ordering harsh treatment of suspected radicals, and, finally, Yuan Shih-k'ai's negative response to Niu and T'ang—signaled that those in authority would take a hard line against any show of independent thinking, no matter how patriotic its impulse.

The immediate result of the association's turn to anti-Manchuism was the loss of as many as half the members.[73] For those who remained—and, very likely, for many who did not—the internal threat to China's future in the form of an outmoded, authoritarian regime seemed a more pressing problem than the danger from foreign intrusions. An association position paper, authored by Ch'in Yü-liu, exemplifies the mood of uncompromising anti-Manchuism that came to dominate the group in midsummer 1903. Lest anyone be under an illusion, Ch'in told his audience, the underlying motive of the anti-Russia protesters all along was not to protect the Manchus' northern preserve but to work toward the independence of the Han Chinese. Like Chang Chi in his *Su pao* article, Ch'in cited a history of Manchu oppression of the Chinese people; the recent capitulation to foreign interests was typically part of a stratagem to keep the restive Han populace subdued. "The Manchus are our age-old enemies; we will overthrow them and crush them relentlessly. Alas for [those who] talk of protecting their property."[74]

Act now before all is lost was Ch'in's message to his fellow activists. The Manchurian crisis posed a "no win" situation for China. Russian occupation of the northern region would trigger intervention by the other Powers within China proper. The resulting scenario was a bleak one:

Under the yoke of the barbarian Manchus, our Han race may still hope for independence; crushed by the enlightened foreign powers, we face eternal slavery. Sitting by and waiting to be struck dead is not as good as dying with a struggle. This is why we have established the Association for National Military Education.[75]

In its new radical form, the association took pains to preserve the utmost secrecy. There were no regularly scheduled meetings or definite meeting places. Members were identified by a secret insignia, a round piece of nickel the size of a Mexican silver dollar. On one side was engraved a representation of China's legendary First Emperor, Huang-ti; on the other a motto chosen to indicate Han Chinese affiliation: "Our First Emperor forged five weapons to preside over the 100 clans. This is our ancestor; we submit to him in our hearts and minds."[76]

The association continued to operate out of Tokyo. Among the leading members, in a group that probably numbered fewer than 100, were Huang Hsing, Yang Tu-sheng, Su P'eng, Ch'en T'ien-hua, and Chang Chi.[77] This small group now had a single objective: to oust the Manchus from power. Members vowed to promote the cause through propaganda, to organize rebellion, and to assassinate leading Manchu figures. The adoption of terrorist tactics likely grew out of a knowledge—through Japanese sources—of such Russian extremist groups as Narodnaya Volya (The People's Will). That the students were serious is indicated by their immediate venture into making explosives. Su P'eng gives an account of one abortive bomb-making operation in Yokohama in early 1904 that nearly cost him and Yang Tu-sheng their eyesight.[78] Later that year, Yang and several other students, now better schooled in explosives, went to Tientsin to try to assassinate the Empress Dowager. This time the bomb was constructed, but the Empress was uncooperative and remained in seclusion until finally the students were forced by lack of funds to return to Tokyo.[79]

By midsummer 1903, the outburst of student patriotism so puzzling to the "old fogies" in Peking had subsided and in its place was heard the rising voice of anti-Manchuism. The transformation of the association into a small terrorist squad that bungled most of its operations was hardly a threat to the regime. What were real causes for alarm were the increased traffic in intrigue between Tokyo and Shanghai beginning that summer, the fact that a growing number of dissidents among overseas students were willing to take the risk of organizing frankly anti-Ch'ing activities once they returned to China, and the ease with which they were able to infiltrate educational institutions and other segments of society. Quite clearly after 1903, many of China's "best and brightest" were using their talents to defy rather than shore up the regime in power.

Japanese naval officer defanging "John Chinaman"; Meiji political cartoon, May, 1895. (Noyes Collection, Library of Congress)

Main street in Peking, 1902. (Library of Congress)

Right: A busy street in old Shanghai, 1900. (Library of Congress)

Classroom scene, Peking University, 1902. (Library of Congress)

Three graduating Chinese students and their Japanese teachers, 1899.
Included are Kanō Jigorō (front row center) and T'ang Pao-ngo (far right).
(Sanetō Keishū, *Kindai Nisshi bunka ron*; Tokyo: Daitō, 1941)

Tokyo's Shimbashi Station in the era of the horse trolley, 1882. The station
scene was little changed when the first Chinese students arrived in 1896.
(Kyōdo Photo Service, Tokyo)

Main thoroughfare in
Tokyo, 1905. (Library
of Congress)

Tokyo schoolroom, 1905. Scenes like this drew admiring comments from
Chinese visitors on the effectiveness of Japan's approach to mass
education. (Library of Congress)

Chinese students in Japan around 1902, including Wu Lu-chen (front row, fourth from left), Chang Tsung-hsiang (back row, second from right), and Ts'ao Ju-lin (back row, far right). (Sanetō Keishū, *Kindai Nisshi bunka ron*; Tokyo: Daito 1941)

Su Man-shu (1884–1918). (Library of Congress)

Wu Yü-chang (1878–1966) as a student at Seijō Gakkō. (Wu Yü-chang, *Hsin-hai ko-ming*; Beijing: People's Publishing House, 1961)

T'ang Pao-ngo (b.1877), as a
student at Waseda University,
around 1903. (Sanetō Keishū,
Kindai Nisshi bunka ron;
Tokyo: Daitō, 1941)

Ch'iu Chin (1875–1907) as a student at
Shimoda Utako's Women's Practical
Arts School. (New York Public Library)

Ch'en T'ien-hua (1874–1905).
(*Hsin-hai ko-ming*, vol. 2;
Shanghai: People's Publishing
House, 1957)

Above: Sung Chiao-jen (1882–1913). (*Hsin-hai ko-ming yü min-kuo chien-yuan*, vol. 1; Taipei: Chengchung, 1961)

Right: Lin Ch'ang-min (1876–1925). (Waseda University, University History Office)

Lu Hsün (1881–1936) (back row, left) with Kōbun Institute classmates, Tokyo, about 1903. (Fukumura Shuppan, Tokyo)

Tsou Jung (1885–1905). (New York Public Library)

Title cover of the news sheet *Su pao* in the celebrated Shanghai libel case, *The Ch'ing Government v. Tsou Jung and Chang Ping-lin.*

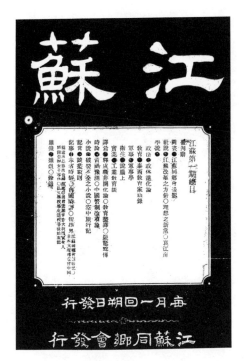

Cover pages of some Chinese student magazines, *Kiangsu* (right), *Hupei Students Circle* (below, left) and *Tide of Chekiang* (below, right), 1903.

Prince Konoe Atsumaro (1863–1904).
(*Konoe Atsumaro nikki*, vol. 1; Tokyo:
Kajima 1968)

Hattori Unokichi (1867–1939).
(*Hattori Sensei koki shukuga kinen
ronbunshu*; Tokyo: Fuzambo, 1936)

Kanō Jigorō (1860–1938). (Kyōdo
News Service, Tokyo)

Shimoda Utako (1856–1936). (Kyōdo News Service, Tokyo)

Shimoda Utako (front center) with the first Chinese women students in Japan, about 1902. Included are Ts'ao Ju-chin, younger sister of Ts'ao Ju-lin, (second from left) and Ch'en Yen-an, later married to Chang Tsung-hsiang (fourth from left). (Fukumura Shuppan, Tokyo)

The Japanese octopus off Port
Arthur; Meiji political
cartoon, October 1904.
(Noyes Collection, Library of
Congress)

Crowds welcoming Admiral
Togo after his victories over
the Russian fleet; Tokyo,
1906. (Library of Congress)

SEVEN

The Formation of Revolutionary Groups, 1903-1905

C H'ING AUTHORITIES sensed the need to head off a crisis as hundreds of free-thinking youth congregated in Tokyo. Yet designing an appropriate package of controls for overseas students was no easy task. A total crackdown was unthinkable. First, it would have required the full cooperation of the Japanese government, which had its own political agenda in China and was not inclined to offend any figures who appeared to have national leadership potential, whether it be Liang Chi'i-ch'ao, Sun Yat-sen, or the students in Japan. Second, even if feasible, harsh repressive measures such as forcing all students to leave Japan would have run counter to the objective of rapidly training large numbers of young people in new skills. Besides, it might have alienated those students who were apolitical or remained pro-Ch'ing. Singling out student leaders for some form of punishment might have seemed a reasonable course, except that it was not entirely clear who those students were and which of the many student clubs and societies were politically dangerous. The very independence of the student movement, the fact that it was not directed by Chinese political exiles or Japanese activists, made it difficult to get a handle on, and so those in power took a stop-gap approach, issuing regulations in ad hoc fashion in the hope of getting the overseas study program back on a conservative track.

It was a vain hope. For Tokyo as early as 1903 had become a base for subverting the Ch'ing regime. The seriousness of the threat posed by the Tokyo-Shanghai connection—two cities out of reach of Ch'ing controls—was starkly revealed in the celebrated *Su pao* trial of December 1903, in which the principal defendants were a

Japan-returned student and a well-known dissident intellectual who had long operated out of Tokyo. As this case was being played out before the public, student activists behind the scenes were organizing revolutionary groups and seeking to build a support network to include not only the educated elite but also members of the secret societies, a traditional source of anti-dynastic sentiment. Even a brief review of these events shows how central the Chinese students in Japan were to the irresistible spread of dissidence in China.

The Su pao Case

The issue in the *Su pao* case was freedom of the press. The principal defendants in the case, which was brought before the Mixed Court in the Shanghai International Settlement, were two of the newspaper's contributors, Chang Ping-lin and Tsou Jung; the plaintiff was the Manchu government; and the charge was libel: "They have intentionally reviled the Emperor and slandered his government. Dangerously seditious and wicked, they seek to incite the citizenry to turn against His Majesty and to hate their own government. Their motives are obscure; their schemes violate the law."[1] In pressing this suit, the government took an unprecedented step: never before had it brought charges against its own subjects in a foreign court.[2]

Chang Ping-lin and Tsou Jung were closely associated with the Chinese student community in Japan. To the students, the thirty-five-year-old Chang must have seemed the epitome of radical virtue and style. A brilliant intellectual steeped in classical philosophy, he was at the same time an activist with flair, a free spirit, and a veteran political outlaw, who had twice now fled to Japan when arrest threatened at home.[3] He was most recently a hero among the students for organizing that gesture of defiance of Manchu rule known as "the 242nd anniversary meeting to commemorate the conquest of China." Though this meeting never got off the ground (this was the rally described in Chapter 5 that had been scheduled for April 26, 1902, and then called off after the Japanese police threatened to intervene), judging from the mention of the incident in both contemporary and later works, even the abortive meeting had the desired effect of promoting Chang's anti-authoritarian views among the Chinese student community.[4]

Following this incident, Chang Ping-lin returned to Shanghai, where he became active in the Chinese Education Association and the Patriotic School. The Education Association, established in April 1902 under the leadership of Ts'ai Yuan-p'ei, was involved primarily in textbook editing and political commentary. Ts'ai was also the principal of the Patriotic School, set up in November 1902 to provide a liberal academic environment for the students who had withdrawn from the Nanyang Academy in protest of administrative restrictions. Wu Chih-hui, recently deported from Japan for his part in the Seijō School affair, was the Patriotic School's supervisor of studies. Chang Ping-lin was on the teaching staff.[5]

In the spring of 1903, the Patriotic School enrolled an eighteen-year-old returned student from Szechuan named Tsou Jung. Keenly intelligent, Tsou had acquired a mastery of the Chinese Classics at an early age. But he was also fiercely independent and refused to use his abilities to strive for success as a civil servant. Instead, his desire to study in Japan sparked by his association with several Japanese in Chungking, Tsou enrolled in the Japanese language program at the Kiangnan Arsenal's foreign language school.[6] Then, in September 1902, with his father's financial support, he set off for Japan to continue his language studies in the recently opened (January) school sponsored by the TDK, the Tōkyō Dōbun Shoin.[7]

As it turned out, Tsou was less interested in study than political activism. He was inspired by accounts of Chang Ping-lin's 242nd anniversary meeting and the Seijō affair, both of which had occurred just before his arrival. Through classmates at the Dōbun Shoin, he met Feng Tzu-yu, a student at the forefront of radical action. He also developed contacts with Niu Yung-chien and Chang Chi, who were to play important roles in the anti-Russia movement the following spring.[8] By all accounts, Tsou was an avid supporter of the Resist-Russia Volunteer Corps.[9] After the corps was disbanded under pressure from the Chinese and Japanese authorities, Tsou, Chang Chi, and three others retaliated by playing a daring prank on the supervisor of military students, Yao Wen-fu. Yao, unpopular among students because of his conservative views, had made himself a particularly choice target by carrying on an affair with the wife of another supervisor. The five youths burst into Yao's bedroom one evening to catch him with his paramour, overpowered him, and cut off his queue, which was then put on display at the Chinese Student Union. Since cutting off the queue was officially viewed as an act of defiance to the government, the shorn civil servant was panicked enough to go public despite his embarrassment at being caught *in flagrante delicto*.[10] He accused Tsou Jung of the deed in a statement to Minister Ts'ai, who in turn informed the Japanese Foreign Office. Both Tsou Jung and Chang Chi left Japan before action could be taken.[11]

The most noteworthy product of Tsou's Japan experience was a tract he wrote in draft form in Tokyo and later polished up for publication in Shanghai under the title *The Revolutionary Army* (Ko-ming chün) in May 1903.[12] Here, Tsou discussed revolution in systematic fashion, defining the concepts "nation" and "race," evaluating China in terms of Western notions of freedom, equality, and national integrity, and outlining a program for revolution aimed at ridding China of its Manchu rulers.[13] Tsou's style of writing was feverish and bombastic:

Let us sweep away the absolute monarchy which has lasted for thousands of years. Let us cast off the slave nature which has lasted for thousands of years. Let us slay and exterminate more than five million of those beastlike Manchus. Let us wipe off the disgrace of this tyranny and cruelty which has been going on for 260 years.[14]

Understandably, Tsou's brand of militant radicalism captivated China's leftist intellectuals. Understandably, also, the Ch'ing authorities added *The Revolutionary Army* to its list of banned publications and issued a warrant for Tsou's arrest.

Other events in Shanghai in the spring of 1903 contributed to the atmosphere of confrontation developing between radical intellectuals and the Ch'ing government. Some fifty students, expelled for political reasons from the military academies at Nanking and Hankow, enrolled in the Patriotic School.[15] Joined by this new radical element, students and faculty of the school organized a series of public meetings at Chang's Gardens to protest Manchu mismanagement and corruption. It was at one of these meetings that the school's students established their own Volunteer Corps in support of the Tokyo anti-Russia effort. During this same period, too, the seven faculty members agreed to contribute a daily article to the Shanghai publication *Su pao* as a means of helping to meet the costs of running the school.[16]

Su pao had undergone several transformations in the years since its founding in 1896, when it was registered at the Japanese consulate in Shanghai to avoid possible government censorship. For the first two years, it was a noncontroversial newssheet peddling the Japanese official line. In 1898, it was bought by Ch'en Fan, a Hunanese who until then had served as a district magistrate in Kiangsi.[17] Ch'en initially sided with the reformist group, then moved further to the left in his thinking. Under his stewardship, in the winter of 1902, *Su pao* introduced a column entitled "Currents from Student Circles," which drew attention to the growing dissidence among Chinese students at home and abroad.[18] In November, Ch'en made a trip to Japan, where along with Huang Hsing and six others, he founded the Hunan Translation Society.[19]

On May 27, 1903, Ch'en appointed a Patriotic School student from Hunan named Chang Shih-chao chief editor of *Su pao*. Chang was a confrere of both Tsou Jung and Chang Ping-lin; the three had talked over possible revisions of *The Revolutionary Army*. The day after Chang took over as editor, he published an editorial, "All Chinese Officials Are Revolutionaries," calculated to pique the interest if not the ire of officialdom. This was followed in the next days by a series of inflammatory articles, including Chang Ping-lin's foreword to Tsou's *The Revolutionary Army* and a piece called "In Refutation of K'ang Yu-wei," also penned by the elder Chang.[20]

"In Refutation of K'ang Yu-wei," for all its discursiveness, offers a full statement of Chang Ping-lin's political views on nationalism, race, and revolution. For Chang, nationalism had its roots in an intense anti-Manchuism. Racial difference provided one justification for attacking the Manchus, political incompetence the other; revolution offered the method—and one stamped with modernity—for ousting the Manchus as a ruling group. In Chang's fulminations against the Manchus as a non-Chinese barbarian group, one hears echoes of Chang's spiritual mentor, the seventeenth-century Ming loyalist Wang Fu-chih. But when he turned to an evaluation of the effectiveness of Manchu rule, his tone moved closer to that of Tsou Jung. Here his invectives were directed against the Manchus as a privileged and incompetent group, firmly entrenched in power and unwilling to relinquish the least measure of control. Singled out for special mention was the Kuang-hsü Emperor. Far from being the paragon of sagelike virtue portrayed by K'ang Yu-wei, Kuang-hsü was the epitome of Manchu debility. As proof of his weakness, consider his behavior after the Hundred Days' reform. How could Kuang-hsü ever become an effective monarch, constitutional or otherwise, Chang asked, when he could not even escape from the clutches of his aunt, the Empress Dowager?

Chang Ping-lin's insulting indictment of the emperor undoubtedly had an arresting effect on the reading public of China in 1903. This was an age when the Throne considered it an outrage even to mention the emperor's personal name, much less to tarnish it. Chang's clever use of the characters of Kuang-hsü's personal name to predict the fall of the dynasty, his description of Kuang-hsü as "a little clown who can't tell the difference between wheat and barley," and his suggestion that Kuang-hsü deserved to be executed for losing Manchuria were all regarded as heinous crimes by the Ch'ing government. As if this was not enough, Chang capped his discussion of Manchu foreignness and political ineptitude with a declaration that ousting the Manchus was the precondition for any improvements in Chinese society: "Unless the Manchus are driven out, it is utterly unreasonable to expect that the gentry and literati will undergo a moral transformation and that the people will be willing to die to rid the country of the hated Western imperialist."[21]

Chang Ping-lin and his fellow radicals at the Patriotic School had been under surveillance for some time. The direct call for revolution in the articles, coupled with the appearance of *The Revolutionary Army*, provoked retaliation from Ch'ing authorities.[22] At the urging of concerned provincial officials, Tuan-fang in particular, the police of the International Settlement arrested Chang Ping-lin on June 30. Tsou Jung gave himself up the next day. The *Su pao* office was closed.

What became known as the *Su pao* trial was a lengthy affair. From the original hearing on July 15, the accused—Chang, Tsou, and four others who were only marginally involved in the publication of the newspaper—languished in jail until December 3, when the trial opened before the Shanghai city magistrate, aided by a British assessor.[23] Their decision was handed down on December 7. Three of the accused were acquitted. A fourth was detained for further inquiries into his activities in connection with the Hankow plot of 1900. Chang and Tsou were held in custody, forced to wait four and a half months longer for their sentencing.

The two delays—from July to December and from December to May—owed to disputes between the Powers and the Ch'ing government over jurisdiction in the case. The first was occasioned by the Ch'ing government's demand that the prisoners be extradited for trial in a Chinese court. The governments of the International Settlement, after much wrangling among themselves, decided to refuse, fearing a replay of the recent case of Shen Chin, a journalist who had been arrested in Peking and cruelly beaten to death without trial.[24] By denying the extradition request, the Powers ensured that if the prisoners were found guilty, they would be jailed inside the foreign-run city.

The delay in final sentencing resulted from a disagreement between the Ch'ing government and Powers over the punishment to be meted out to Chang and Tsou. The top Chinese official in Shanghai insisted on life imprisonment. Foreign representatives argued for leniency. Once again the Powers prevailed. On May 21, 1904, Chang Ping-lin and Tsou Jung, who had pleaded guilty to charges of spreading libel about the emperor, heard the verdict: Tsou Jung was to be imprisoned for two years from the date of his arrest and Chang Ping-lin for three.[25] The mental and physical strain of prison life proved too much for twenty-year-old Tsou. He died just a few months before he was to be set free, in April 1905.[26] Chang served out his term. Immediately on his release in June 1906, he went back to Japan to serve as editor of *Min pao.*

The Ch'ing government's interference in the publication of *Su pao* had reverberations in the student press in Japan, especially among the writers for *Kiangsu.* For them, the arrest of Chang and Tsou and the closing of the *Su pao* office was patent proof of Manchu repression, of Manchu violation of those inalienable freedoms held by people of any civilized nation—freedom of thought, freedom of discussion, and freedom of the press.[27] Yet barely pausing to deplore this fact, these student journalists predicted that whatever the outcome of the case, it would work against the Manchus and further the radical cause. In the first place, the fact that Chang and Tsou were being given a fair trial when the plaintiff in the case was the Manchu government established an unprecedented measure of equality between Han and Manchu. More important, the publicity given the trial would arouse the interest of the general public in the *Su pao* articles and Tsou's *Revolutionary Army,* thus affording the authors a wide audience for their beliefs. Ordinary folk asking themselves why Chang and Tsou were seized could only conclude that it was because they were patriots intent on driving out the Manchu oppressors of the Han people. This would be passed from one person to another, until 400 million Chinese would be imbued with the principle of "expel the Manchu" (*p'ai-man*). "Thereupon we will rid ourselves of this alien race of five million barbarians as easily as pulling up a rotten stump."[28]

Government action against *Su pao* did not in any way silence the opposition press in Shanghai. On August 8, 1903, just a month and a half after Chang Ping-lin's arrest, Chang Shih-chao and Hsieh Hsiao-shih founded *The National People's Daily* (Kuo-min jih-jih pao) to carry on the *Su pao* tradition.[29] In response, the Ch'ing government circulated a notice to provincial authorities in the Yangtze region prohibiting the sale of the paper and even went so far as to request the Customs Office to notify the Postal Bureau not to send copies of it through the mail. The Customs Office, in its reply, pointed out the futility of attempting a check of the mails to find issues of the *Daily* and suggested shutting it down as an effective alternative. Not prepared for another case of *Su pao* proportions, the government declined to take such a step.[30] In the end, quarrels among the staff killed the paper off.[31]

It was not long before another publication in Shanghai accepted the burden of promoting free expression. This was Ts'ai Yuan-p'ei's *Warnings on Russian Affairs* (O-shih ching-wen), a daily issued first on December 15, 1903. *Russian Affairs* was affiliated with the Society of Comrades Against Russia (Tui O T'ung-shih Hui), a group set up by Ts'ai as part of the anti-Russia effort initiated the previous spring.[32] The publication broadcast its anti-Russia message to men in all walks of life: for the scholar there were essays in classical Chinese; for the merchant, an essay in colloquial style; for men in the northern and the western provinces, diatribes incorporating particular Mandarin speech patterns. Even the Fukien and Kwangtung colloquial dialects were represented. Reviewing the new publication, the *North China Herald* observed:

So long as the "Wo-shih Ching-wan" keeps to its present style and abstains from seditious utterings and abrasive addresses to the present rulers of the land, there seems to be no reason why the seed spread by that paper should not bear fruit a hundredfold and the people of China be made to recognize the necessity of paying more intelligent attention to the political condition of their country and by moral force compel the Government to give more heed to public opinion.[33]

Russian Affairs continued publishing daily until February 15, 1904, a total of seventy-three issues.[34]

In the spring of 1904, the paper reemerged under a new name, *The Alarm Bell* (Ching-chung jih-pao). Now its criticisms of the Manchu government did begin to take on an abrasive tone. In response, the government sent a communique through the German consul to the Mixed Court at Shanghai with a warrant for the arrest of two of the editors. They avoided capture, but the paper's sales manager and a proofreader were jailed, and their printing equipment confiscated. *The Alarm Bell* ceased publication in January 1905, after putting out 338 issues.[35]

The China Rise Society

In June 1903, just as the *Su pao* drama was unfolding, there arrived in Shanghai a returned student from Japan, Huang Hsing. Huang, a native of Hunan province, had gone to Japan the year before, at the age of twenty-eight. His background included the standard classical education, with a *hsiu ts'ai* degree won at the age of eighteen, as well as experience in progressive political circles. At the time of the reform movement in Hunan in 1897–98, Huang was a student at the Academy of Hunan and Hupei in Wuchang, a modern-style school financed and designed by Governor-general Chang Chih-tung.[36] According to some sources, Huang played an active role two years later in T'ang Ts'ai-ch'ang's planned uprising.[37] If so, it could not have come to the attention of Chang Chih-tung, for in 1902 Huang was awarded a Hupei provincial government scholarship for teacher training in Japan.

Huang arrived in Japan in June 1902 and enrolled at the Kōbun Institute.[38] Shortly after his arrival, the dispute over Seijō admissions policy began. Huang does not figure in any accounts of this incident, nor is he on the roster of members of the Youth Society formed in the winter of 1902. The first we hear of him is as a founder of the Hunan Translation Society, which began publishing the magazine *Translations of Hunan Students Abroad* in November 1902. A few months later, he was involved in founding another student magazine, the *Hupei Students Circle*.[39] In the spring of 1903, he joined the anti-Russia protesters, signing up as a member of the Resist-Russia Volunteer Corps established in May.[40] He stayed with the diehards when the corps was reorganized as the Association for National Military Education, and it was as a representative of the association that he returned to China on June 4, 1903, following his graduation from the Kōbun Institute.[41]

In the following months, Huang sought to build a revolutionary network, making use of the numerous contacts with student radicals he had developed during his year in Japan.[42] Initially, he paid a visit to old friends at the Academy of Hunan and Hupei. There he talked up revolution and distributed several thousand copies of Tsou Jung's *Revolutionary Army* and Ch'en T'ien-hua's pamphlet *Awake!* (Meng-hui t'ou).[43] Carrying additional copies of these and other anti-Manchu tracts with him, Huang then traveled to Changsha, where he had accepted a teaching position at the Ming-te School. The principal of this school, opened only a few months before,[44] was Hu Yuan-t'an, a fellow provincial of Huang's and himself recently back from a period of study in Japan. Chang Chi, who had fled Japan in late spring with Tsou Jung, was on the teaching staff, as were Su Man-shu,[45] Hsieh Hsiao-shih, and Ch'in Yü-liu. At Ming-te, students were not only offered the standard curriculum but treated to lectures on such revolution-inspiring topics as the Manchu oppression of the Han Chinese.[46]

In Changsha, Huang also developed close connections with the Hunan Industrial School, operated by three Japan-returned students, Weng Hao, Cheng Hsien-ch'eng, and Li Shu-fan.[47] Weng and Cheng were founding members of the Association for National Military Education; they returned to China in the fall of 1903 as propagandists for that organization. Their affiliation with the radical cause must have been successfully disguised—or known and approved—for it was the Hunan student supervisor himself who invited the two to set up an industrial school in Changsha. Opened in February 1904, the school became a focal point of revolutionary intrigue with returned students Chao Sheng, Chang Chi, Ch'in Yü-liu, and Su Man-shu recruited for the teaching staff.[48]

In December 1903, one of Huang Hsing's classmates, Liu K'uei-i, left Japan for Changsha. Shortly thereafter, with the support of Liu, Chang Chi, and others, Huang finalized plans to establish a new revolutionary organization, the China Rise Society (Hua-hsing Hui). At least twenty-one of the twenty-nine founding members recorded by Liu K'uei-i had been or were soon to become students in Japan.[49] According to the list of names compiled by Chang Yü-fa, the group began with a membership base of eighty-nine. At least thirty of the original members were Japan-returned students; fifty-three were Hunan natives.[50] Huang Hsing assumed the post of chairman of the new society, with Ch'in Yü-liu as his deputy. Huang's declared tactic for promoting revolution was to capitalize on the incipient anti-Manchuism emerging within three groups: the students, the army, and the secret societies.[51]

In the case of the students, Huang was notably successful. In the city of Changsha alone, there were about 3,000 students in fifty-seven modern schools, with a teaching staff of around 200 largely recruited from returned students with anti-Manchu leanings. In such circumstances, it is hardly surprising that students were preponderant among the 400–500 society members. Many of these came from the Industrial School, where the society's propaganda won over several hundred students to the revolutionary cause.[52] A society affiliate was set up in Hupei, another appeared spontaneously among Hunan and Hupei students in Tokyo, and contact points were established with new radical groups like the Shanghai Patriotic Society (Ai-kuo Hsieh-hui) and the Changsha Daily Knowledge Society (Changsha Jih-chih Hui).[53]

To create a strike force for armed uprising, Huang Hsing and his colleagues turned to the secret societies, ready-made mass organizations with a strong anti-Ch'ing tradition. Probes into possible collaboration with Hunan's Ko-lao Hui were made through Liu K'uei-i, who had contacts with the secret society's leader, Ma Fu-i. Ma reportedly commanded a network of some 20,000 people over a four-province area. Their talks resulted in a China Rise Society affiliate, the Common Enemy Society (T'ung-ch'ou Hui), whose principal function was to liaise with the secret societies in organizing plans for revolt.[54]

Within a few months, Huang, Liu, and Ma had outlined a strategy for simultaneous uprisings in the provincial capital, Changsha, and five other Hunan districts as the opening salvo in the battle to oust the Manchus. The action was to begin on November 16, 1904, the Empress Dowager's seventieth birthday, when a few judiciously hurled bombs thrown into the crowd of provincial officials gathered for birthday festivities might enable students and sympathizers within the army to seize the capital city as a revolutionary base. Secret society members were to play the major role in taking over outlying districts.

Expecting that the revolt would inspire other provincial uprisings, the leaders stationed Common Enemy Society contact men outside Hunan.[55] Ch'en T'ien-hua and Yao Hung-yeh were to coordinate the uprisings in Kiangsi, Chou Wei-chen and Chang Hsiung-fu in Szechuan, Sung Chiao-jen and Hu Ying in Wuchang, Yang Tu-sheng and Chang Shih-chao in Shanghai, and T'ao Ch'eng-chang in the Chekiang-Anhui region.[56] A strikingly large number of these key activists, most of them long forgotten, were returned students from Japan or—like Sung Chiao-jen and Chang Shih-chao—would find themselves there soon. Whether they could be said to be serious students at this stage is questionable, given the obvious depth of their commitment to other pursuits and the fact that many belonged to several other revolutionary organizations. Sung Chiao-jen and Hu Ying, for example, were key figures in the Hunan front group the Science Study Society, and Yang Tu-sheng, representing the Association for National Military Education, was involved—in the months the Changsha revolt was taking shape—in the plot to assassinate the Empress Dowager in Tientsin.[57]

The China Rise leaders worked diligently through the summer of 1904 arranging arms purchases, training students to use guns, selling dissident tracts, and solidifying their ties with secret society operatives.[58] Not surprisingly, given the scale of activity and the number of people involved, all this could not be kept under wraps for so long a period. By mid-October, it became clear that someone had leaked details of the uprising to already suspicious Hunan authorities. Plans were hastily scrubbed, with a special warning sent to collaborators in the Science Study Society at Wuchang. Huang Hsing managed to elude Changsha police and made his way to Shanghai in early November, accompanied by Chang Chi.[59] There he immediately joined another revolutionary group, the Patriotic Society, formed the previous spring by Yang Tu-sheng to organize uprisings in the Nanking-Shanghai area. But this group was broken up when Huang Hsing, Yang, Chang Shih-chao, and others were arrested in connection with an attempt to assassinate the former governor of Kwangsi, Wang Chih-ch'un. In fact, this plot was not a product of the Patriotic Society but the individual effort of a man named Wan Fu-hua, who was acquainted with some of the society members. Once convinced of this, the police released Huang and his friends. With their names now on file at the police office, however, society members feared arrest for their involvement in the Changsha plot. Most fled to Tokyo.[60]

The Restoration Society

The month that marked the failure of the China Rise Society at Changsha saw the formal founding of a new revolutionary organization in Shanghai, the Restoration Society (Kuang-fu Hui). Like the China Rise Society, the Restoration Society had a regional focus, in this case a five-province area in East and South China. A further similarity was that it was the brainchild of the Chinese students in Japan.

In the fall of 1903, a full year before the Restoration Society declared its existence, some dozen members of the Chekiang Study Society began meeting in secret at the Tokyo lodging of twenty-four-year-old Wang Chia-wei,[61] Waseda student and editor of *Tide of Chekiang*, for the purpose of organizing anti-Ch'ing activities. They decided to form a new group committed not simply to propaganda efforts but to armed uprising. At a meeting held in November 1903, the core members—who included Shen Tieh-min, Hsü Shou-ch'ang, and Lu Hsün, all Kōbun students in their early twenties; the veteran Chekiang radical T'ao Ch'eng-chang; and Kung Pao-ch'uan and Wei Lan of the Association for National Military Education—devised a short-term plan of action.[62] T'ao and Wei were assigned to Chekiang and Anhui, and Kung to Shanghai; Chang Hsiung-fu and Shen Tieh-min were to report to Changsha to assist Huang Hsing, who was at the start of his revolutionary venture there.[63]

During the spring and summer of 1904, the five contact men worked on establishing a reliable network of sympathizers in Chekiang and Anhui. T'ao and Wei solicited the support of the leaders of Chekiang's secret societies. T'ao subsequently met with both Huang Hsing and Ts'ai Yuan-p'ei in Shanghai for the purpose of co-ordinating anti-Ch'ing action in the Chekiang-Anhui area with the planned uprising in Hunan. Chang Hsiung-fu and Shen Tieh-min were on hand with Huang in Changsha, Chang on the staff of the Hunan Industrial School and Shen at Ming-te.

Kung Pao-ch'uan, who returned to Shanghai as planned, fared poorly in his initial efforts to form an assassination squad on the National Military Education model. He sought the advice of T'ao Ch'eng-chang, who counseled against the terrorist approach and proposed instead setting up a revolutionary organization concerned with infiltrating educational institutions and garnering support from the secret societies. The two men agreed that, with Chang Ping-lin in prison, the new organization must seek the endorsement of the noted dissident Ts'ai Yuan-p'ei to establish its credibility within the anti-Ch'ing movement. They decided that Kung should be the one to approach Ts'ai, apparently fearing that the scholarly Ts'ai might balk at overtures from T'ao, with his well-known ties to the underworld.[64] Ts'ai was receptive to Kung's request for support and agreed to head the new group. Aware of T'ao's influence among the secret societies, he then invited T'ao to join.[65] The new group, named the Restoration Society, was formally established in Shanghai in November 1904. Two months later, T'ao made a trip to Tokyo to report to Chekiang students. A Tokyo branch of the society was set up under the leadership of *Tide of Chekiang* editor Wang Chia-wei.[66]

Little is known about the organizational structure of the Restoration Society. Members were bound to the strictest secrecy, to the point that new recruits were not told who their fellow conspirators were until they had worked on several projects, if then. On initiation, they had to sign an oath in blood: "To restore the Han people to power and to recover our land; to sacrifice oneself for the nation and to remain anonymous in the successful completion of a task."[67] Ts'ai Yuan-p'ei was named to head the society, with T'ao Ch'eng-chang and Kung Pao-ch'uan as deputies. But the members soon became dissatisfied with Ts'ai's performance. Though they greatly respected his personal integrity and intellect, they questioned his ability to expand the organization through contacts with the secret societies.[68] Hsü Hsi-lin, who joined the Restoration Society in January 1905, later played a prominent role in directing liaison activities with secret societies from a base in Shaohsing.[69] (Eventually, in 1909, the society moved its central office to Tokyo, and Chang Ping-lin assumed the position of director, with T'ao Ch'eng-chang as his assistant.)[70]

The Restoration Society carried out three types of activities. One important pursuit was to coordinate with the secret societies in planning for an armed uprising against the Ch'ing regime. Efforts were concentrated on the five-province area of Kiangsu, Chekiang, Anhui, Fukien, and Kiangsi.[71] T'ao and company used the same technique as Huang Hsing and Liu K'uei-i for tapping secret society support, namely, setting up third-party organizations incorporating members of both groups. After months of trekking through Chekiang building personal contacts with society leaders, T'ao drew up plans for a liaison group called the Dragon Flower Society (Lung-hua Hui), which he hoped would be palatable to the secret societies in style and at the same time provide the Restoration Society a broad base of support for military action.[72]

A second society pursuit was propaganda. A number of experienced writers and propagandists belonged to the society, including Chang Ping-lin of *Su pao* fame; Wang Chia-wei, Hsü Shou-ch'ang, and Lu Hsün, who wrote for *Tide of Chekiang*; and Ch'iu Chin, ardent feminist and student of Shimoda Utako in Japan, who helped found the *Vernacular Journal* (Pai-hua pao) and *The Chinese Women's Journal* (Chung-kuo nü-pao). T'ao Ch'eng-chang himself actively promoted publications, wrote revolutionary tracts, and distributed dissident literature. Subversive works such as Tsou Jung's *Revolutionary Army* and Ch'en T'ien-hua's *Awake!* were passed from hand to hand along the network of Restoration Society contacts.[73]

Finally, the society put considerable effort into establishing revolutionary front organizations. Just as Huang Hsing worked through the Industrial School and Ming-te, the Restoration Society had as a primary base of operations the Ta-t'ung School in Shaohsing. Ta-t'ung was the joint project of T'ao Ch'eng-chang and Hsü Hsi-lin. To make things look legitimate, they got the proper official permit to establish the school and to offer a six-month military course as part of the curriculum. Though Ta-t'ung was actually a revolutionary training ground for secret society recruits, it was so effective in putting up a front of respectability that its subversive activities went undetected for a long time.[74] The full extent of Ta-t'ung's connection with the revolutionary cause was not discovered by authorities until 1907, brought to light only by Hsü Hsi-lin's ill-conceived attempt on the life of the governor of Anhui, En-ming, as the signal for coordinated uprisings in Anhui and Chekiang. Both Hsü and his fellow conspirator Ch'iu Chin were captured and executed.[75] Many Restoration Society members fled to Japan. With this, the society's heyday of intrigue came to an end.

Both the China Rise Society and the Restoration Society from conception to active life had vital ties with the student group in Japan. The former was the brainchild of Huang Hsing acting as China agent for the Japan-based Association for National Military Education. Other association activists joined Huang, and when plans took shape for revolt in Hunan's capital city, it was returned students who were sent to surrounding provinces to coordinate the action. The failure of the uprising meant eventual escape to Japan for a regrouping of forces. The Restoration Society's growth followed much the same pattern. The original group was similarly linked to the Tokyo-based association, especially to its assassination squad, as well as to the dissident Chekiang students in Japan. Once embarked on its work for revolution in East and South China, the leaders shuttled back and forth between Shanghai and Tokyo. And when the uprising was crushed, many of its members likewise fled to Japan.

Revive China Society

What role, if any, did the students in Japan play in the oldest of the revolutionary organizations, Sun Yat-sen's Revive China Society (Hsing-Chung Hui), which dated back to 1894? After all, in most of the period under discussion, Sun was living within easy access, in Yokohama. With the aid of Japanese supporters, he had even designed a plan for armed uprising in Kwangtung from that base.

During these years, Sun centered his recruitment efforts on the overseas Chinese community and the secret societies, making little attempt to enlist the support of disaffected intellectuals. It may be that Sun thought these two groups alone would provide a viable base for his revolutionary apparatus. Or—more likely—he recognized that the intellectual stratum was simply not available for recruitment in these years, gravitating as it was around the K'ang/Liang camp and viewing Sun as déclassé at best. We are reminded of Wu Chih-hui's oft-cited first impression of Sun as an "uncultured bandit," and Chang Ping-lin's remark that, for the most part, the students who made the trip to Yokohama to visit Sun in this period went not out of political sympathy, but as curiosity seekers eager to see the rebel in residence.[76] In fact, an analysis of Revive China Society membership reveals only sixteen students among the 325 people who belonged to the group in 1904.[77] With around 1,500 students in Japan by then and the numbers ever rising, Sun's failure to tap into this source appears in hindsight a gross missed opportunity.

At least until 1903 and to a large extent up to 1905, Sun's contacts with the Chinese students in Japan tended to be personal and unsystematic; that is, the relationship was between Sun as an individual and individual students, rather than between the Revive China Society and student organizations. Both Feng Tzu-yu and Ch'in Li-shan played pivotal roles in keeping Sun in touch with Chinese students and intellectuals. Ch'in, himself an early K'ang/Liang supporter who moved further left following the Hankow revolt, was instrumental in introducing Sun to Chang Chi and Chang Ping-lin, among others. Sun, in turn, as noted in Chapter 4, gave a measure of financial aid to Ch'in and Chang Chi in their journalistic venture, *The Chinese National*, in 1900; he offered his support as well to Chang Ping-lin's 242nd anniversary meeting in 1902. Feng Tzu-yu, a Revive China Society member, Waseda University student, and reporter for the Hong Kong *China Daily*, introduced Sun to thirty students or so. Some were fellow Cantonese, members of the short-lived Kwangtung Independence Association that Feng helped to organize in the spring of 1902; the group sought Sun's advice and support.[78] Among the other students Feng took to Yokohama for visits with Sun were Ch'eng Chia-sheng (Anhui), Yeh Lan (Chekiang), Tung Hung-wei (Chekiang), Weng Hao (Fukien), and Yang Tu-sheng (Hunan),[79] names we have seen elsewhere in connection with the anti-Russia organizations. Sun, it will be remembered, was out of Japan during the first half of 1903, when the anti-Russia agitation among students was at its height.

In any case, in 1903 Sun seems to have begun to think in terms of a new revolutionary organization to replace the Revive China Society, one that would have as its mainstay the student-intellectual group.[80] One thing that may have set his imagination to work was his dismay at finding that while he was in Hanoi in the spring of 1903, the Yokohama Society regulars had dwindled down to about ten.[81] Undoubtedly Sun was at the same time sensitive to the fact that 1902–3 was seeing a shift to the left on the part of students and intellectuals, as evidenced by the Seijō incident, the establishment of radical student magazines, the anti-Russia movement, and the *Su pao* case.

Sun's first attempt to organize students took place in the summer of 1903. Since, in the aftermath of the Seijō incident, self-supporting students were restricted from entering Japanese military schools, Sun decided to establish his own military training facility at Aoyama. With him in the project was a Major Hino, reputedly an expert military strategist. Fourteen students, all but two of them Sun's fellow provincials, entered the first class.[82] Shortly after, Sun left Japan on a speaking and fund-raising tour, and the school folded within a few months. Sun's tour of Honolulu, the United States, England, and the Continent kept him out of touch with the student movement in Japan from September 1903 to July 1905, when he returned to found the T'ung-meng Hui (Alliance Society).[83]

In an interesting twist, it was Chinese students in Europe who sponsored Sun Yat-sen's comeback to the Tokyo political stage and the cast of Chinese student radicals there. Of course, as just mentioned, Sun's efforts to reach the student constituency, building on a small core of contacts maintained over several years, had by now intensified. Thus he responded eagerly to an invitation, along with travel money and expenses, from Chinese studying in Brussels and Berlin to direct discussions preliminary to forming a national revolutionary organization. Several months of hard-fought arguments in three European capitals eventually won Sun fourteen students (out of the 100 then in Europe) fully committed to his political program, which included his first full articulation of the Three People's Principles and the Five Power Constitution. Fourteen seems a startlingly small number indeed, but it was enough for this remarkable politician to face with confidence the potential Tokyo constituency of as many as 10,000 students.[84]

Sun arrived in Japan on July 19, 1905, to make a bid for leadership of the Tokyo anti-dynastic movement. His timing was excellent. This was just two months after Japan had inflicted a crushing blow on Russia's naval forces in the final scene of the Russo-Japanese War. That defeat of a modern European power had an electrifying effect on nationalist movements throughout Asia, including China. The climate of domestic opinion thus supported a mood of anti-imperialism, anti-foreignism, and anti-Manchuism. A telling example of this upsurge in nationalist sentiment is the Chinese boycott of U.S. goods beginning in June 1905, in retaliation for discriminatory treatment of Chinese laborers.[85] Moreover, the China Rise Society, one of the two new anti-dynastic groups (the Restoration Society was the other), had struck out at Changsha the previous fall and its members, now in Tokyo, were looking for a way to regroup for a second attempt at revolt.

Beyond this, Sun's curriculum vitae had much to commend it, including as it did fifteen years of revolutionary experience and extensive contacts among diverse overseas Chinese communities, secret societies, and Japanese political activists. Not least, there was the man himself. All contemporary accounts attest to Sun's forceful personality, his persuasive powers, and his charm. Sun had charisma.[86]

Still, for all these political advantages, Sun's assumption of leadership of the student movement was by no means a foregone conclusion when he landed in Japan in July. It took him a couple of weeks of tough negotiations to launch the T'ung-meng Hui (TMH), with himself as *tsung-li* (director).[87] Noteworthy, first of all, is the fact that the initial contacts with the student community were made through Sun's longtime Japanese supporter, Miyazaki Torazō, an indication surely that Sun at this point was essentially out of touch with the Tokyo Chinese students.[88] Moreover, some student leaders, including Liu K'uei-i, were flatly opposed to uniting under Sun's leadership, and others, Huang Hsing chief among them, were unwilling to put all their eggs in one basket. They wanted to join Sun's group formally without disbanding the existing anti-Ch'ing organizations.[89]

Sun's persuasive powers ultimately prevailed. At a preliminary meeting held on July 30 and attended by seventy to 100 students representing at least ten provinces,[90] the participants decided to create a new revolutionary group, officially titled the Chung-kuo T'ung-meng Hui or China Alliance Society, and endorsed Sun's four-point program: "Expulsion of the Manchus, restoration of Chinese rule, establishment of a republic, and equalization of land rights." On August 13, Sun's new student associates arranged a reception in his honor, reportedly attended by 600–700 people. The formal inaugural meeting of the T'ung-meng Hui was held a week later, on August 20. Though no precise figures are available, sources estimate that between 200 and 300 people—the majority of them students—accepted formal membership in the new organization.[91] Sun was named director, with Huang Hsing his second in command; and an organizational structure was set up that consisted of three departments, manned by thirty officers in the Tokyo headquarters, and five regional offices in China.[92] A plan to adopt *Twentieth Century China* as the official TMH literary organ had to be abandoned when the Japanese government put the journal out of business on August 28. Subsequently, *Min pao* was created for that purpose; the first issue was published on November 26, 1905.

What kind of organization was the T'ung-meng Hui in the first months of its existence? For a start, it was an organization with a factional bias from the outset. Though the China Rise Society had agreed to merge into the new trans-provincial group, from the pulling and hauling that attended the decision to give command to Sun rather than Huang Hsing, it is clear that China Rise members had reservations about giving up their independence. Yet in view of their failed uprising, it seemed politically wise to do so, even at the cost of losing the top leadership position. The Restoration Society did not disband as a group at all; in fact, unlike the China Rise people, at the time the TMH was getting off the ground, most Restoration activists were still in China, plotting their next move. Eventually, most of the key people joined the TMH, but on an individual basis.[93] The presence of these two societies as shadowy structures within the fledgling TMH eroded the strong and direct leader-follower relationship Sun had enjoyed with the Revive China membership.[94]

In terms of structure, the TMH owed much to the practice of earlier student organizations. A hierarchy of officers, a propaganda arm, research departments, branches in China, trans-provincial operations—all had already been tried and tested in one way or another by the students in Japan. The strength of the TMH, and an outstanding difference from earlier revolutionary groups, was that it offered a clearly articulated program in which ousting the Manchus became not the end but the beginning of a process of change.

It is important to bear in mind, too, that student membership in the TMH in its first months—as we will see in the next chapter—represented but a small percentage of the total student community in Japan. The approximately 200 students at the August inaugural meeting were a tiny fraction of the 8,600 Sun hoped to attract. The apparent failure of students to surge to the TMH and its cause was not a measure of the weakness of what Sun and his cohorts had to offer. It was a measure of the strength and integrity of a student movement that over the years had created many different channels—provincial clubs, student magazines, the Student Union, school clubs, avowedly revolutionary groups—through which students might express newfound interests and ideas. The TMH in its first bloom, in other words, was simply one of many groups contending for student support. Nothing more clearly attests to the inner momentum of the student movement than the fact that right on the heels of the formation of the TMH, some 4,000 students became embroiled in an anti-Japanese protest. This did more ultimately to attract people to the new revolutionary group than anything Sun Yat-sen, who was not in Japan at the time, could have done on his own.

EIGHT

A Climax of
Student Protest, 1905

S TUDENT AGITATION reached a peak in late 1905 in a clash
with the Japanese government over issuance of new school
regulations. In some senses, the protest was merely a restaging
of the past. Students and government authorities raised the same
issues and reacted with the same apprehensions as in previous confrontations. And also as before, the flames of protest, fanned by a
militant few, came to touch the entire student group. What makes
this incident stand out in our story of student dissent is the simple
fact of numbers—some 8,600 potential agitators, as opposed to 500
at the time of the Seijō incident. Over 2,000 students leaving Japan
"in a body," as happened in late 1905, was a crisis of major proportions for both the Chinese and the Japanese government. And it was
those governments, one accused of oppressive domestic policies, the
other of imperialistic aggression, that were the targets of attack of
protesting students.[1]

The Tightening of Student Controls

What aroused the ire of the Chinese students was an official decree
issued by Japan's Education Ministry on November 2, 1905, entitled
"Regulations Regarding Public and Private Schools Admitting Chinese Students." Referred to as Ordinance 19, this fifteen-clause document, designed to standardize enrollment procedures for the expanding Chinese student population, put the burden of controlling
students squarely on the Chinese consulate while leaving the supervision of schools to the Ministry of Education. Evidence suggests

that in issuing the new regulations, the Japanese government proceeded with a cautious eye to Chinese student reactions. As a first step, discussions were held with the Chinese Minister to Japan, Yang Shu. He, in turn, circulated a draft copy to representatives of the Chinese Student Union.[2] When he reported that student representatives mildly objected to clause 9, the Education Ministry agreed to modify it.

The formal release of the document on November 2 drew little comment, in large part because the full version was not initially released to the press. It was not until the end of the month that student attention was riveted to the new regulations. This was the result of an order issued on November 26 through the schools that, in conformity with Ordinance 19, students must produce records confirming their place of origin, present residence, age, and previous schools attended.[3] Failure to comply, the directive warned, would result in unfortunate consequences for the student. This strictly worded command for apparently routine information drew students to look more closely at Ordinance 19, which began to be referred to in the Japanese press as "Regulations to *Control* [*torishimaru*] Chinese Students." Student Union leaders consulted with the heads of the provincial clubs. On December 1, a general student letter was sent via Minister Yang Shu to the Education Ministry expressing opposition in particular to clauses 9 and 10. The first sought to put limits to the number of students domiciled—unsupervised—off-campus, and the second prohibited students expelled from one school for "bad conduct" from entering another.

The political climate of the time served to make this a more volatile issue than it might otherwise have been. On the international scene, this was the month of the Peking Conference (November 22-December 22), the meeting that was to confirm the fruits of Japan's victory over Russia—the territories Russia had earlier seized from China. Student indignation over this issue was expressed in a cable sent to China's Grand Councilors on December 14. This cable was reportedly signed by 3,000 students and had to be sent through Minister Yang, since the Tokyo cable office refused to transmit it under the students' names.[4] Whether that was actually the case matters little. What is important for our understanding of the 1905 protest is that this was a period of humiliation for Chinese youth as their government appeared helplessly pliant in the wake of Japanese success.

There was another, purely internal matter that likely spurred students on to voice their anger against the Education Ministry: its dispute with members of the faculty of Tokyo University (Tōdai) over the issue of academic freedom. The essentials of the case were these. That September, after six professors at Tōdai had attacked what they considered to be their government's concessionary behavior at the Portsmouth peace talks, the Education Ministry had responded by calling for the resignation of one of the six. Thereupon, the university's president, Yamakawa Kenjirō, assailing the abuse of academic freedom, had sent in his own letter of resignation. The ministry initially refused to act on Yamakawa's letter. Then suddenly, on December 2, his resignation was accepted. This decision triggered resignations from eight professors, a protest letter to the ministry signed by 190 lecturers, and a general outcry that Education Minister Kubota Yuzuru himself should resign for his mishandling of the incident. It was just at this juncture, when the ministry was in a vulnerable position, that the students decided to voice their own objections to the ministry's Ordinance 19.[5]

The course of the Sino-Japanese talks and the Education Ministry-Tōdai controversy were undoubtedly reinforcing factors in the students' decision to launch a protest movement. Equally important was the fact that, by 1905, students had become extremely sensitive to any attempt to restrict their personal freedoms. The Seijō incident of 1902 was only the first of a string of protests by Chinese students chafing at school regulations and generally asserting their independence. In the spring of 1903, for example, students at the Kōbun Institute staged a strike over a minor issue of school policy. As a harbinger of the anti-Japanese mood of 1905, the institute's director, Kanō Jigorō, came under verbal attack as an agent of Japanese oppression.[6] Kanō, we will recall, was the mentor of the first thirteen Chinese students and the founder of the Kōbun overseas student program, a man who had a career-long interest in improving China's educational system.

The rise in numbers of Chinese students, particularly of those disposed to dissident, even revolutionary activities (the TMH had been established in August), is precisely what concerned both the Chinese and the Japanese government and led them to draw up a new set of regulatory measures in the first place. In Chang Chih-tung's case, the need to assert control over students even as he continued to promote the study-abroad program was a key element in his thinking from the time he issued warnings to offenders after the Hankow debacle in 1900. Chang's was the awful dilemma that study abroad, the chance for a modern education and training in new techniques essential to China's development, could only be got at the cost of exposure to new ideas potentially disruptive of the status quo. As we have seen, in 1903, following the Seijō incident, Chang and Minister Uchida issued a document standardizing school admissions procedures and warning students against involvement in political activities. Ordinance 19 reinforced this policy.

Official Japanese thinking had for years supported Chang and his progressive approach to China's development: primary emphasis on educational reform but without excluding elements of Chinese learning. Neither Chang nor the Japanese who supported the study-abroad program envisioned Chinese students as the vanguard of a new political order. Their role was to deliver new skills, pedagogic, legal, technical, organizational, that would enable China to tap its national resources and move along paths to wealth and power. Ordinance 19 was consistent with this approach; quite simply, it was designed to force Chinese youths to "keep their noses to the grindstone," so to speak, rather than dissipating their energies in extracurricular frivolities or, worse still, subversive politics.

The Japanese had other motives for issuing the new regulations. However accommodating Meiji society was in terms of new ideas, it was still a law-and-order society concerned above all with maintaining stability. The Education Ministry was thus hardly likely to countenance so large a group of foreign students living and learning within ill-defined boundaries. It was to forestall potential chaos that the regulations sought, as the title of the ordinance indicates, to control the schools attended by Chinese students, many of which were, in fact, "fly-by-night" institutions set up merely to make money as they saw the number of students swelling into the thousands. The regulations sought to improve educational standards through accreditation procedures and to step up the surveillance of Chinese students by requiring that periodic reports on their numbers and course schedules be submitted to the ministry.[7] Considering the additional staff time needed to carry out the new procedures, one suspects that school administrators must have reacted with as much frustration as their Chinese charges.

The Student Reaction

Very likely, the caution with which the regulations were released—consultation with the Chinese side, only printing the ordinance in official papers at first—was intended to forestall sharp reaction from Chinese students. The stern demand for information issued on November 26 undid all this. Sensing that there was more to the new regulations than they had bargained for, students at once took a careful look at Ordinance 19. On December 1, Student Union leaders and representatives of the provincial clubs submitted a joint letter to the Education Ministry outlining their objections to the new policy.[8]

The student argument at this point dispassionately and logically addressed the practical implications of clauses 9 and 10: forcing students into school-administered dormitories and private houses would be an economic blow to the self-supporting students, who were likely to be in Japan on limited funds and thus needed to shop around for the best possible bargain in living arrangements. Such a policy would also curtail the academic opportunities of a great many students who were taking courses at several schools and needed to locate their living quarters accordingly. In the case of clause 10, said the students, the Education Ministry's failure to define "bad conduct" allowed all schools, even the worst diploma mills, to ignore often-justified complaints from the student side.

During the first week of December, as this letter was making its way to the Education Ministry through the good offices of Minister Yang and the Japanese Foreign Office, students representing the major schools attended by Chinese met at the Student Union. Registering dissatisfaction with the mildly worded letter of December 1, they called instead for a boycott of classes in order to bring added pressure to bear on the Japanese government. On December 4, school strikes were launched at the Railroad and Mining School and the Kōbun Institute.[9] Strike activity quickly spread to nine other schools, including Seijō Gakkō and Waseda University's Chinese student division. Striking students formed picket lines around their schools, attempting to persuade or intimidate their classmates into joining the boycott. Those who persisted in attending classes were denounced as "public enemies of the student world."[10]

As disruption spread, certain students tried to maintain a degree of order by issuing regulations to govern strike behavior: (1) individual Japanese were not to be harassed; (2) students were not to create disturbances at inns, dormitories, or lodging houses; and (3) during the period of the strike, students were to boycott restaurants and shops, but were not to turn the strike into a lark.[11] Minister Yang's attempts to get the students to call off the strikes through the intercession of Student Union leaders were unsuccessful. Instead, strikers began to organize, setting up the Rengōkai (in full, Kakkō Rengōkai, or United League of Schools), a group representing the various school clubs and calling for a mass exodus of Chinese students unless Ordinance 19 in its entirety was withdrawn.[12]

The Rengōkai protest was in marked contrast to the logical argument of the December 1 union-sponsored letter. Cries of discrimination replaced pleas for understanding. Ordinance 19, charged Rengōkai members, was in toto discriminatory because Chinese students were subjected to restrictive measures not applied to Japanese or other foreigners attending school in Japan. It was a "grave national insult" and a violation of international law:

China exists on a basis of equality with Japan internationally. In terms of rights, apart from specially stipulated exceptions, we ought to be accorded the same treatment as Japanese nationals. Provided Japan is a country where slavery does not exist, we also ought to enjoy our freedom. In [the case of] the present regulations, to control our extracurricular activities is to deprive us of our physical freedom. To restrict those who have been expelled from schools is to take away their spiritual freedom.[13]

Such acts of prejudice against Chinese students, the Rengōkai students asserted, revealed Japan's arrogance toward fellow Asians and signaled its ultimate desire to enslave Chinese generally as part of a grand scheme for self-aggrandizement in Asia. Again and again, Rengōkai spokesmen pointed to the example of Korea. We have seen before that Chinese youths were extremely sensitive about being compared with Koreans. The point was especially telling in late 1905, for Itō Hirobumi had just devised an administrative scheme that made Korea a Japanese mandate.[14]

As cynical as the Rengōkai was about Japan's real intentions, it did not view Ordinance 19 as an attempt to pressure Chinese students to leave Japan altogether. Quite to the contrary, Rengōkai writers claimed that Japan stood to gain from the foreign student presence: Japan not only welcomed the income from the thousands of resident Chinese, but prized its reputation of taking the lead in Asian education. It was the Chinese government, concerned about mounting revolutionary activity, that wanted to see students either rigorously controlled in their Japanese setting or forced to return to China, where they could be kept under strict surveillance. What the Chinese authorities failed to comprehend, in the Rengōkai view, was that the students abroad were the key to China's future, and that defending them against the discriminatory policies of a foreign government was a necessary assertion of China's independence and strength.[15]

Throughout the Rengōkai essays, the students are portrayed as a vanguard of the politically conscious, a new force whose actions would have a profound impact on China's present course and ultimate fate:

It is precisely because of the Chinese students abroad that China, as the twentieth century unfolds, is able to maintain its position as an equal nation in a world where the Powers are poised rapaciously, ready to attack. The students, above all, have freedom, enthusiasm, group unity. They urge on our 400 million countrymen, "Stride boldly, heads erect. Don't become slaves!"[16]

Aware of their potential as a new leadership group, students were emboldened, too, by what the sheer fact of their numbers implied for China's future:

In Japan's case, only a few dozen people had a firsthand look at the progress of Western civilization, and one by one advocated [elements of this tradition for Japan]. Our Chinese students abroad number more than 10,000; we represent a collective force. When, for all that, our ability to develop a new educational system and organize a new world is brought into question, we find it unacceptable.[17]

Several events lent dramatic appeal to Rengōkai arguments and gained supporters for the group. First of all, student representations to Minister Yang did not yield the hoped-for results. After an all-night vigil, he agreed to see the Rengōkai members, but simply to inform them that he would intercede with the Ministry of Education on their behalf only so far as to present the case for the withdrawal of clauses 9 and 10. A request that the entire set of regulations be rescinded was out of the question.

When we compare Minister Yang with his predecessor Ts'ai Chün in terms of style and approach, Yang appears much the wiser and more accessible. After all, from the first he had made sure that student leaders were given advance warning of the new regulatory measures and then, when objections to clauses 9 and 10 arose, he readily transmitted them with a cover letter in his own name to the Ministry of Education.[18] Yet Rangōkai leaders chose to interpret Yang's statement as a major rebuff. They complained of a conspiracy of Chinese and Japanese authorities to oppress the overseas students. This seemed to be further confirmed when the Japanese Foreign Office, which had learned from other sources of the "return-to-China" group's demands, made it plain that withdrawing Ordinance 19 altogether was not even a matter for discussion.

What aroused student tempers even more than the apparent immovability of Yang and the Foreign Office, however, was the protest suicide of the well-known revolutionary Ch'en T'ien-hua. Ch'en's action was in direct response to Japanese press accounts that were contemptuously critical of the student strikers, calling them "self-indulgent and small-minded." Undoubtedly for Ch'en, whose volatile personality ran to pessimistic statements about the unlikely survival of the Chinese "race," it was a terrible blow to hear China's students described as dissolute rabble. Suicide apparently seemed to him the sole means of dramatizing to protesters that only by a display of high-minded behavior could they give the lie to Japanese criticisms.[19]

If that was his intent, Ch'en certainly achieved a measure of success. By December 10, few students could not have heard of his suicide, which was widely reported in the Japanese press. BODY OF THIRTY-YEAR-OLD CHINESE STUDENT FOUND FLOATING IN MORI CANAL ran the *Asahi Shimbun* headline. Students now became even more unyielding in their demands, the number of Rengōkai supporters increased, and those who had raised the threat of a "return in body" actually began to leave Japan. The *Asahi Shimbun* of December 16 reported that 204 Chinese students had departed the afternoon of the 14th for Yokohama, and that Shanghai-bound vessels were fully booked for the 17th, 20th, and 23rd.[20] By December 21, according to the *Kokumin Shimbun*, only twenty Chinese students were left at Shinbu Gakkō, twelve at the Kōbun Institute, and a mere two at Seijō Gakkō.[21]

The total figures on returnees varied—and indeed were difficult to calculate at this juncture—but *Asahi*'s estimate of upward of 2,000 was probably close to the final mark.[22] According to a *Miyako Shimbun* survey, the many lodging houses in Kanda catering to a Chinese clientele feared a huge loss of income if students left en masse. Chinese restaurants, noodle shops, and sundry goods' stores were already feeling the pinch of the boycott that was being systematically enforced by student strikers.[23]

But as scores of students vied for reservations out of Yokohama, a counter movement began gathering momentum. The turning point came with the issuance of an explanatory document by the Ministry of Education on December 16, followed by a memorandum eight days later. In the earlier piece, ministry officials argued that the intent of Ordinance 19 was not to restrict but to protect Chinese students. With the recent increase in numbers of Chinese seeking study opportunities in Japan, they pointed out, not unreasonably, providing school facilities had become a problem. Many of the schools that had sprung up catering to Chinese were for-profit operations offering a substandard curriculum. It was to rectify this situation and thus ensure that Chinese students were receiving a quality education that Ordinance 19 stipulated new reporting requirements for schools as the basis for continued accreditation. Other provisions were likewise designed for the benefit of the Chinese student of serious bent. Clause 9, which provided for supervised dormitory life, aimed to protect him from the influence of "bad elements"—presumably Japanese—outside school. Clause 10, which restricted school transfers, was meant not to curb the freedom of expression of legitimate students but to silence troublemakers. Decisions on which students had justifiable grievances and which did not were put squarely on the shoulders of the Chinese minister to Japan. In the follow-up document, a memorandum sent to Minister Yang on December 24, the Ministry of Education, backing off slightly from its original position on school transfers, now left it entirely up to the minister to authorize reentrance as he saw fit. He was also empowered to grant exceptions in cases of students applying for nonsupervised housing.

The Education Ministry's arguments and attempt to conciliate struck a responsive chord among those students who from the beginning had favored moderation and viewed the exodus of their classmates with alarm. The mid-December documents thus acted as a catalyst in the formation of a new group, the Iji Dōshikai (in full, Ryūgakkai Iji Dōshikai, or Students Abroad Common Cause Society). By late December, it claimed a membership of over 2,000.[24]

The crux of the Dōshikai argument was that considerations of the long-term benefits of study abroad to the Chinese nation must far outweigh any immediate concern about limitations on students' personal freedoms. From this premise, Dōshikai members countered the Rengōkai demand for a total rejection of Ordinance 19 with a call for examining the regulations on a clause-by-clause basis. Their conclusions were, first of all, that the regulations were not meant to discriminate against Chinese in particular. Similar measures had been drawn up in recent years to apply to all foreigners studying in Japan. Besides, the word "control" (*torishimaru*) did not carry the pejorative meaning in Japanese that it took on in Chinese translation.[25]

Moreover, the Dōshikai claimed, the new measures were directed as much to Japanese schools as to Chinese students. In a statement reminiscent of the Ministry of Education's line, a Dōshikai writer asserted:

We are opposed to complete abolition [of the regulations], not only because it cannot be done but because certain portions should not be abolished. Those fellow students who urge complete abolition do so entirely on the grounds that it is not [appropriate] for our overseas students to be under the special control of the Japanese government. They have not calmed down enough to examine the relative advantages or disadvantages of the regulations themselves. Their premise that they ought not be under the special control of the Japanese government is greatly mistaken and brings the situation to an impasse. Furthermore, the ministry ordinance is not meant to control the students but to control the schools they are entering. . . . Are the schools the Japanese set up specially for us Chinese students really allowing us to fulfill our goals? If not, should we not hope that the Ministry of Education will look into it and intervene? . . . The Japanese government is not [issuing controls on schools] solely out of a devout interest in the students but particularly because it feels responsible [for seeing that any] actions by its countrymen not bring shame on a civilized nation.[26]

Continuing in this coolheaded vein, the author turned to an analysis of current Japanese China policy. There were two schools of thought, he asserted. One supported outright aggression (*ch'in-lueh chu-i*) on the mainland. This position ran the grave risk of heightening anti-Japanese feeling among Chinese and arousing suspicion among the Powers and thus had remained the minority view. The prevailing school of thought supported a "policy of wooing" (*hsi-shou chu-i*); this approach came in two forms, economic and psychological. Psychological wooing was the tack taken by such major figures as Konoe and Ōkuma, and involved the use of peaceful means to win over the hearts and minds of the Chinese people. Economic wooing was tantamount to economic imperialism: "Those Japanese who are attracted by money drool over China's wealth. With slogans of same culture, same race, they publicly pledge assistance to the wholesale export of civilization (*bummei*) [to China]. In reality, the goal is to accumulate money."[27] But, as long as China benefited from such a policy, the author said, why should it be concerned about ultimate Japanese motives?

For example, if we come to Japan to study we must enter schools. If the schools are good, there is no need to question whether the goal in setting up the school was making money. By entering those schools, we have derived that much benefit. At present, though schools are being established in China, there is a shortage of teachers. If the Japanese surpass us in learning, what difference does it make if their motive for coming to China is profit? We are deriving an advantage from inviting these teachers to China.[28]

In the practical sphere, the Dōshikai aim was to restore order among the student body and effect a return to classes. To this end, meetings were held with concerned parties on all sides—the Chinese principals, TDK representatives, and members of Japanese political parties. Not surprisingly, such conciliatory activity produced an angry reaction from Rengōkai extremists. A vigorous "poster war" ensued, with each group denouncing the other's position.[29] In an attempt to mediate between the warring factions, two additional student groups were formed, small in membership but a sign of the urgency felt in many quarters that the issues be resolved.

The Storm Abates

As the year drew to a close, the drift was toward compromise. In a memorandum to students issued on December 31, Minister Yang highlighted the conciliatory action taken by the Ministry of Education as a result of his month-long bargaining sessions with officials there and at the Foreign Office. According to the Education Ministry's explanatory document of December 24, the Chinese minister to Japan or his duly authorized representative was to act as final arbiter in cases falling within the limits of clauses 9 and 10. Counting this a major concession to student demands, the minister expressed the hope that students would return to classes on January 11, following the winter holiday.[30]

For many students, the ministry's decision to concede a point, to allow that the clauses at issue need not necessarily apply to everyone without exception, clearly tipped the balance. Not only that, by late December, as many as 2,000 of the most radical students had departed. This selection-out process left a Chinese student group by definition more amenable to settlement. Yet to stop here in our analysis of how a settlement ultimately came about would be to give short shrift to what was in fact a *process* of negotiations revealing numerous special interests among people in high places.

Key players in the process were high-level Chinese officials who functioned as mediators between student leaders and Japanese officialdom. We have seen something of the action of the Chinese minister, Yang Shu, as he shuttled protest letters and replies between students and Education Ministry personnel, all the while attempting through attached memorandums to interpret student demands for the ministry and to convey the ministry's reasoning to students. Yang was not, it appears, unsympathetic to certain of the students' objections. Another figure involved in the dispute who likewise—judging by the number of dinners and gatherings held in his honor—enjoyed the trust of many students was Li Tsung-t'ang. This was the same Li who played a mediating role during the Seijō disturbances. By 1905, he was a veteran reporter on Chinese student affairs, having made four previous trips to Japan in that capacity.[31] His 1905 account offers information on the financial and academic status of students from Anhui, Kiangsi, and Kiangsu, as well as a well-documented record of the protest events of December. Li held numerous meetings with students, particularly those from Anhui, trying to convince them of the long-term advantages of continuing their education.[32]

According to a January newspaper report, another official who played a role was a Chinese vice-minister of education sent out by the Peking government on a fact-finding cum mediating mission. This emissary helped form an arbitration group comprising both Dōshikai and Rengōkai representatives that not only made peace with Japanese authorities, but also sought, through a cabled appeal, to persuade students who already had returned "in a body" to change their minds and come back.[33]

On the Japanese side, too, several leading intellectuals and politicians bent their efforts to smooth things out. School principals, including the redoubtable Kanō Jigorō, held a series of meetings with students over the month of December, trying to persuade them to return to classes.[34] Political parties got involved in the issue. Seiyūkai representatives met with Student Union head Chang Chi and others on December 18 for a briefing on the school strikes. Shimpotō (Progressive Party) officials likewise held talks with students and Count Nagaoka of the TDK; their conclusion was that if the regulations were not withdrawn, the issue should be submitted as a parliamentary question.[35]

The Japanese press gave wide coverage to the protest, seeking out student leaders to get their side of the story. For example, on December 17, some dozen reporters met with student spokesmen Chang Chi and Ch'eng Chia-sheng to get clarification of the student position.[36] Not all of the resulting articles were unsympathetic. Some suggested that the Education Ministry reappraise the regulations. Others wondered—wisely—if Japan had simply gotten caught in the middle of a conflict between the Ch'ing government and its own nationals.[37] The bulk of the editorials and analyses, however, had nothing good to say about the students. One writer in *Nihon Shimbun*, after identifying diverse causes of the protest, ranging from the concern over security on both the Chinese and the Japanese side to the fact that students had become bored and homesick, recommended that strong measures be taken in dealing with protesters.[38]

Other writers were less temperate in tone, expressing their indignation and outrage at the students' ingratitude toward their Japanese hosts, who had provided them with a fine opportunity to learn about modern civilization. The students were labeled unreasonable in equating academic freedom with an absence of controls, and "soft" in their inability to put up with the least inconvenience for the sake of the nation.[39] Typical was this statement in the *Chūō Shimbun* of December 15, 1905:

Eight thousand Chinese students (some reports say 10,000), claiming as unjust the regulations to control overseas students issued by the Education Ministry, took joint action to boycott the schools. Since then several weeks have elapsed and still the issue has not been resolved. We cannot help deeply deploring this from the standpoint of the students. The Chinese students came to Japan of their own volition to absorb the new atmosphere of Western civilization. We [Japanese] were pleased that China, our fellow East Asian nation in culture and race, had [at last] awakened and was on the road to great progress in accordance with world trends. Our Empire today, rapidly overtaking the Great Powers, has entered the ranks as a first-class nation. If one searches for the origins [of our present strength], it all derives from the fact that our students went to the advanced countries of Europe and the United States, bore any kind of inconvenience, difficulty, insult, for the sake of their studies, for the sake of their nation, and endured all sorts of hardships in order to capture the essence of world civilization and apply it at home. We have welcomed the Chinese students, believing them to be pioneers, a vanguard to bring their country to enlightenment. However, many of the students coming to Japan tend to grow irresponsible and gradually slip into unrestrained behavior. Bad elements in our country, taking advantage of the students' unfamiliarity with our ways, pander to their desires and they become corrupt beyond salvation. Is this not an extremely worrisome situation for the students? And further, is it not Japan's responsibility to clearly differentiate on the basis of quality the schools students select and let them know when they have made a bad choice? Clearly it is, and it is equally clear that the Education Ministry, in stipulating a select list of schools and in establishing regulations to control extracurricular activity, has as its sole wish improving the lot of the Chinese student, not in the least inflicting him with excessive restrictions. . . . We suspect that the Chinese students have misinterpreted our true intentions when they stand up in a body, abandon their studies, and cry noisily about the injustice of the regulations. Saying that imposing regulations on students is the first step in annexing China is a laughable supposition.[40]

This kind of sharp rebuke obviously had a devastating effect on certain students, notably Ch'en T'ien-hua. Others probably found compromise the better part of discretion in the face of severe criticism from their Japanese hosts.

Perhaps the most effective player in the settlement process was the TDK's Count Nagaoka. At the time of the Seijō incident in 1902, the TDK had taken on a mediating role, though an informal and tentative one. In fact, it was the TDK's overtures to some students in the hope of settling the dispute that deepened the rift between moderates and radicals. At the time of the 1905 incident, the TDK in the person of Nagaoka was a more visible part of the process of coming to terms with students. The press quickly pinpointed him as the Ministry of Education's arbiter. Nagaoka himself, however, was reluctant to be too closely identified with the ministry's position, evidently preferring to maintain an independent hand in the negotiations. A spokesman for the count sought to make it clear that Nagaoka's role as mediator derived as much from his TDK and Tō-A Seinenkai functions and from his Chinese student contacts as from his connections within the Ministry of Education.[41]

Indeed, Nagaoka projected an impartial image. For example, he had attended the students' mid-December meeting with Shimpotō delegates, where it was resolved to urge the Education Ministry to withdraw the regulations.[42] The following day found him at the ministry discussing the students' demands. One might reasonably assume that Nagaoka had considerable input into the ministry's clarifications of December 16 and 24.

Nagaoka's guiding hand was evident also in the organizing of the Sino-Japanese Student Society immediately after the students' return to classes. Though ostensibly formed "to plan for the friendship of Chinese and Japanese students,"[43] the group met only once, and the tone of that unique event suggests that its sole purpose was to publicize and legitimate the informal agreement reached between Chinese students and Japanese negotiators. Present at the January 28 inaugural meeting were some 1,500 students and fifty honored guests, most of them Japanese. Principal guests on the Chinese side were the special envoy Li Tsung-t'ang (Yang Shu, surprisingly, is not listed) and the former student Ch'eng Chia-sheng. Several Japanese notables attended, including besides Count Nagaoka, Count Ōkuma Shigenobu, Count Aoki (who had succeeded to the presidency of the TDK after Konoe's death in 1904), Kanō Jigorō, and Baron Umazaki. Nezu Hajime, a long-time promoter of East Asia projects, and his colleague Fukumoto Nichinan were also on hand. Among the Chinese students were Chang Chi, representing Meiji University, and several former Rengōkai members.

Various speeches delivered for the occasion bore the TDK stamp. Ōkuma, for example, traced the course of Japan's modernization as an object lesson for China. Eastern culture began to stagnate while the West advanced. When Western nations began to penetrate into

East Asia, Japan at first resisted, then, forced to yield, initiated a rational process of change in all areas of public life by sending thousands of special emissaries and students abroad and hiring foreign consultants. The result of this masterly policy was the rapid introduction of new technology that supplemented rather than supplanted the indigenous culture. Present-day China, Ōkuma pointed out, was Japan of forty years ago—on the brink of change—the difference being that now an advanced Japan could pass on the new learning and thus ease the transition.[44]

For those Chinese students who remained in Japan, it was back to studies in an atmosphere of harmony and restraint. Of those who had returned to China, some drifted back to Tokyo. Others sought to set up a new school and, ironically, applied to the Peking government for financial aid. When this was not forthcoming, they used their own funds and established a school called the China Public Institute. Hu Shih was one of its more distinguished graduates.[45]

The protest produced a marked reduction in the total number of students in Japan. From upwards of 9,000, the figure dipped to 7,000. Though there was some reverse flow, the heyday of the Chinese student movement to Japan was over. The regulations, slightly modified but still in force, made study in Japan less attractive: not only did they create a more restrictive social life for students; they prevented the instant diploma sought by many. By 1909, student numbers had dropped to 5,000. Two years later, the call of revolution led to a massive "return in a body," an ironic finale to the Ch'ing study-abroad program.

Students and the T'ung-meng Hui

An unprecedented number of students were active in the 1905 protest, boycotting classes, producing reams of petitions and opinion papers, and, even, as the ultimate act of defiance, returning home to China. Most of these students were Rengōkai supporters. But the Dōshikai, with a claimed membership of 2,000, though less militant, was also resolutely against some features of Ordinance 19. All told, then, some 4,000 students—half the total group—were willing to voice open opposition to the new restrictive policies.

The student response, as it unfolded between November and January, appears to have been carefully organized and planned. Accounts are clear on the role of the Student Union, the provincial and school clubs, and the two political action groups, the Rengōkai and Dōshikai. Less clear is whether there were links between the student leaders and the TMH, newly formed in August and soon to take center stage in the movement to overthrow the Ch'ing.

Identifying the protest leaders and early TMH members requires a bit of detective work. The names of ninety-six protesters may be gleaned from Saneto Keishu's extensive compilation of documents on the 1905 incident. By the mere fact of the publicity surrounding them as signers of manifestos, speakers at protest meetings, and mediators in the final stages, one may assume that they were in some sense the "leaders" of the movement.

On the TMH side, membership numbers and names are problematic for what was a frankly anti-Ch'ing organization; one can understand the reluctance of many students, particularly those on government scholarship, to have their names recorded on the TMH roster. Chang Yü-fa, in his research through early records and post-1911 reminiscences (when the reluctance had worn off), has unearthed 101 possible members as of July 30, 1905. But he has been unable to fully verify the membership of twenty-nine of these, so the real total may have been well under 100.[46] By the August 20 inaugural meeting, and definitely by December 1905, when the Education Ministry protest was at its height, membership figures were much higher, perhaps 200–300,[47] but the actual names are not available. In other words, though the 101 figure is much on the conservative side for December, it is likely accurate as far as actual names are concerned.

Comparing the 96 names on the leadership list with the 101 on the TMH list reveals a surprisingly low overlap of 15 percent.[48] Though this is only a rough indicator at best, there are other grounds for concluding that the 1905 incident was not TMH-inspired. To begin with, both Sun Yat-sen and Huang Hsing, the key decision makers in the new group, were out of the country, and in their absence the second-level leaders were in a complete quandary about what position to take. The only thing they were sure of was that Sun, who had spent years building up Japanese contacts, would be chary of too close a connection with an avowedly anti-Japanese protest. An article in the *Asahi Shimbun* of December 16, 1905, purportedly submitted by "a close friend of Sun's in Tokyo," denied that the revolutionary chief was in any way involved in the current disturbance. In the first place, Sun's friend informed readers, Sun had left the country in early October for a trip to Southeast Asia. In any case, he said—and this was a telling point—Sun's sole goal was to oust the Manchus; he had no anti-foreign inclinations whatever. Far from it; in the case of Japan particularly, Sun had consistently stressed the importance of unity and friendship.[49] To many in the fledgling TMH, the anti-Japanese demonstrations and the resultant publicity must have seemed at least an embarrassment, if not a potential threat to the group's very existence. November 26, the day Student Union representatives first registered objections to the Education Ministry's regulations, marked the debut of *Min pao*, the propaganda arm of the TMH. To the editors, who were running a suspect operation anyway, launching a protest at that juncture must have seemed to be asking for trouble.

Still, how to respond to the turmoil within the student community was clearly an important issue for the TMH, which split along Rengōkai-Dōshikai lines. According to Hu Han-min's account, one clique, centering around Sung Chiao-jen and Hu Ying, advocated that the entire Chinese student body return home to China and focus on engineering a revolution. This, he says, was the more popular position. The second clique, which he himself subscribed to, along with Wang Ching-wei and several other Kwangtung compatriots, strongly opposed the return-in-a-body tack as irresponsible and risky. For one thing, they said, it would jeopardize the existence of *Min pao*. There was also a practical consideration in taking the path of compromise: those students about to graduate wanted their diplomas and thus preferred a policy of negotiating with the various school principals to a precipitous departure from Japan.

A striking feature of Hu Han-min's account of this event far in his past is the passion with which he reenacted the scene, his acrimonious exchanges with Ch'iu Chin and Hu Ying in particular.[50] Disagreement over how to respond to the Education Ministry regulations clearly provided a springboard for debate over the fundamental issue of how to run a revolution. A similarly emotional account of divisiveness among student TMH members is found in the reminiscences of Liao Chung-k'ai's wife, Ho Hsiang-ning.

Ho's account is even stronger testimony than Hu Han-min's that the controversy within the student community—between, as she characterized them, timorous souls eager for compromise and firm oppositionists—had immediate repercussions on the TMH, testing the strength of the new organization. Hers was the majority position, that of unremitting resistance to the regulations, to the point, if necessary, of leaving Japan. She acknowledged that the return of the entire group was fraught with difficulties, not the least of which was the danger of arrest for those TMH members whose names were on the Ch'ing wanted list. She also admitted that Sun Yat-sen had not put his imprimatur on the return-in-a-body policy. But what she faulted Hu Han-min and Wang Ching-wei for was not so much their unwillingness to carry protest to this extreme point as their halfhearted support for the protest activities then taking place in Japan. In her view, Hu, Wang, and others like them were guilty of gross self-interest: enrolled in short-term courses awaiting entry to regular universities, they feared that joining a boycott of classes might jeopardize their chances of getting government scholarship aid. For this selfish reason, they preferred to compromise with Japanese authorities rather than support the school strikes.[51] Except for the personal slur, Ho's version differs only slightly from Hu's own contention that students of more studious bent were the ones eager for negotiations.

In spirit and form, the 1905 movement hews to the pattern of previous student disturbances, notably the Seijō incident and the protest against Russian aggression in Manchuria. Characteristic of each was the politicization of what were essentially student social clubs—the Student Union and the various provincial and school associations—and the simultaneous appearance of issue-oriented groups such as the Rengōkai bent on effecting a change in policy. Policy change was as far as it went for most students, even by 1905 and even among those most outspoken in their criticism of Ch'ing officialdom. Their demonstrations, in other words, were not in original intent moves to overthrow the government. In reviewing the series of confrontations over the 1902–5 period, one is struck by a sense of missed opportunities on the part of the Ch'ing, that a strong stance vis-à-vis the Powers or a declaration of support for the overseas students, for example, might at some point have turned the creative energies of China's educated youth in favor rather than implacably against the regime.

As it was, seemingly minor grievances were allowed to fester and grow into painful clashes between students and authorities. In the 1905 protest, as in the Seijō incident, the original issue was what the students considered to be unfair school regulations. Appeals for change were made through the Chinese minister to Japan. Working together, Chinese and Japanese officials sought to effect a compromise without backing off from the intent of tightening controls over students. The students reacted angrily toward both sides, labeling Chinese officials incompetent and unpatriotic and Japanese officials arrogant imperialists. But in both cases, the action groups they formed rather quickly fell apart. In 1902, fissures appeared over the role the TDK should play as mediator. In 1905, the divisive issue was whether students should leave Japan in protest or put up with discriminatory policies for the sake of a good education. The degree of commitment to the cause was also a point of disagreement among students in the 1903 resist-Russia movement. In that case, the most militant students went underground and reemerged to help form the China Rise Society and the Restoration Society. The Ch'ing government retaliated by issuing more stringent regulations to govern study abroad.

In 1902 and 1905, student disputes with authorities were more or less settled in a process involving the same key elements—the TDK and important figures on both the Japanese and the Chinese side, including Li Tsung-t'ang, who was sent out on a fact-finding mission on both occasions. From the pages of his journal, it appears that Li was in frequent contact with students, especially those from his home province, Anhui. One can speculate that talks with Li helped persuade Ch'eng Chia-sheng, a graduate from Anhui and a TMH member (could Li have known this?),[52] to work toward negotiating a settlement of the disturbance. A point that comes through more clearly in the mediation process in 1905 than in 1902 is that old-timers among the Chinese students like Ch'eng, who had been in Japan for six years, had their own contacts among Japanese quite separate from those developed by Sun Yat-sen. As prominent a figure as Konoe Atsumaro records a meeting with Ch'eng in November 1902, though the reason for the get-together is unexplained.[53]

The long-term impact of the 1905 protest was to feed more youth into the radical fringe that had been growing in numbers since Hankow in 1900 and in solidarity through such organizations as the Restoration Society and the T'ung-meng Hui. The publicity surrounding the protest of thousands drew the sympathy of thousands more. Sun Yat-sen was able to ride the crest of a wave. This very likely accounts for the great upsurge in TMH membership during the first year of its existence.

NINE

The Student Political Awakening, 1900-1905

S TUDENT ACTION in the disturbances of 1902–5 was spontaneous and improvised. Politically unsophisticated, Chinese
youths did not mount their protests to make a doctrinal point;
they did not act on the basis of a defined ideology or explicit political program. Instead, protests arose as ad hoc responses to specific,
often minor grievances—like the objectionable school regulations
that triggered the Seijō and 1905 incidents. Rebuffed by authorities,
students became disenchanted with the possibility of working
through established channels; and broader issues, fundamental political issues related to the competence of the regime in power, became a new focal point of protest. For many students what started
as a demand for change from within turned into an external assault
on the entire system of governance. Peaceful confrontations were
replaced with conspiracies to overthrow the regime.

This process of radicalization tempered and shaped a student political outlook. In other words, action tended to crystallize views
rather than the reverse in the case of the Chinese students in Japan.
This is not to downplay the force of ideas. Quite to the contrary.
Though the Chinese students acted without thinking in consciously ideological terms, their disposition to perceive particular-
ized disputes in universal political terms—to make the incompetent bureaucrat Ts'ai Chün, for example, into a symbol of Ch'ing
bureaucratic incompetence generally—was precisely the result of
the new ideas and beliefs they were being exposed to in Japan. The
Japan experience, which for most students represented nothing less
than an intellectual awakening, provided a new frame of reference

from which to view Chinese politics and politicians. The curious part of this transmission of ideas is that it was not bilateral between China and Japan, but trilateral, the third party being an undifferentiated "West." Gaining knowledge of the West was, after all, the primary and explicit objective of China's study-in-Japan program. THE CHINESE STUDENTS' MECCA OF WESTERN LEARNING was how the *North China Herald* described Tokyo in 1904 when the influx of students was reaching major proportions.

Passage to a World of New Ideas

The Chinese students in Japan represented a transitional generation intellectually. They were born into the Confucian world as it existed before the Sino-Japanese War, a world still dominated by traditional cultural-moral beliefs. Confucianism, that system of ethical precepts joined to political philosophy, was still the touchstone of socially acceptable values and the route to career success. And the Confucian Classics, the distillation of a centuries-old way of life, were still the focus of study in a Chinese youth's first years at school.

At the same time, it was a world that was slowly changing, accommodating to the Western advance eastward, all the faster after the Sino-Japanese War, when those students soon to go to Japan were in their middle teens. Educational opportunities were expanding, especially at the middle-school level and above. Modern schools were being planned and built; "Western" subjects, primarily in technical fields and foreign languages, were being inserted into the standard Confucian curriculum. Chinese teenagers who found themselves in this progressive educational environment—and in the coastal and central regions this was a sizable percentage of those in school—likely warmed to alien ideas and ferreted out whatever they could of the "new learning."

The chief guru of Western thought in the late 1890's was the noted scholar Yen Fu. To what extent youths still in school could handle such intellectual giants as Mill, Huxley, Darwin, and Spencer via the translations of Yen Fu, who prided himself on his recondite style, is difficult to gauge.[1] More likely, they were introduced to Western currents of thought through the pen of the political exile Liang Ch'i-ch'ao, himself greatly influenced by Yen Fu. Liang wrote in a more popular style than Yen; his writing, touching on a broad range of topics, reached a wide audience through the Yokohama publications *Public Opinion* and *New People's Miscellany*.

The intellectual baggage that a Chinese youth typically carried with him to Japan, then, comprised the ABCs of Confucianism combined with a smattering of knowledge of, or at least curiosity about, Western thought. It was his entire Japan experience that capped his educational career, that schooled him in the works of Western thinkers and their applicability to what we today would term a developing country.

This intellectual growth involved several distinct phases. Undoubtedly what first captured the student's attention was Tokyo itself, that "modern" city with its street lamps and trolleys and gentlemen in European dress sporting short hair styles. A longer stay familiarized him with those aspects of Japanese society—an active press, political parties, a constitution—that showed the imprint of Western concepts and models. Once he was enrolled in the Japanese school system, he was exposed in a more direct sense to Western theories. His initial task was to learn Japanese. Mastery of written Japanese opened the door to Japanese translations of Western works, to the writing of the Meiji intelligentsia, much of it derived from Western politico-philosophical convictions, and to the output of Meiji journalists, which to Chinese around 1900 seemed a singularly impressive window to the world. In the classroom, too, the Chinese student became painfully aware of what low ratings were given to Chinese-related subjects in the school curriculum. "Mostly injurious," the newspaper *Jiji Shimpo* termed the influence of Chinese-language teachers in Japanese schools. Conservative in outlook, they were said to preach Confucian, out-of-date notions that were "opposed to the spirit of civilization Japan supports."[2] How ironic, this divorce in Japanese minds between Chinese learning and "civilization."

Chinese youth primed for new ideas were captivated by the vibrancy of Meiji intellectual life and the variety of Western thinkers whose writings were the stuff of discussion and debate. It was no monolith, Western thought in its Japanese presentation. There was no single bias toward one Western country of the sort that many former colonies have shown for the intellectual traditions of their colonizers. Nor did the Japanese embrace any one school of thought to the exclusion of others. Instead, Meiji Japan was influenced by a succession of American, British, French, and German thinkers, representing a range of ideologies from liberalism to statism to socialism.

A contemporary assessment of the relative influence of various Western thinkers on Meiji society is found in the July 1900 issue of

Sociology Magazine (Shakai zasshi). In the political field, the writer
stated, the views of Rousseau, Bentham, Mill, and Spencer had prevailed in the years immediately following the Restoration, only to
give way to German influences in the framing of the Meiji Constitution. In law, the study of the French and English legal systems was
being superseded by an emphasis on German law. In economics, the
current trend was toward American and German protectionist writers and away from Japan's first mentors, Adam Smith and the free
trade school. And in sociology, the Americans were coming to the
fore after years of relying solely on Spencer. The writer conceded
that in literature the English still held sway, though Mori Ogai had
done much to familiarize the Japanese public with German authors.[3] However one might agree or disagree with this review—the
Japan Weekly Mail, which offered a summary of the article, con-
tended that it overemphasized the German influence[4]—it does indicate the range of Western thinkers whose views caught the attention of Meiji Japanese.

Nor was this interest confined to the intellectual giants of the
Western world. A perusal of the *Japan Weekly Mail*'s "Monthly
Summary of Japanese Current Literature" shows that the works of
many lesser lights were being translated as well. Among the recently published translations mentioned in two issues in 1900, for
example, were *A History of English Literature* (Eibugakushi), an English work translated by the noted scholar Tsubouchi Shōyū; *Understanding International Law* (Kokusaihō yoron), the work of a Professor Westlake; *China's Relation to the Other Powers* (Kokusai
Shina), from a series of articles by Desjardins appearing in French
periodicals; and *German Commercial Law* (Doitsu shōhōron) and *A
History of European Politics in the Nineteenth Century* (Juku seiki
Oshū seijishōron), works whose original authors went unmen-
tioned.[5]

Amid this potpourri of ideas, the body of thought that elicited the
greatest interest was Spencerianism, the application of Darwinist
theories of biological evolution—the struggle for existence, natural
selection, survival of the fittest—to the development of human society. It is difficult for us today, just now emerging from the age of
Marx and Lenin, to feel the excitement generated by prosaic-
sounding phrases out of Social Darwinism. Yet at the turn of the
century, these phrases had a fresh and meaningful ring, not only in
Japan, where thirty-three translations of Spencer's works were issued between 1878 and 1896,[6] but in the West as well, especially in
the United States, where:

Spencer's variation upon the theme of inevitable progress fell in with the general optimism of American life, the sanguine views of a people who had won their independence and spread to the Pacific. When, at the close of the nineteenth century, the national aspirations were breaking upon foreign shores, John Fiske and others could invoke Spencerian formulas about the survival of the fittest to put the stamp of the cosmos upon the advance of the Anglo-Americans to world dominion over the lesser breeds.[7]

For the Japanese, concerned with East-West competition, Social Darwinism had added appeal: it not only made Japan the equal of Western nations by judging all on an objective scale of societal development (i.e., whoever survived was the fittest regardless of racial stock), but held out the hope that, if the Japanese as a people were in fact superior, Japan was on an inevitable course toward national strength and, ultimately, imperial power. Japanese Westernizers and Japan purists alike could find solace in a philosophy that at once offered universal principles and gave free rein to the nationalistic impulse. Furthermore, the personal doctrine of Social Darwinism, which set store by frugality and self-discipline, fit in as much with traditional Japanese values as it did with the prevailing ethic in Protestant America.[8] So, too, in the Japanese mind, was there comfort in the Spencerian vision of the ties between individual and community: the individual must exert his energies to the utmost, not for personal fulfillment, but for the benefit of the species. "In Social Darwinism no one was free to 'be himself,' only to be what survived."[9]

Where Spencer's views were at variance with Japanese reality, namely, his belief that the state must not play an intrusive role in regulating industry, establishing tariffs, supervising schools, and the like, Japanese thinkers simply rewrote Spencer. For example, Katō Hiroyuki, apostle of Social Darwinism in Japan, paid greater heed to Spencer's depiction of the nationalistic phase—the so-called militant society—in the progress of the human species than did Spencer himself, who regarded this stage as but a way station in the ascent to the peaceful industrial society at the pinnacle of civilization.

During these years when the Chinese students were immersing themselves in Japanese intellectual life, Darwin's *On the Origin of Species* remained on the best-seller lists, and Dr. Katō continued to hold forth with Social Darwinist interpretations of Japan's national growth pattern.[10] In a pamphlet issued in April 1904 entitled *The Destiny of Russia and Japan from an Evolutionary Point of View*, for instance, Katō pronounced that higher types of civilization—namely, Japan—were slated to vanquish lower types should conflict occur between them. Katō was joined in his use of evolutionary language by other contemporary scholars who focused their attention on the phenomenon of imperialism, a topic of much discussion and debate in Japan at the turn of the century. As the *Japan Weekly Mail* observed in February 1902: "The fever of imperialism has evidently reached Japan if we may judge from the lengthy discussions which are taking place on the subject in certain journals."[11]

A leading apologist for imperialism was Ukita Kazutami, whose book *Teikoku-shugi* (Imperialism) appeared just after the Sino-Japanese War and was translated into Chinese soon after.[12] In 1901–2, Ukita and like-minded colleagues brought the topic before a larger forum in a series of lengthy articles in *Kokumin Shimbun*. Imperialism was presented here not only as part of a worldview that posited an irresistible historical course for the human species after the fashion of Katō or, later, Lenin, but as a policy issue that demanded public attention. In other words, whether or not Japan "went imperialist" was not an inevitability, but a matter of wise policy. Thus while Katō and others paid heed to an evolutionist premise—"Competition and the survival of the fittest are nature's law"[13]—they also urged the Japanese public to "take a stand" on the matter, since imperialism had been "adopted" already by Russia, England, Germany, and America, and "it look[ed] as if it would be the leading principle of the twentieth century." As policy, imperialism could be the means to the end of gaining national strength, not simply the inescapable result of such strength: "If we are desirous of more real union among ourselves, there is no better principle for a nation to rally around than this modern imperialism. As a promoter of the very highest state interests there is nothing to be compared to it."[14]

Still, Japan could choose what style of imperialism to adopt. It should not, in Ukita's view, be in the aggressive military mode of Germany, but of the civilizing-mission variety, in which enlightenment, emigration, and colonization would move peacefully hand in hand.

The Imperialism we wish to see promoted must begin with educating our people so that wherever they may go or in whatever capacity they may act they may produce a good impression on outsiders. We should like to see our nationals flocking to neighboring countries, engaging in diverse enterprises, and carrying the light of civilization wherever they go. A mere military imperialism is bound to be comparatively short-lived.[15]

This was part of Ukita's reply to those who attacked imperialism on the grounds that it was immoral. He also refuted the charge that imperialism interfered with individual freedom by pointing to the United States and England, imperialist nations that were the fountainhead of individual liberties as well.[16] Besides—and this part of the answer harked back to deterministic themes—ultimately an infinitely superior cosmopolitan morality would replace parochial national versions: "The nations are all engaged in furthering the same great ends—the development and amelioration of the world, materially, mentally, and morally in every case preparing the way for the higher principle of cosmopolitanism."[17]

Facets of a Student Political Outlook

Much like their counterparts today, the Chinese overseas students at the turn of the century were drawn to the diversity of "modern" ideas, technologies, and institutions in the world outside China. Exposed to what was new, they wanted not only to learn but to inform the Chinese reading public; clear evidence of this is the zeal with which students who had just acquired a working knowledge of Japanese took up translation. As we saw in Chapter 4, both the Translation Society and the Hunan Translation Society, in conjunction with their literary organs, were responsible for bringing out a long list of articles and books on topics Western and Japanese, either translations of Japanese originals or retranslations of foreign works. Even when students branched out from pure translation to magazines of discussion and political commentary, translations from the Japanese press continued as a regular feature.

In the manner of Liang Ch'i-ch'ao's magazines, *Public Opinion* and *New People's Miscellany*, the student publications were dedicated to disseminating new information and ideas. The provincial magazines had an eclectic character something like today's *Reader's Digest*. An essay on the Russian anarchist movement might be followed by articles on the Meiji banking system, the functioning of the brain, and the relationship of geography to national character. A count of topics in *Tide of Chekiang* and *Kiangsu* shows two-thirds of all articles falling in a miscellaneous category covering such things as current events, the arts, and science, as opposed to purely political themes.[18]

In writing style, the students, again like Liang Ch'i-ch'ao, favored a straightforward, colloquial variant of Chinese, sometimes boringly repetitive but seldom obscure. They also turned their efforts to popularizing a new terminology, the language of liberalism, socialism, more often of nationalism and Social Darwinism. It was just at the turn of the century that such terms as "race" (*chung-tsu*), "people" or "nation" (*min-tsu*), "society" (*she-hui*), "international" (*kuo-chi*), "capital" (*tzu-pen*), "economics" (*ching-chi*), and "imperialism" (*ti-kuo chu-i*) were being introduced or reintroduced into Chinese from Japanese.[19] This fascinating process of language accommodation to new vocabulary may be shown in the example of the term *ko-ming*, now rendered "revolution." In its original definition in the Chinese historical lexicon, "ko-ming" literally meant "cutting off the skin of the Mandate of Heaven" or, by extension, "revoking the Divine Right," and thus referred to a form of dynastic change. When nineteenth-century Japanese were searching for an equivalent for the Western word "revolution," the ancient term "ko-ming," or *kakumei* in Japanese, was chosen as closest in meaning and given new definitional value. In turn, after the Japanese fashion, it was adopted by Chinese writers. Much of the students' literary energy was directed to coming to grips with new terminology, defining it, explaining it to the Chinese public.

If the student articles sometimes have the quality of school reports or only partially understood class notes, it is probably because they were just that. If they seem short on analysis and long on emotional fervor, that, too, fits in with the youthful embrace of new ideas. In short, the students were not innovators but popularizers. Their magazines, like those of Liang Ch'i-ch'ao and other mainland publications, supplied the small (two to four million) but rapidly growing literate public with much new information—simplified versions of Western political concepts, descriptions of institutions, reportage on current events—along with polemics against Manchu rule. The net effect was a growing public awareness of the world outside China and alternatives to the traditional cultural-political order.[20]

PERSPECTIVES ON NATIONAL POWER

The fascination of China's intellectuals and students with Western technology and ideas was no mere faddism, but an attempt to account for the origins of Western power made manifest in Europe's expansion into Asia. The burning question—still unanswered—was how China, too, could become a modern nation, capable of checking the West and competing on the international scene. At the turn of the century, Social Darwinism with its credo of human progress seemed at least to explain the rules of the game. To the Chinese students, as to Meiji modernizers concerned with Japan's development, the evolutionist vision had special appeal: China and Japan could be compared with the West not in terms of some arbitrary standard of worth, but according to their performance on an objective and all-inclusive scale of societal development. For Chinese, the theory offered a rationale—the struggle for survival—for resisting both the West and Japan as representatives of the highest form of nationalist development, imperialism.

Whether writing on political theory or foreign policy, the students used the language of Social Darwinism, the terms and concepts of international competition. They adopted a comparative outlook, seeking to derive lessons from the experience of Western nations and Japan. Though from our perspective much of the discussion seems schoolboyish and simplistic, to the contemporary Chinese reader, this undoubtedly seemed a fresh and exciting way to view world politics. The typical article on nationalism described the growth of civilization as a struggle for survival in which more intelligent peoples (*min-tsu*) bested the less endowed, who fell by the wayside in the process of natural selection. The superior peoples— Germans, English, Italians, Japanese, in the student example—were those capable of generating national spirit (*kuo-hun*), a driving faith in their cultural distinctiveness, historical continuity, and irresistible advance toward unity. Nationalism (*min-tsu chu-i*), in the student definition, was the force that "unites those of the same race, segregating aliens, thereby creating a nation-state [*kuo-chia*] of a single people."[21]

Once formed, a nation must grow and expand in order to keep its place in the ranks of the fittest. "If a race [*chung*] is not able to unify, it will not become a nation and the race will perish. If a nation is incapable of further consolidation, it will no longer constitute a nation; it will perish and the race will follow it to destruction."[22] The nations of Europe, student writers informed their readers, had demonstrated a continued capacity for growth and, therefore, survival. The nineteenth century witnessed the will to national power on the part of the European peoples. Nations emerged; constitutional governments were set up. Tempered into strong stuff in the struggle for nationhood, Europeans had the drive to advance in science, communications, and industry. As a better life was achieved, population and production increased. The capitalist element (*tzu-pen chia*) within each nation, in search of new markets, set its sights on colonization abroad. "The magnitude of natural forces pushes [the nation] on this inevitable course."[23]

The drive toward foreign expansion, the prime indicator of ongoing national strength, implied a strong military establishment. This, in the minds of student writers, was a feature to laud, not deplore. Thus, students wrote admiringly of Germany precisely because it could boast a well-stocked arsenal and a citizenry thoroughly imbued with military spirit. The Japanese, too, were cited for their willingness to take up arms to defend the nation. By contrast, complained one writer, dying for one's country seemed a concept alien to Chinese thinking. Reform in the Chinese setting, another asserted, must include both the training of a professional military and the promotion of military virtues among the populace generally, so that each citizen would consider it his duty to defend the nation in time of crisis.[24]

An effective military capability acting to facilitate the export of capital marked the highest stage of nationalist development, imperialism. "Imperialism has nationalism as its father and the tide of economic expansion as its mother."[25] Delving more deeply into the subject, the writer of an article with the heady title "A Discussion of the Development of Imperialism and the Course of the World in the Twentieth Century" found the roots of imperialism in the advancement of science, the expansion of racial groups, the inability of the strong and the weak to co-exist, and the revolutions that had allowed countries to gain Great-Power status. In the case of science, readers were told, advances among European nations led to improved means of production, which in turn led to surpluses. Hence these nations sought an expanded market for their goods; they turned to foreign areas such as China and staked out spheres of influence.[26]

Imperialism would prove to be the dominating force of the twentieth century, students forecast, echoing the sentiments of Meiji writers. However, student writers departed from their Meiji mentors in one respect: they spent less time discussing the "whether or not to" of imperialism as policy. Student writers showed a general lack of interest in such questions as the fate of individual rights in an imperialist era, questions troubling certain Meiji intellectuals. For Chinese students, wondering about the morality of it all probably seemed quite beside the point, if not blatantly hypocritical. For them, China's very survival was the critical issue. And given current political realities—the ascendancy of Western nations and the rise of Japan—survival necessarily seemed to mean progress along similar paths to vigorous nationalism and, finally, imperialism. The Social Darwinist model in its simplest outlines was an accepted premise, not arguable theory, a descriptive tool to render more comprehensible the intricacies of international relations.

In these terms, the Far Eastern Question was projected as a struggle-for-survival drama played among the Powers, with China at center stage. "When China became the great market in the commercial war among the Powers, the Powers introduced capital in order to exploit commercial-industrial advantages either by opening up China's resources, or by demanding rights to lay railroads, or by extorting the right to exploit mines. And the so-called peaceful war becomes ever more severe."[27]

Reflecting the extent to which foreign policy had become a matter of public concern in late Ch'ing China, numerous student writers focused on the comparative policies of the Powers, describing the manner of their convergence on the Pacific region. A typical account, entitled "The Pacific Area in the Twentieth Century," identified Great Britain as the first nation to make a major push into the Pacific, stamping its colonial pattern initially on Australia and New Zealand, then extending its influence to Hong Kong, the Yangtze Valley, and the port of Weihaiwei. Britain's present protestations of faith in the integrity of China, the student writer warned, belied a keen desire to equal Russian gains there.[28] The United States, then Germany, had followed the British model of developing trade, securing concessions and colonies, and promoting the growth of sea power to protect their interests. The United States and Russia would emerge as the two major powers in the twentieth century, predicted another student writer, the United States as the dominant commercial nation, Russia on the basis of its military might.[29] The French, in the student view, were less aggressive imperialists, the reasons for this being slower population growth and an all-too-pleasant life at home.[30] But Japan was as enterprising as the most ambitious of its imperialist colleagues. Proving its mettle in the Sino-Japanese War and the Boxer uprising, Japan in a two-front Asia policy was seeking to establish Fukien as a sphere of influence and to secure Korea against a Russian southward advance.[31]

If ever there was a case of distrust and hostility, it was in the Chinese students' attitude toward Russia and its imperialist designs; this, of course, clearly mirrored the feelings of Meiji Japanese. Chinese foreign policy was much in error, student writers warned, to bank on the Anglo-Japanese alliance as the sole bulwark against the Russian advance, for the Russians were wily operators. Picking up on national character themes, one article depicted Russia's tactics in the domain of foreign policy as a direct projection of its people's personality traits, chief among them deviousness or opportunism (*yin*), tenaciousness (*nai*), and flexibility (*jou*). For example, students saw evidence of Russian *yin* in the aftermath of the Boxer incident, when Russia slipped an invasion force into Manchuria while the Powers were preoccupied with securing Peking. Again, the young writers accused Russia of opportunism in initiating military moves against the Balkans while world concern was focused on the Manchurian problem.[32] They would have agreed with a prominent journalist writing in 1980: "It is the Soviet style . . . to move with sudden stealth and to move massively for the shock effect, throwing adversaries on their heels with little recourse but to protest and accept the fait accompli."[33]

This attitude, colored by Japanese press and public opinion, was energetically expressed in the course of the anti-Russia movement of 1903. Here the issue was clear-cut. Russia was encroaching on Chinese territory; Russia therefore received the immediate brunt of anti-imperialist sentiment. As Russia and Japan hovered on the brink of war, the students were in a dilemma about what posture they—and China—should take. After all, Japan, too, had been identified as an imperialist power. And in August 1903, as Russo-Japanese negotiations over the Manchurian crisis began, students reminded readers that Japan was acting in its own self-interest in threatening to oust the Russians from Manchuria. Its motive was not pure friendship for China.[34] In any case, said the student writers, China stood to lose no matter what the outcome of war between Japan and Russia. If Russia won, Japan would seek compensation in South China; even with Japan the victor, Russia still would demand a favorable settlement in the North.[35]

Yet for several reasons the students favored alliance with Japan over neutrality. For one thing, as they saw it, a Japanese victory seemed likely in the impending war with Russia. An official pledge of support for Japan prewar would surely gain China a better position at the bargaining table than passive neutrality. For another thing, aligning with Japan in a showdown with the Russian aggressors seemed a more honorable course than policies of watchful waiting or continued appeasement. This, as we saw in Chapter 6, was the major argument of the anti-Russia protesters. Finally, for many students, the racial argument had a convincing sound.

The coming war, it was asserted, was not the usual international conflict, but represented a struggle between the yellow and white races. And Japan at this juncture was the standard bearer of the yellow race, the sole Asian nation fully awake to the dangers of the white peril, yet sanguine about its leadership role: "Japan, through unrelenting effort, hopes to defeat the white race in the world of the future."[36] But even as student writers echoed the common culture themes currently popular among Japanese, they stressed the crucial role China must play in the victory of Asian peoples. "Japan's territory is small, its people few, and despite wholehearted efforts, [Japan] is barely able to hold its own with the white race, thereby to preserve the yellow race. Therefore, the continued existence of the yellow race bears a close relationship to the fortunes—rise or decline, order or chaos—of our fatherland."[37] In racial "we-they" terms, then, China was duty-bound to cast its lot with Japan. In fact, in February, as war began, reports circulated that large numbers of students had subscribed to the Japanese war fund and had even requested the Japanese government for permission to join the Japanese army as volunteers.[38] When Japan began recording victories over Russia in the spring of 1904, Chinese students wrote admiringly of Japan's achievements since the Meiji Restoration. Japan's military superiority, they said, demonstrated the capabilities of an Asian nation; it showed as well the efficacy of constitutional government over autocratic rule.[39]

This rising tide of popularity was not enough to dispel an undercurrent of distrust of Japan's ultimate motives. In fact, the new evidence of Japanese power soon contributed to a heightening fear in student circles of Japanese imperialist designs. We saw in the previous chapter how quick the students were to cry discrimination, how sure they were, even the moderates, that self-interest was the sole dictate of Japan's China policy. Thus, while students called for joint Sino-Japanese action against Russia and made passing mention of yellow peoples versus the whites, they did not extend this to a vision of Asian alliance. They never embraced pan-Asianism as Liang Ch'i-ch'ao did for a while and as Sun Yat-sen did for a lifetime.

China's Weakness and Its Causes

The agonizing question for turn-of-the-century Chinese trying to understand world politics from a Social Darwinist perspective was why China had deviated from the national-imperialist model, why it had failed to develop the kind of economic-military complex that allowed Japan to compete with the West. After all, China, like Japan, had faced the relentless Western push into Asia, an external threat that, according to evolutionary theory, should have acted as a unifying force creating the foundation for national power.[40] As a British author of the 1920's, Rodney Gilbert, put it succinctly in the title of his book: *What's Wrong with China?*

In searching for answers, the student writers turned not to institutional, economic, or geopolitical factors—they lacked the analytical skills for that—but to Chinese tradition, national character, and the kinds of personal-moral concerns familiar from their Confucian upbringing. One thing wrong with China, most agreed, was a tendency toward passivity and servility in the Chinese personality that almost invited foreign encroachment. The Chinese, one writer asserted, too easily assumed the posture of "docile citizens": the unresisting populace that greeted the allied armies entering Peking after the Boxer siege, the ready collaborators with the Russians in Manchuria.[41] The Russian army, a writer for *Kiangsu* informed readers, had even been able to recruit Chinese soldiers to serve in its occupying force.[42] The Chinese government saw advantages in this docility as well; it used "obedient people," in contrast to "rebellious people," as a term of praise for those willing to suffer silently the cruelties of autocratic rule.[43] Subservience, in the student view, was a disease permeating every aspect of Chinese life:

Scholars are slaves to book learning, those who worship wealth are slaves to money, the people are at the mercy of officials, youths are servile before their teachers, wives are in bondage to their husbands, sons are slaves to their fathers, and [all] are subservient to an autocratic ruler and in the iron grip of an alien race.[44]

A related character deficiency working to the advantage of intruding foreigners was the tendency to put self or private interests above the welfare of the community at large. As the student writers saw it, the concept of public spirit was lacking in Chinese tradition. People thought of China not as "my China" but as the ruler's China; they did not see the fate of the nation as a personal concern. The basic error, said the young writers, lay in considering private and public as contradictory terms, whereas they were, in fact, complementary, with the sense of privateness or special interests both preceding and generating public spiritedness.[45]

Other writers focused on the China-as-culture versus China-as-nation theme, identifying the lack of national consciousness as another thing "wrong" with China. An article on the role of the military in the modern nation state made the following claim, not without a note of cynicism:

A nation that loves war reaps the fruits of battle; a nation that abhors war is brought to the calamity of defeat. A nation that enjoys killing is looked up to by others; one that abstains from killing is plundered by others. A national military [system] creates a citizenry possessed of a bellicose spirit, thereby ensuring that the nation exists with peace in the region. A country that demeans its military and esteems the genteel arts is not able to take a commanding position as a nation and protect the rights of its citizens. [An example is China], an ancient country with a civilization thousands of years old. Various Tungusic-Manchu peoples on its northern borders, mounting forays unparalleled in their use of daring and ruthless tactics, galloped their horses over the mainland and destroyed it. Millions of their officials and concubines were in command in the Chinese territory, subjugating children and officials of our race, [treating them] as slaves and animals. That our race was visited by this acute misfortune, which had not happened in the hundred years previous, was due to the fact that [China's] military men at that time, in all their knowledge, years of service, and proven abilities, had never been imbued with the concept of nationhood.[46]

The ambivalence felt by Chinese youth toward China-as-culture shows forth in this passage. Theirs was by no means a full-scale attack on China's cultural heritage. There was nothing in the student magazines of 1903 to parallel the uncompromising "down with Confucius" spirit activating the May Fourth generation. To the contrary, in many instances, China's heritage was stressed as a positive element in national development, and the Chinese were taken to task for—unlike the Japanese—failing to pay it sufficient heed.[47] The writer of the above article, for example, cited the need to glorify the heroes of Chinese history as an emotional stimulus to the spread of nationalism.[48] Other writers held up Chinese civilization as second to none; the Chou dynasty, a writer for *Kiangsu* argued, was characterized by freedom and diversity of thought and an original penetrating scholarship on a par with the intellectual output of present-day Europe and America.[49]

China's mistake was a failure to be selective about what elements of its tradition to preserve, and what to cull out. The development of national consciousness, claimed a Chekiang student, depended on discarding negative attitudes from the past, such as passivity and an insensitivity to public interests. The frustration students felt at being part of "old" China facing the "modern" West is typified in the following avowal: "Foreigners upbraid us, saying that we lack [a sense] of community, calling us an outworn empire, and speaking about the peculiar characteristics of the Chinese. I hate their words, but for all that, I cannot help being shamed by them."[50]

What added salt to the wound was that the foreigners so contemptuous of China and the Chinese included the Japanese. Many of the articles from the Japanese press that student journalists chose to translate for their readers hammered the themes of Chinese political immaturity, lack of patriotism, irresponsibility, and general spinelessness.[51] As brought out earlier, the students' self-image as Chinese was molded in large part by seeing themselves through Meiji Japanese eyes.

Manchu Politics and Politicians

In their disposition to cast off certain elements of Chinese tradition and personality, the students in Japan were much in accord with Yen Fu and particularly Liang Ch'i-ch'ao and his notion of a "new people," a breed of Chinese who would combine the best of the old and the new. When it came to assigning blame for China's present deficiencies, however, the students departed from both Yen, who looked to weaknesses in Chinese scholarship, and Liang, who saw the problem in institutions rather than men and thus came to espouse a kind of constitutionalism designed to accommodate rather than eliminate the Manchu ruling group. For the student activists, short on political experience and inclined toward simple solutions, responsibility for China's condition lay full square on the Manchus. Rid China of the Manchus, they argued in the pages of their Tokyo publications, and the march toward national strength could begin.

This uncompromising anti-Manchuism, which in concert with anti-imperialism became the driving force of Chinese nationalism before 1911, rested on the basic premise that the Manchus were political incompetents, incapable of preventing or, worse still, guilty of aiding and abetting foreign encroachment in China. Since capitulation to Great Power dominance was seen as the major cause of arrested national development in the contemporary world, it followed that China's very survival necessitated removing the Manchus and their style of government. These were the arguments advanced by the Seijō and anti-Russia protesters. The Seijō disturbances, it will be recalled, turned on the issue of the competence and integrity of the Manchu representative to Japan, Ts'ai Chün. Ts'ai's professional abilities were brought into question over his inept handling of the matter of school entrance requirements. What really aroused student antagonism, however, was the minister's eventual resort to the Japanese police to oust Chinese student demonstrators from their own legation. Ts'ai at once became a symbol of a Manchu betrayal of the Chinese or, in more neutral terms, of a Manchu failure to represent Chinese interests in confrontations with foreigners.

Similar doubts about the Manchus were raised in the course of the anti-Russia movement. Students who had hoped initially and with apparent sincerity to enlist government support for their stand against Russia viewed the suspicious response to their overtures as evidence of political ineptitude and weakness at best; at worst, as unpatriotic. When China declared neutrality on the eve of the Russo-Japanese War, the students launched undisguised attacks on the Manchus, "the old Buddha and other high-class slaves."[52] The neutrality policy, in their view, simply reflected fear on the part of the Manchu rulers that China's direct involvement in war might mean a loss of personal wealth and power. It was not a policy based on national concerns.[53]

Certain officials were repeatedly singled out for attack in the pages of the student magazines. Han officials in the employ of the Ch'ing government—Ts'ai Chün, Chang Chih-tung, Yuan Shih-k'ai—were labeled Manchu slaves. Ts'ai, accused of personal and political misconduct, was held responsible for the allegedly diminishing respect accorded Chinese diplomats by their Japanese counterparts.[54] Chang and Yuan were charged with being more concerned with the rewards of office than with the lives of their fellow countrymen.[55] Yuan was further portrayed as a great dissembler, playing both the liberal and the conservative game so as to enhance his own power.[56] The Court favorite Jung-lu appeared as the epitome of the villainous Manchu bureaucrat, a man who would sell out his country for personal gain.[57] Implicit if not explicit in all of the attacks on prominent officials was that such men had no sense of patriotism, that the all-consuming nature of their own selfish aims rendered them incapable of thinking in broadly national or statesmanlike terms.

The attack on the Manchus as political incompetents was reinforced by a related attempt to get them on racial grounds. Increasingly in 1903, especially at the time of the *Su pao* trial, which gave publicity to the racist writings of Chang Ping-lin and Tsou Jung, articles penned by students deploring Manchu ineffectiveness in the face of foreign encroachment stressed as well the racial division between Han and Manchu. The Manchus, student writers took pains to point out, were essentially an inferior breed, a product of a primitive nomadic existence in which "religion and government were lacking, [in which] they did not know how to cultivate the soil and, only skilled in riding and shooting, spent their days in pursuit of wild animals."[58] Forever tainted by their rude origins, the Manchus remained, as one writer put it, "monkeys dressed in men's clothing."[59] In fact, by mid-1903 the word "Manchus" seldom appeared without a derogatory label attached to it—"barbarians," "aliens," "thieves"—or without mention made of the unbridgeable gap and implacable hatred between the Han people and the Manchu rulers. Still, there is nothing in the student discussions to parallel the elaborate attempt to demonstrate racial difference found in Chang Ping-lin's "In Refutation of K'ang Yu-wei." The student writers had accepted Chang's proof, as it were, and incorporated it into what evolutionary theory had taught them about struggles among races and nations.

Yet racially inferior as the Manchus were, in the student view, they had the wherewithal—the fighting ability and ruthless disregard for human life that marked them as barbarians in the first place—to sweep down from the north and wrest control of China from a weakened Ming dynasty. The Manchus as oppressors was the guise they most often appeared in in the pages of the student magazines. The Han Chinese victims, "sunk in a hell on earth," had become over several generations politically inert and ignorant of their own racial superiority.[60] In this sense, the Manchus were held partly responsible for the Chinese character defects the students so deplored: slavishness, passivity, and blind conservatism.

The portrait of the Manchus as oppressors took on vivid immediacy when the students cited their own grievances. Protesting the attempt to suppress the Association for National Military Education, one young writer charged, "The government has used the Association for National Military Education, an organization of the students abroad, to test its butcher knife, which will swiftly kill the people of our country."[61] Another article describing government attempts to restrict the activities of returned students spoke of the "pernicious plans of this murderous, traitorous government."[62] Again, the Manchu regime was described as cruel, rapacious, and arbitrary in the flogging to death of the journalist Shen Chin, an event as we saw in Chapter 8 that affected the course of the *Su pao* case. The major student objection was that Shen was summarily executed without trial.[63] Significantly enough, the argument here, as in various other protests over the government's denial of a free press,[64] was in terms of Western standards of justice and freedom. The Manchus were charged with both racial difference and the inability to approximate Western ideals of progress.

The student writers argued that Manchu acts of repression—from the persecution of the 1898 reformers to the recent restrictions on anti-Russia protesters—had forged the Han Chinese into revolutionaries.[65] "Alas! The Manchu government is daily arresting and executing people. In the future, it will effect a total transformation of 400 million Han Chinese into revolutionary groups that will resist its rule. I pity [the Manchus'] stupidity; I take joy in their stupidity."[66] Likewise, students forecast that Manchu pressure on secret societies would serve to unite them, and that attempts to silence the opposition press would intensify radical expression.[67] In the same vein, a *Kiangsu* article claimed that Chang Chih-tung's stringency toward the self-supporting student was a boon to the revolutionary cause. It would persuade the constitutionalists among the Chinese students in Japan of the reasonableness of the revolutionaries' outcry against Manchu repression.[68] Elsewhere, an emotional appeal was made for revolution over constitutionalism: "To die begging for freedom is not as good as dying in a struggle for freedom. Ineffectual talk about a constitution and in the end not escaping death is not as good as carrying out revolution and perhaps not dying in vain."[69]

Examples from Western history (and occasionally, from Japanese) invited the discussion of revolution in China. When speaking of evading literary controls and defying autocracy, the students drew on the experience of the Russian nihilists.[70] When describing the tide of revolution in China as resembling "the irresistible force of 10,000 horses galloping abreast," they cited the French Revolution.[71]

China's Political Options

Student discourse on revolution was more fervent than analytical. The focus was more on the *necessity* of revolution, with its presumed cleansing effect on Chinese society, than on how to accomplish it. When strategy and tactics were brought up at all, it was generally done by indirection. An article on Russia's Nihilist Party, for example, cites the critical importance of grass-roots organization to building an effective revolutionary power base, and the reader knows that the lesson is meant to apply to the Chinese case as well. Discussions of China's economy and social structure, the setting for the revolutionary event, were also short of real analysis or even good descriptive material. In fact, the majority of articles on economics, commerce, and industry were not on China at all, but on other countries and their economic institutions—a history of banking in Meiji Japan, for example—or somewhat theoretical pieces that looked at the international scene through Social Darwinian eyes.

Of course, there were occasional and interesting exceptions in which writers ventured a more penetrating look into Chinese realities. An entry in the final issue of *Kiangsu* offered a breakdown of Kiangsu society by trades and occupations, arguing that the province's rich resources should be developed by local entrepreneurs exclusively, without resort to foreign investment.[72] Another article, featuring the Kiangsu silk industry, attempted to account for China's declining share of the world market. The writer recommended that the Chinese government undertake research and development efforts in sericulture based on Japan's experience.[73] Japan, not surprisingly, was often the point of comparison in discussions of China's economy. A writer for *Hupei Students Circle*, calling for the expansion of agricultural and industrial output in order to reduce foreign imports, lauded the Japanese example in agricultural education: Japan had a college of agricultural science, each prefecture and district had established an agricultural preparatory school, and over 100 magazines were available in the agricultural field.[74]

Social analysis of China's vast population was given short shrift in the pages of the student magazines. To be sure, there were repeated references to "the Chinese people," "the Han Chinese," and "China's 400 millions" as the ultimate beneficiaries of change, but just who these people were, what their present condition was, precisely how their lives might be altered for the better, and so forth were not issues confronted by student writers. Articles in the agriculture sections tended to focus not on the peasant economy and institutions but on the need for technical advances in soil science, fertilizer application, cropping patterns, and the like.[75]

This inattention to sociological factors is hardly surprising. Far from being trained social scientists, the student writers, with rare exceptions, lacked even an elementary knowledge of peasant life. As noted in Chapter 3, the average Chinese student in Japan was a child of the educated elite; his family might be down on its fortunes, but it was hardly part of the toiling peasant masses. When the student writers registered a concern for China's 400 millions, it was out of a conviction that the sole route to national strength for China lay in galvanizing the wills of each and every Chinese. The focus was on political education, rather than economic and social development. Yet, even here, there was nothing of the "to the people" impulse that took Chinese students and intellectuals into the countryside two decades later.

The students were only slightly more expansive and explicit in their vision of a post-revolutionary world. Presumably, the evils of Manchu rule would disappear with the Manchus. The Han Chinese, freed from the oppression of domestic aliens, would be able to withstand their external enemies by bringing their national potential to full flower. Such demanding questions as what system of government would best be able to translate these nationalistic goals into policy and projects and what the respective roles of state and individual would be in the future body politic were not fully addressed in student writings. The largely descriptive student essays stopped short at a simplistic, idealized attachment to representative institutions and an occasional nod in favor of a republican form of government.

To cite a typical example, a writer for *Kiangsu*, in a review of modern political forms, postulated that mankind was evolving toward ever more democratic forms of government—in other words, the more democratic, the better. Thus, among the constitutional monarchies, Britain ranked first because its laws and institutions had been created in response to a demand from below and its representative body exercised strong authority. Germany was in second place: though its constitution was a grant from the throne rather than a prize wrested by the masses, the fact that constitutional revisions were the responsibility of a representative institution allowed a respectable score on the democratic scale. Japan fell below Germany because the Meiji Constitution was not only handed down from above but depended on imperial consent for revision. While each of these political models had something to recommend it, the *Kiangsu* writer called for a leap forward within the decade to what he considered the ultimate in representative government, democracy on the American model. He forecast for China: "The twentieth century will see the emergence of an integrated and complete national republic."[76]

Student writings on current political issues and structures usually followed the same format as this *Kiangsu* article. That is, the focus was on informing readers about the functioning of modern political institutions in a general sense, with China brought in only by inference or in an occasional aside. Deriving lessons for China in this fashion, from a review of the workings of politics in other national settings, was less a conscious technique than a reflection of most students' inability to offer comprehensive analyses of China's political present and, from this, to prescribe a program of political change. A second feature of many of the student writings on political themes is that the example of Japan, parvenu to the ranks of modernized nations, was cited as giving comforting certainty to China's own future success. Here was the same refrain, oft-repeated from the 1880's on, that if Japan, poorly endowed and weak, could make the grade, China, with its wealth of natural and human resources, undoubtedly would achieve more in less time.

An article in *Tide of Chekiang* on the role of the Japanese political parties exhibits both features. Japan, the author reminded his readers at the outset, had emerged on the world scene as a first-class nation boasting a constitutional system of government; this was in marked contrast to China, sadly lacking in political maturity and failing to rank among the Powers. Nevertheless, Japan had not enjoyed its constitutional status for long—a mere thirteen years, during which time parliament had met seventeen times and been dissolved six. Yet in the fierce clashes between the government's party (the Seiyūkai), supporter of the principle of transcendental cabinets, and the popular parties, working toward the establishment of responsible party cabinets, the *Tide of Chekiang* writer saw evidence of the future good health of the Japanese political system. This interpretation and, at a general level, the view that, in politics, evolution toward higher forms implied a steady move toward more broadly representative or democratic systems, come out in the following passage:

Now the progressive development of a nation's politics generally depends on whether victory in decisive [political] battles rests with the government's party or the opposition parties; this becomes an index of the waxing or waning of popular rights. If victory rests with the government's party, then the power of the government advances a step, and popular rights are correspondingly reduced. If the opposition parties emerge victorious, then the power of political parties rises slightly, and popular rights are likewise expanded. Therefore, if a government takes an action or issues an order and its citizens do not dare to offer a counterproposal or to strongly disagree or to attack offending points, we must conclude that they lack political consciousness. For citizens to develop political consciousness, whenever a government action [is perceived as being] in any way disadvantageous to them, they must whip up their emotions, join shoulders in the fight, and in this way put such pressure on the old government that it will not be able to carry out its harsh measures, and that will be the end of it. This is why, in the case of the world's civilized nations, as the clashes between the government's party and the opposition parties inevitably grow more frequent and intense, [that nation's] politics necessarily moves to a more advanced level. Conversely, then, if there is increasing accommodation and harmony between the government's party and opposition parties, politics unavoidably stagnates and becomes incapable of improvement. Thus it is that if we wish to judge the state of progress of a nation's politics, we must first take a look at the maturity of [that] nation's political parties.[77]

Japanese institutional development along Western lines was the usual model cited in student discussions of how to get the Chinese people to participate in their own political life. An article in *Tide of Chekiang* on the topic of local self-government, for example, took as its starting point the views of Rudolph von Gneist, German political scientist and adviser to the Japanese leader Itō Hirobumi. Quoting von Gneist, the writer pointed out that in order to develop public spirit, people must be encouraged to participate in public affairs, particularly in local governing bodies. Broadening participation at the local level had the advantages of relieving the central government of some of its burdens, especially tax collection, and training people in the workings of representative government as preparation for establishing a national constitution. Local self-government had some precedent in China, the writer claimed, in the gentry's traditional role in local affairs. But it was Japan's recent experience in setting up local assemblies and advisory committees in each prefecture and district that provided lessons in modern political systems.[78] As a *Kiangsu* writer explained: "Once the Japanese decided to establish constitutional government, they first promulgated the system of local self-government to give people practice in the functions of government and thereby mature their capabilities. . . . If our people wish to attain popular rights, they must take note of the system of self-government."[79]

Reformers and Revolutionaries Reconsidered

This discussion of local self-government, with its argument that participation at the grass-roots level was the key to political progress for Chinese, might well have come from the pen of Liang Ch'i-ch'ao or even Yen Fu. Declaring for revolution, in other words, ultimately put distance between the overseas students and Liang but could not erase the fact that the Meiji environment had helped make enthusiastic liberals of them all. Thus it was that the student writers, for all their revolutionary outbursts, often sounded more like propagandists for a liberal cause, pure and simple. Consistently, they professed their beliefs in human progress, in the strength of representative government, in the obligation of modern governments to work for the happiness of the greatest number, and in intellectual freedom as the right of every citizen of a civilized nation. They were true believers in the notion that Chinese should have more control over their lives.

In the liberal vein, too, students spoke often and long about the necessity of expanding educational opportunity and what we today would call curriculum development. Not only mass education but women's education excited student comment. The goal in all this, said one writer citing Herbert Spencer, was producing a generation of self-reliant citizens.[80] Along with their call for increased school enrollments, students argued for curriculum changes: placing greater emphasis on the study of economics, on technical education,

on scientific research, and on all the other elements that characterized the broad-based liberal arts programs available in Western
school systems.[81] A Chinese education, they said, continued to be
deficient: it gave too much emphasis to moral cultivation, too little
to the cultivation of the intellect, the acquisition of modern knowledge, and physical education. Japan, the inevitable contrast, had
made great strides in revamping its educational system, wisely following the advice of Western educators, whose works were all available in Japanese translation.[82]

Introducing curriculum changes and gaining acceptance of the
principle that everyone, whatever his origins, had the right to an
education were not considered ends in themselves but means to an
end. The ultimate objective of educational reform was to develop
national consciousness, power, and prestige. This line of thought, as
brought out in Chapter 2, was shared by Chinese official observers
of the contemporary Japanese educational scene and certainly by
Meiji educators themselves.

The overseas students, of course, were not simply advocates of
this approach. They were its emerging products, youth schooled in
modern subjects, politically aware, vitally concerned about the well-
being of the Chinese people. They were, at the same time, a transitional group, questioning traditional values, yet not prepared to
abandon Tradition—inclined, instead, to revitalize elements of it in
their glorification of a distinctly Han heritage. The overseas students were, in short, living examples of Liang's "new people."

And they saw themselves as such. A striking characteristic of the
Chinese students was their perception of their uniqueness as a
group. Like the Communist cadres three decades later, they viewed
themselves as the most politically conscious members of Chinese
society and therefore qualified to act as agents of enlightenment and
change. Their own role was to be the element of free will in an otherwise deterministic world, in which superior races evolved into
strong nations and imperialist powers, leaving the less fit to fall into
oblivion. The role of political vanguard, students claimed, was
theirs by default: the upper class eschewed intellectual pursuits in
favor of money and power; for the lower classes, toiling for the basic
necessities of life left no time for the realm of ideas. It was thus the
burden of the middle class, or that small element within it not com-
promised by a desire for personal gain, to awaken the Chinese people
to a realization of their perilous balance between imminent nationhood and total destruction.[83] "Twentieth-century China is the stu-

dents' China. If China rises, it is only because they made it rise; if China is destroyed, it is because they let it be destroyed."[84]

This affirmation of responsibility was motivated by a deep concern for China's ability to survive in the face of multiple foreign pressures, coupled with the conviction that only a broad public commitment to political change could give it the strength to do so. In this attitude, reformers and revolutionaries alike spoke with the voice of modern nationalism. Nationalists all, they shared also the liberal mentality referred to above. They believed in democratic participation through representative institutions, increased educational opportunity, freedom of thought and discussion. They subscribed to the logic of Social Darwinist notions of human progress. The idea that political and economic development proceeded in a series of stages, that the modernization process obeyed objective, universal laws, appealed particularly to those driven to catch up and catch up quickly. It allowed for a great leap forward, the optimistic vision put forth by Chinese political critics from Huang Tsun-hsien to the radical students, that China possessed the requisite human and natural resources to become a major world power overnight.

Yet, ironically, new perspectives on China gained from the vantage point of a vigorous Japan brought the final disillusionment with Manchu rule. Lessons from history reinforced critical judgments of the Manchus, but current events sounded the original indictment, exposing the Manchus' deference to the Powers, laying them open to charges of expropriating for themselves, rather than developing for all, China's resource potential.

Obviously, overseas students parted company with a generation of reformers when they began to preach revolution, call for a republic, and flirt with terrorist techniques.[85] Uncompromising anti-Manchuism and anti-imperialism became the new look in Chinese nationalism. Nevertheless, until 1905 at least, student revolutionaries were not acting from a well-developed ideology or platform, or even a unified plan of action. After 1905 and the appearance of the TMH, differences in revolutionary and reformist positions were more clearly articulated, especially in the series of debates between Liang Ch'i-ch'ao and the staff of the TMH's *Min pao*. Even so, there was enough common ground in their liberal assumptions for reformers to slip in easily under the revolutionary label when the time came in 1911.

Student participation in politics, under whatever label, signaled a deeper public involvement in the problems facing China and increased the likelihood of nontraditional solutions. To look at it from a slightly different angle, what the students had to say reflected the mood of this increasingly concerned public. The *North China Herald*'s wise commentary on the *Su pao* defendants could apply equally well to the student writers: "What these men have said in print is what thousands have probably said in conversation."[86]

The students were more than spokesmen. They were propagandists. Faced with the West's claim to a monopoly on truth, supported by an evident monopoly on power, they half accepted, half chafed against it, urging their countrymen to rally in pursuit of new strength. In student hands, such themes as the survival of the fittest became political slogans, a way to sound a warning to the Chinese public about China's possible fate. All in all, student writings represent an expanded use of journalism to inform, to educate, to popularize, to publicize. Where the student writers contributed to the widening alienation between the Chinese public and the regime in power was in bringing before a larger forum the messages of liberalism, a new nationalism sharply focused on anti-Manchu and anti-imperialist themes, and finally, revolution.

Epilogue

THE FIRST DECADE of the study-in-Japan program projects fast-moving images of change: a few effete-looking Chinese graduates queued and gowned versus rows of Chinese schoolboys smartly outfitted in Japanese school uniforms; lonely youngsters counseled by kindly Japanese professors versus thousands of protesting students erecting strike barriers and shouting anti-Japanese slogans; proud recipients of clan or provincial scholarships versus intense youths constructing bombs to hurl at Ch'ing officials. On this group of young people were pinned the hopes of reform-minded pragmatists within the Ch'ing regime and Japanese politicians committed to "Asia for the Asians" notions of solidarity against the West. In the immediate aftermath of the Sino-Japanese War, support for study in Japan seemed wise policy from both sides. Chinese students would get low-cost lessons in how to modernize, how to plumb the secrets of Western technology and institutions. Their new skills, applied at home, would strengthen China and safeguard the regime in power. For Japan, nagging concerns over national security would be eased by a strengthened China able to hold off the West. There was the promise of long-term benefits, too, of producing a generation of pro-Japanese Chinese leaders. (That was the hope if not the outcome.)

The 15,000 or so Chinese students who swept in the open door to Meiji Japan in the years 1895–1905 played out a different drama. For them, exposure to the outside world created the desire to participate in China's political life, to help chart out a course for China's future. For them, Asia for the Asians came to mean China for the Chinese, national independence and the strength to ward off all imperialists of whatever origin. In this key decade were articulated dilemmas still plaguing China's rulers and ruled nearly a century later: how to compete in the international community, how far to open the door to Western influences, how to relate to an economically strong Japan, how much political reform should accompany technological-economic change, what balance to strike between central authority and local participation, and, above all, how to become modern and remain distinctively Chinese.

The Maturing of a Nationalist Mentality

Chapters 1 and 2 documented how study in Japan emerged as a rational, well-conceived policy measure endorsed by both the Chinese and the Japanese government. That the Ch'ing regime failed to enlist the support of its youth educated in Japan was due in part to the difficulties in administering this overseas program once it was launched. The initial screening process was obviously inadequate, since some of those selected for government scholarship aid were already involved in anti-government activities. Nor was there any overall plan, beyond the issuance of degree equivalencies, for using the skills of the newly trained once they returned to China; this very likely was a source of frustration for many. Of course, within five years, there was not so much a program to administer as a migration to control. Allowing privately funded students to study abroad might have made financial sense from the government's standpoint, but it raised the difficult problem of supervision. Increasingly, it was the disaffected who chose to go to Japan. Whether the Ch'ing government could have done things differently in this first-ever study-abroad program is debatable: it had neither the experience nor a workable system of controls.

Probably the gravest miscalculation on the part of Ch'ing officials like Chang Chih-tung was that it was possible to send students to Japan with blinders on, their field of vision limited to new techniques, unaware of the larger panorama of change. They may also have assumed that the Meiji government, as host, would keep the visiting students under tight rein. In fact, Meiji Japan, absolutist state though it was, provided a far more liberal environment than Ch'ing China. Simply being away from home gave Chinese youths additional freedoms. More important, it gave them new perspectives on themselves as Chinese, on China's prospects for development, and on how to meet the challenge of the West.

What they learned about themselves as Chinese was harsh: that the rest of the world, including their "backward" cousins the Japanese, viewed them with a condescending eye as substandard on the scale of modern civilization, in the same category, incredibly, with the Koreans. It came as a shock to Chinese youth abroad for the first time to find themselves regarded as quaintly outmoded by the average Japanese. It came as a rude awakening, too, to see the China of the Japanese press, a nation seemingly without recourse before the bullying of the Foreign Powers.

For our understanding of later dissension within the T'ung-meng Hui over what posture to take toward Japan, it is important to note that the unpleasantries the students faced in everyday encounters with Japanese were not experienced by Sun Yat-sen. For one thing, Sun was already a veteran expatriate when he first arrived in Japan and well aware of what the rest of the world thought of China. For another, he had Japanese friends in Tokyo who took care of such practical matters as house rental for him, unlike the students, who had to fend for themselves in often trying circumstances. Sun's bitter memories of discrimination against Chinese derived from his experiences in Britain, not Japan.[1] For the Chinese students, Japanese arrogance was what was most immediately offensive, and they came to harbor a resentment toward the Japanese as a people and a distrust of Japan's aims that Sun did not share.

Still, there were lessons to be learned from a firsthand look at a successfully modernizing nation. Pride, of course, prevented unqualified admiration. Student commentaries on Japan were laced with "anything you can do, I can do better" phrases and an occasional scornful aside to the effect that Japan's achievements were but a pale reflection of the Western original. Yet even in these emotional reactions, one detects the almost reflexive turn to self-analysis, the key question being why China was weak compared with the West and, now, with Japan as well.

What came out of the students' attempts to understand Japan's success, to analyze the ingredients of national power, was nothing so grand as a new ideology, but it was a new outlook involving a common set of assumptions. First, the overseas students—as represented by the writers among them—came to believe that changes of some kind in orthodox modes of thinking were fundamental to the building of a new China. The most telling feature of student journalism was not its originality but the receptiveness it showed to a range of views and theories available through Japanese selection, translation, and interpretation. This new cosmopolitanism was not pursuit of knowledge for its own sake. Always, in any discourse, the overriding question was: how does this piece of information apply to the China problem? In this sense, the quest for outside ideas sprang from a nationalist impulse, a concern for ensuring China's continued existence and independence as a nation.

What the Chinese students chose to highlight from that unwieldy category "Western learning"—and this reflected the Meiji selective bias—were current politics, theories of institution building, and comparative history, rather than purely technical, scientific subjects or the arts and literature. Of course, there were science articles and short stories in the student magazines, but almost invariably an essay on biology would have a Social Darwinist slant, and a story a political moral. A second common assumption growing out of this intense political interest was that to ensure national survival, the Chinese people must gain more control over their lives. A constitutional government of some kind, representative assemblies, local self-government, political parties, were all subscribed to by the great majority of students. Not only that, the students' very actions demonstrated a commitment to political organization and propaganda, as well as to free expression, as essential mechanisms for change.

Faith in human progress, the Social Darwinist belief that the races of mankind were ever changing for the better, or at least the stronger, was a third assumption accepted by students. Japan's success, the Meiji economic miracle that the students knew firsthand, seemed to verify the Spencerian interpretation. A people that had been lagging behind might catch up if the proper stimulus were given—in this case, creation of an intense nationalism. What made this notion particularly appealing was the presumption of most Chinese, beginning with K'ang Yu-wei in the 1880's, that for all Japan's remarkable strides along the road to modernization, China, possessed of superior human and material resources, could surely outstrip this small island neighbor. China, too, could take the nationalist-imperialist path, the better to stave off foreign interference. Given credibility by Western theory, the "leap forward" conviction now became part of the outlook of a generation of potential new leaders.

As for how this was to be brought about, the students acted from the belief that they, as the modern-educated and politically conscious, must be in the vanguard of change, that they could make the difference in propelling China forward to a position of international strength. This element of voluntarism had obvious links to both the past and the future—to the scholar-official with his deep sense of community responsibility and to the Communist cadre, free agent in an otherwise deterministic picture.

Assumptions about the desirability of change and how it should necessarily proceed involved taking a critical view of China's past. As noted in Chapter 9, turn-of-the-century students did not take an anti-traditional stance. Theirs was a preliminary step in reevaluating Chinese traditional modes of thinking and behaving, sometimes echoing Japanese criticisms, often pointing to the bedrock strengths of China's as-yet-to-be-tapped resources. In other words, they accepted the need to grapple with the issue without going the "down with Confucius" route of the May Fourth generation.

This common body of assumptions—that openness to Western ideas was the only way to stay competitive, that an improved future required increased popular participation in national life and the elimination of foreign interference, that China was capable of a "great leap forward" under the guidance of the newly educated, that Chinese tradition must be reassessed—is at the core of China's modern nationalist mentality and has supplied the thematic background to its ongoing revolution during the twentieth century. During the first stage, 1900–1911, a consensus developed among the reform-minded that China's survival in a world of rapacious imperialists could only be ensured by a fundamental change in political form. The Manchus moved to open up the decision-making process from 1905 on, but they were too halfhearted about it, too concerned with maintaining their hold on power to satisfy the expectations of China's new social elites—student-intellectuals, businessmen, and modern-trained military. Increasingly, the question posed was not whether a fundamental change in dynastic system would occur, but when.

Returned Students and the Revolution of 1911

We have seen how, in a few short years, the students in Japan, in the grip of a new Chinese nationalism, matured in political vision and developed the tactics of expressing dissent. The creation of national organizations, the issuing of propaganda and polemical writing specifically designed to influence public opinion, the launching of protest demonstrations, with such features as the sit-in, the school strike, even the protest suicide, were all part of the overseas students' repertoire after 1900. By 1903–4, some activists, working with sympathetic elements within schools and secret societies in China, had engineered the formation of small, regionally based revolutionary organizations, notably the China Rise Society and the Restoration Society. At the end of 1905, Chinese students in Japan lent the force of their numbers to the first all-China revolutionary organization, the T'ung-meng Hui, which for all its problems with factionalism, gave new focus to anti-Ch'ing energies.

Evidence suggests that students, particularly Japan-educated students, continued to be the dominant element in the TMH, accounting for as much as 90 percent of the total membership in the years 1905–7 and supplying the core leadership. Student names were prominent on the roster of those involved in the numerous insurrectionary and terrorist activities sponsored by the TMH and other known groups before 1911—uprisings in Szechuan, Kwangtung, and Yunnan in 1907–8, for example—and in the 1911 Revolution itself.[2] In their professional life, many of these returned students cum revolutionaries held teaching posts in the new schools or officer's rank in the new army: an estimated 10 percent of the 1,000 or so listed members of the TMH in 1906 were graduates of Japan's Army Officers School.[3] They thus found themselves strategically placed to sign up new revolutionary recruits and pass on dissident literature, much of it originating in the thirty-odd publications sponsored by Chinese students in Tokyo in the period 1906–11.[4] Another group of returned students reportedly involved in anti-government activities of one kind or another were those employed as clerks and accountants in new businesses along the coast, where their extracurricular pursuits were difficult to track.[5] The net effect of the reabsorption of these student radicals was that dissidence spread like an infection, quietly, rapidly, defying Ch'ing attempts at a cure.[6]

Of course, not all in the Japan group put themselves on the TMH active list. Some pursued with serious intent careers in the new technical and financial agencies the Ch'ing government established after 1901 as part of its strategy of reforming the central administration. Of the 1,388 foreign-educated students who passed the new civil service examinations in the years 1906–11, fully 90 percent (1,252) were graduates of Japanese institutions. Sixty-five percent were graduates in politics and law; 22 percent had specialized in commerce and industry. Most were given official appointments, some under the Ministry of Education as directors of new institutions, many others as bank managers or department heads within the Ministry of Commerce and Ministry of Posts and Communications. However, even this group, which appeared to put professional above political interests, was viewed with suspicion by Ch'ing conservatives as TMH-inspired uprisings involving a large returned student element followed one after another in the years 1906–8.[7]

Another important segment of the Japan-educated group figured prominently in the provincial assemblies organized in 1909 as part of the government-sanctioned move toward constitutional rule. Additional research, cross-checking assembly lists with records of Japan graduates, is needed to determine the percentages of returned students in each provincial assembly, but available evidence suggests that the proportion was fairly high. For example, a background check of sixty-six of the 112 Chekiang assemblymen reveals that at least fourteen of them, or 21 percent, had studied in Japan. A number of sources, in addition, cite instances of assembly leaders who were former students in Japan.[8]

In other words, what makes the student migration to Japan a key episode in the drama of the 1911 Revolution is not simply that it produced a relatively small group of avowed revolutionaries. Its real importance lies at a broader level: that it hastened the emergence of a new social force in China, a youthful elite equipped with a modern education and full of nationalist fervor. A safe estimate is that some 20,000 Chinese passed through Japanese halls of learning between 1900 and 1911.[9] Whether these people are termed radicals, revolutionaries, constitutionalists, or moderates, their return meant a significant and sudden swelling of the ranks of the modern-spirited. These Japanese-trained young people, the bulk of them still in their twenties, were reinserted into Chinese life at a time when enrollments in China's expanding school system—public schools offering a modern curriculum—were multiplying at a startling rate. Data on public school attendance indicate roughly a fiftyfold increase between 1903 and 1909, when the figure reached about 1.5 million.[10] Messages about the urgency of political and economic reform were broadcast to receptive ears. As a particularly dramatic example, twenty-five million people are said to have signed petitions in 1910 calling for an early convening of a national representative assembly.[11]

That the Manchus would not survive became ever more apparent after 1905 as insurrection and terrorism increased, the army was rent by subversive activities, merchants complained about foreign economic pressures, and the provincial assemblies with which the Manchus hoped to neutralize leftist opposition demanded more and more decision-making power.[12] The dynasty was not felled by a single revolutionary blow in 1911. It simply crumbled under the weight of a growing national consensus among various elite groups on the need for fundamental change. That is why the 1911 Revolution—much like the Meiji Restoration, and for the same reasons of consensus within the class that traditionally supplied leadership—

involved little bloodshed and few reprisals. There were few enemies of the Revolution.

Japan and the Revolution of 1911

What position did official Japan take in this Revolution, engineered in part by products of its halls of learning? It equivocated, attempted to follow the British lead, toyed with support for a divided China, with a Manchu regime in the North and a republic in the South, and in the end failed to make the gains that a proximity to the scene and its players would seem to have promised. Yet this approach was consistent with Japanese China policy during the decade we have been focusing on. Recall, for example, Japan's behavior during China's reform movement and subsequent coup in 1898, of trying to keep channels open to all political figures, including K'ang Yu-wei, Liang Ch'i-ch'ao, and at the fringes, through the good offices of Miyazaki, Sun Yat-sen. Or again, think of Japan's position in 1900 at the time of the Boxer disturbances, when Japanese China hands from Konoe Atsumaro to Tōyama Mitsuru joined forces in a move to strengthen bonds with China's progressive governors even as top-level army officers were laying plans for a military expedition into Fukien province.[13] In this connection, Japan's official reaction to Sun is also worth noting, not only because he was expelled in 1907, but because he was let into the country in 1905 and even allowed to construct on Japanese soil an organization dedicated to the overthrow of the Ch'ing government.

In short, official Japan in 1911 showed no deviation from previous patterns of behavior: a consistent strategy of seeking to advance a special position in China through tactics that might alternatively be described as flexible or poorly coordinated. The Japanese nonofficial reaction—the press, educators, the business community, such lobbyist organizations as the Tō-A Dōbunkai—to the Revolution needs closer study. Certainly, it has been pointed out often enough that most of the foreigners who played a direct role in the Revolution were Japanese.[14] Yet considering the number of years Sun spent building Japanese contacts and the number of revolutionaries who were Japan-educated, one might wonder why there were so *few* Japanese—less than 150—directly involved. The explanation lies in part in a habitual caution about supporting anti-Ch'ing forces, an attitude more pronounced after 1905, when Japan's priorities in foreign policy were to solidify its contacts with the Powers and to advance its own claims in Korea and Manchuria. Such a scenario assumed a politically stable China—hence greater interest in shoring up the Ch'ing regime and less in establishing links with Chinese dissidents. The Tokyo TMH, though tolerated, was under strict surveillance; student members risked expulsion from school for too active an involvement.[15] At the end of the day, on the issue of personal commitment to China and its Revolution, most Japanese long associated with such concerns showed themselves to be not professional idealists but professional politicians and "Japan-firsters."

Furthermore, the fact that the Japanese who did take an active part were mostly personal followers of Sun Yat-sen's highlights again what was brought out in Chapter 3: namely, that in most cases student contacts with Japanese were limited in variety and extent. Teachers and educators such as Kanō Jigorō and Shimoda Utako were the only points of interaction with students on a day-to-day basis. People like Count Nagaoka kept their distance, stepping in as the need arose to intercede in crisis situations. Prince Konoe, strong advocate of Sino-Japanese political-cultural solidarity, was a more distant figure still in his role of distinguished patron of the Chinese student program. Student contacts with the general public—Japanese students, shopkeepers, landlords—were casual and superficial. Few friendships were formed. To the contrary, contact often produced undisguised hostility both ways, hardly the basis for common cause in revolution. The only area of sympathetic contact between Chinese students and Japanese after 1905 was between members of the *Min pao* staff and certain Japanese leftists who shared an interest in current socialist-anarchist trends.[16]

The Waxing and Waning of Japanese Influence

Factors other than growing hostility toward their Japanese hosts made the lure of Japan less attractive to Chinese students after 1905. For one thing, staying at home and receiving a modern education was increasingly a real possibility. As mentioned earlier, school facilities were rapidly expanding, with enrollments jumping from about 30,000 in 1903 to 1.5 million by 1909. Many of the teachers at these new institutions had been educated abroad, which for some young people was almost as good as—and certainly cheaper than—going overseas themselves. For another thing, for those who still had their sights set on foreign training, other options were available. One was the United States, which in the years after the Russo-Japanese War increasingly assumed the role of Japan's chief rival in the Pacific area, not only for the China market but for the hearts and minds of Chinese. CHINESE DON'T WANT JAPANESE TEACHERS was the lead for a New York *Daily Tribune* story in June 1907. Its thrust was that the Chinese had come to realize that they were getting what they had paid for, that while teachers from Japan could be gotten cheaply, they were correspondingly substandard; the current trend was thus to replace Japanese with Western instructors. This article, promptly translated into Japanese, caused considerable consternation among Japanese educators.[17] Figures for Japanese teachers in China were indeed on the decline, from 461 in 1906 to sixty-three in 1914 and a mere twenty-seven in 1916.[18]

As friendship with China blossomed, Americans warmed to the idea of offering study opportunities to Chinese youth. As the president of the University of Illinois put it: "The Chinese are in many points jealous of the Japanese, and, other things being equal, would often prefer to send their young people to other countries. Among all these countries the United States would be the most natural one to choose."[19] Those sentiments were echoed by other U.S. educators, businessmen, and policy makers and, with President Theodore Roosevelt's backing, the decision was made to establish a scholarship program for Chinese financed by Boxer indemnity funds. The result was a steady increase in numbers of Chinese attending U.S. institutions, from a total of fifty in 1903, to 239 in 1909, to 650 in 1911 and 1,124 in 1918. France, too, played host to considerable numbers of Chinese students financed through various work-study arrangements; by some estimates, the program attracted as many as 6,000 in 1920–21. The British government did not choose to use Boxer funds for scholarships until the 1930's; and the Chinese students studying in Britain never reached more than a couple of hundred until the mid-1940's.[20]

Still, for reasons of both proximity and the pocketbook, substantial numbers of Chinese students continued to enroll in Japanese schools during the entire period from 1911 to the outbreak of the second Sino-Japanese War. Attendance figures for any given year were a barometer of political unrest at home and tension in relations with Japan. For example, virtually all students left Japan at the call to revolution in 1911. This was followed by a reverse flow, so that by 1913 an estimated 2,000 were once again counted on the rolls of Japanese schools. The figure had swelled to 5,000 by 1914 as opposition mounted to Yuan Shih-k'ai's actions to crush the pro-democracy movement at home. As in an earlier day, Japan functioned not only as a center for modern studies, but as a convenient haven for political exiles.

Japan's presentation of the infamous 21 Demands to the Yuan government in 1915 produced an angry student reaction, climaxing in a return-in-a-body movement reminiscent of the 1905 protest. The 21 Demands underwrote Japanese special interests in Shantung, Kwantung, South Manchuria, Inner Mongolia and Fukien, and called for inserting Japanese advisers in key positions in Chinese government agencies. In short, by ultimatum, a quick strike that capitalized on the preoccupation of the Western powers with war in Europe, China was to become a protectorate of Japan.

Two aspects of this notorious event, which did the Sino-Japanese relationship irreparable harm, are relevant to our study of the decade 1895–1905. First, what Marius Jansen aptly terms "guidance by force" had interesting antecedents in turn-of-the-century politics: namely, the presence of Japanese advisers in educational, legal, and military capacities, *and* by Chinese request. Second, Sun Yat-sen's reaction to the Demands again points up how much he and his followers differed in their attitude toward Japan from most of the overseas students. Sun's energies by 1915 were totally consumed by his power struggle with Yuan Shih-k'ai. Some evidence suggests that Sun, eager to capitalize on his special Japanese contacts in his bid to oust Yuan, went so far at one point as to offer Japan even better terms than it was demanding in return for its support.[21] By contrast, those students and revolutionaries who had fled to Tokyo after 1913 to escape Yuan's repressive regime found an aggressive Japan a distasteful alternative and began to return to China. By the time the Sino-Japanese Agreement incorporating most of the Demands was signed in May 1915, as many as 2,000 of the total overseas group of 5,000 had left Japan. Others followed the next year, when news of Yuan's death signaled a more liberal atmosphere at home.[22]

The number of Chinese students in Japan continued to decline until 1920. The year 1918 witnessed another return-in-a-body, by now a standard tactic of protest. This time students were demonstrating against the pro-Japanese stance of the Tuan Ch'i-jui government, which was allegedly striking deals with Japan to provide military bases in North Manchuria and Outer Mongolia. Once back in China, students busied themselves establishing such publications as the *Save-the-Nation Daily* and launching the Young China Association. Student-led demonstrations and boycotts of Japanese goods were carried out in a number of Chinese cities and won the support of merchant groups.[23]

These events were a prelude to the outpouring of anti-Japanese sentiment that marked the May Fourth incident of 1919. Shattered by news from the Paris Peace Conference that Japan had been awarded former German rights in Shantung province, students organized a mass rally to coincide with the fourth anniversary of the 21 Demands. Once again hundreds of Chinese students left Japan for home, this time to join nationwide demonstrations, unprecedented in size, against Japanese aggression in China and the warlord regime that had capitulated to Japan's demands.[24] By the end of 1919, according to a contemporary account, the student group in Japan had shrunk by 80–90 percent in the course of two or three years. Of those who had returned to China, about 40 percent had done so in protest, the other 60 percent because, in the turmoil of warlord politics, fewer scholarships were available for study abroad.[25]

But still students chose to go to Japan. Even after the Manchurian Incident in 1931, a militarist move that made Manchuria a Japanese puppet state, student numbers edged upward. In 1936–37, on the eve of war, Chinese students in Japan numbered 5,000–6,000, the highest level since 1913–14. In part, the buildup of this large a group at the height of anti-Japanese sentiment among Chinese in general reflected a continuation of the curious love-hate relationship in which resentment smoldered beneath the surface of an attraction for an easily accessible modern education. Present, too, was the feeling of know thy enemy: in order to resist Japan and save China, Chinese must penetrate the Japanese psyche. The pocketbook issue also figured large. The exchange rate in 1935 was highly favorable to Chinese visitors.[26]

Not to be overlooked also is the fact that certain Japanese wanted to keep Chinese students coming to Japan. Particularly after 1915, when Japan became a prime target of student protests, Japanese businessmen, politicians, and educators showed concern about their country's waning influence in China. For instance, in 1919 a Japanese businessman made a special grant to the Seijō School for the purpose of encouraging Chinese student enrollments. His immediate motive for the gift stemmed from a visit to the United States, where he had observed Chinese students welcomed with open arms and noted their enthusiastic response to American overtures.[27] This concern about the United States as competitor both politically and culturally in East Asia was intensified at the time of the May Fourth movement, which many Japanese saw as an American-instigated plot to fan the flames of Chinese anti-Japanism. The question of Japan's role in educating Chinese students was considered important enough to be submitted for formal discussion in the Japanese Diet in 1918, then again in sessions 43–45, 1920–22.[28]

There is considerable irony in the fact that once China at last engaged in full-scale war against imperialism, the enemy was Japan, the newest imperialist, the nation that had stepped in to fill the breach after a recession of Western power in the Pacific during the First World War. To be sure, there were those like Wang Ching-wei, former student in Japan, who, claiming allegiance to Sun's true pan-Asianist principles, took the path of collaboration with the Japanese. But for the majority of Chinese, gripped by a resurgent Chinese nationalism, Japan's designs for East Asian community with itself in the lead were unacceptable. Bonds from a shared Asian past provided no restraints in the fundamental clash of national interests.

What all of this suggests is that pragmatism has far outweighed any sense of Asian kinship in shaping China's relationship with Japan, both in that unusual period of harmony, 1895–1905, and today, when Japan is the leading contributor of bilateral assistance to China, and every Chinese taxi driver wants a Toyota. If anything is a holdover from the past, it has been China's consistent concern about its ranking vis-à-vis Japan. Fascination with the Japanese model of development is still tinged with envy, as it has been for a century or more. Witness this complaint in a wall poster of 1977. The figures may differ, but the sentiments are those of our late Ch'ing critics:

In 1957 . . . Japan produced about 10 million tons of steel, approximately the same amount as China. But in 1972, Japan's steel production was more than 100 million tons while ours was only 20 million tons. . . . Does this mean the Chinese people are less intelligent than the Japanese, that we are less diligent? Does it mean that Chinese natural resources are inferior to those of Japan or that our social system is somehow lacking?[29]

Reflections on the Present

Can China catch up with Japan? Steady economic progress after 1979 seemed to portend a rosy future, but a decade later China faltered, slowed by problems of inflation, corruption, and an aging leadership clinging to power through traditional mechanisms of control. The *t'i-yung* dilemma has come to the fore once again: Is it possible to import Western technology and ideas and retain a Chinese "essence"—cultural perspectives and a style of governing that are uniquely Chinese? Is it possible to achieve rapid economic modernization under authoritarian rule—or, conversely, without intense concern for social order—given a billion people and the tremendous diversity that is China today?

The present scene and its players bear an uncanny likeness to turn-of-the-century counterparts. In 1979, as in 1895, the Chinese leadership of its own will opened the door to outside influences and for similar reasons: to bring in new technology that would pull China out of economic stagnation and to strengthen the hand of the regime in power. What we see today is a new set of Chang Chih-tungs and Manchu hard-liners, jockeying for power within the system but in agreement, for the short-term at least, that the "Empress Dowager" and her supporters should retain command over unchanging political institutions. We have, too, a repeat appearance of the K'ang Yu-weis, intellectuals in exile, who have reinterpreted the prevailing political ideology and proposed a blend of old and new. The featured performers, the students, represent as before the hope of the future; their role, according to the official script, is to absorb what is modern and useful—the technology of developed countries—for the sake of economic growth and political stability. And so young people have been encouraged over the past decade, as they were after 1900, to go abroad for study in increasing numbers—18,000 in Japan alone in 1990 and more than 40,000 in the United States—increasingly on their own funds.[30]

The parallels are striking: overseas students forming student unions, writing articles critical of the reform process at home, sponsoring protest demonstrations. It is a reenactment of the scenes of confrontation between China's students and, in the words of the *North China Herald*, "the old fogies in Peking." The reaction of the latter, in the face of mounting radicalism, was to introduce a few incentives—special recognition of Japanese degrees—and, above all, to institute controls. The reaction of top officials in the State Education Commission in 1989 was to propose that China put a screen in its window to the outside word to prevent "flies and worms" from entering freely.[31] It is a statement out of the lexicon of the Ch'ing leadership, perhaps the Empress Dowager herself. The problem at the turn of the century was, as we have seen, that controlling dissident students and noxious foreign influences was impossible.

Before becoming trapped in the too-easy conclusion that revolution is the inevitable climax of this drama starring students in an anti-authoritarian mood, we must note some key differences in China then and now. First, and most important, China's social revolution, the struggle of the past forty years, has brought a crowd of new players to the scene. The nation may still be populous and poor in relative terms, but a much greater percentage of the total population is now literate and informed, and participates in local, if not national, decision making. A 1911-style, elitist, student/intellectual-led revolution that in fact leaves out most of the population is no longer feasible. Second, the student unrest that erupted in 1989 was spearheaded by the students in China, not those overseas,[32] though the latter may play an increasingly important role in the future, given the tightening of controls at home. Third, until now at least, anti-imperialism has not surfaced as a battle cry of youth. Whatever concern there is about foreign influence has come from the leadership itself, in statements, for example, decrying bourgeois liberalization. Fourth, there is nothing comparable now to the anti-Manchu bias of turn-of-the-century youth, though, as we have noted, this ultimately was more political sloganeering than real racial hatred. Finally, until the Tiananmen protest of June 1989, there was no sense of a gathering consensus on the need for fundamental political reform, the kind of oppositionist mood that swept out the Manchus in 1911. The driving force of the decade after 1979 was economic reform, including such profound changes as sanctioning the transfer of private property, and here rulers and ruled appeared to be marching in step.

In the final analysis, history is made by human beings, and human nature is unpredictable. The element of unpredictability is particularly strong in the Chinese setting, where personal relationships still hold sway over the rule of law and institutions. Bearing in mind the hazards of forecasting, we may still find some lessons worth pondering in China's first study-in-Japan experience. To begin with, sending young people overseas for the sole purpose of learning advanced techniques or technology is a risky business from the standpoint of the sender. Inevitably, the foreign student in an advanced country absorbs at least again as much about the prevailing ideologies and institutions in his new setting and begins to compare the workings of his host society with how things operate at home. His outlook and expectations change, making it difficult for him to accept his own society as it is. If "home" is restrictive, repressive, and offers no perceived outlet for his new ideas, the student may become disaffected, a partisan of radical change. This is, in simple terms, what happened in our story. Could there have been an outcome other than total alienation? At some points in the story, for example, we are left with a feeling of missed opportunities, accommodation that might have been possible had it not been for an obsessive fear of dissenting views and a reflexive resistance to change on the part of the old-style Ch'ing bureaucrats clinging to power. We have the same feeling of missed opportunities, of a tragedy that might have been averted, when we review the events of April–June 1989.

At the simplest level, what the Chinese students in Japan were demanding was participation in the political process, a chance to choose, to dissent, and to share in decision making. The parallels with 1989 are unmistakable. Once this demand was articulated, it refused to go away, but boiled up to the surface again and again, culminating finally in the national consensus that ousted the Ch'ing. Yet looking at the 1911 Revolution and its aftermath, and in fact at the past century of revolution in China, leads one to question whether dissent (or, more neutrally, political pluralism) has ever been a workable notion in Chinese politics. Priority has always been given to consensus building, with a special premium placed on ideological conformity, not on the concept of a loyal opposition. The result is vague yearnings for democracy that survive but find no legitimate institutional outlet.

This brings us to a final point well worth keeping in mind, namely, that any long-term solution to problems of succession and systemic change will assuredly be a Chinese solution, the Western *yung* accommodating to the Chinese *t'i*. If history is any guide, the *t'i* itself will change, but slowly, as China, ever self-conscious about the "outside," Western world, seeks its own ideology of economic growth. The impulse of China's modernizing drive is Asia for the Asians still.

Reference Material

Notes

For complete authors' names, titles, and publication data on the works cited in short form in these Notes, see the Bibliography, pp. 265–80. The following abbreviations are used:

CCC	*Che-chiang ch'ao*
CNRS	Sanetō Keishū, *Chūgokujin Nihon ryūgaku shi*
HHKM	*Hsin-hai ko-ming*
HMTP	*Hsin-min ts'ung-pao*
HP	*Hupei hsueh-sheng chieh*
JWM	*Japan Weekly Mail*
KMCCT	*Ko-ming chih ch'ang-tao yü fa-chan*
KMHL	*Ko-ming hsien-lieh hsien-chin chuan*
KMIS	Feng Tzu-yu, *Ko-ming i-shih*
KS	*Kiangsu*
NCH	*North China Herald*
NHR	Sanetō Keishū, *NitChū hi-yūkō no rekishi*
SC	Sanetō Collection, Tokyo Hibiya Library archives
TDK	Tō-A Dōbunkai, *Taishi kaiko roku*

Introduction

1. The standard source for these figures, Sanetō Keishū, calculated a figure of 8,600 for 1905–6. See *CNRS*, pp. 15, 58–60, 87, 107. See also Kuo Mo-jo's estimate, in *CNRS*, p. 143, that from 1896 to 1937 Japan played host to some 300,000 Chinese students. Recent researchers have revised the figures for student totals for various years, but the order of magnitude remains the same. See, for example, Tung Shou-i, pp. 196–97; and Futami and Satō. It is impossible to arrive at a precise figure for any given year, particularly after 1903, since a large number of students were enrolled at more than one school and in a variety of short-term courses.

2. The themes touched on in this paragraph—the emergence of new social groupings as both a response and a further stimulus to economic/political change and the question of state versus elite group power—are examined in a number of recent studies, notably Rankin, *Elite Activism*;

Schoppa, *Chinese Elites and Political Change*; Su Yun-Feng, *Chung-kuo hsien-tai-hua-ti ch'ü-yü yen-chiu*; Bastid-Bruguière, "Currents of Social Change"; Lee and Nathan, "Beginnings of Mass Culture"; and Cohen, "Post-Mao Reforms."

3. By the turn of the century, reform had become an issue in ruling-class politics. MacKinnon, *Power and Politics*, demonstrates convincingly how Yuan Shih-k'ai used reform as a source of power, playing to the interests of both local elites and central officials in pushing through key reform measures. If this piece of adroit political maneuvering also enhanced the centralizing influence of the Dowager and the Court, as MacKinnon suggests, it was short-lived. Though the Court evaded forming a cabinet and managed to "retire" Yuan from his provincial post in 1909, the center was losing out. As Fincher, p. 93, observes, "For all its efforts at reform since 1901, the Qing government was still slipping behind in its race with disorder when it published the Nine Year Plan in 1908."

4. For a particularly insightful discussion of *ch'ing-i*, see Kwong. Kwong argues that while the *ch'ing-i* practitioners of the 1890's differed from their earlier counterparts in being more outspoken in their critical commentaries on current affairs, they did not form any kind of coherent opposition force that might be identified as a faction or party, and still "posed as defenders of moral principles and government integrity" (p. 234). It is possible, he notes, that the Ch'ing government actually encouraged the *ch'ing-i*–style show of critical opinion as a means of developing a consensus on major decisions.

5. There are some exceptions, notably Marius Jansen and Joshua Fogel. Jansen's many and extremely important contributions over the last 35 years include *The Japanese and Sun Yat-sen*; "Japanese Views of China During the Meiji Period"; *Japan and China*; and the chapter in the *Cambridge History of China*, "Japan and the Revolution of 1911." See also Jansen's article "Chung-kuo liu-Jih hsueh-yun yü Hsin-hai ko-ming-ti kuan-hsi" in *Chi-nien Hsin-hai ko-ming ch'i-shih chou-nien hsueh-shu t'ao-lun-hui lun-wen-chi*, which footnotes an earlier unpublished version of the present work, "Asia for the Asians." Fogel has recently published a succession of excellent works, two of which are unique feats of scholarship embracing both cultures: *Politics and Sinology* and *Nakae Ushikichi in China*. Two recent articles, also extremely useful, are Douglas Reynolds's "Chinese Area Studies in Prewar China" and "A Golden Decade Forgotten."

Chapter 1

1. Y. C. Wang, *Chinese Intellectuals*, pp. 42–49; LaFargue, pp. 33–34.

2. Toby, *State and Diplomacy*, suggests that the Tokugawa *sakoku* (closed-country) style of foreign policy was not so much reactive and isolationist as a calculated attempt to assert Japan's independence in Asia by establishing Japan as an alternative power center competing with the Sino-centric world order.

3. Sanetō, *Kindai NitChū kōshō shiwa*, pp. 55–65. On *Senzai Maru* traveler Takasugi Shinsaku's reactions to China of the 1860's, see Harootunian, pp. 33–35; and Fogel, *Politics and Sinology*, pp. 14–15. Takasugi, sent to Shanghai in 1862 as part of a mission to investigate trade prospects, came

away from his trip despairing of China's impoverishment and inability to resist Western incursions, and conscious of the lessons Japan might derive from China's inept handling of the foreign powers.

4. Wang Hsiang-jung, pp. 22–23, points out that before the Meiji period Western culture was transmitted to Japan via books in Chinese. Japanese of the period were not well versed in Western languages except for some Dutch. For a full discussion of the *kangaku-kokugaku* issue, see Webb, pp. 142, 168, 209–10. Harootunian, p. 29, argues that in the late Tokugawa period China lost its central place as the subject of discussion for Japanese thinkers and in this sense "disappeared from discourse."

5. Chow Jen Hwa, pp. 90–99; Sanetō, *Meiji Nisshi*, pp. 99–102, 166–69, 359–62; *CNRS*, p. 243.

6. Kamachi, pp. 26–27, 32–33, 104–9; Sanetō, *Meiji Nisshi*, translation of Ho Ju-chang's diary, pp. 5–64.

7. Hō Takushū, pp. 176–77. Huang's contacts included the prominent scholars Oka Senjin, and Shigeno Yasutsugu and Meiji political leaders Itō Hirobumi and Ōkuma Shigenobu.

8. Particularly in the years after the Satsuma Rebellion in 1877, when the noble failure of rebels in service of traditional values fired up the imaginations of many, sales of Chinese books—the K'ang-hsi dictionary, the *Tso-chuan*—increased markedly (Sanetō, *Meiji Nisshi*, pp. 158–60).

9. Kamachi, pp. 50–52.

10. Sanetō, *Kindai NitChū*, pp. 143–235; Fogel, *Politics and Sinology*, p. 11. Oka's disillusionment with China dated from this China trip, particularly the discovery that the noted scholar Wang T'ao, whom he met in Shanghai, was an opium smoker. Japan, Oka concluded, needed to "secede from" (*ridatsu*) China.

11. Sanetō, *Meiji Nisshi*, pp. 104, 167.

12. Ibid., pp. 113–47.

13. Ibid., pp. 180, 362–69. For additional examples of Chinese commentaries on Japanese barbarisms and Japan's slavish imitation of the West, see Cohen, *Between Tradition and Modernity*, p. 106.

14. Sanetō, *Meiji Nisshi*, pp. 134–36, 169, 193. Yao's eight-volume work, the first modern Chinese geography of Japan, drew much of its material from a Japanese Army Ministry publication on the subject. One may assume that as an official publication of the Tsungli Yamen, it enjoyed wide use.

15. Ibid., pp. 181–82.

16. Ibid., p. 195.

17. Kennedy, p. 89; Chirol, *Far Eastern Question*, pp. 138, 140. One official who argued that China should not underestimate Japan was Li Shu-ch'ang, China's minister to Japan in the years 1882–84. In impassioned memorandums to his home government, he argued that war should be averted. As Sino-Japanese relations deteriorated, so, apparently, did Li's mental health, and he died in 1897, two years after retiring to his native Kweichow (Sanetō, *Meiji Nisshi*, pp. 106–7). Liu Hsueh-chao and Fang Ta-lun, pp. 131–32, point out that both the "attack Japan" and the "ally with Japan" groups were contemptuous of Japan.

18. Except as otherwise noted, all quotations are from Hō Takashū. Sanetō is of the opinion that substantial portions of Huang's highly influential

compendium were actually translations from a variety of Japanese works. Huang himself mentions having consulted over 200 sources, as well as expending eight or nine years' effort on the 40-volume work, which he completed in 1887. (Sanetō, *Meiji Nisshi*, pp. 135–36.) See also Kamachi, p. 50.

19. Hō Takashū, p. 179.

20. Cited in Cohen, *Between Tradition and Modernity*, pp. 105–6.

21. Hō Takashū, pp. 178–79.

22. Ibid., pp. 174–75.

23. Cited in Cohen, *Between Tradition and Modernity*, p. 107.

24. Hō Takashū, p. 154.

25. Cited in Pyle, p. 149.

26. Pyle, p. 152.

27. The arrival in Tokyo in 1878 of the new Chinese minister, the first envoy since the Restoration, was the occasion for forming a Sino-Japanese group called the Shin-A Kai (Promote Asia Society). This was superseded by the Kō-A Kai. See TDK, 1: 674–75, Kokuryūkai, 1: 414–16; and Satō.

28. Kokuryūkai, 1: 417–19; TDK, 1: 676–78; Nakayama, 8: 83.

29. Kokuryūkai, 3: 561–63; Okamoto, p. 27.

30. Kokuryūkai, 1: 337–42; 3: 658–60; TDK, 2: 1–12; Tō-A Dōbun Shoin, pp. 3–4.

31. Kokuryūkai, 1: 326; Jansen, "Japanese Views."

32. *Tō-A Dōbun Shoin*, p. 4.

33. Kokuryūkai, 1: 332–35, 397–98, 400–404, 3:609–11; *Tō-A Shoin*, pp. 6, 10–13; TDK, 1: 700–701; Jansen, "Japanese Views," pp. 185–86.

34. For an excellent and provocative reassessment of K'ang Yu-wei's role in the Hundred Days Reform, see Kwong. Kwong argues (1) that the reforms did not incorporate any really radical innovations; and (2) that the inspiration for the Hundred Days came from a range of diverse sources, not simply K'ang and his colleagues.

35. Clearly, for a man of Chang's vision, *t'i-yung* was not rigid formula but merely a guideline for action. In practice, Chang's educational policy even in the 1880's and certainly postwar shows great flexibility in what was admitted under the rubric Western learning; Chang, after all, was instrumental in dismantling the civil service examination system. Nevertheless, *t'i-yung* at bottom did imply a kind of cultural separatism between what was new, reformist, and Western and what was traditional, unchanging, and Chinese, and a determination to preserve as much of the Chinese *t'i* intact as possible.

36. Chang Yü-fa, *Chung-kuo hsien-tai cheng-chih-shih lun*, p. 15, points out that K'ang advocated both Western *t'i* and Western *yung*.

37. Chang Yü-fa, *Li-hsien tuan-t'i*, pp. 179–98, 190–99; Hō Takushū, p. 155.

38. Quoted in Hō Takushū, p. 158.

39. Ibid., pp. 159–60. For an interesting assessment of K'ang's document on Japan, see Kwong, pp. 192–94. The author points out that it is not known how the Emperor reacted to the document.

40. Ayers, pp. 105, 139–42, 150; Lo Jung-pang, p. 43; Bays, pp. 42–45, 48, 108.

41. Shu Hsin-ch'eng, pp. 41–48.

42. Ibid., pp. 24–26; CNRS, p. 49.

43. Hō Takushū, pp. 163–64.

44. Wang Shu-huai, pp. 152–53. For an account of the China specialist Col. Kamio Kōshin's visit with Chang Chih-tung in Hupei in 1897 to discuss Sino-Japanese contacts, see TDK, 2: 256–59; and Kokuryūkai, 3: 243–44. On Utsunomiya Tarō, who contacted Chang and Liu K'un-i in early 1898, see TDK, 2: 797–99; and Kokuryūkai, 3: 390–91. Reportedly, Chang replied in "same race, same culture" terms when Kamio advanced arguments about Asian solidarity against the whites. For a detailed discussion of Chang's postwar contacts with Japanese, see Kobayashi, pp. 4–5. Kobayashi notes that Chang was inclined to look to Japan for assistance because he was annoyed by the arrogance of German instructors. Also, note in *CNRS*, p. 207, that Utsunomiya and Fukushima Yasumasa made overtures to Chang Chih-tung, Liu K'un-i, and Yuan Shih-k'ai, urging them to send students to Japan for military training. It is interesting, as Kobayashi points out, that all these contacts were being made at the provincial/local rather than the central level.

45. By 1898, Chang Chih-tung, Liu K'un-i, Ch'en Pao-chen, and other officials who in the immediate postwar years had favored an alliance with Russia to control Japan had become sanguine about the possibilities of détente with Japan. The Tsungli Yamen nevertheless could not be sold on the idea of an alliance with England and Japan; too much suspicion of Anglo-Japanese motives existed, coupled with uncertainty about the effectiveness of such an alliance in the event of a Russian threat. (Wang Shu-huai, pp. 154–55, 157–67.)

46. Shu Hsin-ch'eng, pp. 50–51; Ayers, p. 14; Ch'iao Chih-ch'iang, pp. 116–17; Tung Shou-i, pp. 202–4.

47. *JWM*, Feb. 22, 1902, p. 207.

48. Ibid.

49. *TDK*, 2: 888. For a similar statement, see *Tō-A Dōbun Shoin*, p. 16. Contemporary Western observers discussed the prospect of Japanese regional dominance under the heading "Asia for the Asiatics" or "the Orient for the Orientals." See, for example, Henry Norman, pp. 398–99, and Millard, p. 47.

50. *TDK*, 1: 679; *Tō-A Dōbun Shoin*, pp. 16–17; *Konoe nikki*, 2: 147, supplementary vol.: 401–2.

51. *Konoe nikki*, 2: 175; Kokuryūkai, 1: 610; Jansen, *Japanese and Sun*, p. 37; *Tō-A Dōbun Shoin*, p. 17; Kokuryūkurabu, p. 179.

52. For a full treatment of the origins and range of activities of the Tō-A Dōbunkai, see Reynolds, "Chinese Area Studies."

53. *Konoe nikki*, 2: 83–84. Until his death in January 1904, Konoe Atsumaro (b. 1863), president of the TDK, worked actively with people like Nezu Hajime to determine its policies and projects. He was regarded as an influential figure by a number of leading Chinese of the day: he held talks with Chinese governors-general in his capacity as TDK president, and was approached for aid by K'ang Yu-wei and Liang Ch'i-ch'ao directly and Sun Yat-sen indirectly through Miyazaki. Konoe's diary is an extremely useful source on Meiji politics and Sino-Japanese relations. Konoe may have edited his accounts, but the last entry is dated March 1903, *before* Japan's victory in the Russo-Japanese War or the rise to prominence of Sun Yat-sen and his group. Thus the reader is given a genuine picture of how liberal nationalists

like Konoe assessed such figures as K'ang, Liang, and Sun and progressive Chinese officials such as Chang Chih-tung who were instrumental in promoting the study abroad program.

54. For a complete list of members, see TDK, 1: 682–83.

55. Nakayama, 10: 308–9.

56. Konoe offers a clarifying footnote at this point, saying the question in his mind was that, even if the Dowager was ousted, who was to say whether this would mean the Emperor's return to power or the establishment of a republic (*Konoe nikki*, 2: 195–97).

57. Ibid., pp. 247, 292–94. See also Miyazaki, pp. 127–31, 247, n. 31, on K'ang's attempts to set up a place of exile in Japan.

58. *Konoe nikki*, 2: 456.

59. Ibid., pp. 426, 456.

60. On Konoe's contacts with and comments on Miyazaki, see ibid., pp. 123, 426, 427, 434, and 3: 259. For Miyazaki's biography, see Kokuryūkai, 3: 684.

61. On TDK activities during the Boxer disturbances, see *Konoe nikki*, 3: 184–85, 199, 201–2, 208–9, 211, 213, 237, 248, 266, and 4: 229.

62. Jansen, *Japanese and Sun*, pp. 106–7.

63. *Konoe nikki*, 2: 455.

64. For references to the Nanking school and its later incarnation, the Tō-A Dōbun Shoin set up in Shanghai in August 1900, see Reynolds, "Chinese Area Studies; Tō-A Dōbun Shoin, pp. 22–24, 110–66; Kokuryūkai, 3: 755–57; TDK, 1: 707–8; *Konoe nikki*, 2: 489, 514, 529, 3: 117–18, 4: 174, 178, 5: 67–71; and Nakayama, 11: 322. In the period from the first graduating class in 1904 to the 42d and last in 1945, over 4,000 students passed through the Tō-A Dōbun Shoin's three-year course (*Tō-A Dōbun Shoin*, pp. 1, 35). These China experts were particularly active in the fields of diplomacy and research during a most tragic period in Sino-Japanese relations. For examples of their careers, listed by profession, see *Tō-A Dōbun Shoin*, pp. 110–66.

65. *Konoe nikki*, 4: 239–40, 5: 67–71; Nakayama, 11: 369; *JWM*, Nov. 22, 1902, pp. 576–77.

66. For example, Hōsei, Meiji, and Waseda universities set up special divisions for Chinese students in 1904 and 1905. See *CNRS*, pp. 64–75, for a brief overview of schools for Chinese; and Sanetō, *Chūgoku*, pp. 36–102, for a detailed account of the educational programs and student experiences at one of the earliest, the Nikka Gakudō, a private school established in 1898. Another good overview of Japanese schools catering to Chinese is found in Huang Fu-ch'ing, *Ch'ing-mo liu-Jih hsueh-sheng*, pp. 121–46. Also very useful is the shorter assessment in Li Hsi-so, "Hsin-hai ko-ming," pp. 643–47. According to 1907 Japanese Foreign Office records, Chinese students attended 43 institutions (Futami and Satō, p. 104).

67. TDK, 2: 273–76; *CNRS*, p. 65; Matsumoto, p. 13.

68. *CNRS*, pp. 66–67; Matsumoto, pp. 11–12; *Konoe nikki*, 4: 174.

69. Kanō Sensei Denki Hensankai, p. 169 (see pp. 166–68 for details on schooling for the first 13). See also Yokoyama, pp. 158–59 and Sang P'ing, "Liu-Jih hsueh-sheng fa-tuan." Sang argues that the first 13 were not really "students" but interpreter-trainees brought over at the express request of the Chinese minister to Japan, Yü-keng. The Japanese accounts depict them as pioneers in the study-in-Japan program and emphasize the care that was

taken in their training. Certainly the program designed for them included more than language studies. See, for example, Sanetō's interview with one of the 13, T'ang Pao-ngo, in *Kindai Nisshi*, pp. 175–93.

70. Kanō Sensei Denki Hensankai, pp. 176–79; Yokoyama, pp. 210–23.

71. Matsumoto, pp. 6–9; *CNRS*, pp. 67–68.

72. *CNRS*, pp. 93–97; Abe Hiroshi, *NitChū kyōiku*. Abe offers the fullest treatment to date on Japanese teachers in China, including names, numbers, contract terms, and courses. On the subject of Japanese assistance to China, the *Japan Weekly Mail* of Sept. 27, 1907, reported that 10 Japanese railway engineers had been hired in the construction of the Hankow–Canton railway and concluded: "If Japan has to supply to China teachers for schools and experts for industrial enterprises, the resources of this country will be strained."

73. *CNRS*, p. 88. An American observer, writing in 1906, offers an interesting perspective: "Within the last few years thousands of Japanese, many of them Buddhist priests, have come to China and are now scattered to the remotest parts of the country, where other foreigners are seldom, if ever, seen. Some estimates place the number of these Japanese now in China as high as fifty thousand, although this is probably a mere guess. However, it is certain that thousands of Japanese tradesmen and commercial agents have settled in various remote parts of the empire, adopting the life of the people and often their dress." (Millard, *New Far East*, p. 247.)

74. For a contemporary account of China's receptiveness to hiring Japanese teachers and advisers, see Nakayama, 11: 460. The three Wuhan schools were the Self-Strengthening School, the Agricultural Affairs School, and the Technical School (*Konoe nikki*, 2: 452–53).

75. Hattori was hired on a four-year contract beginning in September 1902. For an account of Hattori's China service, see Abe Hiroshi, *NitChū kyōiku*, pp. 11–14. For additional notations on Hattori's career, see *JWM*, March 21, 1903, p. 317; and Nakayama 10: 146, 175, 392.

76. *JWM*, Sept. 27, 1902, p. 330.

77. "Tō-A Dōbunkai yōshi," pp. 65–66; Abe Hiroshi, *NitChū kyōiku*, pp. 24–26.

78. *JWM*, July 5, 1902, p. 4.

79. *JWM*, Jan. 25, 1902, p. 95.

80. *Konoe nikki*, supplementary vol.: 402; Sanetō, *Shikō*, pp. 153–61, 210; *CNRS*, pp. 89–90.

81. *Konoe nikki*, 4: 82–85. The actual salaries paid to Japanese teachers were much higher, ranging from 200 to 400 yen a month (Abe Hiroshi, *NitChū kyōiku*, p. 26).

82. Sanetō, *Shikō*, pp. 154–56; TDK, 1: 709–10. Sanetō offers a list of names of 56 Japanese teachers at the school, 1901–6, along with information on their backgrounds, length of stay, and later activities. Most teachers spent only a semester at the school. The bulk of them thereafter continued to be involved in China/Manchuria activities as teachers, journalists, and businessmen. In 1906, the school was transferred from Nakajima's management—at his request—to that of the Chihli educational authorities.

83. Sanetō, *Shikō*, pp. 163–68. *JWM*, Sept. 27, 1902, p. 338, reported that 12–15 teachers from the Higher Normal School were to go to China to work in Yuan's schools (Abe Hiroshi, *NitChū kyōiku*, pp. 15–16).

84. *JWM*, Aug. 30, 1902, p. 221. For a collection of Japanese newspaper

accounts of Wu's trip to China (translated into Chinese), see Wu Ju-lun *Tung-yu Jih-pao*; Sanetō, *Shikō*, p. 167; and Sanetō, *Meiji Nisshi*, pp. 340–46.

85. For two of Huang's accounts, see SC 55 and 56.

86. Sanetō, *Shikō*, pp. 158–59; Strand, pp. 66–68.

Chapter 2

1. Ch'iao Chih-ch'iang, pp. 116–19; Abe Hiroshi, "Borrowing from Japan," pp. 60–67.

2. Sanetō, *Meiji Nisshi*, p. 359.

3. Despite this inauspicious beginning, Lo Chen-yü became one of the greatest scholar-antiquarians of his time, well known as the founder of oracle bones study in China.

4. Mu Ch'üan-sun.

5. Chang Chien.

6. Ho Pin-sheng.

7. On Kanō Jigorō, see Yokoyama, *Kanō Sensei den*; *Kanō Sensei Denki Hensankai*; Kanō, *Watakushi*; and Hasegawa, *Kanō Jigorō no kyōiku to shisō*. Kanō had a lifelong passion for judo and always emphasized the importance of physical education in his discussions with the Chinese. See also index entries on Kanō in Nakayama, 15: 91.

8. An attempt to arrange a personal meeting between Shimoda and Tz'u-hsi was made by Hattori Unokichi, who was on assignment in Peking. Hattori, himself much interested in women's education, brought up the issue with Manchu Prince Kung (grandson of the powerful Prince Kung who headed the Tsungli Yamen in 1861), who said that the only way to get some action on the matter was to get the Empress Dowager's support. Hattori could not think of a better spokesperson than Shimoda; the plan was to conduct the meeting with Hattori's wife acting as interpreter. (*Shimoda Utako Sensei den*, pp. 415–16.) See also Ishii. There are numerous articles on both Hattori and Shimoda in Nakayama.

9. Wu Ju-lun, SC 52 and 53. The language of communication with visiting groups was Chinese. The Foreign Ministry routinely assigned interpreters. Of course, virtually all the Japanese with whom the Chinese visitors had appointments had at least a reading knowledge of Chinese. For a biographical sketch of Wu Ju-lun, see Hummel, pp. 870–72.

10. Chu Shou, pp. 38a–40.   11. Chou Hsueh-hsi, intro.

12. Lin Ping-chang, p. 30b.   13. Wang Ching-hsi, p. 43b.

14. Ch'ang Po-wen, p. 16b.   15. Mu Ch'üan-sun, pp. 10a–b.

16. Ch'ang Po-wen, pp. 11a–b.

17. Lin Ping-chang, p. 26b. For an excellent analysis of the Rescript on Education, including an account of the original drafting of the document and its use as a moral basis for Japanese education to the end of the Second World War, see Gluck, pp. 120–27, 146–56.

18. Lin Ping-chang, p. 4b.   19. Ch'ang Po-wen, p. 8b.

20. Lin Ping-chang, p. 4b.   21. Hu Yü-chin, pp. 48–49.

22. Mu Ch'uan-sun, p. 4a.

23. Sanetō, *Kindai NitChū kōshō shiwa*, pp. 243–48.

24. Hu Yü-chin, p. 24.

25. Mu Ch'üan-sun, pp. 10a–b.
26. Hu Yü-chin, p. 106.
27. Wang Ching-hsi, p. 16b.
28. Hu Yü-chin, pp. 41–42.
29. Ch'ang Po-wen, p. 16b.
30. Wu Ju-lun, SC 53, p. 15a.
31. Ibid., pp. 13b–14a.
32. Ibid., p. 10a.
33. Wu Ju-lun, SC 52, p. 20a.
34. Wang Ching-hsi, pp. 51b–52a.
35. Ibid., p. 51b.
36. Chu Shou, p. 40a.
37. Lin Ping-chang, p. 20b.
38. Chang Chien, pp. 23b–24a.
39. Ibid., p. 14b.
40. Ting Yuan-fang, p. 10.
41. Hu Yü-chin, p. 14.
42. Ting Yuan-fang, p. 18.
43. Mu Ch'üan-sun, p. 8a.
44. Hu Yü-chin, p. 29.
45. Ibid., pp. 27–78.
46. Ch'ang Po-wen, p. 16a.
47. Chang Chien, pp. 25b–29b.
48. Hu Yü-chin, pp. 67–70.
49. Wang Ching-hsi, p. 45a.
50. Ibid., p. 45a; Hu Yü-chin, pp. 67–70; Lin Ping-chang, p. 15a; Ling Wen-yuan, pp. 9a–b.
51. Chou Hsueh-hsi, p. 18b.
52. Ibid., postface, p. 1.
53. Hu Yü-chin, pp. 42–43, 116–19.
54. Wang Ching-hsi, p. 17b.
55. Ling Wen-yuan, pp. 12a–b.
56. Chou Hsueh-hsi, p. 7a.
57. Hu Yü-chin, pp. 55–59.
58. Hu Yü-chin, pp. 80–83; Wang Ching-hsi, pp. 48a–49a; Lin Ping-chang, pp. 21b–23a.
59. Hu Yü-chin, pp. 83–84.
60. Ibid., pp. 52–53.
61. Lin Ping-chang, pp. 16a–18b.
62. Chou Hsueh-hsi, pp. 12a–b; Ling Wen-yuan, p. 8b.
63. Kuo Chung-hsiu, p. 26a.
64. See, in this connection, Philip Kuhn's pathbreaking article "Local Self-Government Under the Republic."
65. Chou Hsueh-hsi, intro.
66. Ibid., postface, p. 1.
67. Mu Ch'üan-sun, p. 5a.
68. Chu Shou, p. 41a.
69. Hu Yü-chin, p. 10.
70. Ho Pin-sheng, p. 84.
71. Hu Yü-chin, pp. 105–6.
72. Ibid., pp. 13, 39.
73. Huang Ching, SC 55, pp. 34b–35a.
74. Chang Chien, p. 24a.
75. Chou Hsueh-hsi, p. 13a.
76. Wang Ching-hsi, p. 12b.

Chapter 3

1. *JWM*, Oct. 19, 1901, p. 394.
2. Fang Chao-ying. Ages are given for only 618 of the 663 students.
3. The time between qualification and appointment could stretch out over many years, though *chin-shih* degreeholders had less of a wait than *chü-jen* recipients, for whom the average span, in a sample analyzed by Watt (pp. 34–35, 45–58), was 20 years. See also Rawski, pp. 29–33; and D. Johnson, pp. 55–59.
4. Chang Tsung-hsiang (1877–1940?) served as a Minister of Justice in the early Republican period, and later, in 1916, as minister to Japan. During

the May Fourth movement in 1919, he was labeled a traitor by protesting students (Fang Chao-ying, p. 1; Boorman, 1: 127–29).

5. On his return to China, Hu Yuan-t'an (1872–1940) founded the Ming-te School, where he sought to put into practice the principles of liberal education he had learned in Japan. Hu devoted most of his subsequent career through the 1920's to developing the facilities at Ming-te (*Yu-hsueh i-pien*, no. 10, list of Hunan students in Japan; Boorman, 2: 182–83).

6. Tung Hung-wei was born in Chekiang province in 1880. After obtaining the *chü-jen* degree, he went to Japan in 1901. During the Republican period, he served in various posts in the Education Ministry. (Fang Chao-ying, p. 3; *Gendai Shinajin meikan*, pp. 89–90.)

7. Lin Ch'ang-min (1876–1925), a Fukien native, went to Japan in 1902 and first enrolled in an English-language school in Tokyo. On his graduation from Waseda University, Lin returned to China to become secretary of the Fukien provincial assembly. In the May Fourth period, Lin became a leader of the Progressive Party and a supporter of the student movement. (Fang Chao-ying, p. 7; Boorman, 2: 368–72.)

8. Generally considered China's greatest modern writer, Lu Hsün (1881–1936) through his short stories and essays exerted a profound influence on the direction of literary reform and the spread of new ideas in the May Fourth period. In the 1930's, he was active in the League of Left-wing Writers (Fang Chao-ying, p. 27; Boorman, 2: 416–24).

9. *KMIS*, 3: 139–40. Hu Han-min (1879–1936) was one of seven children. His father died when Hu Han-min was 12; his mother died two years later. Nevertheless, he succeeded in earning the *chü-jen* degree in 1902 at the age of 22. In 1902, he was among a group of students sent to Japan by Governor T'ao Mo under the supervision of Wu Chih-hui. Hu studied briefly at the Kōbun Institute, then returned to China. He revisited Japan in 1904. Active in the T'ung-meng Hui and a close associate of Sun Yat-sen's, Hu was a prominent figure in China after 1911. He was the first Republican governor of Kwangtung, became a top-ranking member of the Kuomintang's Central Executive Committee in 1924, and served as head of the Legislative Yuan from 1928 until 1931, when a policy conflict with Chiang Kai-shek resulted in his being placed under house arrest. Although freed by the end of the year, Hu remained at odds with the Nanking regime until his death in 1936. (*KMHL*, pp. 639–74; Boorman, 2: 159–66.)

10. Chang Shih-chao (b. 1881) studied the Classics at a local private school, then entered the Military Academy at Nanking in 1902. Fleeing to Japan in late 1904 as a suspect in an assassination plot, Chang was so impressed with Japan's modernization that he abandoned his radical views in favor of a gradualist approach. He refused to join the T'ung-meng Hui in 1905. In 1908, Chang went to Scotland for study. During the 1920's, he held various posts in the Education Ministry and was a Minister of Justice. In 1934, he became president of the Shanghai Law College. (Boorman, 1: 105–9.)

11. Feng Tzu-yu (1882–1958) was sent back to the family's native province, Kwangtung, for schooling. But he returned to Japan at the age of 14 for his high school years, and in 1900 he entered the political science department at Waseda University. Feng was active in the early Chinese radical groups in Japan and, later, in the Kuomintang until its reorganization in 1924. From that time on, he devoted himself to historical writing, especially

accounts of the 1911 Revolution. In 1949, Feng became national policy adviser to Chiang Kai-shek, a post he held until his death. (*KMHL*, p. 535; Boorman, 1: 30–32.)

12. Later, in 1903, Chou began to receive scholarship aid (*Yu-hsueh i-pien*, no. 10, list of Hunan students in Japan).

13. Yin Yüan-i later attended the Tokyo Fifth Higher School, from which he graduated in 1909. He then entered the engineering school at Tokyo University. (Fang Chao-ying, p. 30. *Nihon ryūgaku Shina yōjin roku*, p. 1, gives Yin's birth date as 1886, which would have made him only 15 when he started at the Kōbun Institute in 1901.)

14. On Li Wen-fan (1882–1953), see *KMHL*, pp. 934–35; and *Nihon ryūgaku Shina yōjin roku*, p. 223.

15. *KMHL*, p. 236. This source and others (see Y. C. Wang, *Chinese Intellectuals*, p. 287; and Hsiao P'ing, ed., *Hsin-hai ko-ming lieh-shih shih-wen hsüan* [Literary selections from revolutionary heroes, Beijing: China Press, 1962], p. 192) indicate that Wu arrived in Japan in 1896–97. But according to Fang Chao-ying, p. 9, Wu arrived in fall 1899 and was 20 years old when the roster was made up (1903).

16. Sanetō, *Meiji Nisshi*, p. 309; Tung Shou-i, p. 206.

17. Yokoyama, pp. 175, 189–90.

18. Lee and Nathan, p. 373; D. Johnson, pp. 57–60.

19. See Y. C. Wang, *Chinese Intellectuals*, pp. 78–79, 155. In 1925, a Chinese government student in the U.S. got $80 a month, or 143 Chinese dollars. A student in Japan got 70 yen, or about 50 Chinese dollars.

20. Ts'ao Ju-lin, p. 16. Ts'ao Ju-lin (1876–1966) was born in Shanghai and went to Japan in 1900, where he enrolled as a self-supporting student first at Waseda and then at the Tokyo Law Academy (part of Chūō University). Returning to China in 1904, he won the *chin-shih* degree in the special imperial examinations in 1905, joined the civil service, and by 1911, had become Vice-Minister of Foreign Affairs in both the Ch'ing government (1911) and the Yuan Shih-k'ai regime (1915). In that capacity, he managed the negotiations over Japan's 21 Demands and the resultant Sino-Japanese Treaty. Ts'ao was a target of attack of protesting students during the May Fourth incident. (Fang Chao-ying, p. 6; Ts'ao Ju-lin; Sanetō, *Kindai Nisshi*, pp. 204–6; Chow Tse-tung, pp. 102–3; Boorman, 1: 299–302.)

21. Tung Shou-i, p. 204. According to Fang Chao-ying's roster, over half of those on scholarship were provincial scholarship holders.

22. V. K. Ting.

23. *NCH*, Sept. 24, 1902, pp. 630–31.

24. Y. C. Wang, *Chinese Intellectuals*, pp. 60–61; Ch'iao Chih-ch'iang, p. 117.

25. Huang Fu-ch'ing, *Ch'ing-mo liu-Jih*, pp. 65–82; Chang Yü-fa, *Li-hsien tuan-t'i*, p. 82.

26. *JWM*, Oct. 26, 1901, p. 434.

27. Ts'ao Ju-lin, p. 16. See also n. 20, above.

28. Sanetō, *Meiji Nisshi*, p. 308. Those who went to Japan with an eye to the main chance were probably chagrined to find themselves in a scramble for high grades with their countrymen—a competition as bad as that for ranking within the civil service examination from which Chinese youth supposedly had been freed, according to the 1905 diarist "So Kauman."

29. Shen Hsiang-yün (d. 1913), a native of Chekiang, was in Japan be-

tween 1898 and 1901. He was a victim of Yuan Shih-k'ai's assassins in 1913 (*KMHL*, pp. 332–33). Ch'in Yü-liu (1879–1937) was born in Kiangsu. His father, a *chü-jen* degreeholder, was a copyist at the Historical Records Office. Ch'in himself lost interest in taking the civil service examination when he became convinced, from his contact with reformist publications of the 1890's, that such institutions needed to be changed. On the urging of Wu Chih-hui, Ch'in went to Japan early in 1902 to enroll in the political science program at Waseda University. Active in radical groups in Japan, Ch'in was also a key figure in Huang Hsing's China Rise Society from 1904 on. After 1911, he served for a while as Sun Yat-sen's secretary. Ch'in was subsequently imprisoned for opposing Yuan Shih-k'ai's bid for power. On his release and until his death in 1937, Ch'in Yü-liu held various posts in the Kiangsu provincial government. (*KMHL*, pp. 906–17; *KMIS*, vol. 1.) Ch'en T'ien-hua (b. 1874), a scholarship student from Hunan, went to Japan in April 1903 to study at the Kōbun Institute (*Yu-hsueh i-pien*, no. 10, list of Hunan students in Japan). He committed suicide in 1905.

30. Lu Hsün, p. 78.
31. Wu Yü-chang, pp. 50–55.
32. See Lin Te-cheng, p. 399, for examples.
33. Sung Chiao-jen (b. 1882) studied first at Hōsei University, then transferred to Waseda in 1905. He returned to China in 1910. In 1912, he was instrumental in forming the Kuomintang, which was highly critical of the increasing repression under the Yuan Shih-k'ai regime. Sung was shot and killed by Yuan's hired assassins in 1913. (*KMHL*, pp. 293–310.)
34. Yokoyama, pp. 174–78; Kanō Sensei Denki Hensankai, pp. 170–72; Yang Cheng-kuang, pp. 110–11; *CNRS*, pp. 80–82.
35. *Ryūgakuseibu shusshinsha meibo.*
36. Shu Hsin-ch'eng, pp. 55–62.
37. Ibid., pp. 58–62; Y. C. Wang, *Chinese Intellectuals*, pp. 67–68.
38. Tung Shou-i, pp. 212–13; Sanetō, *Kindai Nisshi*, pp. 236–37.
39. Shu Hsin-ch'eng, p. 55; Futami and Satō, p. 101.
40. *JWM*, March 1, 1902, p. 227.
41. See Kuo T'ing-i, 2: 17–44, for a list of governors by province. On Hsü Ying-kuei (given as Hsü Ying-ch'i), see Chung, p. 106.
42. *JWM*, Jan. 30, 1904, p. 120; *NCH*, March 16, 1906, pp. 569–70.
43. *CNRS*, pp. 75–79; Ishii, pp. 32–36; *Shimoda Utako Sensei den*, pp. 398–405 (p. 401 reproduces the graduation speech that Ms. Ch'en delivered in fluent Japanese). For a very useful account of women *liu hsueh-sheng*, which also highlights the progress of women's education in China, see Huang Fu-ch'ing, *Ch'ing-mo liu-Jih*, pp. 55–64.

44. Lu Hsün, p. 79.   45. *CNRS*, p. 419.
46. Ibid., p. 173.   47. Chang Tsung-hsiang, SC 49.
48. *Liu hsueh-sheng chien*, SC 117.
49. Ibid., p. 13; *CNRS*, p. 176.
50. Chang Tsung-hsiang, pp. 22–23; *Liu hsueh-sheng chien*, pp. 71–80.
51. *Liu hsueh-sheng chien*, pp. 22–40.
52. Ibid., sec. 26.
53. Ibid., p. 64; for a discussion of fees, see also *CNRS*, pp. 178–82 (translation of Chang Tsung-hsiang, SC 49).

54. Y. C. Wang, *Chinese Intellectuals*, p. 517.

55. *Liu hsueh-sheng chien*, p. 69.   56. Ibid., p. 71.

57. Ibid., p. 63.   58. Chiang Monlin, p. 66.

59. Ts'ao Ju-lin, p. 28.   60. Chirol, *Fifty Years*, p. 193.

61. Chirol, *Far Eastern Question*, pp. 116–17.

62. Ts'ao Ju-lin, p. 27.   63. Sanetō, *Meiji Nisshi*, p. 310.

64. Ibid., p. 326.   65. Chou Tso-jen, pp. 114–15.

66. *Shimoda Utako Sensei den*, p. 404; Ishii, p. 34.

67. Lu Hsün, p. 80.

68. Sanetō, *Meiji Nisshi*, p. 307; Ts'ao Ju-lin, p. 26.

69. Lu Hsün, p. 85.   70. Ibid., p. 86.

71. *CNRS*, pp. 193–95.   72. *Liu-tung wai-shih*, p. 10.

73. Ibid., pp. 30–32.   74. Sanetō, *Meiji Nisshi*, p. 310.

75. Masada, p. 129.   76. Ibid., pp. 122–23.

77. Lu Hsün, p. 87.

78. Ts'ao Ju-lin, p. 31. In one of life's ironies, when Ts'ao Ju-lin's house was attacked by protesting students during the May Fourth movement (1919), he was entertaining Nakae Chōmin's journalist son, Nakae Ushikichi (Chow Tse-tsung, pp. 112–13). For a wonderful account of Nakae Ushikichi, which relates this incident in some detail, see Fogel, *Nakae Ushikichi*, pp. 38–41.

Chapter 4

1. Sanetō, *Meiji Nisshi*, pp. 256–57.

2. Biggerstaff, *Modern Government Schools*, pp. 165–76; Spence, *To Change China*, pp. 129–60.

3. Nakamura, pp. 95–96.

4. Schwartz, chap. 4, passim.

5. *CNRS*, p. 249.

6. Howard, pp. 289–91, 307, n. 44; *CNRS*, pp. 255–56.

7. *Chūyaku Nichibunsho mokuroku*, pp. 4–5; *CNRS*, p. 251; Nakamura, pp. 99–100.

8. *CNRS*, pp. 251–54.

9. Ibid., p. 256.

10. Chi I-hui, a native of Hupei and a close associate of Sun Yat-sen's, was also active in the Translation Society, the Promote Determination Society, the Hankow plot, and the magazine *Chinese National* (Kuo-min pao; *KMIS*, 3: 45; *CNRS*, pp. 38–39).

11. Ariga Nagao (1860–1921), professor of international law at Waseda, served as an adviser to Yuan Shih-k'ai in 1914–15 at the time of the 21 Demands. Ariga's secretary was Nakae Ushikichi, who got the job through his mother's former boarder Ts'ao Ju-lin (Fogel, *Nakae Ushikichi*, pp. 27–29).

12. *I-shu hui-pien*, no. 2, p. 161.

13. *CNRS*, pp. 264–65; *Chūyaku Nichibunsho mokuroku*, pp. 16–17.

14. *Chūyaku Nichibunsho mokuroku*, p. 10.

15. Nakamura, p. 101.

16. *HMTP*, no. 26, p. 32; *CNRS*, p. 264.

17. *Chūyaku Nichibunsho mokuroku*, p. 23.

18. *CNRS*, p. 283. Based on the level of translation activity we can document, it seems safe to say that most of the translating from Japanese in this period was done by Chinese students. The student journals abound with advertisements of recent releases.

19. Smythe, p. 54; *NCH*, Aug. 29, 1900, pp. 437–38.

20. Kuo T'ing-i, 2: 1083.

21. *NCH*, Aug. 29, 1900, pp. 435–36.

22. On Japan's role in the Hankow affair, the *North China Herald* correspondent commented: "Through their natural affinity for the Chinese and their connection with many of His Excellency Chang's pupils who were educated here, the Japanese are thoroughly au fait of the Reform movement in Central and Southern China and are only surprised that it cannot give a better account of itself." (Sept. 19, 1900, p. 598.)

23. *NCH*, June 24, 1904, p. 1331. For example, an edict offering amnesty to those involved in the 1898 reform movement specified that it did not extend to K'ang, Liang, and Sun, "who have organized societies hostile to the dynasty."

24. Chang Chih-tung, 166: 10a–b.

25. Ibid., 9a–10a.

26. Ibid., 34a–b.

27. By "Shanghai National Assembly," Chang has reference to the National Assembly set up at a meeting of T'ang's followers in Shanghai in July 1900 (Kuo T'ing-i, 2: 1090).

28. Chang Chih-tung, 104: 1a–9b.

29. *KMIS*, 1: 122; *KMHL*, p. 333.

30. *KMIS*, 1: 151. Feng lists the students in each faction.

31. Ibid., pp. 146–47, 151.

32. Ts'ao Ju-lin, pp. 21–23.

33. *Su pao*, p. 241.

34. *KMIS*, 1: 151–54.

35. *Yu-hsueh i-pien*, no. 4, p. 5.

36. Nakayama, 12: 31–32; *Su pao*, p. 241. The *Su pao* account says some 200 attended this meeting. I would give greater credence to the Japanese newspaper figure of 1,000 simply because the reporter attended the meeting. See also *JWM*, March 14, 1903, p. 276, mentioning that a daughter and a niece of K'ang Yu-wei were passing through Japan en route to the U.S.

37. *HMTP*, no. 5, pp. 117–20.   38. Ts'ao Ju-lin, p. 18.

39. *HMTP*, no. 11, p. 65.   40. Sanetō, *Meiji Nisshi*, p. 261.

41. *KMHL*, p. 755.

42. Sanetō, *Meiji Nisshi*, pp. 259–61; Li Hsi-so, "Hsin-hai ko-ming," pp. 636–37.

43. Sanetō, *Meiji Nisshi*, p. 258.

44. Ibid., pp. 267–71.

45. Hu Han-min, p. 358.

46. *Yueh-chang ch'eng-an hui-lan*, 32: 35.

47. *HP*, no. 1, p. 128.

48. S. H. Cheng, p. 106.

49. *KS*, no. 1, pp. 197–201; *CCC*, no. 2, p. 4 (see the last 10 pages—unnumbered—for the charter of the intelligence department).

50. *HP*, no. 1, pp. 137–51.

51. The Chihli Provincial Society started up a monthly magazine called *Chih-shuo* (Chihli Speaks) in February 1903. Apparently only two issues have survived (Chang Nan and Wang Jen-chih, 2: 967).

52. Tseng Hsü-pai, p. 191. For a review of the late Ch'ing press, see Lee and Nathan, pp. 361–68.

53. Tseng Hsü-pai, p. 194.

54. Ibid., pp. 201–3.

55. Ibid., pp. 203–5.

56. Chang Nan and Wang Jen-chih, 1: 59–60.

57. Ibid., 2: 966; *KMIS*, 1:142.

58. *KMIS*, 1: 122–23, 143; Chang Chi, *Chang P'u-ch'uan*, p. 216.

59. Lee and Nathan, pp. 371–72. Per-copy readership of all magazines and papers is estimated at about 15 people.

60. Chang Chih-tung, 185: 19a–b

61. *Su pao*, April 11, 1903, p. 250.

62. Ko Kung-chao, p. 167. This statement reflects the overall policy toward the opposition press. For example, an edict of February 1900 prohibited the sale and possession of the writings of Liang Ch'i-ch'ao and K'ang Yu-wei (*NCH*, Feb. 21, 1900). From that time on, the Ch'ing government kept a careful watch on students' literary pursuits, forbidding them to "write heretical books and publish newspapers" or even to read such publications. (Ko Kung-chao, pp. 167–69).

63. *KMHL*, p. 533; *KS*, no. 5, unnumbered page.

64. See Nakayama, 12: 476, for the official Japanese complaint against the magazine.

65. V. K. Ting, p. 52. For slightly differing lists of student-sponsored publications, see *CNRS*, pp. 418–19; and Wang Hsiang-jung, pp. 65–70. Exactly how many magazines there were cannot be determined. Many folded after a couple of issues and vanished without trace.

Chapter 5

1. Kwong, pp. 23, 70–73, 305, nn. 16, 20.

2. Shu Hsin-ch'eng, p. 24; *Kuang-hsü-ch'ao Chung-Jih chiao-she shih-liao*, 52: 3735.

3. *JWM*, Nov. 30, 1901, p. 568.

4. *NCH*, Aug. 21, 1901. This may well have been more than rumor. The charges against Ts'ai were later investigated (*NCH*, Aug. 20, 1902, June 11, 1903).

5. Ts'ao Ju-lin, p. 19.   6. *Konoe nikki*, 5: 66.

7. *HMTP*, no. 5, p. 87.   8. Ibid., pp. 85–88.

9. *Konoe nikki*, 5: 66; Nagai, "Kyoga gakuseigun," p. 68.

10. *Konoe nikki*, 5: 66. From his diary, we see that Konoe had had regular contact with the minister from the start, so his visit to the legation was not unusual (for example, see ibid., pp. 79, 110). Furthermore, as TDK head, Konoe had a special interest in the education of the Chinese students. The TDK-sponsored Tokyo Dōbun Shoin held its opening ceremonies in January 1902 with Minister Ts'ai attending (ibid., p. 17).

11. *JWM*, May 3, 1902, p. 471.

12. Foreign Ministry to Ts'ai Chün, Kuang-hsü 28/14/12, Ts'ai Chün file, 1902–3, Foreign Ministry Archives, Institute of Modern History, Nankang, Taiwan.

13. *JWM*, April 12, 1902, p. 390.

14. Nagai, "Kyoga gakuseigun," p. 68; *HMTP*, no. 5, p. 89.

15. *JWM*, April 12, 1902, p. 390.

16. *JWM*, May 10, 1902.

17. Wang Chia-chü (b. 1879) was a graduate of the law faculty of Hōsei University. At the time of the May Fourth incident in 1919, he was chancellor of Peking University's College of Law and Political Science (*Nihon ryūgaku Shina yōjin roku*, p. 17; Chang Yü-fa, *Ko-ming tuan-t'i*, p. 289; Chow Tse-tung, p. 124). Ch'eng Chia-sheng (1873–1914), a native of Anhui, arrived in Japan on a Hupei scholarship in October 1899 to pursue agriculture studies at Tokyo Imperial University (Fang Chao-ying, p. 2; *KMHL*, pp. 350–61).

18. *KMIS*, 1: 84.

19. According to Feng Tzu-yu (ibid., p. 89), about 100 people showed up anyway, unaware of the police ban.

20. Feng Tzu-yu, *Erh-shih-liu nien tzu-chih shih*, pp. 60–61.

21. *JWM*, May 3, 1902.

22. *Kuang-hsü-ch'ao Chung-Jih chiao-she shih-liao*, 66: 4755.

23. Shu Hsin-ch'eng, p. 24 (from an 1898 Tsung-li Yamen document); *NCH*, Sept. 25, 1901.

24. Shu Hsin-ch'eng, pp. 48–50.

25. Nagai, "Iwayuru Go-Son jiken," p. 49.

26. *Meiji iko kyōiku*, 4: 665.

27. *CNRS*, p. 186.

28. *HMTP*, no. 13, pp. 1–5, 62–67.

29. Price Tsai Chen to Foreign Ministry, Kuang-hsü 28/8/21, Tsai Chen file, 1902, Foreign Ministry Archives, Institute of Modern History, Nankang, Taiwan.

30. *JWM*, Aug. 9, 1902, p. 136.

31. *CNRS*, p. 65. In 1898, when the first Chinese students were admitted, the chief of the General Staff Office was the school head.

32. Ibid.

33. Wu Yü-chang, pp. 60–61.

34. *Ryūgakuseibu shusshinsha meibo*, pp. 2–3. See *Meiji gakusei enkaku shi*, p. 1260, for the major schools attended by Chinese students in this period. The principal schools accommodating Chinese military students were, as of 1906, Shinbu Gakkō, Rikugun Yunen Gakkō, and the Army Officers School (Rikugun Shikan Gakkō). Other schools with large numbers of Chinese students were Tokyo Imperial University, Tokyo Higher Commercial School, Tokyo Higher Engineering School, Kōbun Institute, Tokyo Dōbun Shoin, Waseda University (Chinese students division), and Keio Academy. Tokyo Dōbun Shoin and the Kōbun Institute were set up specially for Chinese students. See, in the same source, pp. 1265–1267 for a breakdown of Chinese students by school (72 schools are listed: 151 Chinese students were attending Shinbu in 1906); and pp. 1267–1273 for detailed information on the course of study at the Kōbun Institute.

35. Nakayama, 11: 425.

36. Nagai, "Iwayuru Go-Son jiken," pp. 56–57, n. 3. In a telegram to the Foreign Ministry of Kuang-hsü 28/6/27, Minister Ts'ai states that nine self-supporting students expelled from the Nanyang school were seeking to pursue military studies in Japan.

37. *KMHL*, p. 731.

38. *HMTP*, no. 13, p. 105.

39. Ibid., pp. 106–7.

40. *Kuang-hsü-ch'ao Chung-Jih chiao-she shih-liao*, 66: 4785.

41. Grand Council, Kuang-hsü 28/8/21, memo on "Special Envoy Tsai's Report of the Disturbance Among Chinese Students in Japan," Ts'ai Chün files, 1902–3, Foreign Ministry Archives, Institute of Modern History, Nankang, Taiwan.

42. *HMTP*, no. 13, pp. 107–11.

43. Ibid., pp. 112–15.

44. Ibid., pp. 118–19.

45. Ibid, p. 119. Here, as elsewhere, the students used traditional images and allusions: the quoted passage was preceded by a direct reference to Mencius (book 4, part 1, ch. i, 13) on the responsibilities of a ruler's chief counselors.

46. Ibid., pp. 119–20.

47. It is odd, to say the least, that a representative of a host country should step in with a promise of this sort. Very likely, either Kobayashi had instructions from his government to placate the students while still allowing the minister his dignity, or, as the *Japan Weekly Mail* (Aug. 23, 1902, p. 192) asserts, his statement was misconstrued.

48. *HMTP*, no. 14, pp. 105–12. Little information is available on Sun K'uei-chün, who ended up being deported along with Wu Chih-hui. Since from all acounts Wu did almost all the speaking for the student group at the meeting with the minister, Sun's punishment seems curiously harsh. But he did speak out of turn on one occasion at the legation that evening (*HMTP*, no. 13, p. 114), which may explain his arrest.

49. Nagai, "Iwayuru Go-Son jiken," pp. 46, 58, n. 19.

50. *NCH*, Sept. 24, 1902.

51. *Kuang-hsü-ch'ao Chung-Jih chiao-she shih-liao*, 66: 4784.

52. Ibid.

53. *HMTP*, no. 13, pp. 7–8, no. 14, pp. 105–12; *JWM*, Aug. 9, 1902, p. 137. Some doubts were cast on the sincerity of Wu's motives in light of his failed suicide attempt. Chang Ping-lin, his archenemy, later accused him of throwing himself into a mere drainage ditch in a play for notoriety (*HHKM*, 1: 399). In an on-the-scene report, the *North China Herald* slyly suggested that if Wu were really intent on taking his own life, he could easily jump into the sea on the return voyage to China (Sept. 3, 1902, p. 478). *JWM*, Aug. 9, 1902, terms the doubts about Wu's sincerity "baseless."

54. *HMTP*, no. 13, pp. 62–67.

55. *HMTP*, no. 14, p. 64.

56. According to *JWM*, Aug. 23, 1902, 70–80 students made such a decision. See Nagai, "Iwayuru Go-Son jiken," p. 59, for figures from different sources on the number of withdrawals from school resulting from the Seijō incident.

57. *Ko-ming wen-hsien*, 3: 381.   58. *HMTP*, no. 14, pp. 117–18.
59. *HMTP*, no. 15, pp. 62–63.   60. *HMTP*, no. 17, pp. 113–20.

61. Li Tsung-t'ang first went to Japan in 1901 to gather information on the Japanese educational system for the Liang-Kiang governor-general. He made at least nine other trips on fact-finding missions of various kinds. His reports are contained in a six-volume work, *Tung-yu chi-nien* (Record of my Japan trips); see *CNRS*, p. 425. The Seijō account is contained in the second section of vol. 1. Li's first meetings on this trip were with Prince Konoe and Nagaoka of the TDK and Foreign Minister Komura; he also saw some 10 students from Kiangsu, Chekiang, Anhui, and Hupei. Li indicates that the Japanese authorities with whom he conferred—including former Prime Minister (1898) Baron Ōkuma Shigenobu—were not pleased with Minister Ts'ai Chün's handling of the affair (Li Tsung-t'ang, pp. 2b, 8b–9a).

62. Prince Tsai, on a world tour as part of his duties as special ambassador to the coronation of Edward VII, had received the Foreign Ministry order on reaching the United States on August 9. With him the tour was Wang Ta-hsieh—later a key figure in student affairs—of the Foreign Ministry. (*NCH*, Feb. 19, 1903, p. 332.)

63. *JWM*, Sept. 13, 1902.

64. Grand Council memo, Kuang-hsü 28/8/21, Ts'ai Chün files, 1902–3, Foreign Ministry Archives, Institute of Modern History, Nankang, Taiwan.

65. *Kuang-hsü-ch'ao Chung-Jih chiao-she shih-liao*, 66: 4826.

66. Ibid., p. 4827.

67. The translated decree appears in *NCH*, Nov. 5, 1902.

68. *Kuang-hsü-ch'ao Chung-Jih chiao-she shih-liao*, 66: 4826.

69. Ibid., p. 4857.

70. Ts'ao Ju-lin, p. 20. See also *NCH*, July 21, 1905, p. 143.

71. *Kuang-hsü-ch'ao Chung-Jih chiao-she shih-liao*, 66: 4786.

72. *NCH*, Aug. 20, 1902, p. 380.

73. *NCH*, Sept. 3, 1902.

74. See, for example, articles in *JWM*, Sept. 6, 1902; and *NCH*, Oct. 1, 8, 22, 1902.

75. *NCH*, Oct. 23, 1903, p. 852; Chow Jen Hwa, appendix.

76. *Kuang-hsü-ch'ao Chung-Jih chiao-she shih-liao*, 66: 4789.

77. *CNRS*, p. 460.

78. Ts'ai Chün to Foreign Ministry, Kuang-hsü 28/9/9, Ts'ai Chün files, 1902–3, Foreign Ministry Archives, Institute of Modern History, Nankang, Taiwan. Of the 12 clauses, only the first and last dealt with scholarship students. The first clause proposed that, in view of their increasing numbers, Szechuan, Hunan, Fukien, and Kwangtung should send special supervisory officials to Japan. At that time, only Hupei and the Commissioners of the Northern and Southern Ports maintained officials in Tokyo to oversee students. Clause 12 stated that funds to cover the expenses of scholarship students should be remitted to the legation, then passed on to the various supervisors.

79. Ibid., Kuang-hsü 28/10/9.

80. *Yueh-chang ch'eng-an hui-lan*, 32, pp. 35–39.

81. Shu Hsin-ch'eng, pp. 60–61.

82. *CNRS*, pp. 70–71; Wu Yü-chang, pp. 61–62; Okamoto, pp. 58, 63–64.

83. *NCH*, Aug. 27, 1902; *HMTP*, no. 15, p. 101.
84. Nagai, "Kyoga gakuseigun," p. 68. *NCH*, Nov. 19, 1902, says that 200 students withdrew.

Chapter 6

1. *CCC*, no. 2, pp. 133–35.
2. *KS*, no. 1, p. 147.
3. *CCC*, no. 2, pp. 134–35.
4. Ibid., pp. 133–35; *KS*, no. 1, pp. 151–57; *KMIS*, 1: 189–90; *NCH*, March 19, 1903, p. 542.
5. *KS*, no. 1, pp. 151–57.   6. Ibid., p. 147.
7. *HP*, no. 3, pp. 107–8.   8. *KS*, no. 1, pp. 146–51.
9. *NCH*, Jan. 14, 1903, p. 72. Wang Chih-ch'un had been appointed governor of Kwangsi in June 1902, on his assurance that he could deal with the Kwangsi rebels in short order. Wang was an old military man, a ranking general in the army. He had been sent to Japan in 1879 by the Liang-Kiang governor-general Shen Pao-chen as a military observer. His report, *Notes on My Trip Abroad* (T'an ying lu), offered, on the plus side, the first modern survey maps of Japan. But the accompanying description was at best lackluster ("Yokohama is only 30 *ri* from Tokyo by the land route; it is not a defense stronghold. One can go directly by steamboat") and, at worst, in error (as when he landed at Shimonoseki and mistook it for Kagoshima. See Saneto, *Meiji Nisshi*, pp. 172–78.
10. *CCC*, no. 4, pp. 127–30. See also slightly differing versions of the goings-on in *HP*, no. 4, pp. 119–20; and *KS*, no. 2, p. 144.
11. *NCH*, April 30, 1903, pp. 834–36.
12. *NCH*, Feb. 11, 1903, p. 284.
13. *NCH*, March 5, 1903, pp. 431–32.
14. *NCH*, Sept. 25, 1903, p. 655.
15. Kosaka Masataka.
16. Nish, *Anglo-Japanese Alliance*, p. 230.
17. MacMurray, pp. 326–29.
18. See, for example, *NCH*, Feb. 11, 1903, p. 262 (a *Japan Times* report); and *HP*, no. 3, pp. 99–100.
19. *NCH*, May 14, 1903, pp. 943–44.
20. *NCH*, Feb. 11, 1903, p. 262.
21. *NCH*, May 7, 1903, pp. 874–75, May 21, 1903, pp. 985–87; Nakayama, vol. 12 *passim*.
22. *NCH*, April 23, 1903, p. 776; Okamoto, pp. 62–63.
23. *KMCCT*, 2: 111. This statement also ran in both *CCC*, no. 4, p. 130, and *KS*, no. 2, p. 145. *NCH*, April 30, 1903, p. 811, merely paraphrased Planson's remark: "He added that Russia, weary of the trouble resulting from her present undefined status in Manchuria, had determined to add the three provinces definitely to her empire."
24. Nakayama, 12: 57. The abridged version is from *Tokyo jiji shimbun*. The full version of April 29 is from the *Asahi shimbun*; this is the version in *KS*, no. 2, p. 145. Planson was later reprimanded by his government for his intemperance (*KMCCT*, 2: 114).

25. Malozemoff, p. 206. Malozemoff states that China rejected the Demands on April 22. Kuo T'ing-i agrees with April 18 as the date Planson presented the Seven Demands but does not mention that the note was rejected on April 22. The *Asahi* account (Nakayama, 12: 57) says the Demands were rejected on April 25. There is some question, in fact, whether China ever did "reject" Russia's Demands. According to the *North China Herald*, as late as the end of May, Russia had not yet withdrawn them (*NCH*, May 28, 1903, p. 1050). Furthermore, Russia had gone so far as to construe the Chinese Foreign Office's reply that China had no intention of alienating Manchuria to any foreign nation as an acceptance of the Demands. Later, the *Herald* cited a Peking dispatch reporting that though the Chinese government was giving assurances that the Demands had been rejected, top advisers had actually given in to Russia. (*NCH*, June 18, 1903, p. 1209). *KS*, no. 2, p. 140, asserts that one of the top Manchu officials, Prince Ch'ing, feigned illness as a delaying tactic when the Demands were first presented.

26. *KMCCT*, p. 114.

27. *HP*, no. 4, pp. 121–22.

28. T'ang Erh-ho (b. 1877) graduated a few years later from the Kanazawa Medical School, then went to Germany for further training. He went on to prominence in the field of medical education, becoming chancellor of the National Medical College of Peking. Well connected in Peking government circles, T'ang at this time recommended Ts'ai Yuan-p'ei for appointment as chancellor of Peking University and Ch'en Tu-hsiu as dean of the university's School of Letters. In 1922, T'ang was made Minister of Education. (Fang Chao-ying, p. 14; *Gendai Shinajin meikan*, p. 104; Chow Tse-tsung, pp. 52, 138–39.)

29. Niu Yung-chien (1873–1963?) had graduated from a military school in Kiangsi before going to Japan to continue his studies. After the Revolution, he joined the Nanking Provisional Government in an advisory capacity. A member of the anti-Yuan army in 1913, Niu fled to Japan after its defeat. (*Gendai Shinajin meikan*, p. 220.)

30. *KMCCT*, 10: 122.

31. Ibid., p. 111.

32. Ibid., p. 112.

33. *KMIS*, 1: 155. Feng Tzu-yu was not an eyewitness to these events (p. 152); he was out of the country on business and did not return until after the Volunteer Corps had been formed.

34. *HP*, no. 4, p. 122. The list of speakers included Wang Ching-fang, Niu Yung-chien, Yeh Lan, and Chang Chao-t'ung.

35. The extracts from T'ang's speech are drawn from *KS*, no. 2, pp. 146ff.

36. Ibid., p. 148. These figures are corroborated by *CCC*, no. 4, p. 133, and *HP*, no. 4. *KMIS*, 4: 24, is in error in saying that 130 signed up for the army at the April 29 meeting.

37. The telegram to Yuan read: "The Russian crisis is worsening. Partition is imminent. We beg you to offer immediate and firm resistance. We students have formed a Volunteer Corps and are preparing to go to the front. A detailed letter follows" (*KMCCT*, 10: 112).

38. *NCH*, May 7, 1903, p. 885; *Su pao*, May 8, 1903, p. 414.

39. *HMPT*, no. 30, p. 114; *KS*, no. 2, p. 135; *NCH*, April 30, 1903, p. 832. The anti-Russia meeting of the spring of 1903 had a precedent in protest

meetings held at Chang's Gardens in early 1901 over the issue of the Sino-Russian negotiations regarding Manchuria. It is interesting to note that Chang Chih-tung (172: pp. 2a–b) saw the 1901 meetings as a cover-up for subversive operations on the part of T'ang Ts'ai-ch'ang's followers.

40. *CCC*, no. 4, pp. 130–38.

41. *KS*, no. 2, p. 138.

42. *CCC*, no. 4, pp. 130–38.

43. The text of this letter was also sent to Prince Tsai Chen on May 17 (*KMCCT*, p. 116).

44. *CCC*, no. 4, p. 133.

45. Ibid.

46. *HP*, no. 4, p. 125; *KS*, no. 2, p. 148. Wu Yü-chang, recalling his participation in the Volunteer Corps (pp. 55–59), observed that he had been impelled to join not out of firm political commitment, but simply out of a desire to do what so many other students were doing. The decision to join the corps, however, had a profound effect on his life, setting him on the path to revolution.

47. *KS*, no. 6, in *KMCCT*, 10: 96, 97.

48. *CCC*, no. 4, p. 136. In a story headlined PATRIOTIC CHINESE YOUNG LADIES, the *North China Herald* noted that these women students joined the Japanese Red Cross Society "with the expressed determination to volunteer as nurses for the front." This same story reported that "some six or seven hundred young Chinese studying in Japan" had made a decision to form a volunteer battalion." (May 7, 1903, p. 907.)

49. *KS*, no. 2, pp. 149–50; Fang Chao-ying, p. 8; *Su pao*, May 18, 1903, pp. 481–82, in *KMCCT*, 10: 136 (*KMIS*, 5: 37–38, corroborates *Su pao*'s list). Lan T'ien-wei was in the Officers School's second Chinese graduating class. At the time of the Wuchang uprising in 1911, he was commander of the Twentieth Mixed Brigade of the Fengtien Third Division (*Gendai Shinajin meikan*, pp. 682–83).

50. *HP*, no. 4, p. 126.

51. *KS*, no. 2, p. 150; *KMIS*, 5: 39.

52. *KS*, no. 2, p. 150.

53. *Su pao*, May 20, 1903, p. 494.

54. *KS*, no. 2, p. 150.

55. Chang Yü-fa, *Ko-ming tuan-t'i*, pp. 262–72. Most of those on Chang's list of 190 members were from the eastern and southern coastal provinces, though there was considerable regional diversity, with 14 provinces represented. See Yang T'ien-shih and Wang Hsueh-chuang, pp. 127–28, for a list of 208 association members, including 12 women, and pp. 129–33, for a list of the 500-odd contributors to the association and the amounts they gave.

56. "The Association for National Military Education's Appeal for Aid", *KS*, no. 2, pp. 327–28.

57. The speech is quoted in *KMCCT*, 10: 115. Yeh's reference to drill practice suggests that this forbidden activity was being continued. For other accounts of the various send-off meetings, see *HP*, no. 5, p. 134; *KS*, no. 2, p. 155; and *CCC*, no. 5, p. 151.

58. *CCC*, no. 5, p. 151.

59. The *North China Herald* recorded this rumor, "which for the sake of civilization and the future of China we sincerely hope is untrue," on June

11, 1903 (p. 1182). On June 18, readers were informed that the story was baseless (p. 1209).

60. *Su pao*, May 16–17, 1903, in *KMCCT*, 10: 137.

61. *CCC*, no. 6, sec. "Liu-hsueh chieh chi-shih."

62. *KMCCT*, 10: 116. Chang Po-hsi apparently was instructed by top officials in the central government to so advise the students.

63. *NCH*, May 21, 1903, p. 1019.

64. According to Li Shu-fan (p. 1), the informer was a Manchu student named Liang-pi. In his view, though the group was already inclined toward anti-Manchuism, its attitude hardened when the government, acting on Liang-pi's report, ordered certain students expelled from Japan. Feng Tzu-yu (*KMIS*, 1: 155–59) claims that the informer was a Hupei scholarship student and Volunteer Corps member named Wang Ching-fang. Wang had arrived in Japan on a provincial scholarship in the fall of 1899 (Fang Chao-ying, p. 4).

65. Yang T'ien-shih and Wang Hsueh-chuang, pp. 157, 159, 175, 179, 187.

66. Tuan-fang telegram of Kuang-hsü 29/5/29, Telegrams Received, Foreign Ministry Archives, Institute of Modern History, Nankang, Taiwan. Other accounts of Tuan's telegram are given in *Su pao* (*KMCCT*, 10: 133–34); *HMTP*, no. 33, p. 64; and *KS*, no. 3, pp. 145–46.

67. *NCH*, June 11, 1903, p. 1157.

68. *KMIS*, 1: 158.

69. *KMCCT*, 10: 134; *Hsin-hai ko-ming hui-i lu*, 1: 241.

70. Chang Chi, "Tu Yen-na liu-hsueh-sheng."

71. Ibid., p. 133.

72. According to a Japanese Foreign Office document dated July 28, 1903, Wang Chia-chü, Ch'in Yü-liu, Tung Hung-wei, Chang Chao-t'ung, and Yeh Lan gave the Japanese police written assurance that the association was being disbanded and would not be set up again in Japan. When the organization reappeared, it was careful to keep the matter quiet. (Nagai, "Chin Ten-ka," p. 66, n. 44.)

73. See *HHKM*, 1: 470. Wang Ta-hsieh reported on July 23 that 100 people, including Wang Ching-fang, left the group when it turned to anti-Manchuism.

74. *KMIS*, 1: 163.

75. Ibid.

76. Ibid., p. 166.

77. Su P'eng, a new name in the record, was a native of Hunan who went to Japan to study in 1902 (*KMIS*, 3: 108).

78. Su P'eng's account of this episode illustrates the unsophisticated and almost haphazard character of the students' tactics. First they hired a chemistry teacher to instruct them in the art of bomb making. When he proved inadequate to the task, they combed through Japanese chemistry journals for a rumored explosive the Japanese had developed, which was said to be safe to handle and convenient to manufacture. But the Japanese evidently were not publishing defense secrets in chemistry journals, for the search yielded nothing. Nevertheless, the students had somehow acquired enough knowledge of chemistry to make crude explosives. Su recounts how during

a police health check of Yokohama residences, he and his friends, fearing discovery of their operation, dumped all the explosives they had manufactured into a large crock of water. When particles of the compound floated to the surface, one of the group stirred the water with a glass rod thinking to dissolve the powder. There was a terrific explosion. He and Yang suffered eye injuries in the blast, but recovered in a matter of months (Su P'eng, in *KMCCT*, 10: 100).

79. Ibid., pp. 100–101.

Chapter 7

1. *KMCCT*, 10: 533.

2. See Y. C. Wang, "Su-pao Case," pp. 15–21, for an account of the growth of the International Settlement at Shanghai and the extension of the Mixed Court's jurisdiction.

3. Chiang I-hua, pp. 1–17; *KMIS*, 1: 78–84. For two excellent essays on Chang Ping-lin in English, see Chang Hao, *Chinese Intellectuals in Crisis*; and Chi Wen-shun, *Ideological Conflicts*.

4. T'ao Ch'eng-chang, "Che-an chi-lüeh," in *HHKM*, 3: 14–21, sees the 242nd anniversary meeting as an important step in the emergence of a revolutionary apparatus in China. See also *KMIS*, 1: 81.

5. Chiang Wei-ch'iao, "Chung-kuo chiao-yü hui," in *HHKM*, 1: 487.

6. Tu Ch'eng-hsiang, pp. 18, 22.

7. Fang Chao-ying, p. 31.

8. Tu Ch'eng-hsiang, p. 24.

9. Ibid., p. 25; *KMIS*, 2: 52–57. Tsou's name does not appear on the official roster of the Student Army in *KMIS*.

10. Hsü Shou-ch'ang remarks that the wearing of queues was an embarrassment to many of the Chinese students in Japan. The odd effects produced when they attempted to conceal the queue under a hat opened them up to ridicule by Japanese children. But none of the Kiangnan group had shorn them on the orders of Supervisor Yao. Tsou's attack on Yao was probably motivated as much by the queue issue as by Yao's moral lapse. Hsü also mentions that in the period before Wang Ta-hsieh's appointment, the supervisors of students in Japan were ignorant of Japan and the Japanese language and so provided no guidance at all to the students.

11. Tu Ch'eng-hsiang, pp. 25–26.

12. Hummel, 2: 769.

13. Y. C. Wang, *Chinese Intellectuals*, pp. 237–38.

14. The translation here is from *NCH*, July 17, 1903, pp. 144–45. For the original work, see Tsou Jung, *Ko-ming chün*, in *HHKM*, 1: 331–64; and for a recent translation, see John Lust, *The Revolutionary Army: A Chinese Nationalist Tract of 1903* (1968). Also useful are Abe, "Sū Yō no [Kakumeigun]," pp. 150–64; and Pusey's playful translation of Chiang Chih-yu's poem "How good to be a slave," which Tsou ran in his tract (*China and Charles Darwin*, pp. 184–85).

15. S. H. Cheng, p. 77.   16. *HHKM*, 1: 367–68.

17. Ko Kung-chen, pp. 153–62.   18. *HHKM*, 1: 367.

19. See announcement in *Yu-hsueh i-pien*, no. 1, no page number.

20. *HHKM*, 1: 368.

21. Chang Ping-lin, pp. 752–64.

22. Wu Chih-hui recalled that he, Chang Ping-lin, and Ts'ai Yuan-p'ei were questioned by the police several times that month (Chou Chia-jung, pp. 48–49).

23. London *Times*, Dec. 4, 1903, p. 3; Y. C. Wang, "Su-pao Case," pp. 26–28, 32–38.

24. London *Times*, Aug. 5, 1903, p. 3.

25. *NCH*, May 27, 1904, p. 1121.

26. Ts'ai Yuan-p'ei visited Chang and Tsou in prison once a month, as often as he could under official visiting privileges (Chou Chia-jung, p. 71).

27. *KS*, no. 4, pp. 120–21.

28. Ibid., pp. 119–20. This same article by way of footnote rejected the contention that foreigners sitting in judgment in the *Su pao* case represented a national humiliation. After all, the Manchus were aliens, too, and among civilized nations, a third party commonly stepped in to arbitrate disputes between different people.

29. Chang Chi, "Hui-i lu," p. 57.

30. Ko Kung-chen, pp. 155–56.

31. Tseng Hsü-pai, p. 213.

32. S. H. Cheng, p. 81.

33. *NCH*, Dec. 18, 1903, p. 1295.

34. Gasster, p. 43, n. 33.

35. Ibid.; Ko Kung-cheng, p. 156.

36. Hsueh Chün-tu, *Huang Hsing*, pp. 2–4, 12.

37. S. H. Cheng, p. 73; Nagai, "Chin Ten-ka," p. 50.

38. Fang Chao-ying, p. 26.

39. Hsueh Chün-tu, *Huang Hsing*, p. 9.

40. Liu K'uei-i, pp. 1–2. Liu, a native of Hunan, arrived in Japan in April 1903 to study at the Kōbun Institute (*Yu-hsueh i-pien*, no. 10, list of Hunan students in Japan).

41. Kuo T'ing-i, 2: 1181. Huang was not present when the association was reorganized into a militant group in July. But in view of his later activities, he very likely had a guiding hand in the revised strategy outlined at that time.

42. In addition to their active role in the anti-Russia organizations, Huang and other Hunan students formed a radical group at Kōbun, the Saturday Society, which called for direct action against the Ch'ing (P'eng Kuo-hsing, p. 677).

43. Li Shu-fan, p. 2.

44. The Ming-te School was founded April 26, 1903. In October or November, it installed a teacher training course; this was the course Huang Hsing was invited to administer (Ting Chih-p'ing, p. 12).

45. Su Man-shu, a native of Kwangtung, spent his formative years in Yokohama, where he was a close friend of Feng Tzu-yu's. Su attended the Ta-t'ung School and then Waseda University. The rolls of Seijō Gakkō show him as a self-supporting student in military studies in early 1903. He was then 17 or 18 years old. Later Su became a poet and Buddhist priest (Fang Chao-ying, p. 16; *KMIS*, 1: 235–42).

46. Liu K'uei-i, p. 2; Shen Tieh-min, p. 133.

47. Weng Hao, a native of Fukien, arrived in Japan in early 1903 at the age of 27 (Fang Chao-ying, p. 43). Cheng Hsien-ch'eng was also from Fukien (*KMIS*, 3: 79).

48. Li Shu-fan, pp. 1–3. Chao Sheng, a native of Kiangsu, was in Japan for a brief time in 1903 (*KMHL*, p. 560).

49. Liu K'uei-i, p. 3. According to P'eng Kuo-hsing, pp. 680–81, an initial, formative meeting of the Hua-hsing Hui was held in November 1903 by 12 radicals, 10 of whom were from Hunan. The formal inaugural meeting was held Feb. 15, 1904.

50. Chang Yü-fa, *Ko-ming tuan-t'i*, pp. 276–82.

51. *KMIS*, 1: 183; Hsueh Chün-tu, *Huang Hsing*, p. 18.

52. Li Shu-fan, p. 3; P'eng Kuo-hsing, pp. 679–80; *KMIS*, 1: 183.

53. P'eng Kuo-hsing, pp. 681–84.

54. Wei Chien-yu, pp. 530–33; P'eng Kuo-hsing, pp. 683, 685–86; Nagai, "Chin Ten-ka," p. 50; Chu Shou-p'eng, ch. 190: 2b. Sometime in December, Peking sent a telegram to Minister Yang Shu requesting him to look into the connection between the T'ung-ch'ou Hui and the Chinese students in Japan.

55. Hsueh Chün-tu, *Huang Hsing*, p. 19.

56. Yao Hung-yeh (b.1886) of Hunan went to Japan in 1904. He committed suicide in 1906 (*KMHL*, pp. 50–51). Chou Wei-chen, a returned student from Szechuan, had been carrying out the society's propaganda work in his native province (*KMIS*, 3: 106). Chang Hsiung-fu was also a returned student. A Chekiang self-supporting student, he was only 17 or 18 when he went to Japan in the winter of 1902 to enroll in the Seijō Gakkō military course (*CCC*, April 1903, list of Chekiang students). *KMIS*, 3: 105, lists Hu Ying as a student in Japan but gives no particulars. The identification of Chang Shih-chao as a Shanghai contact is from Nagai, "Chin Ten-ka," p. 51. T'ao Ch'eng-chang's student status is questionable. Feng Tzu-yu mentions T'ao's failed attempt to enter the Army Officers School in 1902 (*KMIS*, 3: 98). He appears as a self-supporting student in Seijō Gakkō's military course on the April 1903 *Tide of Chekiang* list of students, but Rankin, *Early Chinese Revolutionaries*, pp. 169–70, refers to another try at gaining admission to military school in 1905 or 1906. On T'ao's talks with Huang Hsing and Ts'ai Yuan-p'ei about his role in the planned revolt, see Shen Tieh-min, p. 133.

57. Chang Chi, "Hui-i lu," p. 58.

58. P'eng Kuo-hsing, pp. 687–89.

59. Hsueh Chün-tu, *Huang Hsing*, p. 23. P'eng Kuo-hsing, pp. 690–94, offers a detailed account of the disclosure to authorities of plans for uprising.

60. S. H. Cheng, pp. 34–35.

61. Wang Chia-wei arrived in Japan in 1901 at the age of 22 as a self-supporting student (Fang Chao-ying, p. 3; Chang Yü-fa, *Ko-ming tuan-t'i*, pp. 290–92).

62. Hsü Shou-ch'ang (b. 1882) arrived in Japan in September 1902 on a Chekiang scholarship. After his stint at the Kōbun Institute, he entered the Tokyo Higher Normal School, from which he graduated in 1908 (Fang Chao-

ying, p. 28; *Nihon ryūgaku Chūkaminkoku jimmei shirabe*). We know nothing more about Wei Lan than that he was a native of Chekiang, was in Japan in the summer of 1903, and had joined the association (*KMIS*, 3: 99).

63. Shen Tieh-min, pp. 131–32.

64. Ibid., pp. 133–34.

65. *HHKM*, 3: 14–21; Wei Chien-yu, p. 535.

66. Shen Tieh-min, p. 134. Ho Tse-fu, pp. 277–78, doubts that the Tokyo branch amounted to much, since it is not mentioned in the reminiscences of T'ao Ch'eng-chang and others.

67. Ch'en Wei, p. 127. For a discussion of the Kuang-fu Hui's political orientation, see Hu Kuo-shu, pp. 716–21.

68. Ibid. *KMIS*, 5: 83, voices the same view.

69. Ch'en Wei, p. 127. Hsü Hsi-lin (1873–1907), a native of Chekiang, first went to Japan in 1903 to see the Osaka Exhibition. He returned in the winter of 1905 and attempted without success to enter various military schools (*KMHL*, pp. 57–67).

70. Shen Tieh-min, p. 134.

71. Ibid.

72. Rankin, *Early Chinese Revolutionaries*, pp. 150–157; Shen Tieh-min, p. 133; Hu Kuo-shu, pp. 723–24; Wei Chien-yu, p. 535.

73. Hu Kuo-shu, pp. 722–23. Ch'iu Chin (1875?–1907) was born and grew up in Fukien province, though the family's home base was in Chekiang. Ch'iu's father was some kind of minor official, possibly a *chü-jen* degree-holder, whose postings took him to Taiwan and Hunan; her mother was a well-educated woman who apparently encouraged her daughter's independent ways. In the liberalizing atmosphere following the Sino-Japanese War, the spirited Ch'iu Chin came to champion women's rights and citizen action for national salvation. These new pursuits put further pressure on her already strained arranged marriage. She and her husband separated, and Ch'iu went to Japan in 1904. After studying Japanese at the Chinese Student Union, she enrolled in the teacher training course at the Women's Practical Arts School. During her two years in Japan, Ch'iu emerged as a leading political agitator for the cause of anti-Ch'ing revolution. (*KMHL*, pp. 70–79; Rankin, *Early Chinese Revolutionaries*, pp. 38–47; Ono, pp. 59–65.)

74. Rankin, *Early Chinese Revolutionaries*, pp. 164–67.

75. *KMHL*, pp. 70–79; Rankin, *Early Chinese Revolutionaries*, p. 44; Ono, p. 65.

76. Wang Te-chao, "T'ung-meng Hui," pp. 69, 94.

77. See Chang Yü-fa, *Ko-ming tuan-t'i*, pp. 199–200, for an occupational breakdown of the 325 Revive China Society members as of 1904. Only about 100 lived in Japan, a lamentably small number from Sun's standpoint, considering that the overseas Chinese community numbered around 10,000 by that time (ibid., p. 202). See also *Jih-pen hua-ch'iao chih*, p. 113, which shows 5,498 Chinese living in Japan in 1890 and 6,890 in 1900.

78. *KMIS*, 1: 146.

79. Ibid., pp. 192–93.

80. Wang Te-chao, "T'ung-meng Hui," pp. 70, 74.

81. *KMIS*, 1: 192.

82. Hsueh Chün-tu, *Huang Hsing*, p. 197, n. 37.

83. Ibid., p. 35.

84. Schiffrin, pp. 347–55.

85. Thomas Millard, writing in 1905, claimed that the boycott was not a spontaneous outburst of popular feeling in response to the American exclusion act but the product of a campaign mounted by the Japanese-controlled press in China and supported by paid Japanese-political agitators among the returned students from Japan (*New Far East*, pp. 236–55).

86. Chang Yü-fa, *Ko-ming tuan-t'i*, pp. 316–17; Schriffrin, pp. 363–64.

87. The point is well attested. See especially Chang Yü-fa, *Ko-ming tuan-t'i*; Schiffrin; and Jansen, *Japanese and Sun*.

88. Chang Yü-fa, *Ko-ming tuan-t'i*, pp. 305–6.

89. Ibid., p. 307.

90. Ibid., pp. 307–14. See also Ho Tse-fu, pp. 275–76.

91. Tung Shou-i, p. 297; Chang Yü-fa, *Ko-ming tuan-t'i*, pp. 317–18. Reported attendance figures for the August 13 meeting vary widely. Ch'en T'ien-hua claimed 1,300 people were present. Sources agree on the 200 to 300 sworn in at the August 20 meeting. According to *Min pao*, 5,000–6,000 attended the TMH meeting at the end of 1906, again the great majority students.

92. Schiffrin, p. 362. For charts of the central leadership group, see Chang Yü-fa, *Ko-ming tuan-t'i*, pp. 343–56.

93. Chang Yü-fa, *Ko-ming tuan-t'i*, p. 463; P'eng Kuo-hsing, pp. 698–99; Chin Ch'ung-chi and Hu Sheng-wu, pp. 742–44.

94. Chang Yü-fa, *Ko-ming tuan-t'i*, p. 181. On the quality of Sun's leadership of the TMH, see Schiffrin, pp. 363–66.

Chapter 8

1. This chapter is based primarily on materials in *NHR*. Also useful were Sanetō, *Nihon bunka*, pp. 84–111; *CNRS*, pp. 461–94; and Nagai, "Ryūgakusei torishimaru kisoku jiken," pp. 11–34.

2. *NHR*, p. 76.

3. *NHR*, p. 25.

4. *NHR*, pp. 230, 263–65.

5. Sanetō, *Nihon bunka*, p. 91; *NHR*, p. 263. One of the six was Professor Terao, the organizer of the Tōhin School, which provided military studies to Chinese self-supporting students. See Chap. 5; and Okamoto, pp. 66–67.

6. *JWM*, April 4, 1903, p. 366; *HP*, no. 4, pp. 116–19 (the same text appeared in *KS*, no. 1, p. 158).

7. *NHR*, p. 80.	8. *NHR*, pp. 25, 80–85.
9. *NHR*, pp. 32, 94.	10. *NHR*, pp. 17, 100, 219–20.
11. *NHR*, pp. 27, 95.	12. *NHR*, p. 77.
13. *NHR*, pp. 99, 103.	14. *NHR*, p. 104
15. *NHR*, pp. 104–5.	16. *NHR*, p. 102.
17. *NHR*, p. 105.	18. *NHR*, p. 112.
19. Young, pp. 210–47.	20. *NHR*, p. 238.
21. *NHR*, p. 246.	22. *NHR*, p. 24.
23. *NHR*, pp. 216, 219–20.	24. *NHR*, p. 161.
25. *NHR*, pp. 133–40.	26. *NHR*, p. 127.
27. *NHR*, p. 128.	28. Ibid.
29. *NHR*, pp. 162–64, 255.	30. *NHR*, p. 119.

31. *NHR,* pp. 192–93. See Li Tsung-t'ang's diaries (1901–8) in SC 46 and a Japanese translation of the 1905 portion in *NHR.*
32. See, for example, *NHR,* pp. 188–94.
33. *NHR,* p. 256.
34. *NHR,* pp. 98 (talks between students and Kanō held on 12/9), 160–61, 177.
35. *NHR,* pp. 243–44.
36. *NHR,* pp. 239–40.
37. *NHR,* pp. 217–18, 221, 230, 261–65.
38. *NHR,* pp. 227–28.
39. *NHR,* pp. 202, 226–27, 232–33, 251.
40. *NHR,* pp. 225–26.   41. *NHR,* pp. 215, 219.
42. *NHR,* p. 244.   43. *NHR,* p. 257.
44. *NHR,* pp. 183–84, 257.
45. *NHR,* p. 35; Sanetō, *Nihon bunka,* p. 106; Chow Tse-tsung, p. 34; Hu Shih.
46. Chang Yü-fa, *Ko-ming tuan-t'i,* pp. 304–14. More recent research on different aspects of the same topic is based on Chang's figures. See, for example, Lin Te-cheng. Ho Tse-fu has arrived at a figure of 72 for the July 30 meeting after searching through many of the same original sources Chang Yü-fa used, including, especially, *KMIS.* This is the figure one would get by eliminating all of Chang's "unverifieds."
47. Chang Yü-fa, *Ko-ming tuan-t'i,* p. 317.
48. Of the 96 names extracted from Sanetō's material, 47 signed the original protest document sent to the Education Ministry on December 1. Only seven of these students are on Chang Yü-fa's lists as core members of the TMH. Nine of the 47 show up on membership lists of other organizations: the Hua-hsing Hui (2), the Kuang-fu Hui (1), and the Association for National Military Education (6). Of 24 Dōshikai members, three, including the later renowned Wang Ching-wei, were on the early TMH roster. Two on the Dōshikai list were also listed as Kuang-fu Hui members, including Lu Hsün's friend and biographer Hsü Shou-ch'ang. Finally, among 27 Rengōkai adherents, seven were definitely TMH members. Allowing for overlap—three were both original signers and later Rengōkai members—we can trace certain TMH membership to a mere 14 of the total 96, or about 15%. Though the figure is undoubtedly low, it is probably fair to say that the majority of those in the forefront of the 1905 protest action were not TMH members.
49. *NHR,* pp. 238–39.
50. Hu Han-min, pp. 390–92. Ch'iu Chin, instigator of protest activity among the small contingent of women students, was one of those who departed Japan in mid-December (Ishii, pp. 35–36).
51. Ho Hsiang-ning, pp. 18–19.
52. Liew, p. 48; Chang Yü-fa, *Ko-ming tuan-t'i,* p. 321.
53. *Konoe nikki,* 4: 316.

Chapter 9

1. Schwartz, *Wealth and Power;* Y. C. Wang, *Chinese Intellectuals,* pp. 206, 209–11; Pusey, pp. 155–75.

2. Cited in *JWM*, May 25, 1901, p. 556. Many of the notes to follow are likewise drawn from *JWM*'s discussions of and translated extracts from Japanese newspaper and journal articles.

3. Cited in *JWM*, July 28, 1900, pp. 92–94.

4. *JWM*, Oct. 6, 1900, p. 354.

5. *JWM*, June 30, 1900, p. 643, Oct. 5, 1902, p. 347.

6. Ike, p. 117, n. 17.   7. Fleming, p. 126.

8. Ibid., p. 127.   9. Meyer, p. 85.

10. *NCH*, Jan. 22, 1902, p. 121; *JWM*, March 22, 1902, p. 316. In the U.S., by now, anti-Spencerian theories were on the rise (Fleming, pp. 123–46).

11. *JWM*, Feb. 22, 1902, p. 207.

12. Chow Tse-tsung, p. 354, note g.

13. As quoted in *JWM*, March 22, 1902, p. 318.

14. As quoted in *JWM*, Feb. 22, 1902, p. 207.

15. As quoted in *JWM*, June 29, 1901, pp. 290–91.

16. *JWM*, March 22, 1902, p. 318.

17. As quoted in *JWM*, Feb. 22, 1902, p. 207.

18. Chang Yü-fa, *Ko-ming tuan-t'i*, pp. 16–21.

19. For an extended discussion of language borrowings, see *CNRS*, chap. 7, pp. 331–404. See also Wang Li-ta, p. 93. A *Tide of Chekiang* article entitled "The Translation of New Terms" (no. 2, pp. 181–90) deals with this problem at an earlier date. In a prefatory note, the writer explained that the Japanese had adopted certain character compounds as equivalents for Western terms. An inadequate knowledge of these compounds and of the real meaning of the terms they were meant to convey had led to confusion on the part of some students. On the subject of translated articles from Japanese, see, for example, the section "Current Topics from Japanese Newspapers," *CCC*, no. 2, p. 121, which pointed out that the articles extracted and translated from Japanese periodicals would help to bring a new perspective to the people back home.

20. Wang Hsiang-jung (pp. 65–70) has located over 90 student-managed newspapers and magazines (including Liang Ch'i-ch'ao's two journals) from the period 1898–1937, nearly all of them published in Tokyo and Yokohama. He estimates that this represents about a third of the total actually published. As many as 30 student magazines appeared in the years before 1911, some sponsored by provincial clubs or women's groups, others concentrating on technical subjects like law or medicine. On the growth of a mass audience in the late Ch'ing period, see Lee and Nathan, pp. 368–75.

21. "A Discussion of Nationalism," *CCC*, no. 1, p. 3; "On National Spirit," *CCC*, no. 1, pp. 1–17.

22. "A Discussion of Nationalism," *CCC*, no. 1, p. 7.

23. "On National Spirit," *CCC*, no. 1, p. 13.

24. "On Self-Esteem," *HP*, no. 4, pp. 1–5; "The Story of Being Torn Asunder," *KS*, no. 2, pp. 107–13; "The Relationship Between Military Affairs and the Nation," *HP*, no. 4, pp. 49–57; "The New Popular Spirit," *KS*, no. 5, pp. 1–9.

25. "On National Spirit," *CCC*, no. 1, p. 13.

26. *Enlightenment Journal*, 1901, in *Hsin-hai ko-ming wu-shih chou-nien chi-nien lun-wen*, 1, part 1, pp. 53–58.

27. "The Pacific Area in the Twentieth Century," *CCC*, no. 2, p. 71.

28. Ibid., pp. 65–75. See also "The Far Eastern Question," *CCC*, no. 4, pp. 93–98.

29. "World Corporation," *CCC*, no. 3, pp. 136–37.

30. "The Past and Future of the Chinese People," *KS*, no. 3, pp. 1–11.

31. "Notes on Travel in Fukien," *HP*, no. 3, pp. 105–6; "Japan's Designs on China," *CCC*, no. 1, p. 98; "The Question of the Outbreak of War Between Japan and Russia," *KS*, no. 5, pp. 127–28.

32. "Russia's New East Asian Policy," *CCC*, no. 1, pp. 1–11.

33. Hedrick Smith, "The U.S.-Soviet Crisis in Asia: Some See Start of Cold War II," *International Herald Tribune* (Paris), Feb. 2–3, 1980, p. 7.

34. "The Question of the Outbreak of War Between Japan and Russia," *KS*, no. 5, pp. 127–28.

35. "Actions of the Manchu Government Toward the Three Eastern Provinces," *KS*, no. 8, pp. 151–52.

36. "On Education," *KS*, no. 3, p. 41.

37. Ibid.

38. Peking officials instructed Minister Yang Shu to punish the instigators of such a trend among students. Yang demurred, suggesting that the students had chosen to support Japan out of loyalty to China, not rebelliousness (*NCH*, Feb. 18, 1904, p. 338). See also "Implications for China of the Opening of Hostilities Between Japan and Russia," *KS*, no. 8, pp. 11–17.

39. "Russo-Japanese War News," *KS*, no. 11–12, 150–51. *Kiangsu*, which ran until June 1904, records much of the excitement among Chinese students generated by the outbreak of war between Russia and Japan. The other major magazines—*Hupei Students Circles (Voice of Han)* and *Tide of Chekiang*—were gone by the time the war began.

40. "Letter Urging Our Nanking Comrades to Take Up Foreign Study," *KS*, no. 2, pp. 158–61.

41. "Russia's Docile Citizens in Manchuria," *CCC*, no. 8, pp. 122–23.

42. "Chinese Soldiers in the Employ of Russia," *KS*, no. 2, pp. 139–40.

43. Ibid., p. 141.

44. "The Pain of Slavery," *HP*, no. 4, p. 98.

45. "On Private and Public," *CCC*, no. 1, pp. 1–14.

46. "The Relationship Between Military Affairs and the Nation," *HP*, no. 4, pp. 49–50.

47. "The True Image of the Chinese," *HP*, no. 5, pp. 113–17.

48. "The Relationship Between Military Affairs and the Nation," *HP*, no. 4, pp. 49–57.

49. "On Education," *KS*, no. 3, p. 42.

50. "Introductory Notes," *HP*, no. 1, pp. 1–16. For other examples, see "Ts'ai Chün Brings Dishonor and Shame Upon the Nation," *KS*, no. 6, pp. 149–51; and "More Than Forty Yokohama Chinese Merchants Become Naturalized Japanese Citizens," *KS*, no. 7, pp. 152–53.

51. For examples, see "A Dying China and a Living China," *HP*, no. 3, pp. 79–84; and "The Chinese People's Political Movement," *KS*, no. 2, pp. 91–94.

52. "Actions of the Manchu Government Toward the Three Eastern Provinces," *KS*, no. 8, pp. 151–52.

53. Ibid.; "China's Position in the Event of War Between Japan and Russia," *CCC*, no. 10, pp. 25–31.

54. "Ts'ai Chün Brings Dishonor and Shame Upon the Nation," *KS*, no. 6, pp. 149–51.

55. For example, see "The Question of the Outbreak of War Between Japan and Russia," *KS*, no. 5, pp. 126–27; and "Chang Chih-tung and the Overseas Students," *KS*, no. 4, pp. 130–31.

56. "Yuan Shih-k'ai's Incompetence," *KS*, no. 4, pp. 131–33.

57. "Alas! Jung-lu," *KS*, no. 1, p. 133.

58. "Pain Begets Pain," *KS*, no. 3, p. 122.

59. "Demands of the German Envoy," *KS*, no. 4, p. 134.

60. Ibid. See also "An Analysis of [the Charge] 'Dangerously Seditious and Wicked,'" *KS*, no. 5, pp. 124–26.

61. "Political Intrigue Again," *CCC*, no. 5, p. 127.

62. "What Price the Revolutionary Parties and the Students in Japan," *KS*, no. 4, p. 128.

63. "The Question of the Cruel Death of Shen Chin," *KS*, no. 5, pp. 120–21.

64. See, for example, "Be Alerted! Ch'ing Maritime Customs Will Not Accept *Hsin-min ts'ung-pao* and the Ch'ing Post Office Will Not Transmit *Kuo-min jih-jih-pao*," *KS*, no. 6, pp. 145–47.

65. "Revolutionary Factory," *KS*, no. 5, pp. 121–24.

66. "The Economics Special Course—A Device for Creating a Revolutionary Party," *KS*, no. 4, pp. 129–30.

67. "Be Alerted!" as cited in n. 64, above; "Seize and Deal with the Secret Societies," *HP*, no. 6, p. 117.

68. "Chang Chih-tung's Recent Great Enterprise," *KS*, no. 6, pp. 151–52.

69. "Be Alerted!," as cited in n. 64, above.

70. "Chang Chih-tung's Recent Great Enterprise," *KS*, no. 6, pp. 151–52. See also "The Russian Nihilists," *KS*, no. 4, pp. 51–60. Nihilism was equated in student minds with anarchism, revolution, and populist terrorism.

71. "Chang Chih-tung's Recent Great Enterprise," *KS*, no. 6, p. 151.

72. "The Future of Kiangsu Industry," *KS*, no. 11–12, pp. 129–41.

73. "Notes on Experiments in Sericulture," *KS*, no. 5, pp. 77–82.

74. "Varieties of World Agriculture," *HP*, no. 1, pp. 39–43.

75. See, for example, "China Practices Agriculture But Not Scientific Agriculture," *HP*, no. 5, pp. 23–30.

76. "A Discussion of the Development of Systems of Government," *KS*, no. 3, pp. 27, 32.

77. "Japan's Modern Political Parties and Their Clash with the Government," *CCC*, no. 1, p. 2.

78. "A Respectful Piece of Advice to My Fellow Provincials," *CCC*, no. 2, pp. 1–12.

79. "A Definition of Self-Government," *KS*, no. 4, p. 20. For analyses of late Ch'ing attitudes toward the local-autonomy issue, see Kuhn; and Fincher. See Rankin, *Elite Activism*, pp. 241–47, for a discussion of current scholarship on the issue.

80. "Narratives on Western Educators: Herbert Spencer," *KS*, no. 1, pp. 39–47; "A Statement to the Young Ladies of the Women's World," *KS*, no. 5, pp. 132–33; "On Education," *KS*, no. 3, pp. 37–50.

81. See, for example, "Remarks on Technical Education," *KS*, no. 1, pp. 69–76; and "General Economics Study," *HP*, no. 1, pp. 31–37.

82. "On Education," *KS*, no. 6, pp. 33–43.
83. "Reform of a Confucian Country," *CCC*, no. 10, pp. 19–23.
84. "The Student Struggle," *HP*, no. 2, p. 5.
85. On the involvement of Chinese students with Japanese leftists in support of socialist-anarchist-terrorist activities, see Bernal, *Chinese Socialism*; and Wilson, *Radical Nationalist*.
86. "The Revolutionary Spirit," *NCH*, Aug. 21, 1903, pp. 423–24.

Epilogue

1. Jansen, *Japanese and Sun*, p. 203.
2. Tai Hsueh-chi, p. 603; Li Hsi-so, "Hsin-hai ko-ming," pp. 641–42; P'eng Kuo-hsing, p. 701; Tung Shou-i, pp. 299–301. As a measure of the degree to which Japanese-educated students were involved in the events of 1911, 31 of the 40 Yunnan military leaders who responded to the call to revolution after the Wuchang uprising were returned students from Japan, 22 of them graduates of Japan's Army Officers School. For a distribution of returned students in the political apparatus set up just after the uprising, see Tung Shou-i, pp. 301–2.
3. Lin Te-cheng, p. 394.
4. Wang Hsiang-jung, pp. 68–69; Tung Shou-i, pp. 286–87.
5. According to Millard, pp. 263–64, it was not just *some* of the Japan-educated students who returned to work in the commercial world but many. "Within the last few years," he wrote in 1905, "China has begun to receive back these young men, many of whom have imbibed little more than a smattering of Western learning, their accomplishments being usually limited to an imperfect knowledge of English, together with a brief course of instruction in some Western business system. With these accomplishments, however, they are able to secure employment in one of the foreign hongs or banks, or with one of the new Chinese corporations organized along modern lines, and can pose before ordinary Chinese as men of advanced ideas." But to this unflattering portrait, Millard adds an intriguing note: "The present agitation for internal reform springs almost entirely from this class. In fact, many of them are paid political agitators, subsidized to promote by both subtle and direct means certain political and commercial interests." (*New Far East*, pp. 263–64.)
6. Ch'ing officials were clearly concerned. In 1906, for example, Tuan-fang, returning from his tour abroad as part of a royal commission to review foreign institutions, warned the Throne about the rapid increase in disaffected elements, urging the adoption of a constitution to preempt their call for greater political participation (quote in Tung Shou-i, p. 283). Chang Chih-tung instructed education officials in June 1907 to be on the lookout for dissident literature, speech, and behavior, and to punish all offenders (Chiao Chih-chiang, p. 126).
7. Huang Fu-ch'ing, *Ch'ing-mo liu-Jih*, pp. 65–82; Y. C. Wang, *Chinese Intellectuals*, pp. 68–71, 478–82. A look at the careers of those listed in the *Nihon ryūgaku Shina yōjin roku* shows a consistent pattern of service in new educational institutions and in technical and financial fields, including railways, communications, and, more rarely, banking; only a few went into the business world at the level of managers of spinning mills, mines, or

commercial presses. Sang Ping, "1905–1912," p. 63, notes the Ch'ing government's difficulty, both administratively and politically, in accommodating the newly trained people whose skills were so desperately needed.

8. Rankin, *Elite Activism*, p. 233; Chang P'eng-yüan, "Constitutionalists," pp. 152–53, 162, 174–75; Chang P'eng-yüan, *Li-hsien p'ai*, pp. 28–29 and appended tables, pp. 248–312; Tung Shou-i, pp. 285–86.

9. *CNRS*, pp. 137–43; Matsumoto, p. 25. The chart in *CNRS*, pp. 138–40, shows a total of 2,831 graduates in the years 1909–11. Add to this Matsumoto's figures for the Kōbun Institute, omitted by Sanetō, and the total comes to 6,641. Sanetō's formula that graduates represent approximately a third of the total numbers studying yields the 20,000 figure for the years up to 1911. Sanetō estimated that 50,000 attended Japanese schools during the entire period 1896–1937. Other estimates go as high as 300,000 (see Intro., n. 1, above).

10. Chang Yü-fa, *Chung-kuo hsien-tai cheng-chih-shih lun*, pp. 9–12. Chang offers two data sources for the years before 1911. It is worth noting that in 1903, with their numbers at around 1,000, Chinese students in Japan accounted for about one of every 30 Chinese students receiving a modern education; by 1905, when there were as many as 10,000 students in Japan, the ratio was 1:15–25. Sang Ping, "1905–1912," pp. 60–62, puts the figures for the number of schools at 4,222 in 1904 and 52,348 in 1909, and notes that the period 1902–9 produced 82,769 graduates from all levels of schools in China, including 38,961 normal school graduates. Though school enrollments remained very low as a percentage of the school-age population, there was a tremendous increase in absolute terms of people being trained under a "modern" curriculum.

11. Chang P'eng-yüan, "Constitutionalists," p. 161.

12. For excellent analyses of late Ch'ing administrative reforms and moves towards constitutional government, see Chang Yü-fa, *Chung-kuo hsien-tai cheng-chih-shih lun*, pp. 17–50; and Fincher, pp. 32–51. Chang compares Japan's systematic approach with Ch'ing footdragging in the process of introducing constitutional rule.

13. Crowley, "Japan's Military Foreign Policies," p. 18.

14. Chang Yü-fa found 146 Japanese among the 193 foreign participants he traced, but points out that the listing is incomplete (*Ko-ming tuan-t'i*, pp. 131–33).

15. Jansen, *Japanese and Sun*, pp. 105–30. See Kuo T'ing-i, p. 1269, for an example of the Japanese government's "get-tough" policy: the expulsion from Waseda and Chūō universities of 39 Chinese students connected with the TMH (entry for Feb. 1907).

16. Bernal, *Chinese Socialism*; Wilson, pp. 45–48.

17. *CNRS*, p. 102; Morley, pp. 22–25.

18. *CNRS*, pp. 103–4. See also Japanese Foreign Ministry Archives, "Shinkoku yōhei hompō jimmeihyō." Though the number of Japanese advisers in education and training fell from 84 in 1913 to 36 in 1918, the number of "other advisers and technicians" rose from 93 to 394 in this period (Abe Hiroshi, *NitChū kyōiku*, p. 7).

19. Iriye, *Pacific Estrangement*, pp. 196–97.

20. Y. C. Wang, *Chinese Intellectuals*, pp. 106, 110, 140–41, 158, 513.

21. Wilbur, pp. 28, 83; Jansen, *Japanese and Sun*, pp. 175–201; Morley,

pp. 30–39. More recent evidence has cast some doubt on the authenticity of the document outlining Sun's position on the 21 Demands (personal communication, C. Martin Wilbur, Dec. 1980).

22. *CNRS*, pp. 115–16.

23. Chow Tse-tsung, pp. 77–83; *CNRS*, p. 116.

24. Many of the emotional statements made at this time are reminiscent of student outbursts in 1903. For example, see Chow Tse-tsung, p. 106.

25. *CNRS*, p. 116.   26. *CNRS*, pp. 126–32.

27. *CNRS*, pp. 117–18.   28. *CNRS*, pp. 119–26.

29. Washington *Post*, Feb. 5, 1977.

30. *Japan Times Weekly International Edition*, Feb. 18–24, 1991, p. 6, citing an Education Ministry report on 1990 foreign enrollments. The 18,000 figure represents a better than 60% increase over 1989 and accounts for about 44% of the total of 41,000 foreign students in Japan in 1990. About 85%, or 35,000, of these Chinese students were financing their study through private funding or assistance from their own governments; the rest were on Japanese government scholarships. The figure of 40,000 Chinese students in the U.S. is well known; see, for example, *Washington Post*, May 2, 1989, p. 3.

31. *China Daily*, Sept. 2, 1989, p. 4.

32. Most China-watchers believe this to be the case, though many Chinese officials claimed that the upheaval was foreign-instigated.

Character List

Ai-kuo Hsieh-hui　　愛國協會
Ai-kuo hsueh-she　　愛國學社
Ajia Kyōkai　　亞細亞協會
Arao Kiyoshi (Sei)　　荒尾精
Ariga Nagao　　有賀長雄
Chang Chao-t'ung　　張肇桐
Chang Chi　　張繼
Chang Chien　　張謇
Chang Hsiung-fu　　張雄夫
Chang Ping-lin　　章炳麟
Chang Shih-chao　　章士釗
Chang Tsung-hsiang　　章宗祥
Ch'ang Po-wen　　長白文
Chao Sheng　　趙聲
Che-chiang ch'ao　　浙江潮
Ch'en Fan　　陳範
Ch'en T'ien-hua　　陳天華
Cheng Hsien-ch'eng　　鄭憲成
Ch'eng Chia-sheng　　程家檉
Chi I-hui　　戢翼翬
Chiang-su　　江蘇
Ch'in Li-shan　　秦力山
Ch'in Yü-liu　　秦毓鎏
Ching-chung jih-pao　　警鐘日報
Ching-wu Hsueh-t'ang　　警務學堂
Ch'ing-i pao　　清議報
Ch'ing-nien Hui　　青年會
Ch'iu Chin　　秋瑾

Chou Hsueh-hsi　　周學熙
Chou Hung-yeh　　周宏業
Chou Shu-jen　　周樹人
Chou Tso-jen　　周作人
Chou Wei-chen　　周維楨
Chü-O I-yung-tui　　拒俄義勇隊
Chu Shou　　朱綬
Ch'üan-hsueh p'ien　　勸學篇
Chung-kuo jih-pao　　中國日報
Chung-kuo Liu-hsueh-　　中國留學
　sheng Hui-kuan　　　生會館
Dōbunkai　　同文會
Erh-shih Shih-chi chih　　二十世紀
　Chih-na　　　之支那
Feng Tzu-yu　　馮自由
Fujita Toyohachi　　藤田豊八
Fukushima Yasumasa　　福島安正
Hattori Unokichi　　服部宇之吉
Ho Hsiang-ning　　何香凝
Ho Ju-chang　　何如璋
Ho Pin-sheng　　河賓笙
Hsieh Hsiao-shih　　謝曉石
Hsin-min ts'ung-pao　　新民叢報
Hsing-Chung Hui　　興中會
Hsü Hsi-lin　　徐錫麟
Hsü Shou-ch'ang　　許壽裳
Hsü Ying-kuei　　許應騤
Hu Han-min　　胡漢民

Hu Ying	胡瑛	Lin Ping-chang	林炳章
Hu Yü-chin	胡玉縉	Liu Ch'eng-yü	劉成禺
Hu Yuan-t'an	胡元倓	Liu Hsueh-hsün	劉學詢
Hua-hsing Hui	華興會	*Liu-hsueh-sheng chien*	留學生鑑
Huang Ch'ao-tseng	黃超曾	Liu K'uei-i	劉揆一
Huang Ching	黃璟	Lo Chen-yü	羅振玉
Huang Hsing	黃興	Ma Chün-wu	馬君武
Huang Tsun-hsien	黃遵憲	Ma Fu-i	馬福益
Huang Tsung-yang	黃宗仰	*Meng-hui t'ou*	猛回頭
Hupei hsueh-sheng chieh	湖北學生界	*Min pao*	民報
		Miyazaki Torazō	宮崎寅藏
Ide Saburō	井手三郎	Mu Ch'üan-sun	繆荃孫
I-shu hui-pien	譯書彙編	Munekata Kotarō	宗方小太郎
I-shu Hui-pien She	譯書彙編社	Nagaoka Moriyoshi	長岡護美
Inukai Tsuyoshi (Ki)	犬養毅	Nakae Chōmin	中江兆民
Jih-pen yu-hsueh chih-nan	日本遊學指南	Nakajima Saishi	中島裁之
		Nakanishi Masaki	中西正樹
K'ai-chih lu	開智錄	Nezu Hajime	根津一
Kakkō Rengōkai	各校連合會	Nikka Gakudō	日華學堂
Kanō Jigorō	嘉納治五郎	Nisshin Bōeki Kenkyūjo	日清貿易研究所
Kashiwabara Buntarō	柏原文太郎	Niu Yung-chien	鈕永建
Katō Hiroyuki	加藤弘之	Ōi Kentarō	大井憲太郎
Kawashima Naniwa	川島浪速	*O-shih ching-wen*	俄事警聞
Kishida Ginkō	岸田吟香	Rakuzendō	樂善堂
Kitamura Saburō	北村三郎	Rikugun Shikan Gakkō	陸軍士官學校
Kō-A Kai	興亞會		
Kōbun Gakuin	弘文學院	Ryūgakkai Iji Dōshikai	留學界維持同志會
Kojō Teikichi	古城貞吉		
Konoe Atsumaro	近衛篤麿	Seijō Gakkō	成城学校
Kōtō Shihan Gakkō	高等師範學校	Seika Gakkō	清華學校
Kuang-fu Hui	光復會	Seiryoku tōzen	西力東漸
Kung Pao-ch'üan	龔寶銓	Shen Chin	沈藎
Kuo-min jih-jih pao	國民日日報	Shen Hsiang-yün	沈翔雲
Kuo-min pao	國民報	Shen Tieh-min	沈紱民
Lan T'ien-wei	藍天蔚	*Shih-wu pao*	時務報
Li-chih Hui	勵志會	Shimoda Utako	下田歌子
Li Sheng-to	李盛鐸	Shina hozen	支那保全
Li Shu-ch'ang	黎庶昌	Shina Kyōkai	支那協会
Li Tsung-t'ang	李宗棠	Shinbu Gakkō	振武學校
Li Wen-fan	李文範	Shishi	志士
Liao Chung-k'ai	廖仲愷	Su Man-shu	蘇曼殊
Lin Ch'ang-min	林長民		

Su pao	蘇報	Tung Hung-wei	董鴻禕
Su P'eng	蘇鵬	T'ung-ch'ou Hui	同仇会
Sun K'uei-chün	孫揆均	T'ung-meng Hui	同盟会
Sung Chiao-jen	宋教仁	Uchida Ryōhei	内田良平
Ta-t'ung Hsueh-hsiao	大同學校	Ukita Kazutami	浮田和民
Takahashi Ken	高橋謙	Wang Chia-chü	王家駒
Tanabe Yasunosuke	田鍋安之助	Wang Chia-wei	王嘉禕
T'ang Pao-ngo	唐宝鍔	Wang Chih-pen	王治本
T'ang Ts'ai-ch'ang	唐才常	Wang Ching-hsi	王景禧
T'ang Erh-ho	湯爾和	Wang Ching-wei	汪精衛
T'ao Ch'eng-chang	陶成章	Wang Ta-hsieh	汪大燮
Ting Yuan-fang	定遠方	Watanabe Ryōsei	渡邊龍聖
Tō Ajia	東亞細亞	Wei Lan	魏蘭
Tō-A Dōbunkai	東亞同文会	Weng Hao	翁浩
Tō-A Kai	東亞会	Wu Chih-hui	吳稚暉
Tō-A Shōgyō Gakkō	東亞商業學校	Wu Ju-lun	吳汝綸
Tōbun Gakudō	東文學堂	Wu Lu-chen	吳祿貞
Tōbun Gakusha	東文學社	Wu Yü-chang	吳玉章
Tōhōkyōkai	東邦協会	Yang Shu	楊樞
Tōkyō Dōbun Shoin	東京同文書院	Yang Tu-sheng	楊篤生
Torishimaru	取締る	Yao Hung-yeh	姚洪業
Tōyama Mitsuru	頭山滿	Yao Wen-tung	姚文棟
Tōyō hozen	東洋保全	Yeh Lan	葉瀾
Tsai Chen	載振	Yin Yüan-i	尹援一
Ts'ai Chün	蔡鈞	Yūshi	有志
Ts'ai Yuan-p'ei	蔡元培	Yü-keng	裕庚
Ts'ao Ju-lin	曹汝霖	*Yu-hsueh i-pien*	遊學譯編
Tsou Jung	鄒容		

Bibliography

The following student magazines cited in the Notes are available in collection (Taipei: Kuomintang Party Historical Materials Compilation Committee, 1968):

Che-chiang ch'ao (Tide of Chekiang), Feb.-Dec. 1903 (*CCC*)
Erh-shih shih-chi chih Chih-na (20th Century China), 1905
Hupei hsueh-sheng chieh (Hupei Students Circle; later, after no. 5, *Hansheng*, The Voice of Han), Feb.–Oct. 1903 (*HP*)
Kiangsu, April 1903–June 1904 (*KS*)
Kuo-min pao (The Chinese National), 1901
Yu-hsueh i-pien (Translations by [Hunan] Students Abroad), 1902–3

Su pao (Kiangsu Journal; Shanghai, 1903) and *I-shu hui-pien* (Translation Journal) are also available in collection (Taipei: Taiwan hsueh-sheng shu-chu, 1965, 1966). I have used three abbreviations in the Bibliography: *CNHHKM, Chi-nien Hsin-hai ko-ming ch'i-shih-chou nien hsueh-shu t'ao-lun hui lun-wen chi; HHKMHIL, Hsin-hai ko-ming hui-i lu;* and SC, Sanetō Collection. For the abbreviations used in the Notes, see p. 227.

Abe Hiroshi. "Borrowing from Japan: China's First Modern Educational System." In Ruth Hayhoe and Marianne Bastid-Bruguière, eds., *China's Education and the Industrialized World*, pp. 57–80. New York: M. E. Sharpe, 1987.
———, ed. *NitChū kyōiku bunka kōryū to masatsu* (Sino-Japanese educational and cultural exchange and points of friction). Tokyo: Daiichi Shobō, 1983.
Abe Kenichi. "Shinmatsu Chūgokujin ryū Nichi gakusei no dōkō to shinkaron" (Trends among Chinese students in Japan in the late Ch'ing period and the theory of evolution), 2 parts, *Seiji keizai shigaku*, 195.8 (1982): 59–73; 196.9 (1982): 32–53.
———. "Sū Yō no [Kakumeigun] to seiyō kindai shisō" (Tsou Jung's "Revolutionary Army" and modern Western thought), *Seiji keizai shigaku*, 200 (1983): 150–64.
Ayers, William. *Chang Chih-tung and Educational Reform in China.* Cambridge, Mass.: Harvard University Press, 1971.

Bastid-Bruguière, Marianne. "Currents of Social Change." In *The Cambridge History of China*, vol. 11: *Late Ch'ing, 1800–1911*, ed. John K. Fairbank and Kwang-ching Liu, part 2, pp. 535–602. Cambridge, Eng.: Cambridge University Press, 1980.

Bays, Daniel H. *China Enters the Twentieth Century: Chang Chih-tung and the Issues of a New Age, 1895–1909*. Ann Arbor: University of Michigan Press, 1978.

Beardsley, R. K., and John Hall, eds. *Twelve Doors to Japan*. New York: McGraw Hill, 1965.

Beasley, W. G. *The Meiji Restoration*. Stanford, Calif.: Stanford University Press, 1972.

Bernal, Martin. *Chinese Socialism to 1907*. Ithaca, N.Y.: Cornell University Press, 1976.

———. "The Triumph of Anarchism over Marxism, 1906–1907." In Mary C. Wright, ed., *China in Revolution: The First Phase, 1900–1913*, pp. 97–142. New Haven, Conn.: Yale University Press, 1968.

Biggerstaff, Knight. *The Earliest Modern Government Schools in China*. Ithaca, N.Y.: Cornell University Press, 1961.

Boorman, Howard L. *Biographical Dictionary of Republican China*. 4 vols. New York: Columbia University Press, 1967–70.

Borton, Hugh. *Japan's Modern Century*. New York: Ronald, 1970.

Britton, Roswell S. *The Chinese Periodical Press, 1800–1912*. Shanghai: Kelly and Walsh, 1933.

Cameron, Meribeth. *The Reform Movement in China, 1898–1912*. New York: Octagon, 1963.

Chang Chi. *Chang P'u-ch'üan hsien-sheng ch'üan-chi* (Complete works of Chang Chi). Taipei: Chung-yang wen-wu kung-ying she, 1952.

———. "Hui-i lu" (Recollections). In *Kuo-shih-kuan kuan-k'an* (Publications of the National Historical Office), 1.2 (1948): 54–75.

———. [under pseud. Tzu-jan-sheng]. "Tu yen-na liu-hsueh-sheng mi-yü yu-fen" (Anger at reading the secret edict ordering the arrest of the returned students), *Su pao*, June 10, 1903. In *Ko-ming chih ch'ang-tao yü fa-chan* (The advocacy and development of the Revolution). vol. 10, pp. 130–33. Taipei: Chengchung Press, 1964.

Chang Chien. *Kuei-mao Tung-yu jih-chi* (Japan travel diary). 1903. SC 65.

Chang Chih-tung. *Chang Wen-hsiang-kung ch'üan-chi* (The complete works of Chang Chih-tung). Taipei: Ch'u-hsueh ching-lu, 1963.

Chang Hao. *Chinese Intellectuals in Crisis: Search for Order and Meaning (1890–1911)*. Berkeley: University of California Press, 1987.

———. *Liang Ch'i-ch'ao and Intellectual Transition in China, 1890–1907*. Cambridge, Mass.: Harvard University Press, 1971.

Chang Huang-ch'i. "Su pao an shih-lu" (A record of the Su Pao Case). In *Hsin-hai ko-ming* (The 1911 Revolution), vol. 1, pp. 367–86. Shanghai: People's Publishing House, 1956.

Chang K'ai-yuan. "Liu-Jih hsueh-sheng tui Chung-kuo chin-tai-hua-ti ying-hsiang" (The influence of students in Japan on China's modernization), *Shu-lin*, 1985, no. 1: 17.

Chang Kuo-hui. "Hsin-hai ko-ming-ch'ien Chung-kuo tzu-pen-chu-i-ti fa-chan" (The development of capitalism in pre-1911 China). In *CNHHKM*, vol. 1, pp. 184–218.

Chang Nan and Wang Jen-chih, eds. *Hsin-hai ko-ming ch'ien-shih-nien-*

chien shih-lun hsuan-chi (Selected essays on current events from the decade before the 1911 Revolution), vols. 1–4. Hong Kong and Beijing, Sanlien Bookstore, 1962–63.

Chang P'eng-yüan. "The Constitutionalists." In Mary C. Wright, ed., *China in Revolution: The First Phase, 1900–1913*, pp. 143–83. New Haven, Conn.: Yale University Press, 1968.

———. *Li-hsien-p'ai yü Hsin-hai ko-ming* (Constitutionalists and the Revolution of 1911). Taipei: Institute of Modern History, Academia Sinica, 1969.

———. *Liang Ch'i-ch'ao yü Ch'ing-chi ko-ming* (Liang Ch'i-ch'ao and revolution at the end of the Ch'ing Dynasty). Taipei: Institute of Modern History, Academia Sinica, 1964.

Chang Ping-lin. "Po K'ang Yu-wei shu" (In refutation of K'ang Yu-wei). In Chang Nan and Wang Jen-chih, eds., *Hsin-kai ko-ming ch'ien-shih-nien-chien shi-lun hsuan-chi* (Selected essays on current events from the decade before the 1911 Revolution), vol. 1, part 2, pp. 752–64. Hong Kong: Sanlien Bookstore, 1962.

Chang Yü-fa. *Ch'ing-chi-te ko-ming tuan-t'i* (Revolutionaries of the late Ch'ing period). Taipei: Institute of Modern History, Academia Sinica, 1975.

———. *Ch'ing-chi-te li-hsien tuan-t'i* (Constitutionalists of the late Ch'ing period). Taipei: Institute of Modern History, Academia Sinica, 1971.

———. *Chung-kuo hsien-tai cheng-chih-shih lun* (On China's modern political history). Taipei: Tunghua Press, 1988.

Ch'ang Po-wen. *Tung-yu jih-chi* (A Diary of my trip to Japan), 1906. SC 114.

Ch'en Wei. "Kuang-fu Hui ch'ien-ch'i te huo-tung p'ien-tuan" (Miscellany about activities preceding the founding of the Restoration Society). In *HHKMHIL*, vol. 4, pp. 127–30.

Cheng Hai-lin. "K'ang Yu-wei-ti pien-fa ssu-hsiang yü Jih-pen" (K'ang Yu-wei's reformist thought and Japan), *Li-shih chiao-hsueh*, 1989, no. 7: 1–4.

Cheng, Shelly Hsien. "The T'ung-Meng-Hui: Its Organization, Leadership and Finances, 1905–1912." Ph.D. dissertation, University of Washington, 1962.

Chi Wen-shun. *Ideological Conflicts in Modern China: Democracy and Authoritarianism*. New Brunswick, N.J.: Transaction Books, 1986.

Chi-nien Hsin-hai ko-ming ch'i-shih-chou nien hsueh-shu t'ao-lun hui lun-wen chi (*CNHHKM*; Papers from the symposium to commemorate the 70th anniversary of the 1911 Revolution). 3 vols. Beijing: Chunghua Press, 1983.

Chiang I-hua. *Chang T'ai-yen sheng-p'ing yü ssu-hsiang yen-chiu wen-hsüan* (Anthology of research on Chang T'ai-yen's life and thought). Chekiang: Chekiang People's Press, 1986.

Chiang Monlin. *Tides from the West*. Taipei: World Book, 1963.

Chiang Tsung-hsiang. *Jih-pen yu-hsueh chih-nan* (Guide to study in Japan), 1901. SC 49.

Chiang Wei-ch'iao. "Chung-kuo chiao-yü hui chih hui-i," (Recollections of the Education Society). In *HHKM*, vol. 1, pp. 485–96.

Ch'iao Chih-ch'iang. *Hsin-hai ko-ming-ch'ien-ti shih nien* (Ten years before the 1911 Revolution). Shansi: Shansi People's Publishing House, 1987.

Chin Ch'ung-chi and Hu Sheng-wu. "T'ung-meng Hui yü Kuang-fu Hui kuan-hsi k'ao-shih" (The facts behind the relationship between the T'ung-meng Hui and the Kuang-fu Hui). In *CNHHKM*, vol. 1, pp. 735–65.

Chirol, Valentine. *The Far Eastern Question*. London: Macmillan, 1896.

———. *Fifty Years in a Changing World*. London: Jonathan Cape, 1927.

Chou Chia-jung. *Hsin-hai ko-ming-ch'ien-ti Ts'ai Yuan-p'ei* (Pre-1911 Revolution Ts'ai Yuan-p'ei). Hong Kong: Po Wen, 1980.

Chou Hsueh-hsi. *Tung-yu jih-chi* (Diary of my trip to Japan). 1903. SC 62.

Chou Tso-jen. "Jih-pen ti ts'ai jen-shih" (Japan reconsidered). In *Chung-kuo-jen te Jih-pen kuan* (Chinese views of Japan), pp. 110–25. Tokyo: Meguro Shoten, 1937.

Chow Jen Hwa. *China and Japan: The History of Chinese Diplomatic Missions in Japan, 1877–1911*. Singapore: Chopmen, 1975.

Chow Tse-tsung. *The May Fourth Movement: Intellectual Revolution in Modern China*. Cambridge, Mass.: Harvard University Press, 1960.

Chu, Samuel C. *Reformer in Modern China: Chang Chien, 1853–1926*. New York: Columbia University Press, 1965.

Chu Shou. *Tung-yu chi-ch'eng* (A record of my trip to Japan). 1898. SC 35.

Chu Shou-p'eng, ed. *Kuang-hsü-ch'ao Tung-hua hsü-lu* (Tung-hua records continued for the Kuang-hsü reign). Shanghai: Chi-ch'eng t'u-shu, 1909.

Ch'ü Li-ho. *Ch'ing-mo liu-hsueh chiao-yü* (Late Ch'ing overseas study programs). Taipei: Sanmin Press, 1973.

Chung, Sue Fawn. "The Image of the Empress Dowager Tz'u-hsi." In Paul A. Cohen and John E. Schrecker, eds., *Reform in Nineteenth-Century China*, pp. 101–10. Cambridge, Mass.: Harvard University Press, 1976.

Chūyaku Nichibunsho mokuroku (Catalogue of Japanese works in Chinese translation). 1944. SC 662.

Cohen, Paul A. *Between Tradition and Modernity: Wang T'ao and Reform in Late Ch'ing China*. Cambridge, Mass.: Harvard University Press, 1974.

———. "The Post-Mao Reforms in Historical Perspective," *Journal of Asian Studies*, 47.3 (Aug. 1988): 518–40.

Cohen, Paul A., and John E. Schrecker, eds., *Reform in Nineteenth-Century China*. Cambridge, Mass.: Harvard University Press, 1976.

Colquhoun, Archibald R. *China in Transformation*. New York: Harper, 1898.

Conroy, Hilary. *The Japanese Seizure of Korea, 1868–1910*. Philadelphia: University of Pennsylvania Press, 1960.

Crowley, James B. *Japan's Quest for Autonomy: National Security and Foreign Policy, 1930–1938*. Princeton, N.J.: Princeton University Press, 1966.

Duus, Peter, Ramon H. Meyers, and Mark R. Peattie, eds. *The Japanese Informal Empire in China, 1895–1937*. Princeton, N.J.: Princeton University Press, 1989.

Esherick, Joseph. *The Origins of the Boxer Uprising*. Berkeley: University of California Press, 1987.

———. *Reform and Revolution in China: The 1911 Revolution in Hunan and Hubei*. Berkeley: University of California Press, 1976.

Fairbank, John K. *The Great Chinese Revolution, 1800–1985*. New York: Harper, 1986.

Fairbank, John K., Edwin O. Reischauer, and Albert M. Craig. *East Asia, the Modern Transformation*. Boston: Houghton Mifflin, 1965.

Fan Shou-cheng, ed. *Hsin-hai ko-ming ti yen-chiu* (Research into the 1911 Revolution). Taipei: Hsueh-ying wen-hua shih-yeh yu hsien kung-ssu, 1986.

Fang Chao-ying. *Ch'ing-mo Min-ch'u yang-hsueh hsueh-sheng t'i-ming-lu ch'u-chi* (Preliminary listing of students abroad in the late Ch'ing-early Republican period). Taipei: Institute of Modern History, Academia Sinica, 1962.

Feng Tzu-yu. *Chung-hua Min-kuo k'ai-kuo ch'ien ko-ming shih* (A history of the Revolution prior to the founding of the Chinese Republic). 2 vols. Taipei: Shih-chieh shu-chü, 1954.

———. *Chung-kuo ko-ming yun-tung erh-shih-liu nien tzu-chih shih* (Twenty-six-year organizational history of the Chinese revolutionary movement). Shanghai: Commercial Press, 1948.

———. *Ko-ming i-shih* (*KMIS*; Reminiscences of the Revolution). 5 vols. Taipei: Commercial Press, 1965.

Feuerwerker, Albert. *China's Early Industrialization: Sheng Hsuan-huai (1844–1916) and Mandarin Enterprise.* Cambridge, Mass.: Harvard University Press, 1958.

Feuerwerker, Albert, Rhoads Murphey, and Mary C. Wright, eds. *Approaches to Modern Chinese History.* Berkeley: University of California Press, 1967.

Fincher, John H. *Chinese Democracy: The Self-Government Movement in Local, Provincial and National Politics, 1905–1914.* New York: St. Martin's, 1981.

Fleming, Donald. "Social Darwinism." In Arthur M. Schlesinger, Jr., and Morton White, eds., *Paths of American Thought;* pp. 123–46. Boston: Houghton Mifflin, 1963.

Fogel, Joshua A. *Nakae Ushikichi in China: The Mourning of Spirit.* Cambridge, Mass.: Harvard University Press, 1989.

———. *Politics and Sinology: The Case of Naitō Konan (1866–1934).* Cambridge, Mass.: Council on East Asian Studies, Harvard University, 1984.

———. *Recent Japanese Studies of Modern Chinese History: Translations from Shigaku Zasshi for 1983–1986.* Armonk, N.Y.: M. E. Sharpe, 1989.

Fukuzawa Yukichi. *The Autobiography of Yukichi Fukuzawa.* Tr. Kiyooka Eiichi. New York: Columbia University Press, 1968.

Futami Takeshi and Satō Hisako. "Chūgokujin Nihon ryūgakushi kankei tōkei" (Statistics relating to the history of Chinese students in Japan), *Kokuritsu kyōiku kenkyūjo kiyō*, 94 (March 1978): 99–105.

Gasster, Michael. *Chinese Intellectuals and the Revolution of 1911.* Seattle: University of Washington Press, 1969.

Gendai Shinajin meikan (Directory of contemporary Chinese). Tokyo: Gaimushō, 1937.

Gilbert, Rodney. *What's Wrong with China?* London: John Murray, 1926.

Gluck, Carol. *Japan's Modern Myths: Ideology in the Late Meiji Period.* Princeton, N.J.: Princeton University Press, 1985.

Handlin, Oscar. *Truth in History.* Cambridge, Mass.: Harvard University Press, 1979.

Hao Yen-p'ing. "The Abortive Cooperation Between Reformers and Revolutionaries," *Papers on China* (Harvard University) 15 (1961): 91–114.

Harootunian, Harry D. "The Functions of China in Tokugawa Thought." In

Akira Iriye, ed., *The Chinese and the Japanese*, pp. 9–36. Princeton, N.J.: Princeton University Press, 1980.

Hasegawa Junzo. *Kanō Jigorō no kyōiku to shisō* (The educational works and thought of Kanō Jigorō). Tokyo: Meiji Shoin, 1981.

Hearn, Lafcadio. *Japan: An Interpretation*. Tokyo: Tuttle, 1955.

Ho Hsiang-ning. "Wo-ti hui-i" (My reminiscences). In *HHKMHIL*, vol. 1, pp. 12–59.

Ho Pin-sheng. *Tung-yu wen-chien lu* (A record of experiences from my trip to Japan). 1906. SC 94.

Ho Ping-ti. *The Ladder of Success in Imperial China*. New York: Wiley, 1964.

———. *Studies on the Population of China, 1368–1953*. Cambridge, Mass.: Harvard University Press, 1959.

Hō Takushū [P'eng Tse-chou]. "Kō Yū-i no hempō undō to Meiji Ishin" (K'ang Yu-wei's reform movement and the Meiji Restoration), *Jimbun gakuhō* (Kyoto University), 30 (1970): 149–93.

Ho Tse-fu. "T'ung-meng Hui ch'eng-li hsin-lun" (A new view of the founding of the T'ung-meng Hui). *Chin-tai-shih yen-chiu*, 2 (1985): 267–78.

Hobson, J. A. *Imperialism*. Ann Arbor: University of Michigan Press, 1965.

Howard, Richard. "Japan's Role in the Reform Program of K'ang Yu-wei." In Lo Jung-pang, ed., *K'ang Yu-wei: A Biography and a Symposium*, pp. 280–312. Tucson: University of Arizona Press, 1967.

Hsin-hai ko-ming (*HHKM*; The 1911 Revolution). Ed. Chinese Historical Association. 8 vols. Shanghai: People's Publishing House, 1957.

Hsin-hai ko-ming hui-i lu (*HHKMHIL*; Recollections of the 1911 Revolution). Ed. Historical Materials Research Committee. 5 vols. Beijing: Chunghua Press, 1961–63.

Hsin-hai ko-ming wu-shih chou-nien chi-nien lun-wen chi (Collection of articles commemorating the fiftieth anniversary of the 1911 Revolution). 2 vols. Ed. Philosophical Society and Scientific Society of Hupei Province. Beijing: China Press, 1962.

Hsin-min ts'ung-pao (*HMTP*; New people's miscellany: Yokohama, 1902–7). Ed. Feng Tzu-shan. 17 vols. Taipei, 1966. Originally published in Yokohama, 1902.

Hsü Shou-ch'ang. *Wang-yu Lu Hsün yin-hsiang chi* (Impressions of my departed friend Lu Hsün). Beijing: People's Literature Publishing House, 1953.

Hsueh Chün-tu. *Huang Hsing and the Chinese Revolution*. Stanford, Calif.: Stanford University Press, 1961.

———, ed. *Revolutionary Leaders of Modern China*. New York: Oxford University Press, 1971.

Hu Han-min. "Tzu-chuan" (Autobiography). In Kuomintang Party Historical Materials Compilation Committee, ed., *Ko-ming wen-hsien* (Documents of the Revolution), vol. 3, pp. 373–442. Taipei, 1953.

Hu Kuo-shu. "Lun Kuang-fu Hui" (A discussion of the Restoration Society). In *CNHHKM*, vol. 1, pp. 712–34.

Hu Shih. "An Autobiographical Account at Forty" (tr. William A. Wycoff), *Chinese Studies in History*, 12 (Winter 1978–79): 25–48.

Hu Yü-chin. *Chia-ch'en Tung-yu jih-chi* (A diary of my trip to Japan in 1904). SC 74.

Huang Ching. *Tung-ying ch'ang-ho lu* (Harmonies from the Eastern Sea). 1902. SC 56.

———. *Tung-yu jih-chi* (A diary of my trip to Japan). 1902. SC 55.

Huang Fu-ch'ing. *Chin-tai Jih-pen tsai-Hua wen-hua chi she-hui shih-yeh-chih yen-chiu* (Research into modern Japanese cultural and social activities in China). Taipei: Institute of Modern History, Academia Sinica, 1982.

———. *Ch'ing-mo liu-Jih hsueh-sheng* (Chinese students in Japan in the late Ch'ing period). Taipei: Institute of Modern History, Academia Sinica, 1975.

———. "Shinmatsu ni okeru ryū Nichi gakusei haken seisaku no seiritsu to sono tenkai" (The formulation and development of policy on the dispatch of Chinese students to Japan in the late Ch'ing), *Shigaku zasshi*, 18.7 (July 1972): 37–66.

Huang, Philip C. C. *Liang Ch'i-ch'ao and Modern Chinese Liberalism.* Seattle: University of Washington Press, 1972.

Hummel, Arthur W. *Eminent Chinese of the Ch'ing Period, 1644–1912.* 2 vols. Washington, D.C.: U. S. Government Printing Office, 1943–44.

Ichiko Chūzō. "Political and Institutional Reform, 1900–1911." In *The Cambridge History of China*, vol. 11: *Late Ch'ing, 1800–1911*, ed. John K. Fairbank and Kwang-ching Liu, part 2, pp. 375–415. Cambridge, Eng.: Cambridge University Press, 1980.

Ike Nobutaka. *The Beginnings of Political Democracy in Japan.* Baltimore, Md.: Greenwood, 1950.

Iriye, Akira. *Pacific Estrangement: Japanese and American Expansion, 1897–1911.* Cambridge, Mass.: Harvard University Press, 1972.

———, ed. *The Chinese and the Japanese.* Princeton, N.J.: Princeton University Press, 1980.

Ishii Yōko. "Shingai kakumeiki no ryū Nichi joshigakusei" (Chinese women students in Japan in the 1911 Revolution period), *Shinron*, 36 (1983): 31–54.

Ishizuki Minoru. *Kindai Nihon no kaigai ryūgaku shi* (A history of modern Japanese study abroad). Kyoto: Minerva Shobō, 1972.

Jansen, Marius. "Chung-kuo liu-Jih hsueh-yun yü Hsin-hai ko-ming-ti kuan-hsi" (The Chinese study in Japan movement and its relationship to the 1911 Revolution). In *CNHHKM*, vol. 3, pp. 2600–2615.

———. *Japan and China: From War to Peace, 1894–1972.* Chicago: Rand McNally, 1975.

———. "Japan and the Revolution of 1911." In *The Cambridge History of China*, vol. 11: *Late Ch'ing, 1800–1911*, ed. John K. Fairbank and Kwang-ching Liu, part 2, pp. 339–74. Cambridge, Eng.: Cambridge University Press, 1980.

———. *The Japanese and Sun Yat-sen.* Cambridge, Mass.: Harvard University Press, 1954.

———. "Japanese Views of China During the Meiji Period." In Albert Feuerwerker, Rhoads Murphey, and Mary C. Wright, eds., *Approaches to Modern Chinese History*, pp. 168–89. Berkeley: University of California Press, 1967.

———, ed. *Changing Japanese Attitudes Toward Modernization.* Princeton, N.J.: Princeton University Press, 1965.

Japanese Foreign Ministry Archives, Library of Congress, Microfilm Section. "Shinkoku yōhei hompō jimmeihyō (List of Japanese employed in China), 1909–10. Reel sp. 110.

———. "Tō-A Dōbunkai kankei zassan" (Miscellaneous documents relating to the East Asia Common Culture Society). MT 3.10.1, 13, Reel 773.

Jih-pen hua-ch'iao chih (A record of the overseas Chinese in Japan). Taipei: Committee for the Compilation of Records of Overseas Chinese, 1965.

Johnson, Chalmers A. *Peasant Nationalism and Communist Power.* Stanford, Calif.: Stanford University Press, 1962.

Johnson, David. "Communication, Class and Consciousness in Late Imperial China." In David Johnson, Andrew J. Nathan, and Evelyn S. Rawski, eds., *Popular Culture in Late Imperial China*, pp. 34–72. Berkeley: University of California Press, 1982.

Kamachi, Noriko. *Reform in China: Huang Tsun-hsien and the Japanese Model.* Cambridge, Mass.: Harvard University Press, 1981.

Kanō Jigorō. *Watakushi no shōgai to jūdō* (My life and judo). Ed. Otaki Tadao. Tokyo: Shinjinbutsu Ōraisha, 1972.

Kanō Sensei Denki Hensankai (Committee to Compile the Biography of Professor Kanō), comp. *Kanō Jigorō.* Tokyo: Kōdōkan, 1964.

Kayano Nagatomo. *Chūka minkoku kakumei hikyū* (Secret memoirs of the Chinese Revolution). Tokyo: Kōkoku Seinen Kyōiku Kyōkai, 1941.

Keene, Donald. "The Sino-Japanese War of 1894–5 and Its Cultural Effects in Japan." In Donald H. Shively, ed. *Tradition and Modernization in Japanese Culture*, pp. 121–81. Princeton, N.J.: Princeton University Press, 1971.

Kennedy, Thomas L. *The Arms of Kiangnan: Modernization in the Chinese Ordnance Industry, 1860–1895.* Boulder, Colo.: Westview Press, 1978.

Kim, K. H. *Japanese Perspectives on China's Early Modernization.* Ann Arbor: University of Michigan Press, 1974.

Kimiya Yasuhiko. *Nikka bunka kōryūshi* (History of Sino-Japanese cultural relations). Tokyo: Fuzambō, 1955.

Kita Ikki. *Shina kakumei gaishi* (An unofficial history of the Chinese Revolution). Tokyo: Daitōkaku, 1921.

———. "Shina kakumeitō oyobi kakumei no Shina" (The Chinese revolutionary party and China in revolution), 1915. Japanese Foreign Ministry Archives, Library of Congress, microfilm reel sp. 110.

Ko Kung-chen. *Chung-kuo pao-hsueh shih* (A history of Chinese journalism). Taipei: Hsueh-sheng shu-chü, 1964.

Kobayashi Tomoaki. "Shoki no Chūgoku tai Nichi ryūgakusei haken ni tsuite" (On the early dispatch of students from China to Japan), *Shingai kakumei kenkyū*, 4 (1984): 1–17.

Kokuryūkai. *Tō-A senkaku shishi kiden* (Records and biographies of pioneer patriots in East Asia). 3 vols. Tokyo: Hara Shobō, 1966.

Kokuryūkurabu, ed. *Kokushi Uchida Ryōhei den* (Biography of Uchida Ryōhei). Tokyo: Hara Shobō, 1967.

Ko-ming chih ch'ang-tao yü fa-chan (KMCCT; The advocacy and development of the Revolution). *Chung-hua Min-kuo k'ai-kuo wu-shih nien wen-hsien* (Documents on the first fifty years of the Chinese Republic), vols. 9 and 10. Taipei: Chengchung Press, 1964.

Ko-ming hsien-lieh hsien-chin chuan (*KMHL*; Biographies of revolutionary martyrs and pioneers). Taipei: Chungyang Wenwu Kungying She, 1965.

Ko-ming wen-hsien (Documents of the Revolution). Comp. Lo Chia-lun. 61 vols. Taipei: Kuomintang Party Historical Materials Compilation Committee, 1953.

Konoe Atsumaro nikki (Diary of Konoe Atsumaro). Ed. Konoe Atsumaro Nikki Kankōkai. 5 vols. and suppplemental volume of selected writings. Tokyo: Kajima Kenkyūjo Shuppankai, 1968.

Kōsaka Masaaki, ed. *Japanese Thought in the Meiji Era*. Tokyo: Pan Pacific Press, 1958.

Kosaka Masataka. "Ch'ing Policy Over Manchuria, 1900–1903," *Papers on China* (Harvard University), 16 (1962): 126–53.

Koyūkai, ed. *Tō-A Dōbun Shoin Daigaku shi* (A history of the East Asia Common Culture Academy-University). Tokyo: Koyūkai, 1955.

Kuang-hsü-ch'ao Chung-Jih chiao-she shih-liao (Historical materials on Sino-Japanese relations, Kuang-hsü Period). 88 chuan. Beiping: Beiping National Museum, 1932.

Kuhn, Philip A. "Local Self-Government Under the Republic: Problems of Control, Autonomy, and Mobilization." In Frederic Wakeman and Carolyn Grant, eds., *Conflict and Control in Late Imperial China*, pp. 257–98. Berkeley: University of California Press, 1975.

Kuo Chung-hsiu. *Tung-yu jih-chi* (A diary of my trip to Japan). 1906. SC 99.

Kuo Jung-sheng. *Ch'ing-mo Shansi liu-hsueh-sheng* (Shansi overseas students during the late Ch'ing). Taipei: Shansi wen-hsien she, 1983.

Kuo T'ing-i. *Chin-tai Chung-kuo shih-shih jih-chih* (Daily record of events in modern Chinese history). 2 vols. Taipei, 1963.

Kwong, Luke. *A Mosaic of the Hundred Days: Personalities, Politics, and Ideas of 1898*. Cambridge, Mass.: Harvard University Press, 1984.

La Fargue, Thomas E. *China's First Hundred*. Pullman: State College of Washington, 1942.

Langer, William L. *The Diplomacy of Imperialism, 1890–1902*. New York: Knopf, 1951.

Lee, Leo Ou-fan, and Andrew J. Nathan. "The Beginnings of Mass Culture: Journalism and Fiction in the Late Ch'ing and Beyond." In David Johnson, Andrew J. Nathan, and Evelyn S. Rawski, eds., *Popular Culture in Late Imperial China*, pp. 360–95. Berkeley: University of California Press, 1982.

Levenson, Joseph R. *Revolution and Cosmopolitanism*. Berkeley: University of California Press, 1971.

Lewis, Charlton M. *Prologue to the Chinese Revolution*. Cambridge, Mass.: Harvard University Press, 1976.

Li Hsi-so. *Chin-tai Chung-kuo-ti liu-hsueh-sheng* (Modern Chinese overseas students). Beijing: People's Press, 1987.

———. "Hsin-hai ko-ming-ch'ien-ti liu-Jih hsueh-sheng yun-tung" (The pre-1911 Chinese student movement to Japan). In *CNHHKM*, vol. 1, pp. 606–47.

Li Shu-fan. "Chia-ch'en chü-O i-yung-tui yü Changsha chih ko-ming," *Chien-kuo yüeh-k'an* (Reconstruction monthly), 14.1 (1936): 1–3.

Li Tsung-t'ang. *Tung-yu chi-nien* (Record of my Japan trips). 6 vols. n.d. SC 46.

Liew, K. S. *Struggle for Democracy: Sung Chiao-jen and the 1911 Revolution*. Canberra: Australian National University Press, 1971.

Lin Ping-chang. *Kuei-mao Tung-yu jih-chi* (A diary of my trip to Japan in 1903). SC 67.

Lin Te-cheng. "Liu-Jih shih-kuan hsueh-hsiao hsueh-sheng yü T'ung-meng Hui" (The T'ung-meng Hui connection of Chinese students who attended Japan's Army Officers School), *Kuo-li Ch'eng-kung Ta-hsueh Li-shih Hsueh-pao* (Bulletin of the History Department of Ch'eng Kung University), 13 (March 1987): 377–411.

Lin Yü-sheng. *The Crisis of Chinese Consciousness*. Madison: University of Wisconsin Press, 1979.

Ling Wen-yuan. *Tung-yu jih-chi* (A diary of my trip to Japan). 1904. SC 64.

Lipset, Seymour Martin. *Student Politics*. New York: Basic Books, 1967.

Liu Ch'eng-yü. "Hsien Tsung-li chiu-te lu" (Accounts of Sun Yat-sen's character), *Kuo-shih-kuan kuan-k'an* (Bulletin of the National Historical Bureau), 1 (Dec. 1947): 44–56.

Liu Hsueh-chao and Fang Ta-lun. "Ch'ing-mo Min-ch'u Chung-kuo-jen tui Jih kuan-ti yen-pien" (Evolution of Chinese views toward Japan in the late Ch'ing-early Republican period), *Chin-tai-shih yen-chiu*, June 1989: 124–43.

Liu-hsueh-sheng chien (Handbook for students abroad). Ed. Tokyo Chinese Student Union. 1906. SC 117.

Liu K'uei-i. *Huang Hsing chuan-chi* (Biography of Huang Hsing). Taipei: Pamir Bookstore, 1952.

Liu-tung wai-shih (An unofficial history of study in Japan), 1914. SC 153.

Lo Chia-lun, ed. *Su pao an chih-shih* (Record of the *Su pao* Case). Taipei: Kuomintang Party Historical Materials Compilation Committee, 1968.

Lo Jung-pang, ed. *K'ang Yu-wei: A Biography and a Symposium*. Tucson: University of Arizona Press, 1967.

Lu Hsün. *Dawn Blossoms Plucked at Dusk*. Tr. Yang Hsien-yi and Gladys Yang. Beijing: Foreign Language Press, 1976.

Lust, John. "The Su-pao Case," *Bulletin of the School of Oriental and African Studies*, 27 (1964): 408–29.

MacKinnon, Stephen. *Power and Politics in Late Imperial China: Yuan Shih-kai in Beijing and Tianjin, 1901–1908*. Berkeley: University of California Press, 1980.

MacMurray, John V. A. *Treaties and Agreements with and concerning China, 1897–1919*, vol. 1. New York: Oxford University Press, 1921.

Malozemoff, Andrew. *Russian Far Eastern Policy, 1881–1904, with Special Emphasis on the Causes of the Russo-Japanese War*. Berkeley: University of California Press, 1958.

Martin, W. A. P. *The Awakening of China*. New York: Doubleday, 1907.

———. *A Cycle of Cathay*. New York: Fleming H. Revell, 1896.

Maruyama Masao. "Japanese Thought." In Irwin Scheiner, ed., *Modern Japan, an Interpretive Anthology*, pp. 208–15. New York: Macmillan, 1974.

Masada Wataru. *Ro Jin no inshō* (Impressions of Lu Hsün). Tokyo: Kadokawa Shoten, 1970.

Matsumoto Kamejirō. *Chūka ryūgakusei kyōiku shōshi* (A short history of the education of Chinese students in Japan). Tokyo, 1931.

May, Ernest P., and James C. Thomson, eds. *American-East Asian Relations: A Survey*. Cambridge, Mass.: Harvard University Press, 1972.

Meiji gakusei enkaku shi (The historical development of the Meiji educational system). Tokyo: Kinkōdō Publishers, 1906.

Meiji iko kyōiku seido hattatsu shi (History of the development of the educational system from the Meiji period). 12 vols. Tokyo: Kyōikushi Hensankai, 1938–39.

Meisner, Maurice. *Li Tao-chao and the Origins of Chinese Marxism*. Cambridge, Mass.: Harvard University Press, 1967.

Meyer, Donald. "The Dissolution of Calvinism." In Arthur M. Schlesinger, Jr., and Morton White, eds., *Paths of American Thought*, pp. 71–85. Boston: Houghton Mifflin, 1963.

Millard, Thomas F. *The New Far East*. New York: Scribner's, 1906.

Miwa Kimitada. "Fukuzawa Yukichi's 'Departure from Asia': A Prelude to the Sino-Japanese War." In Edmund Skrzypezak, ed., *Japan's Modern Century*, pp. 1–26. Tokyo: Sophia University, 1968.

Miyazaki Tōten (Torazō). *Sanjū-sannen no yume* (The thirty-three-year dream). Tokyo, 1943.

Morley, James W., ed. *Japan's Foreign Policy, 1868–1941: A Research Guide*. New York: Columbia University Press, 1974.

Morris, Ivan. *Nationalism and the Right Wing in Japan*. London: Oxford University Press, 1960.

Mu Ch'üan-sun. *Jih-yu hui-pien* (Collected essays from a trip to Japan). 1903. SC 60.

Nagai Kazumi. "Chin Ten-ka no shōgai" (The life of Ch'en T'ien-hua), *Shigaku zasshi*, 66 (Nov. 1956): 37–71.

———. "Iwayuru Go-son jiken ni tsuite" (On what is known as the Wu-Sun Incident), *Shigaku zasshi*, 7 (July 1953): 43–62.

———. "Iwayuru Shinkoku ryūgakusei torishimaru kisoku jiken no seikaku" (The character of what is known as the incident concerning regulations to control Chinese students abroad), *Shinyū Daigaku*, March 18, 1953: 11–34.

———. "Kyoga gakuseigun o megutte" (On the anti-Russia student army), *Shigaku zasshi*, 4 (1954): 57–83.

Nakamura Tadayuki. "NitChū bungaku kōryū no isshiten" (A view of literary exchange between Japan and China). In Tam Yue-him, ed., *Sino-Japanese Cultural Interchange: Aspects of Literature and Language Learning*, pp. 91–109. Hong Kong: Institute of Chinese Studies, Chinese University, 1985.

Nakayama Yasuaki, ed. *Shimbun shūsei Meiji hennenshi* (Meiji history through newspapers), vols. 7–12. Tokyo: Zaisei Keizai Gakkai, 1936.

Nihon ryūgaku Chūkaminkoku jimmei shirabe (Survey of the Japan-trained in Republican China). Tokyo, Toritsu Universitiy, Matsumoto Collection.

Nihon ryūgaku Shina yōjin roku (A record of important Chinese figures who studied in Japan). 1942. SC 1144.

Nish, Ian. *The Anglo-Japanese Alliance: The Diplomacy of Two Island Empires, 1894–1907*. London: University of London Press, 1967.

———. "Japan's Indecision During the Boxer Disturbances," *Journal of Asian Studies*, 20.4 (Aug. 1961): 449–61.

Norman, E. Herbert. "The Genyōsha: A Study in the Origins of Japanese Imperialism," *Pacific Affairs*, 17.3 (Sept. 1944): 261–84.

———. *Japan's Emergence as a Modern State*. New York: Institute of Pacific Relations, 1940.

Norman, Henry. *Peoples and Politics of the Far East*. London: T. F. Unwin, 1895.

Oka Yoshitake. "Kokuminteki dokuritsu to kokka risei" (National independence and national interests). In *Kindai Nihon shisōshi kōza* (Series on the history of modern Japanese thought), vol. 8, pp. 9–79. Tokyo: Chikuma Shobō, 1961.

Okamoto, Shumpei. *The Japanese Oligarchy and the Russo-Japanese War*. New York: Columbia University Press, 1970.

Ōkuma Shigenobu, comp. *Fifty Years of New Japan*. 2 vols. New York: Dutton, 1909.

Ono Kazuko. *Chinese Women in a Century of Revolution, 1850–1950*. Ed. Joshua A. Fogel. Stanford, Calif.: Stanford University Press, 1989.

Onogawa Hidemi. "Shō Heirin no minzoku shisō" (The nationalist thought of Chang Ping-lin), part 2, *Tōyōshi kenkyū*, 13.3 (Aug. 1954), 14.3 (Nov. 1955).

O-shih Ching-wen (Warnings on Russian affairs). 1903–04. Taipei: Kuomintang Party Historical Materials Compilation Committee, 1968.

P'eng Kuo-hsing. "Hua-hsing Hui chi-ko wen-ti-ti yen-chiu" (Research into some questions about the Hua-hsing Hui). In *CNHHKM*, vol. 2, pp. 674–711.

Pittau, Joseph. *Political Thought in Early Meiji Japan*. Cambridge, Mass.: Harvard University Press, 1967.

Price, Don C. *Russia and the Roots of the Chinese Revolution*. Cambridge, Mass.: Harvard University Press, 1974.

Pusey, James Reeve. *China and Charles Darwin*. Cambridge, Mass.: Harvard University Press, 1983.

Pyle, Kenneth. *The New Generation in Meiji Japan*. Stanford, Calif.: Stanford University Press, 1969.

Rankin, Mary Backus. *Early Chinese Revolutionaries: Radical Intellectuals in Shanghai and Chekiang, 1902–11*. Cambridge, Mass.: Harvard University Press, 1971.

———. *Elite Activism and Political Transformation in China*. Stanford, Calif.: Stanford University Press, 1986.

Rawski, Evelyn S. "Economic and Social Foundations of Late Imperial Culture." In David Johnson, Andrew J. Nathan, and Evelyn S. Rawski, eds., *Popular Culture in Late Imperial China*, pp. 3–33.

Reynolds, Douglas R. "Chinese Area Studies in Prewar China: Japan's Tōa Dōbun Shoin in Shanghai, 1900–1945," *Journal of Asian Studies*, Nov. 1986: 945–70.

———. "A Golden Decade Forgotten: Japan-China Relations, 1898–1907," *Transactions of the Asiatic Society of Japan*, 1987: 93–153.

Ryūgakuseibu shusshinsha meibo (Alumni of the Seijō Gakkō Students Abroad Division). 1937. SC 1143.

Said, Edward W. *Orientalism*. London: Routledge, 1978.

Sanetō Bunko Mokuroku (Catalogue of the Sanetō Collection). Tokyo: Hibiya Library, 1966.

Sanetō Keishū. *Chūgokujin Nihon ryūgaku shi* (A history of Chinese students in Japan). Tokyo: Kuroshio Shuppan, 1960.

—. *Chūgokujin Nihon ryūgaku shikō* (Draft history of Chinese students in Japan). Tokyo: Nikka Gakkai, 1939.

—. *Chūgoku ryūgakusei shidan* (Accounts of Chinese overseas students). Tokyo: Muraguchi, 1981.

—. *Kindai Nisshi bunka ron* (A discussion of contemporary Sino-Japanese culture). Tokyo: Daitō Shuppansha, 1941.

—. *Kindai NitChū kōshō shiwa* (Historical notes on modern Sino-Japanese relations). Tokyo: Shunjūsha, 1973.

—. *Meiji Nisshi bunka kōshō* (Cultural relations between Japan and China in the Meiji period). Tokyo: Kōfūkan, 1943.

—. *Nihon bunka no Shina e no eikyo* (The influence of Japanese culture on China). Tokyo: Keisetsu Shoin, 1940.

—. *NitChū hi-yūkō no rekishi* (*NHR*; A history of unfriendly relations between China and Japan). Tokyo: Asahi Shimbunsha, 1973.

Sang Ping. "Liu-Jih hsueh-sheng fa-tuan yü Chia-wu Chan-hou-ti Chung-Jih kuan-hsi" (The dispatch of students to Japan and Sino-Japanese relations after the war of 1895), *Hua-chung Shih-fan Ta-hsueh hsueh-pao*, 1986, no. 4: 25–29.

—. "1905–1912-nien-ti kuo-nei hsueh-sheng ch'ün-t'i yü Chung-kuo chin-tai-hua" (The emergence of China-trained students and Chinese modernization, 1905–12), *Chin-tai-shih yen-chiu* (Institute of Modern History, Chinese Academy of Social Sciences), 1989, no. 5: 55–76.

Satō Saburō. "Kō-A Kai ni kansuru ichi kōsatsu" (A study of the Kō-A kai), *Yamagata Daigaku kiyō jimbun kagaku*, 1.4 (Aug. 1951): 399–411.

Scalapino, Robert A. *Democracy and the Party Movement in Prewar Japan: The Failure of the First Attempt*. Berkeley: University of California Press, 1962.

Scalapino, Robert A., and George T. Yu. *The Chinese Anarchist Movement*. Westport, Conn: Greenwood, 1980.

Scheiner, Irwin, ed. *Modern Japan, an Interpretive Anthology*. New York: Macmillan, 1974.

Schiffrin, Harold Z. *Sun Yat-sen and the Origins of the Chinese Revolution*. Berkeley: University of California Press, 1968.

Schlesinger, Arthur M., Jr., and Morton White, eds. *Paths of American Thought*. Boston: Houghton Mifflin, 1963.

Schoppa, R. Keith. *Chinese Elites and Political Change*. Cambridge, Mass.: Harvard University Press, 1982.

Schrecker, John E. *Imperialism and Chinese Nationalism*. Cambridge, Mass.: Harvard University Press, 1971.

Schwartz, Benjamin. *In Search of Wealth and Power: Yen Fu and the West*. Cambridge, Mass.: Harvard University Press, 1964.

Seidensticker, Edward. *Low City, High City*. New York: Knopf, 1983.

Shen Tieh-min. "Chi Kuang-fu Hui erh-san shih" (Two or three reminiscences about the Restoration Society). In *HHKMHIL*, vol. 4, pp. 131–42.

Shen Yun-lung, comp. *Ch'ing-mo Min-ch'u liu-Jih Lu-chün Shih-kuan Hsueh-hsiao jen-ming-pu* (A listing of Chinese students at Japan's Army Officers School in the late Ch'ing-early Republican period). Modern China Historical Materials Series (Tokyo), 67 (1943).

Shih Chin. "Tsao-ch'i Chung-kuo liu-Jih hsueh-sheng-ti huo-tung yü tsu-chih" (The activities and organizations of Chinese students in Japan in the early period), *Szu yü yen* 6.1 (May 15, 1968): 27–35.

Shimoda Utako Sensei den (Biography of Professor Shimoda Utako). Tokyo: Ko Shimoda Kōchō Sensei Denki Hensanjo, 1943.

Shu Hsin-ch'eng. *Chin-tai Chung-kuo liu-hsueh shih* (A history of Chinese students abroad in modern times). Shanghai: Chung-hua Bookstore, 1929.

Smith, Thomas C. *Political Change and Industrial Development in Japan: Government Enterprise, 1868–1880.* Stanford, Calif.: Stanford University Press, 1965.

Smythe, E. Joan. "The Tzu-li Hui: Some Chinese and Their Rebellion," *Papers on China* (Harvard University), 12 (1958): 51–69.

Sotsugyōsei ni kansuru shorui: Shinkoku gakusei kanri-iin (Documents related to graduates: Chinese Students Supervisory Committee). 1899–1905. Tōyō Bunko Archives, no. 6942.

Spence, Jonathan D. *The Search for Modern China.* New York: Norton, 1990.

———. *To Change China: Western Advisers in China, 1620–1960.* New York: Little, Brown, 1969.

Stead, Alfred, ed. *Japan by the Japanese.* London: William Heinemann, 1904.

Strand, David. *Rickshaw Beijing.* Berkeley: University of California Press, 1989.

Su I-i. *Chin-tai Chung-kuo liu-hsueh-shih* (A history of modern Chinese study abroad). Taipei: Lung-t'ien Press, 1979.

Su Yun-feng. *Chung-kuo hsien-tai-hua-ti ch'ü-yü yen-chiu: Hu-pei Sheng, 1860–1916* (Regional studies in China's modernization: Hupei Province, 1860–1916). Taipei: Institute of Modern History, Academia Sinica, 1981.

Sung Yueh-lun. *Tsung-li tsai Jih-pen chih ko-ming huo-tung* (Sun Yat-sen's revolutionary activities in Japan). Taipei: Chung-yang wen-wu kung-ying she, 1953.

Tai Hsueh-chi. "Ch'ing-mo liu-Jih je-ch'ao yü Hsin-hai ko-ming" (Late Ch'ing study-in-Japan fever and the 1911 Revolution). In *CNHHKM*, vol. 1, pp. 3–16.

Tam Yue-him, ed. *Sino-Japanese Cultural Interchange: Aspects of Literature and Language Learning.* Hong Kong: Institute of Chinese Studies, Chinese University, 1985.

T'ao Ch'eng-chang. "Che-an chi-lüeh" (A brief account of the revolts in Chekiang). In *HHKM*, vol. 3, pp. 3–111.

Ting Chih-p'ing, ed. *Chung-kuo chin ch'i-shih-nien-lai chiao-yü chi-shih* (A record of the last 70 years of education in China). Taipei: Kuo-li pien-i kuan, 1961.

Ting, V. K. "Chinese Students," *Westminster Review*, 169 (Jan. 1908): 48–55.

Ting Yuan-fang. *Ying-chou kuan-hsueh chi* (Observations on the East). 1903. SC 59.

Tō-A Dōbunkai (TDK), ed. *Taishi kaiko roku* (Memoirs about China). 3 vols. Tokyo: Hara Shobō, 1968.

"Tō-A Dōbunkai yōshi" (From the letterhead of the East Asia Common Culture Society). Tōyō Bunko Archives, no. 5699. Handwritten copy.

Tō-A Dōbun Shoin Daigaku shi (A history of the Tō-A Dōbun Shoin College). Tokyo: Shanghai Friendship Society, 1955.

Toby, Ronald P. *State and Diplomacy in Early Modern Japan.* Stanford, Calif.: Stanford University Press, 1991. Originally published in 1984.

Townsend, James R. *Political Participation in Communist China.* Berkeley: University of California Press, 1967.

Treadgold, Donald W. *The West in Russia and China*, vol. 2: *China, 1582–1949.* Cambridge, Eng.: Cambridge University Press, 1973.

Ts'ao Ju-lin. *I-sheng chih hui-i* (Recollections of a lifetime). Hong Kong: Ch'ün-ch'iu tsa-chih she, 1966.

Tseng Hsü-pai, ed. *Chung-kuo hsin-wen shih* (A history of Chinese journalism). Taipei: National Political Institute, Newspaper Research Section, 1966.

Tsou Jung. *Ko-ming chün* (The revolutionary army). Shanghai, 1958.

———. *The Revolutionary Army: A Chinese Nationalist Tract of 1903.* Tr., with Introduction by John Lust. Paris: Mouton, 1968.

Tu Ch'eng-hsiang. *Tsou Jung chuan* (Biography of Tsou Jung). Taiwan: Pa-mir Books, 1952.

Tung Shou-i. *Ch'ing-tai liu-hsueh yun-tung shih* (A history of the study-abroad movement during the Ch'ing period). Shenyang: Liaoning People's Publishing House, 1985.

Uyehara, George. *The Political Development of Japan, 1867–1909.* London: Constable, 1909.

Wallace, J. A. "Chinese Students in Tokio and the Revolution," *North American Student* June, 1913: 170–75.

Wang Ching-hsi. *Jih-yu pi-chi* (Notes on my trip to Japan). 1904. SC 70.

Wang Hsiang-jung. *Chung-kuo-ti chin-tai-hua yü Jih-pen* (China's modernization and Japan). Hunan: Hunan People's Publishing House, 1987.

Wang Li-ta. "Hsien-tai Han-yü chung ts'ung Jih-yü chieh-lai te tz'u-hui" (Modern Chinese terms of Japanese origin), *Chung-kuo yü-wen*, 68 (Feb. 1958): 90–94.

Wang Shu-huai. *Wai-jen yü Wu-hsü pien-fa* (Foreigners and the 1898 reforms). Nankang: Chung-yang yen-chiu yuan, 1965.

Wang Te-chao. *Ts'ung kai-ko tao ko-ming* (From reform to revolution). Beijing: Chunghua Press, 1987.

———. "T'ung-meng Hui shih-ch'i Sun Chung-shan Hsien-sheng ko-ming ssu-hsiang ti fen-hsi yen-chiu" (An analysis of Sun Yat-sen's thought during the T'ung-meng Hui period), *Chung-kuo hsien-tai-shih ts'ung-k'an*, 1 (1960): 65–188.

Wang, Y. C. *Chinese Intellectuals and the West, 1872–1949.* Chapel Hill: University of North Carolina Press, 1966.

———. "The Su-pao Case: A Study of Foreign Pressure, Intellectual Fermentation, and Dynastic Decline." Paper delivered at Wentworth-by-the-Sea Conference on the 1911 Revolution, Aug. 1965.

Washio Yoshitsugu, ed. *Inukai Bokudō den* (Biography of Inukai Ki). 3 vols. Tokyo, 1938–39.

Watt, John R. *The District Magistrate in Late Imperial China.* New York: Columbia University Press, 1972.

Webb, Herschel. *The Japanese Imperial Institution in the Tokugawa Period.* New York: Columbia University Press, 1968.

Wei Chien-yu. "Hsin-hai ko-ming shih-ch'i hui-tang yun-tung-ti hsin fa-chan" (New developments in secret society movements in the 1911 period). In *CNHHKM*, vol. 1, pp. 530–45.

Wilbur, C. Martin. *Sun Yat-sen, Frustrated Patriot.* New York: Columbia University Press, 1976.

Wilson, George M. *Radical Nationalist in Japan: Kita Ikki, 1883–1937.* Cambridge, Mass.: Harvard University Press, 1969.

Wright, Mary C., ed. *China in Revolution: The First Phase, 1900–1913.* New Haven, Conn.: Yale University Press, 1968.

Wu Hsiao-ju, ed. *Hsin-hai ko-ming lieh-shih shih-wen hsuan* (Literary selections from revolutionary heroes of 1911). Beijing: Chung-hua Bookstore, 1962.

Wu Ju-lun. *Han-cha pi-t'an* (Correspondence and interviews). 1903. SC 52.

———. *Tung-yu Jih-pao i-pien* (Translations from the Japanese press on [Wu's] trip to Japan), 1903. SC 53.

Wu Yü-chang. *Hsin-hai Ko-ming.* Beijing: People's Publishing House, 1961.

Yang Cheng-kuang. *Matsumoto Kamejirō chuan* (Biography of Matsumoto Kamejirō). Beijing: Shihshih Publishers, 1985.

Yang T'ien-shih and Wang Hsueh-chuang, eds. *Chü-O Yun-tung* (Anti-Russia movement). Beijing: Chinese Academy of Social Sciences, 1979.

Yokoyama Kendō. *Kanō Sensei den* (Biography of Professor Kanō). Tokyo: Oda Nobutada, 1941.

Young, Ernest P. "Problems of a Late Ch'ing Revolutionary." In Hsueh Chün-tu, ed., *Revolutionary Leaders of Modern China.* pp. 210–47. New York: Oxford University Press, 1971.

Yü Hsin-ch'un and Li Ts'ai-chen. "Hsin-hai ko-ming shih-ch'i Jih-pen-ti tui Hua cheng-ts'e" (Japan's policy toward China during the 1911 Revolution period). In *CNHHKM*, vol. 3, pp. 1374–1433.

Yueh-chang ch'eng-an hui-lan (A survey of agreements and legal briefs). 52 chuan. Shanghai: Tien-shi ch'i, 1905.

Zai-Shanhai Tō-A Dōbun Shoin ichiran (A look at the Shanghai East Asia Common Culture Academy). Tokyo: Mombushō, 1911–12.

Index

In this index, "f" after a number indicates a separate reference on the next page; "ff," separate references on the next two pages. *Passim* is used for a cluster of references in close but not consecutive sequence.

Library of Congress Cataloging-in-Publication Data

Harrell, Paula, 1939–
Sowing the seeds of change : Chinese students, Japanese teachers,
1895–1905 / Paula Harrell.
     p.   cm.
Includes bibliographical references and index.
ISBN 0-8047-1985-3 (acid-free paper) :
     1. Foreign study—China—History.   2. Chinese students—Japan—
History.   3. Student movements—China—History.   4. Politics and
education—China—History.   I. Title.
LB1696.6.C6H37   1992
378.1'9829951052—dc20   91-39189
                                                                               CIP

♾ This book is printed on acid-free paper